EDUCATION IN TEXAS

Policies, Practices, and Perspectives

Ninth Edition

T5-BCK-333

Charles W. Funkhouser, Editor

The University of Texas at Arlington

Merrill,
an imprint of Prentice Hall

Upper Saddle River, New Jersey   *Columbus, Ohio*

Library of Congress ISSN Number
1526–372X

Editor: Bradley J. Potthoff
Editorial Assistant: Mary Evangelista
Production Editor: JoEllen Gohr
Production Coordination: Carlisle Publishers Services
Design Coordinator: Diane C. Lorenzo
Cover Designer: Thomas Mack
Cover Art: Stephan Schildbach
Production Manager: Pamela D. Bennett
Director of Marketing: Kevin Flanagan
Marketing Manager: Meghan Shepherd
Marketing Coordinator: Krista Groshong

This book was set in Palatino by Carlisle Communications, Ltd., and was printed and bound by The Banta Company. The cover was printed by The Banta Company.

Printed in the United States of America

10 9 8 7 6 5 4 3 2 1

ISBN: 0-13-013152-0

Prentice-Hall International (UK) Limited, *London*
Prentice-Hall of Australia Pty. Limited, *Sydney*
Prentice-Hall Canada Inc., *Toronto*
Prentice-Hall Hispanoamericana, S. A., *Mexico*
Prentice-Hall of India Private Limited, *New Delhi*
Prentice-Hall of Japan, Inc., *Tokyo*
Prentice-Hall (Singapore) Pte. Ltd., *Singapore*
Editora Prentice-Hall do Brasil, Ltda., *Rio de Janeiro*

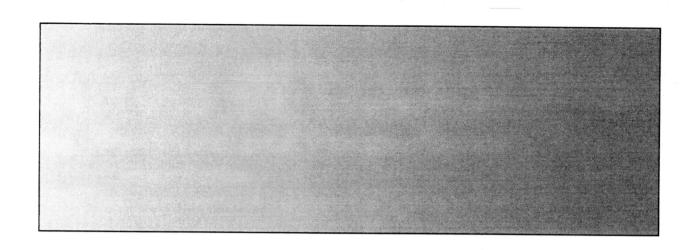

Contents

iv   Contents

SECTION FOUR

The Education Profession 405

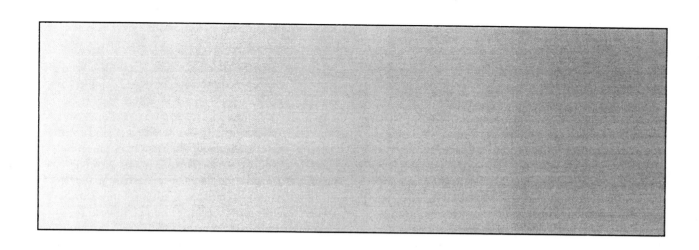

Preface

This ninth edition of *Education in Texas: Policies, Practices, and Perspectives,* like previous editions and any other attempt to record the changes in public education, is a work in progress. While the eighth edition reported the complete statutory overhaul of the Texas Education Code passed as Senate Bill 1 of the 74th Texas Legislature in 1995, the full meaning in the transactions from statutory provisions to administrative interpretation and application had yet to be determined. With the ninth edition, those insights are provided. In addition, the Texas legislature, during the 75th biennial session of 1997 and the 76th of 1999, made appropriate adjustments and "fine tuned" the provisions of the Code, still commonly referred to as Senate Bill 1. The numerous changes in public schooling in Texas which closed out the 20th century took place in the shadow of changes nationwide, allowing the 21st century to usher in dramatic new emphases on accountability for results in student achievement; increased reliance on technology in the school context; more attention to safety and security in schools, including liability for the sexual harassment of students by students; financial equity among schools and districts; and a significant trend toward increasing the alternatives to traditional public schools.

The ninth edition represents the most significant revision of this textbook in the past decade, somewhat of a celebration of the arrival of the new millennium. The same four-section format with detailed overviews was maintained, as were selected chapters of ongoing relevance. Of the 38 chapters in the new edition, 18 are new and 5 have been significantly revised. For the most part, the overviews to each of the sections are new.

The text begins with an overview of recent trends in the governance of public education and in education law. Special emphasis is given to educator liability and immunity, especially important in educational milieu of the 21st century. A review of the expanding list of alternatives to public education is included. Chapter 1 is an update of education law authored by two of the most highly regarded experts on school law in Texas. Like many of the additions to the ninth edition, Chapter 1 is a mini-text on its own merits. Chapter 2 is a complete revision of the chapter on the State Board of Education prepared by a former member of the Board. The new State Board for Educator Certification is the subject of Chapter 3, which was written by the first Executive Director of the Board. School finance, a topic which usually defies understanding, is described simply and effectively in the new Chapter 4. The Academic Excellence Indicator System (AEIS), the state's measure of district and campus achievement for purposes of accreditation, is the subject of Chapters 5 and 6, both new to this edition. Charter schools are the focus of the new Chapter 7. The new

Chapter 8 reprints the Texas Education Code's provisions for student discipline and is appended with an example of a school district's code of conduct. Chapter 9 on classroom management is another new addition to the ninth edition. Authored by distinguished professors from San Houston State University, Wichita State University, and Eastern Kentucky University, this chapter is another one of those which is almost a stand-alone textbook on the subject of practical applications of discipline management techniques. The most recent judicial decisions regarding sexual harassment in the school environment are discussed in the revised Chapter 10. New to this edition is Chapter 11, the most recent *The American School Board Journal* feature entitled "Education Vital Signs 1998." The insights provided therein, and the report of the most recent Gallup Poll on the public's perceptions of their schools in Chapter 16, are essential collections of data for analyses of the full spectrum of conditions affecting America's public schools at the turn of the century.

The new Texas public school curriculum, mandated by the Texas legislature in 1995 and approved by the State Board of Education in 1997, is the subject of Chapter 19, which discusses the Texas Essential Knowledge and Skills (TEKS). Also new is Chapter 20 on the Texas Assessment of Academic Skills (TAAS), the major component of the state *accountability system*. The U.S. Congress "reauthorized" the statutory provisions of the Individuals with Disabilities in Education Act (IDEA) in 1997, and the U.S. Department of Education finalized the "regulations" or administrative law for the revision's implementation in 1999. Those revisions are summarized in the new Chapter 21. Chapter 22 deals with education of the gifted and talented and is new to this edition. Acknowledging that education materials in the 21st century need not be restricted to traditional textbooks, the new Chapter 26 details newly revised guidelines for the selection and purchase of learning materials paid for by state funds. The totally new changes in teacher evaluation are summarized in Chapter 38, which also describes the new teacher appraisal system utilized by over 90% of the state's school districts.

Several of my observations regarding the eighth edition deserve repeating in this preface to the ninth edition.

> According to futurists, change is sometimes difficult to accept. For those who prepare textbooks, or at least this one, change is both exciting and challenging. The flip side of the excitement and challenge is the frustration experienced in attempting to comprehend fully the significance of the changes. Even more difficult is the responsibility for selecting, from an enormous amount of information, that which will be most important to readers' personal interests and professional needs.

Those of us who contribute to this work in progress appreciate the wide acceptance of previous editions and believe that this new edition will meet the high expectations set by those who use it. My personal thanks to all who helped create *Education in Texas* and to those who rely on it in classrooms across the state.

SECTION

I

The Organization and Administration of Education

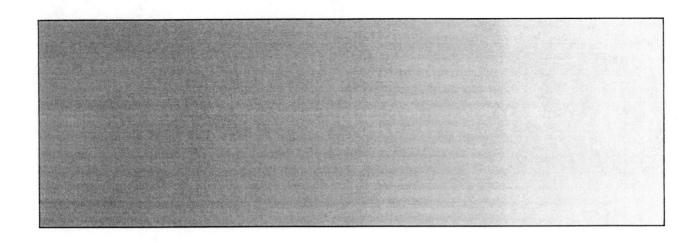

Overview

Public education in Texas is an institution of immeasurable influence and immense responsibility. This multi-billion dollar enterprise is charged with and routinely delivers free, compulsory, and appropriate educational opportunities to approximately four million students. These students bring to their schools an amazing variety of abilities, ethnic backgrounds, religious beliefs, languages, disabilities, economic and psychological needs, interests, abilities, and aspirations. These public school students are enrolled in 1,042 school districts and as many as 160 "charter schools," which vary in enrollment from approximately 200,000 to fewer than a dozen. Each school day over 7,000 public school campuses and 255,000 teachers welcome these students. And the numbers of students, school campuses, and charters are increasing rapidly. In addition, thousands of Texas elementary and secondary students attend private, independent, or religious schools, and a significant number are schooled "at home." The focus of this text is the public school system. That this enormous public school system works, and in fact works reasonably well, is a compliment and should be a comfort to all of the citizens of Texas who support it.

Characteristics of Texas public school students are illustrated in Table 1. The schools they attend are profiled in Table 2 as are their teachers, administrators and other support staff in Table 3.

GOVERNANCE

The United States Constitution does not mention "education" as a federal or Congressional responsi-

bility and, with the Tenth Amendment, leaves public education among the powers "not delegated to the United States . . . , nor prohibited by it to the States, are reserved to the States respectively, or to the people." The Texas Constitution, in Article VII, Section I requires that: "A general diffusion of knowledge being essential to the preservation of the liberties and rights of the people, it shall be the duty of the legislature of the State to establish and make suitable provision for the support and maintenance of an efficient system of free public schools." What constitutes "an efficient system" will be explored later in this text especially in relationship to financial equity. Without question, the major influence and power over Texas public education rests with the legislature. This power is especially evident in the ways the Legislature funds its part of the public education system. School finance is the subject of Chapter 4. Appended to Chapter 4 is an analysis of school district characteristics and expenditures.

State Board of Education

Article VIII of the Texas Constitution directs the legislature to provide "by law for a State Board of Education, whose members shall be appointed or elected in such manner and by such authority and shall serve for such terms as the Legislature shall prescribe not to exceed six years. The said board shall perform such duties as may be prescribed by law." History records shifts from the Legislature providing more autonomy and authority to the State Board of Education (SBOE) to periods of time in

TABLE 1

Students by Ethnicity and Economic Status			
	Number of Students	% of Total	% Increase from 1997
African American	559,708	14.4%	1.9%
Hispanic	1,476,008	37.9%	3.0%
White	1,750,561	45.0%	0.2%
Other	105,600	2.7%	4.7%
Total	3,891,877	100.0%	1.6%
Economic Disadv.	1,886,926	48.5%	2.5%

Students by Grade Span			
	Number of Students	% of Total	% Increase from 1997
Kindergarten & Earlier	425,299	10.9%	1.7%
Elementary (1–5)	1,513,247	38.9%	1.1%
Middle (6–8)	893,915	23.0%	1.0%
High (9–12)	1,059,416	27.2%	3.0%
Total	3,891,877	100.0%	1.6%

Students by Program			
	Number of Students	% of Total	% Increase from 1997
Special Education	466,527	12.0%	4.6%
Bilingual/ESL Edu.	462,379	11.9%	3.4%
Career & Tech. Edu.	676,547	17.4%	2.2%
Gifted & Talented Edu.	313,131	8.0%	3.9%

Source: Texas Education Agency, Snapshot 1998.

which they have provided considerably less. Several Board members admonished their colleagues that if the bickering among members didn't cease (in this particular case over adoption of the Texas Essential Knowledge and Skills [TEKS]), the Legislature may strip them of any remaining authority to make decisions or abolish their positions entirely and replace them with a three-member appointed board. Following passage of House Bill 72, the major reform legislation in 1972, the Legislature delegated significantly more authority to the State Board while reducing that of the Commissioner and the local school districts. Senate Bill 1 of 1995, perhaps the most significant reform bill of the last half century, reversed the earlier trend and assigned more authority to the Commissioner, more autonomy to the districts, and restricted that of the State Board. The more power assigned to the independent school districts and the Commissioner has been accompanied by the imposition of an almost airtight accountability system focusing on student achievement. The State Board of Education is the subject of Chapter 2.

Commissioner of Education

The Commissioner of Education is appointed by the Governor, with the advice and consent of the Texas Senate, for a four-year term. The commissioner is the chief executive officer of the Texas Education Agency, the administrative arm of the public education establishment at the state level. During the period of time when the power over public education

TABLE 2

1,042 School Districts/19 Charters			
District Size	Number of Students	Number of Districts	% of All Students
50,000 and Over	817,405	9	21.0%
25,000–49,999	860,794	24	22.1%
10,000–24,999	749,838	47	19.3%
5,000–9,999	447,769	68	11.5%
3,000–4,999	325,693	84	8.4%
1,600–2,999	285,305	131	7.3%
1,000–1,599	156,150	122	4.0%
500–999	155,484	212	4.0%
Under 500	93,439	364	2.4%
Total	3,891,877	1,061	100.0%
7,053 Campuses			
Campus Type	Number of Students	Number of Campuses	% of Total
High School	1,024,376	1,548	26.3%
Junior High School	231,253	386	5.9%
Middle School	612,581	982	15.7%
Elementary School	1,944,002	3,721	50.0%
Elem. & Secondary	79,665	416	2.0%
Total	3,891,877	7,053	100.0%

Source: Texas Education Agency, Snapshot 1998.

that was delegated the state government was at a high point, for example in 1995, the number of staff members of the bureaucracy at the state level was at 1,144 full-time equivalent, an issue to those who needed explanations and assistance to interpret their policies and requirements, i.e., the local school districts. At the turn of the century, TEA staff members number 834, the smallest number since 1974. With legislative "sunset" directives, State Board of Education rules have been reduced by 55%. According to TEA goals, three principles define the agency's restructured role and operations:

- Fewer employees, with the agency staff clearly focused on its mission and the state goals for public education
- Fewer rules, with the agency working with the State Board to produce a less restrictive environment for local educators
- Fewer burdens on school districts, with the agency reducing paperwork requirements and encouraging innovation at the local level

With a smaller staff and less state regulation over school districts, the TEA has managed to rank high among the states in the amount of state funds received and state funds retained for TEA expenses. The same holds true for federal funds flowing to the state.

The Commissioner also serves as the executive secretary of the State Board of Education. State law delegates the Commissioner with the title of educational leader of the state. In addition, the Commissioner proposes or adopts budgets, reviews and may grant waivers to school districts for exceptions to certain state laws and regulations, and enforces the accountability system, which includes sanctioning low-performing school campuses and districts. The Commissioner, in response to a statutory assignment, has developed an appraisal system for teachers, the Professional Development Appraisal System (PDAS), which is described in Section IV. Over 90% of the state's school districts have adopted the Commissioner's PDAS. Reviewing the 40-some delegations of authority to the Commissioner in

TABLE 3

District Staff by Category			
Category	Full-Time Equivalents	Average Reg. Duty Salary	Average Total Salary
Teachers	254,558	$33,537	$34,133
Campus Administrators	12,287	$52,030	$52,247
Central Administrators	4,139	$62,946	$63,163
Professional Support	33,670	$40,713	$40,962
Total Professionals	304,654	$35,476	$36,015
Educational Aides	48,626	$12,336	$12,406
Auxiliary Staff	136,677	$15,647	$15,647
Total Staff	491,957	$27,601	$27,940

Teacher Profiles		
	Full-Time Equivalents	% of Total
Gender		
Males	57,671	22.7%
Females	196,887	77.3%
Ethnicity		
African American	20,754	8.2%
Hispanic	40,226	15.8%
White	191,485	75.2%
Other	2,093	0.8%
Highest Degree Held		
No Degree	2,473	1.0%
Bachelor's	185,887	73.0%
Master's	65,133	25.6%
Doctorate	1,064	0.4%

Source: Texas Education Agency, Snapshot 1998.

Senate Bill 1 of 1995 and subsequent legislation, it is probably fair to conclude that the legislature preferred to place more authority in a Commissioner appointed by the Governor than in members of the elected State Board of Education. In recent years, the Commissioner's power over public education has become second only to that of the Legislature.

The Commissioner's authority to waive certain statutory and administrative law requirements of school districts is substantial. During the 1998 fiscal year, the Commissioner granted over 2,000 general state waivers. The most frequently requested waiver is for a district to modify its calendar to make additional time for staff development. Types of waiver granted by the Commissioner are listed in Table 4.

Education Service Centers

Although not technically part of the education governance structure, Regional Education Service Centers (ESCs) do provide services at the direction of the Commissioner. With a 1997 change in the Texas Edu-

TABLE 4   Waivers Granted by the Commissioner

Type	Number
Staff Development	631
Course Requirement	384
Certification	132
Modified Schedule	89
Staff Development For Reading/Language Arts	95
Gifted/Talented	54
Student Attendance	35
Early Release Days	384
Other Misc. Waivers	236
Total	**2,040**

Source: Texas Education Agency.

cation Code, the purposes of the ESCs were redefined as follows. "Regional education service centers shall: 1. assist school districts in improving student performance in each region of the state; 2. enable school districts to operate more efficiently and economically; and 3. implement initiatives assigned by the legislature or the commissioner." ESCs are prohibited from performing a regulatory function regarding a school district, more evidence of the Legislature's attempts to hold districts accountable but to remove as much external regulation as possible.

According to ESC literature, centers provide an array of services to school districts. In support of school administration, they provide services in areas such as computer support for business and student services, administrator training, bus driver training, and cooperative purchasing. Centers also provide a wide range of curriculum improvement and staff development opportunities for teachers. Technical assistance and training in instructional technology, programs for special populations, and staff development in instructional improvement are the most common. Centers may operate cooperatives among school districts for programs such as drug abuse prevention, migrant education, accelerated schools, and adult education.

Each ESC is governed by a seven-member lay board who are elected by members of local school district boards of trustees in each region. The state provides 26% and local school districts provide 34% of the ESC operating budget. Through grants and contracts, the remaining 40% comes from federal sources. A directory of the 20 education service centers follows this overview.

Independent School Districts

The Texas Education Code (TEC) in Section 11.151 (b) states that "The trustees as body corporate have the exclusive power and duty to govern and oversee the management of the public schools of the district." Following that pronouncement is the "reserved powers" directive that "All powers and duties not specifically delegated by statute to the agency or to the State Board of Education are reserved for the trustees, and the agency may not substitute its judgment for the lawful exercise of those powers and duties by the trustees." The powers and duties of Superintendents and Principals are also specified in (TEC) Section 11 and will be described in more detail in Chapter 1. Also included in Chapter 1 is a discussion of the relatively new level of educational governance, the "grass roots" campus site–based decision making committees. State law also requires the involvement of a district level committee.

State Board for Educator Certification

Senate Bill 1 of 1995 created a new entity of governance in the State Board for Educator Certification (SBEC). The SBEC replaced the former Commission on Standards for the Teaching Profession. Thirteen of the 15 members of SBEC are appointed by the governor from the following categories: four as teacher representatives, five as citizen representatives, two as school administrator representatives, one counselor representative, and one non-voting dean of a college of education representative. The Commissioner of Education appoints one non-voting member from the staff of the Texas Education Agency (TEA) and the Commissioner of Higher Education appoints one member from the staff of the Texas Higher Education Coordinating Board (THECB). This new board is charged with the responsibility of overseeing all aspects of educator certification, continuing professional development, and enforcement of the Code of Ethics and Standard Practices for Texas Educators.

Specifically, SBEC works with 70 institutions of higher education, 28 alternative teacher certification programs, and six alternative administrator certification programs in the areas of program development, approval, and implementation. The Examination for the Certification of Educators in Texas (ExCET) also falls under SBEC responsibility. Accountability for educator certification likewise rests with the State Board for Educator Certification. The SBEC must submit a copy of each rule it proposes to adopt to the State Board of Education (SBOE) for review. The SBOE may reject a proposed rule by a vote of at least two-thirds of the members present and voting. If the SBOE fails to reject a proposal before the 90th day after the date on which it receives the proposal, the proposal takes effect as a rule and is stated as such in the administrative code. The SBOE may not modify a proposal from the SBEC. SBEC may receive more authority and autonomy in future legislative sessions. SBEC is the subject of Chapter 3, which includes the Code of Ethics and Standard Practices for the Education Profession.

By Texas Constitutional delegation, clearly the most powerful and influential entity in Texas public education is the State Legislature, and session after session the elected members of both houses express their preferences in statutes that provide for more local control and greater accountability for results. Year after year the professional educators of the state plead for more financial support and less state regulations, or as former Lt. Governor Bill Hobby has frequently stated in his advice to members of the Texas Legislature, "just say no to new school regulation."

EDUCATION LAW

Once thought to be a subject of interest only to school attorneys, administrators, local board of education members, and legislators, education law is now of special interest to teachers, students, parents, and the community in general. The news media has developed a special interest in school law just as it has in other highly sensitive areas. In addition to examples of constitutional and statutory law presented above, education law also includes legal precedents established by court decisions and administrative laws created by the State Board and local boards of education. Education law provides the framework for the operation of public education from the State Capitol to the classroom. Texas education statutory law is codified in the Texas Education Code (TEC), which can be found in the Texas School Law Bulletin. The Bulletin is revised every other year following the adjournment of the biennial session of the Texas Legislature. Also included in the Bulletin are excerpts from other "codes" that affect public education such as the Penal Code, the Family Code, Alcoholic Beverage Code, and Transportation Code. The Texas Constitution of 1876 is also reproduced in the Bulletin.

Trends in Education Law. Numerous attempts to determine whether education-related litigation is more or less frequent today than a decade or more ago haven't resulted in data reliable enough to be considered accurate for several reasons. It is recognized that litigants are more interested in compromising out of court than paying the frequently expensive legal fees required in a regular trial. Thus, most cases are "settled" on the courthouse steps or concluded in judgments before or in the early stages of the trial. For those cases that are formally concluded in court, a significant number are never reported. However, there a few discernible trends.

Special Education

There is ample evidence that the fastest-growing area of parent-school district litigation today is special education. The statutory laws and regulations created to implement them include the Individuals with Disabilities Education Act, formerly the Education for All Handicapped Children Act or Public Law 94–142, Section 504 of the Rehabilitation Act of 1973, and the Americans with Disabilities Act (ADA) of 1990. Parents with disabled children have prevailed in a number of cases involving appropriate education opportunities in the least restrictive school environment. One large Texas law firm that represents only public school districts utilizes over half of its attorneys exclusively in special education cases.

Sexual Harassment

Another area of increased litigation and certainly increased media attention is sexual harassment and, the most recent concern to school districts, the potential for liability for peer harassment. Sexual harassment in the public education context is prohibited by Title IX of the Education Amendments of 1972 (20 U.S.C. § 1681 a), which states:

> "No person in the United States shall, on the basis of sex, be excluded from participation in, be denied the benefits of, or be subjected to discrimination under any education program or activity receiving federal funds."

The United States Supreme Court has issued conflicting decisions as to whether a school district can be made to pay damages in the event that a principal, for example, suspected that a teacher and student had engaged in some form of sexual relationship but did not act to investigate or to stop the relationship; that is, acted with deliberate indifference. In the 1998 Supreme Court decision in *Gebser v. Lago Vista Independent School District* the district was not held liable because it could not be proved that any employee of the district was aware of a sexual relationship between an eighth-grade girl and a Lago Vista High School male teacher. Beyond the decision to not hold the district liable was the opinion that if it had been liable, the government's punishment would be limited to a warning of or actual withdrawal of federal funds. That is, the district would not be liable for compensatory or punitive damages. A dissenting Justice observed that the Court's decision ranked the school district's purses above the protection of immature students. In other than public school contexts, the analogous sexual harassment law is Title VII of the Civil Rights Act of 1964. In 1999 the U.S. Supreme Court, in Davis *v.* Monroe County School District, held that a district could be liable when an elementary student sexually harassed a classmate. Sexual harassment is the subject of Chapter 10.

Religion in the Schools

Religion attracts media attention in regards to the school's role in upholding the separation of church and state provided for in the First Amendment to the U.S. Constitution, which states "Congress shall make no law respecting an establishment of religion, or prohibiting the free exercise thereof." Since the Fourteenth Amendment holds the states to the same requirements, the U.S. Supreme Court has periodically ruled on cases in which the schools and parents disagree on what the two clauses, establishment and free exercise, mean in their particular circumstances. For more than half a century these judicial decisions have both clarified and confused what can and can't be legally defensible religious practices in the school context. In relatively homogeneous communities where all or most religious denominations are at least Christian, disagreements may be minimal. When the school enrolls Buddhists, Hindus, Muslims, Jews, Christians, and others, as many do, a stricter adherence to the law is essential. During the Spring of 1995 representatives from each of the major religious groups and interested others, including the American Civil Liberties Union, developed guidelines for public schools entitled "Religion in the Public Schools: A Joint Statement of Current Law." The U.S. Department of Education incorporated those guidelines into recommendations for schools to follow. Those guidelines are summarized below in Table 5.

Educator Liability

Texas public school educators enjoy a degree of statutory immunity from personal liability while performing their professional responsibilities. Chapter 22.051 of the Texas Education Code states that a professional "employee of a school district is not personally liable for any act that is incident to or within the scope of the duties of the employee's position of employment and that involves the exercise of judgment or discretion on the part of the employee, except in circumstances in which a professional employee uses excessive force in the discipline of students or negligence resulting in bodily injury to students." Professionals, as defined by this Chapter of the TEC, include superintendents, principals, teachers, supervisors, social workers, counselors, nurses, teachers' aides, certified bus drivers, college students enrolled in teacher preparation programs and participating in field experiences or internships, and others whose employment requires certification and the exercise of discretion. This immunity does not apply to the operation, use, or maintenance of any motor vehicle.

Texas educators should not believe that Texas statutory immunity ensures that they will never be held liable for negligence or poor judgment. Volume 42, United States Code, § 1983 states the "Every person who, *under color* of any statute, ordinance, regulation, custom, or usage, of any State or Territory, subjects or causes to be subjected, any citizen of the United States or other person within the jurisdiction thereof to the deprivation of any rights, privileges, or immunities secured by the Constitution and laws, shall be liable to the party injured in an action at law, suit in equity, or other proper proceeding for redress." Educators, as employees of the districts and the State, are under "color of law," which means that they are perceived as and in fact are representing the government and must act accordingly. Society has little sympathy or patience with professional employees of the government who enjoy degrees of immunity from civil liability and who violate the public's trust. Beyond public employees such as police officers or tax collectors, the public's tolerance of educators who under "color of law" take advantage of immature students who are taught to respect them is abbreviated or nonexistent. And, just because a teacher, for example, engages in behavior that is not illegal does not mean that the teacher will not be terminated for good cause or simply nonrenewed.

The 1998–1999 academic year recorded some of the most tragic events in the recent history of American public education: students armed with guns and bombs killing other students and educators. The most dramatic incident being the deaths of 12 students, a teacher and the suicides of the 2 student assassins at Columbine High School in the affluent community of Littleton, Colorado in April 1999. This incident followed a number of lesser but still frightening shootings of classmates by students in several states and one reported incident in Canada. "Copycat" incidents detected or suspected and a spate of disruptive bomb threats brought the end of the Spring 1999 semester to a dramatic and even earlier-than-planned conclusion. Observers of these outbursts of violence began to refer to them as either B.C. or A.C., i.e., before Columbine and after Columbine. A flurry of legislative bills proposing limitations on gun sales, gun safety devices, limiting Internet access to bomb making instruction and other measures crowded the U.S. Congress and many of the state legislatures in the days

TABLE 5   Guidelines for Religious Practice in Public Schools

Student prayer and religious discussion: [The U.S. Constitution] does not prohibit purely private religious speech by students. Students therefore have the same right to engage in individual or group prayer and religious discussion during the school day as they do to engage in other comparable activity.

Generally, students may pray in a nondisruptive manner when not engaged in school activities or instruction, and subject to the rules that normally pertain in the applicable setting.

The right to engage in voluntary prayer or religious discussion free from discrimination does not include the right to have a captive audience listen, or to compel other students to participate.

Graduation prayer: Under current [U.S.] Supreme Court decisions, school officials may not mandate or organize prayer at graduation nor organize religious baccalaureate ceremonies. If a school generally opens its facilities to private groups, it must make its facilities open on the same terms to organizers of privately sponsored religious baccalaureate services.

Official neutrality: Teachers and school administrators . . . are prohibited by the [Constitution] from soliciting or encouraging religious activity and from participating in such activity with students. Teachers and administrators also are prohibited from discouraging activity because of its religious content and from soliciting or encouraging anti-religious activity.

Teaching about religion: Public schools may not provide religious instruction, but they may teach about religion . . . the history of religion, comparative religion, the Bible (or other scripture) as literature, and the role of religion in the history of the United States and other countries are all permissible public school subjects.

Although public schools may teach about religious holidays . . . and may celebrate the secular aspects of holidays, schools may not observe holidays as religious events or promote such observance by students.

Student assignments: Students may express their beliefs about religion in the form of homework, artwork, and other written and oral assignments. . . . Such home and classroom work should be judged by ordinary academic standards.

Religious literature: Students have a right to distribute religious literature to their schoolmates on the same terms as they are permitted to distribute other literature that is unrelated to school curriculum or activities.

Religious exemptions: Schools enjoy substantial discretion to excuse individual students from lessons that are objectionable to the student or the student's parents or religious or other conscientious grounds.

Released time: Schools have the discretion to dismiss students to off-premises religious instruction, provided that schools do not encourage or discourage participation. . . . Schools may not allow religious instruction by outsiders on school premises during the school day.

Teaching values: Though schools must be neutral with respect to religion, they may plan an active role with respect to teaching civic values and virtue.

Student garb: Students may display religious messages on items of clothing to the same extent that they are permitted to display other comparable messages.

The Equal Access Act: Student religious groups have the same right of access to school facilities as is enjoyed by other comparable student groups. A school receiving federal funds must allow student groups meeting under the act to use the school media . . . to announce their meetings on the same terms as other noncurriculum-related student groups.

A school . . . trigger[s] equal-access rights for religious groups when it allows students to meet during their lunch periods or other noninstructional time during the school day, as well as when it allows students to meet before and after the school day.

Source: U.S. Department of Education, 1995.

following Columbine. From Hawaii to Montana to Florida and even the small town of Wimberly, Texas, elaborate plans to attack schools with guns and bombs were being investigated.

What remains to be determined is how liable is a school district and its teachers and administrators when these terrorist activities occur on their campuses. Thus far school districts have prevailed in their immunity from compensatory and punitive damages. However, what may materialize is a greater burden for professional educators to report the "signs" of

irrational or destructive behavior whether that behavior is manifested in a student's written composition, choosing bomb-making as a topic for a "how to" presentation in speech class or in other ways. The summer of 1999 was a much needed respite for students, parents, educators, and law enforcement agencies. This time was needed to rethink security arrangements within and surrounding the schools as well as the degree of liability for these tragic acts that reasonably must be assumed by school boards and employees of the school district.

Discipline

Student discipline is frequently cited as the most important problem or challenge to the effectiveness of public schools. Disrespectful behavior of students toward teachers, especially new or relatively new teachers, may very well be one of the most important reasons many of these teachers leave the profession after just a few years. Disrespectful behavior toward classmates continues to increase. Statewide, there were nearly 60,000 student assaults in 1997–1998 compared to 51,000 three years earlier. Enforcement of strict "zero tolerance" policies regarding school district expectations of students may be one of the reasons that students drop out of the public schools, although this hypothesis remains unproved. The Texas Education Code requires that each independent school district adopt a student "code of conduct," which must be posted and prominently displayed at each school campus. Chapter 37 of the Texas Education Code provides the statutory requirements for school discipline policies and is the substance of Chapter 8. Appended to Chapter 8 is a sample Student Code of Conduct adopted by one of the larger school districts of the State. The sample code of conduct is an example of how the sometimes confusing language of statutory law can be simplified by professional educators to school district policies in language that principals, teachers, students, and parents can understand and apply. Chapter 9 features classroom management, the "nitty-gritty" of applying discipline management theory and state and local regulations to the daily routine of the classroom.

Child Abuse and Neglect

Probably not commonly known is the legal obligation of any "... person who has cause to believe that a child's physical or mental welfare has been adversely affected by abuse or neglect by any person shall immediately make a report ..." to the Child Protective Services Division of the Department of Protective and Regulatory Services or to any local or state law enforcement agency. Following the statement above in Chapter 261–101 of the Texas Family Code is a higher standard for professionals, i.e., "If a professional has cause to believe that a child has been or may be abused, the professional shall make a report not later than the 48th hour after the hour the professional first suspects that the child has been or may be abused or neglected." Further, a professional "... may not delegate to or rely on another person to make the report ..." A professional as defined in the Family Code includes teachers, nurses, doctors, day care employees, probation officers,

school administrators, counselors, juvenile detention or correctional officers, and any others who must be licensed or certified to practice by the state. Reports should include the name and address of the child and of the person responsible for the care, custody or welfare of the child and any other pertinent information regarding the suspected abuse or neglect. Failure to report is a Class B misdemeanor punishable by a fine up to $2,000 and/or up to 180 days in jail. The Family Code shown in Table 6 defines abuse and neglect.

Districts may set their own policies within the requirements of the law. For example, one district requires that a teacher notify the campus principal when abuse or neglect is suspected and then file the official report. The principal can not relieve the teacher of the teacher's obligation and, once notified, the principal is bound to report as well. If the principal calls the school district attorney, the attorney also assumes a duty to report.

School law is the subject of Chapter 1.

ACCOUNTABILITY

During the early 1990s, the Texas Legislature directed the State Board of Education to develop a system for determining progress in student achievement, i.e., product or output instead of input or, as some have suggested, the "staff and stuff" of a school district or campus, the traditional criteria utilized in accrediting school districts. From these legislative directives the Academic Excellence Indicator System (AEIS) was produced, with performance indicators that could be used to measure student achievement on the Texas Assessment of Academic Skills (TAAS), attendance rates, and dropout rates. In addition to the those "base" indicators, "additional" indicators include scores from college admissions tests and "report only" results from science and social studies TAAS tests as well as end-of-course examinations, advanced academic courses, and Advanced Placement examinations.

The Public Education Information System (PEIMS) has been streamlined during the first fifteen years of use, and now this computerized data collection and reporting provides state auditors an opportunity for most school districts to be accredited by way of a "paper" or "desk" audit, i.e., if AEIS results are satisfactory, there is no compelling reason for a site visit. Accreditation visits, once mandatory for all school districts, are now conducted only when districts or campuses fail to meet state standards for student performance, dropout rate, and attendance or every five years as is the case with District Effectiveness and Compliance reviews.

TABLE 6   Texas Family Code, Section 261.001

(1)"Abuse" includes the following acts or omissions by any person:

(A) mental or emotional injury to a child that results in an observable and material impairment in the child's growth, development, or psychological functioning;

(B) causing or permitting the child to be in a situation in which the child sustains a mental or emotional injury that results in an observable and material impairment in the child's growth, development, or psychological function;

(C) physical injury that results in substantial harm to the child, or the genuine threat of substantial harm from physical injury to the child, including an injury that is at variance with the history or explanation given and excluding an accident or reasonable discipline by a parent, guardian, or managing or possessing conservator that does not expose the child to a substantial risk of harm;

(D) failure to make a reasonable effort to prevent an action by another person that results in physical injury that results in substantial harm to the child;

(E) sexual contact, sexual intercourse, or sexual conduct, as those terms are defined by § 43.01 of the Texas Penal Code, sexual penetration with a foreign object, incest, sexual assault, or sodomy inflicted on, shown to, or intentionally practiced in the presence of a child, if the child is present only to arouse or gratify the sexual desires of any person;

(F) failure to make a reasonable effort to prevent sexual contact, sexual intercourse, or sexual conduct, as those terms are defined by § 43.01 of the Texas Penal Code, sexual penetration with a foreign object, incest, sexual assault or sodomy being inflicted on or shown to a child by another person, or intentionally practiced in the presence of a child by another person, if the child is present only to arouse or gratify the sexual desires of any person;

(G) compelling or encouraging the child to engage in sexual conduct as defined by § 43.01 of the Texas Penal Code; or

(H) causing, permitting, encouraging, engaging in, or allowing the photographing, filming, or depicting of the child if the person knew or should have known that the resulting photograph, film, or depiction of the child is obscene (as defined by the Texas Penal Code) or pornographic.

(2) "Neglect" includes:

(A) the leaving of a child in a situation where the child would be exposed to a substantial risk of harm, without arranging for the necessary care for the child, and a demonstration of an intent not to return by a parent, guardian, or managing or possessory conservator of the child;

(B) the following acts or omissions by any person:

(i) placing the child or failing to remove the child from a situation that a reasonable person would realize requires judgment or actions beyond the child's level of maturity, physical condition or mental abilities, and that results in bodily injury or a substantial risk of immediate harm to the child;

(ii) the failure to seek, obtain or follow through with medical care for the child, with the failure resulting in or presenting a substantial risk of death, disfigurement or bodily injury, or with the failure resulting in an observable and material impairment to the growth, development, or functioning of the child; or

(iii) the failure to provide the child with food, clothing, or shelter necessary to sustain the life or health of the child, excluding failure caused primarily by financial inability unless relief services had been offered and refused; or

(C) the failure by the person responsible for a child's care, custody, or welfare to permit the child to return to the child's home without arranging for the necessary care for the child after the child has been absent from the home for any reason, including having been in residential placement or having run away.

District Effectiveness and Compliance (DEC) visits, on the other hand, are "preventive" in nature and are conducted on a five-year cycle for every district. In addition to monitoring compliance with state and federal mandates, DEC evaluations review the quality and effectiveness of district programs for all student populations, including those in bilingual education/English as a second language, career and technology education, migrant education, special education, and accelerated education.

Based on the assumption that all students can learn, the results of student performance on the TAAS are reported for individual student populations, i.e., results are disaggregated to reveal how African American, Hispanic, white, other, and economically disadvantaged as well as special education students are achieving. Prior to this practice, an overall passing rate of all students in most districts was sufficient even though students from some groups performed poorly. Current practice dictates

TABLE 7

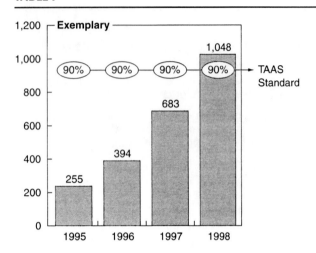

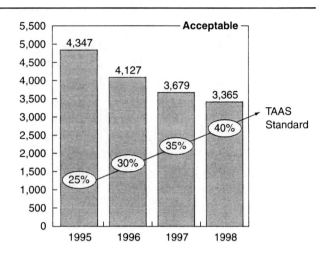

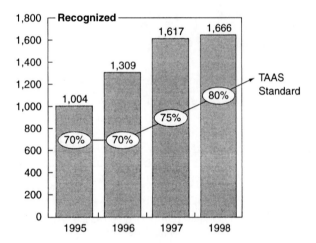

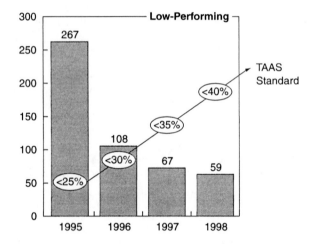

Source: Texas Education Agency.

that when a given number of students in any one of the groups score below expectations, the campus rating suffers. Alternative Education Programs (AEP) are evaluated separately with results either acceptable, needing peer review or not rated.

At the turn of the century, it appears that this higher standard for all groups in all districts has resulted in positive gains. Table 7 records the changes in TAAS scores over a four-year period, and Table 8 records the campus and district accreditation ratings. What remains unanswered is the addition of special education students to the TAAS requirements. Chapter 5 explains the Academic Excellence Indicator System. Chapter 6 provides a "consumer's guide" to AEIS.

SCHOOL CHOICE

The general issues of school choice of public school campuses within school districts is relatively simple

and rarely controversial, unless racial quotas are required. For example, parents may request that their child attend an elementary school where technology is emphasized or a "magnet" high school in which health occupations or fine arts programs are featured. A school district's provision for these special interest campuses may be motivated by the need to desegregate or to consolidate the expertise and special facilities necessary to accomplish specific objectives. When district school boards and administrators consider requests from parents for such transfers, decisions are relatively simple and without controversy. Intradistrict transfers are relatively common.

Parents of children attending "low-performing" schools, defined as those in which 50% or more of the students performed poorly on a TAAS in any two of the previous three years or that in the preceding three years were identified as low-performing by the Commissioner, are eligible to receive a public educa-

TABLE 8

as of November 1, 1998

Campus Ratings	1995	1996	1997	1998
Exemplary	225	394	683	1,048
Recognized	1,004	1,309	1,617	1,666
Acceptable	4,347	4,127	3,679	3,365
Low-Performing	267	108	67	59
Alternative Campus Ratings		1996	1997	1998
Acceptable		157	285	316
Needing Peer Review		106	46	67
District Ratings	1995	1996	1997	1998
Exemplary	14	37	65	120
Recognized	137	209	321	329
Acceptable	860	788	650	585
Academically Unacceptable	34	8	4	6
Academically Unacceptable: SAI		2	3	2

Source: Texas Education Agency.

tion grant (PEG), which allows them to place their children in another school district. However, with many districts, frequently with high levels of student achievement, space needs do not permit the acceptance of PEG students. More about this topic is provided in Chapter 1.

Texas parents were able to choose charter schools after the Texas legislature authorized creation of these alternative schools under three different arrangements: home rule school districts (none have been approved thus far), campus or program charters (far fewer than expected have been approved by local school districts to date), and a minimum of 160 open enrollment charters, which have been approved by statutory law with specific applications requiring approval by the State Board of Education. At the beginning of 1999, the State Board had approved 159 open enrollment charters serving an estimated 11,500 students. Charter schools are the subject of Chapter 7. At the beginning of 1999, characteristics of approved charter schools were as indicated in Table 9.

The issuance of vouchers to parents who can cash them in at the campus of their choice has gained popularity in recent years. Although there are a number of "hot button" issues in public education, vouchers are close to the top and among the most divisive. For example, if the average per-student cost of public education is $5,500, parents would receive a voucher in that amount for each eligible child and could submit or cash in that voucher on the first day of school at the campus of choice, public, private, or even sectarian. Texas court decisions in 1987, and the Texas Supreme Court's decision in *Texas Education Agency v. Leeper* in 1994, held that home schools can be considered private schools, which suggests that a home schooling mother could pick up $5,500 and deposit it her personal bank account. These and other issues have yet to be resolved, although a voucher plan for economically disadvantaged students in Milwaukee, in operation since 1992 and including sectarian schools, was upheld by the Wisconsin Supreme Court in 1998. The majority of the Wisconsin Supreme Court agreed that the voucher law did not violate the establishment clause of the First Amendment. Other favorable aspects of the law, according to the court, included (1) provision for aid to a broad class of students, not merely adding religious schools to a range of pre-existing educational choices, (2) student eligibility was based on nonsectarian criteria, and (3) the aid was paid directly to the student and not the school, subject to the parents' individual choices. The U.S. Supreme Court refused to review the case, leaving intact vouchers in Wisconsin, which has become a model for duplication by other states. For example, Florida's legislature approved a state-wide voucher program in 1999.

As proponents of vouchers promise, vouchers would bring an end to the stagnant monopoly of public education and create a competitive and creative

TABLE 9   Approved Charters

	Regular Charters	Charters Serving At-Risk Students
Number Approved by SBOE:	117	42
Number in Operation:	55	0
Enrollment:	11,520	0

Characteristics of Charter Schools in Operation

	State*	Charter Schools
STUDENTS		
Ethnicity		
African American	14.4%	36.3%
Hispanic	37.9%	40.7%
White	45.0%	20.7%
Other	2.7%	2.3%
Special Populations		
At-Risk	36.9%	61.2%
Special Education	12.0%	7.4%
Bilingual/ESL	11.%	7.3%
Gifted/Talented	8.0%	3.4%
STAFF		
Ethnicity		
African American	8.2%	26.6%
Hispanic	15.8%	20.1%
White	75.2%	49.8%
Other	0.8%	2.6%
Certification		Yes–48%
		No–52%

*Source: State data from Public Education Information Management System, 1997–98.

free-market system for the delivery of education. They believe that vouchers would equalize educational opportunity, reform school finance, facilitate desegregation, and improve education for low-income and minority children. It is probably not possible to be either pro- or anti-voucher because vouchers can be adapted to serve many ends. And vouchers for parents to select from only public education campuses removes the controversy of government aid to a religious school. More on this is provided in Chapter 1.

The 1980s and 1990s were years of dramatic changes, some heralded as reforms, in Texas and throughout the nation. Prompted or spurred by the report entitled "A Nation at Risk," in 1983, the federal and state governments responded with the passion of the post-Sputnik years, which introduced the 1960s with revolutions in civil rights legislation, revolt against the Vietnam War, and the implementation of dramatic new role for the federal government in programs such as the Elementary and Secondary Education Act of 1965. In Texas, the Legislature attempted and sometimes abandoned programs such as the teacher career ladder, which rewarded fewer and fewer teachers as the pyramid narrowed. Attempts to standardize a state evaluation system were introduced, modified, and continued with changing emphases. In the face of teacher shortages, alternatives to traditional college and university-based teacher certification programs were initiated. Attention to and abolition of social promotion became politically popular despite the psychological consequences. A truly significant legislative advancement was to limit class size to 22 students to 1 teacher in the primary grades. The "no pass–no play," requirement prioritized academics over extracurricular activities but also has had a downside in the pressure placed on teachers to make exceptions in their grading of needed-to-win athletes "in the best interests of the school." Legislative mandates for discipline management programs, for alternative education placements and programs for students with behavior problems either in or outside of the school environment, for the authority of teachers to get rid of constantly disruptive students, site-based decision making, technology allotments to the district from the state treasury, and prekindergarten programs have been giant steps forward and, in many cases, positive examples and models for other states to emulate.

Section One is concluded with a new addition to this edition of the text. "Education Vital Signs" is prepared annually by the editors of *The American School Board Journal* with a target audience of local school board members, administrators, and interested others from around the nation. This most recent report acknowledges the "hot topics" of, for example; a new teacher shortage that is not likely to subside, safe schools following shootings by troubled adolescents in Arkansas, Kentucky, Mississippi, Oregon, and Colorado the status of student achievement including international comparisons made available with the Third International Mathematics and Science Study (TIMSS), and other demographics including state-by-state comparisons on enrollments, expenditures, teacher salaries, per-pupil expenditures and a myriad of other information. Vital Signs is featured in Chapter 11.

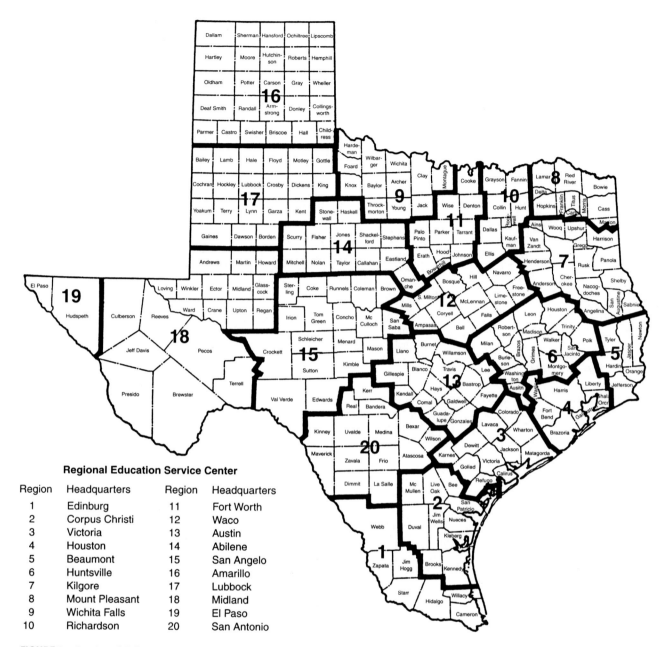

Regional Education Service Center

Region	Headquarters	Region	Headquarters
1	Edinburg	11	Fort Worth
2	Corpus Christi	12	Waco
3	Victoria	13	Austin
4	Houston	14	Abilene
5	Beaumont	15	San Angelo
6	Huntsville	16	Amarillo
7	Kilgore	17	Lubbock
8	Mount Pleasant	18	Midland
9	Wichita Falls	19	El Paso
10	Richardson	20	San Antonio

FIGURE 1 Regional Education Service Centers

Region I
Education Service Center
1900 West Schunior
Edinburg, Texas 78539
Telephone: (512) 383-5611

Region II
Education Service Center
209 North Water Street
Corpus Christi, Texas 78401
Telephone: (512) 883-9288

Region III
Education Service Center
1905 Leary Lane
Victoria, Texas 77901
Telephone: (512) 573-0731

Region IV
Education Service Center
7145 W. Tidwell
Houston, Texas 77092
Telephone: (713) 462-7708

Region V
Education Service Center
2295 Delaware Street
Beaumont, Texas 77703
Telephone: (713) 835-5212

Region VI
Education Service Center
Route 2, Box 33A
Huntsville, Texas 77340
Location: FM 1374
(Possum Walk Road)
Telephone: (713) 295-9161

Region VII
Education Service Center
P.O. Drawer 1622
Kilgore, Texas 75662
Location: 818 East Main St.
Telephone: (214) 984-3071

Region VIII
Education Service Center
P.O. Box 1894
Mt. Pleasant, Texas 75455
Telephone: (903) 572-8551

Region IX
Education Service Center
P.O. Box 4417
Wichita Falls, Texas 76305
Location: 301 Loop 11
Telephone: (817) 322-6928

Region X
Education Service Center
P.O. Box 831300
Richardson, Texas 75083
Location: 400 E. Spring Valley Rd.
Telephone: (214) 231-6301

Region XI
Education Service Center
3001 North Freeway
Fort Worth, Texas 76106
Telephone: (817) 625-5311

Region XII
Education Service Center
P.O. Box 1249
Waco, Texas 76703
Telephone: (817) 756-7494

Region XIII
Education Service Center
5701 Springdale
Austin, Texas 78723
Telephone: (512) 929-1313

Region XIV
Education Service Center
Rt. 1, Box 70A
Abilene, Texas 79601
Telephone: (915) 676-8201

Region XV
Education Service Center
P.O. Box 5199
San Angelo, Texas 76903
Telephone: (915) 658-6571

Region XVI
Education Service Center
P.O. Box 30600
Amarillo, Texas 79120
Location: 1601 South Cleveland
Telephone: (806) 376-5521

Region XVII
Education Service Center
1111 West Loop 289
Lubbock, Texas 79416
Telephone: (806) 792-4000

Region XVIII
Education Service Center
P.O. Box 60580
Midland, Texas 79711
Telephone: (915) 563-2380

Region XIX
Education Service Center
6611 Boeing Drive
El Paso, Texas 79997
Telephone: (915) 779-3737

Region XX
Education Service Center
1314 Hines Avenue
San Antonio, Texas 78208
Telephone: (512) 299-2400

FIGURE 2   Education Service Centers Directory

CHAPTER 1

Overview of Texas Education Law

IN THIS CHAPTER, we begin by examining the sources of school law and describing the basic roles of the state and federal governments in the establishment and operation of the Texas school system. We also look at how the legislature restructured the Texas schooling system in 1995 and review the culmination of the long-running lawsuit over the financing of Texas schools. The chapter ends by examining parent rights, including the right to have their children educated in another district, in private schools, or at home.

SOURCES OF LAW

Constitutional Law

Since education is not a power specifically delegated to the federal government by the U.S. Constitution, it is a state function. The Tenth Amendment to the Constitution declares that all powers not delegated to the federal government are reserved to the states. This amendment gives state governments their traditional power over schools. Viewing the school as an important socialization device, states gradually expanded public education in the nineteenth century. By 1918 all states had compulsory school laws.

Reprinted with permission from THE EDUCATOR'S GUIDE TO TEXAS SCHOOL LAW, 4th Edition, by Frank Kemerer and Jim Walsh, Copyright © 1996. Courtesy of the University of Texas Press.

It is important to note that states do not have to set up public school systems. The U.S. Supreme Court decided in a 1973 case, *San Antonio I.S.D. v. Rodriguez*, that education is not a fundamental right available to all persons. When a state decides to provide public education, as all the states have done, it has established an important benefit, which, as we will see later, it cannot take away from students without following due process procedures.

Consistent with the Tenth Amendment, the Texas Constitution of 1876 establishes the legal basis for a public school system in the state. Section I of Article VII reads: "A general diffusion of knowledge being essential to the preservation of the liberties and rights of the people, it shall be the duty of the legislature of the State to establish and make suitable provision for the support and maintenance of an efficient system of free public schools." The long-running Texas school finance case, *Edgewood I.S.D. v. Kirby*, centered on whether a finance system resulting in substantial inter-district disparities is "efficient" within the meaning of this constitutional provision.

Since the mid-1960s, the Bill of Rights and the Fourteenth Amendment to the U.S. Constitution also have furnished a basis for litigation against public schools. Claims to freedom of speech, press, religion, and association, due process, and other rights have a constitutional basis, just as the state's power to establish and operate schools stems from the Constitution. The Bill of Rights of the Texas Constitution, which protects many of these same civil liberties, also is being asserted more frequently in litigation against schools. Constitutional law at both the federal and state levels thus is an important source of education law.

Statutory Law

A *statute* is a law enacted by a legislative body. Most of the statutes passed by the Texas Legislature that directly affect education are grouped together in the Texas Education Code (TEC). The code is an important source of law because it applies to the daily operation of schools, detailing the responsibilities and duties of the State Board of Education (SBOE), the Texas Education Agency (TEA), school boards, and school personnel.

Since the early 1980s, the Texas Legislature has taken an increasing interest in improving an educational system that it regards as deficient. The result has been a plethora of reform laws. At first, the reforms were top-down in nature. For example, the legislature in 1981 mandated that all schools offer a well-balanced curriculum consisting of specifically designated subjects and in 1984 passed House Bill 72, a massive reform package that changed much of the operation of Texas public schools. By the late 1980s, the legislature began shifting authority and responsibility back to school districts and district personnel in the face of evidence that top-down mandates were having only marginal effects on increasing educational quality. Indeed, some commentators argued that the mandates were having a negative effect. In 1995 the legislature embarked on a complete reworking of the Texas Education Code—the first major overhaul since 1949. Not only did the legislature produce a more systematic, readable code, it took the opportunity to change, and in some cases streamline, many features of the Texas schooling system. Thus, the legislature significantly downsized TEA, gave local districts and school personnel more independence, and provided parents with more authority over the education of their children.

Many other state statutes besides the Texas Education Code affect the activities of the local schools, and we will discuss them in the succeeding chapters. One point worth emphasizing now is that, despite their essentially local character, public school districts are legally part of state government. The present system of some 1,045 Texas school districts and nearly 6,200 individual school campuses could be changed should the legislature desire, given the latter's authority over public education under the Texas Constitution.

Federal statutes also have significant influence over the operation of public schools in the state.

Some of the more important are described later in this chapter. Since establishing and operating schools is not a power that the U.S. Constitution delegates to the federal government, most federal laws affecting education are passed pursuant to the Congress's power to collect taxes and spend for the general welfare. As the late Supreme Court Justice William O. Douglas noted in a famous case, *Lau v. Nichols* (1974), "the Federal Government has power to fix the terms on which its money allotments . . . shall be disbursed" (p. 569). Thus, these laws contain the "strings" the federal government attaches to the use of its money. Schools receiving direct or indirect federal assistance must comply with the conditions the government attaches.

Administrative Law

A third, often overlooked, source of law is administrative law, which consists of the rules, regulations, and decisions that are issued by administrative bodies to implement state and federal statutory laws. Special education personnel, for example, are familiar with the extensive "regs" accompanying the Individuals with Disabilities Education Act, as developed by the administering agency, the Office of Special Education Programs. These regulations are designed by the implementing agency to apply the law to the realities of day-to-day schooling and of necessity must be quite detailed in order to eliminate as much ambiguity as possible. The length of a statute's regulations often exceeds that of the statute itself.

Administrative law also includes the rules and regulations that state agencies establish to carry out their responsibilities. When promulgating rules, administrative agencies are said to be acting in a quasi-legislative capacity. In the education context, this responsibility lies with the State Board of Education. The rules that it enacts are grouped together in volume 19 of the Texas Administrative Code (TAC). As a result of the downsizing of the Texas Education Agency in 1995 and the recodification of the Texas Education Code, the state board rules previously adopted had to be readopted or deleted in areas where state board authority was curtailed.

The policy manuals and handbooks developed by local school districts are excellent close-to-home examples of administrative law. TEC § 11.151(d) provides that school trustees "may adopt rules and by-laws necessary to carry out [their] powers and duties. . . ." Board policies and administrative directives represent the law of the district, and it is a condition of employment that all personnel observe them.

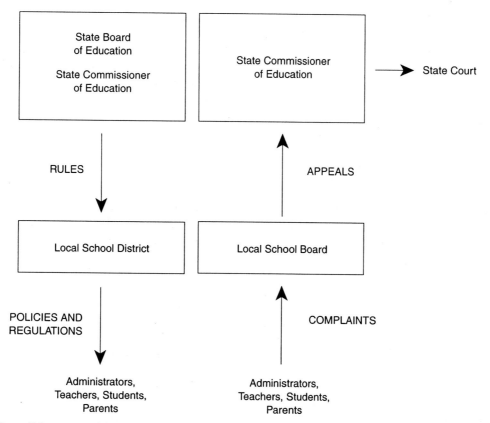

FIGURE 1   The Overall Structure of Texas Administrative Law

Administrative law also has a quasi-judicial character. State law provides that anyone aggrieved by the school laws of the state or the actions or decisions of any school district board of trustees that violate the school laws of the state or that violate a provision of a written employment contract, causing possible monetary harm to the employee, may appeal in writing to the commissioner of education (TEC § 7.057). This section does not apply to student disciplinary actions, however, nor to the termination or nonrenewal of professional employee contracts. These matters have their own appeal procedures. In the past, the majority of the cases appealed to the commissioner annually have involved certification and employment.

Before appealing to the commissioner, the person first must exhaust administrative remedies within the school district. As the commissioner noted in 1992, this includes seeking redress before the school board (*Havel v. Gonzales I.S.D.*). When the commissioner hears an appeal against an action or decision by a school district, the commissioner most often reviews the written record of the school district hearing to determine if there was substantial evidence to support the board's decision. In some instances, the commissioner conducts an evidentiary hearing and has much the same authority as a

state district judge to issue subpoenas, take depositions, and order production of documents in an effort to determine the facts. However, unlike those of a judge, the powers of the commissioner are limited to directing districts to comply with state law. The commissioner cannot issue restraining orders, assess fines, or order contested items removed from a personnel file. Also unlike a judge, the commissioner does not hear the cases personally. Rather, licensed attorneys acting as TEA hearing officers conduct the hearings and draft decisions for the commissioner to review and sign.

The commissioner has developed a set of rules governing these hearings and appeals in the interest of efficiency and fairness. Both the rules and the hearing decisions from the local board on up are classified as administrative law. Figure 1 illustrates the overall structure of Texas administrative law.

Judicial Law

A fourth source of law is composed of state and federal court decisions. When disputes arise under constitutions, statutes, and administrative law, some authority must have final say. The courts serve this function. As we have noted, when a person wants to contest a decision of a local school board, that person has a statutory right of appeal to the commissioner. If, after appeal to the commissioner, the matter still is not resolved to the appellant's satisfaction, that person may appeal to a district court in Travis County, Texas (TEC § 7.057(d)). As noted earlier, employment and student discipline appeals are handled differently.

Before filing an appeal in state district court, the aggrieved party must pursue administrative remedies. Courts generally refuse to become involved until all administrative remedies are exhausted. The reason for the exhaustion requirement is obvious. Administrative agencies are staffed by persons familiar with the educational setting and, theoretically, more qualified than judges to arrive at satisfactory and workable solutions to disputes that arise within that setting. In fact, judges are not educators and, generally, will be the first to admit that the resolution of educational disputes is best left to educational professionals. Further, the exhaustion requirement has the effect of channeling and resolving most conflicts before they reach the judiciary. Only approximately 10 percent of the cases filed with the Texas Commissioner of Education are appealed to state district court.

There are, however, exceptions to the general exhaustion requirement. For example, student expulsion decisions are not appealed to the commissioner but instead must be taken directly to the state district court of the county in which the school district's administration building is located (TEC § 37.009(f)). Further, in 1984 a Texas appeals court ruled that exhaustion of administrative remedies is required only when there is a factual question to resolve. When there are no facts in dispute or when a school board acts outside its statutory authority, a party may proceed directly to state district court without first pursuing administrative remedies before the commissioner of education (*Benavides I.S.D. v. Guerra*). Indeed, TEC § 7.057(b) recognizes that the commissioner appeal process is not intended to deprive a person of a legal remedy. As a practical matter, however, most disputes involve some factual questions, and the commissioner provides the initial forum for most litigation involving school laws and school district actions.

Regardless of whether litigation is filed initially in a state district court or as an appeal from a decision of the commissioner, the state court system plays an important role in the resolution of educational disputes. Therefore, it is important to review the composition of the Texas judiciary. District courts are the major trial courts in the state judicial system, having jurisdiction over major criminal and civil matters. From a district court, an appeal goes to one of the fourteen courts of appeal located throughout the

state and, finally, to the Texas Supreme Court. An appeal from a Travis County district court goes to the Third Court of Appeals in Austin. The Third Court, by virtue of its jurisdiction over appeals from the district courts of Travis County, has great influence over the development of educational and other public law matters. Only the Texas Supreme Court, however, can speak for the entire state in civil matters. For criminal matters, the highest court is the Texas Court of Criminal Appeals. Thus, in Texas we have two supreme courts, one concerned with civil matters and one with criminal matters.

Although the Texas judicial system provides a theoretically efficient structure for adjudicating disputes, frivolous lawsuits present a generally recognized problem. In an effort to deal with this problem, the legislature enacted two provisions providing that a person who files a frivolous lawsuit under state law against a school district or an officer or employee of the district who is pursuing official duties may be liable for court costs and the defendants' attorney fees (TEC §§ 11.161, 22.055). It is important to note, however, that state law provides specific protection for persons who report suspected violations of law.

If the matter in dispute involves a *federal question*, individuals often can avoid administrative law procedures and state courts altogether and go directly to a federal district court in the state. Federal questions are those involving some provision of the U.S. Constitution (e.g., freedom of speech), a federal statute, or a federal treaty. Since many disputes involve constitutional or federal statutory rights, the number of disputes going directly to the district courts in Texas's four federal judicial districts continues to increase. Figure 2 illustrates the geographic jurisdictions of the four Texas federal judicial districts.

The most important function of federal courts is to adjudicate disputes arising under the Constitution and statutes of the United States. As a general rule, disputes arising under state law must be tried in state courts. Decisions of the Texas federal district courts are appealable to the U.S. Court of Appeals for the Fifth Circuit in New Orleans, one of thirteen circuit courts in the nation. Prior to 1981, the Fifth Circuit encompassed six southern states and the Canal Zone. But the population growth in this region of the country convinced Congress to create another federal court of appeals—the Eleventh, with headquarters in Atlanta—to hear the increasing volume of cases coming from Georgia, Alabama, and Florida. The present jurisdiction of the Fifth Circuit includes Louisiana, Mississippi, and Texas. Decisions of the old Fifth Circuit constitute binding precedent in both the current Eleventh and Fifth circuits unless these courts decide to the contrary. On

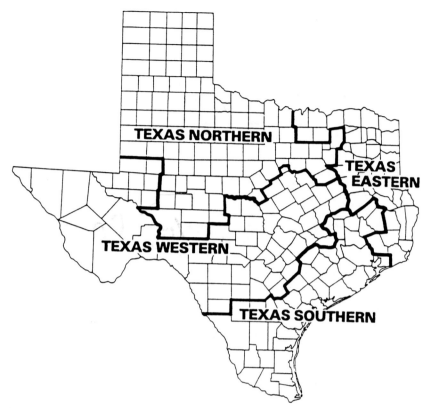

FIGURE 2   Geographic Jurisdiction of U.S. District Courts in Texas

occasion, a decision of the Fifth Circuit will be reviewed by the U.S. Supreme Court in Washington, D.C., which, of course, has the last word for the entire country. Unlike most other courts, the U.S. Supreme Court has the authority to decide which cases it wishes to hear. From as many as eight thousand cases filed annually for review, the justices will select fewer than two hundred for a full hearing. Thus, most federal questions are resolved by the U.S. Courts of Appeals. For this reason, the precedents established by the U.S. Courts of Appeals for the Fifth Circuit are particularly important in the context of Texas schooling.

One might assume that state and federal case law has relatively little impact on Texas public education, compared with state statutes and administrative rules and regulations. Up until the last twenty years or so, this was generally true. Since the late 1960s, however, courts have been increasingly involved in a maze of litigation involving the day-to-day management of schools. The rulings they hand down have become an important part of school law and are ignored at one's peril.

Other sources of law besides the four primary types discussed above also have an impact on education law. For example, contract law plays an important role in the context of employment. For our purposes,

however, separating school law into the four previously discussed types—constitutional, statutory, administrative, and judicial—will help us understand how the system works. Table 1 provides an outline of the four types, and Table 2 shows how they interrelate.

THE STRUCTURE AND GOVERNANCE OF THE TEXAS PUBLIC SCHOOL SYSTEM

Texas Legislature

The Texas Legislature, acting pursuant to the Tenth Amendment to the U.S. Constitution and Article VII of the Texas Constitution, is responsible for the structure and operation of the Texas public school system. The nearly continuous flow of reform legislation since 1980 makes it readily apparent that the legislature is the biggest player in Texas education. Thus, those wanting to influence the way Texas education is structured and conducted are well advised to focus their efforts on the Texas Legislature. Both school districts and educators are becoming increasingly sophisticated in this regard. However, TEC § 7.103(c) prevents a person who registers as a professional lobbyist from serving as a school board member or acting as the general counsel to the board.

TABLE 1   Basic Components of Texas Education Law

Types of Law	Source	Impact on Texas Schooling
Constitutional	Tenth Amendment to U.S. Constitution	States that "the powers not delegated to the United States by the Constitution, nor prohibited by it to the States, are reserved to the States respectively. . . Since education is not delegated to the federal government, it is a power reserved to the states.
	The Bill of Rights and the Fourteenth Amendment to the U.S. Constitution	Protects certain civil liberties of employees and students in the public schools.
	Texas Constitution of 1876, Art. 7, § 1 and Bill of Rights	Authorizes the state legislature to support and maintain an efficient system of public free schools and provides for individual civil liberties.
Statutory	Acts of the U.S. Congress	Acts of Congress guarantee various civil rights and establish the conditions upon which states and political subdivisions may receive federal funds.
	Acts of Texas Legislature; most pertaining to education are found in the Texas Education Code	Sets up the State Board of Education and the Texas Education Agency to carry out limited educational functions. Actual operation of schools is left to school districts. School districts and school personnel are a part of the state.
Administrative	Federal administrative regulations	Both TEA and local school districts must comply with the regulations promulgated by federal educational agencies implementing federal statutes.
	Policies and rulings by school boards, Texas Commissioner of Education, and State Board of Education	Boards of trustees develop policies to be utilized in operating their schools. State board and commissioner have the authority to establish rules that govern school district activity in areas designated by the legislature. Any person aggrieved by the school laws of Texas or actions of school districts involving school laws or impairing employment contracts can appeal to the commissioner. Policies, rules, and appeal decisions are classified as administrative law.
Judicial	Decisions of state courts	Any aggrieved person can appeal an adverse administrative ruling from the commissioner into state courts. Highest state court (civil) is the Texas Supreme Court, which has the last word on matters of state law, subject, of course, to the ultimate authority of the U.S. Supreme Court to review questions of state law in light of federal statutes and the U.S. Constitution.
	Decisions of federal courts	Any person alleging state interference with a right granted by the U.S. Constitution or federal law can bring an action in a federal court. The lowest federal court is the district court. There are thirteen intermediate appellate federal courts (ours is the U.S. Court of Appeals for the Fifth Circuit). At the top is the U.S. Supreme Court, which has the last word on matters of federal law. The U.S. Constitution provides that any state action, law, or constitutional provision that conflicts with the Constitution or a federal law is null and void.

State Board of Education and the Texas Education Agency

Formerly the policy-making body of the Texas Education Agency, the State Board of Education was separated from TEA by the Texas Legislature in 1995 and given a reduced role in the public school system. An elected body of fifteen members, the state board is limited to performing only those duties assigned to it by the state constitution or by the legislature. While many of its functions have shifted in recent years to the Texas Commissioner of Education, the state board is still a powerful entity. Among its designated duties as set forth in TEC § 7.102 are establishing a state curriculum and graduation requirements, determining the standard for satisfactory student performance on assessment instruments, adopting and purchasing state textbooks, adopting rules governing extracurricular activities, and investing the permanent school funds. The board is also charged with granting up to twenty charters for open-enrollment schools, a subject to be discussed later in the chapter, and adopting rules for the accreditation of school districts.

The Texas Education Agency is now composed of the Texas Commissioner of Education and the agency

TABLE 2   Relationship of Law to Establishment and Operation of Texas Public Schools

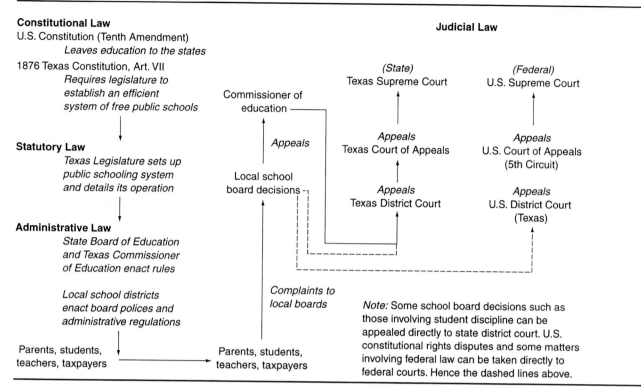

Constitutional Law

U.S. Constitution (Tenth Amendment)
Leaves education to the states

1876 Texas Constitution, Art. VII
Requires legislature to establish an efficient system of free public schools

Statutory Law

Texas Legislature sets up public schooling system and details its operation

Administrative Law

State Board of Education and Texas Commissioner of Education enact rules

Local school districts enact board polices and administrative regulations

Parents, students, teachers, taxpayers

Judicial Law

Commissioner of education

Appeals

Local school board decisions

Complaints to local boards

Parents, students, teachers, taxpayers

(State) Texas Supreme Court

Appeals Texas Court of Appeals

Appeals Texas District Court

(Federal) U.S. Supreme Court

Appeals U.S. Court of Appeals (5th Circuit)

Appeals U.S. District Court (Texas)

Note: Some school board decisions such as those involving student discipline can be appealed directly to state district court. U.S. constitutional rights disputes and some matters involving federal law can be taken directly to federal courts. Hence the dashed lines above.

---

staff. Like the state board, TEA can perform only those duties specifically assigned to it by the legislature. The legislature's disenchantment with top-down control is clearly evident in the wording of TEC § 7.003: "An educational function not specifically delegated to the agency or the board [of education] under this code is reserved to and shall be performed by school districts or open-enrollment charter schools." TEC § 7.021 lists fourteen educational functions that TEA is to perform. Included among them are monitoring district compliance with federal and state programs, conducting research to improve teaching and learning, developing a teacher recruitment program, and maintaining an electronic information system. TEA is also authorized to enter into agreements with federal agencies for such activities as school lunches and school construction. In addition, TEA administers the capital investment fund established by the legislature to provide grants to school districts for improving student achievement. With the downsizing of TEA has come a reduction in staff. By the start of the 1996–1997 school year, TEA will employ 889 people, down nearly 200 from the year before.

Other than the legislature, the most powerful state-level player is the Texas Commissioner of Education, whom the governor appoints and removes with the advice and consent of the Texas Senate. Like the governor, the commissioner serves a four-

year term. The only qualification for serving as commissioner is U.S. citizenship. The legislature designates the commissioner to be the educational leader of the state. The commissioner also serves as the executive officer and executive secretary of the State Board of Education. Included among the forty responsibilities the legislature has assigned the commissioner are adopting an annual budget for the Foundation School Program, reviewing school district waiver requests, adopting rules for optional extended year programs, performing duties in connection with the public school accountability system, and reviewing school district audit reports (TEC § 7.055). Other sections of the Code give the commissioner added responsibilities, e.g., taking sanctions against low-performing campuses and school districts including closure (campuses) and annexation (districts) (TEC § 39.131). Several of the commissioner's current responsibilities previously belonged to the state board, such as adopting a recommended state appraisal process for teachers and administrators and performing duties associated with the guaranteed bond program.

A necessary adjunct to the activities of the Texas Education Agency are the twenty Regional Education Service Centers located throughout the state. Operating under the auspices of the agency, the service centers assist school districts in improving student achievement and increasing the effectiveness of school operations (TEC § 8.001(b)). Their core services include teacher training, assistance in providing specialized programs like compensatory and special education, assistance to low-performing districts and campuses, training in site-based management, and assistance in complying with state law. Funding for these services is provided by the state through the Foundation School Program. The centers provide additional services under contract to school districts and, in partnership with school districts, seek grant support for various purposes. Each service center is governed by a seven-member board as established under rules developed by the commissioner of education. The commissioner also approves the selection of service center executive directors. Districts increasingly are relying on the service centers for computer and media services, staff training, and technical assistance.

Local School Districts

The governance of schools is clearly left to local boards of trustees. Section 11.151 of the Texas Education Code states that "the trustees as a body corporate have the exclusive power and duty to govern and oversee the management of the public schools of the district. All powers and duties not specifically designated by statute to the agency or to the State Board of Education are reserved for the trustees, and the agency may not substitute its judgment for the lawful exercise of those powers and duties by the trustees." Accordingly, the local school board may acquire and hold real and personal property, sue and be sued, receive bequests and donations, levy and collect taxes, sell minerals and property belonging to the district, and condemn property for securing school sites. While the school board also has the authority to make employment decisions, the board by policy must accord the superintendent the sole authority to make recommendations to the board regarding the selection of all personnel other than the superintendent (TEC § 11.163). The board may delegate final authority for hiring to the superintendent. Taken together, these provisions give the local school board a status very similar to that of a municipality.

TEC § 11.157 allows districts to contract with a public or private entity to provide educational services for the district. Sherman I.S.D. became the first Texas school district to take advantage of this provision to contract with the Edison Project to operate one of its elementary schools starting in the fall of 1995. The Edison Project is a for-profit corporation started by entrepreneur-businessman Chris Whittle to revolutionize the schooling process through a rig-

orous curriculum, increased time in school, and the innovative use of technology. When a district contracts with a private vendor to provide educational services, the district must ensure that the vendor complies with state statutory requirements applicable to public school districts (*Att'y. Gen. Op. DM-355,* 1995). The Texas Attorney General noted that nothing in the contracting statute exempts the private vendor from complying with these statutory requirements, nor denies to participating students the benefits the statutes provide.

TEC § 11.158 allows school boards to charge fees for a number of activities such as membership dues in voluntary student organizations, security deposits for return of materials, and parking. The board may not charge fees for school lockers, required field trips, and library books, to name a few. TEC § 11.162 allows school boards to require school uniforms, provided that the uniforms are furnished free of cost to the "educationally disadvantaged" and that children of parents who have a religious or philosophical objection to the requirement are exempted.

One of the more interesting provisions of the Code is TEC § 11.160, which allows the board of trustees to change the name of the district. All kinds of interesting name changes have been proposed in jest, such as "Way Above Average I.S.D.," "Schools-R-Us I.S.D.," and "The Fiercely Independent School District."

The majority of Texas school districts elect their board members in at-large elections. Increasingly, however, minority voters are asserting that single-member districts should replace the at-large system. In a single-member system, the school district is divided into five or more separate election districts, each with its own trustee position. Thus, each election district will be assured at least one trustee who is from that area and represents the special concerns or needs of that election district. TEC §§ 11.052–11.053 governs the changing of an at-large system to a single-member system. A single-member system must be submitted to the U.S. Justice Department for approval under the 1965 Voting Rights Act.

School board trustees serve a term of three or four years (TEC § 11.059). Elections for trustees with three-year terms are held annually, with one-third expiring each year. Elections for trustees with four-year terms are held biennially, with one-half expiring each biennium. The staggered terms assure continuity to school board functioning. A person must be an eligible voter to be qualified for office as a trustee. Trustees serve without compensation. The state board is required to provide a training program for school board members through the regional service centers. Other training programs are offered through professional associations such as the Texas Association of School Boards (TASB). TASB is a comprehensive organization that provides a host of services to school boards, including model school board policies that most districts have adopted. TASB also is influential in the legislative arena on behalf of its members and provides financial support to districts embroiled in expensive litigation.

Charter Schools

Freeing up public schools from state regulation and giving parents more influence over the education of their children have become major legislative agenda items in the 1990s. Texas is no exception. In his 1994 election campaign, Governor George Bush promoted the concept of "home-rule school districts," which would allow local communities to shape the functioning of their schools. Key figures within the Texas Legislature also wanted to increase school district and campus autonomy through locally developed "charters" that are granted by school boards or by the State Board of Education. Three forms of charter schools emerged from the 1995 legislative session: home-rule school district charters, campus charters, and open-enrollment charters.

Home-rule school district charters allow school districts to free themselves from most state requirements. A school district is required to appoint a fifteen-member charter commission if at least 5 percent of the registered voters of the district sign a petition or two-thirds of the school board members adopt a resolution. The charter developed by the commission must address such matters as the educational program to be offered, the governance structure of the district and campuses, acceptable levels of student performance, and the budgeting process (TEC § 12.016). If the secretary of state determines that the proposed charter changes the governance structure of the district, the charter must be submitted to the U.S. Justice Department or the U.S. District Court for the District of Columbia for preclearance under the 1965 Voting Rights Act. The charter also has to be submitted to the commissioner of education for a legal review. The proposed charter becomes effective if adopted by majority vote in an election where at least 25 percent of the registered voters in the district participate. The 25 percent requirement will be a significant hurdle for many districts to overcome. The State Board of Education is given authority for revoking or placing a home-rule district charter on probation. Other provisions in the Texas Education Code describe the process for voter amendment or rescission of the charter.

TEC § 12.012 provides that home-rule districts are subject only to those state laws and administrative rules that specifically apply to them. Thus, for example, since neither Texas educator employment law nor student discipline law specifically mention home-rule districts, home-rule districts arguably are exempt from these provisions. In addition, home-rule aschool districts may determine their own curriculum. However, home-rule districts are not autonomous. In addition to federal law requirements for such matters as special education and nondiscrimination, TEC § 12.013 sets forth a list of state requirements that must be followed. Included are those pertaining to educator certification, student admissions and attendance, high school graduation requirements, class size restriction for low-performing schools, public school accountability, state purchasing, and accreditation sanctions.

Under the second charter option, a school district board of trustees or governing body of a home-rule school district may grant a charter to parents and teachers to operate a campus or campus program free from most regulation including district instructional and academic requirements if presented with a petition signed by the majority of parents and teachers at the school (TEC § 12.052). Cooperative charters involving two or more campuses may also be approved. A school board may not arbitrarily deny approval of a charter. This means that, while boards have discretion in approving proposed campus charters, they can only reject a charter for cause. It will be interesting to see how school boards handle innovative proposals that might be competitive with the district's existing schools and programs. Considerable tension and infighting have occurred in Minnesota and other states where local school boards have the authority to grant charters.

The proposed campus charter must describe the educational program, acknowledge that continuation of the charter is dependent upon satisfactory student performance, specify the conditions under which the charter may be placed on probation or revoked, prohibit various forms of discrimination, describe the governing structure, specify health and safety measures, and provide for an annual audit (TEC § 12.058). The governing body of the campus or program is subject to the provisions of the Texas Open Meetings and Public Information acts. These statutes are discussed in Chapter 9. While the campus charter school has a good deal of autonomy within the district, the school board retains legal responsibility for its activities.

Campus charter schools and programs remain public schools and are subject to federal law and to those state statutes that specifically apply to them. Among matters specified by the latter are the Public Education Information Management System (PEIMS), high school graduation requirements, special education and bilingual education requirements, prekindergarten programs, extracurricular activity provisions, and health and safety measures (TEC § 12.056). But charter schools are exempt from most other provisions of the Code. TEC § 12.064 provides that geography and residence are to be given first priority in student admissions, thus preserving the concept of the nonelite neighborhood school. Age, grade level, and academic qualifications are secondary considerations.

How responsive campus parent bodies and teachers will be to the opportunity campus charters afford for innovative approaches to schooling remains to be seen. For some time, the annual Gallup Poll of Education has shown that most parents give high marks to the public schools their children attend, even if they also express dissatisfaction with public schooling in general.

Open-enrollment charter schools constitute the third charter option. The State Board of Education is given authority to grant up to twenty charters for the operation of these schools in a facility of a commercial or nonprofit entity, a school district, a public or private college or university, or governmental entity (TEC § 12.101). Open-enrollment charter schools are public schools that may attract students from either within or across school district lines in competition with existing public and private schools. Open-enrollment charter schools can provide instruction at one or more elementary or secondary grade levels as long as students perform satisfactorily. They operate much like new school districts, except that they do not have authority to impose taxes. Revenue in the form of state and local funding follows the student. Open-enrollment charter schools may not charge tuition and must provide transportation on the same basis as existing school districts.

Like the other two forms of charter schools, open-enrollment charters are exempt from most state laws and rules other than those specified in the TEC. A list of the latter is provided in TEC § 12.104 and is similar to those for the other forms of charters, except that open-enrollment charter schools must offer the state-required curriculum. The components of the charter are also similar, with the addition of such items as specification of grade levels, qualifications of professional employees, facilities, and enrollment criteria. Open-enrollment charter schools may not discriminate in admissions on the basis of sex, national origin, ethnicity, religion, disability, academic or athletic ability, or school district the student would otherwise attend. Charter schools may reject students who have committed criminal offenses or have a history of disciplinary problems.

Senate Bill I required the State Board of Education to develop approval criteria and procedures for the open-enrollment chartering process. The board took little time doing so, with a set of criteria and procedures in place by the fall of 1995. The criteria address student performance, innovative programs, and potential impact on existing districts. In addition, the legislature also requires the state board to select an impartial organization with experience in evaluating school choice programs to conduct an annual evaluation of open-enrollment charter schools. The evaluation is to encompass costs, student performance, and impact on existing school districts (TEC § 12.118). Previous research on school choice consistently shows that choosing parents are different from nonchoosing parents. They are more likely to have higher incomes, more education, fewer children, and greater ambition for their children's education.[1] At the same time, there is little reliable research on how school choice affects student performance, controlling both for the socioeconomic characteristics of families and the bias inherent in the act of choosing. Open-enrollment charter schools may provide an opportunity to learn more about the impact of school choice on students, parents, and schools. The fact that they must follow the state-mandated curriculum, however, diminishes their ability to be innovative.

School Administrators

The superintendent is the chief operating officer of the district, responsible for implementing the policies of the board. TEC § 11.201 lists eleven superintendent duties. Included among them are responsibility for the operation of the educational programs, services, and facilities of the district and appraisal of the staff; assigning and evaluating personnel; and making personnel recommendations to the school board. The superintendent also is responsible for developing a budget, organizing the district's central administration, overseeing the development of administrative regulations to implement board policies, and performing other duties assigned by the board of trustees.

The school principal is the front-line administrator, with statutory responsibility under the direction of the superintendent for administering the day-to-day activities of the school. Principals have

1 See, for example, Valerie J. Martinez, R. Kenneth Godwin, Frank R. Kemerer, and Laura Perna, "The Consequences of School Choice: Who Leaves and Who Stays in the Inner City," *Social Science Quarterly,* September 1995. See also Valerie J. Martinez, Kay Thomas, and Frank R. Kemerer, "Who Chooses and Why: A Study of Five School Choice Programs," *Phi Delta Kappan,* May 1994.

seven major functions, as listed in TEC § 11.202. Based on criteria developed in consultation with the faculty, they have approval power for teacher and staff appointments to the campus from a pool of applicants selected by the district or of applicants who meet the district's hiring requirements. However, the superintendent or the superintendent's designee can override the principal regarding teacher placement resulting from enrollment shifts or program changes. Principals set campus education objectives through the planning process, develop budgets, and have responsibility for student discipline. They also assign, evaluate, and promote campus personnel, as well as make recommendations to the superintendent regarding suspension, nonrenewal, and termination of personnel. Finally, they perform other duties assigned by the superintendent.

The certification requirements for principals developed by the State Board for Educator Certification—a topic addressed in more detail in Chapter 4—must be sufficiently flexible so that an outstanding teacher may substitute approved experience and professional training for part of the educational requirements (TEC § 21.046). Further, qualifications for certification as a superintendent or principal must allow the substitution of management training and experience for part of the educational requirements. The legislature has increasingly emphasized the importance of recruiting and retaining the highest caliber of personnel for the principalship. School boards are required to institute multilevel screening processes, validated comprehensive assessments, and flexible internships with successful mentors to determine whether a candidate for certification as a principal is qualified.

Believing principals to be the persons with the most responsibility for school improvement, the legislature has given them more authority to operate their schools. At the same time, principals are held more accountable for their work. The appraisal of a school principal must include consideration of the performance of the campus on the academic indicators set forth in TEC § 39.051 and on the campus objectives established under TEC § 11.253. The legislature appears particularly serious about administrator appraisal. School district funds cannot be used to pay an administrator who has not been appraised in the preceding fifteen months. In addition, TEC § 39.054 provides that the campus performance report assembled each year by school districts shall be a primary consideration of superintendents in evaluating principals. Likewise, the district performance report is to be a primary consideration of school boards in evaluating school superintendents. These reports will be discussed in more detail in the next chapter. With increased re-

sponsibility also comes increased liability. For example, principals must be familiar with employment law in order to carry out their personnel responsibilities effectively and without legal liability.

While local school boards and administrators have substantial power, they must manage and govern the public schools in accordance with both federal and state law—law that is constantly changing. And they must do so economically. TEC § 42.201 directs the Texas Commissioner of Education to determine annually a cost ratio of administrative to instructional expenses and to require school district compliance. Failure of a district to reduce administrative costs to the desired ratio can result in a reduction of state aid or a requirement to remit the amount in excess of the ratio to the state comptroller.

District-and Campus-Level Decision Making

Despite the authority given to local school boards, the Texas Legislature since 1990 has increasingly sought to "flatten the decision-making pyramid" by involving others in district and campus governance. Over the years, these requirements have become more complex. TEC § 11.251 requires the establishment of committees at the district and campus level to participate in establishing and reviewing educational plans, goals, performance objectives, and major classroom instructional programs. The committees are to be broadly representative of professional staff, parents, community members, and business representatives. The latter need not reside in the district. In partnership with the district-level committee, the board is also required to delineate the roles of those involved in planning, budgeting, curriculum, staffing, staff development, and school organization at both the district and campus level.

TEC § 11.251 requires each board to have a procedure for the nomination and election of professional staff representatives to the district-level committee (two-thirds must be classroom teachers; one-third must be professional staff) and to establish procedures for selecting the other members and for holding meetings periodically with the board or board designee. The statute stipulates that the committee process is not intended to limit the power of the board to manage and govern the schools and is not to be construed as a collective bargaining statute. Nor is it to restrict the board from conducting meetings with teacher groups or receiving input from students, paraprofessional staff, and others.

A companion statute, TEC § 11.253, requires that the school principal regularly involve the campus committee in planning, budgeting, curriculum, staffing, staff development, and school organization.

Otherwise advisory, the committee does have approval power over the portion of the improvement plan addressing staff development. The membership of the campus committee and its selection are sim-ilar to that of the district-level committee. Like the district-level process, campus-level decision making is not to be construed as any form of collective bargaining. Whether or not mandated site-based decision making will be any more effective than centralized decision making in improving student achievement remains to be seen. At present, there are no reliable research findings on the issue.

Utilizing the deliberative processes set forth in these statutes, school boards and campus administrators are required to engage in an annual planning and improvement process linked to student achievement. Each district's improvement plan is to encompass such matters as a comprehensive needs assessment addressing student performance on the academic excellence indicators set forth in TEC § 39.051, performance objectives, and strategies for improving student achievement. Among the strategies to be discussed are the need for special programs, dropout reduction, integration of technology in instructional and administrative programs, discipline management, and staff development (TEC § 11.253). Each campus's improvement plan must assess each student's performance using the academic excellence indicator system, identify how campus goals will be met, determine the resources and staffing needed, set timelines, and establish a periodic assessment process (TEC § 11.253). At least every two years, school districts are required to evaluate the impact of their planning and decision-making processes on improving student achievement.

That the site-based decision process remains essentially advisory appears clear both from the wording of the current statutes and from early commissioner decisions predating Senate Bill I. In three 1995 decisions, the commissioner rejected teacher contentions that they had been illegally excluded from decision making. The first case involved the hiring of a new principal without involvement by the campus-level committee. The commissioner noted that TEC § 21.931 (now TEC § 11.253) gives school districts considerable discretion in deciding the role of the campus committee. Here, the committee had not been given a direct role in the selection of a principal. This being the case, the district did not violate its own policy by electing not to consult the committee (*Clear Creek Educators Association TSTA/NEA v. Clear Creek I.S.D.*). Similarly, the commissioner determined that the statutes did not require a school district to involve either district- or campus-level committees in the restructuring of the district's junior high schools, since the matter was more a mat-

ter of location and less a matter of instruction (*La Porte Education Association v. La Porte I.S.D.*). In the third decision, the commissioner concluded that the school board retained authority under its plan to reject the school committee's block scheduling proposal, which would have varied the schedules and instructional time at the district's two high schools. The commissioner noted that site-based decision making is not designed to limit the board's governance authority in such matters (*Shoffner v. Goose Creek C.I.S.D.*). In a fourth decision, the commissioner determined that a district's existing policies and procedures met the statutory requirements for implementing site-based management (*Classroom Teachers of Dallas/TSTA/NEA v. Dallas I.S.D.*). All four decisions involved pre-Senate Bill I provisions, and thus are not necessarily indicative of future decisions involving the slightly altered wording of the current statutes.

HOW THE U.S. CONSTITUTION AND FEDERAL GOVERNMENT AFFECT TEXAS SCHOOLS

Key Provisions of the U.S. Constitution

Until recently, the role of Congress and the federal courts in education matters was quite limited. However, the quest for individual rights and greater procedural safeguards triggered by the civil rights movement of the 1960s spilled over into the schools. In the past twenty years, a new generation of constitutional rights law has evolved. The changes have been significant and are discussed in detail in subsequent chapters. Nonetheless, the advent of a more conservative majority on the Supreme Court, led by Chief Justice William Rehnquist, has tempered the Court's recent extension of constitutional protections to students and school district employees. As a result, plaintiffs are beginning to bring suits on these issues in state rather than federal court.

We begin with the Bill of Rights of the U.S. Constitution. Most of our basic civil liberties are included among its provisions. The First Amendment is particularly important, for it lists several liberties inherent in a democratic society: the right to be free from governmental control in the exercise of speech, publication, religious preference, and assembly. However, the First Amendment, like the other nine in the Bill of Rights, applies only to the federal government (the first word in the First Amendment is *Congress*).

To determine what U.S. Constitutional rights we enjoy in the state setting, we must look to the Fourteenth Amendment. For our purpose, two clauses from the first section of that amendment are important: "nor shall any State deprive any person of life, liberty, or property without due process of law, nor deny to any person within its jurisdiction the equal protection of the laws." These two clauses—the due process clause and the equal protection clause—together with the federal laws that implement them, provide the basis for constitutional rights suits against public educational institutions and personnel. Congress passed a statute after the Civil War to enforce the Fourteenth Amendment by enabling aggrieved persons to pursue their claims in federal court. That statute, known as 42 U.S.C. § 1983, is one of the major sources of litigation against both school districts and school personnel. The statute provides that "Every person who, under color of any statute, ordinance, regulation, custom, or usage, of any State or Territory, subjects, or causes to be subjected, any citizen of the United States or other person within the jurisdiction thereof to the deprivation of any rights, privileges, or immunities secured by the Constitution and laws, shall be liable to the party injured in an action at law, suit in equity, or other proper proceedings for redress [in federal court]." As will be noted often in this book and particularly in the last chapter on legal liability, the consequences can be severe.

One may wonder how schools can be affected by the Fourteenth Amendment, phrased as it is in terms of states. As we already have noted, local school districts are legally viewed as state political subdivisions. Therefore, the Fourteenth Amendment applies to public school districts and personnel, but not to private schools, since they are not state related. Neither the Bill of Rights, the Fourteenth Amendment, nor most provisions of the Texas Education Code apply to private schools. This is an important point, for many educators assume they are entitled to the same rights in the private school setting as in the public. In reality, the "rights" that a person has in private schools depend to a large extent on the wishes of the private school. For the private school, contract law is of great importance, since it defines not only the teacher-institution relationship but also the relationship of the student to the school. Thus, it is important that contractual provisions be carefully developed and reviewed.

Over the years the U.S. Supreme Court has held that almost all provisions of the Bill of Rights are binding on the states through the Fourteenth Amendment. In other words, the Supreme Court has gradually incorporated these rights into the Fourteenth Amendment, specifically through the "liberty" provision of the due process clause, thereby ensuring that neither the federal government nor the states can abridge them. Courts have differed, however, on the extent to which teachers and, particularly, students in the public schools enjoy the same protections as do other persons.

Neither liberty rights nor property rights are without limits. They can be regulated, even denied, provided that the state or school follows due process: "nor shall any State deprive any person of life, liberty, or property without due process of law," meaning that, if due process *is* followed, the curtailment of rights *can* occur.

Behavior that is not constitutionally protected as a liberty or property right can be regulated relatively easily. Smoking and the possession and/or use of hallucinogenic drugs fall into this category. The legislature has banned smoking by all persons at school-related or school-sanctioned activities on or off campus (TEC § 38.006) and has made student possession or use of hallucinogenic drugs an expellable offense if punishable as a felony (TEC § 37.007).

Of course, the fact that the U.S. Constitution does not protect certain types of behavior does not mean that a state legislature or school district cannot decide to do so. For example, some school districts grant students personal grooming rights, though they are not legally required to do so.

In sum, the Fourteenth Amendment protects persons from state government repression of basic civil liberties guarantees, such as those in the Bill of Rights to the U.S. Constitution. Since public schools are part of state government, the Fourteenth Amendment applies to them and to their employees, but not to private schools. Exactly what constitutional rights students and teachers have in the public school setting will be discussed in subsequent chapters.

A second major source of constitutional litigation in the public school setting relates to the Fourteenth Amendment equal protection clause: "nor [shall any state] deny to any person within its jurisdiction the equal protection of the laws." This amendment, coupled with civil rights laws designed to enforce it, has furnished the grounds for antidiscrimination suits against schools. While desegregation suits have abated in recent years, so-called second-generation equal protection issues have arisen over such matters as in-school tracking and competency-based testing.

Important Federal Laws

There are a number of federal statutes that directly affect the day-to-day operation of Texas public schools. Several also apply to private schools. The most important are briefly set forth here and will be referred to periodically in later chapters.

42 U.S.C. § 1981 accords all persons the right to make and enforce contracts free of racial discrimination in both the public and private sectors. This law recently has been amended to apply to discrimination occurring during the contract term as well. Thus, a minority child subject to discrimination after being admitted to a private school would have a cause of action. Penalties include both injunctive relief and compensatory damages.

42 U.S.C. § 1983 allows suits for injunctive relief and compensatory damages against public school districts that through policy or practice deprive persons of U.S. Constitutional and federal statutory rights. Public employees are also subject to suit under this statute. This law is very important in the enforcement of federal rights under the Fourteenth Amendment.

Title VI of the 1964 Civil Rights Act prohibits intentional discrimination in the context of race, color, or national origin in federally assisted programs. Injunctive relief and monetary damages are available. This law was instrumental in the desegregation of schools during the 1960s and '70s.

Title VII of the 1964 Civil Rights Act prohibits discrimination on the basis of race, color, religion, sex, or national origin in all aspects of public and private employment. In addition to equitable relief such as back pay and reinstatement, this law has been amended to allow money damages for intentional discrimination.

Americans with Disabilities Act of 1990 accords persons with disabilities meaningful access to the programs and facilities of public and private schools as well as most businesses in the country. The statute also prohibits discrimination against persons with disabilities in public and private employment, and requires employers to make reasonable accommodation for disabled persons to enable them to perform the job. Money damages are available for intentional discrimination.

Title IX of the 1972 Education Amendments prohibits discrimination against persons on the basis of sex in any federally assisted education program. Penalties against school districts under this statute can encompass compensatory damages as well as termination of federal funding. Title IX has gained major significance in the context of student and employee sexual harassment. For example, the school district can be liable when an administrator sexually harasses a teacher or when a principal fails to act when a student complains about unwelcome sexual advances from a teacher.

Individuals with Disabilities Education Act requires public schools to identify and provide children with disabilities a free appropriate public education in the least restrictive environment. Together with § 504 of the 1973 Rehabilitation Act, IDEA provides a comprehensive legal framework for serving children with disabilities.

In addition to these, there are a number of other important federal laws that will be discussed in subsequent chapters. Included among them are the Equal Access Act, the Family Educational Rights and Privacy Act (Buckley Amendment), and the Equal Pay Act.

SCHOOL FINANCE

School finance is a complex subject, generally beyond the scope of this book. However, it is important to have an overview of the subject since it is central to the operation of the school system and remains contentious. In recent years the issue of equalization in school finance has been the focus of a dramatic struggle between the Texas judicial and legislative branches of government.

As previously noted, the 1876 Texas Constitution left to the legislature the duty to establish an efficient system of public education. That same year the Texas Legislature established the Available School Fund, with monies for education apportioned on a per capita basis. The Available School Fund consisted of revenue from an endowment and from designated state taxes. Funding was to be provided on a per capita basis, though for many years the amounts distributed were meager. Most of the funding for public education originated at the local level.

With the growth of population centers, the imbalance between urban and rural districts created by reliance on local property taxation became increasingly apparent. But it wasn't until the enactment of the Gilmer-Aikin Bill in 1949 that substantial reform occurred. The Gilmer-Aikin Bill later became the focus of the *San Antonio I.S.D. v. Rodriguez* equalization lawsuit filed in federal court in the late 1960s. The bill established a Minimum Foundation Program (MFP), whereby state funds for personnel and operations were distributed via a complicated economic index that established a basic minimum below which no district could go. The MFP involved both local and state contributions to a special fund. Eighty percent of the funding came from the state, with the rest coming from local districts on an ability-to-pay basis. Thus, each local district had to levy a property tax to support its contribution. But inequities continued because local districts remained free to enrich their contributions for their schools beyond the MFP local fund assignment. At the time of the *San Antonio I.S.D.* suit, all districts did so, though the amounts raised varied considerably. For example, in 1967–1968, Edgewood I.S.D., one of the parties to the suit, contributed $26 per student above its MFP local fund assignment at a property tax rate of $1.05 per $100 of valuation. Alamo Heights I.S.D., serving an affluent portion of San Antonio, was able to raise $333 per student above its local fund assignment at a tax rate of $0.85 per $100 of valuation. Similar interdistrict differences occurred elsewhere in Texas and, indeed, throughout the nation.

The plaintiffs in the *San Antonio I.S.D. v. Rodriguez* lawsuit tried to convince the courts that this system of educational finance violated the equal protection clause of the Fourteenth Amendment. While the lower court agreed, the U.S. Supreme Court did not. In a five-to-four decision, the Court ruled that the plan had a rational purpose, did not deprive anyone of a fundamental constitutional right, and did not discriminate against any particular group in violation of the Fourteenth Amendment equal protection clause. The high court noted that, while not perfect, the Texas MFP program did alleviate some of the vast differences in school finance among districts. For example, Alamo Heights I.S.D. derived almost thirteen times as much money from local property taxes as Edgewood did in 1967–1968, but the MFP reduced the ratio to approximately two-to-one.

While ruling against the plaintiffs, the majority on the Court urged the Texas Legislature to end the glaring discrepancies between rich and poor districts. Despite some legislative attempts to improve the existing system of educational finance after 1973, significant inequities remained and, in fact, increased. These inequalities persisted despite the passage of House Bill 72 during the special session in the summer of 1984. House Bill 72 fundamentally changed the school finance system by establishing a basic allotment for each student in the state and by introducing other mechanisms intended to foster equalization.

After *Rodriguez*, the next episode in the Texas equalization fight was *Edgewood v. Kirby*, filed in state district court in Travis County. The property-poor districts, having failed to find an enforceable

right under the U.S. Constitution in *Rodriguez*, sought to find such a right under the Texas Constitution in *Edgewood*. The case was tried before Judge Harley Clark, and in 1987 Judge Clark declared the existing system of school finance in Texas unconstitutional. Judge Clark ruled that, because education is a fundamental right and because wealth is a suspect classification under provisions of the Texas Constitution, disparities between property-rich and property-poor districts violate the equal rights provision of the Texas Constitution, Article I, § 3. That provision provides in part that "All free men, when they form a social compact, have equal rights. . . ." Judge Clark enjoined state officials from enforcing the challenged school finance statutes but "stayed" the injunction until September 1, 1989. His intention was to give the 1989 legislature an opportunity to enact a constitutional school finance system.

The defendants appealed the district court decision to the Texas Court of Appeals in Austin. In December 1988, the court of appeals, closely following the reasoning of the U.S. Supreme Court majority in *Rodriguez*, reversed Judge Clark's district court decision. With this development, the legislature was off the hook and, predictably, failed to address equalization in any significant manner.

The plaintiffs, having won in the district court and lost in the court of appeals, filed a further appeal in the Texas Supreme Court. The Supreme Court handed down a decision reversing the Third Court of Appeals on October 2, 1989. The court noted in *Edgewood I.S.D. v. Kirby (Edgewood 1)* that "if the system is not 'efficient' or not 'suitable,' the legislature has not discharged its constitutional duty. . ." Thus, the Texas Supreme Court mandated that the Texas Legislature remedy the inefficiencies in the Texas school financing system by May 1, 1990, although the court purposely provided no guidelines as to how this should be achieved. Finding the present system in violation of the Texas Constitution, the court did offer this guideline:

> Efficiency does not require a per capita distribution, but it also does not allow concentrations of resources in property-rich school districts that are taxing low when property-poor districts that are taxing high cannot generate sufficient revenues to meet even minimum standards. There must be a direct and close correlation between a district's tax effort and the education resources available to it; in other words, districts must have substantially equal access to similar revenues per pupil at similar levels of tax effort. . . . Certainly, this much is required if the state is to educate its populace efficiently and provide for a general diffusion of knowledge statewide.

The Texas Legislature struggled mightily to address the court's objections in enacting yet another finance plan during the sixth called special session in the summer of 1990. In January 1991, the Texas Supreme Court once again unanimously declared the plan unconstitutional because it did not correct the deficiencies noted in *Edgewood I*. The court suggested in *Edgewood II* that the legislature could effect systemic change by consolidating school districts, thus removing duplicative administrative costs, and by consolidating tax bases. Nothing in the state constitution, the court noted, prohibits tax base consolidation. The justices reinstated the injunction against continued state funding of education but delayed the order until April 1, 1991.

Shortly thereafter, the high court was faced with a motion for rehearing filed by property-poor districts. The motion asked the court to overrule its 1931 *Love v. City of Dallas* decision holding that local property taxes could not be used to educate students outside the district. The property-poor districts argued that since local districts are creatures of the state, local property revenue could be considered a state tax and thus could be used to fund other school districts. In an order of February 25, 1991 (known as *Edgewood II* $\frac{1}{2}$ and appended to the court's published *Edgewood I.S.D. II* decision), the court refused to overrule *Love*, noting that tax base consolidation could be achieved through the creation of new districts with the authority to generate local property tax revenue for all of the other districts within their boundaries.

But then, interestingly, five members of the court went further. Noting that property-rich districts as defendants had filed a brief in which they urged the court to clarify whether unequalized local enrichment was still possible under the state constitution, Chief Justice Thomas R. Phillips responded, for the five, in the affirmative. "Once the Legislature provides an efficient system in compliance with Article VII, § 1, it may, so long as efficiency is maintained, authorize local school districts to supplement their educational resources if local property owners approve an additional local property tax." This comment set off a scathing attack by Justice Lloyd Doggett, with whom two other members concurred. Doggett accused the five of responding to newspaper editorials decrying the effect of equalization on wealthy districts, which would see their locally generated revenues siphoned off for use elsewhere. "Today a judge expounds on social policy preferences rather than resolving a motion," he wrote. "The underlying need for writing arises from the fear that the Legislature may otherwise fail to satisfy certain judicial desires, not that it may inadvertently pursue some further unconstitutional

course. The restraint observed by a unified court has become the activism promoted by a majority of a divided one."

The Texas Legislature once again tried to reform the system by enacting Senate Bill 351 in the 1991 regular session. That measure sought to consolidate school district tax bases by creating 188 county education districts (CEDs) to levy, collect, and disburse property taxes in a way to minimize interdistrict disparities. But the Texas Supreme Court was not impressed. In January of 1992, Senate Bill 351 was declared unconstitutional in *Carrollton–Farmers Branch I.S.D. v. Edgewood I.S.D. (Edgewood III)*. The central problem was that the county education districts violated constitutional provisions requiring local voter approval of local property taxes and prohibiting a state property tax. The court, however, did allow the county education district plan to operate for the 1992–1993 school year and gave the legislature until June 1, 1993, to reform the finance system. After that date, all state funding for education would cease. Three justices favored no extension of time. A fourth, Justice John Cornyn, took the opportunity to shift the discussion to a different level. He noted the absence of evidence showing a direct correlation between expenditures and student achievement and suggested the time had come to focus more on ways to achieve equalization of educational results.

Now expressing considerable frustration and uncertainty, the Texas Legislature opted to let the voters have a chance to pass a constitutional amendment upholding the CED plan, which effectively would moot the Supreme Court decision. The voters rejected that measure in the spring of 1993, along with two others designed to help financially strapped districts. With time running out before the June 1 deadline, the legislature passed Senate Bill 7. The law required school districts above a certain wealth level to engage in tax base reduction by transferring wealth to poorer school districts. Five options for school districts were listed: (1) consolidate with one or more districts, (2) detach territory with another district, (3) purchase attendance credits from the state, (4) contract to educate nonresident students, or (5) consolidate tax bases with other districts. The last three options required voter approval. No sooner was the ink dry than lawsuits were filed by both property-poor and property-wealthy school districts. Finally, late in 1994, the Texas Supreme Court upheld Senate Bill 7 as constitutional "in all respects." The Court found that the plan provided an efficient system of education. However, the Court cautioned that "Our judgment in this case should not be interpreted as a signal that the school finance crisis in Texas has ended." The basic provisions of Senate Bill 7 remain in effect.

PARENT RIGHTS

In 1923 the U.S. Supreme Court noted that parents have a constitutionally protected right to control their children's upbringing (*Meyer v. Nebraska*). While the parameters of the right in the education context have remained unclear, growing pressure has been evident in recent years to increase parental influence and control. In this section, we examine how Texas law protects parent rights in public schools, the right of parents to choose private schools, and the right of parents to educate their children at home.

Rights within Public Schools

In the recodification of Texas school law in 1995, the legislature added a section identifying parent rights and responsibilities. TEC § 26.001 recognizes parents as partners in the educational process and encourages their participation in "creating and implementing educational programs for their children." To that end, the statute requires boards of trustees to support the establishment of at least one parent-teacher organization in each school of the district and to establish a parent complaint procedure. The term "parent" means anyone standing in a parental relationship to a child. Excluded are individuals whose parental rights have been terminated or who do not have access to or possession of a child under court order.

While TEC § 25.031 gives school officials the authority to assign students to particular schools and classrooms within a district, parents have the right to petition the board to have their child placed at a particular school or to contest the assignment to a particular school under TEC § 26.003. That section of the Code also gives parents the right to ask the school principal to have the child reassigned from a particular class or teacher within a school if the change would not affect the assignment of another student. Parents have a right to request, with the expectation that the request will not be unreasonably denied, the addition of an academic class to the curriculum if it would be economical to do so, the right to request placement of their child in a class above the child's grade level, and the right to have their child graduate early if all course requirements have been completed. If the child graduates early, the child has a right to participate in graduation ceremonies. The board's decision in these matters is final and nonappealable. This curtails the ability of parents to enforce the statutory provisions against a recalcitrant school board unless they can convince the commissioner or a judge that the board has acted illegally—for example, by engaging in illegal discrimination. As we noted earlier, in this sense nothing is ever truly "final and nonappealable."

Parents of children attending low-performing schools are entitled to a public education grant so that their children may attend a school in another district (TEC § 29.201). This provision is a watered-down version of a voucher plan that did not pass in the 1995 legislative session. The voucher would have enabled parents to choose private, as well as public, schools. Under the public education grant program, a low-performing school is defined as one having 50 percent or more of the students performing less than satisfactorily on state assessment tests or as one identified as low performing by the commissioner of education. The education grant consists of the state and local funding the student is entitled to in the residential district. The chosen district may not charge additional tuition. If the chosen district's expenditure per student is less than the public education grant, the difference remains with the residential district. Districts have the right not to accept students from other districts under this program, but they may not refuse to accept them for reasons of race, ethnicity, academic achievement, athletic abilities, language proficiency, sex, or socioeconomic status. This essentially leaves available space as the selection criterion. If there are more applicants than places, the district must select by lottery, giving preference, first, to choosing students from the same family or household and then to at-risk students. The residential district is required to provide transportation to the school the child would have attended. The parent is responsible for transportation beyond this point. It will be interesting to see how many parents take advantage of this school choice provision once it becomes better known and whether school districts will be willing to accept children from other districts. It is likely that the legislature will expand parental choice options in the future, particularly if parents are frustrated in their attempts to have their children escape low-performing schools.

Texas law reinforces federal law in giving parents access to all written records concerning their child, including attendance records, test scores, disciplinary records, psychological records, and teacher and counselor evaluations (TEC § 26.004). It is important to point out that the federal provisions require that parent rights in this context transfer to the student when the student turns eighteen or is attending a postsecondary institution, though parents do not lose their right of access if they claim their child as a dependent. In addition, parents have a right to see state assessment instruments administered to their children. However, TEA is not required to release questions that are being field-tested and are not used to compute a student's score on a particular test.

Parents also have a right to review all classroom teaching materials and tests previously administered to their child. School districts are required to make these materials readily available to parents and may charge a reasonable copying fee. While parents have always had the right to attend school board meetings, TEC § 26.007 reinforces the right and requires school boards to hold public meetings within the boundaries of the district, with two exceptions: joint meetings with another district and meetings outside the district required by law. This provision restricts the ability of school boards to hold retreats where public business is conducted.

With the exception of child abuse reporting (discussed in the next chapter), parents have a right to all information concerning the activities of their child at school. School employees who encourage or coerce a child to withhold information from the child's parents are subject to contract termination or suspension without pay.

TEC § 26.009 requires school employees to obtain written parental consent before conducting a psychological examination, test, or treatment unless related to child abuse reporting. This right extends a right accorded parents under federal law regarding evaluations and assessments (see Chapter 9). Students cannot be referred to an outside counselor without written parental consent. The district must tell the parent about any relationship between the counselor and the district, and must provide the parent with information about other sources of treatment in the area. Referral also requires approval of appropriate school personnel (TEC § 38.010). The purpose of this statute is to prevent collusion between districts and outside counselors. Written consent is also required under TEC § 26.009 before making a videotape of a child or recording the child's voice unless for safety purposes in common areas of the school or on school buses, for purposes related to cocurricular or extracurricular activity, or for classroom instruction. However, it is important to note that videotape and audiotape recordings may constitute protected records under federal law and cannot be released without parental consent. TEC § 33.004 requires districts to retain signed consent forms in the student's permanent record.

One of the more notable provisions emerging from the 1995 legislative session is TEC § 26.010, which accords parents the right to request temporary exemptions for their child from a class or activity "that conflicts with the parent's religious or moral beliefs if the parent presents or delivers to the teacher of the parent's child a written statement authorizing the removal of the child from the class or

other school activity." Note that both religious *and* moral beliefs are recognized. The right is limited to the extent that a parent cannot remove the child from a class or activity to avoid a test or to prevent the child from taking a subject for the entire semester. Nor does the provision exempt a child from satisfying grade level or graduation requirements.

Choosing Private Schools

The right to control a child's upbringing identified by the U.S. Supreme Court in the 1923 *Meyer* decision does not restrict the state from requiring all children to attend school. However, the state cannot require all children to attend *public* school. In 1925, a unanimous Court ruled that an Oregon statute to this effect was unconstitutional because it deprived private school operators of their property right to operate a business under the Fourteenth Amendment (*Pierce v. Society of Sisters*). Citing the earlier *Meyer* decision, the Court also noted that the Oregon statute "unreasonably interferes with the liberty of parents and guardians to direct the upbringing and education of children under their control." The justices observed that the concept of liberty "excludes any general power of the State to standardize its children by forcing them to accept instruction from public teachers only. The child is not the mere creature of the State; those who nurture him and direct his destiny have the right, coupled with the high duty, to recognize and prepare him for additional obligations" (p. 535). For this reason, the Texas compulsory public school attendance law provides an exemption if the child "attends a private or parochial school that includes in its course a study of good citizenship" (TEC § 25.086).

In the past several years, private schooling has received considerable attention from educational reformers who view the public school system as too resistant to change to be successfully improved. Rather than provide money directly to public schools, these commentators urge the adoption of some type of voucher system whereby public money goes to parents, who then choose a public or private school for their children. Not only would such a system stimulate healthy competition within the educational system, proponents assert, it would give parents a greater stake in their children's education. Critics assert that a voucher system would destroy the common learning experience fostered by the public schools and would be both economically and racially discriminatory. They also point out that private schools likely would experience an increase in state regulation. While the debate rages, some states are moving toward such a system. Voucher measures have been introduced into recent Texas legislative sessions but have yet to garner sufficient support for passage.

Educating Children at Home

A critical problem with the Texas compulsory education statute is that the word *school* is not defined. This uncertainty led to the dispute surrounding what generally is called "home schooling." A state district judge ruled in 1987 that in Texas a home in which students are instructed qualifies as a private school, subject to certain conditions. Chief among them are that the students actually are taught by parents or those standing in parental authority, that there is a specific curriculum consisting of books and other written materials, and that the curriculum is designed to meet basic educational goals of reading, spelling, grammar, mathematics, and a study of good citizenship. The court further held that TEA lacked the authority to enforce a more restrictive interpretation of the compulsory education law previously adopted by the State Board of Education. The decision was affirmed by the Texas Supreme Court in 1994 (*Texas Education Agency v. Leeper*). The high court recognized that TEA has the authority to set guidelines for enforcement of the compulsory attendance law, including requesting achievement test results to determine if students are being taught "in a bona fide manner." The Court then added this confusing statement: "While administration of such tests cannot be a prerequisite to exemption from the compulsory attendance law, we do not preclude the TEA from giving this factor heavy weight." To date, the State Board of Education has not promulgated rules relating to home schooling.

Since the case was brought as a class action lawsuit, the holding applies in all Texas public school districts. Attendance officers are prohibited from initiating charges against parents simply because they are instructing their children at home. The trial court did recognize, however, the legitimate need of attendance officers to make reasonable inquiry of parents to determine whether a child is in attendance in a home school that meets the requirements approved by the court. Thus, information can be requested about the students, the curriculum being offered, and student test scores, if they exist.

In 1992 the Texas Commissioner of Education was confronted with a case in which a parent who home-schooled his daughter requested the local high school to enroll the girl in a one-period choir class. When the request was denied, the parent appealed to the commissioner. Noting that the school required all students except seniors to be enrolled in a seven-period school day, the commissioner denied the appeal. "This policy is rationally grounded to foster several goals of Respondent's board of trustees, including, among other things, maintaining discipline and obtaining state funding," the commissioner observed. The school district had argued that the girl's enrollment would cause complications with choir competition under University Interscholastic League (UIL) rules and would cause logistical problems in student supervision. The commissioner upheld the board's decision, concluding that it was not arbitrary or capricious (*Michelle S. v. Beeville I.S.D.*).

While permitting part-time enrollment of home-schooled students is left to the discretion of the district, such is not the case if the student has a disability. The Individuals with Disabilities Education Act (IDEA) requires school districts to provide special education and related services designed to meet the needs of private school handicapped students who are living in the district. Since home schooling qualifies as private schooling in Texas, school districts have an obligation to serve these students if parents request special education services and agree to allow the student to be dually enrolled in the public school for the amount of time identified in the student's Individual Education Plan.

When home-schooled students seek to return to the public school, placement decisions are left to the school. There is no requirement that school districts recognize the previous grade-level placements of home-schooled children.

SUMMARY

In this chapter we have reviewed the several sources of education law and their relationship to the structure and operation of the Texas public school system. It is apparent that local school districts have considerable authority to operate schools. Included in this authority is the right to develop local policy manuals and handbooks. School employees are required to follow these rules and regulations as they go about their assignments. At the same time, both federal and state law impose restraints on school boards and personnel by requiring compliance with certain constitutional and statutory provisions.

Education reform has been a central concern of the Texas Legislature since the early 1980s. At first, the legislative focus was on establishing state-level mandates that all districts and personnel had to follow. More recently, the legislature has sought to return greater decision-making authority to local districts and educators. At the same time, the legislature has recognized the need for innovation in schooling. A system of charter schools was enacted in 1995 to give local communities, campuses, and entrepreneurs the opportunity to develop new educational approaches and thereby stimulate reform across the education landscape.

While the U.S. Supreme Court has ruled that interdistrict disparities in per-pupil expenditures do not violate the federal constitution, the Texas Supreme Court and the Texas Legislature have spent years addressing the matter. Though the current financial system has been upheld by the Texas high court, the issue of equity in school finance remains a central concern.

Parent rights have increasingly come to the forefront of the policy-making agenda. The Texas Legislature has given parents more influence over the schooling of their children, including the right to request exemptions from programs and activities they find objectionable on religious or moral grounds. Further, parents with children in low-performing schools can take advantage of a public education scholarship to enroll their children in the schools of another district. Constitutional law accords parents the right to choose a private school for their children, though the state has no obligation to finance the choice. Texas law affords parents the right to educate their children at home.

In short, the trend in Texas is decentralization of the educational enterprise, together with parental empowerment.

The Texas State Board of Education

Should educational policymakers be skilled politicians in order to be successful? Can effective school reform occur outside of the political arena? While many educators resist the characterization of their role as political, an examination of recent Texas State Board of Education (SBOE) actions and policy decisions provides relevant insight into the influence of politics in educational policymaking and administration.

History and Background

Since 1898, when the first SBOE consisted of the Governor, the Secretary of State and the Comptroller, the State Board has undergone many configurations in response to popular political thought. In 1929, the SBOE was expanded to a nine-member board appointed by the Governor, and then in 1949 it was converted to an elected board in the Gilmer-Aiken Act. As a result of House Bill 72 in 1984, the SBOE positions once again became gubernatorial appointments. Following approval of a referendum by a majority of the people of Texas, partisan elections returned in 1988 to the current arrangement of elected representatives from fifteen districts to staggered four-year terms.

Representing more than one million constituents, each member of the SBOE serves as the district representative on the state education policy-

making body for public schools. The administrative component is the Texas Education Agency (TEA), which is headed by the Commissioner of Education appointed by the governor for a four-year term. TEA is charged with implementing the approved Board policies and overseeing the state's public prekindergarten through the twelfth grade education system.

Like local school boards throughout Texas, State Board members are not paid to serve, and although some of them are former or current educators, members bring the perspectives of varied educational and vocational backgrounds. In addition, a few have previous experience as local school board trustees. Some consider the position to be a stepping-stone to higher political aspirations, and in fact, several previous members currently serve or have served as members of the Texas Senate or House of Representatives.

Candidates for the Texas State Board of Education must meet the following eligibility requirements: U.S. citizen, minimum of 26 years of age, and resident of the State Board district for the year immediately preceding the election, as well as a qualified voter. Candidates run for a four-year term of office on a partisan slate, and if a Board vacancy occurs, the Governor appoints the replacement. After the 1994 election, members of the Republican party made up the majority of the Board for the first time, reflecting election trends across the nation. Elections in 1996 resulted in a political composition of nine Republicans and six Democrats, and a gender breakdown of ten male and five female members.

Prepared for inclusion in this text by Diane Patrick, 1999.

Typically elections to the SBOE have generated little interest, with candidates spending relatively little money in election campaigns, but strategies used in 1994 and 1996 changed the picture dramatically. Several political action committees that support ultraconservative candidates contributed hundreds of thousands of dollars to help candidates defeat and/or challenge incumbents in several State Board districts (Wallstin, 1997).

Personal and political reputations were at stake, as the campaigns associated with these races were considered by many to be the dirtiest seen at any political level. Literature that was distributed on behalf of the challengers suggested that incumbents who supported the adoption of controversial high school health textbooks were in favor of the legalization of marijuana and featured a photo of a white man and a black man kissing, "exploiting latent racial and sexual fears" (Wallstin, 1997).

Although Republican party members currently dominate the State Board, factions among the members have been created due to differences in educational philosophies ranging from ultraconservative to liberal. For example, the five ultraconservative Republicans typically vote as a block, oftentimes leaving the majority vote to be comprised of the six Democrats plus the remaining Republicans.

Organizational Structure

The organizational structure within the State Board is fairly simple. The Chair, limited to two 2-year terms in the position of leadership, is appointed by the Governor from among the fifteen State Board members. The other officers, consisting of the Vice-chair and the Secretary, are elected by the Board itself. There are five standing SBOE committees appointed by the Chair, and each committee elects its own Committee Chair. These committees are Students, Personnel, Finance, Permanent School Fund, and Long Range Planning.

Required by law to meet a minimum of four times annually, the State Board holds about six meetings annually in Austin at the William B. Travis Building at 1701 N. Congress on Thursday and Friday before the second Saturday of the month. Committee meetings are generally held the day before the regular board meetings. Meetings are open, and members of the public may testify before the Board by registering their intent. Agendas are published in advance and available to interested parties.

The SBOE also appoints special task forces or ad hoc committees to examine particular issues in depth. Examples of these committees are the Students with Disabilities and the Literacy Task Forces.

Usually resulting in major Board policy statements, the membership of these committees is broad based and includes members of the general public as well as educators.

Duties and Responsibilities

The State Board of Education works as an advocate for schoolchildren in partnership with the Governor, the legislature, and local school boards to see that an effective system of public education is established and maintained in Texas. Reporting results to the public and facilitating the flow of information is part of the ongoing goal of communication that is a necessary part of the entire process of accountability for education in the state.

The State Board of Education has duties ranging from establishing the essential elements of the curriculum (Texas Essential Knowledge and Skills, or TEKS) to approving rules concerning extracurricular activities and school district accreditation. They also determine high school graduation requirements and standards for satisfactory student performance on statewide assessment instruments, as well as adopt and purchase state textbooks. Furthermore, the State Board writes rules and guidelines for the implementation of specific statutory education requirements enacted by the legislature, an example being granting open-enrollment charter schools.

Another duty, and perhaps the most important, is the management of the Permanent School Fund (PSF) as authorized under the Texas Constitution. Created in 1854, this task is a rather awesome one, considering that the corpus of the fund has a market value of over $14 billion dollars, making it one of the largest endowments in the country. Revenue generated from the fund is used to offset the cost of textbooks by providing over $300 for each of the state's almost four million schoolchildren.

The Board is charged to exercise fiscal prudence in the investment of the PSF, a philosophy that has historically resulted in conservative internal money management by TEA staff. Recently, however, the Board hired external managers from the private sector to oversee more aggressive investment of a portion of the money. This has been a point of controversy between Board members who favored such actions and those who felt such a move was too risky. Time will determine the wisdom of this course of action.

Legislative actions over the last few sessions have gradually decreased the responsibilities of the Texas State Board of Education, and there are indications that this trend will continue. For example, educator preparation and certification was moved to the new State Board for Educator Certification created under 1995 legislation. Furthermore, several other duties were shifted to the Commissioner of Education or to local school districts. Texas Education Code § 7.003 states "An educational function not specifically delegated to the agency or the board under this code is reserved to and shall be performed by school districts or open-enrollment charter schools."

One reason for this shift of power from the state to the local school district level is the current national movement toward decentralization, and Texas has followed the lead of other states in the establishment of charter school laws. Charter schools have created opportunities for educational entrepreneurs to establish public schools outside many of the rules and regulations of state and local education agencies.

Some long-time observers of the dynamics of state politics have suggested that legislators have become increasingly upset with various actions of the State Board. Public comments and proposed legislation during the 1997 session of the legislature support this claim. Key state legislative educational leader Senator Bill Ratliff, R-Mount Pleasant, stated that he was ready to do away with the whole state school board, and subsequent bills were filed that attempted to abolish the State Board (Kennedy, 1997).

Following several contentious board meetings in the spring of 1997, then Lt. Gov. Bob Bullock, a Democrat, threatened a return to an appointed board, admonishing the elected body, "They need to behave. Texas government needs to get on with educating our children" (Bullock may back, 1997). State Representative Ron Lewis, D-Orange, proposed reducing regular meetings from 10 to four times a year (Ramos, 1997).

Another bill filed by the Chair of the House Public Education Committee Representative Paul Sadler, D-Henderson, would have drastically curtailed the power of the Board only to oversight of the Permanent School Fund and the Texas Growth Fund. However, most of these attempts at further reduction of the Board's power were unsuccessful.

In recent years the Board has been mired in various political controversies. Particularly rancorous issues dominated the meetings during the adoption process of the Texas Essential Knowledge and Skills (TEKS), a curriculum rewrite that stretched over almost three years. Developed with input from thousands of parents and educators across the state, criticism of the TEKS by the ultraconservative members included the accusation of undue influence of the federal government and/or national special-interest groups (Stutz, 1997 b).

Furthermore, some members have challenged 1995 laws that specifically limited the powers of the SBOE to reject textbooks only for the following reasons: factual errors that the publisher cannot change, failure to meet essential elements (now TEKS), or defective binding. This strict interpretation was upheld by Attorney General Opinion DM–424 (1996). Arguments over textbook content have revolved around evolution versus creationism in science textbooks, birth control and homosexuality in health textbooks, and phonics versus whole language in reading textbooks. No longer able to reject a book on the basis of content, reactionary tactics have included a member who stood up at a meeting and ripped off the cover of a textbook to demonstrate "worthless" binding (TEA, 1997).

The five Republican Board members aligned with religious conservatives have recently called for the elimination of the Texas Assessment of Academic Skills (TAAS), the statewide assessment instrument that is the underpinning of the state's accountability system for education. Republican Governor Bush, key bipartisan legislative leaders, and other members of the State Board of Education do not agree with this proposal (Stutz, 1997 a).

Although conflicting educational philosophies have managed to coexist for many years, questions remain as to the amount of political theatrics that are appropriate in educational decision-making. For the time being, however, recent actions of the State Board of Education suggest that indeed, partisan politics appears destined to play an increasingly significant role in educational policymaking and administration in Texas. Although typically the State Board election is of little interest during the primary and general elections, the decision as to the degree of politics that will be tolerated ultimately rests in the hands of Texas voters. They are the ones who will decide the outcome of future elections to the Texas State Board of Education.

REFERENCES

Op., Atty. Gen. No. DM–424, (November 21, 1996).

"Bullock may back appointing school panel." (1997, March 25). *The Dallas Morning News,* p. 28A.

Kennedy, B. (1997, March 20). "Calling Dr. Neill: Public schools still need a hero." *Ft. Worth Star Telegram,* p. B2.

Ramos, C. (1997, March 10). "School board meeting cut eyed." *San Antonio Express-News,* pp. 8A, 13A.

Stutz, T. (1997 a, February 21). "Five state education board members urge abolishing TAAS." *The Dallas Morning News*, p. 17A.

Stutz, T. (1997 b, March 5). "Member warns State Board of Education." *The Dallas Morning News*, p. 14A.

Texas Education Agency (November/December 1997). *Texas Education Today.* (Vol. XI, No. 2). Austin, Texas: Author.

Wallstin, B. (1997). "Basic Ballard," *Houston Press.* Houston, Texas: NewTimes, Inc.

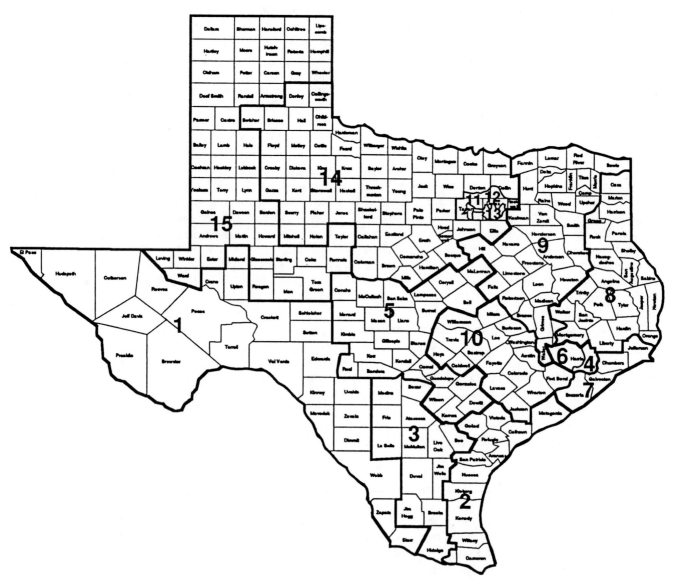

FIGURE 1   State Board of Education Districts

CHAPTER 3

The Texas State Board for Educator Certification

The desire to self-govern is not uniquely Texan, but self-governance is an educational freedom that permeates the history of public education in Texas. As early as 1871, the Texas State Board of Education provided a three-member panel of examiners to serve as the oversight body for the certification of teachers. (The Handbook of Texas School Law, 1948). The panel of examiners was the initial body to serve in an advisory capacity to the commissioner of education or another governing body. However, it was not until the passage of Senate Bill 1 in 1995 that educators in Texas were recognized as professionals with the authority to govern all aspects of their profession.

In 1995, the 74th Legislature passed Senate Bill 1, the state's most recent significant educational reform legislation. Primarily due to the efforts of the Chairman of the Senate Education Committee, Bill Ratliff, and the Chairman of the House Committee on Public Education, Paul Sadler, the State Board for Educator Certification (SBEC) was established "to recognize public school educators as professionals and to grant educators the authority to govern the standards of their profession." (Texas Education Code, §21.031)

The 15-member board was the first educator-dominant board in Texas to have regulatory oversight for the practice of educator certification. Twelve members of the board are voting members,

of which seven (a clear majority) must be educators practicing in Texas public schools. Of those educators, four must be classroom teachers, two must be administrators, and one a school counselor. Of the five remaining voting members, three must never have been employed as public school educators. The Governor of the State of Texas appoints all voting members to the board for six-year terms. Three non-voting members serve on an advisory basis. One is an employee of the Texas Education Agency and is appointed by the Commissioner of Education. Another is an employee of the Texas Higher Education Coordinating Board and is appointed by the Commissioner of Higher Education. The third advisory member is a dean of education in Texas appointed by the Governor (TEC §21.033).

The SBEC is obligated to perform two functions related to public education. The state legislature charges the SBEC with the responsibility of administering educator certificates and accrediting the state's educator preparation programs. Most citizens are aware of the function of issuing and renewing educator certificates. Through this function, the SBEC provides a means for examining prospective Texas educators through the Examination for the Certification of Educators in Texas, or ExCET tests. Additionally, the SBEC is responsible for the investigation and administrative prosecution of educators who have transgressed the "safe to practice" creed by violating statutory (usually criminal) law or who have violated the Educator's Code of Ethics.

A function of the SBEC that is emerging as noteworthy is the task of providing oversight for the

Prepared for inclusion in this text by Mark Littleton, 1999.

accreditation of the state's educator preparation programs. Shifting from an accreditation process based primarily on process, SBEC has taken the national lead in establishing accreditation based on outcomes, or on the performance of the graduates of the educator preparation programs.

The Certification of Educators

As was noted earlier, the most public function of SBEC is the issuance and renewal of educator certificates. The mere volume of certificates issued on an annual basis (approximately 25,000) is remarkable. But, as provided by Senate Bill 1, the SBEC was charged with instituting a certificate renewal system. Beginning with certificates issued on or after September 1, 1999, all certificates issued are on a renewable basis. (Prior to the administrative rules adopted by the SBEC requiring the issuance of renewable certificates, Texas was one of three states that issued initial "lifetime" certificates.) The adoption of those rules did not occur without fanfare. Teacher organizations vigorously contested proposed rules that called for the elimination of all lifetime certificates. However, through negotiations between teacher organizations and prominent legislators, SBEC rules were adopted allowing for certificates issued prior to September 1, 1999 to be "grandfathered" from the renewal requirement.

Unfortunately, upon occasion an educator violates state law or the educator's code of ethics, which may lead the state to question the educator's ability to effectively educate the public school students of Texas. As an arm of the state, the SBEC issues certificates to individuals who can only be reprimanded, or whose certificates can be suspended or revoked after being given adequate due process of law. Consequently, the SBEC also serves as the investigative/disciplinary arm for certified educators. Although educators who are reported for suspected violation represent less than 1% of the practicing certified educators in Texas, that small percentage translates into approximately 2,000 reports annually that require an investigation.

Examination of the Certification of Educators in Texas.   Teacher testing has historically led to considerable debate. Educators and policy makers often take opposing sides and engage in emotional disagreements. Many policy makers insist that standardized tests provide assurances to the public regarding the overall competency of the teaching force, while some educators counter that a paper-and-pencil test is not a valid measure of professional competence. Texans often point to the Texas Exami-

nation for the Certification of Educators in Texas, or TECAT, as a prime example. Although it is debatable, educators often comment that the administration of the TECAT created a backlash that led to the political downfall of a once-popular governor.

However, teacher testing became a part of the certification process in 1987 and continues to the present day. The Examination for the Certification of Educators in Texas (ExCET) is administered to approximately 55,000 educators each year. With very few exceptions, individuals wishing to become certified in Texas must successfully complete one or more ExCET tests. To qualify for a teaching credential, a candidate must achieve a passing score on a test of professional practice and a test of knowledge in a chosen academic field or specialization.

When the SBEC decides that an ExCET test must be developed or revised, an ExCET development committee composed of Texas educators is convened. The ExCET development committee relies upon research and subject area experts to develop a set of objectives to be used in the test development. Once the objectives are created and the test items developed, the ExCET development committee reviews the test items for alignment with the objectives and relevance to the subject area. The examination items are then field-tested, and the data collected from the field-test are reviewed by the ExCET development committee. The ExCET development committee reviews the results for bias, difficulty, and validity. Only after the ExCET development committee conducts a rigorous review and field-testing of the test items are they placed into the test bank.

Accreditation of Educator Preparation Programs

Although normal schools, which had the primary purpose of preparing teachers, existed in Texas in the early 1900s, accreditation of teacher preparation was not a function of the state until the 1950s. Accreditation was left to organizations such as the Association of Texas Colleges, the Southern Association of Colleges and Secondary Schools, and the American Association of Colleges for Teacher Education (Evans, 1955). However, in 1955, state accreditation took center stage and led to the development of the 1955 Standards for Teacher Education in Texas. Like the accreditation standards of the national organizations, the state accreditation process focused on the "inputs" of a teacher education program. Faculty training, teaching load, library holdings, specified semester hours of course work, and a prescription of laboratory experiences were areas investigated to determine the accreditation status of a teacher education program.

Since the development of the 1955 standards, revisions have been frequent and fragmented. Standards were revised in 1972, 1977, 1984, and again in 1987. Primarily because of the prescriptive limitations contained in the 1987 standards, national organizations such as the National Council for the Accreditation of Teacher Education (NCATE) became skeptical of the ability of colleges and universities to ensure the quality of the graduates of educator preparation programs (Watts, 1994). Many state institutions reluctantly chose to withdraw from NCATE rather than face the prospects of having their accreditation denied because of limitations imposed by the 1987 standards.

As a part of the revision of the 1987 standards, Texas moved toward a system of identifying the performance outcomes expected of teachers, administrators, and counselors. These outcomes, better known as learner-centered proficiencies, have become the basis of initial program approval for educator preparation programs, as well as the foundation on which all ExCET tests are developed. The proficiencies have become the focal point of educator evaluations, including pre-service examinations and in-service assessments, as the state has moved toward the development of a new system of accreditation and accountability.

An outgrowth of the state's successful public school accountability system was the Accountability System for Educator Preparation (ASEP). To ensure high quality in educator preparation, the legislature directed the SBEC to institute an accountability system, which takes into consideration:

1. The results of students on the ExCET, and
2. The performance of the beginning teachers based on an SBEC-adopted appraisal system. (TEC §21.045)

The consequence of an institution's failure to address the deficiencies identified by the ASEP may lead to program dissolution within a three-year period. Obviously, the stakes are quite high, and legal challenges are inevitable. Nonetheless, Texas has chosen to take the lead in holding institutions accountable for the performance of their graduates.

Funding

The State Board for Educator Certification is considered a self-funding state agency. Although the state legislature must appropriate funds to operate the agency, the fees for issuance and maintenance of educator certificates must be sufficient to cover the ad-

ministration of the agency. The fees are deposited into the state's general fund, from which the legislature makes its appropriation.

Approval of Rules

The SBEC was granted authority by the Texas legislature to "adopt rules as necessary for its own procedures." The SBEC can adopt rules to: (TEC § 21.041)

1. Provide for the regulation of educators
2. Specify the classes of educator certificates and the period of time for which each is valid
3. Specify requirements for the issuance and renewal of certificates
4. Provide for the transfer for certificates issued outside of the state
5. Provide for special certificates
6. Provide for disciplinary proceedings for the reprimand of educators
7. Provide for an educator's code of ethics
8. Provide for continuing education requirements
9. Certify individuals performing appraisals

As with other state regulatory boards, the SBEC must follow the Texas Government Code in the development of rules. However, to ensure the creation of the SBEC as the law navigated through the legislative process, a unique approval process for SBEC-generated rules was created. Upon proposal of rules by the SBEC, the Texas State Board of Education has 90 days in which to reject the rules by two-thirds majority. Upon the expiration of the 90-day review period, the SBEC must then formally adopt the rules prior to submission to the Secretary of State, at which time the rules become a part of the Texas Administrative Code. Should the State Board of Education reject the rules, the rules are rejected as submitted. Essentially, the State Board of Education does not possess the authority to reject, modify, or amend portions of the submitted rules. It is because of this process that the SBEC is said to be a "semiautonomous" board.

REFERENCES

Evans, C. E. (1955). *The Story of Texas Schools.* Austin, TX: Steck.

TEXAS EDUCATION CODE, SUBCHAPTER B. CERTIFICATION OF EDUCATORS (1996).

The Handbook of Texas School Law (ed. 2) (1948). Austin, TX: Steck.

Watts, D. (1994). NCATE and Texas Eyeball to Eyeball: Who Will Blink? *Phi Delta Kappan.* December, pp. 311–318.

CODE OF ETHICS AND STANDARD PRACTICES FOR TEXAS EDUCATORS

19 Texas Administrative Code Chapter 247.

Statutory Authority: *The provisions of this Chapter 247 are authorized under Texas Education Code, §21.041(b)(8), which requires the State Board for Educator Certification (SBEC) to propose rules providing for the adoption, enforcement, and amendment of an educators' code of ethics, and Section 63(i) of the conforming amendments to Senate Bill 1 (74th Legislature, 1995), which provides for a code of ethics proposed by the SBEC and adopted by the State Board of Education.*

§247.1. Purpose and Scope.

In compliance with the Texas Education Code, §21.041(b)(8), the State Board for Educator Certification (the board) adopts an educators' code of ethics as set forth in §247.2 of this chapter. The board may amend the ethics code in the same manner as any other formal rule. The board is solely responsible for enforcing the ethics code for purposes related to certification disciplinary proceedings.

§247.2. Code of Ethics and Standard Practices for Texas Educators.

(a) Professional responsibility. The Texas educator should strive to create an atmosphere that will nurture to fulfillment the potential of each student. The educator shall comply with standard practices and ethical conduct toward students, professional colleagues, school officials, parents, and members of the community. In conscientiously conducting his or her affairs, the educator shall exemplify the highest standards of professional commitment.

(b) Principle I: Professional ethical conduct. The Texas educator shall maintain the dignity of the profession by respecting and obeying the law, demonstrating personal integrity, and exemplifying honesty.

   (1) Standard 1.   The educator shall not intentionally misrepresent official policies of the school district or educational institution and shall clearly distinguish those views from personal attitudes and opinions.

   (2) Standard 2.   The educator shall honestly account for all funds committed to his or her charge and shall conduct financial business with integrity.

   (3) Standard 3.   The educator shall not use institutional or professional privileges for personal or partisan advantage.

   (4) Standard 4.   The educator shall accept no gratuities, gifts, or favors that impair professional judgment.

   (5) Standard 5.   The educator shall not offer any favor, service, or thing of value to obtain special advantage.

   (6) Standard 6.   The educator shall not falsify records, or direct or coerce others to do so.

(c) Principle II: Professional practices and performance. The Texas educator, after qualifying in a manner established by law or regulation, shall assume responsibilities for professional administrative or teaching practices and professional performance and shall demonstrate competence.

   (1) Standard 1.   The educator shall apply for, accept, offer, or assign a position or a responsibility on the basis of professional qualifications and shall adhere to the terms of a contract or appointment.

   (2) Standard 2.   The educator shall not deliberately or recklessly impair his or her mental or physical health or ignore social prudence, thereby affecting his or her ability to perform the duties of his or her professional assignment.

   (3) Standard 3.   The educator shall organize instruction that seeks to accomplish objectives related to learning.

   (4) Standard 4.   The educator shall continue professional growth.

   (5) Standard 5.   The educator shall comply with written local school board policies, state regulations, and other applicable state and federal laws.

(d) Principle III: Ethical conduct toward professional colleagues. The Texas educator, in exemplifying ethical relations with colleagues, shall accord just and equitable treatment to all members of the profession.

   (1) Standard 1.   The educator shall not reveal confidential information concerning colleagues unless disclosure serves lawful professional purposes or is required by law.

   (2) Standard 2.   The educator shall not willfully make false statements about a colleague or the school system.

   (3) Standard 3.   The educator shall adhere to written local school board policies and state and federal laws regarding dismissal, evaluation, and employment processes.

   (4) Standard 4.   The educator shall not interfere with a colleague's exercise of political and citizenship rights and responsibilities.

(5) Standard 5.   The educator shall not discriminate against, coerce, or harass a colleague on the basis of race, color, religion, national origin, age, sex, disability, or family status.

(6) Standard 6.   The educator shall not intentionally deny or impede a colleague in the exercise or enjoyment of any professional right or privilege.

(7) Standard 7.   The educator shall not use coercive means or promise of special treatment in order to influence professional decisions or colleagues.

(8) Standard 8.   The educator shall have the academic freedom to teach as a professional privilege, and no educator shall interfere with such privilege except as required by state and/or federal laws.

(e) Principle IV: Ethical conduct toward students. The Texas educator, in accepting a position of public trust, should measure success by progress of each student toward realization of his or her potential as an effective citizen.

(1) Standard 1.   The educator shall deal considerately and justly with each student and shall seek to resolve problems including discipline according to law and school board policy.

(2) Standard 2.   The educator shall not intentionally expose the student to disparagement.

(3) Standard 3.   The educator shall not reveal confidential information concerning students unless disclosure serves lawful professional purposes or is required by law.

(4) Standard 4.   The educator shall make reasonable effort to protect the student from conditions detrimental to learning, physical health, mental health, or safety.

(5) Standard 5.   The educator shall not deliberately distort facts.

(6) Standard 6.   The educator shall not unfairly exclude a student from participation in a program, deny benefits to a student, or grant an advantage to a student on the basis of race, color, sex, disability, national origin, religion, or family status.

(7) Standard 7.   The educator shall not unreasonably restrain the student from independent action in the pursuit of learning or deny the student access to varying points of view.

(f) Principle V: Ethical conduct toward parents and community. The Texas educator, in fulfilling citizenship responsibilities in the community, should cooperate with parents and others to improve the public schools of the community.

(1) Standard 1.   The educator shall make reasonable effort to communicate to parents information that lawfully should be revealed in the interest of the student.

(2) Standard 2.   The educator shall endeavor to understand community cultures and relate the home environment of students to the school.

(3) Standard 3.   The educator shall manifest a positive role in school-public relations.

CHAPTER
4

Financing Schools in Texas

Knowledge of school finance is important for all citizens; however, an in-depth understanding of the subject is critical for educators. No area of school management is more critical to the success of day-to-day operations of the school or to the long-range plans for the district than informed resource management.

This chapter provides a general overview of the development and current state of school funding in Texas public schools. Part I reviews the history and context of school finance. Part II explains the basic school finance theories, while Part III looks at the school district budget. Part IV concludes with a discussion of future school finance issues. A glossary of terms and a chronology of important dates related to school finance are included in the Appendices.

I. HISTORY

In accordance with the Tenth Amendment to the United States Constitution, all powers not delegated to the federal government are reserved for the states. Since education is not addressed in the Constitution, states are therefore individually responsible for the education of their citizens. In response, state systems of school finance have evolved as a reflection of prevalent political philosophies of the historical period.

The development pattern of school finance in Texas has progressed much like that of other states:

from complete local funding, to various alternatives increasing state responsibility, to present-day plans emphasizing equality of student educational opportunity and greater taxpayer equity. Later trends toward opportunity for a public education to all students support the practice of the ideals of democracy in the United States (Burrup, Brimley, & Garfield, 1996). Over the last 150 years, Texas public school financing has had a colorful history. Beginning with the accusation in 1836 that the Mexican government had failed to provide public schools, improvement of education has been the battle cry for many political and/or physical battles since that time.

The Permanent School Fund (PSF) was established in 1854 as a permanent educational endowment to be distributed to districts on a per capita basis. With a current market value of approximately 14 billion dollars, today the fund provides approximately $300 per student annually, depending on the revenue from investment returns. Rated in the highest category as a AAA investment, the PSF is also used to guarantee Texas school bonds.

Written in 1876, Section I, Article VII of the current Texas Constitution requires "the legislature . . . to establish and make suitable provision for the support and maintenance of an efficient system of public schools." During this time period, the term *public schools* was interpreted to mean private and community enterprises, while *free schools* were for orphans and paupers. Of further historical interest is the early use in Texas of vouchers for students enrolled in local schools during the mid-1800s (Walker & Casey, 1996).

Prepared for inclusion in this text by Diane Patrick, 1999.

Walker and Casey (1996) describe Texas school finance as simple in the extreme prior to 1949, and conversely, complex in the extreme in subsequent years. From the Gilmer-Aiken Act of 1949, to House Bill 72 in 1984, the finance formula in 1993 Senate Bill 7 of 1993, to the current provision of Senate Bill 4 of 1999, attempts at equity in school funding coupled with weighted pupil and district allowances have resulted in increasingly complicated school funding plans.

Traditionally local school districts have determined the level of school funding through property taxes, which remain the primary source of school funding in Texas and in most other states. Renchler (1992) describes this system as "de facto economic determinism," where wealthy districts are able to generate high levels of revenue with minimum taxing effort compared with low-wealth districts where very high property tax rates result in low levels of school funding. As a percentage of all state and local taxes, Texas is positioned eleventh among all states in reliance on property taxes (Clark & England, 1997).

More than thirty state Supreme Court decisions have been issued in cases contesting school funding formulas since the early 1970s (NASBE, 1997). Financing plans were overturned in about half of the cases on the basis that they violated either the education clause or the equal protection clause of the state's Constitution, but clear guidelines for addressing the inequities have not been provided, resulting in repeated legislative remedies, followed by second and third rounds of court tests (Renchler, 1992).

The history of litigation over equity issues in Texas began in 1971 with *Rodriguez v. San Antonio*, in which the Supreme Court upheld the state's system as constitutional under the U. S. Constitution. Later lawsuits, known as the *Edgewood I, II, IIa, III and IV*, were filed in state courts from 1984 until 1995, when the Texas Supreme Court ruled as constitutional the equity provisions in school funding under Senate Bill 7 (1993).

II. EQUALIZATION THEORIES AND METHODS

There are three basic equalization finance theories: foundation programs, percentage equalizing or guaranteed yield programs, and power equalizing. All states combine or recombine factors within these theories: district wealth, district needs, district tax effort, district tax yield, and state assistance. According to Clark and England (1997), "all of the models are mathematically equivalent," . . . but . . . "emphasize different aspects or types of equity" (p. 4).

Foundation programs rely on a concept in which state funds are provided to enable districts to receive state funds for a minimum program. Local districts may increase expenditures above the foundation program.

Percentage equalizing, or guaranteed yield formulas, are based on a local-state partnership approach. A foundation level is established, and the percentage of state and local funds is based on the wealth of the district.

Power equalizing or recapture combines the principles of equalization and reward for effort. The state provides differing amounts of equalized aid, and there is recapture of local dollars in excess of a certain level (Burrup et al., 1996; Walker & Casey, 1996).

As shown in Figure 1, in order to achieve greater equalization of school funding, Texas has two tiers that use a combination of the foundation program model and an adaptation of the guaranteed yield model. The third tier is based on locally approved bonds and the subsequent local taxes for debt service. Debt service taxes may exceed the $1.50 cap imposed by statute.

Clark and England (1997) describe Tier I as a basic foundation program model where: (1) the state supports a uniform minimum level of expenditures in each district in the state, (2) the program is equalized based on the taxable wealth of the school district, (3) there is a required minimum effective tax rate of 86 cents per 100 dollars of property values for 1996–1997, (4) the foundation level is based on a basic allotment ($2,396 in 1997) and a series of formulas intended to measure district needs, and (5) districts may not enrich the foundation program except for voter-approved bonded indebtedness. Based on the principles of a guaranteed yield, Tier II ensures equitable availability of monies for district tax effort above the required rate of 86 cents.

Sometimes called the "Robin Hood Plan," Texas Senate Bill 7 (1993) established equalization through redistribution of funds generated by the state's wealthiest districts. By exercising one of five options shown in Figure 2, school districts with property values that exceed $280,000 in property value per weighted student must divest this portion of their wealth. Sometimes described as "Five Ways to Pick Your Poison," Option 4 has been exercised by some districts; however, incentives added by the state in 1995 appear to have influenced the majority of districts to choose Option 3. Therefore, most districts simply write a check to the state (Funkhouser, 1996; Walker & Casey, 1996).

TIER III	(**State** Share)
FACILITIES IMPROVEMENT (Optional Taxes)	(**Local**) Voter-Approved Bonds for Capital Improvement

EQUALIZED PORTION

TIER II	(**State** Share) Based on Tax Effort Above $0.86
GUARANTEED YIELD (Optional Taxes)	(**Local**)

TIER I	(**State** Share) Available School Fund
	(**State** Share) Per Capita Apportionment
FOUNDATION SCHOOL PROGRAM (Required Tax Effort)	**Local Fund Assignment** $0.86 Applied to State Values of Local Property Basic Entitlements and Special Allotments Equalized according to property wealth per WADA

FIGURE 1 Basic School Finance Structure in Texas
Source: Walker & Casey, 1996, p. 45; S. Brown, personal communication, March 25, 1998.

Option	Action Required
1. Consolidation with another district	School board approval
2. Detachment of tax base and annexation to another district	School board approval
3. Purchase of attendance credits from state	Voter approval
4. Contracting for education of nonresident students	Voter approval
5. Tax base consolidation with another district	Voter approval

FIGURE 2 Senate Bill 7 (1993) Wealth-Reduction District Options and Action Required
Source: Walker & Casey, 1996.

III. THE SCHOOL DISTRICT BUDGET

Revenue

Figure 3 illustrates the proportions of federal, state, and local sources of revenue for the public schools in Texas. The largest portion, approximately 52% comes from the local district, followed by the state's share at 44.5%, with the remaining 3.6% coming from the federal government (TEA, 1997). Of particular note is the fact that, although the total dollar amount increased in 1996–1997, the percentage of federal dollars decreased from approximately 8% to less than 4%, thus increasing the state and local percentages from previous years.

Most revenue from the federal government goes directly to school districts as categorical funds designated to supplement programs such as the education of students with disabilities, low-achieving and disadvantaged students, and vocational programs. Texas was granted special Ed-Flex status in 1996, which will allow more flexibility in implementation of federal programs.

The major source of local school revenue is property taxes, the only tax available to school districts (Clark & England, 1997). Levied by the locally elected district Board of Trustees, property taxes are set at a rate per hundred dollars of valuation. The property valuation is determined by the local

County Appraisal District. Upon request, home-owners are entitled to automatic homestead exemptions, and there are additional exemptions for eligible taxpayers, e.g., disabled veterans. The school taxes of senior citizens are frozen at age 65.

As illustrated in the Figure 4 calculation, if the local school district tax rate is $1.498 (the average Texas school effective tax rate), the owner of a $85,000 house with a $15,000 homestead exemption would owe $1,048.00 annually for taxes to that particular school district.

While obviously popular with recipients of the benefit, exemptions actually have the effect of shifting the tax burden to the remaining taxpayers. Two types of business exemptions substantially impact school tax revenues throughout the state: abatements and freeport goods exemptions.

Abatements have been used as an incentive for business location in Texas communities by giving a waiver from some or all of the local taxes. After 1993, abatements approved by the local school district Boards of Trustees create a "double whammy" effect due to decreased state aid as the new business increases property values, and this is then combined with the lack of local tax revenue due to the abatement.

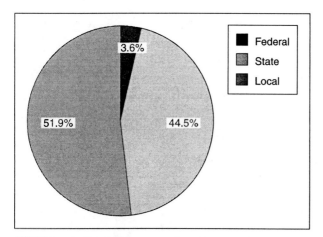

FIGURE 3   Sources of Revenue for Texas Public Schools
Source: Texas Education Agency, 1997.

Freeport goods exemptions are granted by local School Boards for goods in transit. Similar to the effect of abatements, school districts have to consider if the decreased tax revenue created by freeport goods exemptions will be offset by increased economic activity.

Expenditures

About 28% of all state expenditures go to public education in Texas. The cost is about $5,000 per student or approximately 20 billion dollars annually. With 1,059 school districts, Texas has more districts than any other state. Many of these districts are small, with over half (about 55%) enrolling fewer than 1000 pupils. There are almost 4 million students in prekindergarten through grade 12, with an annual 2% growth rate, which has implications for both state and local budgets.

Figure 5 reflects the ethnic makeup of Texas public schools, where students who are minorities make up 54% with 14.3% African American, 37.4% Hispanic, and 2.6% other. Students who are white comprise 45%.

Approximately 48% of Texas students are considered economically disadvantaged, which is determined by participation in the free and reduced lunch program (TEA, 1997).

School district budgets are divided into two general categories: Maintenance and Operations (M & O) and Interest and Sinking (I & S). A labor-intensive industry, over three fourths of the school district's M & O budget is determined by salaries for personnel. The authority of the local school board to raise the tax rate is limited by law. For example, if the M & O effective tax rate is increased by more than 8 cents over the previous year, a rollback election is automatically triggered. Passage of a rollback measure would mean that tax rates would be rolled back to the current effective M & O rate. Furthermore, M & O is capped statewide at $1.50 maximum (Clark & England, 1997).

Formula: Tax Rate times Appraised Property Value (APV) less Exemptions and divided by 100

$$\frac{\text{Tax Rate} \times (\text{APV less Exemptions})}{100} = \frac{1.498 \times (\$85,000 - \$15,000)}{100}$$

$$\frac{1.498 \times \$70,000}{100} = \frac{\$104,860}{100} = \$1,048.60$$

FIGURE 4   Tax Calculation Example

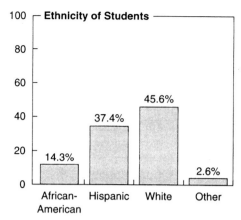

FIGURE 5 Ethnicity of Students in Texas Public Schools
Source: Texas Education Agency, 1997.

I & S is that portion of the budget used to retire debt created through financing capital improvements. Authorized by voters in local bond elections, I & S funds may not be used for district operating expenses. In terms of voter-approved debt burden, Texas ranks first at 11 billion dollars, mainly due to an increasing need for buildings and capital improvements (TASB, 1996).

IV. FUTURE FINANCE ISSUES

In a typical community, three out of four taxpayers do not have children in school. With an ever-increasing number of districts at or near the statutory $1.50 cap on maintenance and operations, a school funding crisis is looming. While some speculate that the pressure from local school districts will persuade lawmakers to raise the cap, some legislators have indicated a strong preference that voters have their say on any increases in tax rates. The practice of voting on a mill levy increase occurs in some other states.

Various plans to relieve the burden on local property taxes have been discussed; however, previous attempts to revise the existing tax structure have met with limited success. Options include sales tax increase, statewide property tax, value-added or business activity tax, gross receipts tax, franchise tax, and income tax. Texas is one of a few states without a state personal income tax, but historically, this option has not been considered viable in Texas, primarily due to political ramifications.

The choice concept has emerged in the last decade as a response to concerns about school quality. This approach to public education has the potential to dramatically affect school funding. A variety of school choice plans exist in which funding follows the student, providing varying degrees of choice.

Texas charter schools were authorized in 1995 legislation that created three charter types: open-enrollment charters across or within districts, campus or program charters within districts, and home-rule charters for entire districts. Over 160 open-enrollment charter schools were up and running or approved in 1999. Held accountable to PEIMS and accountability data, the money follows the child to the charter schools. Most of these schools, both in Texas and across the nation, are small in size, but they have reduced operating expenses by flattening the organizational hierarchy, in some cases eliminating administration all together.

Public education grants (PEGs) provide the right of transfer for a student enrolled in a low-performing school. Funds follow the student from the home district to the receiving district. Subject to the approval of the receiving school board, limited use has been made of this option throughout the state.

Privatization efforts have been in effect for a number of years in certain areas of the school budget. For example, districts have contracted for services for maintenance, buses, or food service. New on the privatization scene is contracting for management services. For example, in 1996, Sherman I.S.D. hired Chris Whittle's Edison Project to run Washington Elementary School. Other educational entrepreneurs are creating similar for-profit corporations to manage schools throughout the nation.

Vouchers are given to families for the education of their children. Although legislation has been attempted in several states, at this writing only Ohio, Michigan and Florida have laws permitting vouchers. With the prospect of using public money for private religious education, the constitutionality of such an arrangement has been questioned. However, the voucher option is slowly gaining favor as more questions are being raised about the quality of public schools, especially in urban areas.

At the same time that equalization of school funding is gradually being accomplished throughout Texas, many districts have established local educational foundations to fund items that they would not otherwise be able to afford. Since educational foundations are largely dependent on resources in the local area, some are concerned that these local initiatives will undermine statewide equalization efforts (Burrup, et al., 1996).

In looking at the future of Texas school funding, many issues have yet to be resolved. Among questions ahead for policymakers are:

1. How to raise the money? What taxes are used and who levies them?
2. How to distribute the money? Who gets how much?

3. How to determine how much to spend on public schools? What portion of available public resources should be spent on schools as opposed to highways, prisons, health and human services?
4. How to decide what the money should be spent on? School buildings, teacher salaries, textbooks, extracurricular programs? (Lane, 1997).

Attempts to answer these questions create a dynamic political tension. The solutions have not been found in the current century, and as the next millennium approaches, policymakers will continue to struggle with these issues affecting the future of school funding in Texas.

REFERENCES

Burrup, P. E., Brimley, V., Jr., & Garfield, R. R. (1996). *Financing Education in a Climate of Change* (6th ed.). Boston: Allyn & Bacon.

Clark, C. P., & England, C. (1997, October). Educational Finance. *Briefing Paper: Texas Public School Finance and Related Issues.* Austin, TX: Texas Center for Educational Research.

Funkhouser, C. W. (Ed.). (1996). *Education in Texas: Policies, Practices, and Perspectives* (8th ed.). Scottsdale, AZ: Gorsuch Scarisbrick.

Lane, R. B. (1997, October 17). *Solutions within the system.* Presentation to the Business of Education Policy Conference. Dallas, TX: Federal Reserve Bank of Dallas.

NASBE Study Group on Funding Education in the 21st Century. (1997, October). *Financing student success: Beyond equity and adequacy.* Alexandria, VA: National Association of State Boards of Education.

Renchler, R. (1992, December). Financial equity in the schools. ERIC Digest, Number 76 [online]. Available HTTP: http://www.ed.gov/ databases/ERIC_Digests/ed350717.html

Texas Association of School Boards (TASB). (1996). *Benchmarks.* Austin, TX: Texas Association of School Boards. Research and Development.

Texas Education Agency (TEA). (1997, December). *Pocket Edition: 1996–97 Texas Public School Statistics.* (TEA Publication No. BR8 602 02). Austin, TX: Texas Education Agency.

Walker, B., & Casey, D. T. (1996). *The Basics of Texas Public School Finance* (6th ed.). Austin: TX: Texas Association of School Boards.

APPENDIX

A

Glossary of School Finance Terms

Abatement Provision whereby a business may be given a waiver from paying property taxes for a given period of time to the city, and/or the county, and/or the school district.

ADA Average Daily Attendance; daily attendance of students during a specified period of time.

ADM Average Daily Membership; the average number of students enrolled.

Basic Allotment (BA) Foundation program allocation based on average daily attendance per unweighted student.

Budget-balanced or **Chapter 41 district** Wealthy district that receives no State Foundation funds.

Categorical aid Dedicated funds (usually federal dollars) for a specific purpose that must be spent in this budget category.

Fiscal year September 1–August 31 in Texas public schools.

Freeport goods tax exemption Goods in transit that are not being taxed, as approved by a local taxing authority.

FTE Full-Time Equivalent; student enrolled six hours a day for five days a week that earns the state basic allotment plus the district cost adjustments.

I&S Interest and Sinking Funds (debt service); portion of the budget used to retire debt created by capital expenditures.

M&O Maintenance and Operations; portion of the budget used to operate the district.

PEG Public Education Grant; authorized under Senate Bill 1 (1995); students may transfer from low-performing schools or districts to a different school or district.

PEIMS Public Education Information Management System; required standards and procedures for school district data submission.

PSF Permanent School Fund; established in 1854 as a permanent endowment to fund Texas public education.

Robin Hood Plan Slang expression used to describe redistribution of money taken from the state's richest districts and given to the poorest in an effort to achieve equalization.

WADA Weighted Average Daily Attendance; ADA with extra weights for programs with higher costs (special education, vocational).

August 20 The date by which the school district budget must be presented to the local school board.

September 1 The beginning of the fiscal year; school district budgets should be adopted by this date.

January 31 Property taxes are due and delinquent after this date.

Chronology of Texas School Finance Events

1836 Republic of Texas established with a Constitution that provided for public education not provided by the Mexican government.

1845 Texas becomes a state with a Constitution mandating state taxes to support free public schools.

1854 Permanent endowment established for schools; later became Permanent School Fund.

1876 Current Constitution that requires legislature to establish and make suitable provision for the support and maintenance of an efficient system of public schools.

1918 State funding for free textbooks.

1949 *Gilmer-Aiken* Law; widesweeping reform bill that established the Minimum Foundation Program.

1973 *Rodriguez v. San Antonio I.S.D.* Supreme Court decision: Texas school funding constitutional under Federal Constitution; education is not a fundamental right.

1984 House Bill 72: reduced class sizes, pre-K program, career ladder, equalization.

1993 Senate Bill 7 established provisions for school funding equity in which any district over $280,000 in property wealth per child would divest their wealth.

1995 SB 7 found constitutional, thereby ending over a decade of litigation over school funding equity.

Texas Association of School Boards TASB Bench Marks 1997–98

Actual Expenditures by School Districts for 1996–1997
(100 Largest School Districts)

Actual Expenditures by School District for 1996–97 (100 Largest School Districts)

Amount per Student Enrolled (1997)

District Name	County Name	Fall 1995 enrollment	% Econ. disadv.	Central admin	Campus admin	Instruct. services	Instruct. related	Pupil services	Cocurricular activities	Transportation	Plant M & O	Community services	Total COE	Admin. ratio	Debt service	Capital outlay	Payroll
(1)	(2)	(3)	(4)	(5)	(6)	(7)	(8)	(9)	(10)	(11)	(12)	(13)	(14)	(15)	(16)	(17)	(18)
STATE AVERAGE		3,834,670	48	$312	$283	$2,949	$147	$515	$124	$135	$593	$24	$5,083	8.29	$385	$764	$4,113
AVG.-50 LARGEST DISTRICTS		2,000,644	50	283	291	2,914	160	517	86	123	594	28	4,997	7.19	411	688	4,132
AVG.-100 LARGEST DISTRICTS		2,552,090	50	290	287	2,909	158	521	95	126	591	28	5,006	7.51	411	752	4,120
HOUSTON	HARRIS	209,610	65	255	329	2,893	171	536	35	170	641	17	5,046	6.04	310	281	4,253
DALLAS	DALLAS	154,933	75	283	323	3,045	205	530	41	21	713	69	5,229	6.31	272	873	4,272
AUSTIN	TRAVIS	76,101	51	298	314	2,844	132	589	47	178	602	54	5,059	7.78	575	339	4,228
FORTH WORTH	TARRANT	75,838	59	273	311	2,847	160	547	73	134	678	33	5,057	7.72	237	129	4,209
EL PASO	EL PASO	64,568	67	342	306	2,957	160	500	89	140	493	6	4,995	9.70	337	696	4,176
SAN ANTONIO	BEXAR	61,420	91	295	337	3,366	262	682	75	78	623	105	5,822	6.67	177	324	4,999
NORTHSIDE	BEXAR	59,394	43	259	243	3,037	156	538	84	190	510	25	5,042	6.68	575	762	4,251
ARLINGTON	TARRANT	53,410	31	191	249	2,758	99	393	60	98	518	9	4,375	4.83	554	1,133	3,681
CYPRESS-FA	HARRIS	53,139	18	231	247	2,802	120	450	101	187	610	13	4,761	5.57	502	597	4,023
YSLETA	EL PASO	47,433	68	281	292	2,872	205	516	107	89	587	22	4,971	7.90	173	493	4,068
ALDINE	HARRIS	47,291	63	295	317	3,190	111	558	87	236	478	2	5,274	6.31	245	533	4,292
FORT BEND	FORT BEND	47,038	20	287	276	2,528	133	434	109	147	612	4	4,530	8.02	592	1,347	3,721
NORTH EAST	BEXAR	45,325	35	287	345	3,099	201	507	88	157	568	27	5,279	6.31	366	972	4,388
GARLAND	DALLAS	45,040	30	234	247	2,675	112	439	91	129	481	24	4,432	5.56	645	702	3,695
CORPUS CHRISTI	NUECES	41,606	52	317	282	2,945	136	500	126	105	549	45	5,006	8.60	349	574	4,016
PLANO	COLLIN	41,076	10	284	277	3,214	255	466	85	92	614	7	5,295	5.92	699	1,246	4,237
PASADENA	HARRIS	40,565	53	236	276	2,717	163	526	96	78	557	5	4,654	6.94	233	781	3,734
BROWNSVILLE	CAMERON	40,521	85	279	270	3,162	189	635	111	129	525	49	5,349	7.02	141	631	4,412
ALIEF	HARRIS	38,448	42	252	229	2,897	115	476	50	156	482	18	4,676	6.74	610	670	4,009
RICHARDSON	DALLAS	34,166	28	377	374	2,891	188	449	108	43	871	6	5,306	8.30	407	773	4,194
LUBBOCK	LUBBOCK	30,464	52	279	298	3,029	199	514	148	122	648	72	5,308	7.25	262	344	3,724
LEWISVILLE	DENTON	30,368	11	242	260	2,976	85	461	98	130	473	36	4,762	6.62	621	1,510	3,766
KLEIN	HARRIS	30,313	15	306	304	2,792	101	491	102	132	625	10	4,862	6.68	624	258	4,037
MESQUITE	DALLAS	30,037	27	268	246	2,422	146	448	131	51	736	5	4,453	9.01	858	1,158	3,528
SPRING BRANCH	HARRIS	29,914	49	420	302	3,173	185	542	99	129	632	43	5,526	10.17	522	1,335	4,618

Amount per Student Enrolled

Contracted instruction (19)	Contracted Prof. services (20)	Social security (21)	Health insurance (22)	Workers' Comp. (23)	Other benefits (24)	Total benefits (25)	Tax appr. collection (26)	Utility (27)	Interest (28)	Travel (29)	Library books (30)	TRS revenue (31)	Bond proceeds (32)	Chpt. 41 revenue adj. (33)	Total revenue (34)	District Name (1)
$36	$144	$48	$178	$47	$234	$507	$32	$156	$177	$39	$13	$192	$483	-85	$5,891	STATE AVERAGE
2	118	53	184	47	235	519	25	150	190	27	13	190	435	-12	5,709	AVG.-50 LARGEST DIST
10	124	51	182	49	234	516	25	150	191	30	13	189	485	-40	5,755	AVG.-100 LARGEST DIST
3	101	31	242	57	254	585	28	136	80	12	7	203	295	0	5,538	HOUSTON
0	111	35	112	54	239	440	24	163	203	14	22	194	0	0	5,564	DALLAS
0	175	260	169	56	220	705	31	120	278	21	10	181	1	0	5,960	AUSTIN
5	102	39	127	99	246	510	24	153	59	32	9	179	0	0	5,623	FORT WORTH
0	82	36	255	40	219	550	33	140	183	31	10	172	0	0	5,777	EL PASO
1	141	305	213	42	260	821	18	113	36	16	18	217	50	1	6,364	SAN ANTONIO
6	72	40	160	76	251	527	28	88	217	27	21	208	845	1	5,640	NORTHSIDE
0	79	33	121	35	209	399	25	158	307	16	12	181	1,224	0	4,869	ARLINGTON
3	101	34	187	32	221	475	25	170	266	25	17	196	345	9	5,616	CYPRESS-FA
0	85	33	268	70	249	621	21	138	69	56	11	192	126	0	5,725	YSLETA
0	86	41	112	29	249	430	15	130	98	22	5	207	1,290	0	5,754	ALDINE
1	118	34	166	24	213	436	18	184	228	19	24	197	24	0	5,423	FORT BEND
3	138	40	166	32	251	488	49	89	127	26	19	212	1,489	0	5,972	NORTH EAST
0	94	35	122	42	210	410	10	137	253	19	6	181	474	0	5,282	GARLAND
0	188	28	92	34	249	404	27	172	159	52	11	196	0	0	5,687	CORPUS CHRISTI
0	200	41	261	37	213	553	50	198	491	23	13	176	2,878	0	6,932	PLANO
0	74	30	175	0	154	358	23	157	102	22	14	129	263	0	5,417	PASADENA
0	70	37	295	70	258	660	14	164	19	33	16	209	0	0	6,221	BROWNSVILLE
0	41	36	161	23	219	440	0	140	291	20	11	182	0	0	5,653	ALIEF
0	119	31	249	54	207	541	23	201	93	17	5	181	1,414	-160	6,228	RICHARDSON
42	785	57	167	39	209	472	38	139	124	59	19	181	0	5	5,814	LUBBOCK
0	200	35	124	13	230	402	33	151	320	19	11	205	1,976	0	5,333	LEWISVILLE
1	54	34	148	9	248	440	26	206	363	20	5	206	99	0	5,689	KLEIN
0	107	33	89	38	204	364	16	177	361	25	22	176	331	2	5,347	MESQUITE
0	106	43	174	20	263	500	38	175	251	49	15	203	770	0	6,245	SPRING BRANCH

Amount per Student Enrolled (1997)

District Name	County Name	Fall 1995 enrollment	% Econ. disadv.	Central admin	Campus admin	Instruct. services	Instruct. related	Pupil services	Cocurricular activities	Transportation	Plant M & O	Community services	Total COE	Admin. ratio	Debt service	Capital outlay	Payroll
(1)	(2)	(3)	(4)	(5)	(6)	(7)	(8)	(9)	(10)	(11)	(12)	(13)	(14)	(15)	(16)	(17)	(18)
STATE AVERAGE		3,834,670	48	$312	$283	$2,949	$147	$515	$124	$135	$593	$24	$5,083	8.29	$385	$764	$4,113
AVG.-50 LARGEST DISTRICTS		2,000,644	50	283	291	2,914	160	517	86	123	594	28	4,997	7.19	411	688	4,132
AVG.-100 LARGEST DISTRICTS		2,552,090	50	290	287	2,909	158	521	95	126	591	28	5,006	7.51	411	752	4,120
CONROE	MONTGOMERY	29,705	26	326	283	2,864	80	461	156	248	576	4	4,999	7.71	581	889	4,325
AMARILLO	POTTER	29,656	49	264	252	2,794	125	491	93	56	458	29	4,562	6.93	274	273	3,742
ECTOR COUNTY	ECTOR	28,763	64	327	262	2,491	151	446	109	124	603	6	4,520	9.25	121	477	3,683
KILLEEN	BELL	28,438	48	235	277	2,772	304	446	118	132	520	13	4,817	5.46	187	500	3,843
CLEAR CREEK	GALVESTON	27,552	8	233	239	2,750	110	420	80	142	550	3	4,527	6.88	527	817	3,756
KATY	HARRIS	26,837	11	255	265	2,692	127	391	79	156	525	15	4,504	7.70	793	1,221	3,870
IRVING	DALLAS	26,759	49	301	297	2,887	118	508	88	10	566	4	4,780	8.44	650	220	4,023
ROUND ROCK	WILLIAMSON	26,395	20	286	278	2,856	117	462	108	96	542	17	4,762	7.46	948	1,732	3,956
MIDLAND	MIDLAND	23,354	44	213	279	2,689	159	461	99	146	530	29	4,605	5.77	199	282	3,856
LAREDO	WEBB	22,987	87	344	305	3,043	200	597	76	56	591	28	5,240	9.08	112	414	4,537
HUMBLE	HARRIS	22,701	14	274	296	2,876	178	538	74	141	608	16	5,002	6.80	662	465	4,277
MCALLEN	HIDALGO	21,704	62	355	246	3,075	249	666	205	76	568	55	5,496	9.18	363	196	4,530
UNITED	WEBB	21,413	70	311	287	2,620	110	503	77	157	526	13	4,602	9.56	638	546	3,759
CARROLLTON-FA	DALLAS	21,287	29	268	312	2,857	253	526	70	83	572	4	4,944	6.11	744	1,502	4,142
SOCORRO	EL PASO	21,126	70	280	308	2,810	142	565	156	128	700	36	5,125	7.69	498	1,312	4,038
SPRING	HARRIS	21,078	30	280	312	3,009	156	483	100	189	570	12	5,111	7.22	515	92	4,279
BIRDVILLE	TARRANT	20,469	27	278	258	2,850	81	430	101	86	525	0	4,609	8.05	553	1,336	3,870
PHARR-SAN JU	HIDALGO	20,377	87	383	278	3,212	167	659	110	109	526	49	5,492	9.70	155	1,166	4,560
BEAUMONT	JEFFERSON	20,021	61	340	308	3,125	121	610	101	159	624	67	5,455	8.89	143	1,130	4,511
ABILENE	TAYLOR	19,671	51	282	268	3,276	141	609	146	86	498	27	5,333	6.93	267	172	4,599
HURST-EU	TARRANT	19,227	24	309	219	3,019	114	483	115	64	551	1	4,875	8.31	442	1,051	4,085
EDINBURG C	HIDALGO	19,159	86	305	234	3,122	149	627	142	180	570	28	5,358	8.55	253	692	4,457
GRAND PRAIRIE	DALLAS	18,413	45	381	264	2,775	146	514	107	74	597	32	4,888	7.43	456	1,281	3,816
GOOSE CREEK	HARRIS	17,921	44	348	283	2,892	95	547	161	141	730	32	5,228	9.48	612	1,299	4,218
GALENA PARK	HARRIS	17,610	52	322	252	2,569	123	516	111	103	639	6	4,640	10.56	275	187	3,596

Amount per Student Enrolled

District Name (1)	Contracted instruction (19)	Contracted Prof. services (20)	Social security (21)	Health insurance (22)	Workers' Comp. (23)	Other benefits (24)	Total benefits (25)	Tax appr. collection (26)	Utility (27)	Interest (28)	Travel (29)	Library books (30)	TRS revenue (31)	Bond proceeds (32)	Chpt. 41 revenue adj. (33)	Total revenue (34)
STATE AVERAGE	$36	$144	$48	$178	$47	$234	$507	$32	$156	$177	$39	$13	$192	$483	-85	$5,891
AVG.-50 LARGEST DIST	2	118	53	184	47	235	519	25	150	190	27	13	190	435	-12	5,709
AVG.-100 LARGEST DIST	10	124	51	182	49	234	516	25	150	191	30	13	189	485	-40	5,755
CONROE	0	71	39	203	28	239	509	32	181	478	34	0	198	545	0	5,678
AMARILLO	3	79	32	223	25	212	493	30	108	95	45	7	183	1,422	18	5,181
ECTOR COUNTY	0	60	29	192	66	215	502	27	128	47	49	8	181	0	0	5,055
KILLEEN	0	47	36	226	19	214	495	17	144	83	31	18	190	0	0	6,330
CLEAR CREEK	0	122	24	235	25	231	515	29	204	313	21	4	190	0	0	5,128
KATY	3	64	39	119	30	231	420	32	158	339	19	22	0	2,162	0	5,703
IRVING	0	122	33	255	67	217	572	0	136	174	24	22	180	0	2	5,604
ROUND ROCK	6	148	41	214	31	193	478	48	154	461	31	14	177	189	0	6,090
MIDLAND	0	100	32	202	44	268	546	33	123	71	51	17	176	856	0	5,046
LAREDO	3	93	26	244	44	243	556	7	146	45	48	9	201	0	0	5,584
HUMBLE	0	108	41	107	42	263	453	0	209	346	18	8	238	969	1	5,837
MCALLEN	12	125	40	180	82	256	558	51	166	60	45	13	209	0	0	5,942
UNITED	3	81	42	179	36	212	470	20	167	326	39	23	171	0	1	5,350
CARROLLTON-FA	0	92	42	224	66	214	546	25	178	406	30	18	184	75	-969	6,229
SOCORRO	0	178	45	199	46	219	509	29	128	239	46	14	186	947	0	5,742
SPRING	2	84	36	154	41	267	499	23	194	264	24	12	213	0	0	5,800
BIRDVILLE	0	110	33	101	44	256	434	23	151	249	18	17	216	2,526	0	5,500
PHARR-SAN JU	5	60	107	186	78	261	632	10	142	59	51	16	197	0	0	6,527
BEAUMONT	5	163	37	295	53	243	628	0	150	121	41	8	204	0	0	6,172
ABILENE	0	94	38	297	62	252	649	22	120	75	67	19	217	0	0	5,712
HURST-EU	0	67	36	159	80	219	494	1	156	133	16	10	198	253	0	5,544
EDINBURG C	8	94	42	203	78	245	568	24	160	150	49	14	203	0	0	6,082
GRAND PRAIRIE	0	136	35	204	67	217	523	10	127	253	29	23	191	0	0	5,529
GOOSE CREEK	0	153	30	156	34	414	634	35	226	409	41	15	196	0	0	6,230
GALENA PARK	0	187	38	136	36	208	417	19	158	160	40	7	180	1	1	5,817

Amount per Student Enrolled (1997)

District Name (1)	County Name (2)	Fall 1995 enrollment (3)	% Econ. disadv. (4)	Central admin (5)	Campus admin (6)	Instruct. services (7)	Instruct. related (8)	Pupil services (9)	Cocurricular activities (10)	Transportation (11)	Plant M & O (12)	Community services (13)	Total COE (14)	Admin. ratio (15)	Debt service (16)	Capital outlay (17)	Payroll (18)
STATE AVERAGE		3,834,670	48	$312	$283	$2,949	$147	$515	$124	$135	$593	$24	$5,083	8.29	$385	$764	$4,113
AVG.-50 LARGEST DISTRICTS		2,000,644	50	283	291	2,914	160	517	86	123	594	28	4,997	7.19	411	688	4,132
AVG.-100 LARGEST DISTRICTS		2,552,090	50	290	287	2,909	158	521	95	126	591	28	5,006	7.51	411	752	4,120
SAN ANGELO	TOM GREEN	17,361	44	342	257	2,714	88	422	177	71	462	3	4,535	10.88	241	388	3,840
TYLER	SMITH	16,559	45	273	245	2,851	126	534	120	106	497	12	4,764	7.57	232	285	3,922
HARLINGEN CONS	CAMERON	16,234	66	234	262	2,875	107	504	136	105	497	41	4,762	6.80	255	1,010	3,978
WACO	MCLENNAN	16,233	71	315	314	2,729	128	599	115	163	621	104	5,089	8.74	153	279	3,754
WICHITA FALLS	WICHITA	15,627	46	301	277	2,986	185	497	200	107	556	2	5,110	8.23	241	365	3,995
JUDSON	BEXAR	15,502	36	287	277	2,963	92	498	60	176	533	18	4,904	7.26	583	1,167	4,172
HARLANDALE	BEXAR	15,150	83	324	450	3,254	195	718	91	54	707	50	5,843	7.04	188	499	4,659
VICTORIA	VICTORIA	14,663	48	283	220	2,982	173	531	152	88	587	19	5,035	7.64	251	72	3,978
EDGEWOOD	BEXAR	14,551	93	376	324	3,243	297	805	104	52	655	35	5,892	7.64	148	920	4,789
LAMAR CON	FORT BEND	14,221	49	306	261	2,783	92	569	96	221	677	16	5,022	9.93	274	2,123	4,108
LA JOYA	HIDALGO	14,185	93	254	303	2,857	159	645	116	227	483	37	5,082	9.72	187	1,027	4,125
NORTH FOREST	HARRIS	13,758	65	467	270	3,042	164	553	71	299	527	0	5,393	7.71	244	198	4,522
BRYAN	BRAZOS	13,189	58	305	231	3,153	96	588	114	170	558	54	5,268	12.74	502	1,673	4,110
BRAZOSPORT	BRAZORIA	12,990	36	288	303	2,784	140	535	107	98	732	1	4,988	7.16	253	737	4,026
WESLACO	HIDALGO	12,963	87	307	288	3,032	274	648	127	110	508	105	5,399	7.50	228	480	4,413
KELLER	TARRANT	12,676	13	276	238	2,161	87	305	120	108	447	4	3,745	7.69	684	3,113	3,115
DENTON	DENTON	12,507	31	332	246	2,817	152	481	108	155	652	1	4,944	10.69	959	1,342	4,041
GRAPEVINE-COL	TARRANT	12,398	6	351	293	3,007	179	431	211	106	687	26	5,292	9.38	795	753	4,232
MISSION CONS	HIDALGO	11,948	83	358	196	3,144	178	682	142	110	491	81	5,383	9.15	119	614	4,400
EAGLE PASS	MAVERICK	11,851	87	300	285	2,836	112	593	106	107	455	85	4,880	9.73	104	997	4,041
PORT ARTHUR	JEFFERSON	11,592	72	310	355	2,981	101	570	125	171	646	14	5,273	9.36	13	226	4,348
DEER PARK	HARRIS	11,503	20	285	282	3,077	188	571	126	142	770	2	5,444	8.44	605	641	4,542
ALVIN	BRAZORIA	11,055	42	286	253	2,719	92	440	128	197	719	6	4,840	7.22	200	933	3,783
MANSFIELD	TARRANT	10,945	19	189	348	2,697	107	406	91	166	591	0	4,596	7.00	692	2,472	3,758
PFLUGERVILLE	TRAVIS	10,744	15	160	276	2,547	115	379	113	149	395	1	4,135	5.89	848	828	3,313

Amount per Student Enrolled

Contracted instruction (19)	Contracted Prof. services (20)	Social security (21)	Health insurance (22)	Workers' Comp. (23)	Other benefits (24)	Total benefits (25)	Tax appr. collection (26)	Utility (27)	Interest (28)	Travel (29)	Library books (30)	TRS revenue (31)	Bond proceeds (32)	Chpt. 41 revenue adj. (33)	Total revenue (34)	District Name (1)
$36	$144	$48	$178	$47	$234	$507	$32	$156	$177	$39	$13	$192	$483	–85	$5,891	STATE AVERAGE
2	118	53	184	47	235	519	25	150	190	27	13	190	435	–12	5,709	AVG.-50 LARGEST DIST
10	124	51	182	49	234	516	25	150	191	30	13	189	485	–40	5,755	AVG.-100 LARGEST DIST
0	61	32	204	38	216	490	28	106	91	42	11	182	1,253	0	5,055	SAN ANGELO
0	128	29	90	65	206	389	49	133	2	33	5	183	0	0	5,263	TYLER
0	62	35	164	48	230	476	26	152	57	53	10	189	0	1	6,052	HARLINGEN CONS
26	441	34	181	28	244	487	32	138	70	57	6	179	0	0	5,784	WACO
0	351	30	188	0	247	465	25	149	12	57	11	193	0	50	5,594	WICHITA FALLS
3	97	40	156	56	231	483	21	128	284	32	10	193	638	0	5,786	JUDSON
6	105	40	108	104	269	521	0	97	56	33	14	211	0	0	6,567	HARLANDALE
14	253	31	180	62	225	497	28		54	72	7	198	0	0	5,528	VICTORIA
5	126	39	146	62	300	547	7	132	70	25	15	235	344	0	6,745	EDGEWOOD
0	153	37	253	60	300	651	21	181	164	26	12	203	0	27	5,967	LAMAR CON
0	68	40	201	111	229	580	9	172	65	57	22	189	0	0	6,536	LA JOYA
0	196	37	353	116	31	537	16	149	119	14	3	0	0	0	5,491	NORTH FOREST
0	96	43	195	38	233	509	26	177	376	39	16	201	0	0	6,182	BRYAN
0	130	34	184	47	271	536	35	191	112	25	5	239	1,448	0	5,429	BRAZOSPORT
0	63	36	188	88	253	565	16	167	139	56	16	198	0	0	6,642	WESLACO
0	94	35	75	75	173	358	19	125	513	33	5	0	0	0	4,961	KELLER
5	124	40	214	85	214	553	37	176	416	37	10	190	6	28	6,118	DENTON
0	225	42	204	68	279	593	46	218	580	46	18	237	0	–787	6,442	GRAPEVINE-COL
1	69	41	165	69	252	527	8	161	22	57	13	206	138	0	6,393	MISSION CONS
1	69	31	198	47	216	492	40	132	48	45	11	174	0	–5	5,458	EAGLE PASS
7	107	255	306	72	221	854	52	154	0	31	7	181	0	0	5,674	PORT ARTHUR
1	104	37	206	47	264	553	40	248	340	28	6	223	0	–3,519	6,420	DEER PARK
3	118	34	141	46	231	451	27	239	143	28	10	156	0	0	5,466	ALVIN
0	105	35	191	47	155	428	22	137	308	29	11	137	4,613	0	5,808	MANSFIELD
0	250	36	119	16	190	361	17	128	453	22	12	173	2,125	0	5,293	PFLUGERVILLE

Amount per Student Enrolled (1997)

District Name	County Name	Fall 1995 enrollment	% Econ. disadv.	Central admin	Campus admin	Instruct. services	Instruct. related	Pupil services	Cocurricular activities	Transportation	Plant M & O	Community services	Total COE	Admin. ratio	Debt service	Capital outlay	Payroll
(1)	(2)	(3)	(4)	(5)	(6)	(7)	(8)	(9)	(10)	(11)	(12)	(13)	(14)	(15)	(16)	(17)	(18)
STATE AVERAGE		3,834,670	48	$312	$283	$2,949	$147	$515	$124	$135	$593	$24	$5,083	8.29	$385	$764	$4,113
AVG.-50 LARGEST DISTRICTS		2,000,644	50	283	291	2,914	160	517	86	123	594	28	4,997	7.19	411	688	4,132
AVG.-100 LARGEST DISTRICTS		2,552,090	50	290	287	2,909	158	521	95	126	591	28	5,006	7.51	411	752	4,120
DUNCANVILLE	DALLAS	10,433	31	328	311	2,663	194	527	134	82	553	11	4,803	4.88	558	391	3,948
SOUTH SA	BEXAR	10,413	92	369	329	3,357	126	689	141	75	558	54	5,699	10.01	307	283	4,766
SAN FELIPE-D	VAL VERDE	10,318	70	302	217	2,763	203	529	120	85	504	108	4,833	9.92	1	336	3,987
GALVESTON	GALVESTON	10,056	60	392	249	3,247	135	605	119	145	701	28	5,622	7.11	261	179	4,491
LEANDER	WILLIAMSON	9,813	20	306	247	2,571	189	452	136	250	556	16	4,724	9.66	858	1,346	3,796
DONNA	HIDALGO	9,717	86	433	208	2,998	277	656	130	153	650	67	5,571	8.51	240	357	4,536
SOUTHWEST	BEXAR	9,241	74	339	325	3,227	132	566	101	140	508	15	5,353	11.24	222	880	4,264
COMAL	COMAL	9,156	31	351	283	2,938	75	550	109	199	641	51	5,196	8.72	627	1,814	4,056
PEARLAND	BRAZORIA	8,899	16	284	224	2,411	89	376	139	152	663	3	4,340	10.65	719	2,092	3,461
TEMPLE	BELL	8,662	46	339	263	2,973	166	516	138	161	577	8	5,143	9.99	395	1,865	4,188
SAN BENITO	CAMERON	8,657	85	390	217	2,894	111	605	157	125	632	50	5,182	9.99	184	886	4,089
LONGVIEW	GREGG	8,387	49	268	216	2,953	133	576	119	215	522	17	5,019	9.84	334	1,222	4,143
LUFKIN	ANGELINA	8,186	51	316	246	2,651	114	478	117	161	498	3	4,585	8.05	527	1,402	3,785
ALLEN	COLLIN	8,133	5	349	235	2,539	129	371	147	61	685	76	4,592	10.46	961	2,617	3,724
RIO GRANDE	STARR	8,066	93	397	236	3,004	202	633	121	198	826	63	5,681	9.67	425	1,840	4,517
MCKINNEY	COLLIN	7,967	26	359	239	2,606	173	434	118	152	531	8	4,620	11.00	820	1,245	3,300
CROWLEY	TARRANT	7,620	19	154	266	2,958	110	394	93	138	523	9	4,643	10.10	676	1,675	3,777
COPPERAS C	CORYELL	7,560	36	355	236	3,073	168	478	149	80	471	7	5,017	4.85	320	745	4,229
SEGUIN	GUADALUPE	7,394	54	362	272	3,062	145	538	124	153	498	0	5,155	7.94	555	322	4,084
LA PORTE	HARRIS	7,353	23	426	307	3,246	137	497	142	187	758	8	5,708	9.01	424	408	4,480
COPPELL	DALLAS	7,142	4	326	286	2,870	135	505	129	52	784	23	5,109	10.15	864	1,363	4,001
CANYON	RANDALL	7,029	19	193	207	2,395	110	366	146	111	429	12	3,969	8.51	388	226	3,268
EANES	TRAVIS	6,967	3	358	277	3,206	126	528	117	122	645	0	5,379	6.58	1,382	2,277	4,222
COLLEGE ST	BRAZOS	6,958	24	336	265	2,681	186	462	183	91	542	19	4,763	8.58	981	1,590	3,845
EAST CENT	BEXAR	6,914	47	296	280	2,889	225	595	126	156	600	19	5,185	9.73	446	1,670	4,292

Amount per Student Enrolled

Contracted instruction (19)	Contracted Prof. services (20)	Social security (21)	Health insurance (22)	Workers' Comp. (23)	Other benefits (24)	Total benefits (25)	Tax appr. collection (26)	Utility (27)	Interest (28)	Travel (29)	Library books (30)	TRS revenue (31)	Bond proceeds (32)	Chpt. 41 revenue adj. (33)	Total revenue (34)	District Name (1)
$36	$144	$48	$178	$47	$234	$507	$32	$156	$177	$39	$13	$192	$483	-85	$5,891	STATE AVERAGE
2	118	53	184	47	235	519	25	150	190	27	13	190	435	-12	5,709	AVG.-50 LARGEST DIST
10	124	51	182	49	234	516	25	150	191	30	13	189	485	-40	5,755	AVG.-100 LARGEST DIST
0	145	34	97	48	249	428	17	169	214	37	17	195	0	4	5,581	DUNCANVILLE
1	96	25	174	109	250	559	8	119	94	29	21	211	0	24	6,551	SOUTH SA
0	77	31	163	34	263	490	16	130	0	69	8	176	0	0	5,629	SAN FELIPE-D
3	73	35	275	29	249	588	23	187	140	63	15	205	0	0	5,876	GALVESTON
5	291	37	171	46	212	466	39	146	462	36	8	197	3,732	0	5,913	LEANDER
0	64	46	241	91	254	633	8	160	78	54	12	205	0	0	5,785	DONNA
5	149	47	141	40	246	475	10	100	60	20	22	198	0	6	5,963	SOUTHWEST
0	147	41	266	29	222	559	64	97	369	50	53	194	0	0	6,113	COMAL
1	152	33	147	28	201	409	21	217	417	41	7	181	2,801	0	5,650	PEARLAND
0	135	40	214	34	243	531	55	187	207	62	10	208	4,431	0	6,047	TEMPLE
0	160	32	201	106	236	575	12	139	79	50	17	184	0	0	6,543	SAN BENITO
0	120	39	98	45	243	424	52	134	110	38	9	207	817	2	5,641	LONGVIEW
38	122	74	81	44	186	385	33	128	322	35	7	156	0	8	5,420	LUFKIN
0	73	43	163	22	206	434	13	172	688	36	24	178	3,298	68	5,946	ALLEN
0	202	48	141	121	252	563	59	181	164	63	6	200	0	0	6,759	RIO GRANDE
44	342	35	173	30	177	415	44	191	318	46	17	158	1,989	-40	5,968	MCKINNEY
0	72	38	39	51	218	345	24	183	388	27	16	198	4,882	10	5,761	CROWLEY
0	67	37	192	51	231	511	20	146	157	50	24	203	0	0	6,411	COPPERAS C
0	308	34	194	29	228	485	37	123	168	59	15	194	0	0	6,074	SEGUIN
1,840	122	31	264	50	282	628	62	240	121	66	7	209	2,584	-1,840	7,493	LA PORTE
681	251	45	190	57	229	521	24	205	516	38	17	193	0	-681	6,224	COPPELL
0	161	65	97	39	184	385	26	130	138	57	12	167	0	2	4,661	CANYON
0	156	41	193	12	258	503	50	170	422	29	29	213	0	-1,459	6,877	EANES
0	109	38	176	18	229	461	53	178	424	50	54	192	4,238	0	6,016	COLLEGE ST
5	97	40	129	128	281	577	21	109	178	31	11	246	171	0	6,120	EAST CENT

CHAPTER 5

Academic Excellence Indicators

This chapter presents the progress the state is making on the Academic Excellence Indicators established in law and/or adopted by the Commissioner of Education or the State Board of Education (SBOE). Analysis of TAAS results and dropout rates can be found in greater detail in Chapters 1 and 2 (of the cited Biannual Report). Other measures and indicators in the Academic Excellence Indicator System (AEIS) State Performance Report on pages 31 to 40 (Biannual Report) include:

- cumulative percent of students passing the exit-level TAAS;
- percentage of students taking end-of-course tests;
- participation of students in TAAS testing (i.e., percentages of students tested and not tested);
- attendance rates;
- completion rates;
- completion of advanced courses;
- completion of the recommended high school program;
- results of Advanced Placement (AP) and International Baccalaureate (IB) examinations;
- equivalency between performance on exit-level TAAS and the Texas Academic Skills Program (TASP) test;

Reprinted with permission from "Evaluating the Performance of Texas Public Schools, A Guide to the Academic Excellence Indicator System Report, 1997–1998". This document is produced by John H. Stevens, Executive Director for the Texas Business and Education Coalition in Austin, Texas.

- results from college admission tests (SAT I and ACT); and
- profile information on students, programs, staff, and finances.

CUMULATIVE PERCENT PASSING EXIT-LEVEL TAAS

Students must pass the exit-level TAAS in order to receive a high school diploma. The exit- level TAAS is first administered in the spring of the tenth grade. Students have seven additional opportunities to retake the test until their graduation date.

This measure reports the percent of students passing all tests taken on the exit-level TAAS for the class of 1998 cohort and the class of 1997 cohort. For example, the TAAS cumulative passing rate for the class of 1998 shows the percentage of students who first took the exit-level test in spring 1996 when they were sophomores, and eventually passed all tests taken by the end of their senior year, May 1998. The measure only includes those students who took the test in the spring of the tenth grade and continued to retake the test, if needed, in the same district.

Statewide, 88.7 percent of the class of 1998 and 86.6 percent of the class of 1997 passed the exit-level TAAS. Passing rates were higher for all student groups in the class of 1998 compared to the class of 1997, except for Native American students (85.5 percent in 1998 compared to 87.5 percent in 1997). The greatest gains were for African American students

(82.4 percent compared to 78.9 percent) and Hispanic students (82.6 percent compared to 79.3 percent).

PERCENTAGE TAKING END-OF-COURSE EXAMINATIONS

Students completing a Biology I or Algebra I course must take an end-of-course examination. The AEIS shows the percent of students who took the test in either December or May of each school year (summer school test takers are not included). For Biology I, the percent of students who took the test in Grades 8-12 is reported. For Algebra I, the percent of students who took the test in Grades 7-12 is reported.

Statewide, 19.7 percent of students in Grades 8-12 in the 1997-98 school year took the Biology I test, which is the same percent as the prior year. In 1997-98, 18.5 percent of students in Grades 7-12 took the Algebra I test, up slightly from the 18.3 percent taking this test the previous year. For Biology I, the percent taking varied from 23.4 percent for Native American students to 18.5 percent for African American students. Only 18.4 percent of economically disadvantaged students took the Biology I end-of-course test. For Algebra I, the range was from 21.3 percent for Native American students to 18.2 percent for African American students; 17.6 percent of economically disadvantaged students took this test.

The AEIS will report the percentage of students taking end-of-course examinations in English II and United States History when the tests are fully implemented.

TAAS PARTICIPATION

Every student enrolled in a Texas public school in grades 3, 4, 5, 6, 7, 8, and 10 must be given the opportunity to take the TAAS test. However, there are circumstances under which some students are not tested. In addition, not all test results are included when evaluating test performance for accountability ratings purposes. The TAAS Participation section of the AEIS reports provides the percentages of students tested and not tested. The percentages are based on the number of answer documents submitted; districts are required to submit an answer document for each student enrolled at the time of the spring TAAS administration in the grades tested.

In 1998,

- 91.1 percent of students were tested. The results of 76 percent of students were included for accountability ratings purposes. The results of 15.1 percent were excluded for the following policy reasons: 4.4 percent were students not

enrolled in the fall in the district where they tested in the spring, 8.7 percent were tested students enrolled in special education programs, and 2 percent were students who took the Spanish version of the TAAS. Beginning in 1999, results for students served in special education who take the TAAS and students taking the Spanish version of the TAAS were included in the results for accountability purposes.

- 8.9 percent of students were not tested. Of those, 0.8 percent were absent on all days of testing, 5.2 percent were students served in special education who were exempt from all the tests by their Admission, Review, and Dismissal (ARD) Committee, 2.3 percent were exempt from all tests due to limited English proficiency (LEP), and 0.7 percent had answer documents coded with a combination of the "not tested" categories or had their testing disrupted by illness of other similar events.

The limited English proficiency (LEP) exemption is not an option for exit-level students. Beginning in 1997, the Spanish TAAS was available for Spanish-speaking students in Grades 3-6 who otherwise might have been exempted due to limited English proficiency.

Special education (ARD) exemptions were highest among African Americans at 9.6 percent, followed by economically disadvantaged (7.8 percent), Native American (5.8 percent) and Hispanic students (5.5 percent).

While there was little variance between males and females in the rate of exemptions for limited English proficiency, a much higher percentage of male students received special education exemptions compared to female students. The special education exemption rate for males was 6.7 percent, while only 3.6 percent of females were ARD-exempt.

STUDENT ATTENDANCE

The commissioner of education has established a student attendance standard of 94 percent for all students in grades 1 through 12 in all Texas public schools. The statewide attendance rate rose slightly to 95.2 percent in the 1996-97 school year from 95.1 percent in 1995-96. Rates for all student groups were above the 94 percent standard for both years, except for students served in special education who had a statewide attendance rate of 93.9 percent in 1996-97, and 93.8 percent in 1995-96.

COMPLETION RATE

Completion rates were calculated and included for the first time on the 1997-98 AEIS reports. This longitudinal measure tracks a group (or cohort) of students enrolled as 9th graders through the following four school years to determine if they completed their high school education. For example, the Class of 1997 completion rate includes those students who were in the 9th grade in 1993-94 and graduated (either on time or early), received a GED, or were still enrolled during the 1997-98 school year. The completion rate for the Class of 1997 was 90.7 percent. This is an increase over the completion rate for the Class of 1996, at 89.3 percent. The lowest completion rates for the Class of 1997 were for students served in special education (83.6 percent) and economically disadvantaged students (84.7 percent).

PERCENTAGE COMPLETING ADVANCED COURSES

This indicator is based on a count of the number of students who complete and receive credit for at least one advanced course in Grades 9-12. The course list includes all advanced courses as well as the College Board Advanced Placement (AP) courses, and the International Baccalaureate (IB) courses.

In 1996-97, the most recent year for which data are available, 19.6 percent of students in Grades 9-12 completed at least one advanced course. This rate is over 2 percentage points higher than that for the previous school year (17.3 percent). All student groups demonstrated improved performance on this indicator.

PERCENTAGE COMPLETING RECOMMENDED HIGH SCHOOL PROGRAM

This indicator shows the percentage of graduates reported as having satisfied the course requirements for the State Board of Education Recommended High School Program. It also includes those who met the requirements for the Distinguished Achievement Program.

For the class of 1997, 1.4 percent of students statewide met the requirements for the Recommended High School Program, up from the 0.5 percent reported for the class of 1996. Performance on this measure is low for several reasons. The Recommended High School Program, which was originally adopted by the State Board of Education in November 1993, underwent a number of changes before being finalized in 1996. It is still very early for significant numbers of students to have qualified for the program. Most districts continue to report their advanced students as having completed either the

"Advanced High School Program," or the "Advanced High School Honors Program" which will no longer be reported beginning with the class of 2001 graduates. As shown in the profile section of the 1997-98 state AEIS report, of the class of 1997 graduates, 71,602 (39.4 percent) were reported as having advanced seals on their diplomas. This compares with 68,944 (40.1 percent) in the class of 1996.

ADVANCED PLACEMENT (AP) AND INTERNATIONAL BACCALAUREATE (IB) RESULTS

This indicator reports the results of the College Board Advanced Placement (AP) and the International Baccalaureate (IB) examinations taken by Texas public school students in a given school year. High school students may take these examinations, usually upon completion of AP or IB courses, and may receive advanced placement or credit, or both, upon entering college. Generally, colleges will award credit or advanced placement for scores of 3, 4, or 5 on AP examinations and scores of 4, 5, 6, or 7 on IB examinations. These are referred to as the "criterion scores" in the points below.

- The percent of 11th or 12th graders taking at least one AP or IB examination rose from 8.6 percent in 1996-97 to 9.7 percent in 1997-98. The percentages of students participating in these examinations rose across all student groups between 1996-97 and 1997-98.
- The percent of examinations with scores above the criterion declined statewide from 59.2 percent to 57.4 percent. African American and Asian/Pacific Islander students were the only groups that improved on this measure between 1996-97 and 1997-98.
- The percent of examinees with at least one score above the criterion decreased statewide from 62.0 percent to 59.6 percent. All student groups declined on this measure between 1996-97 and 1997-98.

The decline in the percentage of AP/IB examinations and examinees with high scores should be considered in the context of increased participation in AP/IB examinations.

TAAS/TASP EQUIVALENCY

The Texas Academic Skills Program (TASP) is a test of reading, writing, and mathematics, required of all persons entering undergraduate programs at Texas public institutions of higher education for the first time. This indicator shows the percent of graduates who did well enough on the exit-level TAAS to have a 75 percent likelihood of passing the Texas Academic Skills Program (TASP) test.

Equivalency rates for the class of 1997 showed that 42.4 percent of graduates statewide scored sufficiently high on the TAAS (when they first took the test) to have a 75 percent likelihood of passing the TASP. This is an improvement over the equivalency rate for the class of 1996, at 40.0 percent. For the class of 1997 the rates varied from a high of 56.4 percent for Asian/Pacific Islander students to a low of 21.1 percent for African American students.

COLLEGE ADMISSION TESTS

Results from the SAT I of the College Board and the Enhanced ACT of the American College Testing Program are included in this indicator.

- The percentage of examinees who scored at or above the criterion score on either test (1,110 on the SAT I or 24 on the ACT) was 26.6 percent for the class of 1997, up slightly from 26.3 percent for the class of 1996.
- The percentage of graduates who took either the SAT I or the ACT declined from 64.7 percent for the class of 1996 to 63.6 percent for the class of 1997; however, the number of graduates taking at least one test increased by over 3,700.
- The average SAT I score for the class of 1997 was 992, a one-point decline from the average for the class of 1996.

- The average ACT composite score was 20.1 for both the classes of 1997 and 1996.

PROFILE INFORMATION

In addition to performance data, the AEIS State Performance Report also provides descriptive profile statistics (counts and percentages) on a variety of data relating to students, programs, staff, and finances.

AGENCY CONTACT PERSON

Senior Director of Performance Reporting, Department of Policy Planning and Research, (512) 463-9704.

OTHER SOURCES OF INFORMATION

AEIS Performance Reports and Profiles for each public school district and campus, available from each district, the agency's Division of Communications, (512) 463-9000, or online at www.tea.state.tx.us/perfreport/.

Pocket Edition, 1997-98: Texas Public School Statistics, published by the Division of Performance Reporting, Department of Policy Planning and Research, available in December 1998.

Snapshot '98: School District Profiles, published by the Division of Performance Reporting, Department of Policy Planning and Research, available in early 1999.

TEXAS EDUCATION AGENCY
Academic Excellence Indicator System
1997-98 State Performance Report

Indicator:

TAAS % Passing Grade 3

		State	African American	Hispanic	White	Native American	Asian/ Pac.Is.	Male	Female	Econ. Disadv.	Special Educ.
Reading	1998	86.2%	76.4%	81.1%	92.1%	85.0%	94.9%	84.4%	88.0%	79.0%	56.9%
	1997	81.5%	69.3%	73.8%	89.3%	79.4%	92.4%	78.9%	83.9%	72.0%	49.8%
Math	1998	81.0%	65.7%	75.0%	89.1%	80.8%	93.7%	81.8%	80.3%	72.2%	52.2%
	1997	81.7%	66.8%	75.6%	89.4%	78.1%	94.2%	81.9%	81.5%	73.3%	53.0%
All Tests	1998	76.6%	60.2%	69.2%	85.7%	75.6%	91.3%	76.1%	77.0%	66.2%	44.0%
	1997	74.2%	57.6%	65.4%	84.0%	70.7%	89.6%	72.8%	75.6%	62.8%	41.1%

TAAS % Passing Spanish Grade 3

		State	African American	Hispanic	White	Native American	Asian/ Pac.Is.	Male	Female	Econ. Disadv.	Special Educ.
Reading	1998	65.6%	60.0%	65.6%	59.5%	75.0%	*	59.3%	71.6%	65.4%	39.3%
	1997	44.6%	33.3%	44.6%	60.0%	50.0%	*	39.2%	50.0%	44.3%	27.5%
Math	1998	66.4%	55.6%	66.4%	70.7%	62.5%	*	65.4%	67.3%	66.3%	43.2%
	1997	53.5%	33.3%	53.5%	60.0%	50.0%	*	53.0%	53.9%	53.2%	35.0%
All Tests	1998	55.2%	40.0%	55.3%	50.0%	56.3%	*	51.3%	59.1%	55.0%	30.2%
	1997	37.2%	22.2%	37.2%	56.0%	50.0%	*	33.9%	40.5%	36.9%	21.4%

TAAS % Passing Grade 4

		State	African American	Hispanic	White	Native American	Asian/ Pac.Is.	Male	Female	Econ. Disadv.	Special Educ.
Reading	1998	89.7%	80.3%	85.3%	95.0%	88.2%	97.0%	88.3%	91.1%	83.4%	56.6%
	1997	82.5%	69.5%	75.5%	90.2%	84.3%	92.5%	80.5%	84.3%	73.0%	46.6%
Writing	1998	88.7%	81.1%	85.2%	92.7%	87.0%	96.3%	86.0%	91.2%	83.0%	52.6%
	1997	87.1%	76.7%	83.3%	92.1%	86.3%	95.2%	84.7%	89.3%	80.4%	52.5%
Math	1998	86.3%	73.3%	82.4%	92.1%	84.6%	96.7%	86.6%	86.0%	79.5%	51.4%
	1997	82.6%	66.3%	77.1%	90.2%	83.8%	94.7%	83.3%	81.9%	73.9%	46.9%
All Tests	1998	78.6%	63.6%	72.3%	86.4%	77.0%	93.0%	76.7%	80.3%	68.9%	36.9%
	1997	72.0%	53.5%	63.5%	82.0%	73.7%	88.1%	70.3%	73.6%	59.8%	31.9%

TAAS % Passing Spanish Grade 4

		State	African American	Hispanic	White	Native American	Asian/ Pac.Is.	Male	Female	Econ. Disadv.	Special Educ.
Reading	1998	39.5%	85.7%	39.3%	52.6%	63.6%	*	33.6%	45.2%	39.4%	18.0%
	1997	36.8%	*	36.8%	18.2%	*	–	31.8%	41.9%	36.5%	14.8%
Writing	1998	64.2%	*	64.1%	81.0%	86.4%	*	58.1%	70.2%	64.3%	36.9%
	1997	59.5%	*	59.4%	83.3%	95.5%	*	58.1%	60.9%	59.5%	30.6%
Math	1998	48.0%	*	48.0%	54.5%	*	–	48.2%	47.9%	48.0%	22.9%
All Tests	1998	33.1%	85.7%	33.0%	52.4%	63.6%	*	28.3%	37.9%	33.2%	14.8%
	1997	29.6%	*	29.6%	18.2%	*	–	26.9%	32.4%	29.5%	10.8%

continued

Indicator:

		State	African American	Hispanic	White	Native American	Asian/ Pac.Is.	Male	Female	Econ. Disadv.	Special Educ.
TAAS % Passing Grade 5											
Reading	1998	88.4%	80.1%	83.3%	94.0%	91.5%	95.9%	86.8%	90.0%	81.7%	52.1%
	1997	84.8%	72.8%	77.4%	92.4%	86.2%	94.0%	82.6%	86.8%	75.7%	47.5%
Math	1998	89.6%	78.2%	86.6%	94.5%	91.5%	97.5%	89.3%	89.9%	84.0%	54.2%
	1997	86.2%	71.6%	81.5%	92.7%	87.2%	96.4%	86.0%	86.3%	78.7%	48.7%
All Tests	1998	83.9%	70.8%	78.0%	91.1%	87.2%	94.7%	82.5%	85.1%	75.3%	42.4%
	1997	79.2%	62.6%	70.8%	88.6%	79.6%	92.4%	77.6%	80.6%	68.2%	37.0%
TAAS % Passing Spanish Grade 5											
Reading	1998	50.2%	*	50.1%	50.0%	*	*	45.4%	55.0%	50.0%	20.7%
Math	1998	57.7%	*	57.8%	87.5%	*	*	57.4%	58.1%	57.9%	28.4%
All Tests	1998	41.9%	*	41.9%	50.0%	*	*	38.9%	44.9%	41.9%	15.4%
TAAS % Passing Grade 6											
Reading	1998	85.6%	78.1%	75.8%	94.6%	90.5%	92.5%	83.7%	87.5%	75.8%	48.5%
	1997	84.6%	74.1%	75.4%	93.7%	88.4%	92.3%	82.4%	86.8%	74.3%	47.6%
Math	1998	86.1%	74.3%	79.8%	93.6%	88.1%	95.6%	85.1%	87.1%	78.4%	46.3%
	1997	81.8%	66.4%	73.6%	91.1%	85.0%	93.7%	81.2%	82.4%	71.7%	40.5%
All Tests	1998	79.9%	67.0%	69.2%	90.8%	83.8%	90.8%	78.0%	81.7%	68.2%	36.1%
	1997	76.8%	59.9%	65.7%	88.5%	81.3%	89.6%	75.1%	78.4%	63.8%	33.0%
TAAS % Passing Spanish Grade 6											
Reading	1998	28.2%	*	28.2%	*	*	—	22.1%	33.9%	28.0%	10.0%
Math	1998	38.2%	*	38.2%	*	*	—	33.8%	42.2%	38.4%	15.0%
All Tests	1998	22.2%	*	22.2%	*	*	—	18.1%	26.1%	22.3%	9.1%
TAAS % Passing Grade 7											
Reading	1998	85.5%	75.1%	76.9%	94.2%	87.9%	92.1%	83.2%	87.8%	75.5%	47.7%
	1997	84.5%	74.8%	75.0%	93.6%	87.1%	90.5%	81.6%	87.3%	74.0%	45.1%
Math	1998	83.7%	67.9%	75.6%	93.2%	86.3%	94.0%	83.5%	83.9%	73.7%	41.7%
	1997	79.7%	63.3%	70.6%	89.8%	82.0%	93.1%	79.0%	80.3%	68.8%	35.9%
All Tests	1998	78.5%	61.3%	67.7%	90.4%	80.8%	89.6%	77.1%	79.9%	65.5%	33.4%
	1997	75.1%	57.9%	63.3%	87.4%	78.1%	87.6%	73.1%	76.9%	61.4%	29.0%

TAAS % Passing
Grade 8

Reading	1998	85.3%	76.2%	94.2%	86.8%	91.1%	82.6%	87.9%	74.8%	45.3%
	1997	83.9%	74.0%	93.0%	85.6%	91.3%	81.3%	86.4%	72.7%	44.4%
Writing	1998	84.0%	75.6%	91.7%	83.9%	90.5%	79.8%	87.9%	74.7%	37.1%
	1997	80.7%	69.9%	90.0%	80.4%	88.4%	76.3%	85.0%	69.4%	33.6%
Math	1998	83.8%	71.6%	92.2%	85.5%	94.5%	83.3%	84.3%	74.6%	40.1%
	1997	76.3%	58.8%	87.9%	79.9%	91.7%	77.1%	75.7%	63.6%	30.8%
Science	1998	84.3%	70.0%	94.4%	86.6%	92.3%	84.8%	83.8%	73.2%	48.2%
	1997	84.6%	69.3%	94.6%	87.5%	92.3%	85.6%	83.6%	73.7%	52.7%
Social S.	1998	69.9%	53.3%	84.7%	75.5%	84.0%	71.0%	68.9%	52.8%	30.5%
	1997	67.4%	50.0%	82.4%	71.1%	80.6%	68.8%	66.1%	49.5%	27.8%
All Tests	1998	61.8%	42.3%	78.1%	65.8%	78.9%	60.9%	62.7%	43.5%	16.5%
	1997	57.3%	36.3%	74.1%	59.9%	74.2%	56.8%	57.8%	38.2%	13.8%

TAAS % Passing
Grade 10

Reading	1998	88.3%	80.0%	95.4%	91.3%	88.8%	87.5%	89.1%	78.3%	52.2%
	1997	86.1%	75.7%	94.4%	86.9%	87.2%	85.6%	86.9%	73.9%	50.5%
Writing	1998	89.9%	82.5%	95.9%	91.5%	91.0%	88.3%	91.5%	81.7%	49.8%
	1997	88.5%	79.6%	95.4%	91.7%	89.6%	86.1%	90.7%	78.6%	49.0%
Math	1998	78.4%	61.8%	88.5%	82.3%	89.3%	81.1%	75.9%	66.6%	35.0%
	1997	72.6%	54.0%	84.9%	74.8%	87.3%	75.1%	70.2%	57.9%	29.4%
All Tests	1998	73.1%	56.2%	85.2%	78.1%	81.5%	74.1%	72.2%	58.2%	25.3%
	1997	67.8%	49.2%	81.8%	71.7%	79.4%	68.5%	67.1%	50.3%	22.6%

TAAS % Passing
Sum of 3-8 & 10
Accountability Subset

Reading	1998	87.0%	78.2%	94.2%	88.7%	93.0%	85.1%	88.7%	78.4%	51.1%
	1997	84.0%	73.2%	92.4%	85.3%	91.3%	81.8%	86.1%	73.7%	47.1%
Writing	1998	87.4%	80.4%	93.4%	87.2%	92.4%	84.5%	90.1%	79.7%	46.0%
	1997	85.3%	76.1%	92.5%	85.9%	90.8%	82.1%	88.2%	76.0%	44.5%
Math	1998	84.2%	70.5%	91.9%	85.7%	94.3%	84.4%	84.0%	76.1%	46.7%
	1997	80.1%	64.1%	89.5%	81.6%	92.8%	80.5%	79.8%	70.5%	41.8%
All Tests	1998	77.7%	62.6%	87.9%	79.6%	89.3%	76.3%	79.0%	66.4%	35.1%
	1997	73.2%	55.7%	84.9%	74.7%	86.7%	71.7%	74.6%	60.2%	31.1%

continued

	State	African American	Hispanic	White	Native American	Asian/ Pac.Is.	Male	Female	Econ. Disadv.	Special Educ.
1999 Preview Indicator **TAAS % Passing** **(Includes Spec. Ed. & Spanish 3-4)** **Sum of 3-8 & 10**										
Reading 1998	83.3%	74.8%	74.8%	91.3%	84.7%	92.2%	80.6%	86.1%	73.7%	51.0%
Writing 1998	84.2%	77.0%	77.4%	90.1%	82.6%	91.7%	80.2%	88.0%	75.6%	46.0%
Math 1998	80.4%	67.0%	73.3%	88.6%	81.2%	93.4%	79.7%	81.2%	71.5%	46.6%
All Tests 1998	73.1%	58.8%	63.1%	83.6%	74.0%	88.1%	70.6%	75.7%	61.2%	35.0%
2000 Preview Indicator **TAAS % Passing** **(Includes Spec. Ed. & Spanish 3-6)** **Sum of 3-8 & 10**										
Reading 1998	83.2%	74.8%	74.4%	91.3%	84.6%	92.2%	80.4%	85.9%	73.4%	50.9%
Writing 1998	83.8%	77.0%	76.7%	90.1%	82.7%	91.7%	79.8%	87.7%	75.1%	45.9%
Math 1998	80.3%	67.1%	73.0%	88.6%	81.1%	93.4%	79.5%	81.0%	71.3%	46.6%
All Tests 1998	72.9%	58.8%	62.7%	83.6%	74.0%	88.1%	70.4%	75.7%	60.9%	34.9%
TAAS Cumulative **Pass Rate - Exit**										
Class of 1998	88.7%	82.4%	82.6%	93.9%	85.5%	91.8%	88.1%	89.2%	n/a	n/a
Class of 1997	86.6%	78.9%	79.3%	92.7%	87.5%	90.5%	86.2%	87.0%	n/a	n/a
End-of-Course Exam **(% Taking)** **Biology I**										
Grades 8-12 1998	19.7%	18.5%	19.3%	20.0%	23.4%	20.4%	19.6%	19.8%	18.4%	11.1%
1997	19.7%	18.0%	19.1%	20.0%	22.5%	20.6%	19.5%	19.9%	18.0%	10.8%
Algebra I										
Grades 7-12 1998	18.5%	18.2%	18.7%	18.0%	21.3%	18.7%	18.4%	18.5%	17.6%	7.6%
1997	18.3%	18.0%	18.2%	18.1%	21.6%	18.5%	18.2%	18.4%	17.1%	7.2%

1997 & 1998 TAAS Participation Report for All Students (Grades 3-8, & 10)
All Tests - % Answer Documents

1997 TAAS Participation Grades 3-8 & 10	State	African American	Hispanic	White	Native American	Asian/ Pac.Is.	Male	Female	Econ. Disadv.
Tested	91.1%	88.5%	87.2%	95.0%	91.0%	89.2%	89.3%	92.9%	86.4%
Accountability	76.0%	74.9%	69.9%	81.2%	69.2%	82.7%	71.9%	80.4%	68.8%
TAAS Mobile	4.4%	5.1%	3.8%	4.2%	10.0%	3.7%	4.2%	4.5%	3.9%
Special Education	8.7%	8.5%	8.0%	9.6%	10.9%	2.8%	11.3%	5.9%	9.7%
Spanish (gr. 3-6)	2.0%	0.0%	5.5%	0.0%	1.0%	0.0%	2.0%	2.1%	4.0%
Not Tested	8.9%	11.5%	12.8%	5.0%	9.0%	10.8%	10.7%	7.1%	13.6%
Absent	0.8%	0.9%	0.8%	0.7%	0.8%	0.4%	0.8%	0.7%	0.8%
ARD Exempt	5.2%	9.6%	5.5%	3.8%	5.8%	1.8%	6.7%	3.6%	7.8%
LEP Exempt	2.3%	0.2%	5.4%	0.1%	1.2%	7.9%	2.3%	2.2%	4.1%
Other	0.7%	0.8%	1.0%	0.4%	1.1%	0.7%	0.8%	0.6%	1.0%
Total Answer Documents	2,052,472	289,287	753,013	947,170	5,978	50,888	1,051,417	999,500	972,809

1997 TAAS Participation Grades 3-8 & 10	State	African American	Hispanic	White	Native American	Asian/ Pac.Is.	Male	Female	Econ. Disadv.
Tested	90.6%	88.4%	86.2%	94.8%	90.6%	88.0%	88.7%	92.5%	85.6%
Accountability	76.0%	75.6%	69.6%	81.2%	69.8%	81.5%	71.9%	80.3%	68.7%
TAAS Mobile	4.5%	5.2%	3.9%	4.3%	9.9%	3.8%	4.3%	4.6%	4.0%
Special Education	8.2%	7.6%	7.4%	9.3%	10.4%	2.7%	10.6%	5.6%	9.0%
Spanish (gr. 3-4)	2.0%	0.0%	5.3%	0.0%	0.5%	0.0%	1.9%	2.0%	3.9%
Not Tested	9.4%	11.6%	13.8%	5.2%	9.4%	12.0%	11.3%	7.5%	14.4%
Absent	0.8%	1.0%	0.9%	0.7%	1.0%	0.4%	0.8%	0.7%	0.8%
ARD Exempt	5.3%	9.6%	5.7%	4.0%	6.0%	1.8%	6.9%	3.7%	8.0%
LEP Exempt	2.4%	0.2%	5.8%	0.1%	1.3%	8.9%	2.5%	2.4%	4.4%
Other	0.9%	0.9%	1.4%	0.4%	1.2%	0.9%	1.0%	0.7%	1.2%
Total Answer Documents	2,028,676	283,225	735,435	948,748	5,718	48,857	1,039,863	987,043	950,764

TEXAS EDUCATION AGENCY
Academic Excellence Indicator System
1997-98 State Performance Report

Indicator:	State	African American	Hispanic	White	Native American	Asian/ Pac.Is.	Male	Female	Econ. Disadv.	Special Educ.
Attendance Rate										
1996/97	95.2%	94.7%	94.7%	95.6%	94.4%	97.3%	95.2%	95.2%	94.8%	93.9%
1995/96	95.1%	94.5%	94.6%	95.6%	94.2%	97.2%	95.1%	95.1%	94.8%	93.8%
Dropout Rate										
1996/97	1.6%	2.0%	2.3%	1.0%	1.9%	0.8%	1.7%	1.5%	1.6%	1.9%
1995/96	1.8%	2.3%	2.5%	1.1%	2.0%	1.1%	1.9%	1.6%	1.7%	2.1%
Completion Rate										
Class of 1997	90.7%	87.2%	85.6%	94.5%	89.0%	95.7%	89.9%	91.6%	84.7%	83.6%
Class of 1996	89.3%	85.5%	83.4%	93.8%	88.9%	94.2%	88.4%	90.3%	82.5%	81.6%
% Adv. Courses										
1996/97	19.6%	14.0%	14.9%	23.4%	20.6%	35.7%	18.0%	21.2%	13.2%	4.2%
1995/96	17.3%	11.7%	12.3%	21.2%	17.0%	32.8%	15.8%	18.8%	10.9%	2.9%
% Rec. HS Pgm.										
Class of 1997	1.4%	1.1%	1.1%	1.6%	1.9%	1.7%	1.3%	1.4%	1.2%	1.0%
Class of 1996	0.5%	0.2%	0.6%	0.5%	0.0%	0.3%	0.5%	0.5%	0.6%	0.4%
AP/IB Results										
% Tested										
1997-98	9.7%	3.7%	6.5%	11.9%	9.8%	27.2%	8.5%	10.7%	n/a	n/a
1996-97	8.6%	3.3%	5.3%	10.8%	7.8%	25.5%	7.6%	9.5%	n/a	n/a
% Scores = Crit.										
1997-98	57.4%	29.9%	42.8%	60.9%	56.1%	70.1%	60.1%	55.2%	n/a	n/a
1996-97	59.2%	29.5%	45.5%	62.5%	60.8%	69.8%	61.2%	57.6%	n/a	n/a
% Examinees = Crit.										
1997-98	59.6%	30.5%	50.0%	63.1%	53.3%	72.9%	61.3%	58.3%	n/a	n/a
1996-97	62.0%	31.5%	52.2%	65.3%	66.2%	74.5%	63.5%	60.8%	n/a	n/a

TAAS/TASP Equiv.

										5I W
Class of 1997	42.4%	21.1%	26.4%	54.4%	43.5%	56.4%	45.4%	39.7%	24.1%	8.5%
Class of 1996	40.0%	19.2%	24.1%	51.2%	45.9%	53.1%	42.5%	37.7%	22.0%	7.4%

SAT/ACT Results

% At/Above Crit.

Class of 1997	26.6%	7.1%	10.9%	34.6%	28.5%	44.2%	29.5%	24.2%	n/a	n/a
Class of 1996	26.3%	6.8%	10.1%	34.6%	25.4%	42.7%	29.0%	24.1%	n/a	n/a

% Tested

Class of 1997	63.6%	58.2%	46.9%	70.6%	88.3%	88.9%	61.0%	66.0%	n/a	n/a
Class of 1996	64.7%	60.1%	48.8%	71.1%	90.9%	86.9%	62.4%	66.9%	n/a	n/a

Mean SAT I Score

Class of 1997	992	849	907	1044	967	1067	1011	976	n/a	n/a
Class of 1996	993	852	908	1043	973	1066	1013	976	n/a	n/a

Mean ACT Score

Class of 1997	20.1	17.2	18.0	21.4	20.8	21.8	20.1	20.1	n/a	n/a
Class of 1996	20.1	17.1	17.9	21.4	20.2	21.7	20.0	20.1	n/a	n/a

CHAPTER

6

Academic Excellence Indicator System Report

How does your school perform against state standards? How does your school compare to similar schools? Are students making progress from one year to the next? **The answers to these and other questions are in the Academic Excellence Indicator System (AEIS) reports** published annually by the Texas Education Agency. When used appropriately, these reports are a powerful tool for evaluating school performance and focusing improvement efforts.

The AEIS provides information about the performance of 1,042 school districts, more than 7,000 schools, more than 300,000 professional staff, and 3.9 million students. The Texas Business and Education Coalition (TBEC) publishes this guide to help you understand your school's AEIS report.

Student Achievement as Measured On the Annual Texas Assessment of Academic Skills (TAAS) Test is the Centerpiece of AEIS. The reports contain student test results by subject and grade level for districts and campuses. In addition, the reports provide several **useful comparisons.**

- District performance is compared to the state and the entire region of its Education Service Center (ESC).

Reprinted with permission from "Evaluating the Performance of Texas Public Schools: A Guide to the AEIS Reports, 1997–1998." Produced by John H. Stevens, Executive Director for the Texas Business and Education Coalition, Austin, 1999.

- Campus performance is compared to a group of 40 similar campuses in the state.
- Performance among student groups is compared on each campus and within each district.
- Campus and district performance are compared to their own previous year's performance.

Important New Indicators are reported for the first time in the 1997–98 AEIS Reports.

Spanish TAAS Results. This year's AEIS reports include results on the expanded Spanish TAAS. New assessments include writing at the 4th grade, and reading and mathematics at 5th and 6th grades.

Comparable Improvement. Campus AEIS reports include a new section that compares the performance of each campus to that of 40 other Texas campuses serving similar student populations. Campuses are assigned a quartile ranking according to how much student reading and math scores improved from 1997 to 1998.

TAAS Participation Report. District and campus reports include this important new indicator that shows student participation in TAAS for 1997 and 1998.

Completion Rate. (District Report only) The current year (class of '97) completion rate looks at the group of students who were enrolled as 9th graders in the 1993–94 school year, and follows them through the following four school years. Completers are any students who during those years graduated, either on time or early; or received a GED; or were found to be enrolled in school during the 1997-98 school year. **The reports also contain profile information** about:

- **students,** including enrollment, ethnicity, and economic status;
- **finances,** including revenues and expenditures;
- **staff,** including number and types, years of experience, degree held, salaries and turnover rates; and
- **programs,** including student enrollments, teacher counts, and operating expenditures.

TBEC believes the information in the AEIS reports can help improve public schools. However, no information system can answer every question or explain every aspect of school performance. If used incorrectly, some information in the report could lead to invalid conclusions or inappropriate actions. This guide will help explain both the usefulness and the limitations of the 1997–98 AEIS reports.

<u>**To obtain an AEIS report for any district or campus in Texas, go to the Division of Performance Reporting website at http//www.tea.state.tx.us/ perfreport.**</u>

EXPLANATION OF PERFORMANCE SECTION FOR 1997-98

This part of the guide explains the technical aspects of the performance section of the 1997-98 AEIS report. The sample is excerpted from a district report because it includes all the indicators and information found on reports for elementary, middle, and high schools. Please understand that all indicators do not apply to all schools. Your school's report shows results for the indicators that apply, depending on the school's grade span. Definitions and Descriptions of items found in the Performance and Profile Sections of the AEIS report are explained in the abbreviated *Glossary* at the end of this publication.

Currently **the AEIS report includes the following student performance indicators:** Texas Assessment of Academic Skills (TAAS); TAAS participation; Percentage of Students Taking End-of-Course Exams; Attendance Rate; Annual Dropout Rate; Percent Completing Advanced Courses; Percentage of Graduates Completing the Recommended High School Program; AP/IB Results; TAAS/TASP Equivalency; and College Admissions Tests Results (SAT I and ACT). Note that both current and prior year data are shown for most indicators.

The Texas Assessment of Academic Skills (TAAS) Program includes: tests in reading and math in grades 3 through 10 (exit-level), writing in grades 4, 8 and 10 (exit-level), and science and social studies in grade 8.

The 1997-98 AEIS report includes additional student results on the **expanded TAAS in Spanish:** writing in grade 4, reading and math in grades 5 and 6.

School districts and campuses are assigned an accountability rating according to their performance. **District ratings** are *Exemplary, Recognized, Academically Acceptable, and Academically Unacceptable.* **Campus ratings** are *Exemplary, Recognized, Academically Acceptable, and Low-Performing.* **Alternative education schools** are rated *AE: Acceptable,* or *AE: Needs Peer Review.* The Accountability Manual published annually by the Texas Education Agency contains information about how the accountability ratings are determined.

TEXAS EDUCATION AGENCY
Academic Excellence Indicator System
1997-98 District Performance
Accountability Rating: Academically Acceptable

Section I - Page 1

District Name: Your ISD
District #: 999999

Indicator:		State	Region 04	District	African American	Hispanic	White	Native American	Asian/ Pac. Is.	Male	Female	Econ. Disadv.	Special Educ.
TAAS % Passing Grade 3													
Reading	1998	86.2%	88.5%	82.0%	84.8%	74.4%	83.5%	-	*	77.6%	86.7%	80.5%	27.8%
	1997	81.5%	84.9%	78.2%	70.4%	78.6%	81.7%	-	*	67.7%	87.0%	75.2%	33.3%
Math	1998	81.0%	83.9%	82.2%	78.7%	81.4%	83.8%	-	*	83.2%	81.2%	82.0%	44.0%
	1997	81.7%	84.7%	80.3%	67.3%	82.8%	84.9%	-	*	73.2%	86.2%	79.4%	33.3%
All Tests	1998	76.6%	79.8%	73.6%	74.5%	67.4%	75.2%	-	*	72.0%	75.2%	71.9%	11.5%
	1997	74.2%	78.2%	70.9%	54.5%	75.9%	77.0%	-	*	59.8%	80.2%	67.3%	26.7%
TAAS % Passing Spanish Grade 4													
Reading	1998	39.5%	48.0%	29.0%	-	29.0%	-	-	-	14.3%	41.2%	30.0%	-
	1997	36.8%	40.7%	28.6%	-	28.6%	-	-	-	33.3%	25.0%	28.6%	*
Math	1998	59.5%	67.4%	14.3%	-	14.3%	-	-	-	7.7%	20.0%	14.3%	-
	1997	48.0%	52.8%	21.4%	-	21.4%	-	-	-	50.0%	0.0%	21.4%	*
Writing	1998	64.2%	71.1%	37.1%	-	37.1%	-	-	-	31.3%	42.1%	82.0%	57.7%
All Tests	1998	33.1%	39.8%	19.4%	-	19.4%	-	-	-	23.5%	15.8%	20.0%	-
	1997	29.6%	33.0%	7.1%	-	7.1%	-	-	-	16.7%	0.0%	7.1%	*
TAAS % Passing Grade 8													
Reading	1998	85.3%	86.4%	82.0%	75.0%	73.4%	90.7%	-	80.0%	77.5%	86.7%	77.0%	33.3%
	1997	83.9%	85.1%	81.1%	65.6%	78.0%	90.5%	-	*	77.6%	84.9%	72.8%	38.9%
Writing	1998	84.0%	84.5%	80.2%	76.4%	74.6%	84.4%	-	100.0%	74.2%	86.6%	72.9%	28.6%
	1997	80.7%	81.4%	82.9%	77.8%	80.0%	86.8%	-	*	76.8%	89.3%	79.3%	28.9%
Math	1998	83.8%	84.3%	78.4%	68.5%	73.4%	86.1%	-	80.0%	76.3%	80.5%	76.7%	38.5%
	1997	76.3%	76.7%	66.3%	53.1%	62.0%	74.2%	-	*	68.3%	64.2%	58.0%	19.4%
Science	1998	84.3%	85.1%	74.3%	60.7%	67.2%	85.6%	-	80.0%	74.1%	74.5%	72.6%	27.3%
	1997	84.6%	85.1%	78.7%	57.8%	76.0%	90.5%	-	*	80.0%	77.3%	72.5%	31.4%
Social S.	1998	69.9%	70.8%	48.1%	36.4%	37.5%	59.8%	-	60.0%	50.8%	45.1%	40.2%	11.5%
	1997	67.4%	68.9%	57.2%	38.1%	50.0%	69.0%	-	*	56.5%	58.0%	48.1%	16.7%
All Tests	1998	61.8%	63.2%	42.2%	33.9%	29.7%	52.7%	-	60.0%	42.3%	42.1%	33.3%	3.4%
	1997	57.3%	58.7%	48.4%	29.2%	42.0%	59.5%	-	*	46.9%	50.0%	39.3%	7.7%

There are three **district-level indicator only indicators**: TAAS Cumulative Pass Rate - Exit shown on the previous page, AP/IB Results and Completion Rate on this page.

For accountability ratings, __Annual Dropout Rate standards__ must be met for all students and each student group as follows: 1.0% or less for *Exemplary*, 3.5% or less for *Recognized*, and 6.0% or less for *Acceptable*.

These indicators show the percent of 11th and 12th graders taking at least one **Advanced Placement (AP) or International Baccalaureate (IB) exam**, and the percent of scores from 3 to 5 on the AP, or 4-7 on the IB, and the percent of examinees scoring from 3 to 5 on the AP or 4-7 on the IB. It is included only on the AEIS district reports.

This indicator shows the percentage of students whose score on the exit-level TAAS predicts that they will pass the Texas Academic Skills Program (TASP) test required of entering freshmen in Texas postsecondary institutions.

Indicator:	State	Region 04	District	African American	Hispanic	White	Native American	Asian/ Pac. Is.	Male	Female	Econ. Disadv.	Special Educ.
Attendance Rate												
1996-97	95.1%	95.0%	95.3%	96.0%	94.8%	95.4%	94.9%	97.6%	95.4%	95.3%	95.5%	94.9%
1995-96	95.1%	95.0%	95.5%	96.1%	95.1%	95.5%	94.5%	97.8%	95.6%	95.4%	95.7%	95.0%
Dropout Rate												
1996-97	1.8%	1.4%	1.8%	1.6%	2.4%	1.5%	-	-	2.0%	1.6%	1.2%	2.4%
1995-96	2.6%	2.0%	3.2%	2.8%	4.2%	2.6%	2.1%	4.7%	4.0%	2.4%	2.9%	2.9%
Completion Rate												
Class of 1997	1.8%	1.4%	1.8%	1.6%	2.4%	1.5%	-	-	2.0%	1.6%	1.2%	2.4%
Class of 1996	2.6%	2.0%	3.2%	2.8%	4.2%	2.6%	2.1%	4.7%	4.0%	2.4%	2.9%	2.9%
% Advanced Courses												
1995-96	15.1%	17.3%	17.0%	10.5%	12.4%	20.3%	12.0%	30.4%	16.3%	17.5%	11.7%	1.1%
1995-96	13.2%	15.3%	12.5%	9.4%	8.2%	14.8%	0.0%	21.2%	10.4%	14.3%	6.3%	0.3%
% Rec. HS Program												
Class of 1997	0.3%	0.6%	0.0%	0.0%	0.0%	0.0%	0.0%	0.0%	0.0%	0.0%	0.0%	0.0%
Class of 1996												
AP/IB Results												
% Tested												
1997-98	7.6%	10.9%	3.0%	1.5%	1.5%	4.5%	22.0%	1.5%	2.5%	3.5%	n/a	n/a
1996-97	6.8%	9.7%	1.5%	2.0%	0.5%	1.5%	12.5%	3.5%	1.0%	2.0%	n/a	n/a
% Scores > = crit.												
1997-98	60.6%	63.3%	59.0%	*	54.6%	60.0%	*	*	56.6%	60.4%	n/a	n/a
1996-97	60.0%	63.4%	41.0%	14.2%	40.0%	44.0%	*	66.6%	76.4%	18.6%	n/a	n/a
% Examinees > = crit.												
1997-98	62.6%	65.6%	60.0%	*	44.4%	65.0%	*	*	65.2%	56.2%	n/a	n/a
1996-97	62.4%	66.8%	48.0%	*	*	50.0%	*	*	77.8%	31.2%	n/a	n/a
TAAS/TASP Equiv.												
Class of 1997	39.9%	44.2%	41.9%	16.7%	31.0%	51.2%	0.0%	40.5%	46.5%	37.6%	19.1%	0.0%
Class of 1996												
SAT I/ACT Results												
% At/Above Crit.												
Class of 1997	18.0%	22.2%	16.2%	7.2%	5.9%	21.8%	*	20.9%	17.5%	14.8%	n/a	n/a
% Tested												
Class of 1997	64.8%	65.9%	59.6%	59.4%	42.5%	63.9%	*	83.7%	57.1%	62.0%	n/a	n/a
Class of 1996	64.8%	65.5%	56.4%	64.7%	42.1%	59.0%	42.9%	68.4%	54.6%	58.1%	n/a	n/a
Mean SAT I Score												
Class of 1997	891	918	935	886	953	891	*	938	954	916	n/a	n/a
Class of 1996	885	908	991	908	956	1023	*	929	1013	972	n/a	n/a
Mean ACT Score												
Class of 1997	20.0	20.7	20.0	8.6	19.4	21.1	*	17.9	19.8	20.3	n/a	n/a
Class of 1996	20.1	20.7	20.0	17.8	19.1	21.0	19.8%	20.4	19.5	20.5	n/a	n/a

For accountability ratings, the __state standard for attendance__ is a rate of 94.0 percent or higher for all students in grades 1 through 12.

This indicator shows the percentage of students receiving credit for at least one __advanced course.__

This indicator shows the percentage of graduates who have completed the 24 credit course requirements of the __Recommended High School Program.__

These indicators show the percentage of students who scored at or above 24 on the ACT (composite) or 1110 on the SAT I (total); the percentage of students taking college entrance tests; and the average scores on ACT and the SAT I.

A *dash* (-) indicates that fewer than 5 students were in this classification.

An *asterisk* (*) indicates that fewer than 5 students were in this classification.

n/a - indicates that the data are not available this year or are not applicable.

A *question mark* (?) indicates data that are statistically improbable or were reported outside of a reasonable range.

Texas public schools administer state developed end-of-course exams in Biology I and Algebra I. This indicator shows the percent of students taking these exams.

District-wide performance is reported for each of these student groups.

District performance is compared to the state and the regional education service center with which the district is associated. **Campus performance** is compared to the state and a group of 40 similar campuses.

Students must pass all three sections (reading, writing and math) of the 10th grade exit-level TAAS to meet **minimum high school graduation requirements.** This indicator shows the results for students who took these tests as sophomores in the spring of 1998.

This indicator, the "sum of all students" tested by subject area (accountability subset), is used to determine **district and campus accountability ratings.**

This preview indicator, that includes TAAS results for special education students and those students who took the tests in Spanish, is most important. It will be used to determine accountability ratings beginning with the 1998-99 school year.

This indicator includes those students who passed the 10th grade exit-level TAAS test on subsequent attempts. The Class of 1998 includes students who first took the exit-level TAAS as sophomores in 1996 and finished testing in the same district in May 1998. It is included only on the AEIS district reports.

Indicator		State	Region 04	District	African American	Hispanic	White	Native American	Asian/ Pac. Is.	Male	Female	Econ. Disadv.	Special Educ.
TAAS % Passing Grade 10													
Reading	1998	88.3%	88.4%	83.1%	83.9%	64.3%	94.0%	-	*	82.2%	84.0%	74.2%	45.5%
	1997	86.1%	86.5%	78.5%	71.9%	69.0%	86.2%	-	100.0%	76.5%	80.6%	72.9%	33.3%
Writing	1998	89.9%	89.5%	80.5%	83.6	62.5%	89.3%	-	*	79.0%	82.0%	68.9%	25.0%
	1997	88.5%	87.7%	87.3%	79.4%	78.0%	96.8%	-	80.0%	83.3%	91.2%	83.1%	42.1%
Math	1998	78.4%	78.8%	68.8%	52.7%	62.5%	81.9%	-	*	67.7%	70.0%	63.9%	27.3%
	1997	72.6%	73.0%	64.4%	59.4%	53.7%	71.6%	-	80.0%	60.8%	68.0%	54.1%	35.0%
All Tests	1998	73.1%	73.4%	60.9%	48.2%	47.4%	76.2%	-	*	61.8%	60.0%	50.0%	16.7%
	1997	67.8%	68.0%	59.4%	53.1%	45.2%	68.8%	-	80.0%	58.3%	60.6%	45.9%	14.3%
TAAS % Passing Sum of 3-8 & 10 (Accountability Subset)													
Reading	1998	87.0%	88.4%	84.0%	80.7%	77.6%	88.5%	*	89.5%	80.2%	87.6%	79.8%	46.2%
	1997	84.0%	85.8%	82.2%	77.2%	76.0%	87.1%	*	82.8%	77.8%	86.3%	77.9%	39.7%
Writing	1998	87.4%	88.3%	82.4%	81.5%	73.2%	86.7%	-	100.0%	78.0%	86.5%	75.6%	39.4%
	1997	85.3%	86.2%	86.5%	82.2%	79.3%	92.1%	-	84.6%	82.7%	90.1%	84.8%	43.0%
Math	1998	84.2%	85.3%	78.1%	69.7%	75.5%	83.0%	*	89.5%	77.3%	78.9%	74.3%	37.2%
	1997	80.1%	81.3%	76.5%	64.3%	74.2%	82.9%	*	86.2%	75.5%	77.3%	72.3%	30.4%
All Tests	1998	77.7%	79.4%	70.9%	62.8%	65.3%	76.8%	*	89.5%	78.2%	73.4%	65.2%	21.3%
	1997	73.2%	75.1%	69.0%	58.4%	62.7%	76.3%	*	79.3%	65.9%	71.8%	63.1%	18.4%
1999 Preview Indicator — TAAS % Passing (Includes Spec. Ed. & Spanish 3-4) Sum of 3-8 &10													
Reading	1998	83.3%	85.6%	78.6%	76.4%	69.0%	84.6%	*	85.7%	73.2%	83.9%	71.9%	46.5%
Writing	1998	84.2%	86.0%	78.3%	77.5%	69.7%	82.0%	-	100.0%	72.7%	84.0%	71.9%	39.4%
Math	1998	80.4%	82.5%	72.3%	65.2%	66.9%	77.9%	*	90.5%	70.3%	74.2%	66.4%	37.5%
All Tests	1998	73.1%	75.9%	63.8%	57.5%	56.2%	70.2%	*	85.7%	59.7%	67.9%	56.1%	21.7%
TAAS Cumulative Pass Rate-Exit (note: district-level only indicator)													
Class of 1998		88.7%	88.1%	86.1%	85.1%	79.2%	88.9%	-	100.0%	82.1%	89.7%	n/a	n/a
Class of 1997		86.6%	85.6%	83.3%	93.2%	81.0%	80.0%	-	*	82.5%	84.3%	n/a	n/a
End-of-Course Exam (% Taking)													
Biology I													
Grades 8-12	98	19.7%	18.9%	16.9%	15.2%	12.8%	19.8%	-	19.0%	16.8%	17.1%	15.5%	8.7%
	97	19.7%	18.7%	19.1%	22.3%	21.3%	16.1%	-	20.0%	18.8%	19.3%	19.5%	9.9%
Algebra I													
Grades 7-12	98	18.5%	17.9%	23.5%	26.8%	25.0%	20.6%	-	22.7%	23.9%	22.9%	25.7%	18.0%
	97	18.3%	17.3%	17.3%	16.6%	16.3%	18.0%	?	19.2%	16.6%	18.1%	14.2%	2.8%

TAAS PARTICIPATION REPORT—AN IMPORTANT NEW INDICATOR FOR 1997-98

This page explains the TAAS Participation Report, a new indicator that replaces the "percentages of students exempted from TAAS" that appeared in previous years' AEIS reports. The report is shown for both the 1997-98 and 1996-97 school years. Percentages shown for each category are calculated against the total enrollment in the grades tested.

State policy requires that every student enrolled in grades 3 through 8 and 10 be given an opportunity to take the TAAS tests. Although the intention is to test every student in these grades, there are circumstances under which some students are not tested. This report shows the percentages of various categories of students who participated in the TAAS assessments for 1997-98 as well as those who did not.

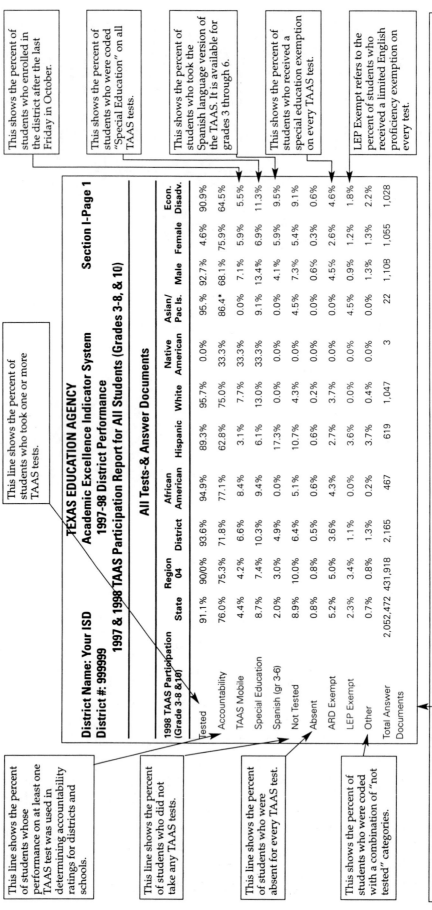

This shows the percent of students who enrolled in the district after the last Friday in October.

This shows the percent of students who were coded "Special Education" on all TAAS tests.

This shows the percent of students who took the Spanish language version of the TAAS. It is available for grades 3 through 6.

This shows the percent of students who received a special education exemption on every TAAS test.

LEP Exempt refers to the percent of students who received a limited English proficiency exemption on every test.

This line shows the percent of students who took one or more TAAS tests.

This line shows the percent of students whose performance on at least one TAAS test was used in determining accountability ratings for districts and schools.

This line shows the percent of students who did not take any TAAS tests.

This line shows the percent of students who were absent for every TAAS test.

This shows the percent of students who were coded with a combination of "not tested" categories.

TEXAS EDUCATION AGENCY
Academic Excellence Indicator System
1997-98 District Performance **Section I-Page 1**

District Name: Your ISD
District #: 999999

1997 & 1998 TAAS Participation Report for All Students (Grades 3-8, & 10)

All Tests-& Answer Documents

1998 TAAS Participation (Grade 3-8 &10)	State	Region 04	District	African American	Hispanic	White	Native American	Asian/ Pac Is.	Male	Female	Econ. Disadv.
Tested	91.1%	90/0%	93.6%	94.9%	89.3%	95.7%	0.0%	95.%	92.7%	4.6%	90.9%
Accountability	76.0%	75.3%	71.8%	77.1%	62.8%	75.0%	33.3%	86.4%*	68.1%	75.9%	64.5%
TAAS Mobile	4.4%	4.2%	6.6%	8.4%	3.1%	7.7%	33.3%	0.0%	7.1%	5.9%	5.5%
Special Education	8.7%	7.4%	10.3%	9.4%	6.1%	13.0%	33.3%	9.1%	13.4%	6.9%	11.3%
Spanish (gr 3-6)	2.0%	3.0%	4.9%	0.0%	17.3%	0.0%	0.0%	0.0%	4.1%	5.9%	9.5%
Not Tested	8.9%	10.0%	6.4%	5.1%	10.7%	4.3%	0.0%	4.5%	7.3%	5.4%	9.1%
Absent	0.8%	0.8%	0.5%	0.6%	0.6%	0.2%	0.0%	0.0%	0.6%	0.3%	0.6%
ARD Exempt	5.2%	5.0%	3.6%	4.3%	2.7%	3.7%	0.0%	0.0%	4.5%	2.6%	4.6%
LEP Exempt	2.3%	3.4%	1.1%	0.0%	3.6%	0.0%	0.0%	4.5%	0.9%	1.2%	1.8%
Other	0.7%	0.8%	1.3%	0.2%	3.7%	0.4%	0.0%	0.0%	1.3%	1.3%	2.2%
Total Answer Documents	2,052,472	431,918	2,165	467	619	1,047	3	22	1,108	1,055	1,028

Total Answer Documents: Typically, only one answer document per student is counted, so this represents the number of students who were in school during the spring TAAS administration and is roughly equivalent to enrollment in the grades tested. The official "enrollment" numbers in grades 3-8 & 10 will not match exactly the number of answer documents submitted because enrollment is taken in the fall and students are tested in the spring.

COMPARABLE IMPROVEMENT: A NEW FEATURE OF THE CAMPUS AEIS REPORTS FOR 1997-98

This year's AEIS campus reports contain an important new two-page section called *Comparable Improvement*. This important new "value-added" accountability indicator shows the impact of the campus on the learning results of their students and is a *supplemental indicator* in the accountability system. Each campus is compared to a unique group of 40 other schools that serve a similar student population. Reading and mathematics performance of the campus is evaluated based on the year-to-year improvement (or loss) is TAAS scores. This section contains other information that will enrich your understanding of how the school in which you have an interest performs against similar schools in Texas. This page provides an example and explains how the campus groups are formed. The following page explains how improvement is evaluated and highlights other new information provided to the user.

To begin, the 100 most similar campuses are selected based on the most dominant characteristic for the target school. That group is refined by removing the 10 campuses most distant from the target campus according to the second most dominant characteristic. The same process is repeated in order for the other characteristics, leaving a group of 50 schools. The final step is to remove the 10 schools that are least similar to the target school according to the least dominant characteristic. This leaves a group of 40 comparison schools, all of the same type—elementary, middle, or high school—that serve student populations very much like that of the target campus.

The characteristics used to construct the campus comparison groups include those defined in statute and others that are statistically significant. The six campus-level characteristics used in 1997-98 are listed across the top of the example.

A unique comparison group of 40 campuses is identified for each school. The target school is identified with an asterisk. The group is selected on the basis of the most dominant characteristics of the target campus. The order of dominance is determined by ranking the characteristics from highest to lowest percent. In the example, % economically disadvantaged is the most dominant characteristic and % limited English proficient the least dominant.

TARGET CAMPUS NAME: SAMPLE MIDDLE SCHOOL
TARGET CAMPUS #: 22790104 6
DISTRICT NAME: SAMPLE ISD
CAMPUS TYPE: MIDDLE SCHOOL

TEXAS EDUCATION AGENCY
CAMPUS COMPARISON GROUP FOR 1997-98

CAMPUS NUMBER	CAMPUS NAME	DISTRICT NAME	% ECON	% WHITE	% HISPANIC	% MOBILITY	% AFR. AMER.	% LEP
003905041	DIBOLL JH	DIBOLL ISD	55.9	41.2	38.7	17.6	20.1	3.4
004901042	ROCKPORT INT	ARANSAS COUNTY ISD	54.7	60.5	29.1	16.9	2.2	3.1
020905042	FREEPORT INT	BRAZOSPORT ISD	55.4	41.8	44.1	20.4	3.5	4.2
025902108	BROWNWOOD INT	BROWNWOOD ISD	53.7	67.3	24.5	15.5	7.9	4.1
028902041	LOCKHART JH	LOCKHART ISD	51.6	49.9	41.3	15.2	8.0	3.3
028903041	LULING JH	LULING ISD	54.0	45.4	46.7	13.7	7.6	4.7
045905041	WEIMAR JH	WEIMAR ISD	56.0	52.8	26.4	13.4	0.8	13.6
047901041	JEFFERIES JH	COMMANCHE ISD	54.4	63.2	35.5	14.6	0.9	6.9
049901041	GAINSVILLE MIDDLE	GAINESVILLE ISD	51.3	70.5	17.9	21.9	9.6	4.6
057907109	HARDIN INT	DUNCANVILLE ISD	51.8	45.4	18.5	18.7	32.4	4.4
057910041	ADAMS MIDDLE	GRAND PRAIRIE ISD	51.4	42.3	38.6	28.4	16.4	5.0
068901042	BONHAM JH	ECTOR COUNTY ISD	51.6	48.7	44.9	23.3	5.8	7.5
071902045	CHARLES MIDDLE	EL PASO ISD	52.0	31.0	50.5	19.8	16.0	6.7
083903041	SEMINOLE JH	SEMINOLE ISD	53.0	58.5	38.1	12.3	3.4	10.9
085902041	POST ISD	POST ISD	52.5	47.5	42.8	13.0	9.3	2.1
089901042	GONZALES JH	GONZALES ISD	54.6	39.1	46.2	16.0	14.4	2.2
093904042	NAVASOTA JH	NAVASOTA ISD	53.3	47.0	24.4	12.1	28.3	2.6
096904041	MEMPHIS MIDDLE	MEMPHIS ISD	52.8	44.8	42.4	19.3	12.0	8.8
099903041	TRAVIS MIDDLE	QUANAH ISD	51.9	63.4	29.0	16.0	7.6	2.3
101903141	KLENTZMAN INT	ALIEF ISD	52.8	11.3	25.0	24.6	39.0	22.3
101903142	YOUNGBLOOK INT	ALIEF ISD	51.9	15.9	26.9	26.3	36.7	18.0
101911041	BAYTOWN JH	GOOSE CREEK ISD	54.9	32.5	52.5	22.7	14.5	15.5
101917043	PARK VIEW INT	PASADENA ISD	52.1	53.8	42.0	31.6	2.7	12.7
114901041	GOLIAD MIDDLE	BIG SPRING ISD	54.3	46.8	45.7	16.6	6.5	5.9
133903104	TIVY UPPER EL	KERRVILLE ISD	53.1	63.5	32.1	13.6	3.7	2.2
146901041	CLEVELAND MIDDLE	CLEVELAND ISD	53.8	58.6	19.1	21.9	21.5	8.5
152901047	SLATON JH	LUBBOCK ISD	52.7	49.1	40.3	32.2	8.4	3.4
158901041	BAY CITY JH	BAY CITY ISD	52.4	46.4	44.8	15.0	7.2	2.2
158901043	MACALLISTER JH	BAY CITY ISD	54.3	44.2	26.7	16.6	27.8	4.5
161914041	LAKE AIR MIDDLE	WACO ISD	53.2	41.0	23.7	28.9	34.6	3.7
174904041	THOMAS RUSK MIDDLE	NACOGDOCHES ISD	51.3	52.5	18.2	15.1	28.6	7.9
188901045	HOUSTON MIDDLE	AMARILLO ISD	53.9	63.2	18.3	20.5	16.9	1.4
206901041	SAN SABA JH	SAN SABA ISD	51.3	67.3	31.3	14.1	1.3	6.7
217901041	ASPERMONT JH	ASPERMONT ISD	55.7	71.4	25.7	14.9	1.4	2.9
220910041	N A HOWRY MIDDLE	LAKE WORTH ISD	52.2	59.8	32.6	23.2	5.8	3.8
220917041	MARSH MIDDLE	CASTLEBERRY ISD	54.2	69.2	29.0	22.4	0.9	6.3
221901041	FRANKLIN MIDDLE	ABILENE ISD	54.5	50.4	40.5	21.7	7.2	4.0
221901047	CLACK MIDDLE	ABILENE ISD	54.3	55.9	25.1	25.7	16.7	1.6
227901046	*SAMPLE MIDDLE	SAMPLE ISD	53.7	39.3	36.6	27.6	20.8	12.3
227901049	PORTER MIDDLE	AUSTIN ISD	53.7	37.5	53.7	21.7	8.2	12.3
243905048	KIRBY MATH-SCIENCE CTR	WICHITA FALLS ISD	55.8	50.1	18.2	24.0	29.4	2.3
GROUP AVERAGE			53.2	47.2	34.4	23.9	15.3	7.0

This page shows an example of the performance part of Comparable Improvement. It explains how "improvement" is calculated and how the campuses are ranked. It also highlights other significant information shown on this page that did not appear in previous years' AEIS reports, including the percentage of students who achieved a 5 point or greater increase in their TLI scores and those who scored 84 TLI or higher in reading and mathematics.

Column 1—the "number of matched students"—shows how many students have test results from schools in the same district during both the current and the previous school years.

Column 2 shows the average Texas Learning Index (TLI) score for those students on the current year's TAAS. Column 3 shows the average TLI score for those same students on the previous year's TAAS. Column 6—TLI Average Growth—is the difference between these two scores. A negative number indicates students made less than a year's gain.

The target campus—Sample Middle School—is identified by an asterisk.

Column 7—Quartile—shows how the schools in the group rank for reading and math separately. Q1 is the highest group and Q4 the lowest. Note that the target school—Sample Middle—ranks in the 4th quartile in both reading and math.

Column 4 shows the percentage of students at each school who achieved 5 or more points of growth in their TLI scores from the previous to the current school year.

Column 5 shows the percentage of students whose TLI score was 84 or higher on the previous year's TAAS. NOTE: These students are not included in the growth calculation shown in column 6.

TARGET CAMPUS NAME: SAMPLE MIDDLE SCHOOL
TARGET CAMPUS #: 227901046
DISTRICT NAME: SAMPLE ISD
CAMPUS TYPE: MIDDLE SCHOOL

TEXAS EDUCATION AGENCY
1997-98 COMPARABLE IMPROVEMENT
ADDITIONAL ACKNOWLEDGEMENT: DOES NOT QUALIFY

READING

CAMPUS NAME	(1) Number Matched Students	(2) Current Year Avg. TLI	(3) Prior Year Avg. TLI	(4) % > 5 Pts. Growth	(5) % > 84 On prior Yr. TLI	(6) TLI Avg. Growth	(7) Quartile
DIBOLL JH	180	75.46	72.11	41.1	36.8	3.35	Q4
ROCKPORT INT	214	78.04	69.32	61.2	42.5	8.72	Q1
FREEPORT INT	192	78.99	73.11	51.0	50.1	5.88	Q1
BROWNWOOD INT	227	76.87	69.66	57.3	52.8	7.21	Q1
LOCKHART JH	249	75.51	71.27	49.4	49.1	4.24	Q3
LULING JH	179	73.11	70.47	40.8	39.1	2.63	Q4
WEIMAR JH	19	83.26	77.21	68.4	67.8	6.05	Q1
JEFFERIES JH	113	72.92	72.11	35.4	51.5	0.81	Q4
GAINSVILLE MIDDLE	167	77.62	71.99	50.3	57.1	5.62	Q2
HARDIN INT	177	73.23	69.19	46.3	52.9	4.04	Q3
ADAMS MIDDLE	183	77.04	71.22	53.6	57.9	5.83	Q2
BONHAM JH	299	73.28	69.57	47.2	46.0	3.71	Q3
CHARLES MIDDLE	437	77.41	71.81	49.0	48.3	5.60	Q2
SEMINOLE JH	257	77.37	70.75	55.6	40.1	7.72	Q1
POST MIDDLE	89	77.33	71.93	42.7	46.0	5.44	Q2
GONZALES JH	289	73.15	68.16	47.1	35.2	4.99	Q2
NAVASOTA JH	320	73.28	68.42	47.8	38.8	4.87	Q2
MEMPHIS MIDDLE	45	75.87	73.47	37.8	45.1	2.40	Q4
TRAVIS MIDDLE	40	83.33	75.68	60.0	56.5	7.65	Q1
KLENTZMAN INT	320	79.82	70.47	65.6	46.8	9.35	Q1
YOUNGBLOOK INT	297	80.31	72.08	60.9	47.2	8.22	Q1
BAYTOWN JH	303	78.15	69.31	63.4	47.8	8.84	Q1
PARK VIEW INT	361	75.96	69.95	51.0	46.4	6.01	Q2
GOLIAD MIDDLE	290	76.63	71.58	47.2	47.8	5.06	Q2
TIVY UPPER EL	202	78.33	73.56	49.5	59.5	4.77	Q2
CLEVELAND MIDDLE	295	70.66	67.12	44.7	38.5	3.54	Q3
SLATON JH	149	67.60	67.93	30.9	65.2	0.33	Q4
BAY CITY JH	171	75.95	71.20	47.4	48.6	4.75	Q2
MACALLISTER JH	211	75.01	71.80	45.0	50.1	3.21	Q3
LAKE AIR MIDDLE	258	72.96	68.56	46.1	45.2	4.40	Q3
THOMAS RUSK MIDDLE	363	71.68	67.78	45.7	45.8	3.90	Q3
HOUSTON MIDDLE	351	72.60	71.14	36.5	52.8	1.46	Q4
SAN SABA JH	53	74.45	70.32	37.7	41.1	4.13	Q3
ASPERMONT JH	34	77.21	72.68	50.0	37.0	4.53	Q3
N A HOWRY MIDDLE	125	71.14	68.80	32.8	37.5	2.34	Q4
MARSH MIDDLE	257	76.87	72.41	46.7	48.6	4.46	Q3
FRANKLIN MIDDLE	279	76.78	71.41	48.7	55.3	5.38	Q2
CLACK MIDDLE	230	75.90	72.54	37.8	46.1	3.36	Q4
*SAMPLE MIDDLE	376	70.62	68.29	40.4	44.9	2.32	Q4
PORTER MIDDLE	449	68.84	67.22	39.2	38.6	1.63	Q4
KIRBY MATH-SCIENCE C	148	77.41	73.22	47.3	60.9	4.20	Q3
GROUP AVERAGE	8822	75.25	70.39	48.2	48.0	4.79	

MATH

CAMPUS NAME	(1) Number Matched Students	(2) Current Year Avg. TLI	(3) Prior Year Avg. TLI	(4) % > 5 Pts. Growth	(5) % > 84 On Prior Yr. TLI	(6) TLI Avg. Growth	(7) Quartile
DIBOLL JH	210	71.94	70.08	29.5	25.5	1.86	Q3
ROCKPORT INT	215	79.76	72.07	60.9	42.5	7.69	Q1
FREEPORT INT	216	77.87	72.63	46.3	44.8	5.24	Q1
BROWNWOOD INT	278	77.16	71.73	47.8	42.7	5.43	Q2
LOCKHART JH	303	75.45	72.35	35.0	38.4	3.10	Q4
LULING JH	194	72.11	71.25	25.3	33.1	0.86	Q4
WEIMAR JH	31	79.29	76.19	25.8	47.5	3.10	Q2
JEFFERIES JH	137	70.32	70.25	23.4	40.7	0.07	Q4
GAINSVILLE MIDDLE	203	76.02	72.28	38.4	47.3	3.74	Q2
HARDIN INT	236	74.50	71.44	36.9	37.9	3.05	Q2
ADAMS MIDDLE	256	73.36	71.05	30.1	41.1	2.31	Q3
BONHAM JH	345	68.69	69.22	22.3	37.7	0.53	Q4
CHARLES MIDDLE	600	73.99	70.55	37.2	28.5	3.44	Q2
SEMINOLE JH	288	76.08	70.37	50.7	32.9	5.71	Q1
POST MIDDLE	97	77.05	73.36	38.1	41.6	3.69	Q2
GONZALES JH	310	73.31	70.59	34.8	31.4	2.72	Q3
NAVASOTA JH	381	73.50	69.06	41.7	25.7	4.44	Q1
MEMPHIS MIDDLE	46	75.46	71.35	43.2	43.2	4.11	Q1
TRAVIS MIDDLE	58	79.22	76.48	27.6	34.8	2.74	Q3
KLENTZMAN INT	377	78.11	71.21	54.6	37.2	6.90	Q1
YOUNGBLOOK INT	310	76.86	72.18	45.0	45.0	4.68	Q1
BAYTOWN JH	370	74.92	70.93	39.7	36.8	3.99	Q2
PARK VIEW INT	483	71.19	69.48	29.0	27.5	1.71	Q3
GOLIAD MIDDLE	408	74.22	71.37	36.0	28.2	2.85	Q3
TIVY UPPER EL	223	78.30	74.04	41.3	55.0	4.25	Q1
CLEVELAND MIDDLE	386	67.09	66.75	28.0	17.7	0.94	Q4
SLATON JH	196	67.10	68.69	19.4	54.5	1.60	Q4
BAY CITY JH	179	73.89	71.72	35.2	46.1	2.17	Q3
MACALLISTER JH	242	71.84	69.42	34.7	42.8	2.42	Q3
LAKE AIR MIDDLE	321	70.84	68.10	34.0	34.0	2.74	Q3
THOMAS RUSK MIDDLE	409	73.60	68.17	48.2	38.9	5.43	Q1
HOUSTON MIDDLE	475	70.27	70.61	23.2	36.3	0.34	Q4
SAN SABA JH	56	72.93	71.84	25.0	39.1	1.09	Q4
ASPERMONT JH	41	75.05	74.17	26.8	24.1	0.88	Q4
N A HOWRY MIDDLE	159	70.03	66.47	38.4	19.7	3.56	Q2
MARSH MIDDLE	325	72.47	70.90	30.5	34.6	1.57	Q3
FRANKLIN MIDDLE	365	74.92	71.73	37.0	41.5	3.19	Q2
CLACK MIDDLE	282	74.30	71.00	26.4	34.1	3.30	Q2
*SAMPLE MIDDLE	470	67.49	66.82	29.8	31.4	0.67	Q4
PORTER MIDDLE	554	67.76	66.92	23.8	24.4	0.84	Q4
KIRBY MATH-SCIENCE C	189	73.52	73.52		50.4	0.40	Q4
GROUP AVERAGE	10754	73.31	70.43	35.9	36.6	2.85	

Note: All values are based on students who can be matched from current to prior year TAAS. Values in columns 1,2,3,4,6, and 7 are based on those matched students with a TLI of 84 or less in the prior year. Values shown in column 5 are based on all matched students in the prior year. Current year is 1998 while prior year is 1997 for grades 3-8 and 1996 for grade 10 (exit level).

84

INTERPRETING THE DATA

This part of the guide explains how to look at the data. There are two sections in the AEIS report. This first contains information about student performance; the second provides profile information about the district or campus. Everyone is naturally more interested in test scores and other measures of student performance than in the data about student demographics, the instructional staff, or school finance. The bottom-line performance information is the most important part of the AEIS report, but to understand the district or campus situation more completely, it is necessary to examine and understand the profile data to gain a context for interpreting performance.

HOW TO EVALUATE PERFORMANCE DATA

The following section explains how to look at indicators of student performance. The example below is part of the AEIS report for an elementary school. It shows the TAAS results for grades 3 and 4. The statements in italics below suggest what these data show about this school's performance for the 1997-98 school year.

District Name: SAMPLE ISD
Campus Name: SAMPLE ELEMENTARY SCHOOL
Campus #: 55555888

TEXAS EDUCATION AGENCY
Academic Excellence Indicator System
1997-98 Campus Performance
Accountability Rating: Acceptable

Section I - Page 1
Total Enrollment: 425
Grade Span: PK-5
School Type: Elementary

Indicator:	State	District	Campus Group	Campus	African American	Hispanic	White	Native American	Asian/ Pac. Is.	Male	Female	Econ. Disadv.	Special Educ.
TAAS % Passing Grade 3													
Reading 1998	86.2%	82.0%	90.0%	87.8%	100.0%	63.6%	89.8%	*	-	84.2%	91.7%	88.9%	42.9%
Reading 1997	81.5%	78.2%	88.0%	71.6%	56.3%	66.7%	77.4%	-	-	61.9%	80.4%	69.2%	18.2%
Math 1998	81.0%	82.2%	84.0%	85.1%	92.9%	81.8%	83.7%	*	-	92.1%	77.8%	88.9%	30.0%
Math 1997	81.7%	80.3%	87.4%	76.7%	52.9%	80.0%	82.3%	*	-	72.1%	80.9%	78.0%	18.2%
All tests 1998	76.6%	73.6%	80.3%	78.4%	92.9%	54.5%	79.6%	*	-	81.6%	75.0%	77.8%	10.0%
All tests 1997	74.2%	70.9%	80.0%	65.6%	41.2%	50.0%	72.6%	-	-	58.1%	72.3%	63.4%	9.1%
TAAS % Passing Grade 4													
Reading 1998	89.7%	90.1%	90.7%	94.6%	85.7%	100.0%	95.7%	-	-	90.9%	97.6%	93.9%	58.3%
Reading 1997	82.5%	81.0%	87.0%	88.1%	100.0%	81.8%	84.2%	*	*	86.4%	88.9%	93.1%	40.0%
Writing 1998	88.7%	86.9%	93.3%	93.2%	78.6%	91.7%	97.9%	*	-	90.6%	95.2%	91.2%	45.5%
Writing 1997	87.1%	90.5%	91.1%	95.6%	94.4%	90.9%	97.4%	-	-	95.5%	95.7%	96.8%	47.1%
Math 1998	86.3%	79.6%	89.3%	84.9%	78.6%	91.7%	84.8%	-	-	84.4%	85.4%	75.8%	42.9%
Math 1997	82.6%	75.4%	87.8%	82.4%	72.2%	72.7%	89.5%	-	*	82.6%	82.2%	74.2%	27.8%
All tests 1998	78.6%	75.1%	84.8%	80.0%	66.7%	91.7%	80.9%	-	-	75.8%	83.3%	70.6%	33.3%
All tests 1997	72.0%	61.3%	77.8%	71.4%	72.2%	45.5%	77.5%	-	*	70.8%	71.7%	64.5%	11.1%

- This campus has an accountability rating of *Acceptable*. Readers should observe that its performance on all indicators exceeds the minimum Acceptable standard of 40% by a comfortable margin, but *it needs to improve considerably and stabilize results to move up to a Recognized accountability rating.*

- *Campus performance generally exceeds that of the state and district in both 3rd and 4th grades.* The campus lags behind its campus group in 3rd grade reading, but exceeds the group at 4th grade. The campus exceeds the campus group in 3rd grade math, but lags behind at the 4th grade. Fourth grade writing scores match those of the campus group almost exactly. Notice that the percentage of *students passing all tests is always the lowest figure.* Of course, it cannot be higher than the lowest performance on the individual tests. The lower performance on the math test pulls the overall results down.

- There is no clear pattern on this campus regarding the performance of the various student groups, except that African-American and Hispanic students lag behind Whites. African-American students did much better at the 3rd grade level in 1998 than they did in the same grade in 1997, but African American 4th graders did better in 1997 than in 1998. Hispanic 4th graders did better in 1998 compared to the same grade in 1997. White students did better at both grade levels in 1998 than in 1997, except in 4th grade math.

THE IMPORTANCE OF ANNUAL TESTING

Since 1994, the TAAS tests are taken by students in grades 3 through 8 and 10 (exit-level). It is now possible to look at the year-to-year progress of the same students through elementary and middle schools. For this school, it is interesting to look at the 4th grade scores for 1998 compared to the 3rd grade scores for 1997 (see table below). This gives a different perspective about the school's performance rather than looking only at a single grade level because it shows scores for basically the same group of students as they move through the school. Annual testing also makes possible the kind of performance analysis that is found in the Comparable Improvement section now included in campus AEIS reports.

Schools should aim at improved performance at each higher grade level to prepare as many students as possible for a successful experience in the next grade or school. The desirable pattern is for 4th grade performance to show improvement over 3rd grade, like that achieved by this campus in both reading and math for all student groups. Schools should always aim at improving student performance from every grade level to the next. In the end, perhaps the best indicator of campus performance is how many students it prepares for success at the next school level.

			District	Group	Campus	Afr.Am.	Hispanic	White	Native Am.	As./Pc. Is.	Male	Female	Econ. Dis.	Spec. Ed.
Reading	1998	4th gr.	90.1%	90.7%	94.6%	85.7%	100.0%	95.7%	-	*	90.9%	97.6%	93.9%	58.3%
	1997	3rd gr.	78.2%	88.0%	71.6%	56.3%	66.7%	77.4%	-	*	61.9%	80.4%	69.2%	18.2%
Math	1998	4th gr.	79.6%	89.3%	84.9%	78.6%	91.7%	84.8%	-	*	84.4%	85.4%	75.8%	42.9%
	1997	3rd gr.	80.3%	87.4%	76.7%	52.9%	80.0%	82.3%	-	*	72.1%	80.9%	78.0%	18.2%
All tests	1998	4th gr.	75.1%	84.8%	80.0%	66.7%	91.7%	80.9%	-	-	75.8%	83.3%	70.6%	33.3%
	1997	3rd gr.	70.9%	80.0%	65.6%	41.2%	50.0%	72.6%	-	*	58.1%	72.3%	63.4%	9.1%

LOOK AT THE OTHER INDICATORS

Repeat this process with the other indicators and grade levels. Remember, the idea is to identify patterns or trends. You should be able to form a good idea of where your district or campus stands. The most important step, of course, is to use the information constructively to develop plans for improvement in specific performance areas, or for particular groups of students and even individual students who are not doing as well as they should.

UNDERSTANDING THE INSTRUCTIONAL ENVIRONMENT

The Profile Section has information about students, staff, budgeted revenues and expenditures, and programs. Selected portions of the student information for a sample middle school report are explained below.

TEXAS EDUCATION AGENCY
Academic Excellence Indicator System
1997-98 Campus Profile

Section II - Page 1

District Name: **SAMPLE ISD**
Campus Name: **SAMPLE MIDDLE SCHOOL**
Campus #: **55555777**

Total Enrollment: **697**
Grade Span: **06-08**
School Type: **Middle**

STUDENT INFORMATION

		Campus Count	Campus Percent	Campus Group	District	State
Total Students		638	100.0%	22,729	18.383	3,828,975
Students By Grade	Grade 7	334	52.4%	36.0%	8.5%	7.8%
	Grade 8	304	47.6%	34.1%	7.8%	7.5%
Ethnic Distribution:	African American	144	22.6%	19.6%	22.5%	14.4%
	Hispanic	170	26.6%	26.7%	27.4%	37.9%
	White	317	49.7%	50.7%	49.0%	45.0%
	Asian/Pac. Islander	7	1.1%	2.8%	1.0%	2.4%
	Native American	0	0.0%	0.2%	0.1%	0.3%
Mobility (1996-97)		133	19.2%	19.3%	24.2%	22.1%
Economically Disadvantaged		271	42.5%	42.5%	47.2%	48.5%
Limited English Proficient (LEP)		35	5.5%	4.5%	10.6%	13.4%
Number of Students Per Teacher		14.8	n/a	15.0	15.3	15.3

Retention Rates by Grade:

	Non-Special Education rates				Special Education Rates			
	Campus	Campus Group	District	State	Campus	Campus Group	District	State
Grade 7	0.8%	2.9%	0.8%	2.6%	7.3%	3.0%	7.3%	3.0%
Grade 8	1.2%	1.7%	1.2%	1.8%	7.1%	2.6%	7.1%	3.2%

Looking at enrollment per grade suggests an increasing student population because there are greater numbers of students in grade 7 than grade 8. An examination of elementary enrollment figures would show whether or not this is a long-term trend that needs to be accommodated in the future.

It is helpful to look at the comparisons. Overall, this campus is a microcosm of the district as a whole. It, of course, looks much like the campus group. The student population has smaller percentages of mobile and LEP students than the district and the state.

The Retention Rates at this campus are identical to those of the district. Retention rates for non-special education students are lower than the campus group and the state, but considerably higher for special education students. The campus should be sure that its grading policies are consistent with state standards so that students are promoted based on real academic achievement as measured by their performance on the TAAS. The Comparable Improvement section might give some idea about whether or not the lower retention rates are the result of better academic performance at this campus than others in the campus group.

Another part of the Profile Section provides information about the school staff. NOTE: The AEIS report includes more information than is shown in this excerpt, including the average teacher salary by years of experience and the numbers of contracted instructional staff.

STAFF INFORMATION	Campus Count	Campus Percent	Campus Group	District	State
Professional Staff:	51.6	92.8%	87.9%	61.8%	61.9%
Teachers	43.1	77.4%	77.3%	49.4%	51.7%
Professional Support	5.6	10.0%	6.5%	8.0%	6.8%
Campus Administration (School Leadership)	3.0	5.4%	4.1%	2.7%	2.5%
Educational Aides:	4.0	7.2%	12.1%	6.0%	9.9%
Total Staff:	55.6	100.0%	2,615.0	517.2	491,957.1
Total Minority Staff	11.0	19.8%	16.8%	22.3%	35.9%
Teachers by Ethnicity and Sex:					
Females	30.3	70.4%	72.3%	80.2%	77.3%
Males	12.8	29.6%	27.7%	19.8%	22.7%
African American	8.0	18.6%	6.9%	12.8%	8.2%
Hispanic	1.0	2.3%	4.8%	7.4%	15.8%
White	34.1	79.1%	87.6%	79.8%	75.2%
Asian/Pacific Islander	0.0	0.0%	0.4%	0.0%	0.5%
Native American	0.0	0.0%	0.3%	0.0%	0.3%
Teachers by Years of Experience					
Beginning Teachers	4.0	9.3%	8.1%	7.0%	7.0%
1-5 Years Experience	20.6	47.7%	31.0%	28.0%	26.6%
6-10 Years Experience	2.0	4.6%	15.2%	12.9%	17.5%
11-20 Years Experience	8.0	18.7%	27.0%	24.3%	28.7%
Over 20 Years Experience	8.5	19.7%	18.8%	27.8%	20.1%

	Campus	Campus Group	District	State
Average Years Experience of Teachers:	9.2 Yrs.	11.1 Yrs.	12.8 Yrs.	11.8 Yrs.
Average Years Experience of Teachers with District:	5.2 Yrs.	7.2 Yrs.	8.8 Yrs.	8.0 Yrs.
Average Actual Salaries (excluding supplements):				
Teachers	$32,019	$32,521	$34,543	$33,537
Professional Support	$37,914	$39,641	$37,799	$40,713
Campus Administration (School Leadership)	$49,594	$51,001	$50,204	$52,030

- The percentage of Hispanic staff at the campus is very low, especially considering the large percentage of Hispanic students at the school, although the percentages of African-American students and staff are much closer (see previous page). The district-wide numbers show more Hispanic staff, but fewer African-Americans than this campus. Almost three-fourths of the staff are female.

- The campus has a relatively young teaching staff with over 50% having less than six years experience. The overall average experience of teachers is greater than their time in the district indicating that several have moved to the campus from outside the district. Total years teaching experience and experience with the district is lower than the state and the district. As older teachers retire, an effort should be made to recruit more Hispanic teachers.

- Average salaries for all staff at this campus are lower than the district reflecting the younger staff. Salaries are lower than the campus group and the state.

88

District reports include staff information not found on the campus reports, including: permits by type, turnover rate, and class size by subject area. The Profile Section also includes financial information.

The following sample is from a middle school campus report. The information in the campus group, district, and state columns show total expenditures for campuses in the group, all campuses in the district, and all campuses in the state. Other costs not reported at the campus-level—such as central office administrative expenditures—are not included. The district and state columns include expenses for elementary and high schools, not just other middle schools. **Note: these are budgeted figures not actual expenditures.**

BUDGETED OPERATION EXPENDITURE INFORMATION

	Campus		Campus Group		District		State	
	Amount	Pct.	Amount	Pct.	Amount	Pct.	Amount	Pct.
Total Campus Budget	$3,060,005	100.0%	$116,656,734	100.0%	$18,308,805	100.0%	$15,628,506,927	100.0%
By Function:								
Instruction	$1,932,635	63.2%	$82,603,959	70.8%	$12,315,079	67.3%	$11,177,315,322	71.5%
Instruct. Leadership	$62,706	2.0%	$1,603,985	1.4%	$390,154	2.1%	$247,497,091	1.6%
School Leadership	$211,430	6.9%	$8,797,102	7.5%	$1,083,792	5.9%	$1,132,287,552	7.2%
Other Campus Costs	$853,234	27.9%	$23,651,688	20.3%	$4,519,780	24.7%	$3,071,406,962	19.7%

Average Costs per Campus

Per Pupil:	Campus	w/in Campus Grp	w/in District	w/in State
Total	$4,796	$3,853	$4,675	$4,017
Instruction (inc. Inst. Admin.)	$3,127	$2,781	$3,244	$2,936
School Leadership	$331	$291	$277	$291
Other Campus Costs	$1,337	$781	$1,154	$789

- *The percentage of expenditures on instruction at this campus (63.2%) is lower than the campus group (70.8%), lower than the district (67.3%) and lower than the state (71.5%). School Leadership costs are about the same as the campus group and the state, but higher than the district. The "other campus costs" are higher than the campus group, the district, and state. Some investigation would be required to determine just what causes this disparity.*

- *Per pupil expenditures at this campus are generally higher in all categories than those of the campus group, the district, and the state.*

The Profile Section also includes important information about campus programs, including student enrollment, staffing, and expenditures. The example below is for the student enrollment portion only.

PROGRAM INFORMATION

Student Enrollment by Program:	Campus		Campus Group	District	State
	Count	Percent			
Special Education	80	12.5%	15.5%	10.4%	12.0%
Career & Technology Education	0	0.0%	17.6%	11.0%	17.4%
Bilingual/ESL Education	35	5.5%	3.9%	10.6%	11.9%
Gifted & Talented Education	54	8.5%	8.7%	7.4%	8.0%

- *Student enrollment data are not provided for the "regular" program. Students can participate in more than one of these special programs, so these percentages are not additive.*

- *This campus apparently has no Career and Technology Education courses. Special Education enrollment at this campus is about the same as the campus group, the district and the state. Bilingual/ESL enrollment is higher than the campus group, but lower than the district and the state. A campus should look much like the campus group, because the Comparable Improvement methodology is based on similar student demographics.*

- *The campus AEIS report also contains information for staffing and expenditures by program.*

This page shows some of the additional financial information contained in the District AEIS Report. Other financial details include: The local tax base Value by Category (business, residential, land, oil and gas, and other) as well as Total Expenditures by Object (payroll, professional and contracted services, supplies and materials, debt service, and capital outlay). The numbers in parentheses refer to the state accounting code.

TAX INFORMATION

	District		State	
	Amount	Percent/Rate	Amount	Percent/Rate
Total Adopted Tax Rate (calendar year 1996)	n/a	$ 1.520	n/a	$ 1.497
Standardized Tax Rates (Comptroller Valuation)				
Maintenance and Operations	n/a	$ 1.420	n/a	$ 1.305
Interest and Sinking Fund	n/a	$ 0.100	n/a	$ 0.191
Total Rate (sum of above)	n/a	$ 1.520	n/a	$ 1.496
Standardized Local Tax Base (Comptroller Valuation)				
Value (after exemptions)	$ 1,583,072,044	n/a	$ 708,921,744,666	n/a
Value Per Pupil	$ 404,257	n/a	$ 182,154	n/a

BUDGETED REVENUE INFORMATION

	District		State	
	Amount	Percent/Rate	Amount	Percent/Rate
Total Revenues	$24,015,398	n/a	$ 21,483,063,493	n/a
Total Revenue per Pupil	$ 6,133	n/a	$ 5,520	n/a
Revenues by Source				
Local Tax	$ 20,099,390	83.7%	$10,101,854,657	47.0%
Other Local & Intermediate	$ 1,252,401	5.2%	$945,522,633	4.4%
State	$ 1,908,987	7.9%	$9,716,447,548	45.2%
Federal	$ 754,620	3.1%	$ 719,238,655	3.3%

BUDGETED EXPENDITURE INFORMATION

	District		State	
	Amount	Percent/Rate	Amount	Percent/Rate
Total Expenditures	$ 25,080,471	100.0%	$ 21,783,918,315	100.0%
Total Operating Expenditures by Function	$ 22,059,709	100.0%	$ 19,465,285,020	100.0%
Instruction (11, 95)	$ 12,315,079	55.8%	$ 11,245,811,208	57.8%
Instruction-Related Services (12, 13)	$512,074	2.3%	$ 562,761,247	2.9%
Instructional Leadership (21)	$ 390,154	1.8%	$ 265,584,022	1.4%
School Leadership (23)	$ 1,083,792	4.9%	$ 1,137,476,933	5.8%
Support Services - Student (31, 32, 33)	$ 913,365	4.1%	$ 849,752,434	4.4%
Student Transportation (34)	$ 905,167	4.1%	$ 550,716,637	2.8%
Food Services (35)	$ 1,363,668	6.2%	$ 1,088,906,943	5.6%
Cocurricular/Extracurricular Activities (36)	$ 550,829	2.5%	$ 490,126,870	2.5%
Central Administration (41, 92)	$ 1,024,861	4.6%	$ 801,049,679	4.1%
Plant Maintenance and Operations (51)	$ 2,693,218	12.2%	$ 2,183,072,112	11.2%
Security and Monitoring Services (52)	$ 197,849	0.9%	$ 103,877,919	0.5%
Data Processing Services (53)	$ 109,653	0.5%	$ 186,149,016	1.0%

Per Pupil Expenditures:	District	State
Total Expenditures	$ 6,405	$5,597
Total Operating Expenditures by Function:		
Instruction (11, 95) & Instruct. Leadership (21)	$5,633	$ 5,002
School Leadership (23)	$3,244	$ 2,958
Central Administration (23)	$277	$292
Central Administration (41, 92)	$262	$206
Other Operating (12, 13, 31-36, 51, 53)	$ 1,850	$ 1,546
Total Expenditures for Athletic Programs	$ 1,081,213	$, 304,156,322

GLOSSARY

Accountability Rating   The public school accountability system assigns ratings for districts and campuses based on performance levels on TAAS, dropouts, and attendance. The four levels of ratings are:

- **Exemplary** for both districts and campuses
- **Recognized** for both districts and campuses
- **Academically Acceptable** for districts, **Acceptable** for campuses
- **Academically Unacceptable** for districts, **Low-performing** for campuses

Alternative Education campuses are rated **AE: Acceptable** or **AE: Needs Peer Review.**

Advanced Courses   This indicator is based on the number of students who complete and receive credit for at least one advanced academic course (Advanced Placement or International Baccalaureate courses) in grades 9-12.

AP/IB Results   These are the results of the College Board Advanced Placement (AP) examinations and the International Baccalaureate (IB) examinations taken by Texas public school students in a given school year. High school students may take these examinations, ideally upon completion of AP or IB courses, and may receive advanced placement or credit, or both upon entering college. Generally, colleges will award credit or advanced placement for scores of 3, 4, or 5 on AP examinations and scores of 4, 5, 6, or 7 on IB examinations. Three values are calculated for this indicator:

1. The percent of students in grades 11 and 12 taking at least one AP or IB exam,
2. The percent of AP scores 3 to 5 and IB scores 4-7, and
3. The percent of examinees with at least one AP score above 3 or IB score above 4.

Attendance Rate   Attendance rates are based on student attendance for the entire school year. Attendance is calculated as follows for 1996-97:

$$\frac{\text{total number of days students were present in 1996-97}}{\text{total number of days students were in membership in 1996-97}}$$

Attendance rates are shown for 1996-97 and 1995-96. Note that only students in grades 1 through 12 are included in the calculations.

Campus Group   Each school has a unique campus group of 40 schools that closely match the school demographically. Six demographic variables are used:

1. Percent of economically disadvantaged students for 1997-98
2. Percent of limited English-proficient students for 1997-98
3. Percent of African American students for 1997-98
4. Percent of Hispanic students for 1997-98
5. Percent of White students for 1997-98
6. Percent of mobile students from 1996-97 cumulative attendance

The number in the Campus Group column is the performance of the middle campus (median) in the group. Median is defined as the middle number, not the average, in any given distribution of values. Group information in the Profile Section shows totals or averages rather than median values.

College Admissions Tests   These include the College Board's SAT I and ACT, Inc's ACT assessment. Three values are calculated for this indicator:

1. Percentage who scored at or above the criterion score on either test (1110 on SAT I or 24 on ACT).
2. Percentage of graduates who took either test.
3. Average score for each test.

Completion Rate   (Districts only): This longitudinal measure is new for 1998. The current year (class of 1997) completion rate looks at the group of students who were enrolled as 9th graders in the 1993-94 school year, and follows them through the next four school years. Completers are any students who during those years:

- graduated, either on time or early; or
- received a GED; or
- were enrolled in school during the 1997-98 school year.

Dropout   A student is identified as a dropout if the individual is absent without an approved excuse or documented transfer and does not return to school by the fall of the following year, or if he or she completes the school year but fails to enroll the following school year.

Dropout Rate   The dropout rate is the number of dropouts summed across all grades, 7 through 12, divided by the number of students summed across all grades, 7 through 12. It is calculated as follows:

$$\frac{\text{number of students who dropped out during the school year}}{\text{number of students who were in membership at any time during the school year}}$$

Economically Disadvantaged   The percentage of economically disadvantaged students is calculated as the sum of students eligible for free or reduced-price lunch or eligible for other public assistance, divided by the total number of students.

Ethnic Distribution   Students are reported as White, African American, Hispanic, Asian/Pacific Islander, and Native American.

Graduates (Class of 1997)   This is the total number of graduates (including summer graduates) for the 1996-97 school year reported in the Fall of 1997. It includes 12th graders who graduated as well as graduates from other grades. Special education graduates are included in the totals and reported as a separate group. Counts of graduates receiving advanced seals are also shown.

Limited English Proficient (LEP)   These are counts of students identified as limited English proficient by the Language Proficiency Assessment Committee (LPAC), or a designated professional. Pupils identified as LEP do not necessarily receive bilingual or English as a second language instruction, though most do.

Mobility   A student is considered to be mobile if he or she has been in attendance at the school for less than 83% of the school year (i.e., has missed six or more weeks at a particular school).

Paired Schools   Schools that reported enrollment but did not have grades in which the TAAS test is given (e.g., 9th grade centers, K-2 schools, etc.) are paired with schools with which they have a "feeder" relationship to determine accountability ratings.

Recommended High School Program   This indicator reports the percentage of graduates who satisfied the course requirements for the Texas State Board of Education Recommended High School Program. Distinguished Achievement Program graduates are also included.

Retention Rates by Grade   The retention rate, which is reported in the profile section, shows the percentage of students in the Texas public school system who enrolled the following year in the same grade as their grade in the last

reported six-weeks period of the prior year. Special education rates are calculated separately.

School Type   For purposes of demographic grouping, schools are divided into four classifications based on lowest and highest grades at the school: Elementary, Middle, Secondary, and both Elementary/Secondary (K-12).

Special Education   This refers to the population served through programs for students with disabilities. Performance of special education students on assessments such as TAAS, End-of-Course exams, and on the TAAS/TASP equivalency is reported separately and not included in the calculation of campus or district values. For all other indicators where special education information is available, values for these students are included in the calculation of campus and district values.

TAAS (Texas Assessment of Academic Skills)   This criterion-referenced test measures student achievement in reading and mathematics in grades 3 through 8 and 10; writing in grades 4, 8, and 10; and science and social studies in grade 8. Spanish versions of the test are administered in grades 3-6. Passing rates are calculated and reported in two ways:

By Grade—As in previous AEIS reports, TAAS passing rates are shown by grade for each subject area and for all tests taken. Two years of information are available—for tests administered in the spring of 1997 and the spring of 1998.

Summed Across All Grades—The accountability system uses TAAS pass rates summed across all grades tested at a school. For example, the passing rate for reading in an elementary school with a grade span of K-5 is calculated as follows:

$$\frac{\text{number of students who passed the reading test in grades 3, 4, \& 5}}{\text{number of students who took the reading test in grades 3, 4, \& 5}}$$

Note that not all test takers are included in the values shown on the AEIS reports.

- Only test takers who were enrolled in the district as of the last Friday in the previous October are included. This is referred to as the "October subset" or the "accountability subset."
- For exit-level, only 10th graders tested are included in the count. This includes 10th graders who are repeating the grade and may have previously taken the exit-level TAAS.
- Students coded as Special Education, and students taking the Spanish TAAS are also

not included in this year's accountability subset.

TAAS End-of-Course Exams   Students completing a Biology I or Algebra I course must take an End-of-Course exam. The AEIS shows the percent of students who took the test in either December or May of the 1997-98 school year.

TAAS Exit-level Cumulative Pass Rate   The TAAS cumulative pass rate for the class of 1998 shows the percent of students who first took the exit-level test in spring 1996, and eventually passed all tests taken (in the same district) by May 1998. This measure is intended to show the relative success of districts in their efforts to help all their students pass the exit-level TAAS, which is a requirement for graduation from Texas public schools.

TAAS Participation Report   Every student enrolled in grades 3 through 8 and 10 must be given the opportunity to take the TAAS tests. Although the intention is to test every student in these grades, there are circumstances under which some students are not tested. Also, of the students tested, not all students' test scores are considered for accountability purposes. This report provides a breakdown of what was reported on each student: whether they took the test, were absent, were exempted, etc.

TAAS, Passing Standard   The standard for passing (or meeting minimum expectations) on the exit-level TAAS test is equivalent to correctly answering 70% of the items based on the October 1990 exit-level test. In the spring of 1994, the passing standards in reading and mathematics at grades 3-8 were aligned with the exit-level standard in order to measure student achievement across time. Students in grades 3-8 and 10 achieving a Texas Learning Index (TLI) score of 70 or higher meet minimum expectations in reading and mathematics. On the writing test, students must achieve a scale score of 1500 or higher to meet minimum expectations. The passing standard for the Spanish TAAS in reading and mathematics at grades three and four is a score of 1500 or higher.

TAAS/TASP Equivalency   This indicator shows the percent of graduates from the classes of 1996 and 1997 who did well enough on the exit-level TAAS to have a 75% likelihood of passing the Texas Academic Skills Program (TASP) test. To be counted for this indicator a student must have a TLI of X-81 on the reading test, and a TLI of X-77 on the mathematics test. On the writing test, a scale score of 1540 or higher is required.

TASP   The Texas Academic Skills Program is a basic skills test measuring reading, writing, and mathematics skills. It is required of persons entering Texas public institutions of higher education for the first time, unless they are exempted based on their levels of performance on the Exit-level TAAS, SAT or ACT college entrance tests.

POINTS TO CONSIDER WHEN USING THE AEIS REPORT

The 1997-98 AEIS report will not give you a complete picture of student learning or school performance. The information in AEIS does provide a factual foundation for a discussion about the performance of your district or campus. Keep the following thoughts in mind when reviewing the AEIS report for your school district or campus.

1. **Much of the information in the AEIS report is self-reported** by schools, i.e., salaries and dropouts, and has not been verified independently at the time of reporting.
2. **Tests have limitations as measurement tools.** Standardized assessments, like the TAAS, should be understood as good indications of student academic achievement rather than precise and complete measures.
3. **Do not rely on a single indicator,** such as test scores, to draw absolute conclusions about student learning or school performance. A review of student test scores should be the beginning of the discussion about school performance. There are other important factors to be considered, such as the numbers of students completing rigorous courses in the core subject areas.
4. Student **participation rates may affect performance data** considerably. Look at the new section of the AEIS report that shows the extent to which various student groups participated in the TAAS at your school. Question data when participation rates are low.
5. Student learning and school performance should be analyzed in **the context of each school's unique environment.** The environmental factors of a school and its students affect learning to a great extent. Consider the information in the Profile Section of the AEIS report when looking at your school.

6. The new **Comparable Improvement section should be used extensively.** It shows how schools perform in terms of year-to-year student gains, and includes other useful information, such as the percentage of students scoring a TLI of 84 or better in reading and math.

7. **Use both objective and subjective information** when making judgments about student learning and school performance. The opinions of parents, school staff and students can be very helpful in understanding the strengths and weakness of schools.

8. **Beware of explanations or solutions that seem too simple.** There is no easy cure or *magic bullet* that will dramatically improve school performance. A correlation is not the same thing as a cause. Be skeptical when anyone states that something directly and predictably caused some result to occur.

9. **Remember to look at school performance over time.** The best measure of success is found in continuous progress and improvement. Look at year-to-year changes and long-term trends.

It is not enough for a district or campus to do better than the neighboring district or other schools with similar characteristics. Such comparisons often lead to a false sense of satisfaction. It is also not enough for parents to know that their child is doing well when other students are not showing good results. It is in everyone's interest that all students perform to their potential. Texas schools will not have fulfilled their mission until all students learn what is necessary for them to compete favorably in the world community of the 21st century.

QUESTIONS AND ANSWERS

1. **Why should I be interested in the AEIS report?**
   AEIS is the best single source of information about the performance of Texas public schools. It will help you to answer the tough question: How well does my public school perform?

2. **What is the purpose of the AEIS report?**
   The AEIS report is an important part of the Texas school accountability system. State policy makers,

district and campus educators, the media, and the general public to evaluate the performance of public schools use the information.

3. **What is contained in the AEIS?**
   The district and campus reports have two sections. The <u>Performance Section</u> includes student performance information such as test scores, attendance, dropout rates, and more. The <u>Profile Section</u> contains student demographics, staff, and financial information.

4. **What does AEIS mean to parents?**

   * *AEIS compares their campus to the district and to 40 other similar campuses across the state. Schools must seek to match the performance of the best schools, rather than only aim to match or beat the average.*
   * *It allows parents to evaluate the performance of different groups of students within their local school. Schools are expected to close performance gaps between student groups.*
   * *It compares school performance for the last school year to the previous one. Everyone should expect year-to-year improvement.*

5. **Is more information available about school performance in Texas public schools?**
   More information on the AEIS and other information about your school is available at the district administration office and on most campuses.

   All 1998 AEIS reports are available on the Performance Reporting Section of the Texas Education Agency's web site. The address is: **http//www.tea. state. tx.us/ perfreport.**

   If you are interested in a historical perspective of your campus's or district's performance, this site includes AEIS reports beginning with the 1993-94 school year. The site also includes a list of the accountability ratings of all campuses in any district for the past several school years.

   The TEA's site also offers links to many other excellent sources of information about Texas public schools and significant national education groups.

   Several companies and/or education vendors have developed powerful information management software that will help educators analyze the performance and efficiency of their schools. Call TBEC at 512/480-8232 for more information.

Charter Schools

American public education is primed for reinvention. The lack of confidence in the nation's public schools has reached such a nadir that only 22% of respondents in the most recent Phi Delta Kappa/Gallup Poll give a grade of "A" or "B" to the public schools as a whole. One-fifth of those surveyed say that they have very little or no confidence in the public schools. Perhaps the most significant finding, however, is that almost three-fourths of respondents believe that improvement should come through reforming the existing system rather than through seeking an alternative system (Rose, Gallup, and Elam, 1997).

One promising response to reform of the existing system is the publicly-controlled charter school. Judging by the intense interest of the media and policymakers, charter schools are being recognized as having the potential to simultaneously provide "dramatically different schools . . . and incentives for districts to follow with changes in their own schools" (Kolderie, 1994, p. 36).

What role will these charter schools play in the reinvention of public education? This chapter will review the brief history of charter laws, examine the implementation of charter schools in four states, and delineate issues and concerns. The purpose is to suggest educational practices within charter schools

which are pertinent to the successful reinvention of America's public schools.

CHARTER SCHOOL HISTORY, LAWS, AND COMPONENTS

The literature defines charter schools as one of the variations of school choice options in which autonomous public schools operate under a contract, free from most local and state education regulations and direct control but are held accountable for achieving outcomes in student performance or other specified areas. The resulting leadership philosophy results in a more child-centered curriculum in which the innovative talents of teachers are fully mobilized (Biller, 1995; Hanushek, 1995). While charter schools are profoundly different from compulsory attendance schools, they typically include (a) an instructional plan, (b) specific educational results and how they will be measured, (c) a management or governance plan, and (d) a financial plan (Hill, 1996).

Charter contracts are granted for a specified period of time, usually three to five years. Although there are procedures for revoking a charter if there are material violations of the contract, the charter generally remains in effect if student academic performance is satisfactory (McGree, 1995). Furthermore, the significance of the school's accountability lies in its charter contract, not under regulations established by the state. Based on free-market concepts reflecting local parental desires for their children's education, schools that do not provide

Reprinted with permission from "The Role of Charter Schools in the Reinvention of Public Education," by Diane Patrick. *Teacher Education and Practice*, Fall/Winter 1997.

programs that satisfy parents and children will lose students and the accompanying funding (Cookson and Weiher, 1996). Unlike conventional public schools, charter schools must be customer-oriented in order to remain in the business of education.

Kolderie (cited in Bierlein and Mulholland, 1994) identifies common characteristics of a model charter school as the reasons for the likelihood of its success. These elements are as follows:

1. At least one other public authority besides the local school board is able to sponsor the school (for example, a state board or university).
2. The state allows a variety of public or private individuals/groups the opportunity to organize, seek sponsorship, and operate a charter school.
3. The charter school is a discrete legal entity.
4. The charter school, as a public entity, embraces the ideals of the common school. It is nonsectarian in programs and operation, tuition-free, nonselective in admissions, nondiscriminatory in practices, and accountable to a public body.
5. Each charter school is accountable for its performance, both to parents and to its sponsoring authority.
6. In return for stricter accountability, states exempt charter schools from all state and local laws and regulations except those related to health, safety, and nondiscrimination practices, and those agreed to within the charter provisions.
7. A charter school is a school of choice for students, parents, and teachers; no one is forced to be there.
8. Each charter school receives the full operating funds associated with its student enrollment (that is, fiscal autonomy).
9. Within a charter school, teachers may be employees or owners and/or subcontractors. If previously employed in a district, they retain certain "leave" protections (seniority, retirement benefits, and so on) should they choose to return within a designated time frame. (p. 35)

The significance of these nine components is that they all center around the two essential qualities of a charter school: autonomy and choice. Each is an important aspect if the school is going to have the independence necessary to be educationally innovative so that parents and students will have meaningful choices (Cookson and Weiher, 1996).

Although the charter school movement is a relatively new educational choice in the United States that has developed over the past six years, Great Britain's charter schools were authorized as grant-maintained schools under the Parliament's Education Reform Act of 1988. All British schools are funded from the national government Department of Education, while U.S. charter schools are funded primarily from state and local funds. In both countries, however, charter schools are free schools paid for out of public funds and share the same vision of improving education by becoming self-governing. Evidence suggests that British grant-maintained schools are well regarded by parents, and the number has increased dramatically since the beginning of the program. In comparing the newer grant-maintained schools with the traditional district-controlled schools, one can make the argument not so much that they are different, but that the British schools are "institutions at different points on the same management continuum" (Wohlstetter and Anderson, 1994, p. 488).

Based on the notion of Henry Hudson's charter with the East India Company to find a new passage to the orient, school district organization expert Ray Budde is credited with introducing the idea of charter schools in the United States in the late 1980s. The concept was bolstered when American Federation of Teachers president Albert Shanker proposed that teachers be allow to charter their own schools (Bierlein and Mulholland, 1994). More recently, Budde has proposed chartering all schools to replace the centralized bureaucracy with a "services-oriented unit" (1996). In other words, school site-based management is redefined as a more meaningful form of school organization.

The first United States charter school law was passed in 1991 in Minnesota and was followed by California charter legislation in 1992, with six more states joining the list the next year: Colorado, Massachusetts, Michigan, Wisconsin, New Mexico, and Georgia. In 1994, Arizona, Kansas, and Hawaii passed charter laws, and Wyoming, Texas, Arkansas, Alaska, Delaware, New Hampshire, Rhode Island, and Louisiana authorized charters in 1995. Subsequent legislation has brought the 1997 total to 28 states plus Washington, D.C. (Manno, Finn, Bierlein, and Vanourek, 1997). This rapid growth may be attributed to the appeal of charter features such as: guaranteed results, public school entity, more educational options, true decentralization, and market-driven (Bierlein and Mulholland, 1994).

No two state charter laws are alike. Laws vary in components such as sponsors of charters being either local boards or state boards of education, but the majority of states require local board approval. Charters are granted to teachers, parents, universities, community members, business leaders, and other interested groups (Medler 1996; McGree, 1995). A charter may be self-contained in its own facilities, part of an existing school, or it may be an entire school.

Stronger state statutes are those considered closer to a true charter concept with greater potential impact on all public schools. Using criteria of (a) who grants the charter, (b) who can organize the charter, (c) degree of fiscal and legal autonomy, (d) maximum number of charters, and (e) personnel qualifications to measure relative strength, states with stronger charter law components are Arizona, Michigan, Delaware, and New Hampshire, while those on the weaker end of the continuum include Rhode Island, Georgia, Kansas, and Arkansas. Stronger statutes are considered closer to a true charter concept that challenges the status quo system with greater potential impact on all public schools (Bierlein and Mulholland, 1994; Bierlein, 1995). The result has been the proliferation of charter schools in those states with strong charter school laws, with few or no charters being created in states with weak laws.

A LOOK AT CHARTER SCHOOLS IN FOUR STATES: CALIFORNIA, COLORADO, MINNESOTA, TEXAS

Most of the charter sites could be described as either a variation of progressive education or traditional or both; however, many of them are distinct and innovative. Smaller than most traditional schools, charter schools are organized in a variety of grade configurations from the entire span of kindergarten-grade 12 to various combinations such as elementary and middle school or middle and high school. The leadership of charter schools includes teachers, principals, chief executive officers, directors, non-profit or for-profit groups; however, the principal-assistant principal model is not typical. Furthermore, deregulation has resulted in a broad approach to school decision-making about issues such as staffing, where educators may include professionals who are not graduates of conventional educator preparations entities (Manno et al., 1997). Examples from the following four states highlight the variety of possibilities within the concept of charter schools.

California

California's charter law is considered to be relatively strong primarily because applicants are released from most local and state regulations, including the ability to hire noncertified staff. Although the 1992

law caps the number of charter schools at 100, the California State Board of Education has used its waiver authority to exceed the cap. There are three main types of charter schools in California: conversion of conventional public schools, new start-up schools, and independent study programs, with school size ranging from 20 to over 1,000 students (Finn, Bierlein, and Manno, 1996).

One of the most unique charters operates in Kingsburg, California, where the entire K-8 district has become a charter district, freeing the 1,800 pupil district from rigid state requirements and policies intended for larger districts. Oakland Charter Academy is a middle school created by parents with the help of the Pacific Research Institute specifically to provide a safe school environment (Manno et al., 1997).

Diamond's (1994) report on the charter schools in California concludes that the success of the charter school movement "will require a covenant among all segments of the educational community—unions, boards, teachers, and administrators—to do the business of education in a new way, focused on the needs of children, not on the needs of old bureaucracies" (p. 45).

Colorado

Although Colorado was in its fourth year in 1996–97, relatively few charters existed (approximately 30) due to key difficulties embedded within the law. Barriers seem to center around the requirement that only the local board may be the charter sponsor, and although appeals may be made to the state board, that body does not have the authority to grant charters. The resulting governance tension appears to have restrained charter school development.

Sweeney (1994) has listed the following organizational lessons learned from experiences in establishing the Community Involved Charter School in Colorado (CICS): (a) envision the school with all participants, (b) define new roles for students, teachers, and parents, (c) decide on the administrative structure, (d) decide on specifics for size, growth, and curriculum, and (e) gain power in numbers by seeking collaborative partnerships. Additional findings from evaluations of two of the first charter schools in Colorado included the fact that the 200-pupil back-to-basics Jefferson Academy had a waiting list of 350 elementary students for the next fall after the first three months of its existence. Under the leadership of the principal's authoritarian management style, teacher morale is high, even though they are on year-to-year contracts, and their salaries are lower than in the surrounding district.

Established for kindergarten through grade 12, CICS has a completely different atmosphere, but it is equally well received. Built around personalized learning plans for each student, CICS has a more diversified student body, and at over 400 students, has more than twice the students of Jefferson Academy. The basics are covered, but there is a range of nontraditional offerings, as well.

Both of these Colorado charters appear to be well established and meeting the intent of the charter school law: providing an innovative educational approach which meets the needs of the school community (Raywid, 1995).

Minnesota

Currently 20 charters operate in Minnesota, where charter school legislation is part of a menu of innovative public school choice initiatives that have been widely replicated across the nation. The state's charter law is considered to be medium-strong, but subsequent revisions to the original 1991 legislation have increased the cap to 40, allowed appeals to the state board, and provided for more than one entity to sponsor charters. One of the major stumbling blocks which remains is the reduced funding formula (Manno et al., 1997).

An unusual personnel arrangement can be found in LeSeur, where the teacher-dominated governing board of the Minnesota New Country School has contracted with EdVisions Cooperative for all educational and management services, giving teachers dual roles as employers and employees. Cited as a model for charter accountability, Minnesota holds the significant distinction of revoking a charter when the Dakota Open Charter School for American Indian students near Redwood Falls was closed due to lack of student achievement (Manno et al., 1997).

Interesting partnerships abound in Minnesota, including the St. Paul Parks and Recreation Department, the Minneapolis Urban League, the Minnesota Business Partnership, the Minnesota Teamsters Service Bureau, as well as universities, parents, teachers and community citizens (Manno et al., 1997). These charter schools show promise for systemic school reform, such as the rural Minnesota district which found that the locally granted charter spurred improvements throughout the district, an example being the use of instructional technology (Thomas, 1996).

Texas

Charter laws passed in 1995 in Texas expand charter options beyond what has been seen in most other states. There are three types of charters available: home rule district charters, campus/program charters, and open-enrollment charter schools. The most innovative among these is the home-rule charter, which allows an entire district to reorganize as a charter. However, this type of charter is viewed as difficult to obtain because of the requirement for a voter turnout of 25 percent, which is more than twice the typical local election turnout. At this point none of the over 1,000 school districts in Texas indicate their intent to follow this course of action.

Campus-based charters may be granted by the local school board upon receipt of a petition signed by over half of the teachers and parents of children attending that school. This exempts campuses from most non-management state laws except those pertaining to high school graduation, prekindergarten, bilingual, and special education programs, no pass-no play, and student testing and campus accountability. The number allowed is unlimited, but few campus-based programs have been created under this provision. Statutory revisions in 1997 required local school boards to have procedural policies for establishing local campus charters by January of 1998.

The third type of charter available in Texas is the open-enrollment charter. Originally limited to 20 chartered by the State Board of Education, all of the available charters were awarded in the spring of 1996. Recent 1997 legislation allows up to 100 more, with no cap if 75 percent of the population served is at-risk. Exempt from the same state laws as campus charters, they may be operated in school district or non-school district facilities by public or private higher education institutions, non-profit organizations, or governmental entities. Open-enrollment charter schools are eligible to receive the same amount of state and local funding that would be spent from the student's resident district (Cookson and Weiher, 1996).

The majority of the open-enrollment charter schools in Texas focus on at-risk students. Formerly a privately run non-profit operation, Dallas Can! Academy Charter is a drop-out recovery program which has seen a growth in enrollment from 300 to 500 students during its first year of operation. A similar conversion, the American Institute of Learning Charter has combined academic foundation with project-based education for career preparation using a certificate of mastery model.

ISSUES AND CONCERNS

There are a number of unresolved issues surrounding charter schools. One overriding concern for charters in all states is that the schools must comply with state accounting and accountability systems, which typically require sophisticated knowledge and equipment; therefore, the degree of autonomy is still somewhat limited. The philosophy of leaving the process to innovative educators is critical to the success of the charters, but some state and local educational agencies are reluctant to share authority. For example, in California evidence shows that districts were the least supportive of those charter schools wishing to be the most independent (Dianda and Corwin, 1994). Such issues can affect the ability of charter schools and districts to work together for the education of their students.

Some barriers to charter schools center around negative attitudes coming from the traditional educational establishment. For example, a recent survey indicated that local school board presidents are lukewarm about granting more charters, with 43 percent in favor and 43 percent opposed, and 14 percent with no opinion. Sixty-seven percent of school board members believe that grants for charters should be given to public schools only (DeSpain and Livingston, 1996). School administrators in California have not been viewed as supportive of charter schools (Schneider and Dianda, 1995). However, studies show that some boards are collaborating with charter schools as institutions of action research and beginning to recognize the value of having local charter schools (Finn et al., 1996).

Wohlstetter and Anderson (1994) report some disturbing findings that some British schools obtain grant-maintained status to preserve existing situations. Early evidence from Minnesota suggested a similar pattern since several rural schools scheduled for closing were among those applying for charters.

Among other issues are financial concerns since state per-pupil funds that would have gone to the local district follow the students to the charter school; however, in most states the funding is negotiated between the school and the sponsoring district. States where the funds flow directly to the charter schools experience far greater autonomy (McGree, 1995).

McGree also points out that, like traditional schools, funding is allocated based on enrollment; however, unlike other public schools, charter schools have no taxing authority or ability to sell bonds. Sustainability has been identified as a problem due to the intense efforts required in setting up a charter school. Charter schools find that the unusual timing of state funding formulas can create problems as well, such as Michigan's school funding not beginning until October and Arizona's payment cycle which skips months.

There can be further financial strain in states such as Texas where start-up and facility funds are not available; however, studies show that although almost all of the facilities would be described as minimal, and in some cases, actually dilapidated, this is not a deterrent to charter school participants (Finn et al., 1996). According to a survey of California charters, nearly half of the respondents stated that lack of start-up funding was a major obstacle, and at least one school failed to obtain the start-up funds needed and subsequently relinquished its charter (Diamond, 1994). In response to these challenges, the federal government now provides grant funds for charter schools targeting at-risk students, and some states are now beginning to include start-up grants much like the British system.

Another concern is voiced by teachers who feel that their efforts are being undermined; however, evidence in Massachusetts indicates that teacher applications for some charter schools have outnumbered positions by 100 to one (National Association of the State Boards of Education, 1995). Likewise, Finn et al. (1996) found that outstanding teachers are attracted to charter schools, and most do not want to be affiliated with teachers' unions. They conclude that the teachers are willing to make trade-offs for personal and professional fulfillment.

Legal problems have plagued charters in some states. Colorado had lawsuits dealing with the equity issue, but they were ultimately dismissed by a federal district judge citing the state's legitimate interest in educational innovation. Michigan issues centered around the promotion of religion through a charter requested by a home school network called Noah Webster Academy. From a Constitutional perspective, the applicable test for evaluating whether state action has violated the Establishment Clause is that established by *Lemon v. Kurtzman,* (1971). Known as the "Lemon test," three conditions must be met to avoid excessive entanglement: a secular purpose, neither advance nor inhibit religion, and must not foster excessive entanglement between government and religion (Kemerer and Walsh, 1994). Because of the practical limitations on monitoring, attorney Martin Semple (1995) predicts similar conflicts whenever religious groups or home schools are involved in the charter process.

Although equity for all students, especially those who are disadvantaged, is promoted as one of the advantages, the reality continues to be a concern, as evidence comes in from states such as Colorado, where only a few of the state's charter schools serve at-risk populations. Travers (1996) cites studies from Europe where data shows that middle and higher income students took advantage more often of educational choice. Further, Tovey (1995) points to studies which reveal a disturbing trend: choosing families tend to choose on the basis of similarity in culture, location, and ethnic mix;

therefore, uncontrolled choice programs could exacerbate racial and socioeconomic segregation.

Contrary to this concern, data indicates that charter schools enroll almost one-third again as many minority students, who make up 40 percent of the charter school enrollments in six states, higher than the 31 percent in the regular public schools. However, Kemerer (1996) points out that this finding may be somewhat skewed since about half of the charter schools operating in 1995 targeted "at risk" students, a population which tends to have an over-representation of minorities.

Issues of transportation have created problems in some states. In Minnesota, the district is required to provide transportation to students who live within the district, while parents must assume the responsibility if the student resides outside the district. This has impacted charter schools which must adapt to the district's bus schedule, as well as district concerns about the additional time and costs associated with bussing students from all over the district.

Special education is particularly challenging for the charter schools, which are often unprepared for the demands of the identification processes and accompanying services. However, students with special needs are choosing charter schools. One such example is the Metro Deaf School in Minnesota, where American Sign Language is the main language. Lange and Ysseldyke (1994) caution against regression to segregated special education settings with negative student outcomes. Other studies suggest that the entire issue of special education individualized education plans (IEPs), while a federal law, may be a moot point since this personalized approach is typical in charter schools (Finn et al., 1996).

Evaluation is critical if the overall effectiveness of charters is to be determined. However, oftentimes, there is no funding for this effort although the process is required by law, such as in Texas. Hlebowitsh (1995) raises the question, "To what extent will charter schools contribute to the revitalization of the essential core purposes and functions of public education" (p. 9)? Currently, there are no guidelines to determine if in fact this occurs. Furthermore, there are no consistent reporting requirements. Additional findings suggest other problems due to a "double standard" evaluation system where more is expected from charter schools than of traditional schools (Finn et al., 1996).

IMPLICATIONS FOR THE FUTURE OF PUBLIC EDUCATION

Research findings are beginning to emerge from the charter sites, but it is still too early to determine the outcome of charter schools on students, teachers, parents, and the public education system in general. The limited number of studies have focused on such issues as the degree of parental satisfaction and demographics; however, further review of charter schools is needed, particularly in the areas of governance, accountability, and equity. Questions must be answered such as whether external constraints have stifled previous school restructuring efforts. Perhaps the greatest potential for reinvention of public education through charters lies in the various individual school reform ideas which are more likely to be effective because the efforts are integrated (Bierlein and Mulholland, 1994).

Alexander (1993) makes the argument that the promise for charter schools is unlimited and predicts that by the year 2000 school choice will be commonplace because middle- and low-income parents will have demanded it. Given the public's high level of concern about the quality of American schools, accompanied by the strong belief of many to reform education within the existing public school system, customer-oriented charter schools offer one of the most viable options to address these opinions. Among the various school choice options, charter schools are clearly destined to play a major role in reinventing public education for the twenty-first century.

REFERENCES

Alexander, L. (1993, June). School choice in the year 2000. *Phi Delta Kappan, 74,* 762–766.

Bierlein, L. (1995, September). Charter schools: a new approach to public education. *NASSP Bulletin, 79,* 12–20.

Bierlein, L. & Mulholland, L. A. (1994, September). The promise of charter schools. *Educational Leadership, 52,* 34–35, 37–40.

Biller, L. W. (1995, September). School choice: an educational myth or a panacea? *NASSP Bulletin, 79,* 33–40.

Budde, R. (1996). *Strengthen school-based management by chartering all schools.* Andover, MA: The Regional Laboratory for Educational Improvement of the Northeast and Islands.

Cookson, C. & Weiher, G. R. (1996, May). Charter schools in Texas. *Houston Economics.* Houston, TX: University of Houston, Center for Public Policy.

DeSpain, B. C. & Livingston, M. (1996, July). Roads to reform. *The American School Board Journal, 183,* 17–20.

Diamond, L. (1994, September). A progress report on California's charter schools. *Educational Leadership, 52,* 41–45.

Dianda, M. R. & Corwin, R. G. (1994, September). Start-up experiences: a survey. *Educational Leadership, 52,* 42–43.

Finn, C. E., Bierlein, L. A., & Manno, B. V. (1996). Charter schools in action: a first look. *Charter schools in action project.* Washington, DC: Hudson Institute.

Hanushek, E. A. (1995, November). Moving beyond spending fetishes. *Educational Leadership, 53,* 60–64.

Hlebowitsh, P. (1995, September). Can we find the traditional American school in the idea of choice? *NASSP Bulletin, 79,* 1–11.

Hill, P. (1996, June). The educational consequences of choice. *Phi Delta Kappan, 77,* 671–675.

Kemerer, F. R. (1996, July). *What do we know about school choice?* Paper presented at the NSBA/Southern Region Conference, San Antonio, TX.

Kemerer, F. R., & Walsh, J. (1994). *The educator's guide to Texas school law.* Austin, TX: University of Texas Press.

Kolderie, T. (1994, September). Charters: an invitation to change. *Educational Leadership, 52,* 36.

Lange, C. & Ysseldyke, J. E. (1994, November). How school choice affects students with special needs. *Educational Leadership, 52,* 84–85.

Lemon v. Kurtzman, 403 U.S. 602 (1971).

Manno, B. V., Finn, C. E., Bierlein, L. A., & Vanourek, G. (1997, July). How charter schools are different. *Charter schools in action project.* Washington, DC: Hudson Institute.

McGree, K. (1995, July). Charter schools: early learnings. *Insights.* Southwest Educational Development Laboratory: Austin, TX.

Medler, A. (1996, March). Promise and progress. *The American School Board Journal, 183,* 26–28.

National Association of the State Boards of Education [NASBE]. (1995, December). Charter schools. *Policy Update, 3.* Alexandria, VA: Policy Information Clearinghouse.

Raywid, M. A. (1995, March). The struggles and joys of trailblazing. *Phi Delta Kappan, 76,* 555–560.

Rose, L. C., Gallup, A. M., & Elam, S. M. (1997, September). The 29th annual Phi Delta Kappa/Gallup poll of the public's attitudes toward the public schools. *Phi Delta Kappan, 79,* 41–56.

Schneider, J. & Dianda M. (1995, August). Coping with charters. *The School Administrator, 52,* 20–23.

Semple, M. (1995, August). Legal issues in charter schooling. *The School Administrator, 52,* 24–26.

Sweeney, M. E. (1994, September). How to plan a charter school. *Educational Leadership, 52,* 46–47.

Thomas, D. (1996, July). The choice to charter. *The American School Board Journal, 183,* 20–22.

Tovey, R. (1995, September). School choice and racial/class inequities. *The Education Digest, 61,* 14–18.

Travers, P. (1996, Spring). Academic privatization and choice in public education, K-12. *Education, 116,* 471–475.

Wohlstetter, P. & Anderson L. (1994, February). What can U.S. charter schools learn from England's grant-maintained schools? *Phi Delta Kappan, 75,* 486–491.

CHAPTER 8

Discipline Management

This chapter summarizes the statutory provisions for discipline management and alternative programs included in the Texas Education Code. Beyond these statutory provisions, the policies and procedures for discipline management are determined, for the most part, by local boards of education. Campus committees may decide to add requirements unique to that environment and each teacher may formulate classroom protocol, consistent with all of the above, that communicates his or her expectations within the classroom context. An example of a district code of conduct is appended.

SUBCHAPTER A. ALTERNATIVE SETTINGS FOR BEHAVIOR MANAGEMENT

§ 37.001. Student Code of Conduct

(a) The board of trustees of an independent school district shall, with the advice of its district-level committee established under Section 11.251, adopt a student code of conduct for the district. The student code of conduct must be posted and prominently displayed at each school campus. In addition to establishing standards for student conduct, the student code of conduct must:

Reprinted with permission from the Texas Education Code, 1998.

(1) specify the circumstances, in accordance with this subchapter, under which a student may be removed from a classroom, campus, or alternative education program;

(2) specify conditions that authorize or require a principal or other appropriate administrator to transfer a student to an alternative education program; and

(3) outline conditions under which a student may be suspended as provided by Section 37.005 or expelled as provided by Section 37.007.

(b) A teacher with knowledge that a student has violated the student code of conduct shall file with the school principal or the other appropriate administrator a written report, not to exceed one page, documenting the violation. The principal or the other appropriate administrator shall, not later than 24 hours after receipt of a report from a teacher, send a copy of the report to the student's parents or guardians.

(c) Once the student code of conduct is promulgated, any change or amendment must be approved by the board of trustees.

§ 37.002. Removal by Teacher

(a) A teacher may send a student to the principal's office to maintain effective discipline in the classroom. The principal shall respond by employing appropriate discipline management techniques consistent with the student code of conduct adopted under Section 37.001.

(b) A teacher may remove from class a student:

   (1) who has been documented by the teacher to repeatedly interfere with the teacher's ability to communicate effectively with the students in the class or with the ability of the student's classmates to learn; or

   (2) whose behavior the teacher determines is so unruly, disruptive, or abusive that it seriously interferes with the teacher's ability to communicate effectively with the students in the class or with the ability of the student's classmates to learn.

(c) If a teacher removes a student from class under Subsection (b), the principal may place the student into another appropriate classroom, into in-school suspension, or into an alternative education program as provided by Section 37.008. The principal may not return the student to that teacher's class without the teacher's consent unless the committee established under Section 37.003 determines that such placement is the best or only alternative available. The terms of the removal may prohibit the student from attending or participating in school-sponsored or school-related activity.

(d) A teacher shall remove from class and send to the principal for placement in an alternative education program or for expulsion, as appropriate, a student who engages in conduct described under Section 37.006 or 37.007. The student may not be returned to that teacher's class without the teacher's consent unless the committee established under Section 37.003 determines that such placement is the best or only alternative available.

§ 37.003. Placement Review Committee

(a) Each school shall establish a three-member committee to determine placement of a student when a teacher refuses the return of a student to the teacher's class and make recommendations to the district regarding readmission of expelled students. Members shall be appointed as follows:

   (1) the campus faculty shall choose two teachers to serve as members and one teacher to serve as an alternate member; and

   (2) the principal shall choose one member from the professional staff of a campus.

(b) The teacher refusing to readmit the student may not serve on the committee.

§ 37.004. Placement of Students With Disabilities

The placement of a student with a disability who receives special education services may be made only by a duly constituted admission, re-

view, and dismissal committee. A student with a disability who receives special education services may not be placed in alternative education programs solely for educational purposes if the student does not also meet the criteria for alternative placement in Section 37.006(a) or 37.007(a).

§ 37.005. Suspension

(a) The principal or other appropriate administrator may suspend a student who engages in conduct for which the student may be placed in an alternative education program under this subchapter.

(b) A suspension under this section may not exceed three school days.

§ 37.006. Removal for Certain Conduct

(a) Except as provided by Section 37.007(a)(3) or (b), a student shall be removed from class and placed in an alternative education program as provided by Section 37.008 if the student commits the following on or within 300 feet of school property, as measured from any point on the school's real property boundary line, or while attending a school-sponsored or school-related activity on or off of school property:

   (1) engages in conduct punishable as a felony;

   (2) engages in conduct that contains the elements of the offense of assault under Section 22.01(a)(1), Penal Code, or terroristic threat under Section 22.07, Penal Code;

   (3) sells, gives, or delivers to another person or possesses or uses or is under the influence of:

      (A) marijuana or a controlled substance, as defined by Chapter 481, Health and Safety Code, or by 21 U.S.C. Section 801 et seq.; or

      (B) a dangerous drug, as defined by Chapter 483, Health and Safety Code;

   (4) sells, gives, or delivers to another person an alcoholic beverage, as defined by Section 1.04, Alcoholic Beverage Code, commits a serious act or offense while under the influence of alcohol, or possesses, uses, or is under the influence of an alcoholic beverage;

   (5) engages in conduct that contains the elements of an offense relating to abusable glue or aerosol paint under Sections 485.031 through 485.035, Health and Safety Code, or relating to volatile chemicals under Chapter 484, Health and Safety Code; or

(6) engages in conduct that contains the elements of the offense of public lewdness under Section 21.07, Penal Code, or indecent exposure under Section 21.08, Penal Code.

(b) Except as provided by Section 37.007(d), a student shall be removed from class and placed in an alternative education program under Section 37.008 if the student engages in conduct that contains the elements of the offense of retaliation under Section 36.06, Penal Code, against any school employee.

(c) In addition to Subsection (a), a student shall be removed from class and placed in an alternative education program under Section 37.008 based on conduct occurring off campus and while the student is not in attendance at a school-sponsored or school-related activity if:

    (1) the student receives deferred prosecution under Section 53.03, Family Code, for conduct defined as a felony offense in Title 5, Penal Code;

    (2) a court or jury finds that the student has engaged in delinquent conduct under Section 54.03, Family Code, for conduct defined as a felony offense in Title 5, Penal Code; or

    (3) the superintendent or the superintendent's designee has a reasonable belief that the student has engaged in a conduct defined as a felony offense in Title 5, Penal Code.

(d) In addition to Subsection (a), a student may be removed from class and placed in an alternative education program under Section 37.008 based on conduct occurring off campus and while the student is not in attendance at a school-sponsored or school-related activity if:

    (1) the superintendent or the superintendent's designee has a reasonable belief that the student has engaged in conduct defined as a felony offense other than those defined in Title 5, Penal Code; and

    (2) the continued presence of the student in the regular classroom threatens the safety of other students or teachers or will be detrimental to the educational process.

(e) In determining whether there is a reasonable belief that a student has engaged in conduct defined as a felony offense by the Penal Code, the superintendent or the superintendent's designee may consider all available information, including the information furnished under Article 15.27, Code of Criminal Procedure.

(f) Subject to Section 37.007(e), a student who is younger than 10 years of age shall be removed from class and placed in an alternative education program under Section 37.008 if the student engages in conduct described by Section 37.007.

(g) The terms of a placement under this section must prohibit the student from attending or participating in a school-sponsored or school-related activity.

(h) On receipt of notice under Article 15.27(g), Code of Criminal Procedure, the superintendent or the superintendent's designee shall review the student's placement in the alternative education program. The student may not be returned to the regular classroom pending the review. The superintendent or the superintendent's designee shall schedule a review of the student's placement with the student's parent or guardian not later than the third class day after the superintendent or superintendent's designee receives notice from the office or official designated by the court. After reviewing the notice and receiving information from the student's parent or guardian, the superintendent or the superintendent's designee may continue the student's placement in the alternative education program if there is reason to believe that the presence of the student in the regular classroom threatens the safety of other students or teachers.

(i) The student or the student's parent or guardian may appeal the superintendent's decision under Subsection (h) to the board of trustees. The student may not be returned to the regular classroom pending the appeal. The board shall, at the next scheduled meeting, review the notice provided under Article 15.27(g), Code of Criminal Procedure, and receive information from the student, the student's parent or guardian, and the superintendent or superintendent's designee and confirm or reverse the decision under Subsection (h). The board shall make a record of the proceedings. If the board confirms the decision of the superintendent or superintendent's designee, the board shall inform the student and the student's parent or guardian of the right to appeal to the commissioner under Subsection (j).

(j) Notwithstanding Section 7.057(e), the decision of the board of trustees under Subsection (i) may be appealed to the commissioner as provided by Sections 7.057(b), (c), (d), and (f). The student may not be returned to the regular classroom pending the appeal.

(k) Subsections (h), (i), and (j) do not apply to placements made in accordance with Subsection (a).

§ 37.007. Expulsion for Serious Offenses

(a) A student shall be expelled from a school if the student, on school property or while attending a school-sponsored or school-related activity on or off of school property:

  (1) uses, exhibits, or possesses:

    (A) a firearm as defined by Section 46.01(3), Penal Code;

    (B) an illegal knife as defined by Section 46.01(6), Penal Code, or by local policy;

    (C) a club as defined by Section 46.01(1), Penal Code; or

    (D) a weapon listed as a prohibited weapon under Section 46.05, Penal Code;

  (2) engages in conduct that contains the elements of the offense of:

    (A) aggravated assault under Section 22.02, Penal Code, sexual assault under Section 22.011, Penal Code, or aggravated sexual assault under Section 22.021, Penal Code;

    (B) arson under Section 28.02, Penal Code;

    (C) murder under Section 19.02, Penal Code, capital murder under Section 19.03, Penal Code, or criminal attempt, under Section 15.01, Penal Code, to commit murder or capital murder;

    (D) indecency with a child under Section 21.11, Penal Code; or

    (E) aggravated kidnapping under Section 20.04, Penal Code; or

  (3) engages in conduct specified by Section 37.006(a)(3) or (4), if the conduct is punishable as a felony.

(b) A student may be expelled if the student, while on school property or while attending a school-sponsored or school-related activity on or off of school property:

  (1) sells, gives, or delivers to another person or possesses, uses, or is under the influence of any amount of:

    (A) marijuana or a controlled substance, as defined by Chapter 481, Health and Safety Code, or by 21 U.S.C. Section 801 et seq.;

    (B) a dangerous drug, as defined by Chapter 483, Health and Safety Code; or

    (C) an alcoholic beverage, as defined by Section 1.04, Alcoholic Beverage Code; or

  (2) engages in conduct that contains the elements of an offense relating to abusable glue or aerosol paint under Sections 485.031 through 485.035, Health and Safety Code, or relating to volatile chemicals under Chapter 484, Health and Safety Code.

(c) A student may be expelled if the student, while placed in an alternative education program for disciplinary reasons, continues to engage in serious or persistent misbehavior that violates the district's student code of conduct.

(d) A student shall be expelled if the student engages in conduct that contains the elements of any offense listed in Subsection (a) against any employee in retaliation for or as a result of the employee's employment with a school district.

(e) In accordance with federal law, a local educational agency, including a school district, home-rule school district, or open-enrollment charter school, shall expel a student who brings a firearm, as defined by 18 U.S.C. Section 921, to school. The student must be expelled from the student's regular campus for a period of at least one year, except that:

  (1) the superintendent or other chief administrative officer of the school district or of the other local educational agency, as defined by 20 U.S.C. Section 2891,[1] may modify the length of the expulsion in the case of an individual student;

  (2) the district or other local educational agency shall provide educational services to an expelled student in an alternative education program as provided by Section 37.008 if the student is younger than 10 years of age on the date of expulsion; and

  (3) the district or other local educational agency may provide educational services to an expelled student who is older than 10 years of age in an alternative education program as provided in Section 37.008.

(f) A student who engages in conduct that contains the elements of the offense of criminal mischief under Section 28.03, Penal Code, may be expelled at the district's discretion if the conduct is punishable as a felony under that section. The student shall be referred to the authorized officer of the juvenile court regardless of whether the student is expelled.

(g) A school district shall inform each teacher of the conduct of a student who has engaged in any violation listed in this section. A teacher shall keep the information received in this subsection confidential. The State Board of Educator Certification may revoke or suspend the certification of a teacher who intentionally violates this subsection.

(h) Subject to Subsection (e), notwithstanding any other provision of this section, a student who is younger than 10 years of age may not be expelled for engaging in conduct described by this section.

Added by Acts 1995, 74th Leg., ch. 260, § 1, eff. May 30, 1995. Amended by Acts 1997, 75th Leg., ch. 1015, § 5, eff. June 19, 1997.

§ 37.008. Alternative Education Programs

(a) Each school district shall provide an alternative education program that:

(1) is provided in a setting other than a student's regular classroom;

(2) is located on or off of a regular school campus;

(3) provides for the students who are assigned to the alternative education program to be separated from students who are not assigned to the program;

(4) focuses on English language arts, mathematics, science, history, and self-discipline;

(5) provides for students' educational and behavioral needs; and

(6) provides supervision and counseling.

(b) An alternative education program may provide for a student's transfer to:

(1) a different campus;

(2) a school-community guidance center; or

(3) a community-based alternative school.

(c) An off-campus alternative education program is not subject to a requirement imposed by this title, other than a limitation on liability, a reporting requirement, or a requirement imposed by this chapter or by Chapter 39.

(d) A school district may provide an alternative education program jointly with one or more other districts.

(e) Each school district shall cooperate with government agencies and community organizations that provide services in the district to students placed in an alternative education program.

(f) A student removed to an alternative education program is counted in computing the average daily attendance of students in the district for the student's time in actual attendance in the program.

(g) A school district shall allocate to an alternative education program the same expenditure per student attending the alternative education program, including federal, state, and local funds, that would be allocated to the student's school if the student were attending the student's regularly assigned education program, including a special education program.

(h) A school district may not place a student, other than a student suspended as provided under Section 37.005 or expelled as provided under Section 37.007, in an unsupervised setting as a result of conduct for which a student may be placed in an alternative education program.

(i) On request of a school district, a regional education service center may provide to the district information on developing an alternative education program that takes into consideration the district's size, wealth, and existing facilities in determining the program best suited to the district.

(j) If a student placed in an alternative education program enrolls in another school district before the expiration of the period of placement, the board of trustees of the district requiring the placement shall provide to the district in which the student enrolls, at the same time other records of the student are provided, a copy of the placement order. The district in which the student enrolls may continue the alternative education program placement under the terms of the order or may allow the student to attend regular classes without completing the period of placement.

(k) A program of educational and support services may be provided to a student and the student's parents when the offense involves drugs or alcohol as specified under Section 37.006 or 37.007.

(l) A school district is not required to provide in the district's alternative education program a course necessary to fulfill a student's high school graduation requirements other than a course specified by Subsection (a).

(m) The commissioner shall adopt rules necessary to administer the provisions of Chapter 39 for alternative education programs. Academically, the

1. Section 20 of Acts 1997, 75th Leg., ch. 1015 provides: "This Act takes effect beginning with the 1997–1998 school year."

mission of alternative education programs shall be to enable students to perform at grade level. Annually, the commissioner shall define for alternative education programs acceptable performance and performance indicating a need for peer review, based principally on standards defined by the commissioner that measure academic progress of students toward grade level while attending an alternative education program.

Added by Acts 1995, 74th Leg., ch. 260, § 1, eff. May 30, 1995. Amended by Acts 1997, 75th Leg., ch. 1015, § 6, eff. June 19, 1997.

§ 37.009. Conference; Hearing; Review

(a) Not later than the third class day after the day on which a student is removed from class by the teacher under Section 37.002(b) or (d) or by the school principal or other appropriate administrator under Section 37.006, the principal or other appropriate administrator shall schedule a conference among the principal or other appropriate administrator, a parent or guardian of the student, the teacher removing the student from class, if any, and the student. At the conference, the student is entitled to written or oral notice of the reasons for the removal, an explanation of the basis for the removal, and an opportunity to respond to the reasons for the removal. The student may not be returned to the regular classroom pending the conference. Following the conference, and whether or not each requested person is in attendance after valid attempts to require the person's attendance, the principal shall order the placement of the student as provided by Section 37.002 or 37.006, as applicable, for a period consistent with the student code of conduct.

(b) If a student's placement in an alternative education program is to extend beyond the end of the next grading period, a student's parent or guardian is entitled to notice of and an opportunity to participate in a proceeding before the board of trustees of the school district or the board's designee, as provided by policy of the board of trustees of the district. Any decision of the board or the board's designee under this subsection is final and may not be appealed.

(c) Before it may place a student in an alternative education program for a period that extends beyond the end of the school year, the board or the board's designee must determine that:

(1) the student's presence in the regular classroom program or at the student's regular campus presents a danger of physical harm to the student or to another individual; or

(2) the student has engaged in serious or persistent misbehavior that violates the district's student code of conduct.

(d) The board or the board's designee shall set a term for a student's placement in an alternative education program under Section 37.002 or 37.006.

(e) A student placed in an alternative education program under Section 37.002 or 37.006 shall be provided a review of the student's status, including a review of the student's academic status, by the board's designee at intervals not to exceed 120 days. In the case of a high school student, the board's designee, with the student's parent or guardian, shall review the student's progress towards meeting high school graduation requirements and shall establish a specific graduation plan for the student. The district is not required under this subsection to provide in the district's alternative education program a course not specified under Section 37.008(a). At the review, the student or the student's parent or guardian must be given the opportunity to present arguments for the student's return to the regular classroom or campus. The student may not be returned to the classroom of the teacher who removed the student without that teacher's consent. The teacher may not be coerced to consent.

(f) Before a student may be expelled under Section 37.007, the board or the board's designee must provide the student a hearing at which the student is afforded appropriate due process as required by the federal constitution and which the student's parent or guardian is invited, in writing, to attend. At the hearing, the student is entitled to be represented by the student's parent or guardian or another adult who can provide guidance to the student and who is not an employee of the school district. If the school district makes a good-faith effort to inform the student and the student's parent or guardian of the time and place of the hearing, the district may hold the hearing regardless of whether the student, the student's parent or guardian, or another adult representing the student attends. If the decision to expel a student is made by the board's designee, the decision may be appealed to the board. The decision of the board may be appealed by trial de novo to a district court of the county in which the school district's central administrative office is located.

(g) The board or the board's designee shall deliver to the student and the student's parent or guardian a copy of the order placing the student in an alternative education program under Section 37.002 or 37.006 or expelling the student under Section 37.007.

(h) After a school district notifies the parents or guardians of a student that the student has been expelled, the parent or guardian shall provide adequate supervision of the student during the period of expulsion.

Added by Acts 1995, 74th Leg., ch. 260, § 1, eff. May 30, 1995. Amended by Acts 1997, 75th Leg., ch. 1015, § 7, eff. June 19, 1997.

§ 37.010. Court Involvement

(a) Not later than the second business day after the date a hearing is held under Section 37.009, the board of trustees of a school district or the board's designee shall deliver a copy of the order placing a student in an alternative education program under Section 37.006 or expelling a student under Section 37.007 and any information required under Section 52.04, Family Code, to the authorized officer of the juvenile court in the county in which the student resides. In a county that operates a program under Section 37.011, an expelled student shall to the extent provided by law or by the memorandum of understanding immediately attend the educational program from the date of expulsion; provided, however, that in a county with a population greater than 125,000 every expelled student who is not detained or receiving treatment under an order of the juvenile court must be enrolled in an educational program.

(b) If a student is expelled under Section 37.007(c), the board or its designee shall refer the student to the authorized officer of the juvenile court for appropriate proceedings under Title 3, Family Code.[2]

(c) Unless the juvenile board for the county in which the district's central administrative office is located has entered into a memorandum of understanding with the district's board of trustees concerning the juvenile probation department's role in supervising and providing other support services for students in alternative education programs, a court may not order a student expelled under Section 37.007 to attend a regular classroom, a regular campus, or a school district alternative education program as a condition of probation.

(d) Unless the juvenile board for the county in which the district's central administrative office is located has entered into a memorandum of understanding as described by Subsection (c), if a court orders a student to attend an alternative education program as a condition of probation once during a school year and the student is referred to juvenile court again during that school

year, the juvenile court may not order the student to attend an alternative education program in a district without the district's consent until the student has successfully completed any sentencing requirements the court imposes.

(e) Any placement in an alternative education program by a court under this section must prohibit the student from attending or participating in school-sponsored or school-related activities.

(f) If a student is expelled under Section 37.007, on the recommendation of the committee established under Section 37.003 or on its own initiative, a district may readmit the student while the student is completing any court disposition requirements the court imposes. After the student has successfully completed any court disposition requirements the court imposes, including conditions of a deferred prosecution ordered by the court, or such conditions required by the prosecutor or probation department, if the student meets the requirements for admission into the public schools established by this title, a district may not refuse to admit the student, but the district may place the student in the alternative education program. Notwithstanding Section 37.002(d), the student may not be returned to the classroom of the teacher under whose supervision the offense occurred without that teacher's consent. The teacher may not be coerced to consent.

(g) If an expelled student enrolls in another school district, the board of trustees of the district that expelled the student shall provide to the district in which the student enrolls, at the same time other records of the student are provided, a copy of the expulsion order and the referral to the authorized officer of the juvenile court. The district in which the student enrolls may continue the expulsion under the terms of the order, may place the student in an alternative education program for the period specified by the expulsion order, or may allow the student to attend regular classes without completing the period of expulsion.

(h) A person is not liable in civil damages for a referral to juvenile court as required by this section.

Added by Acts 1995, 74th Leg., ch. 260, § 1, eff. May 30, 1995. Amended by Acts 1997, 75th Leg., ch. 1015, § 8, eff. June 19, 1997.

§ 37.019. Emergency Placement or Expulsion

(a) This subchapter does not prevent the principal or the principal's designee from ordering the

2. V.T.C.A., Family Code § 51.01 et seq.

immediate placement of a student in the alternative program if the principal or the principal's designee reasonably believes the student's behavior is so unruly, disruptive, or abusive that it seriously interferes with a teacher's ability to communicate effectively with the students in a class, with the ability of the student's classmates to learn, or with the operation of school or a school-sponsored activity.

(b) This subchapter does not prevent the principal or the principal's designee from ordering the immediate expulsion of a student if the principal or the principal's designee reasonably believes that action is necessary to protect persons or property from imminent harm.

(c) At the time of an emergency placement or expulsion, the student shall be given oral notice of the reason for the action. Within a reasonable time after the emergency placement or expulsion, the student shall be accorded the appropriate due process as required under Section 37.009. If the student subject to the emergency placement or expulsion is a student with disabilities who receives special education services, the term of the student's emergency placement or expulsion is subject to the requirements of 20 U.S.C. Section 1415(e)(3) and 34 CFR 300.513.

(d) A principal or principal's designee is not liable in civil damages for an emergency placement under this section.

§ 37.020. Reports Relating to Expulsions and Alternative Education Program Placements

In the manner required by the commissioner, each school district shall annually report to the commissioner:

(1) for each placement in an alternative education program established under Section 37.008:

(A) information identifying the student, including the student's race, sex, and date of birth, that will enable the agency to compare placement data with information collected through other reports;

(B) information indicating whether the placement was based on:

(i) conduct violating the student code of conduct adopted under Section 37.001;

(ii) conduct for which a student may be removed from class under Section 37.002(b);

(iii) conduct for which placement in an alternative education program is required by Section 37.006; or

(iv) conduct occurring while a student was enrolled in another district and for which placement in an alternative education program is permitted by Section 37.008(j); and

(C) the number of days the student was assigned to the program and the number of days the student attended the program; and

(2) for each expulsion under Section 37.007:

(A) information identifying the student, including the student's race, sex, and date of birth, that will enable the agency to compare placement data with information collected through other reports;

(B) information indicating whether the expulsion was based on:

(i) conduct for which expulsion is required under Section 37.007, including information specifically indicating whether a student was expelled on the basis of Section 37.007(e);

(ii) conduct, other than conduct described by Subparagraph (iii), for which expulsion is permitted under Section 37.007; or

(iii) serious or persistent misbehavior occurring while the student was placed in an alternative education program;

(C) the number of days the student was expelled; and

(D) information indicating whether:

(i) the student was placed in a juvenile justice alternative education program under Section 37.011;

(ii) the student was placed in an alternative education program; or

(iii) the student was not placed in a juvenile justice or other alternative education program.

§ 37.082. Possession of Paging Devices

(a) The board of trustees of a school district may adopt a policy prohibiting a student from possessing a paging device while on school property or while attending a school-sponsored or school-related activity on or off school property. The policy may establish disciplinary measures to be imposed for violation of the prohibition and may provide for confiscation of the paging device.

(b) The policy may provide for the district to:

(1) dispose of a confiscated paging device in any reasonable manner after having provided the student's parent and the company whose name and address or telephone number appear on the device 30 days' prior notice of its intent to dispose of that device. The notice shall include the serial number of the device and may be made by telephone, telegraph, or in writing; and

(2) charge the owner of the device or the student's parent an administrative fee not to exceed $15 before it releases the device.

(c) In this section, "paging device" means a telecommunications device that emits an audible signal, vibrates, displays a message, or otherwise summons or delivers a communication to the possessor.

§ 37.083. Discipline Management Programs; Sexual Harassment Policies

(a) Each school district shall adopt and implement a discipline management program to be included in the district improvement plan under Section 11.252.

(b) Each school district may develop and implement a sexual harassment policy to be included in the district improvement plan under Section 11.252.

SUBCHAPTER D. PROTECTION OF BUILDINGS AND GROUNDS

§ 37.101. Applicability of Criminal Laws

The criminal laws of the state apply in the areas under the control and jurisdiction of the board of trustees of any school district in this state.

§ 37.102. Rules; Penalty

(a) The board of trustees of a school district may adopt rules for the safety and welfare of students, employees, and property and other rules it considers necessary to carry out this subchapter and the governance of the district, including rules providing for the operation and parking of vehicles on school property. The board may adopt and charge a reasonable fee for parking and for providing traffic control.

(b) A law or ordinance regulating traffic on a public highway or street applies to the operation of a vehicle on school property, except as modified by this subchapter.

(c) A person who violates this subchapter or any rule adopted under this subchapter commits an offense. An offense under this section is a Class C misdemeanor.

§ 37.103. Enforcement of Rules

Notwithstanding any other provision of this subchapter, the board of trustees of a school district may authorize any officer commissioned by the board to enforce rules adopted by the board. This subchapter is not intended to restrict the authority of each district to adopt and enforce appropriate rules for the orderly conduct of the district in carrying out its purposes and objectives on the right of separate jurisdiction relating to the conduct of its student and personnel.

[Sections 37.108 to 37.120 reserved for expansion]

SUBCHAPTER E. PENAL PROVISIONS

§ 37.121. Fraternities, Sororities, Secret Societies, and Gangs

(a) A person commits an offense if the person:

(1) is a member of, pledges to become a member of, joins, or solicits another person to join or pledge to become a member of a public school fraternity, sorority, secret society, or gang; or

(2) is not enrolled in a public school and solicits another person to attend a meeting of a public school fraternity, sorority, secret society, or gang or a meeting at which membership in one of those groups is encouraged.

(b) A school district board of trustees or an educator shall recommend placing in an alternative education program any student under the person's control who violates Subsection (a).

(c) An offense under this section is a Class C misdemeanor.

(d) In this section, "public school fraternity, sorority, secret society, or gang" means an organization composed wholly or in part of students of public primary or secondary schools that seeks to perpetuate itself by taking in additional members from the students enrolled in school on the basis of the decision of its membership rather than on the free choice of a student in the school who is qualified by the rules of the school to fill the special aims of

Added by Acts 1995, 74th Leg., ch. 260, § 1, ef. May 30, 1995.

For transition provisions relating to offenses, see note following V.T.C.A., Education Code § 37.102.

the organization. The term does not include an agency for public welfare, including Boy Scouts, Hi-Y, Girl Reserves, DeMolay, Rainbow Girls, Pan-American Clubs, scholarship societies, or other similar educational organizations sponsored by state or national education authorities.

Added by Acts 1995, 74th Leg., ch. 260, § 1, eff. May 30, 1995.

§ 37.122. Possession of Intoxicants on Public School Grounds

(a) A person commits an offense if the person possesses an intoxicating beverage for consumption, sale, or distribution while:

(1) on the grounds or in a building of a public school; or

(2) entering or inside any enclosure, field, or stadium where an athletic event sponsored or participated in by a public school of this state is being held.

(b) An officer of this state who sees a person violating this section shall immediately seize the intoxicating beverage and, within a reasonable time, deliver it to the county or district attorney to be held as evidence until the trial of the accused possessor.

(c) An offense under this section is a Class C misdemeanor.

Added by Acts 1995, 74th Leg., ch. 260, § 1, eff. May 30, 1995.

§ 37.123. Disruptive Activities

(a) A person commits an offense if the person, alone or in concert with others, intentionally engages in disruptive activity on the campus or property of any private or public school.

(b) For purposes of this section, disruptive activity is:

(1) obstructing or restraining the passage of persons in an exit, entrance, or hallway of a building without the authorization of the administration of the school;

(2) seizing control of a building or portion of a building to interfere with an administrative, educational, research, or other authorized activity;

(3) preventing or attempting to prevent by force or violence or the threat of force or violence a lawful assembly authorized by the school administration so that a person attempting to participate in the assembly is unable to participate due to the use of force

or violence or due to a reasonable fear that force or violence is likely to occur;

(4) disrupting by force or violence or the threat of force or violence a lawful assembly in progress; or

(5) obstructing or restraining the passage of a person at an exit or entrance to the campus or property or preventing or attempting to prevent by force or violence or by threats of force or violence the ingress or egress of a person to or from the property or campus without the authorization of the administration of the school.

(c) An offense under this section is a Class B misdemeanor.

(d) Any person who is convicted the third time of violating this section is ineligible to attend any institution of higher education receiving funds from this state before the second anniversary of the third conviction.

(e) This section may not be construed to infringe on any right of free speech or expression guaranteed by the constitution of the United States or of this state.

Added by Acts 1995, 74th Leg., ch. 260, § 1, eff. May 30, 1995.

§ 37.124. Disruption of Classes

(a) A person commits an offense if the person, on school property or on public property within 500 feet of school property, alone or in concert with others, intentionally disrupts the conduct of classes or other school activities.

(b) An offense under this section is a Class C misdemeanor.

(c) In this section:

(1) "Disrupting the conduct of classes or other school activities" includes:

(A) emitting noise of an intensity that prevents or hinders classroom instruction;

(B) enticing or attempting to entice a student away from a class or other school activity that the student is required to attend;

(C) preventing or attempting to prevent a student from attending a class or other school activity that the student is required to attend; and

(D) entering a classroom without the consent of either the principal or the teacher and, through either acts of misconduct or the use of loud or profane language, disrupting class activities.

(2) "Public property" includes a street, highway, alley, public park, or sidewalk.

(3) "School property" includes a public school campus or school grounds on which a public school is located and any grounds or buildings used by a school for an assembly or other school-sponsored activity.

Added by Acts 1995, 74th Leg., ch. 260, § 1, eff. May 30, 1995.

§ 37.125. Exhibition of Firearms

(a) A person commits an offense if the person, by exhibiting, using, or threatening to exhibit or use a firearm, interferes with the normal use of a building or portion of a campus or of a school bus being used to transport children to or from school-sponsored activities of a private or public school.

(b) An offense under this section is a third degree felony.

§ 37.126. Disruption of Transportation

(a) Except as provided by Section 37.125, a person commits an offense if the person intentionally disrupts, prevents, or interferes with the lawful transportation of children to or from school or an activity sponsored by a school on a vehicle owned or operated by a county or independent school district.

(b) An offense under this section is a Class C misdemeanor.

SUBCHAPTER F. HAZING

§ 37.151. Definitions

In this subchapter:

(1) "Educational institution" includes a public or private high school.

(2) "Pledge" means any person who has been accepted by, is considering an offer of membership from, or is in the process of qualifying for membership in an organization.

(3) "Pledging" means any action or activity related to becoming a member of an organization.

(4) "Student" means any person who:

(A) is registered in or in attendance at an educational institution;

(B) has been accepted for admission at the educational institution where the hazing incident occurs; or

(C) intends to attend an educational institution during any of its regular sessions after a period of scheduled vacation.

(5) "Organization" means a fraternity, sorority, association, corporation, order, society, corps, club, or service, social, or similar group, whose members are primarily students.

(6) "Hazing" means any intentional, knowing, or reckless act, occurring on or off the campus of an educational institution, by one person alone or acting with others, directed against a student, that endangers the mental or physical health or safety of a student for the purpose of pledging, being initiated into, affiliating with, holding office in, or maintaining membership in an organization. The term includes:

(A) any type of physical brutality, such as whipping, beating, striking, branding, electronic shocking, placing of a harmful substance on the body, or similar activity;

(B) any type of physical activity, such as sleep deprivation, exposure to the elements, confinement in a small space, calisthenics, or other activity that subjects the student to an unreasonable risk of harm or that adversely affects the mental or physical health or safety of the student;

(C) any activity involving consumption of a food, liquid, alcoholic beverage, liquor, drug, or other substance that subjects the student to an unreasonable risk of harm or that adversely affects the mental or physical health or safety of the student;

(D) any activity that intimidates or threatens the student with ostracism, that subjects the student to extreme mental stress, shame, or humiliation, that adversely affects the mental health or dignity of the student or discourages the student from entering or remaining registered in an educational institution, or that may reasonably be expected to cause a student to leave the organization or the institution rather than submit to acts described in this subdivision; and

(E) any activity that induces, causes, or requires the student to perform a duty or task that involves a violation of the Penal Code.

For transition provisions relating to offenses, see note following V.T.C.A., Education Code § 37.102.

ARLINGTON ISD STUDENT CODE OF CONDUCT

Group I Misbehaviors:

Discipline infraction may include, but are not limited to:

- Actions or misbehaviors interrupting student's right to learn
- Failure to abide by published district, campus or classroom rules and procedures
- Failure to have supplies and/or assignments
- Misconduct: May include, but not limited to: chewing gum, eating candy or food, not being on task, bothering other students, inappropriate or loud talking, cutting in line, throwing paper wads, note writing, sleeping, minor defacing of school property.
- Running or making excessive noise
- Tardiness
- Violation of rules and/or procedures established by teacher

Group I Disciplinary Consequences

- Special Education Student—Refer to Behavior Intervention Plan in Individual Educational Plan (IEP) and Special Education Discipline Handbook
- 504, if applicable review Behavior Intervention Plan
- Denial of classroom privileges
- Detention hall
- In-class discipline: May include, but not limited to: lower citizenship grades, teacher detention, additional assignments
- In-school suspension (limited to three days as a disciplinary management technique)
- Misbehavior warning (verbal or written)
- Other appropriate consequences or activities directed by the teacher, approved *before use*, by the Principal or Assistant Principal
- Parent contact, by written message or by phone

Group II Misbehaviors: Discipline Infractions

Discipline infractions may include, but are not limited to:

- Altering records or forging signature
- Campus possession and/or distribution of magazines, books, or printed material not appropriate for school
- Excessive, repetitive problems from Group I (generally defined to mean 3 or more occurrences of the same misbehavior)
- Exhibiting unacceptable physical contact not resulting in injury (i.e., pushing)
- Failing to abide by school rules at extracurricular or co-curricular activities
- Failure to abide by published campus rules and procedures
- Horseplay
- Improper dress as defined by Student Code of Conduct Dress Code
- Inappropriate public display of affection
- Leaving class/campus without school permission which includes before school and during school hours
- Loitering, littering, trespassing, or abusing residential property on the way to and/or from school
- Misconduct on the bus
- Participating in dishonest, deceitful activities
- Possession of articles inappropriate for school including, but not limited to: radios, matches, lighters, tobacco, or items considered as distractions to the classroom environment, etc.
- Possession of cellular phones or pagers on campus during normal school hours
- Possession of electronic toys at school or on school campus during school hours
- Posting or distributing unauthorized communicative materials at school
- Refusing to allow directions and instructions given by school personnel
- Riding in-line skates, skate boards, roller skates, bicycles, etc., on campus during the school day
- Throwing objects, causing or participating in disturbances in the classroom, cafeteria, hallways, restrooms, or campus
- Violation of Attendance Policy—unexcused absences and tardies

Group II Disciplinary Consequences

- Special Education Student—Refer to Behavior Intervention Plan in Individual Educational Plan (IEP) and Special Education Disciplinary Handbook
- 504, if applicable review the Behavior Intervention Plan
- A zero may be given for dishonest or deceitful actions on class assignments
- Confiscation of inappropriate articles
- Denial of Privileges: Classroom privileges—by teacher; Other privileges—by administrator
- Detention Hall
- Disciplinary reassignment by a principal
- In-school suspension
- Restitution/Restoration

- Saturday School
- Short-term removal from the classroom (less than 1 day) to the principal's office
- Any other disciplinary action deemed appropriate by the principal or assistant principal

Group III Misbehaviors: Disruptive Activities

Disruptive activities may include, but are not limited to:

- Excessive repetitive problems from Group II
- Failure to comply with reasonable request of school personnel
- Failure to comply with school policies
- Fighting
- Gambling
- Hazing
- Obscene gestures or actions
- Possession or distribution of published material that is pornographic or obscene or which threatens others or incites others to violence. (Pornographic is defined as explicit depiction or description of sexual acts.)
- Possession of knives *not* meeting the Penal Code definition of "illegal knife" (Penal Code 46.01)
- Profane language
- Racial, religious, ethnic, demeaning statements or acts
- Serious acts of disobedience or disorderly conduct
- Sexual harassment (that does not include any physical contact)
- Smoking or use of tobacco products in any form at any school-related or school-sponsored activity on or off school property
- Stealing
- Threats to students
- Defiance of authority of school personnel

Group III Disciplinary Consequences

- Special Education Student—Refer to Behavior Intervention Plan in Individual Educational Plan (IEP) and Special Education Discipline Handbook
- 504, if applicable review Behavior Intervention Plan
- Denial of extracurricular activities
- Detention Hall
- Emergency Removal from school
- In-school suspension
- Referral to law enforcement agencies
- Restitution/Restoration
- Saturday School
- Suspension (may be suspended for a period not to exceed 3 school days, and grade adjustment

will be made—suspension only for Alternative Education Program offenses)
- Assignment to CHOICES
- Any other disciplinary action deemed appropriate by the Principal or Assistant Principal and approved by the Executive Director of Student Services

Group IV Misbehaviors: Serious, Persistent Problems or Illegal Acts

Serious persistent problems or illegal acts may include, but are not limited to:

- Activities relating to unapproved organizations (gangs, fraternities, sororities or secret societies)
- Assault or Fighting
- Blocking any building entrance, exit, or passageway
- Excessive repetitive problems from Group III
- Extortion or blackmail
- Fireworks or explosive devices (some explosive devices are expellable offenses)
- Identification with gangs and gang activities (see additional information on page 31)
- Improper use of aerosols
- Look-alike weapons presented as authentic weapons such as stun guns, BB guns or other look-alike weapons. (Starter pistols are an expellable offense)
- Major group student disruption
- Possession, use or sale of controlled substance or look-alike controlled substances
- Possession or use of pepper spray
- Possession or use of weapons
- Rioting, group disobedience, or disturbance
- Sexual conduct
- Sexual harassment (including physical contact)
- Solicitation of immoral or illegal acts
- Stink bombs
- Tampering/setting off a fire alarm
- Theft, robbery, or burglary
- Threats to teacher/staff
- Vandalism (criminal mischief as defined by Penal Code 28.03)—Students may be subject to criminal penalties. If damage exceeds $1,500, it is an expellable offense.

Group IV Disciplinary Consequences

- Special Education Student—Refer to Behavior Intervention Plan in Individual Educational Plan (IEP) and Special Education Discipline Handbook

- Confiscation of inappropriate article
- In-School Suspension
- Referral to appropriate law enforcement agency or other agencies (such as Child Protective Services) for appropriate action
- Restitution/Restoration
- Suspension (for Alternative Education Program offenses only)
- Transfer to another school
- CHOICES
- Alternative school for certain offenses
- Any other disciplinary action deemed appropriate by the principal or assistant principal and approved in advance by the Executive Director of Student Services

Offenses Warranting Expulsion

A student will be EXPELLED if the student engages in the following activities:

Uses, exhibits, or possesses a firearm

Uses, exhibits, or possesses an illegal knife

Uses, exhibits, or possesses a club

Uses, exhibits, or possesses a weapon listed as a prohibited weapon

Engages in aggravated assault or aggravated sexual assault

Aggravated assault

Arson

Murder, capital murder

Indecency with a child

Aggravated kidnaping

Sells, gives or delivers to another person or possesses, uses, or is under the influence of marijuana or a controlled substance, a dangerous drug or an alcoholic beverage

Using abusable glue or aerosol paint or relating to volatile chemicals

Continues to engage in serious or persistent misbehavior that violates the district's Student Code of Conduct criminal mischief

A student will be placed in an ALTERNATIVE EDUCATION PROGRAM if the student engages in any conduct punishable as a felony, or commits the following on school property or while attending a school-sponsored activity on or off school property:

Engages in conduct punishable as a felony

Engages in conduct that contains the elements of the offense of an assault or terroristic threat

Sells, gives or delivers to another person or possesses or uses or is under the influence of marijuana, a controlled substance, or a dangerous drug

Sells, gives or delivers to another person an alcoholic beverage or commits a serious act or offense while under the influence of alcohol, or possesses, uses, or is under the influence

Engages in conduct that contains the elements of an offense relating to abusable glue or aerosol paint or volatile chemicals

Engages in conduct that contains the elements of the offense of public lewdness or indecent exposure

Engages in conduct that contains the elements of the offense of retaliation against any school employee

Persistent and serious misbehavior

Serious violations of the Student Code of Conduct which affect the orderly environment of the school

CHAPTER 9

Classroom Management

What makes teachers quit the profession? For over twenty years, lack of discipline has consistently been listed in the Phi Delta Kappa Gallup Poll of the Public's Attitudes Toward the Public Schools as one of the most pressing school problems. Further, teachers who leave do so most often because they are unable to manage their classrooms effectively. This chapter highlights factors that teachers need to consider as they develop their classroom management plans. These factors include: (a) teaching in a changing society, (b) forming a learning community, (c) preventing management problems, and (d) communicating with students and parents. Focusing on these factors will make your life as a teacher much more pleasant and your skills more effective.

TEACHING IN A CHANGING SOCIETY

Experienced teachers are keenly aware that social and economic conditions have changed in recent decades and continue to do so. Changing families (Seligman, 1989), including poverty stricken, single parent, and blended families (Armstrong, Henson, & Savage, 1997) are part of today's world. High incidence of drug and alcohol use (Johnson, 1986) also alters life in schools. Without understanding students' backgrounds, teachers often become frustrated when Charlie acts defiantly in class or Suzy

Prepared for inclusion in this text by Patricia Williams, Robert Alley, and Ken Henson, 1999.

forgets her math homework again. If teachers know, however, that Charlie is working two jobs to support his five-year-old sister or that Suzy has been kicked out of her house, they may not excuse the behavior, but they may approach the handling of the situation differently. Many students face problems today that are quite different from yesteryear, such as AIDS, fetal alcohol addiction, and cocaine abuse.

FORMING A LEARNING COMMUNITY

To cope with a changing social context, teachers and school administrators have developed the concept of school as a learning community (Williams, Alley, & Henson, 1999), a community wherein all members are partners in creating an understanding of the world around them. As early as 1916, Dewey explained the benefits of a learning community: "If, however, they (a collection of people) were all cognizant of a common end and all interested in it so that they regulated their specific activity in view of it, then they would form a community" (p. 5). Williams, Alley & Henson (1999) suggest six characteristics that all learning communities should possess (p. 10).

- Professional development must be an ongoing process as all teachers research the institutional goals that they agree are important.
- Students must be involved in generating knowledge.
- The climate must be relatively free of fear from the urgency to complete assignments by given deadlines.

117

- Teachers must make research a part of their self-images.
- School administrator support is necessary for a school to build a successful community.
- Community building must be a collaborative process where all members discuss the long-term goals.

These six elements collectively represent the notions of a unified team committed to the same group goals. As Keller (1995) points out, "When these elements are combined to form a community, its members strengthen their images of themselves and their colleagues and are more trusting, and a supportive environment is formed" (p. 12). Students, regardless of age, should be involved in developing common goals to which students, teachers, administrators, and parents can adhere.

Advocates assert that a successful learning community serves as a proactive means to diminish discipline problems. In our present schools "Learners sometimes feel 'lost' or anonymous in secondary schools, especially those with large student bodies" (Manning & Saddlemire, 1996, p. 43). As teachers we need to think of ways to make all students feel a part of the whole. How can students and teachers feel that their contributions are heard when the school enrollment is 3600? What can we, as teachers, do to make every voice heard? Eisner (1994) argues "the natural unit in education is the school. . . . The school stands out as an entity; it is something that secures allegiance and provides students with an identity" (pp. 376–377). A learning environment, if correctly planned, can serve as a proactive means of diminishing discipline problems in both the school and classroom.

Beginning teachers often find themselves isolated—at least they think they are. Others know what's occurring, and neophytes are afraid to ask. They need avenues to analyze their teaching and classroom management practices, reflect upon them, and discuss them with colleagues. Above all, they need clear goals that relate to the school's mission. These goals should be (a) a change from current conditions, (b) perceived as difficult but achievable, (c) clear and concrete, and (d) short-term yet connected to long-term directions of the learning community (Leithwood, Menzies, & Jantzi, 1994). What are your school's mission and goals? Can you restate them in your words? How do you fulfill these each day in your classroom? These are questions that reflective teachers ask and answer. Although teachers must devote time and attention to developing a learning community, they will reap dividends. The community brings a sense of common purpose and organizes the environment so that each member's time is spent engaged in attaining focused goals (Williams, Alley, & Henson, 1999).

PREVENTING MANAGEMENT PROBLEMS

Teachers prepare before the school year starts, as well as during the first week of school, to prevent classroom management problems. Experienced teachers know the importance of starting the year right and will spend time planning for a more effective school year. However, beginning teachers can also take appropriate steps in summer and at the outset of school to help prevent management problems. Schell and Burden (1992) compiled an extensive activity list that teachers might undertake over the sixty days prior to beginning the school year. Their concrete suggestions are an excellent source for all. Having your classroom and yourself organized to begin the school year includes the following.

Before School Starts

Visit your new school and carefully analyze the classrooms in which you'll be teaching. Ask your administrator whether you'll have your own classroom or whether you'll share it with another teacher. If you are sharing, negotiate with that person to have your own storage space along with a section of the bulletin boards and a portion of the chalkboards exclusively for your use. Then you can post assignments, announcements, and other materials for your class.

As you analyze your classroom, note the placement of the furnishings. Will you have the materials and equipment you need? An overhead projector? A computer? An LCD projector? Specialized equipment unique to your teaching field? Also, think about the room arrangement. Is there a central spot to place your materials such as handouts, overheads, and chalk? Are the student desks arranged to facilitate your teaching style? Do you prefer having your desks in rows or in clusters so that students can work cooperatively? Can you see all students from your central teaching spot? As illustrated in Williams, Alley, & Henson (1999), numerous student desk arrangements are possible. Each arrangement has its advantages, and conversely, its limitations. Furthermore, desk arrangements communicate messages about your expectations. Think for a moment. What message are you communicating if you have student desks arranged in a circle? In clusters of four with two facing two? In rows?

Many teachers, especially ones who are fairly close to their students in age, try to be buddies with students. This mistake is especially risky to beginning teachers because they haven't yet established their student expectations. It is best, especially for beginning teachers, to remain in the teacher role rather than trying to become a buddy. You can be a warm, caring, fair teacher and still have control in your classroom.

The First Day of School

You will have only one first day of school each year. If you've been planning as we suggested, you doubtless have many questions. How should I begin class? Will the students like me? Should I start off tough?

The first day, and even the first few minutes of each class period, will help set the tone for your school year (Williams, Alley, & Henson, 1999). Next semester you'll be glad you spent the extra hours preparing. In his research Brooks (1985) found that students come to school with key questions. Those questions might be expressed as follows.

1. Right Room—Am I in the right room? Is this my class? Are you the teacher?
2. The Teacher—Who is this person/teacher? Is this teacher a real human being or Mr. Grouch? Ms. Terminator?
3. The Self—Will this teacher care about me and my problems?
4. Seat Assignment—Where am I supposed to sit? Can I sit with my friends? Can I sit wherever I like?
5. Nature of the Course—What will we be doing in this class? Will it be interesting or boring?
6. Grading—How will this teacher evaluate my work? What kind of grades does this teacher give? Will this teacher be fair?
7. Rules—What rules does this teacher expect me to follow? What are the consequences if I don't?

Brooks further suggests that providing answers to these questions during the first few days should be the teacher's priority. One way to begin is to provide an autobiographical sketch of who you are. For instance, you might say, "Hi! I'm _____ , your ninth-grade history teacher. The bell has rung so please be seated. I'm excited about this year and want you to know about our class, the topics we will be discussing, the assignments, and the school requirements. Plus, not only do I want to meet each of you, but also I want you to know about me. Therefore, our first activity will be to get acquainted. You might be wondering who this person is you've just met.

Let me direct your attention to the 'Who Am I?' bulletin board" (Williams, Alley, & Henson, 1999, p. 76). Then, quickly note the items you've placed on the bulletin board.

Your successes, and maybe your failures (your ninth-grade report card with that D in science lab), your graduation picture, organizational certificates, family, pets, and your ninth-grade photos are but a few items that will interest students. Have you ever wondered what your college professors looked like when they were in high school? What grades did they make? Who is their family? Their friends? Before students really enjoy a class, they must feel a bond toward the teacher. This bulletin board often begins that link.

You can't tell students absolutely everything during the first class. Make yourself two lists, one that details points to address immediately and another for items the class should know later in the week, such as procedures for handing in and returning homework.

In your advance planning, you'll want to think about possible classroom rules and procedures, along with the best way to instruct your students. Will you want student input regarding rules (expectations) and consequences? Which classroom management models will you follow? Will you give each student a 3 × 5 index card to write suggested rules, or will you select the rules and explain them to the class? Answers to these questions will help you in formulating your management plan.

Often schools have shortened class periods for the first day, so you'll need to plan accordingly. Some teachers begin immediately with an activity; others prefer to start actual instruction on the second day because the class roll isn't firm and the time-frame is usually shortened. Which will you do? Two procedures we recommend establishing are entering the room and taking seats (defining "tardy"), and leaving class. Often, teachers require that students not leave their seats until given an appropriate signal.

COMMUNICATING WITH STUDENTS

Visualize a frowning teacher striding quickly and purposefully down a classroom aisle. What is the teacher communicating even though she has not uttered a sound? As you work with students, you'll realize the many ways to communicate. In the example, the teacher is showing displeasure with particular students. She doesn't have to tell them that she is upset with their actions; they can "read" her behavior and know that she is unhappy. She has mastered the "teacher look." Even though we have never been taught that look, all students, regardless of age, know its meaning.

The most common communication between teacher and students is teacher/student talk. Other examples include facial expressions, body movements, and the room arrangement, such as the teacher's desk location, bulletin board materials, colors to decorate, lighting, and plants or other unique touches.

Polite Language

Four types of talk, especially polite language, help establish positive teacher/student relationships. If you direct a student to do a task, such as turning off the lights for a movie, add polite forms of communication such as "please" and "thank you." These expressions are always appropriate, but nowhere more significant than in the classroom.

Supportive/Extending Language

Often a student response is partially correct, and the teacher wishes to elicit a more fully developed answer. To encourage risk-taking, the teacher must accept and value all responses, even incorrect ones, because the student attempted to answer. For example, suppose the history teacher asks students to define mercantilism and receives a partially correct response. The teacher should follow with words such as these: "Thank you, Ann. Yes, it is connected to trade." Then turn to the class and say, "Ann gave us a good start in defining the term. Who can add points to help us more fully define the concept?" The supportive/extending language serves to acknowledge Ann's contribution, and thereby encourages her to make future comments, and moves the discussion forward.

Inclusive Language

Using inclusive language aids students in feeling ownership. When a teacher states, "In my class, I expect you to ask permission to get out of your seat," the teacher has declared possession of the class. Student actions become her responsibility. A more appropriate response in describing class norms is "In this class, we. . . ." Such inclusive language suggests that the teacher sees students as partners rather than subordinates. The comment also implies that both students and the teacher have common responsibilities and that problems are shared. Teachers who use inclusive language such as "our class," "we," and "us" send a powerful message. Inclusive language, even when directed at one student, is implicitly a directive to all.

I-Messages

Another form of common discourse is a You-message (Gordon, 1974). Teachers often respond to student behavior in terms of, "You are. . ." (naming some inappropriate behavior that the teacher dislikes). These teacher messages are inevitably put-downs to students because they appear accusatory. Gordon describes them as criticizing, blaming, name-calling, and stereotyping, among others. He advocates that teachers use I-messages to take responsibility for their own discomfort or inner feelings. Such messages should be used when the student's action affects the teacher. For instance, the message "When I'm interrupted while giving directions, I have a difficult time making the directions clear, and it frustrates me," indicates specifically what has occurred and how the teacher reacted.

Good I-messages have three components (Gordon, 1974). First, they often begin with "when." It is important to let students know the situation being described. Second, I-messages pinpoint the effect of the students' actions in a non-judgmental way. The third part states the feelings generated within the teacher. In the example, the teacher says, "It frustrates me. . . ." According to Gordon, effective I-messages highlight the locus of the feelings—within the teacher. They have a high probability of promoting willingness to change, and they contain minimal negative judgment of the student's actions. Therefore, these messages do not injure the student/teacher relationship.

Use of Praise

Every teacher uses praise. Right? Well, yes, the vast majority do, but is it used appropriately? Carelessly dousing students with praise is ineffective, and most contemporary teachers do not praise very much (Postner & Rudnitsky, 1997). However, when used appropriately, it makes learning more pleasurable (Yelon, 1996). When teachers comment on specific attributes of students' work, the students will attribute the praise to a teacher who really cares. Rather than hearing "good job," students want to know exactly what is good.

Shane's studies revealed that the foremost student desire was for teachers who really care (as cited in Williams, Alley, & Henson, 1999). In addition, the Center for Research's study of the context of secondary schools found that students voice a recurring message: They want teachers to care about them (Phelan, Davidson, & Cao, 1992). What steps can you take to let students know you care?

COMMUNICATING WITH PARENTS

Probably the most neglected teacher support system is parents. Some teachers find communicating effectively with parents a fearful activity that is too demanding on their time. Successful teachers, however, use parent involvement to assist them and, more importantly, to help students whose learning they are trying to facilitate. Keys to successful communication with parents can be identified.

Check with your school administrators. You may find that district and/or school personnel have organized a system-wide plan for contacting and working with parents. Some administrators mandate a minimum number of contacts. If your school does not have a plan, you will want to devise one for your classes. This plan should be written early in the year. Some experts argue that the teacher should contact every parent no later than the end of the first week. As we argued in Williams, Alley, & Henson (1999), "The most important aspect of working to achieve parental involvement is communication. As a general rule, the better informed the parents are, the more often involvement will occur." And, "The earlier the contact with the parents, the better" (p. 108). Some teachers attempt to contact parents before school starts—either by phone, letter, or e-mail. It can be a simple message indicating who you are and that you are looking forward to working with their son or daughter. In that same initial contact, encourage the parents to contact you to voice their compliments and concerns. You may also want to ask if they have special talents that they might share. For example, would Joe's mother, an internal medicine specialist, be willing to speak to your health class about AIDS and HIV? If you contact the parents early, you are much more likely to have supportive parents who volunteer their time for special requests, such as speaking engagements and routine tasks like copying materials for class.

Unfortunately, not every parent contact will be positive. Darby (1979) identified seven types of parents you may encounter. These include non-hostile and cooperative, anxious or overwhelmed, self-absorbed, in denial, resistant, punitive, and hostile. He emphasized that most parents will be friendly and cooperative. They'll look for specific cues about the way you'd like them to relate to you and your class. Don't be afraid to tell them your expectations and invite them to participate in class activities. Negative parent types usually resist advice, and they can be punitive to their own child or openly hostile to you. Sometimes their attitudes were shaped by unpleasant experiences that they had while in school. Darby (as found in Williams, Alley, & Henson, 1999, p. 113) suggests appropriate ways for a teacher to relate to each type.

SUMMARY

This chapter identified numerous strategies that beginning teachers can use to assure that their classrooms are well managed. Adjust your thinking regarding the personal life of your students and formulate learning communities. Prevent management problems by taking action before school starts and during the first few days of school. Communicate effectively with students through polite, extending, and inclusive language. Use I-messages and praise. And, involve parents in school-related activities. Following these suggestions as a beginning teacher will assist you in becoming an effective teacher.

REFERENCES

Armstrong, D. G., Henson, K. T., & Savage, T. V. (1997). *Teaching today: An introduction to education* (5th ed.). Upper Saddle River, NJ: Merrill/Prentice Hall.

Brooks, D. M. (1985). The first day of school. *Educational Leadership, 42*(8), 76–78.

Darby, C. (1979). Parent Conferences. [Handout from summer graduate course].

Dewey, J. (1916). *Democracy and education.* New York: Macmillan.

Eisner, E. (1994). *The educational imagination* (3rd ed.). Upper Saddle River, NJ: Merrill/Prentice Hall.

Glasser, W. (1992). The quality school curriculum. *Phi Delta Kappan, 73*(9), 690–694.

Gordon, T. (1974). *Teacher effectiveness training.* New York: Peter H. Wyden.

Johnson, L. (1986). *Drug use among American high school students, college students and other young adults.* Washington, DC: National Institute on Drug Abuse.

Keller, B. M. (1995). Accelerated schools: Hands-on learning in a unified community. *Educational Leadership, 52*(5), 10–13.

Leithwood, K., Menzies, T., & Jantzi, D. (1994). Earning teachers' commitment to curriculum reform. *Peabody Journal of Education, 69*(4), 38–61.

Manning, M. L., & Saddlemire, R. (1996). Developing a sense of community in secondary schools. *NASSP Bulletin, 80*(584), 41–48.

Phelan, P., Davidson, A., & Cao, H. (1992). Speaking up: Students perspectives on school. *Phi Delta Kappan, 73*(9), 695–704.

Postner, G. J., & Rudnitsky, S. N. (1997). *Course design: A guide to curriculum development for students* (5th ed.). New York: Longman.

Schell, L. M. & Burden, P. (1992). *Countdown to the first day of school.* Washington, DC: National Education Association of the United States.

Seligman, J. (1989). Variations on a theme. *Newsweek, 22*(2), 38–46.

Williams, P. A., Alley, R. D., & Henson, K. T. (1999). Managing secondary classrooms: *Principles and strategies for effective management and instruction.* Needham Heights, MA: Allyn & Bacon.

Yelon, S. L. (1996). *Powerful principles of instruction.* White Plains, NY: Longman.

CHAPTER 10

Sexual Harassment and Sexual Abuse of Students

Sexual harassment and sexual abuse of students are harmful events that can occur in the public schools. The issues of sexual harassment and sexual abuse of students are likely the most notorious issue in education today. Not only are sexual harassment and sexual abuse unlawful, but they also can be emotionally devastating. Finally, it is extremely disruptive to the educational process.

A few of the many questions about sexual harassment and sexual abuse of students are:

- What exactly is sexual harassment?
- Why are sexual harassment and abuse unlawful?
- What are the courts deciding about harassment?
- What should educators and school districts do if allegations arise?

This chapter attempts to answer these questions. Space constraints do not allow treatment of sexual harassment of school employees or student-to-student sexual harassment, both significant topics in their own right.

DEFINITIONS OF SEXUAL HARASSMENT

Sexual harassment and sexual abuse are forms of sexual discrimination. Sexual discrimination is unequal or unfair treatment based solely on an individual's

Prepared for inclusion in this text by JoAnn Seiglar Wright. 1999.

gender. Sexual harassment has many definitions. In its guidelines on sexual harassment, the Office of Civil Rights (OCR) describes sexual harassment; it includes unwelcome sexual advances, requests for sexual favors or other verbal or physical conduct that is gender-based, where submission to such conduct is explicitly or implicitly made a term or condition of the individual's education; or such conduct has the purpose or effect of unreasonably interfering with the individual's education or creating an intimidating, hostile, or offensive environment.

The two types of sexual harassment described by OCR are generally classified as *quid pro quo* and *hostile environment*. *Quid pro quo* harassment is the requirement that sexual favors are exchanged for a thing of value. *Hostile environment* harassment is the creation of an atmosphere that interferes with a student's ability to learn or to derive educational benefit from the school setting.

A mere definition does not answer the question "What is sexual harassment?" Some behaviors that have been found to constitute sexual harassment include:

1. Verbal
   - name calling
   - jokes
   - sexual comments or innuendos
   - comments about appearance or clothing
   - suggestive sounds, wolf whistles
   - flirting, over-familiarity
   - negative gender-based comments
   - obscenities

- discussions about a person's sexual preference or orientation

2. Nonverbal
   - displaying calendars, cartoons, or posters that are sexual or sexist
   - graffiti
   - notes or letters with sexual content
   - sexual surveys

3. Physical
   - touching, patting, stroking, hugging
   - brushing against a person
   - tickling, pinching
   - sitting in a person's lap
   - massages
   - leering, ogling
   - sexual assault, sexual abuse

Some of these behaviors could be innocuous in some situations, yet turn into sexual harassment in another context. A husband massaging a wife's neck is familial affection. A male coach massaging the thigh of a female student could constitute sexual harassment. A brother pinching and tickling a sister is teasing. A principal hugging all the blond senior girls could be sexual harassment.

Another variable determines sexual harassment. Whether a behavior is or is not harassment depends on the perception of the person to whom the behavior is directed. The test is what a reasonable person would believe to be harassment. An elementary student may welcome a teacher's hug. A secondary student may find a teacher's hug unwelcome. In all situations, good judgment must be exercised.

Sexual harassment, then, is difficult to pinpoint at times, because of the context, the situation, and the perceptions of the individuals involved. To determine if behaviors constitute harassment, the totality of the circumstances must be considered.

SEXUAL DISCRIMINATION

Sexual harassment and sexual abuse are both forms of sexual discrimination. Discrimination on the basis of sex, or gender, is like discrimination on the basis of race, color, national origin, age, religion, or disability. Discrimination on any of these bases is unlawful. The laws that make discrimination unlawful also provide remedies to individuals who believe they are the target of discrimination. Those remedies can be exerted in lawsuits against the person or against the institution alleged to have acted in a discriminatory manner. The two major legal authorities that make sexual discrimination unlawful are the U.S. Constitution and federal statute. Other

miscellaneous laws make sexual harassment and abuse unlawful. The following is an overview of the relevant law and interpretation of sexual harassment and abuse.

U. S. Constitutional Authority

The Due Process Clause of the Fourteenth Amendment to the United States Constitution declares:

> No state shall . . . deprive a person of life, liberty or property without due process of law.

Due process has a procedural mechanism and a substantive element. The procedural mechanism requires that before an individual is deprived of an interest in property or liberty, some fundamentally fair process must be followed (*Ingraham v. Wright*, 97 S.Ct. 1401 (1977)). The substantive element of due process protects individual liberty against certain government actions regardless of the fairness of the procedure used to implement them (*Collins v. City of Harker Heights*, 112 S.Ct. 1061 (1992)).

The Fourteenth Amendment goes on to express:

> "No State shall deny to any person . . . the equal protection of the laws."

The equal protection clause of the Fourteenth Amendment is essentially a mandate that all persons similarly situated must be treated alike (*City of Cleburne, Tex. v. Cleburne Living Center*, 105 S.Ct. 3249 (1985)).

To protect constitutional rights and guarantees, subsequent to the Civil War, Congress enacted certain laws known as the Civil Rights Acts of 1866 and 1871 (42 U.S.C. §§1981 et seq.). These statutes guarantee equal rights under the law, protect property rights, and provide remedies in the form of civil action for the deprivation of civil rights. Specifically, 42 U.S.C. §1983 allows that:

> Every person who, under color of any statute, ordinance, regulation, custom, or usage, of any State or Territory or the District of Columbia, subjects or causes to be subjected, any citizen of the United States or any other person within the jurisdiction thereof to the deprivation of any rights, privileges, or immunities secured by the Constitution and laws, shall be liable to the party injured in an action at law, suit in equity, or other proper proceeding for redress.

To state a claim for violation of due process under 42 U.S.C. §1983, three elements must be proven.

1. It must be shown that the individual has a recognized property or liberty interest.
2. The individual must have been deprived of that interest either intentionally or recklessly.

3. The deprivation must occur under color of state law (*Griffith v. Johnson*, 899 F.2d 1427 (5th Cir. 1990)).

Whether a liberty or property interest is a recognized one is a matter of law. The interest must be established and well known at the time of the alleged deprivation. The acts depriving a person of a right must be purposeful or with extreme recklessness, callous unthinking, or deliberate disregard of the individual's rights. "Under color of law" requires the action to have been taken by a governmental entity—state, municipal, or local, such as a school district. In order for a governmental entity to be held liable for a violation of constitutional or civil rights, the violation must have been caused by a custom, practice, or policy. An official policy can be established when the policymaker (typically the governing body) makes a decision, adopts a policy, or allows a custom to develop that is the moving force behind the violation of constitutional rights. To show that a custom violated constitutional or civil rights the plaintiff must show the existence of a continuing, persistent widespread practice of unconstitutional misconduct, deliberate indifference to or tacit approval of such misconduct by policymaking officials, and that the plaintiff was injured by virtue of the unconstitutional acts pursuant to the board's custom, and that the custom was the moving force behind the unconstitutional acts (*Monnel v. New York Department of Social Services*, 436 U.S. 658 (1978)). Damages allowable under these laws for violation of constitutional and civil rights include money damages, injunctive relief, attorney fees, and costs. Punitive damages against a governmental entity are not allowed.

Title IX of Education Amendments of 1972

Title IX of the Education Amendments of 1972 prohibits discrimination on the basis of sex by any educational institution that receives federal funds. This law, found at 20 U.S.C. §1681(a), states:

> [N]o person in the United States shall, on the basis of sex, be excluded from participation in, be denied the benefits of, or be subjected to discrimination under any educational program or activity receiving Federal financial assistance.

Rules that interpret this statute are found in Title 34 of the Code of Federal Regulations, 34 C.F.R. §106.1 et seq. These regulations authorize the U.S. Department of Education to oversee compliance of Title IX. The U.S. Department of Education, Office of Civil Rights (OCR) has jurisdiction to investigate alleged violations of Title IX. OCR also has developed guidelines for addressing complaints lodged under Title IX.

If an alleged violation of Title IX occurs, an aggrieved person is able to file a complaint with OCR. OCR investigates each charge. A voluntary compliance procedure is available to foster resolution of a complaint. If OCR finds a violation of Title IX, it may initiate administrative proceedings against the institution. Such action may affect the institution's federal funding assistance. OCR may route the complaint to the U.S. Department of Justice, which can bring court action against the institution.

A complaint of discrimination under Title IX does not have to be filed with OCR. An aggrieved individual may proceed directly to federal court and file a lawsuit against the institution for unlawful discrimination. Under Title IX the remedies available to a plaintiff in a lawsuit include monetary damages for actual costs, pain and suffering, emotional distress, and attorney fees. The plaintiff also may obtain injunctive relief. An injunction is a court order that would require an institution either to stop a course of action or to take and maintain some endeavor prospectively.

Other Laws

Other laws at the state or local level make sexual discrimination, sexual harassment, and sexual abuse unlawful. These laws include state constitutional provisions such as state Equal Rights Amendments. Other state or local laws may prohibit any form of discrimination. State and local criminal laws make sexual abuse and sexual assault illegal. In addition, remedies are available under the common law. According to *Black's Law Dictionary* (6th ed., 1990), common law is distinguished from statutory law, which is created by the enactments of legislatures. Common law encompasses principles and rules of action derived from historical usages and customs, particularly old English law. Examples of common law actions for sexual harassment or sexual abuse include torts such as civil assault and battery and intentional infliction of emotional distress.

COURT RULINGS

Case Law

The courts have dealt with sexual harassment and sexual abuse in a number of cases. Case law is an important resource, as reviewing court decisions assists in interpreting the law. The cases illustrate how the law would be applied to certain factual situations. The holdings in these cases give some direction to educators, to help them understand allegations of sexual harassment and sexual abuse. Unfortunately, although each case may bring clarification on one issue, many questions remain.

Franklin v. Gwinnett County Public Schools[1]

Facts. A female student in a public high school was coerced into sexual relations by her economics teacher. A student who was a friend of the girl informed another teacher about the activity. This teacher discouraged the girls from taking any action against the economics teacher. The school had no formal sexual harassment complaint procedure. When the principal and other administrators later learned of the incident of sexual abuse, they began a cursory investigation of the complaint. The investigation ceased upon the resignation of the teacher accused of the misconduct and retirement of the teacher who knew of the incident.

The student filed a charge with OCR alleging that the school intentionally discriminated against her on the basis of sex. OCR investigated and found the school district in violation of Title IX. The girl later filed a lawsuit against the school district alleging that she was subjected to sexual harassment and abuse, that teachers and administrators were aware of the conduct but took no action, and that the school closed the investigation conditioned upon the economic teacher's resignation. The cause of action raised by the student was in violation of Title IX. The plaintiff requested monetary damages.

Court Holdings. The lower courts dismissed the plaintiff's claim. The courts held that monetary damages were not available under Title IX, deciding that the statute allowed only prospective relief. The U.S. Supreme Court, however, held that prospective relief would be an inadequate remedy to this plaintiff, as she no longer was a student at that school. The Supreme Court held that since this was a case of intentional sexual discrimination, monetary damages under Title IX were available to this plaintiff. This decision opened the door to a plaintiff's ability to recover money damages from school districts under Title IX. To compound the dilemma, there is no statutory cap or limitation on the damages allowed. A school district may be liable to pay substantial funds to successful plaintiffs.

Stoneking v. Bradford Area School District[2]

Facts. A student alleged that her band instructor had threatened, intimidated, and coerced her to engage in sexual relations, which continued over a period of three years. There were indications that the band teacher had been involved sexually with other female students in prior years. In light of these rumors, the administration took no action against the teacher. Another student complained to the administration that she had been sexually abused by the teacher. An administrator had talked that student into recanting her statement, warning the student that she would be ostracized for making such charges. The female student filed suit against the school district and the administration. Her claim was brought under 42 U.S.C. §1983 and was based on due process violations.

Court Holdings. An earlier case, *Stoneking v. Bradford Area School District* (856 F.2d 594 (3rd Cir. 1988), vacated sub. nom. *Smith v. Stoneking*, 109 S.Ct. 1393 (1989), [*Stoneking I*]), held that schools have an affirmative duty to protect students from the acts of teachers. Failure to provide protection would expose the school district to liability. *Stoneking I* was before the U.S. Supreme Court when the court issued its decision in *DeShaney v. Winnebago County Department of Corrections* (109 S.Ct. 998 (1989)). In *De-Shaney*, a county was sued for damages for failing to remove a child from the home of his abusive father. The father later beat the child so viciously that it caused permanent brain damage, rendering the child profoundly retarded. The Supreme Court held that a county or any governmental entity does not have a duty to protect individuals from the wrongful acts of third parties. In light of the decision in *De-Shaney*, the Supreme Court remanded *Stoneking I* to the trial court. The Supreme Court directed the trial court to reconsider its decision on the school district's duty to protect. The Supreme Court instructed the trial court to render a decision consistent with *DeShaney*.

The lower court refused to dismiss the student's case. A legal theory different from the duty to protect was devised, thus maintaining the student's cause of action. The court's new direction was to determine that sexual abuse and molestation is a violation of a student's right to bodily integrity. This violation was a cognizable claim under the Fourteenth Amendment.

---

1. 112 S.Ct. 1028 (1992) *reversing,* 911 F.2d 617 (11th Cir. 1990).

2. 882 F.2d 720 (3rd Cir. 1989), *cert. denied* 110 S.Ct. (1990) [Stoneking II]

The administrators who had been sued individually claimed that they had qualified immunity from suit. Governmental employees may have immunity from personal liability unless they violate a person's clearly established constitutional right. The court held that the administrators would not be able to enjoy qualified immunity and could be individually liable to the student. The court found that the administrators failed to take the sufficient action in the face of obvious complaints of sexual abuse. Such inaction constituted a policy, practice, or custom of failing to respond to complaints of sexual abuse of students by teachers.

As in *Stoneking,* a claim that a school district has a duty to protect students was struck down in *D.R. by L.R. v. Middle Bucks Area Vocational Technical School* (972 F.2d 1364 (3rd Cir. 1992), *cert.* denied 113 S.Ct. 1045 (1993)). The court held that there is no special custodial relationship between students and schools, even with compulsory school attendance laws. Therefore, the state does not have a duty to protect students from independent acts of third parties. Without a duty to care, there can be no failure to render the duty. Without this element, there can be no cause of action.

Doe v. Taylor Independent School District[3]

Facts. A female high school student, Jane Doe, became involved in a romantic relationship with a teacher/coach. They eventually had sexual relations. The coach had a reputation for flirting with pretty female students, and there were rumors of sexual liaisons. Even when the coach was observed behaving inappropriately intimately with female students, including hugging, dancing, taking girls to lunch, touching, and giving girls excessive attention, no action was taken to stop his behavior. Jane Doe's best friend went to the administration, telling the principal about the relationship between the coach and Jane Doe. The administration took no action. Jane Doe's mother found, in her daughter's room, a valentine, love notes, and photographs with intimate inscriptions written by the coach. After initially denying the relationship, the student finally confessed. The teacher/coach resigned and subsequently pled guilty to criminal charges of sexual assault.

The student filed a lawsuit against the school district and against the high school principal and the superintendent individually. She alleged that the administration knew of the coach's propensity for

sexual harassment and sexual abuse. In the face of substantial information about the coach's behavior, it took no action to protect the student from the harassment and abuse. She claimed that this was a violation of her constitutional rights to due process and brought a lawsuit under 42 U.S.C. §1983.

Court Holdings. The court found that students do have a liberty interest in bodily integrity. Physical sexual abuse by a teacher at school violates that right. The administrators claimed that they had qualified immunity and could not be sued. The court held that school administrators can be sued individually when they act with deliberate indifference to the rights of students. The court defined deliberate indifference as more than gross negligence; instead, deliberate indifference is a lesser form of intent. The school principal, who did nothing after repeated accusations, rumors, reports, and accounts of sexual harassment and abuse, acted with deliberate indifference. He was found not to have qualified immunity and was individually liable to the student. Although this case is controlling in the 5th Circuit only (Texas, Louisiana, and Mississippi), it creates a substantial precedent on how courts may look at the issue of liability for sexual discrimination, sexual harassment, and sexual abuse.

Gebser v. Lago Vista Independent School District, 118 S.Ct.1989 (1998)

Facts. Star Gebser attended school in Lago Vista ISD. At that time, the district had not adopted or issued a sexual harassment policy or formulated a grievance procedure. Star was a ninth grader in 1992 when her teacher, Frank Waldrop, began a sexual relationship with her. The relationship continued throughout the summer and into the following school year. They often had intercourse during class time but never on school property. Star told no one about the matter, she remained silent because she wanted to continue having Waldrop as a teacher. Other parents had complained that the teacher made sexual comments in class. The principal cautioned the teacher about the comments but made no report to the Superintendent, who was also the Title IX coordinator. In January, a police officer discovered Star and Waldrop engaging in sexual intercourse. Waldrop was arrested, terminated, and lost his certification. Star's parents sued the district under Title IX and §1983.

Court Holdings. The district court dismissed the case, stating that the purpose of Title IX was to counter policies of discrimination. School administrators

3. 15 F.3d 443 (1994) [Doe II]; vacating *Doe v. Taylor Independent School District*, 975 F.2d 137 (5th Cir. 1992) [Doe I].

must have some notice of gender discrimination and fail to respond before such conduct is actionable under Title IX. The district court determined that the complaints about the teacher's comments were not sufficient notice to the district that the teacher was involved in a sexual relationship with a student.

The Plaintiffs appealed the Title IX cause of action to the Fifth Circuit, which affirmed the district court's dismissal. The appeals court declined to impose strict liability on a school district for a teacher's conduct and reiterated prior holdings that a school district is not liable under Title IX for teacher-to-student sexual harassment unless an employee with supervisory authority over the harasser knew of the abuse, had the power to end it, and failed to do so. The court determined that the district could not be liable on the basis of constructive notice because there was no evidence to suggest that the district knew or should have known of the teacher's conduct.

The case was appealed to the Supreme Court and certiorari was granted. The Petitioners were joined by the United States as *amicus curiae*. They advanced the theory that liability should be based on the standards used in Title VII employment sexual harassment cases: agency principles of *respondeat superior* and constructive notice. Analogizing to *Meritor Savings Bank, F.S.B. v. Vinson*, 477 U.S. 57 (1986) the Petitioners argued that a teacher is aided in harassment of students by the teacher's authority with the institution, and under agency principles the district should be liable irrespective of whether school officials had notice of the harassment. The Petitioners further argued that the district should be liable on the basis of constructive notice. If the district knew or should have known but failed to discern the harassment, it should be liable. Under either approach, a district would face liability in a broader range of situations than with the rule adopted by the Fifth Circuit.

The court refused to apply agency standards, because there is not the "agent" language in Title IX as there is in Title VII. It further compared Title VII and Title IX and stated that while Title VII contains an express cause of action, a Title IX cause of action is judicially applied. *Cannon v. University of Chicago*, 441 U.S. 677 (1979) Petitioners were asking for not only a finding of a Title IX violation but they sought damages. While in *Franklin v. Gwinette, supra* the court determined that monetary damages are available, it did not set out when liability would lie. In *Franklin*, the school officials knew of the sexual abuse and failed to take any action, making the discrimination intentional. In *Gebser* there is no evidence that the school officials had knowledge and failed to act, thus the court indicated that *Franklin* is not applicable to *Gebser*.

Because a Title IX cause of action is judicially applied the court believed that it could shape a scheme that best comports with the intent of Title IX. To apply Title VII *respondeat superior* principles to student sexual harassment would frustrate the legislative purposes of Title IX. Congress enacted Title IX to avoid the use of federal funds to support discriminatory practices; Title VII is a prohibition of discrimination. Title IX focuses on protecting individuals from discrimination from agencies receiving federal funds; Title VII compensates victims for discrimination.

Title IX violations hinge on an agency's knowledge of the discrimination and failure to eliminate it. To be actionable a school district must have actual notice of the harassment and then fail to take any action. There was no such evidence presented in the case. Even Lago Vista's failure to follow Department of Education guidelines to have a sexual harassment policy and grievance procedure did not rise to actual notice and deliberate indifference to the harassment. There is no implied cause of action for violations of administrative requirements.

The court declared that claims of sexual harassment by teachers is all too common, but to apply a strict liability standard would make schools liable in every case where a teacher sexually harassed a student. The Fifth Circuit holding, that absent actual notice and deliberate indifference a school district would not be liable, was affirmed. Not only did the majority of the Court require that there must be proof of actual knowledge, but the actual knowledge must be on the part of someone having authority over the teacher. If, for example, a fellow teacher had actual knowledge of the abuse, the district would not be liable. If a plaintiff does prove that an authoritative representative had actual knowledge, the next step would be to prove conscious indifference. A school district could avoid liability if it can show that some response was made to stop the abusive behavior, therefore defeating the conscious indifference claim.

RESPONSIBILITIES OF THE SCHOOL

Title IX requires that educational institutions have a policy prohibiting sexual harassment and a published grievance procedure to deal with complaints of harassment. The policy should define the prohibited behavior and give consequences for violations of the policy. A grievance procedure should have informal and formal stages. Designating and publishing the name of the individual at the institution who is responsible for responding to Title IX claims, along with the proper manner to contact that person, are important.

Strong disapproval of sexual harassment has to be communicated to all employees on a continuing basis. Sensitivity training for all staff members who have contact with students is a suitable manner to raise consciousness. Educators must be made aware of what behaviors can constitute harassment. Once they understand what constitutes sexual harassment, most individuals become more sensitive to the issue. A school district must let it be known that sexual harassment will not be tolerated. Taking such a position can be an indication that a school district is acting in good faith to prevent harassment in the event a claim arises. Evidence of either the *quid pro quo* or the *hostile environment* form of sexual harassment must be dealt with immediately. If a hostile environment is apparent, steps must be taken to respond to the behaviors and to remediate them. Allowing such behavior to continue is a violation of Title IX.

Students likewise should be educated regarding sexual harassment. They need to recognize that they do not have to tolerate behavior that makes them feel uncomfortable. Students should be made aware that complaints will be taken seriously and that each complaint will be investigated. Schools should impart to students that complaints will be treated with sensitivity and confidentiality. As was recounted in the lawsuits described above, difficulties occur when a student has no reasonable outlet at school to file a complaint, or if administrators respond initially to the complaints as being trivial or without merit. It should be communicated to students regularly that there will be no retaliation for making a true and honest complaint.

Prior to allegations being made, possible consequences for committing sexual harassment or sexual abuse should be considered. These sanctions should be communicated to educators. Regular training is essential for supervisors who will be enmeshed in sexual harassment situations.

Whether the allegations are true or false, irreparable damage can be caused to the individuals involved—emotional devastation, humiliation, careers destroyed, reputations ruined. Educators must be prepared to face the potential of accusations being made about them, their colleagues, and friends.

RECOURSE TO THOSE ACCUSED

Procedures must be established to manage a harassment complaint prior to a claim arising. Once an allegation is made, emotions and fear may prevent the creation of rational, reasonable procedures.

When a complaint is made, the first step is to document the allegation. Good records may serve many purposes later on. Under child abuse laws an outside agency might have to be notified of a claim of sexual abuse. Such notification should be made immediately. Any internal investigation may be interrupted while the outside agency conducts an investigation.

Many law enforcement agencies take exception to an individual questioning witnesses while its investigation is being conducted. In some jurisdictions it may be considered illegal to interfere.

If only an internal investigation is proceeding or after the outside agency approves, information must be gathered from the complainant, any witnesses, and the purported harasser. Attempts should be made to get statements in writing, signed by the person making the statement. All information must be kept confidential. The Family Rights and Privacy Act (the Buckley Amendment) compels the confidentiality of student records.

The investigator must remain neutral and objective. No value judgments about either the accuser or the accused should be made. The investigator should be sensitive to both. The investigator should not attempt to cross-examine witnesses. The interviewer preferably is the same sex as the witness. During the investigation both the accused and accuser should be protected from interaction with the other.

Parents of the student filing the complaint must be notified of the situation. As the case progresses, the parents must be kept informed. Parents of other students who may act as witnesses should be notified that their child is part of an investigation. The parents should be requested to respect the confidentiality of all persons.

After the investigation is complete, express findings and outcomes must be made and documented. If the employee did behave as alleged, employment status must be determined in accordance with employment laws and contract provisions. If disciplinary action is indicated, it must be commensurate with the seriousness of the offense.

Two recent court cases, *Hickey v. Irving Independent School District*[4] and *Doe v. Petaluma City School District*,[5] indicate that the statute of limitations (the time in which a person has a right to sue) for a student is until two years after the student's 18th birthday. Because of this, records of complaints and investigations must be retained permanently. For confidentiality purposes, the records should not be kept with the student's educational records. Instead, a separate secure file should be preserved.

---

4. 976 F.2d 980 (5th Cir. 1992)
5. 830 F.Supp. 1560 (N.D. Cal. 1993)

CONCLUSION

Human behavior regarding sexuality is a complex matter, which makes the issue of sexual harassment and abuse problematic. What the law has indicated thus far is that educators must be cautious and use good judgment in dealing with students. Additional litigation will be brought to court in the future with a likelihood of expanding plaintiff's ability to recover. The training of educators is the one tool that can protect students, educators, and school districts from the tragedy of sexual harassment and sexual abuse.

CHAPTER 11

Education Vital Signs 1998

FROM TEST SCORES TO TEACHER SHORTAGES, A YEAR OF DIMINISHED EXPECTATIONS

by Lawrence Hardy

"By the year 2000, United States students will be the first in the world in mathematics and science achievement."

Goal Five of the National Education Goals is bold, unequivocal, and—if we are to extrapolate from one of the more disturbing reports of 1998—utterly unreachable.

Released in February, the 12th-grade report from the Third International Mathematics and Science Study (TIMSS) placed U.S. seniors near the bottom of 21 industrialized and semi-industrialized nations—significantly lower than Canada, Australia, and Slovenia and ahead of only Cyprus and South Africa.

It was, perhaps, the signature event of 1998, a year of disappointment and diminished expectations for public education.

"By the year 2000, the nation's teaching force will have access to programs for the continued improvement of their professional skills and the opportunity to acquire the knowledge and skills needed to instruct and prepare all American students for the next century."

Goal Four is equally ambitious, a reminder that student achievement depends foremost on the quality of the nation's teaching force. Yet while many

states made progress on improving teacher training in 1998, one of the year's biggest education stories concerned the apparent failure of one state, Massachusetts, to ensure that a majority of its teacher candidates were even minimally competent. When results were released from Massachusetts' first statewide test of prospective teachers in June, they showed that nearly 60 percent had failed.

"By the year 2000, every school in the United States will be free of drugs, violence, and the unauthorized presence of firearms and alcohol and will offer a disciplined environment conducive to learning."

Experts on our often-violent society say that school remains one of the safest places for young people. Yet no one following the news in 1998 could escape the harrowing images of places like Jonesboro, Ark., where two boys gunned down a teacher and four middle school classmates after luring them outside with a fire alarm. It was one of several school shootings, which led to 40 deaths during the 1997-98 school year.

PROBLEMS AND SETBACKS

It was a sobering year for public education. If anything, 1998 showed that the problems facing the nation's schools would not magically resolve themselves through strong statements or the kind of wishful thinking that accompanies an approaching millennium. Instead, problems such as finding and training competent teachers or preparing high school seniors for a changing technological world proved to be extraordinarily complex and resistant to simple solutions.

There were areas of progress, to be sure, particularly regarding children living in poverty. A September report by the U.S. Department of Education found that 9-year-old students in high-poverty schools were starting to close the more than two-grade-level gap in math scores on the National Assessment of Educational Progress with their counterparts in low-poverty schools. And the Census Bureau reported in June that 86.2 percent of young African Americans ages 25 to 29 had graduated from high school, a rate nearly equal that of whites, though the Hispanic graduation rate remained much lower at 55 percent.

But for every problem solved, or at least confronted, there were new ones appearing on the horizon. Perhaps most ominous was the coming teacher shortage and its potential impact on teacher quality, which U.S. Education Secretary Richard Riley warned about in his annual back-to-school address in September.

"We do not seem to recognize the magnitude of the task ahead," Riley said. "In the next 10 years, we need to recruit 2.2 million teachers. One-half to two-thirds of these teachers will be first-time teachers."

The year was also marked by significant setbacks to some of the major education initiatives of the '60s, '70s, '80s, and '90s. Whether these setbacks were ultimately good or bad for education depended in large part on one's political perspective, but they underscored the depth of the country's divisions.

First to take a hit was affirmative action. In late 1997, the Piscataway, N.J., school board, using money donated from civil rights groups, reached a surprise out-of-court settlement with Sharon Taxman, a white business teacher who was released from her job instead of a black woman whom the district had deemed equally qualified. The board, facing the need to make a staff cut, had chosen to let Taxman go to preserve racial diversity in the business department. That decision led to a pivotal court case that was scheduled to be heard by the U.S. Supreme Court.

"It's obvious to me that they were afraid that affirmative action might be very badly damaged if the Supreme Court had decided the case," Steven E. Klausner, Taxman's attorney, told the Associated Press.

Proponents of bilingual education also suffered a setback when more than 60 percent of California voters approved Proposition 227. The measure requires that children be taught in English, although parents can seek waivers to keep their children in traditional bilingual classes. Students of limited English proficiency are to be placed in one-year English immersion programs.

By early October, school districts throughout California were still struggling to implement the measure—or, as critics of bilingual education claimed, to circumvent it. Thirty-nine of the state's nearly 1,000 districts—including Los Angeles, San Diego, and Oakland—had sought schoolwide or districtwide waivers from the state board of education but had been rebuffed. After a judge ruled that the board had to consider the requests, the board filed an appeal that could take months to resolve, according to the *New York Times*. In the meantime, the districts were required to implement the proposition.

Advocates of a merger between the nation's two largest teacher unions were also handed a defeat when delegates at the New Orleans conference of the 2.4-million-member National Education Association (NEA) rejected a merger with the American Federation of Teachers (AFT) by a margin of 58 percent to 42 percent. Some NEA members who opposed the merger said they did not want a unified organization to fall under the umbrella of the AFL-CIO, with which the AFT is affiliated.

A few weeks later, AFT delegates, in a largely symbolic vote, approved the merger by an overwhelming 1,982 to 46 margin. AFT President Sandra Feldman said her organization planned to continue working on a merger plan with the NEA and was not going to "let the dream die."

A CONSERVATIVE AGENDA

Conservatives, who often criticize the influence of the teachers unions, had much to cheer about in 1998. In June, the Wisconsin Supreme Court ruled that it is constitutional for tax dollars to be used to send poor Milwaukee children to religious schools. It was the first time a state Supreme Court had ruled on the issue of public tax dollars being used to pay for vouchers for private schools. The U.S. Supreme Court is expected to hear an appeal.

School choice advocates also were buoyed by news of individuals and foundations donating funds for private tuition programs. In Louisville, more than 330 students from low-income families began attending private schools on gifts provided by School Choice Scholarships Inc., a nonprofit organization that has raised $1.2 million in contributions from individuals and businesses, according to the Louisville *Courier-Journal*. Officials of the Jefferson County (Mo.) Public schools urged the group to use its money to support public education. "We're very disappointed to lose any child from the public schools," said school spokeswoman Lauren Roberts. "We have programs and services to meet the needs of every child, as well as, if not better than, anyone else."

An even more ambitious program was launched in Texas, where the nonprofit Children's Educational Opportunity Foundation offered vouchers to nearly all 14,000 students in the Edgewood District, in one of the poorest sections of San Antonio. The foundation pledged to provide $5 million for 10 years for Edgewood students to attend the school of their choice.

Sponsors said the competition would boost public education. Critics called the program a stalking horse for an eventual state-funded voucher plan. Vouchers, said John O'Sullivan, secretary-treasurer of the Texas Federation of Teachers, would allow private schools to "cherry pick" the students they want. "It shortens the honor roll [in public schools]. One of the strengths of the public school system is it puts everyone together."

Proponents of private school choice suffered one defeat, however, when President Clinton vetoed legislation that included tax breaks for parents who send their children to private schools. Clinton said the bill would use $3 billion to give tax benefits for richer families while doing "virtually nothing for average families." He said the money could be better spent to improve public schools.

The bill's sponsor, Sen. Paul Coverdell, R-Ga., accused Clinton of reaching "a new low in shameless pandering" to teachers unions. "America's children lose," he said, "and the union bosses win."

That kind of partisan anger was overcome in October, however, when Congress, enjoying an unexpected budget surplus, approved a massive appropriations bill that included a $1.1 billion "down payment" for 100,000 new teachers. It was a key victory for Clinton and the Democrats, who had been shell-shocked in recent weeks by a debilitating impeachment inquiry.

The teacher recruitment money "will make a major down payment toward our goal of an average class size of 18 in the early grades," Clinton said.

Clinton also got most of what he wanted for pet projects such as Goals 2000, Head Start, and School-to-Work, but he backed away from a proposed tax subsidy to build 5,000 schools.

BAD NEWS IN MATH AND SCIENCE

What a difference a year makes. In June 1997, when the second TIMSS report was released, Clinton and Riley announced the results in the White House Rose Garden. The report showed U.S. fourth-graders competing favorably in math and science with 25 other nations. While it was also true that the scores had dropped by eighth grade, the news was encouraging overall.

"This report proves we don't have to settle for second-class expectations or second-class goals," Clinton said at the time. "We don't have to be afraid of the results anymore."

No such fanfare accompanied the 12th-grade report, issued this year. While U.S. fourth-graders had been surpassed only by Korea in science, the nation's high school seniors were bested by students in 11 of the 21 nations tested at the high school level. In math, U.S. fourth-graders were outscored by just seven other nations; the seniors were beaten by 14.

Even more disturbing, the test found that America's "elite" students, who took physics and advanced mathematics, scored near the bottom of 16 nations that were compared on this basis.

"Our best students in math and science are simply not world class," wrote Curtis C. McKnight, a mathematics professor at Oklahoma University, and William H. Schmidt, a Michigan State University education professor and coordinator of the TIMSS study, in the *Boston Globe*. "And arguments that Americans thrive anyway because they are creative thinkers are difficult to support when there is precious little grounding in the sciences from which pragmatic creativity tends to spring."

Schmidt and McKnight cited a number of problems with U.S. math and science curricula. They said too many schools track math students by eighth grade, leading to achievement gaps that many children can never overcome. U.S. fourth-graders score well on math "basics," but they don't move quickly beyond them; their teachers cover similar ground in succeeding years, while instructors in Europe and Asia move on to more advanced material. Moreover, Schmidt and McKnight wrote, U.S. math and science curricula and textbooks tend to be "a mile wide and an inch deep," trying to cover a host of subjects rather than focusing on a few key ones.

The 12th-grade scores prompted Clinton to call on states to raise teacher standards and reduce the number of math and science teachers not specifically trained in those areas. In 1998, more than 30 percent of math teachers were teaching out of field.

"We need a revolution," Clinton said.

TESTING THE TEACHERS

A few weeks after Clinton's talk of a teaching "revolution," some Massachusetts educators were demanding a revolutionary overhaul of their teacher-training system. The outcry was prompted by the results of the first-ever Massachusetts Teacher Test, which was failed by 59 percent of the prospective teachers. A second exam, administered three months later, was failed by 47 percent.

Among the more strident critics was John Silber, chancellor of Boston University and chairman of the Massachusetts Board of Education. In a column in the *New York Times*, Silber listed grammatical mistakes from test-takers that he said "would provide material for Jay Leno." And he cited spelling "casualties," such as "belive," "refere," "messures" and "invation."

"No responsible person would subject anyone's children, much less his own, to such teachers," Silber wrote.

That kind of talk angered state Education Commissioner Frank W. Haydu III, who had initially persuaded the board of education to lower the passing grade of the first test to allow 260 additional teachers to pass. When the board reversed itself at the urging of acting Republican Gov. Paul Cellucci, Haydu resigned.

"Our teachers—because of the governor—are being tarred and feathered with being incompetent and illiterate," Haydu said. "It's so inaccurate and unfair."

Other educators criticized the test itself, saying prospective teachers were told last fall that the test would not affect their ability to get jobs, only to be notified two weeks before the exam that it would.

While Massachusetts battled over the politics of teacher training, California legislators were collaborating on several bills to improve the size and quality of the state's teaching force. One bill provides $10,000 bonuses to as many as 500 teachers who achieve National Board certification. Another law allows undergraduate schools to offer teacher-training programs. For the past 30 years, the state had required that theses programs be crowded into a year of post-graduate study—a policy that didn't always attract the best candidates.

"If you wait until the fifth year, people become teachers by default," said Gary Hart, director of the Institute for Education Reform at California State University, Sacramento, who spoke to the *Sacramento Bee*. "They decide not to become a business major or whatever, and you get whoever's left."

The law also increases state support—at a cost of $68 million—for a popular mentoring program that supports first- and second-year teachers.

MUSIC HATH CHARMS

While Massachusetts and California were worrying about teacher quality, two more unusual controversies were warming up involving a duo not often heard in education debates: Beethoven and Mozart.

It all began when Georgia Gov. Zell Miller—responding to research suggesting that listening to Mozart and other classical composers can improve performance on some cognitive tests—urged the state legislature to spend $100,000 to give each newborn in the state a cassette tape or compact disc of classical music.

As it turned out, the state didn't have to put up the money. Sony Classical compiled a compact disc of 17 classical selections and shipped copies to every hospital in Georgia.

But not everyone was humming the same tune. Psychologist Frances Rauscher was quoted in a British newspaper as saying, "No study shows that listening casually—as opposed to taking lessons—has any effect at all on children."

No matter. The research was enough to persuade Florida State Sen. Bill Turner to come up with his own measure, the so-called Beethoven's Babies Law. Signed into law in May by Gov. Lawton Chiles, it requires the staff of all state-funded child care centers and preschools to play classical music and read to children for a half hour each day.

Betty Bohan, who manages four YWCA child-care centers, told the *St. Petersburg Times* she was not impressed. If the legislators really wanted to help children, she said, they would take a look at the wages paid to childcare workers.

"The people who work in childcare make about the lowest of any wage earner in the nation," Bohan said. "And they are dealing with our most important citizens."

Probing the roots and prevention of youth violence
by Kevin Bushweller

When conflict resolution expert Linda Lantieri ponders the destructive power of youth anger and violence, she often thinks of how her friend Patrick Daly died. Daly was the principal of an elementary school in a troubled neighborhood in New York City. On the morning of Dec. 17, 1992, he went looking for a fourth-grade boy who had run out of the school in anger. As he was heading for a housing development near the school, Daly was shot and killed by a stray bullet, the product of a drug deal gone bad.

Lantieri, head of the Resolving Conflict Creatively Program (RCCP) in New York City, recalls the incident in the preface of a book she coauthored, *Waging Peace In Our Schools*. Daly's violent death illustrates the far reach of youth anger and violence. Yet ironically, Lantieri says, just a few months before he was killed, Daly was interviewed by a television station about how his school was teaching kids not to be violent.

How to prevent violence and improve discipline in public schools has been on everyone's minds this year. And, despite the year's high-profile school shootings, there is some encouraging news. Reports from the U.S. Department of Education and the Department of Justice show modest signs of progress—especially in the nation's poorest schools, in neighborhoods similar to the one where Daly worked.

The reasons for the modest turnarounds are hard to pinpoint. But it's likely that progress is being made because poor urban schools have focused intensely for several years on improving safety and discipline. Some districts have developed programs to teach kids how to resolve conflicts, and others have installed high-tech security systems and hired experienced police officers to patrol the halls. Still others have taken a zero-tolerance stance on school violence, expelling students for up to a year for violating weapons policies.

TRENDS IN SCHOOL VIOLENCE

Violence and Discipline Problems in U.S. Public Schools: 1996-97, a report released this year by the U.S. Department of Education, examined five-year trends by asking school principals to identify problems in their schools. (The complete report is available online at *http://nces.ed.gov.*) Comparing these data with data collected five years earlier, ED found encouraging signs in the nation's poorest schools (those where 75 percent or more of the student population is living in poverty). Areas of improvement included student tardiness and absenteeism, physical conflicts among students, robbery, vandalism, alcohol and drug use, possession of weapons, and verbal and physical abuse of teachers.

Between 1990-91 and 1996-97, fewer principals in high-poverty schools reported problems in the following safety and discipline areas:

- Physical conflicts among students. (The percentage of principals who cited this as a problem declined from 40 percent in 1990-91 to 29 percent in 1996-97.)
- Alcohol use among students. (The percentage declined from 12 percent in 1990-91 to 3 percent in 1996-97.)
- Drug use among students (from 13 percent to 5 percent).
- Physical abuse of teachers (from 6 percent to 1 percent).
- Verbal abuse of teachers (from 24 percent to 13 percent).

And as these areas improved, teachers apparently became more willing to show up for work. During the same five-year period, the percentage of principals who believed teacher absenteeism was a problem in their schools fell from 33 percent to 15 percent.

Although the problems in the nation's wealthiest schools (defined by the report as those with 20 percent or fewer of their students living in poverty) pale in comparison to those in the poorest schools, school officials in wealthier communities nevertheless have reason for concern. According to the report, growing percentages of principals in affluent schools say student tardiness and absenteeism, drug use, tobacco use, and verbal abuse of teachers are a problem.

HEART AND MIND

"I think cities are prophetic about what is going to happen everywhere else over the next five years," Lantieri said in a telephone interview. "That's why we can't keep waiting for kids to get in trouble. We need a new vision of education that includes educating the heart as well as the mind."

Lantieri says efforts to teach kids to lead more peaceful lives seem to be paying off, especially in urban schools and schools in inner suburbs. In *Violence and Discipline,* researchers found that principals in schools with minority populations of 50 percent or more saw improvement in several areas, including:

- Student absenteeism. (The percentage of principals who reported this as a problem dropped from 39 percent in 1990-91 to 35 percent in 1996-97.)
- Physical conflicts among students. (The percentage declined from 40 percent in 1990-91 to 31 percent in 1996-97.)
- Robbery or theft (from 9 percent to 7 percent).
- Vandalism (from 21 percent to 16 percent).
- Alcohol use (from 11 percent to 3 percent).
- Trespassing (from 12 percent to 7 percent).

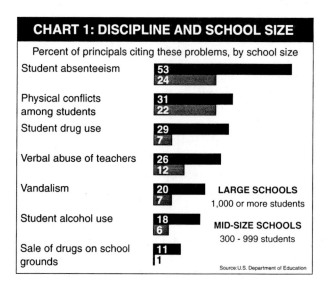

CHART 1: DISCIPLINE AND SCHOOL SIZE

Percent of principals citing these problems, by school size

Student absenteeism	53 / 24
Physical conflicts among students	31 / 22
Student drug use	29 / 7
Verbal abuse of teachers	26 / 12
Vandalism	20 / 7
Student alcohol use	18 / 6
Sale of drugs on school grounds	11 / 1

LARGE SCHOOLS 1,000 or more students

MID-SIZE SCHOOLS 300 - 999 students

Source: U.S. Department of Education

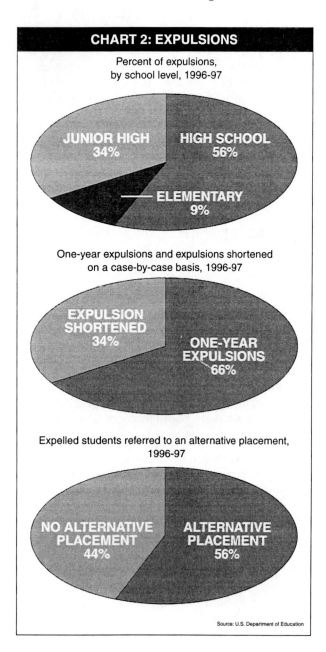

CHART 2: EXPULSIONS

Percent of expulsions,
by school level, 1996-97

JUNIOR HIGH 34%
HIGH SCHOOL 56%
ELEMENTARY 9%

One-year expulsions and expulsions shortened
on a case-by-case basis, 1996-97

EXPULSION SHORTENED 34%
ONE-YEAR EXPULSIONS 66%

Expelled students referred to an alternative placement,
1996-97

NO ALTERNATIVE PLACEMENT 44%
ALTERNATIVE PLACEMENT 56%

Source: U.S. Department of Education

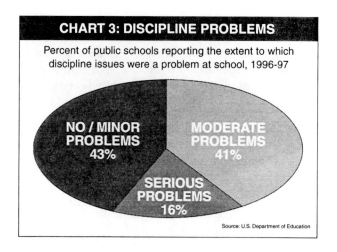

CHART 3: DISCIPLINE PROBLEMS

Percent of public schools reporting the extent to which
discipline issues were a problem at school, 1996-97

NO / MINOR PROBLEMS 43%
MODERATE PROBLEMS 41%
SERIOUS PROBLEMS 16%

Source: U.S. Department of Education

blcak, but he admits schools and communities have a lot of work ahead of them.

For years, he says, schools have tried a number of strategies to improve discipline and make their classrooms safer. In most cases, though, these strategies have been used in isolation, rather than joined into one comprehensive effort. The challenge now, he says, is for schools to combine prevention efforts, early intervention programs, law enforcement partnerships, and punishment programs into one full-scale initiative.

What's more, he says, what works to improve academic achievement often also works to reduce disorderly and disruptive behavior as well. One noteworthy example he cites is the effect of class and school size on student safety—a factor that is also noted in *Violence and Discipline*, which found a direct link between school size and discipline problems. Principals in schools of 1,000 or more students were more likely to cite problems with students in such areas as physical conflicts, drug use, and verbal abuse of teachers, for example, than were principals of mid-size schools with between 300 and 999 students.

What is especially alarming is that between 1990-91 and 1996-97, the percentage of principals at large schools who identified these problems actually increased for several of the problem areas. Among principals of mid-size schools, on the other hand, the percentage citing these student problem areas decreased over five years in all categories except tardiness, drug use, and tobacco use.

"What is promising is that we have a lot of communities talking about the problem," says Modzeleski. "That's really where the promise is. Schools can't do it by themselves."

But Modzeleski cautions that "there are alarming signs, too."

A joint study by the U.S. Department of Education and the Department of Justice, *Students' Reports of School Crime: 1989 and 1995*, identified some of those signs.

- Physical abuse of teachers (from 3 percent to 1 percent).

There was a slight increase, however—from 15 percent to 17 percent—in the percentage of principals who reported a problem with student verbal abuse of teachers.

"Are we getting better? That's a tough question," says Bill Modzeleski, director of the Safe and Drug Free Schools program at the U.S. Department of Education. "Some districts are getting better, some are not."

The media frenzy in the wake of school killings this past spring made it appear as though the nation's educators were losing control of troubled students. Modzeleski says the picture isn't nearly that

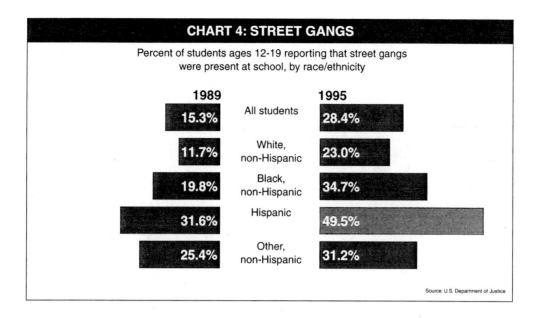

CHART 4: STREET GANGS

Percent of students ages 12-19 reporting that street gangs were present at school, by race/ethnicity

	1989		1995
All students	15.3%		28.4%
White, non-Hispanic	11.7%		23.0%
Black, non-Hispanic	19.8%		34.7%
Hispanic	31.6%		49.5%
Other, non-Hispanic	25.4%		31.2%

Source: U.S. Department of Justice

(The study is available online at *http://nces.ed.gov.*) The number of students who are likely to be victimized by a violent crime—while still relatively small—is on the rise: from 3.4 percent in 1989 to 4.2 percent in 1995, the study found. (The study defined violent crime as a physical attack or a robbery using physical force, a weapon, or a verbal threat.) The percentage of students who reported the presence of street gangs at school has also increased over the same time period, from 15 percent to 28 percent.

PLANNING FOR PREVENTION

Such figures are especially troubling in the wake of school shootings last year in Jonesboro, Ark., Pearl, Miss., West Paducah, Ky., Edinboro, Pa., and Springfield, Ore.

School safety consultant Peter Blauvelt calls those incidents a "wake-up call" for smaller, rural school districts. "They finally realized their level of vulnerability and started paying attention to developing crisis management plans," he says.

But Blauvelt says it's a mistake for schools to wait until they are shocked into action by high-profile incidents. Rather, he says, schools need to concentrate on recurring problems like bullying and harassment—antisocial behavior that sows the seeds of violence.

The difficulty, says New York's Lantieri, is predicting what's around the bend. She recalls visiting Anchorage, Alaska, several years ago to talk to school officials about how the problems of urban America were likely to emerge in places like Alaska. After telling disturbing stories of drive-by shootings and drug-related violence at schools, Lantieri recalls, "One of the teachers just laughed at me and

said, 'How could you think this could happen in Anchorage, Alaska?' Well, five years later, it did." And soon after, Lantieri's group helped create a conflict resolution program in the Anchorage schools.

In addition to crisis planning, conflict-resolution programs, and other prevention strategies, many educators recommend stricter discipline measures.

The U.S. Department of Education's *Report of State Implementation of the Gun-Free Schools Act—School Year 1996-97: Final Report 1998* outlines the results of states' efforts to enforce zero-tolerance policies for weapons violations. (The report is available online at *http://ed.gov.*) According to the report, 6,093 students were expelled in 1996-97 for bringing weapons to school. The majority of the expulsions, 58 percent, were for students who brought handguns to school; 35 percent were for other types of firearms, including bombs, grenades, or starter pistols; and 7 percent involved rifles or shotguns.

In a statement to the press, U.S. Secretary of Education Richard W. Riley said the results of the study showed that "our nation's public schools are cracking down on students who bring guns to school. We need to be tough minded about keeping guns out of our schools and do everything possible to keep our children safe."

Yet Riley cautioned schools not to simply discard the troublemakers: "I urge schools to do everything possible to make sure that expelled students are sent to alternative schools. These young people need to get their lives turned around." (According to the report, about 56 percent of the students who were expelled were referred to an alternative school or program.)

The majority of expulsions (56 percent) were from high schools, 34 percent were from junior high and

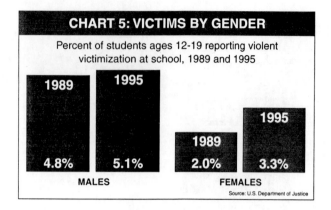

CHART 5: VICTIMS BY GENDER

Percent of students ages 12-19 reporting violent victimization at school, 1989 and 1995

1989: 4.8% 1995: 5.1% (MALES)
1989: 2.0% 1995: 3.3% (FEMALES)

Source: U.S. Department of Justice

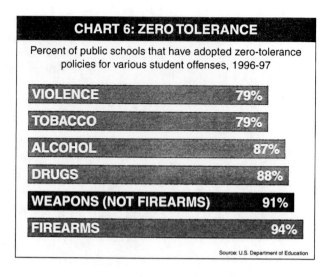

CHART 6: ZERO TOLERANCE

Percent of public schools that have adopted zero-tolerance policies for various student offenses, 1996-97

VIOLENCE	79%
TOBACCO	79%
ALCOHOL	87%
DRUGS	88%
WEAPONS (NOT FIREARMS)	91%
FIREARMS	94%

Source: U.S. Department of Education

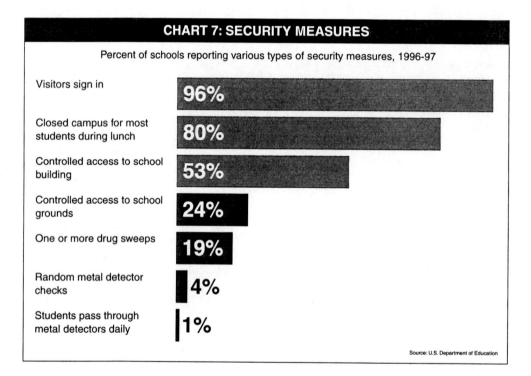

CHART 7: SECURITY MEASURES

Percent of schools reporting various types of security measures, 1996-97

Visitors sign in	96%
Closed campus for most students during lunch	80%
Controlled access to school building	53%
Controlled access to school grounds	24%
One or more drug sweeps	19%
Random metal detector checks	4%
Students pass through metal detectors daily	1%

Source: U.S. Department of Education

middle schools, and 9 percent were from elementary schools. And a growing number of educators say schools are struggling with discipline problems as early as kindergarten. Mary E. Pier, a kindergarten teacher in Aberdeen, Wash., told the Associated Press: "I have students who would fly off the handle at the drop of the hat, throw chairs, and throw tables . . . because they didn't get their way."

Part of the problem, teachers say, is that their schools of education did not teach them enough about how to maintain an orderly classroom. As a result, they must learn on the job how to modify students' behavior and attitudes.

Unfortunately, the nation's education professors apparently do not share this concern. A 1997 survey by Public Agenda found that education professors rated discipline as a low-priority skill for future teachers. If teachers kept students interested, they said, classroom order would take care of itself. (Information on this report—"Different Drummers: How Teachers of Teachers View Public Education"—is available online at *www.publicagenda.org*.)

Additional evidence of the need for teacher training comes from researchers at the Johns Hopkins School of Public Health, who found a link between poor classroom control in the first grade and increased aggression in the middle school years. "These findings suggest that effective behavior management by the first-grade teacher is essential,"

Sheppard G. Kellam, author of the study, told the Associated Press.

ROOT CAUSES

Even with better teacher training, controlling unruly students can be a deeply frustrating task. Some studies say today's students come to school much more defiant and disorderly than kids of previous generations.

What is the root cause of these problems? And what can schools do to improve student behavior?

For years, clinical psychologists and educators have believed that low self-esteem was the underlying cause of much unruly and aggressive behavior. Acting on this belief, schools across the country have designed specific programs to help students build up their self-esteem.

But a recent study by Brad Bushman of Iowa State University and Roy F. Baumeister of Case Western Reserve University suggests that schools might want to take a more careful look at these programs—especially if they unintentionally encourage students to develop inflated views of themselves. The two researchers found that people who hold such views are more likely to react aggressively to criticism or confrontation.

Unfortunately, Bushman says, many teachers and school administrators fail to hold students accountable for their behavior or academic performance. As a consequence, kids don't learn how to deal with normal levels of criticism or confrontation. When someone finally confronts them or denies them something, Bushman says, their anger level spikes far above normal.

Bushman concludes: "If the goal is to decrease violence in schools, then schools should teach self-control, not self-esteem."

Clearly, schools have to look at a myriad of solutions to discipline and violence problems. One way to begin is to keep a close eye on trends emerging in your schools. Are kids more verbally abusive toward teachers? Do they skip school more often? Vandalize school property more frequently? Asking such questions regularly can help keep you out in front of trends—and keep you from having to react to crisis after it strikes.

School leaders focus on standards and achievement

Listen to today's school board members, and you'll hear a growing sense of urgency in their voices. It's easy to understand why: Standardized test scores have been sluggish this year, and U.S. students turned in a disappointing performance on a major international assessment of math and science. A bumper crop of kids is knocking at the school-

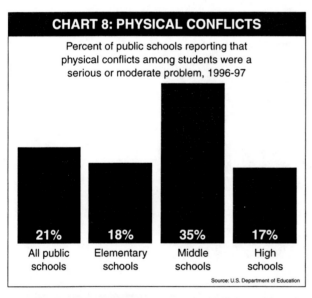

CHART 8: PHYSICAL CONFLICTS

Percent of public schools reporting that physical conflicts among students were a serious or moderate problem, 1996-97

21%	18%	35%	17%
All public schools	Elementary schools	Middle schools	High schools

Source: U.S. Department of Education

CHART 9: DISCIPLINE PROBLEMS AND SCHOOL SIZE

Percent of public school principals reporting these discipline issues were serious or moderate problems, by size of school

DISCIPLINE PROBLEM	1990-91			1996-97		
	under 300	300-999	1,000 or more	under 300	300-999	1,000 or more
Physical conflicts among students	16	25	30	13	22	31
Robbery or theft of items over $10	5	7	16	2	6	12
Vandalism of school property	12	10	24	7	7	20
Student alcohol use	13	7	25	7	6	18
Student drug use	6	3	19	8	7	29
Sale of drugs on school grounds	0	1	4	1	1	11
Verbal abuse of teachers	4	14	17	7	12	26
Physical abuse of teachers	1	1	2	3	1	1
Teacher absenteeism	9	15	26	5	11	25

Source: U.S. Department of Education

CHART 10: DISCIPLINE PROBLEMS AND POVERTY

Percent of public school principals reporting these discipline issues were serious or moderate problems, by percent of students eligible for free- or reduced-price lunch program

DISCIPLINE PROBLEM	1990-91			1996-97		
	under 20%	75% or more	TOTAL	under 20%	75% or more	TOTAL
Physical conflicts among students	15	40	23	13	29	21
Robbery or theft of items over $10	7	8	7	6	6	5
Vandalism of school property	7	25	12	5	17	8
Student alcohol use	13	12	10	11	3	7
Student drug use	7	13	6	12	5	9
Sale of drugs on school grounds	1	0	1	3	1	2
Verbal abuse of teachers	7	24	11	8	13	12
Physical abuse of teachers	0	6	1	0	1	2
Teacher absenteeism	9	33	14	7	15	10

Source: U.S. Department of Education

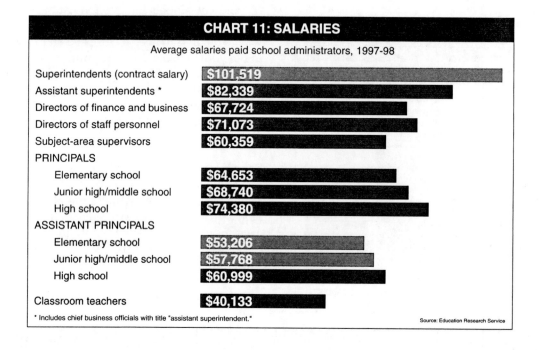

CHART 11: SALARIES

Average salaries paid school administrators, 1997-98

Superintendents (contract salary)	$101,519
Assistant superintendents *	$82,339
Directors of finance and business	$67,724
Directors of staff personnel	$71,073
Subject-area supervisors	$60,359
PRINCIPALS	
Elementary school	$64,653
Junior high/middle school	$68,740
High school	$74,380
ASSISTANT PRINCIPALS	
Elementary school	$53,206
Junior high/middle school	$57,768
High school	$60,999
Classroom teachers	$40,133

* Includes chief business officials with title "assistant superintendent."

Source: Education Research Service

house door, and districts are struggling to find qualified teachers.

It is not surprising, then, that a survey by *The American School Board Journal* and Virginia Tech University found school board members identifying student achievement as their top concern. Board members' concerns about finances and budget issues usually command the top spot on this annual survey's worry list, but this year, that honor went to academics.

Money is still very much on board members' minds, of course: According to the *ASBJ*/Virginia Tech survey, finance and budget issues are their sec-

ond biggest concern, followed by increasing enrollment, curriculum development, facilities, special education, technology, parent involvement, at-risk students, and management issues.

The concerns of local board members mirror those of other elected officials and educators. In a poll of governors, state legislators, chief state school officers, state school board members, and higher education officials conducted by the Education Commission of the States (ECS), researchers identified "standards/assessment/accountability" as the top issue state education leaders are grappling with this year. Finance was number three on the ECS list, behind "charters/choice/vouchers."

Other issues high on the state leaders' priority list, according to the ECS report, include teacher education, technology, school facilities, safety and discipline, and teacher credentials.

WHAT SUPERINTENDENTS SAY

To better understand ways in which districts can raise student achievement, the National School Boards Association (NSBA) conducted a survey of school superintendents from across the country.

The results of the survey—published in NSBA's *Reaching for Excellence: What Local School Districts are Doing to Raise Student Achievement*—identify the biggest roadblock to student achievement as lack of

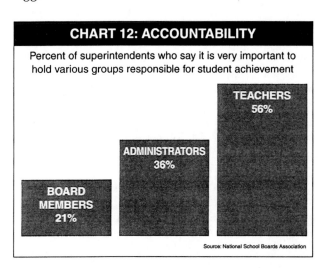

CHART 12: ACCOUNTABILITY

Percent of superintendents who say it is very important to hold various groups responsible for student achievement

TEACHERS 56%

ADMINISTRATORS 36%

BOARD MEMBERS 21%

Source: National School Boards Association

parent involvement. Some 68 percent of the superintendents surveyed say this is a moderate or great problem in their districts. A close second is teachers' resistance to change, cited by 67 percent of superintendents as a moderate or great roadblock to student achievement.

Other significant challenges include lack of funds, state regulations, lack of teacher accountability, negative perceptions of public education, and federal regulations, according to the NSBA survey.

Increasing public demands for accountability are shared by the superintendents NSBA surveyed: More than half say it is very important to hold teachers accountable for student achievement, and more than one-third would hold administrators accountable as well. The call for accountability reaches the boardroom, too: Roughly one-fifth of the superintendents say it is very important that school board members be held accountable for student achievement. (For online information about *Reaching for Excellence, see www.nsba.org.*)

A SHORTAGE OF PRINCIPALS

Raising student achievement and implementing accountability systems will take hard work on the part of a district's leadership team. And the challenge will be even more daunting in the face of a growing shortage of qualified school administrators.

This year, the National Association of Elementary School Principals (NAESP) and the National Association of Secondary School Principals (NASSP) hired the Educational Research Service (ERS) to poll

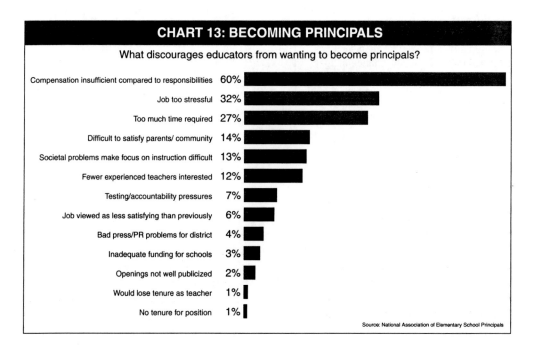

CHART 13: BECOMING PRINCIPALS

What discourages educators from wanting to become principals?

Compensation insufficient compared to responsibilities	60%
Job too stressful	32%
Too much time required	27%
Difficult to satisfy parents/ community	14%
Societal problems make focus on instruction difficult	13%
Fewer experienced teachers interested	12%
Testing/accountability pressures	7%
Job viewed as less satisfying than previously	6%
Bad press/PR problems for district	4%
Inadequate funding for schools	3%
Openings not well publicized	2%
Would lose tenure as teacher	1%
No tenure for position	1%

Source: National Association of Elementary School Principals

CHART 14: SCHOOL BOARD MEMBERS

	1987–88	1997–98
GENDER		
Male	.61.0	54.1
Female	.39.0	39.1
No response	.n/a	6.8
ETHNIC BACKGROUND		
Black	.3.6	6.5
White	.94.4	81.3
Hispanic	.1.5	3.1
American Indian	.0.1	1.0
Asian	.0.2	0.3
Other/No reponse	.0.2	7.8
AGE		
Under 25	.0.1	0.7
25–35	.6.9	3.7
36–40	.19.4	6.1
41–50	.41.8	46.6
51–60	.20.9	24.2
Over 60	.10.9	14.6
No response	.n/a	4.1
INCOME		
Under $20,000	.5.0	0.3
$20,000 - $39,999	.28.0	10.6
$40,000 -$59,999	.32.4	15.3
$60,000 - $79,999	.18.4	21.0
$80,000 - $99,999	.6.3	17.3
More than $100,000	.9.4	28.0
No response	.n/a	7.5
WHERE BOARD MEMBERS LIVE		
Small town	.28.6	24.5
Suburb	.27.6	37.4
Rural area	.25.9	15.7
Urban area	.11.0	7.1
Mixed (combination of reponses checked)	.n/a	13.6
Other	.n/a	0.7
No response	.n/a	0.7

BOARD MEMBERS' WORRIES

1987–88	1997–98
1. Lack of financial support	1. Student achievement
2. Curriculum development	2. School finance/budget
3. State mandates	3. Increasing enrollment
4. Facilities	4. Curriculum development
5. Management/leadership	5. Facilities
6. Collective bargaining	6. Special education
7. Declining enrollment	7. Technology
8. Student use of drugs	8. Parental involvement
9. Parents' lack of interest	9. At-risk students
10. Personnel relations	10. Management issues

Source: The American School Board Journal/Virginia Tech

school district hiring officials about the seriousness of the shortage. The ERS report—"Is There a Shortage of Qualified Candidates for Openings in the Principalship?"—concludes that finding good principals is going to become more and more difficult over the next several years. (To review the report online, see *www.naesp.org/misc/shortage.htm.*)

While the Bureau of Labor Statistics predicts a 10 to 20 percent increase in the need for school administrators through the year 2005, nearly half of the districts ERS surveyed reported a shortage in the pool of candidates for principal positions they were trying to fill last year.

"We've been listening to warnings from state principals associations about serious shortages," says Samuel G. Sava, NAESP's executive director. "The results of this poll point to a national shortage."

Thomas F. Koerner, executive director of NASSP, adds that "schools are going without principals, retired principals are being called back to full-time work, and districts have to go to great lengths to recruit qualified candidates."

According to the ERS report, shortages exist in all types of schools—rural, urban, and suburban—and at all levels, elementary through high school. Even so, the report says, only about a quarter of the districts surveyed have programs to recruit and train teachers to become principals. About half of the districts have formal on-the-job training or mentoring programs for new principals.

Why are teachers shying away from the principalship? The number one reason, the report found, was that would-be school leaders believe that principals don't get paid enough to put up with the responsibilities they must shoulder.

ERS estimates that high school principals earn average annual salaries of $74,380; middle school principals make $68,740; and elementary principals bring in $64,653. The average classroom teacher salary is slightly above $40,100, according to ERS, and superintendents average $101,519.

Salaries aside, there are other reasons for staying out of the principal's chair, according to district hiring officials. Roughly a third say the job is simply too stressful; 27 percent say it requires too much time; and 14 percent say the problem is the difficulty of satisfying parents and the community.

Hiring officials also say teachers don't want to become principals because societal problems make it difficult to focus on learning and because they don't want to have to deal with testing and accountability pressures.

MINORITIES IN THE PRINCIPALSHIP

Minorities—already in short supply in the principalship—will be even more difficult to recruit because of such concerns, the ERS report says. Among the districts surveyed, 64 percent say no qualified minority candidates applied for openings. As it is, only about 16 percent of the nation's public schools

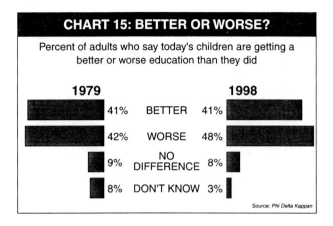

CHART 15: BETTER OR WORSE?

Percent of adults who say today's children are getting a better or worse education than they did

	1979		1998
BETTER	41%		41%
WORSE	42%		48%
NO DIFFERENCE	9%		8%
DON'T KNOW	8%		3%

Source: Phi Delta Kappan

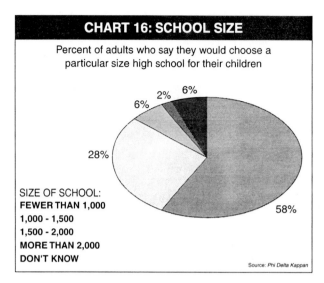

CHART 16: SCHOOL SIZE

Percent of adults who say they would choose a particular size high school for their children

SIZE OF SCHOOL:
FEWER THAN 1,000 — 58%
1,000 - 1,500 — 28%
1,500 - 2,000 — 6%
MORE THAN 2,000 — 2%
DON'T KNOW — 6%

Source: Phi Delta Kappan

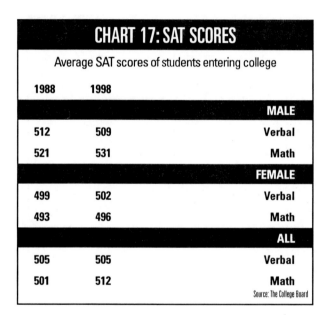

CHART 17: SAT SCORES

Average SAT scores of students entering college

1988	1998	
		MALE
512	509	Verbal
521	531	Math
		FEMALE
499	502	Verbal
493	496	Math
		ALL
505	505	Verbal
501	512	Math

Source: The College Board

have minorities as principals, according to U.S. Department of Education statistics.

Women, on the other hand, are breaking into the administrative ranks in greater numbers than ever before, according to *The Elementary School Principal in 1998*, the report of a study by NAESP. The study, which examines 10-year trends among principals of elementary and middle schools, has been conducted every decade since 1928.

Ten years ago, roughly 20 percent of elementary and middle school principal positions were held by women. Now, about 42 percent of those jobs are held by women. Of those principals with fewer than five years of experience, 65 percent are women.

The authors of the study—James L. Doud of the University of Florida and former NAESP Deputy Director Edward P. Keller—call this a "rather rapid" increase. It suggests, they say, "that, at least for women, employment policies and practices of the past 10 years have proven to be particularly beneficial."

In addition to the gender shift, the NAESP study turned up other illuminating findings. Despite the stress of the job, for example, principals are generally pleased with their relationships with superintendents and school board members. About 85 percent characterize these relationships as excellent or good.

According to the study, the best relationships with superintendents and school boards exist in small towns and rural areas. Also, principals with fewer than five years of experience generally report more positive experiences working with superintendents and school boards.

Here are some other findings of the 10-year study:

- The traditional methods for evaluating teachers are still used by the vast majority of districts. More than 92 percent of principals say they have primary responsibility for evaluating teachers. About 6 percent report sharing this responsibility with teachers or other

administrators in the school, and 2 percent share the responsibility with central office staff.
- Although merit pay is often a hot topic in the media, it is failing to gain popularity across the country. Only 15 percent of principals report they are working under merit pay contracts. That represents a 2 percent drop from 1988.
- The study also expresses serious concerns about leadership in public education. Two of every three principals surveyed say they are worried about the ability of public schools to attract high-quality leaders—both now and in the future.

The study concludes that policymakers at the local, state, and national levels need to take a hard look at whether the authority and salary attached to the principalship balance its work-related stress.

"Today's principal faces more and more issues of increasing complexity and accountability, sometimes without the accompanying authority to balance the extent to which they are held responsible for what happens in their school," the NAESP report says. "The multiplicity and diversity of issues confounds [principals'] ability to find time to do much more than respond to the current crises they face, leaving little time for the type of reflective thinking and planning expected of most organizational leaders."

Indicators of school success—half full, half empty

Are today's kids getting a better education than you did—or a worse one?

The 30th annual Phi Delta Kappa/Gallup Poll of the Public's Attitudes toward Public Schools asked that question this year. What it found was a country almost evenly divided on the answer.

Among the general population, 48 percent say education today is worse, 41 percent say it's better, 8 percent say there's no difference, and 3 percent aren't sure. Parents of children in public school are a bit happier than the general population, with 49 percent saying education is better and 43 percent saying it's worse (6 percent see no difference, and 2 percent aren't able to decide).

Phi Delta Kappa/Gallup researchers first asked this question in 1979. The answers haven't changed much since then, but the slight changes that have occurred aren't encouraging. Since 1979, the percentage of the general population that believes schools have grown worse has increased by 6 percentage points. Among public school parents, the increase is 4 percentage points.

Why do some people see the glass half empty and others see it half full? To a large degree, personal experience drives those opinions. Many of today's parents, for instance, attended smaller schools than their children do. "It is not unusual to hear parents . . . complain that the school their youngsters attend is large and impersonal," the survey says. "The public thinks small is better." More than half (58 percent) of U.S. adults say they would prefer that their child attend a high school with fewer than 1,000 students—and 28 percent prefer a high school enrollment of between 1,000 and 1,500 students. Only 2 percent prefer high schools with more than 2,000 kids.

Parents have other concerns, too, according to the Phi Delta Kappa/Gallup poll—including the push to include students with learning disabilities in regular classrooms. Respondents haven't budged much on that issue since that question was first

---

CHART 18: ACT SCORES

National composite average ACT scores

Year	Score
1989	20.6
1990	20.6
1991	20.6
1992	20.6
1993	20.7
1994	20.8
1995	20.8
1996	20.9
1997	21.0
1998	21.0

Source: The American College Testing Program

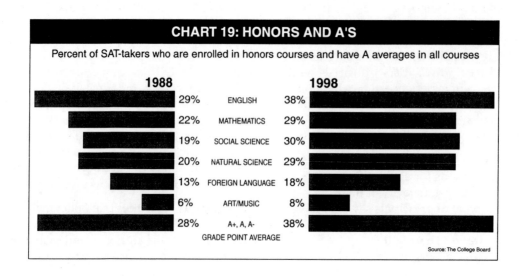

CHART 19: HONORS AND A'S

Percent of SAT-takers who are enrolled in honors courses and have A averages in all courses

	1988		1998
ENGLISH	29%		38%
MATHEMATICS	22%		29%
SOCIAL SCIENCE	19%		30%
NATURAL SCIENCE	20%		29%
FOREIGN LANGUAGE	13%		18%
ART/MUSIC	6%		8%
GRADE POINT AVERAGE (A+, A, A-)	28%		38%

Source: The College Board

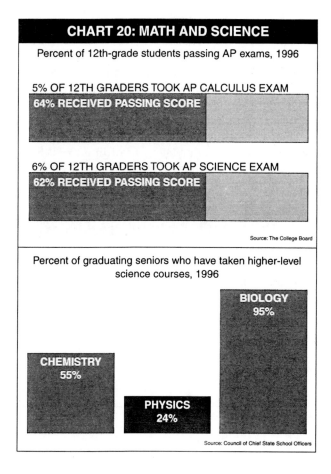

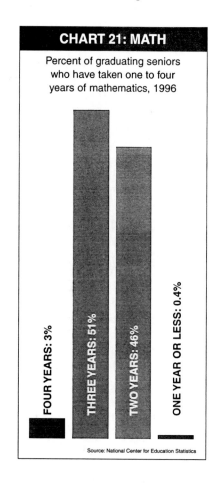

asked in 1995. Sixty-five percent of the general public—and 63 percent of public school parents—believe that students with learning disabilities should not be placed in regular classrooms.

TRENDS IN PERFORMANCE

Among the many factors that influence public opinion is academic performance, and in this area, there were both hopeful signs and troubling trends.

This year's Scholastic Assessment Test results showed reasons for optimism and concern. The average SAT math score (512) is the highest it has been since 1972. But the average verbal score (505) has remained the same for three years—just 6 points above the record lows of 1991 and 1994.

"We can point to increased math and science study as a reason for the current high in the average math score," says Donald M. Stewart, president of the College Board, the organization that administers the SAT. "But the rock-steady verbal scores are more difficult to explain."

Although the verbal scores are above average and rising in many suburban districts, they are 13 points below average for urban kids and 9 points below for rural students.

The good news, Stewart says, is that schools enrolling large populations of African-American and Hispanic students are attempting to better prepare their students for the rigors of higher education. Today, more than 80 percent of college-bound African-American and Hispanic students studied chemistry, 40 percent took physics, 29 to 38 percent had precalculus, and 13 to 19 percent studied calculus.

How academically demanding those courses are is a separate question. And there might be reason to think teachers are handing out more A grades than ever before. This year's SAT results, for instance, showed the possibility of nationwide grade inflation. Since 1988, the percentage of students with grade-point averages of A− to A+ has grown from 28 to 38 percent, while their SAT scores have fallen an average of 12 points on verbal and 3 points on math.

"We don't know why grades are rising," says Stewart. "The trend may reflect positive changes in education, but it may also reflect greater focus on personal qualities instead of academic achievement."

Indeed, there might be serious concerns about grade inflation. But the results of the American College Testing program's achievement test show that students might, in fact, be learning more. This year's average composite score on the ACT, which is taken by nearly 60 percent of the nation's college freshmen, remained at 21.0 (on a scale of 1 to 36).

ACT President Richard L. Ferguson says more students were tested this year than ever before. In fact, about 200,000 more students are taking the test now than in the early 1990s, reaching a record 995,000 for this year's results, compared to 1.2 million who take the SAT.

"Whenever there's a substantial increase in the number of students tested, the additional students must be at least as well-prepared as those tested earlier or the average score will drop," says Ferguson. "So the fact that the national average has remained steady or increased slightly while the tested population has grown is positive.

"This period of steady or increasing scores coincides with nationwide efforts to emphasize the need for more demanding college-preparatory coursework," he says, "and that emphasis seems to be producing results."

Yet just when it seems things are improving, a report is released that challenges your assumptions. This year, the Third International Mathematics and Science Study (TIMSS) issued just such a report. (See "Solving Problems in Math and Science Education," *The American School Board Journal,* July 1998.) Arguably most troubling was the study's finding that American kids lose ground to their international peers as they progress through school.

The survey—which included roughly half a million students in 45 industrialized and semi-industrialized countries—was one of the most comprehensive international comparisons of student achievement ever done. Its results were sobering: According to TIMSS, U.S. fourth-graders performed above the international average in math, but the nation's eighth- and 12th-graders ranked near the bottom. Even the brightest U.S. students scored below advanced students from other countries.

The poor showing by the United States in the upper grades was no mystery, according to TIMSS: The study reported that, while U.S. eighth-graders

1997 STAR ASSESSMENT FINDING:

59%
OF AMERICAN
SCHOOLS ARE
RATED LOW TECH

1997 LOW-TECHNOLOGY SCHOOL:

Limited access to modern computers: The student to computer ratio is 13 to 1, while the average student to multimedia computer ratio is 25 to 1.

Older technology: Only 49% of all computers have processors equal to or greater than an Intel 386. There are over 250 students per CD-ROM drive.

Might have Internet access: 60% of these schools have Internet access.

Limited number of networked computers: 73% of these schools do not have access to a Local Area Network (LAN)

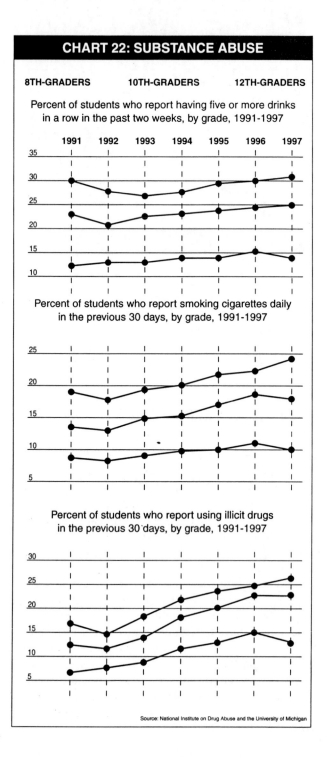

CHART 22: SUBSTANCE ABUSE

Source: National Institute on Drug Abuse and the University of Michigan

are still, by and large, working on arithmetic, their international peers are studying more sophisticated mathematics, such as algebra and geometry.

The TIMSS report sparked widespread debate—including conversations about what makes a good math or science teacher. A report released this year by the U.S. Department of Education sheds some light on the math half of that question. According to "School Policies and Practices Affecting Instruction in Mathematics," in-depth knowledge of complex mathematics isn't vital for elementary school teachers. In fact, elementary teachers who majored in education in college tend to get better results from students than teachers who majored in math.

As mathematics becomes more sophisticated in middle school and high school, though, it becomes more important to have a teacher who majored in math. The highest scoring eighth-graders had teachers who had majored in mathematics—not mathematics education or elementary or middle school education. The same held true for students who achieved the highest in algebra classes.

RAISING EXPECTATIONS

But once you have well-educated teachers in place, how do you raise expectations for all students, particularly in science and math? At the high school level, some educators say, schools need to do a better job encouraging more kids to take Advanced Placement (AP) classes—and giving them the skills to pass the AP tests.

As it is, only 5 percent of the nation's 12th-graders take AP calculus and 6 percent take AP science, according to the College Board. Of those students, 64 percent received passing scores on the math test and 62 percent on the science test. In other words, only a small percentage of all students take and pass AP exams in math and science. Even so, College Board officials say the numbers are increasing, and the population of AP students is growing more diverse. (To review the data online, see *www.collegeboard.org*.)

The College Board reported that more than 635,000 students in roughly half of the nation's high schools took AP placement exams this year. Wade Curry, director of the AP program, says more than 320,000 of those students were seniors with "exceptional academic backgrounds, very high grades, and average SAT verbal and math scores at least 80 points above the national average."

Keep in mind, however, that students who take SAT, ACT, and AP tests represent today's more motivated, college-bound students. Those assessments, therefore, do not present a comprehensive picture of how public school students as a whole are doing.

According to the National Education Goals Panel, the bigger picture has equally mixed results. American students are making some progress in math and science, panel officials report, but falling behind in reading by the time they reach their senior year in high school.

On a positive note, the percentage of fourth-graders who met the panel's standards in mathematics rose from 13 percent in 1990 to 21 percent in 1996. For eighth-graders, the percentage rose from 15 to 24 percent. And for 12th-graders, the passing rate increased from 12 to 16 percent.

Reading achievement, on the other hand, was level for fourth- and eighth-graders alike. But the percentage of 12th-graders meeting the panel's reading standards dropped from 40 percent to 36 percent between 1992 and 1996.

TECHNOLOGY USE

Used wisely, technology can help students become more engaged in their school work and prepare them for a technology-oriented workforce. Yet the majority of America's schools remain seriously unequipped to take advantage of what technology has to offer, according to "School Technology and Readiness Report: From Pillars to Progress," an analysis of school technology programs by the CEO Forum on Education and Technology (*www.ceoforum.org*).

The report defines 59 percent of America's schools as "low technology" schools, which means these schools have limited access to computers, with roughly 25 students for every multimedia computer and 250 students per CD-ROM drive. Furthermore, roughly 40 percent of low-technology schools do not have Internet access, and 73 percent do not have access to a Local Area Network (LAN).

According to the report, 26 percent of American schools are considered "mid technology" schools. These schools have about 15 students per multimedia computer and 90 students per CD-ROM drive; 30 percent of mid-technology schools do not have access to the Internet, and 45 percent are not linked to a LAN.

At "high technology" schools—representing 12 percent of the total—the ratio of students per multimedia computer is 8:1, and there are about 31 students per CD-ROM drive. About 20 percent of these schools do not have Internet access, and 23 percent do not have a LAN.

Only about 3 percent of U.S. schools have achieved the CEO Forum's top designation, "target technology school." These schools have only four students per multimedia computer and nine per CD-ROM drive. Only 7 percent of these schools do not have Internet access, and 16 percent do not have a LAN.

No matter how well-equipped a school might be, making the most of technology as a teaching and learning tool requires intensive staff development. But such training is not widespread: One out of every two teachers cites "lack of time to train" as one of the greatest barriers to integrating the Internet into classroom learning, according to the CEO Forum report. And only 13 percent of all public schools report that technology training is required by the school district or by state teacher certification agencies.

This inattention to professional development is especially troubling in light of a ground-breaking study recently published by the Educational Testing Service (ETS) and *Education Week.*

The study—"Does It Compute? The Relationship Between Educational Technology and Student Achievement in Mathematics"—found that fourth- and eighth-grade students whose teachers had received technology training performed better on standardized mathematics tests than their peers whose teachers had no such training. (To review the study online, see *www.ets.org/research/pic.*)

Harold Wenglinsky, the ETS researcher who conducted the study, also found a link between computer use and improved student achievement—so long as the computers are used to develop rigorous thinking skills through math/learning games in the lower grades and simulations and applications in higher grades. However, if the computers are used simply for drill and practice, the study found, students actually do worse than if there are no computers in the classroom at all. In fact, the study found that students who spent more time on computers in school performed slightly worse than their peers on standardized achievement tests.

In other words, it's not the quantity of computer time that counts—it's the quality of that time.

LIFE AND HEALTH

Concerned for the whole child, educators today need to know about physical and emotional development as well as cognitive development. And when it comes to today's students' lifestyles, there are troubling signs.

To begin with, the percentage of eighth-, 10th-, and 12th-graders who report that they smoke cigarettes daily has increased since 1992, according to the Monitoring the Future Study by the National In-

stitute on Drug Abuse (*www.nida.nih.gov*). Twenty-five percent of 12th-graders say they light up daily, as do 18 percent of 10th-graders and 9 percent of eighth-graders. Prior to 1992, the percentage of 12th-graders who reported smoking daily had been dropping steadily since 1980.

A similar trend is evident in students' alcohol use. The same study found that heavy drinking—that is, drinking five or more alcoholic drinks in a row at least once every two weeks—apparently peaked in 1981, when 41 percent of seniors reported this behavior. The percentage declined to a low of 28 percent in 1993 but rose to 31 percent in 1997.

Equally troubling are the study's findings of significant increases in the use of illegal drugs among high school seniors. Between 1992 and 1997, the percentage of drug users increased from 14 to 26 percent for this group. (Students identifying themselves as drug users use illegal drugs at least once a month.) For eighth- and 10th-graders, drug use increased steadily between 1992 and 1996 but dropped slightly last year, according to the study.

It's not all bad news on the health front, however. For the first time this decade, more than half of high school students are deciding not to have sex, according to the federal Centers for Disease Control and Prevention (CDC; *www.cdc.gov*). And the CDC found that high school kids who are having sex are using condoms at the highest rate reported in the 1990s.

According to the CDC's 1997 survey of 16,262 students ages 15 to 19, 52 percent say they have not had sexual intercourse, compared with 46 percent in 1991. And the report found decreasing levels of promiscuity, too: 16 percent of students report having had sex with four or more partners, a decrease from 19 percent in 1991.

Lloyd Kolbe, director of the CDC's Division of Adolescent and School Health, says the recent declines are the result of better efforts by parents, schools, and health officials to educate kids about safe sex and the risks of teen pregnancy and sexually transmitted diseases. But he encourages parents, schools, and health officials to have higher expectations for what can be accomplished. Says Kolbe: "The worst thing we could do is be lulled into complacency."

State standards under scrutiny

Are your state's academic standards rigorous enough?

That question goes to the heart of a state's commitment to public education. Standards, after all, often drive the discussions about how well a state is educating its children. As Ken Nelson, executive director of the National Education Goals Panel (NEGP), puts it, "Standards are the linchpin of state improvement efforts."

The trouble is, there is little consensus on what makes good academic standards. A 1998 NEGP report found troubling inconsistencies among reviews of state academic standards by three national groups, the American Federation of Teachers (AFT), Council for Basic Education (CBE) and the Fordham Foundation. Each group, the report says, evaluated the standards through a different lens.

Florida, for example, received a grade of A from AFT, C+ from CBE, and D from Fordham, according to the report, while New Jersey was graded D by AFT, A by CBE, and D by Fordham. Kentucky, considered a ground-breaker in the education standards movement, received a C from AFT, a B from CBE, and a D from Fordham.

Only two states, Mississippi and Texas, received exactly the same grades—solid B averages—from all three groups.

The report—*The Reviews of State Content Standards in English Language Arts and Mathematics*— is the first evaluation of how the three groups grade academic standards. (To review the report online, see *www.negp.gov/reports/arch2.htm.*)

CBE, the report says, focused its evaluations on academic rigor, comparing state standards to a CBE-developed framework of what state curricular standards should look like. AFT, on the other hand, rated state standards on how well they offered a "common core curriculum," NEGP says. The "harshest grader" of the three, according to the report, is the Fordham Foundation, which based its evaluation on the clarity of the standards as well as their organization and content.

"By knowing what the different groups were looking for, we can make better judgments about their ratings," says NEGP's Nelson. "States should view these ratings with caution and make sure the reviewer was counting the aspects of these standards that are important to the citizens of their state."

Despite the varying views on quality, the report says, all three groups agree on one thing: Standards need to be improved in most states—something to bear in mind as you consider the state of education in your own state.

THE 'MILLENNIUM GENERATION'

Standards are just one ingredient in the mix, of course. As society and schools grow more complex, it is increasingly important to examine a host of factors in charting the progress of public education in your state.

"The fact that more than 20 percent of children live in poverty, that 26 percent of families are headed by a single parent and that one in six third-graders [has] attended three schools since first grade are things the public does not see," proclaims *Achieving Ambitious Goals*, a report by the Education Commission of the States (*www.ecs.org*). "On the increase is the number of students who cannot speak English when they enter school. . . . All these factors add up to a remarkably complex and challenging environment for education."

Notably challenging is the current enrollment boom, and there is no immediate end in sight. This year, the population of children in the United States surpassed the records set when the baby boomers were coming of age—an increase from 69.9 million in 1966 to 70.2 million today.

These kids are making news demographically as well as numerically: According to the U.S. Census Bureau, there are now more Hispanic children than African-American children in the United States, making Hispanics the largest minority group among kids 18 or younger.

The new group of students—dubbed the Millennium Generation—is expected by many to make a real impact on society as well as schools. "This is a revolution in waiting," Gerald Celente, director of the Trends Research Institute in Rhinebeck, N.Y., told the *Washington Post*. "This generation will redefine society in the 21st century just as baby boomers shaped social, political, and economic changes in the last half of the 20th century."

How the Millennium Generation reshapes the cultural landscape will depend largely on how well the kids of this generation do in school.

For a glimpse of how students—and schools— are doing in your state, see the charts on the following pages.

EDUCATION VITAL SIGNS

CHART 22: NORTHEAST

Finances	Conn.	Del.	Maine	Mass.	N.H.	N.J.	N.Y.	Pa.	R.I.	Vt.
Per-pupil expenditures										
1992-93	$8,188	$6,420	$6,162	$6,505	$5,619	$9,712	$8,525	$7,748	$6,649	$7,172
1997-98	$9,218	$8,576	$7,107	$7,861	$6,556	$10,427	$9,812	$7,752	$8,429	$7,925
Average teacher salaries										
1992-93	$48,343	$36,217	$30,250	$38,223	$33,931	$42,680	$44,999	$41,215	$37,933	$34,824
1997-98	$50,730	$42,439	$34,349	$43,930	$36,640	$50,442	$49,034	$47,650	$44,300	$36,299
Funding percentages 1997-98										
Federal	4.6	7.1	6.3	5.1	3.1	3.1	6.5	5.5	5.2	4.8
State	40.4	67.3	45.9	36.1	6.1	37.7	40.3	41.2	42.4	28.0
Local	55.0	25.6	47.8	58.8	90.8	59.2	53.2	53.3	52.4	67.2
Capital outlay 1997-98 (in thousands)	$246,060	$62,703	$58,970	$200,768	$73,701	$375,271	$1,825,048	$184,227	$13,973	$59,900
State budget allocations for education (percent of total state budget)	13.4	23.3	14.3	14.7	7.4	22.7	18.9	19.9	15.8	17.9
Per-capita income 1997	$36,263	$29,022	$22,078	$31,524	$28,047	$32,654	$30,752	$26,058	$25,760	$23,401
Classroom characteristics										
High school completion rates**	96.1	88.8	91.8	92.0	87.7	87.0	90.9	89.6	87.5	87.0
Students per multimedia computer	11.3	9.4	10.8	9.9	9.3	7.4	15.9	12.8	12.8	9.5
Pupil/teacher ratios										
1991-92	14.0	16.8	14.0	15.1	15.5	13.8	15.4	16.8	14.6	13.6
1996-97	14.4	16.6	13.7	14.5	15.6	13.6	15.4	17.0	14.2	13.7
Enrollment										
Fall, 1992-93										
Elementary	356,908	59,452	156,057	628,321	124,112	799,031	1,509,076	958,123	85,986	59,252
Secondary	132,761	44,869	55,796	231,226	57,135	331,529	1,180,610	759,490	57,057	39,306
Total	489,669	104,321	211,853	859,547	181,247	1,130,560	2,689,686	1,717,613	143,043	98,558
Fall, 1997-98										
Elementary	390,833	60,782	151,879	701,590	134,306	885,644	1,584,000	989,980	88,719	58,065
Secondary	145,263	51,178	56,879	246,746	65,835	355,384	1,256,000	822,900	64,459	47,919
Total	536,096	111,960	208,758	948,336	200,141	1,241,028	2,840,000	1,812,880	153,178	105,984
% Minority enrollment										
Fall, 1996										
Black	13.6	29.9	0.9	8.4	1.0	not	20.3	14.2	7.3	0.8
Hispanic	11.8	4.3	0.4	9.6	1.3	available	17.6	3.7	10.7	0.4
Asian or Pacific Islander	2.5	1.8	0.9	4.0	1.1		5.2	1.8	3.3	1.0
American Indian/Alaskan Native	0.3	0.2	0.6	0.2	0.2		0.6	0.1	0.5	0.6
Total % Minority	28.2	36.2	2.8	22.2	3.6		43.7	19.8	21.8	2.8
% Special education enrollment										
1995-96	12.7	12.0	12.3	14.9	11.5	14.3	11.4	10.0	14.4	9.0
Mean SAT Scores										
1988 Verbal	513	510	508	508	523	500	497	502	508	514
Math	498	493	493	499	511	495	495	489	496	499
1998 Verbal	510	501	504	508	523	497	495	497	501	508
Math	509	493	501	508	520	508	503	495	495	504
% of graduates taking SAT—1998	80	70	68	77	74	79	76	71	72	71

** **High school completion rate:** Percentage of 18 to 24-year-olds who have completed high school.

Per-pupil expenditures, average teacher salaries, funding percentages, and enrollment: National Education Association, *Estimates of School Statistics, 1997-98*; revised 1992-93 figures from 1993-94 edition.
Per-capita income: U.S. Department of Commerce, Bureau of Economic Analysis
Capital outlay: National Education Association, *Estimates of School Statistics, 1997-98*
Pupil/teacher ratios, minority enrollment: U.S. Department of Education, National Center for Education Statistics
High school completion rate: U.S. Department of Commerce, Bureau of the Census
State budget allocations: National Association of State Budget Officers
Special education enrollment: U.S. Department of Education
SAT scores and percentage of graduates taking test: The College Board
Students per multimedia computer: Quality Education Data (QED)

EDUCATION VITAL SIGNS

CHART 23: SOUTHEAST

Finances	D.C.	Fla.	Ga.	Md.	N.C.	S.C.	Va.	W.Va.
Per-pupil expenditures								
1992-93	$7,998	$5,303	$4,544	$6,447	$4,810	$4,573	$5,517	$5,689
1997-98	$8,069	$6,137	$6,177	$7,375	$5,830	$5,555	$6,569	$7,110
Average teacher salaries								
1992-93	$38,702	$31,172	$30,051	$38,753	$29,315	$29,224	$32,306	$30,301
1997-98	$46,350	$34,475	$37,378	$41,739	$33,315	$33,608	$36,654	$33,398
Funding percentages								
1997-98								
Federal	14.8	7.3	6.6	5.7	7.1	7.5	5.4	8.6
State	—	48.5	52.3	40.3	65.8	52.4	37.1	62.8
Local	85.2	44.3	41.2	54.0	27.1	40.1	57.5	28.6
Capital outlay								
1997-98 (in thousands)	$12,663	$2,333,817	$1,508,193	$598,320	$789,664	$453,900	$504,411	$100,631
State budget allocations for education								
(percent of total state budget)	—	18.8	25.3	17.7	25.1	17.3	17.8	31.2
Per-capita income 1997	$35,852	$25,255	$24,061	$28,969	$23,345	$20,755	$26,438	18,957
Classroom characteristics								
High school completion rates**	87.8	80.1	81.3	93.4	87.2	88.4	86.6	89.3
Students per								
multimedia computer	38.6	19.8	14.7	12.0	8.1	11.1	7.0	14.7
Pupil/teacher ratios								
1991-92	12.7	17.6	18.5	16.9	16.8	16.9	15.7	15.3
1996-97	14.9	18.6	17.0	17.1	16.1	15.7	14.7	14.6
Enrollment								
Fall, 1992-93								
Elementary	49,903	1,175,761	891,952	445,631	804,325	459,829	670,830	191,420
Secondary	31,034	804,172	315,638	306,219	302,551	173,159	361,228	126,299
Total	80,937	1,979,933	1,207,590	751,850	1,106,876	632,988	1,032,058	317,719
Fall, 1997-98								
Elementary	52,308	1,323,893	696,091	479,123	897,760	463,568	712,196	186,690
Secondary	27,130	967,952	679,889	351,621	328,533	186,590	399,396	114,047
Total	79,438	2,291,845	1,375,980	830,744	1,226,293	650,158	1,111,592	300,737
% Minority enrollment								
Fall, 1996								
Black	87.3	25.4	37.6	35.6	30.8	42.2	25.5	4.0
Hispanic	7.2	15.9	2.6	3.5	2.3	0.8	3.3	0.5
Asian or Pacific Islander	1.4	1.8	1.7	3.9	1.5	0.8	3.4	0.3
American Indian/Alaskan Native	0.1	0.2	0.1	0.3	1.5	0.2	0.2	0.1
Total % Minority	96.0	43.3	42.0	43.3	36.1	44.0	32.4	4.9
% Special education enrollment								
1995-96	7.6	12.5	8.9	10.9	10.8	11.5	11.3	12.8
Mean SAT Scores								
1988 Verbal	479	499	480	509	478	477	507	528
Math	461	495	473	501	470	468	498	519
1998 Verbal	488	500	486	506	490	478	507	525
Math	476	501	482	508	492	473	499	513
% of graduates taking SAT—1998	83	52	64	65	62	61	66	18

** **High school completion rate:** Percentage of 18 to 24-year-olds who have completed high school.

Per-pupil expenditures, average teacher salaries, funding percentages, and enrollment: National Education Association, *Estimates of School Statistics, 1997-98*; revised 1992-93 figures from 1993-94 edition.
Per-capita income: U.S. Department of Commerce, Bureau of Economic Analysis
Capital outlay: National Education Association, *Estimates of School Statistics, 1997-98*
Pupil/teacher ratios, minority enrollment: U.S. Department of Education, National Center for Education Statistics
High school completion rate: U.S. Department of Commerce, Bureau of the Census
State budget allocations: National Association of State Budget Officers
Special education enrollment: U.S. Department of Education
SAT scores and percentage of graduates taking test: The College Board
Students per multimedia computer: Quality Education Data (QED)

EDUCATION VITAL SIGNS

CHART 24: NORTHCENTRAL

Finances	III.	Ind.	Iowa	Ky.	Mich.	Minn.	Mo.	Neb.	Ohio	Wis.
Per-pupil expenditures										
1992-93	$5,191	$5,641	$5,297	$4,942	$6,402	$5,572	$4,487	$4,950	$5,963	$6,500
1997-98	$6,363	$6,642	$5,713	$6,283	$7,673	$6,727	$5,597	$5,846	$6,539	$7,272
Average teacher salaries										
1992-93	$38,632	$35,066	$30,130	$31,115	$43,604	$35,093	$29,382	$28,768	$34,500	$35,926
1997-98	$43,873	$39,682	$34,040	$34,525	$49,277	$39,106	$33,975	$32,668	$38,977	$39,899
Funding percentages										
1997-98										
Federal	7.0	4.9	3.7	7.5	6.6	3.9	5.9	3.9	6.8	4.3
State	26.7	53.6	54.1	66.0	81.8	57.3	40.0	37.2	43.3	55.0
Local	66.3	41.4	42.2	26.5	11.6	38.8	54.1	59.0	50.0	40.7
Capital outlay										
1997-98 (in thousands)	$865,056	$663,710	$288,859	$164,755	$850,572	$1,042,044	$630,629	$219,016	$1,414,074	$865,892
State budget allocations for education										
(percent of total state budget)	18.3	24.1	21.4	26.4	30.8	25.1	25.4	16.3	17.1	24.5
Per-capita income 1997	$28,202	$23,604	$23,102	$20,657	$25,560	$26,797	$24,001	$23,803	$24,661	$24,475
Classroom characteristics										
High school completion rates**	89.3	88.3	91.6	82.2	89.1	95.3	88.0	93.3	87.7	92.5
Students per										
multimedia computer	10.1	8.6	13.9	14.2	8.8	7.3	11.9	10.8	12.7	6.7
Pupil/teacher ratios										
1991-92	16.8	17.6	15.7	17.2	19.2	17.2	16.0	14.7	17.3	15.7
1996-97	17.0	17.3	16.4	16.7	19.1	17.6	16.1	14.5	17.0	16.1
Enrollment										
Fall, 1992-93										
Elementary	1,343,281	678,247	270,903	441,897	1,163,212	446,666	604,266	169,633	1,177,082	588,162
Secondary	530,286	281,508	223,319	198,580	439,345	346,141	236,143	111,734	625,921	241,253
Total	1,873,567	959,755	494,222	640,477	1,602,557	792,807	840,409	281,367	1,803,003	829,415
Fall, 1997-98										
Elementary	1,438,010	541,483	263,251	431,574	1,209,652	458,727	634,302	155,264	1,195,410	607,743
Secondary	567,945	444,868	237,817	202,127	487,105	401,100	258,939	136,321	651,020	279,429
Total	2,005,955	986,351	501,068	633,701	1,696,757	859,827	893,241	291,585	1,846,430	887,172
% Minority enrollment										
Fall, 1996										
Black	21.2	11.2	3.4	9.9	، 18.9	5.2	18.5	6.0	15.4	9.6
Hispanic	12.8	2.4	2.4	0.5	2.8	2.2	1.1	4.9	1.4	3.5
Asian or Pacific Islander	3.1	0.8	1.6	0.6	1.5	4.1	1.0	1.3	1.0	2.9
American Indian/Alaskan Native	0.1	0.2	0.5	0.1	1.0	1.9	0.3	1.4	0.1	1.3
Total % Minority	37.2	14.6	7.9	11.1	24.2	13.4	20.9	13.6	17.9	17.3
% Special education enrollment										
1995-96	11.5	11.8	11.4	10.2	9.8	10.0	12.3	11.9	10.7	10.1
Mean SAT Scores										
1988 Verbal	540	490	587	551	532	546	547	562	529	549
Math	540	486	588	535	533	549	539	561	521	551
1998 Verbal	564	497	593	547	558	585	570	565	536	581
Math	581	500	601	550	569	598	573	571	540	594
% of graduates taking SAT—1998	13	59	5	13	11	9	8	8	24	7

** **High school completion rate:** Percentage of 18 to 24-year-olds who have completed high school.

Per-pupil expenditures, average teacher salaries, funding percentages, and enrollment: National Education Association, *Estimates of School Statistics, 1997-98*; revised 1992-93 figures from 1993-94 edition.
Per-capita income: U.S. Department of Commerce, Bureau of Economic Analysis
Capital outlay: National Education Association, *Estimates of School Statistics, 1997-98*
Pupil/teacher ratios, minority enrollment: U.S. Department of Education, National Center for Education Statistics
High school completion rate: U.S. Department of Commerce, Bureau of the Census
State budget allocations: National Association of State Budget Officers
Special education enrollment: U.S. Department of Education
SAT scores and percentage of graduates taking test: The College Board
Students per multimedia computer: Quality Education Data (QED)

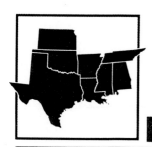

EDUCATION VITAL SIGNS

CHART 25: SOUTHCENTRAL

Finances	Ala.	Ark.	Kan.	La.	Miss.	Okla.	Tenn.	Texas
Per-pupil expenditures								
1992-93	$3,779	$3,838	$5,459	$4,352	$3,390	$4,085	$4,033	$4,933
1997-98	$5,110	$5,222	$6,348	$5,194	$4,732	$4,634	$5,591	$6,291
Average teacher salaries								
1992-93	$26,953	$27,433	$32,863	$27,617	$24,367	$25,918	$28,960	$29,935
1997-98	$32,818	$30,578	$36,811	$29,650	$29,547	$30,606	$35,340	$33,648
Funding percentages								
1997-98								
Federal	9.4	8.3	5.4	12.0	13.0	9.7	7.9	7.7
State	64.5	66.1	58.7	49.8	56.8	62.5	51.5	43.0
Local	26.0	25.6	35.9	38.2	30.2	27.8	40.6	49.4
Capital outlay								
1997-98 (in thousands)	$576,227	$252,498	$202,552	$273,113	$283,263	$330,774	$99,909	$2,836,933
State budget allocations for education (percent of total state budget)	25.6	20.5	29.4	19.2	21.5	26.3	17.4	29.5
Per-capita income 1997	$20,842	$19,585	$24,379	$20,680	$18,272	$20,555	$23,018	$23,656
Classroom characteristics								
High school completion rates**	86.8	86.7	91.6	82.2	83.9	87.0	83.3	79.3
Students per								
multimedia computer	14.6	20.0	12.0	11.5	13.9	16.5	12.3	8.9
Pupil/teacher ratios								
1991-92	17.8	17.0	16.2	16.6	17.9	15.6	19.4	15.8
1996-97	16.6	17.1	15.1	16.6	17.2	15.7	16.5	15.5
Enrollment								
Fall, 1992-93								
Elementary	404,841	242,943	306,526	579,778	318,462	346,800	612,196	2,086,088
Secondary	322,059	197,739	145,010	202,708	185,767	250,300	233,432	1,449,654
Total	726,900	440,682	451,536	782,486	504,229	597,100	845,628	3,535,742
Fall, 1997-98								
Elementary	413,475	251,509	315,148	549,238	326,877	345,190	652,744	2,238,725
Secondary	325,846	207,252	153,596	234,135	177,915	282,570	248,971	1,654,144
Total	739,321	458,761	468,744	783,373	504,792	627,760	901,715	3,892,869
% Minority enrollment								
Fall, 1996								
Black	36.4	23.5	8.6	46.4	51.0	10.5	23.4	14.3
Hispanic	0.7	1.8	6.5	1.2	0.4	4.3	0.9	37.4
Asian or Pacific Islander	0.6	0.7	1.9	1.3	0.6	1.3	1.0	2.4
American Indian/Alaskan Native	0.7	0.4	1.1	0.6	0.2	15.1	0.1	0.3
Total % Minority	38.4	26.4	18.1	49.5	52.2	31.2	25.4	54.4
% Special education enrollment								
1995-96	11.5	9.7	9.8	9.8	11.4	10.3	12.5	10.3
Mean SAT Scores								
1988 Verbal	554	554	568	551	557	558	560	494
Math	540	536	557	533	539	542	543	490
1998 Verbal	562	568	582	562	562	568	564	494
Math	558	555	585	558	549	564	557	501
% of graduates taking SAT—1998	8	6	9	8	4	8	13	51

** **High school completion rate:** Percentage of 18 to 24-year-olds who have completed high school.

Per-pupil expenditures, average teacher salaries, funding percentages, and enrollment: National Education Association, *Estimates of School Statistics, 1997-98*; revised 1992-93 figures from 1993-94 edition.
Per-capita income: U.S. Department of Commerce, Bureau of Economic Analysis
Capital outlay: National Education Association, *Estimates of School Statistics, 1997-98*
Pupil/teacher ratios, minority enrollment: U.S. Department of Education, National Center for Education Statistics
High school completion rate: U.S. Department of Commerce, Bureau of the Census
State budget allocations: National Association of State Budget Officers
Special education enrollment: U.S. Department of Education
SAT scores and percentage of graduates taking test: The College Board
Students per multimedia computer: Quality Education Data (QED)

EDUCATION VITAL SIGNS

CHART 26: NORTHWEST

Finances	Alaska	Idaho	Mont.	N.D.	Ore.	S.D.	Wash.	Wyo
Per-pupil expenditures								
1992-93	$9,290	$4,025	$5,348	$4,404	$6,240	$4,359	$5,528	$5,932
1997-98	$10,650	$4,973	$6,237	$4,978	$6,719	$5,166	$6,488	$6,312
Average teacher salaries								
1992-93	$46,019	$27,011	$27,617	$25,211	$35,880	$24,289	$35,759	$30,080
1997-98	$51,738	$32,775	$30,617	$28,230	$42,150	$27,341	$38,788	$32,022
Funding percentages								
1997-98								
Federal	12.6	6.5	9.9	11.6	7.1	9.3	6.9	6.8
State	63.6	64.7	48.6	41.7	61.7	31.7	68.2	48.0
Local	23.9	28.8	41.5	46.6	31.2	58.9	24.8	45.2
Capital outlay								
1997-98 (in thousands)	$37,393	$156,429	$64,467	$30,786	$402,000	$91,837	$1,776,387	$62,650
State budget allocations for education								
(percent of total state budget)	20.2	28.7	22.5	17.0	16.7	17.5	25.9	21.5
Per-capita income 1997	$26,305	$20,478	$20,046	$20,271	$24,393	$21,447	$26,718	$22,648
Classroom characteristics								
High school completion rates**	87.8	85.2	89.8	93.0	81.1	89.6	86.8	89.4
Students per								
multimedia computer	6.8	9.7	11.3	9.5	8.2	5.5	8.6	6.1
Pupil/teacher ratios								
1991-92	16.7	19.4	15.8	15.3	18.6	14.8	20.2	15.6
1996-97	17.5	18.8	16.0	15.2	20.1	14.9	20.2	14.7
Enrollment								
Fall, 1992-93								
Elementary	91,640	126,562	115,233	84,569	336,390	97,627	513,869	55,448
Secondary	30,847	105,106	44,758	34,165	172,960	36,048	384,134	44,865
Total	122,487	231,668	159,991	118,734	509,350	133,675	898,003	100,313
Fall, 1997-98								
Elementary	94,981	130,753	112,025	78,868	370,220	93,331	540,032	49,106
Secondary	36,659	118,743	50,433	37,945	170,345	42,715	453,346	47,398
Total	131,640	249,496	162,458	116,813	540,565	136,046	993,378	96,504
% Minority enrollment								
Fall, 1996								
Black	4.7	0.7	0.6	0.9	2.6	1.0	4.8	1.2
Hispanic	2.9	8.9	1.5	1.1	7.4	0.8	8.3	6.2
Asian or Pacific Islander	4.5	1.2	0.8	0.7	3.4	0.8	6.7	0.8
American Indian/Alaskan Native	24.8	1.3	9.9	8.1	2.0	13.6	2.7	2.8
Total % Minority	36.9	12.1	12.8	10.8	15.4	16.2	22.5	11.0
% Special education enrollment								
1995-96	11.9	8.2	9.6	8.9	10.7	8.8	9.4	10.5
Mean SAT Scores								
1988 Verbal	518	543	547	572	517	585	525	550
Math	501	523	547	569	507	573	517	545
1998 Verbal	521	545	543	590	528	584	524	548
Math	520	544	546	599	528	581	526	546
% of graduates taking SAT—1998	52	16	24	5	53	5	53	10

** **High school completion rate:** Percentage of 18 to 24-year-olds who have completed high school.

Per-pupil expenditures, average teacher salaries, funding percentages, and enrollment: National Education Association, *Estimates of School Statistics, 1997-98*; revised 1992-93 figures from 1993-94 edition.
Per-capita income: U.S. Department of Commerce, Bureau of Economic Analysis
Capital outlay: National Education Association, *Estimates of School Statistics, 1997-98*
Pupil/teacher ratios, minority enrollment: U.S. Department of Education, National Center for Education Statistics
High school completion rate: U.S. Department of Commerce, Bureau of the Census
State budget allocations: National Association of State Budget Officers
Special education enrollment: U.S. Department of Education
SAT scores and percentage of graduates taking test: The College Board
Students per multimedia computer: Quality Education Data (QED)

EDUCATION VITAL SIGNS

CHART 27: SOUTHWEST & TOTAL

Finances	Ariz.	Calif.	Colo.	Hawaii	Nev.	N.M.	Utah	U.S. Total
Per-pupil expenditures								
1992-93	$4,140	$4,608	$4,969	$5,806	$4,976	$4,643	$3,218	$5,574
1997-98	$4,937	$5,345	$5,704	$6,127	$5,601	$5,865	$3,900	$6,548
Average teacher salaries								
1992-93	$31,352	$40,035	$33,541	$36,470	$34,119	$26,532	$27,239	$35,027
1997-98	$33,850	$43,725	$37,052	$38,377	$37,093	$30,152	$32,950	$39,385
Funding percentages								
1997-98								
Federal	7.8	8.9	5.6	7.5	4.2	8.8	6.3	6.8
State	48.1	56.8	44.5	90.3	31.4	70.4	62.6	49.4
Local	44.1	34.3	49.9	2.3	64.4	20.8	31.1	43.8
Capital outlay								
1997-98 (in thousands)	$756,308	$2,522,056	$554,486	$155,064	$408,243	$535,739	$315,906	$29,131,847
State budget allocations for education								
(percent of total state budget)	17.9	23.0	21.2	14.0	N/A	21.1	34.2	21.7
Per-capita income 1997	$22,364	$26,570	$27,051	$26,034	$26,791	$19,587	$20,432	$25,598
Classroom characteristics								
High school completion rates**	85.8	78.6	87.9	92.6	81.4	82.7	91.3	85.8
Students per								
multimedia computer	17.4	34.3	10.0	9.6	9.2	8.3	10.7	11.7
Pupil/teacher ratios								
1991-92	19.3	22.8	17.9	18.5	18.6	17.6	24.9	17.3
1996-97	19.7	22.9	18.5	17.7	19.1	16.7	24.4	17.1
Enrollment								
Fall, 1992-93								
Elementary	505,977	3,784,861	357,639	103,358	131,315	169,960	326,863	28,008,263
Secondary	177,154	1,410,916	254,996	73,565	91,531	124,701	134,396	14,651,120
Total	683,131	5,195,777	612,635	176,923	222,846	294,661	461,259	42,659,383
Fall, 1997-98								
Elementary	602,579	4,107,161	387,855	108,197	173,962	182,757	323,495	29,241,071
Secondary	219,746	1,579,990	299,312	81,084	122,659	147,585	155,656	16,682,437
Total	822,325	5,687,151	687,167	189,281	296,621	330,342	479,151	45,923,508
% Minority enrollment								
Fall, 1996								
Black	4.3	8.7	5.5	3.3	9.6	2.4	0.7	16.9
Hispanic	30.1	39.7	18.8	4.9	18.8	47.7	6.0	14.0
Asian or Pacific Islander	1.8	11.2	2.6	66.4	4.6	1.0	2.4	3.8
American Indian/Alaskan Native	7.2	0.9	1.1	0.4	1.9	10.2	1.5	1.1
Total % Minority	43.4	60.5	28.0	75.0	34.9	61.3	10.6	35.8
% Special education enrollment								
1995-96	8.5	9.0	9.1	7.6	9.1	12.6	9.7	10.6
Mean SAT Scores								
1988 Verbal	531	500	537	484	517	553	572	505
Math	523	508	532	505	510	543	553	501
1998 Verbal	525	497	537	483	510	554	572	505
Math	528	516	542	513	513	551	570	512
% of graduates taking SAT—1998	32	47	31	55	33	12	4	43

** **High school completion rate:** Percentage of 18 to 24-year-olds who have completed high school.

Per-pupil expenditures, average teacher salaries, funding percentages, and enrollment: National Education Association, *Estimates of School Statistics, 1997-98*; revised 1992-93 figures from 1993-94 edition.
Per-capita income: U.S. Department of Commerce, Bureau of Economic Analysis
Capital outlay: National Education Association, *Estimates of School Statistics, 1997-98*
Pupil/teacher ratios, minority enrollment: U.S. Department of Education, National Center for Education Statistics
High school completion rate: U.S. Department of Commerce, Bureau of the Census
State budget allocations: National Association of State Budget Officers
Special education enrollment: U.S. Department of Education
SAT scores and percentage of graduates taking test: The College Board
Students per multimedia computer: Quality Education Data (QED)

By The Numbers

FACTS AND FIGURES ABOUT CHILDREN AND SCHOOLS

Woman's Work.
73 percent of public school teachers are women.

No Diploma. 11.1 percent of young people 16 to 24 years old are high school dropouts.

Bottom Line. Total education expenditures—$560 billion in 1996-97—account for about 7.4 percent of the U. S. gross national product.
Source: *Mini-Digest of Education Statistics*, 1997, National Center for Education Statistics, 1998.

Troubled Kids. The number of students with serious emotional disturbance who were mainstreamed into regular classes nearly tripled in a decade, increasing from 32,388 in 1985-86 to 93,335 in 1994-95.
Source: *Nineteenth Annual Report to Congress on the Implementation of IDEA*, U.S. Department of Education, 1997.

Birds and Bees. 89 percent of public school parents say schools should include sex education in their instructional program.
Source: "The 30th Annual Phi Delta Kappa/Gallup Poll of the Public's Attitudes toward the Public Schools," *Phi Delta Kappan*, September 1998.

Public vs. Private, I. Public schools have more minority employees than private schools—an average of 12 percent of public school teachers and 16 percent of principals, vs. 9 percent of private school teachers and 8 percent of principals.

Public vs. Private II. Public schools also have more racially and ethnically diverse student populations—28 percent of public school students in grades 1-12, vs. 17 percent of private school students.
Source: *Public and Private Schools: How Do They Differ?* National Center for Education Statistics, 1997.

Mother Tongue. 1.25 million school-age children—some 5 percent of the nation's total enrollment—speak a language other than English at home.

Family Life. 68 percent of U.S. children lived with two parents in 1997, down from 77 percent in 1980.

Starting Early. 45 percent of young children ages 3 to 4 attended preschool in 1996, up from 30 percent in 1980.
Source: *American's Children: Key National Indicators of Well-Being*, Federal Interagency Forum on Child and Family Statistics, 1998.

Call Me 'Doctor'. 44,700 people earned doctorates in 1997, up from 34,041 a decade earlier; by 2008, the number of doctor's degrees conferred in the United States is expected to rise to 49,100.
Source: *Projections of Education to Statistics 2008*, National Center for the Statistics, 1998.

Behind Bars. The juvenile violent crime arrest rate increased from 305 arrests per 100,000 youths ages 10 to 17 in 1985 to 507 in 1995.

Dying Young. 78 percent of all teen deaths in 1995 were due to accident, homicide, or suicide, with accidents accounting for more than twice as many as any other source.
Source: *Kids Count 1998*, The Annie E. Casey Foundation, 1998.

The Foundations
of Public Education

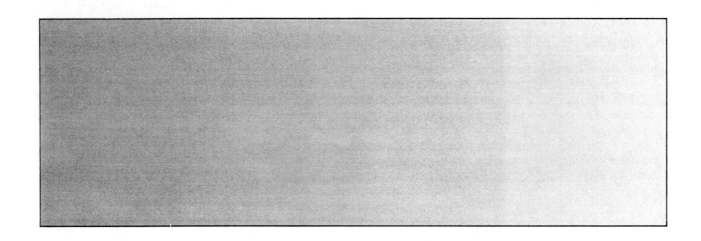

Overview

The U.S. Constitution does not identify education as a responsibility of the federal government. In fact, it does not mention education at all. Thus the power to determine educational policy and practice is reserved to the people and to the governments of the states. In theory, and within the rights assured to individuals by the U.S. Constitution, each state's policy regarding both public and private education can be unique to that state and therefore unlike that of any other state. In practice, however, there are more similarities than differences among the states in what and how they provide for the education of their respective citizens.

The focus of this section is on the foundations of public education. The chapters that follow provide insights into how education nationally and in Texas has developed into what it is today. In many ways the system of education in Texas has evolved somewhat differently from the systems of other states. Yet the development of education in Texas has followed a pattern in common with many other states in the country.

In Chapter 12 the multicultural-multiethnic nature of the Texas school population is explored. Although all states have multicultural-multiethnic citizens, the large minority population in Texas has played an important role in the development of education in this state. The influence of school-age children who are predominantly Spanish-speaking, the growing number of other children with non-English or limited English speaking proficiency, and the issue of free public education for the children of illegal immigrants greatly influenced the unique development of education in Texas. Minority students now account for 55 percent of the total Texas school population, which makes Texas a "majority minority" state.

According to Texas Education Agency data, the growth in student population can be attributed only to the increase in minority students. In 1989–1990 minority students increased by 46,480 while the number of white students decreased by 1,204. In 1986–1987 white students declined 9,687, and in 1987–1988 they declined 3,604. Hispanic students are increasing at a 3.8 percent rate and now constitute 37.9 percent of the student population. African-American students represent 14.4 percent of the total population, with a less than 1 percent growth rate. Asian and American Indian students make up 2.7 percent with a 2.1 percent growth rate.

Nationwide, the 1990 U.S. Census Bureau report revealed that the nature of the 9.8 percent growth in the U.S. population was more significant than the number. According to the Census Bureau figures, the "racial complexion" of the U.S. population changed more dramatically from 1980 to 1990 than during any other decade of the 20th century (see Table 1). In 1990, nearly one in four Americans had African, Asian, Hispanic, or American Indian ancestors; 10 years earlier that number was one in five.

Demographer Harold Hodgkinson describes the "spectacular changes that have occurred in the nature of the children who come to school" in the 1990s in Chapter 13. He estimates that at least one-third of these children are at risk of school failure even before they enter kindergarten.

Chapter 14 identifies and summarizes the major events in American history that have influenced the development of schooling in America. Education since 1960, the theme of Chapter 15, reviews the major developments of that era and places the present educational scene in relatively recent historical perspective. Chapter 16 offers status reports of the public schools.

No study of the development of education would be complete without a "report card" from the consumers and financial supporters of our present-day schools. The Annual Gallup/Phi Delta Kappa poll has provided the results of a national survey administered each year for the past 30 years. This poll has become the authority on the public's perception of its schools, not only within the education profession but also in every media. The public's perceptions of the effectiveness of its public schools usually is based upon what people see on television or read about in the newspapers. They are more positive about their neighborhood school or schools but at times far from confident about schools outside their neighborhoods and districts.

Gerald Bracey, a research psychologist, believes that the national media have focused on the weaknesses of the American educational system, particularly the nation's public schools. He believes that the self-fulfilling prophecy of poor schools should be challenged and that the dozens of studies showing the comparative status of American schools and students among other nations of the world has been portrayed by the media in the most negative of lights. In his *Fourth Bracey Report on the Condition of Public Education*, he continues his "demolition work on the hoaxes and myths that mar the public perception of American education." Bracey's work is the focus of Chapter 17.

CHAPTER 12

Cultural Diversity in Texas Schools

With our nation's changing demographics, today's schools reflect a reality quite different from any other period in our history. Classrooms at the end of this century and beyond will grow increasingly diverse in terms of ethnic, cultural, linguistic, and socioeconomic diversity. As an overview of changes to come, consider the statistics for today's classrooms (Grant & Sleeter, 1989a; "Here They Come," 1986; Hodgkinson, 1988, 1991; *Teacher Magazine*, April 1991):

- 1 in 5 Americans under age 18 live in poverty; for children under 3, the number is 1 in 3
- 14 percent were children of teenage mothers
- 25 percent of pregnant mothers receive no medical care during the first trimester of pregnancy
- 14 percent of children were illegitimate
- 40 percent will be living with a single parent by age 18
- 30 percent were latchkey children
- 15 percent of the children entering school in 1986 were immigrants who spoke no or little English
- 10 percent had poorly educated or illiterate parents
- 15 percent had physical or mental handicaps
- 30 percent will not finish high school; many of these will be members of minority groups (3 in 10 African-Americans, 4 in 10 Hispanics or American Indians, 1 in 10 whites)
- 38 percent of all students will be students of color by 2010.

Prepared for inclusion in this text by Nancy Hadaway, 1995.

This demographic information represents an *average* across the nation. In some areas these figures fall far short of the whole story. For instance, 22 of the 25 largest central city school districts in the nation are predominantly minority. California, Arizona, New Mexico, Texas, and Colorado already have moved to a "majority minority" status in their schools (*From Minority to Majority Education*, 1988; "Teacher, student diversity don't match," 1994).

This portrait of diverse classrooms stands in stark contrast to our homogeneous teaching force. Approximately 90 percent of teachers are Euroamerican, with the percent of teachers of color declining over the last decade (NEA, 1987). Further, most educators are monolingual and middle class. They have never experienced poverty, and few, if any, have ever been in special education programs. Most of today's more experienced teachers grew up in two-parent, single-income families (Grant & Sleeter, 1989b; Armstrong & Savage, 1990). Future teachers simply mirror these findings and reflect limited experience or knowledge of cultures other than their own. One study reported that most education students had not traveled more than 100 miles from home (Zimpher, 1989).

These statistics should heighten our awareness that proceeding with business as usual will not suffice. As the gap between the experiences and personal background of today's educators and those of the children they serve continues to broaden, teachers will feel increasingly challenged and often unprepared to meet students' needs (Grant & Sleeter,

1989b; Hadaway & Florez, 1988). The responsibility for awareness does not rest solely with the teacher, however. The schools have a crucial part to play as well. "The problems our children face in and out of the classroom—racism, poverty, language differences, and cultural barriers—are not adequately addressed in today's typical school" (QEMP, 1990, p. 11). The outmoded curricula of schools contribute to this dilemma as they seek to promote "one language and one dialect, one version of history, one literary tradition, one view of the relationship between people and nature" (Sleeter & Grant, 1988, p. 145). The mainstream-centric or Eurocentric (Banks, 1989) curricular focus has failed to keep pace with the changes in society shaping our schools.

What happens when we combine an outdated, elitist curriculum, teachers unprepared for the demographic shifts in our society, and the new student population? The effects can be devastating. Children who enter school "at risk" never quite make it out of that category. "By third or fourth grade, minority and nonminority achievement levels begin to diverge" (QEMP, 1990, p. 18). The process continues as culturally and linguistically diverse children are more often tracked into lower-ability classes from which they never emerge, and a disproportionately high percent of minority children end up in special education programs. As these students fall further behind, their dropout rates run significantly higher than those of Euroamerican students.

Thus, the curriculum, the teacher, and the school combine to create an inadequate system for many of our children. In recognition of the problem, many states have mandated multicultural training for both preservice and inservice teachers. In a Texas Education Agency memorandum (1977), the state called for prospective teachers to be provided "a study of the cultural patterns and interactions of the several ethnic groups in the Texas society." Such initiatives are a beginning, but attention must be focused on the school and curricular materials as well.

The purpose of this chapter is to chronicle the changing awareness of and reactions to the culturally and linguistically diverse population in the United States; to provide an overview of the historical background and educational experience of the major cultural groups within Texas—the African American, Mexican American, American Indian, and Asian; and to argue for an expanded curricular vision that would encompass the background and experiences of all children.

FROM ASSIMILATION TO PLURALISM— THE LONG ROAD

We did not arrive easily at today's level of awareness, limited though it is. For the diverse populations who came to America, it was a struggle to maintain any type of identity and positive self-concept regarding their roots. Although this nation is one primarily of immigrants, the immigrant experience has differed depending on how much an individual deviated from the dominant group— white, Anglo-Saxon, Protestant. Early in the history of our developing nation, new groups coming to the United States were expected to assimilate into the existing culture. Assimilation is the process "by which diverse ethnic and racial groups come to share a common culture and have equal access to opportunity in the structure of society" (Roberts, 1991, p. 106). Thus, for example, when Irish or Polish immigrants arrived, we hoped that through interaction with the larger population, they would become simply American. White, Anglo-Saxon Protestants wanted "the disappearance of a cultural group that [was] distinct from the dominant culture" (Gollnick & Chinn, 1986, p. 20).

Schools were viewed as a mechanism of assimilation, a means of perpetuating the ideologies and values of the dominant group. The schools' major goal was to "assimilate and amalgamate these [immigrants] as part of our American race, and to implant in their children, as far as can be done, the Anglo-Saxon conception of righteousness, law and order, and popular government, and to awaken in them a reverence for our democratic institutions and for those things in our national life which we as a people hold to be of abiding worth" (Cubberly, 1909, pp. 15–16).

Basically, two differing views of assimilation competed during early immigration to this country: the Anglo conformity and the melting pot theories. Anglo conformity has predominated in our interactions with the culturally and linguistically diverse. According to this theory, an immigrant group was expected to give up its cultural background and conform to the values, beliefs, and behavior of the dominant group, in this case the Anglo-Saxon core group (Gollnick & Chinn, 1986). This viewpoint can be expressed as the basic mathematical formula $A + B + C = A$ (Newman, 1973, p. 53), where A represents the dominant, mainstream culture.

The theory of Anglo conformity worked adequately well for the old immigrants, the white Protestant immigrants from northern and western Europe who perceived themselves as the rightful inhabitants of the United States (Banks, 1988). But for the new immigrants from southern, central, and eastern Europe who flooded into America in the late 1800s, for the Hispanics who were annexed, and for the blacks brought as slaves, Anglo conformity was never a reality. Cultural conflicts and the resulting competition for jobs between waves of old and new immigrants precipitated suspicion, distrust, and discrimination (Banks, 1988). Even with some assimilation over time, the new groups remained distinct and separate from mainstream America.

At the turn of the century, another theory, more generous and appealing to new immigrants, emerged in the work of an English Jewish writer, Israel Zangwill (1900). He proposed that a new unique culture to which *all* groups contributed would evolve, and that America would become a "melting pot" or amalgamation of the diverse cultures and ethnic groups making up the nation. In other terms, this theory would be represented by the equation A + B + C = D, where D is "a synthesis of these groups into a distinct new group" (Newman, 1973, p. 63).

The idea that all people could have input into shaping the culture and face of this nation never truly materialized. Even though "non-English cultural groups have made tremendous contributions to American civilization, the cultural patterns from the various groups have not melted with the patterns of the native Anglos. Instead, the specific cultural contributions of the non-English groups were transformed into the dominant core culture" (Gollnick & Chinn, 1986, p. 22).

In the early 20th century, still others argued against assimilationist theories and instead defended the rights of immigrants. These philosophers and writers believed that neither Anglo conformity nor the melting pot truly characterized the American immigrant experience. What they saw happening was immigrants' and visible minority groups' refusing to assimilate, desiring instead to preserve their ethnic identities, settle in ethnic communities or enclaves for support, maintain their culture, and derive power and services from within-group institutions (Gollnick & Chinn, 1986). Moving away from the melting pot analogy, proponents of immigrant's rights used a "salad bowl" argument; all groups would maintain their own identity but add flavor to the whole (Banks, 1988). Represented by a formula, this idea of classic cultural pluralism would be A + B + C = A + B + C (Newman, 1973, p. 67). In this theory the different cultural groups remain separate entities over time. This scheme, however, did not allow for the inevitable interaction among the distinct subgroups that resulted in some

level of shared culture or macroculture (Gollnick & Chinn, 1986). What more likely occurred was a modified cultural pluralism, or $A + B + C = A_1 + B_1 + C_1$, denoting the impact of group interaction (Newman, 1973, p. 70), which seems to be more consistent with the reality of our society. All groups influence the shared American culture to some extent, but they also remain distinct.

The commitment to cultural pluralism has not been widespread despite a growing awareness of the unique cultures making up the United States. Well into this century, assimilation ideology has been the moving force behind much political, educational, and legislative action. "During the 1940s and 1950s social scientists predicted that ethnic groups would fade from modernized societies as the people in these groups would become assimilated and acculturated" (Banks, 1988, p. 57). This prediction proved incorrect. The Civil Rights movement of the 1960s spurred increased ethnic awareness.

We now are beginning to understand the value of ethnic affiliation in the midst of a modernized but often dehumanized society. Unfortunately, cultural pluralism continues to be assaulted by individuals who argue that diversity and difference cannot be healthy or productive for the United States. These ethnocentric attitudes, reflecting an assimilationist foundation, persist today and fuel debates over the legitimacy of educational endeavors such as bilingual and multicultural programs aimed at broadening our curriculum to meet the needs of all.

ETHNIC GROUPS' STRUGGLE FOR EDUCATIONAL OPPORTUNITY

Multicultural education originated as an outgrowth of cultural pluralism. That "cultural diversity actually exists and should be recognized and taught to all Americans" was an important step forward (Sleeter & Grant, 1989, p. 148). Access to educational opportunity, however, has been a struggle for the various cultural groups that make up Texas and the nation. Understanding the historical background and educational experience of the major ethnic groups in Texas can help preservice and inservice teachers appreciate the need for an expanded curricular vision through multicultural education.

African Americans

African Americans are the largest minority group in the United States today. They account for approximately 12 percent of the total population. Despite being lumped together as one category, African Americans actually represent tremendous diversity and were drawn from many cultures and countries in Africa, as well as from the Caribbean and Central and South America.

Africans had been living in Europe for some time before the first European explorations to America began. The Moors from North Africa invaded Europe in A.D. 711, eventually conquering and ruling Spain for many years. During their reign they brought a high level of prosperity as well as many contributions to literature and art. Historical records note many blacks who accompanied early explorers to America: Diego el Negro with Columbus in 1502, Nuflo de Olano with Balboa in 1513, and Estevanico in 1529 explored much of what is today New Mexico and Arizona (Banks, 1987). Africans were also some of the first non-American Indian settlers, arriving in South Carolina in 1526 and in St. Augustine, Florida, in 1565.

In the late 1500s white European settlers established colonies in Africa and began to engage in slave trade. From that point through 1800, they carried hundreds of thousands of Africans to North and South America (Roberts, 1991). The institution of slavery was harsh. In effect it denied an individual's humanity. Slaves were not allowed to form groups without whites, carry or own firearms, testify in court against whites, own property, or have marriages recognized as legal. Most important, slaves were denied an education; it was illegal to teach them to read and write (Banks, 1987). Despite the oppressive policies of slavery, African Americans managed to survive and have numerous outstanding achievements to their credit.

Many African Americans were instrumental in the development of Texas. Free black colonists as well as black slaves fought to help establish a new republic in Texas. Famous black Texans include William Goyens, wealthy landowner, blacksmith, wagon manufacturer, freight hauler, mill owner, planter, and ally and associate of Sam Houston. In addition, blacks contributed to the political scene in Texas. After the Civil War, Norris Wright Cuney became leader of Texas' Republican party. In more recent times, Barbara Jordan has served as representative from Texas to the U.S. Congress (Roberts, 1991).

Overcoming hardships to participate in the larger society and make a contribution was difficult. The journey to educational equity for African Americans was as arduous as their personal struggle against slavery. After the Civil War, blacks held out great hope for significant changes, but progress remained slow. Institutions such as the Freedman's Bureau and its successor and African-American private education efforts, coupled with the public schools, provided some educational assistance (Roberts, 1991). Furthermore, Carter G. Woodson, founder of the Association for the Study of Negro Life and History; W. E. B. Dubois, noted black scholar and educational philosopher; and Booker T. Washington, founder of the Tuskegee Institute, helped to foster educational opportunity for black Americans (Banks, 1988).

Post World War II was a turning point, however. During the 1940s and 1950s President Harry Truman and the U.S. Supreme Court helped to move civil rights forward. "A landmark decision of this period was the Brown decision of 1954, which ruled that school segregation is inherently unequal" (Banks, 1987, p. 214). Despite this ruling, movement toward school desegregation was painfully slow and uneven. Fueled by the Civil Rights movement of the 1960s, more legal and economic progress was made.

And where are we today? Looking back brings the realization that impressive educational gains have been made in the last 20 years. For example, "in 1960, the average black adult had an 8th grade education; by 1986 the average black adult had a high school diploma" (QEMP, 1990, p. 30). Still, the educational progress of African Americans has been hampered by continued poverty, unequal school situations, and family difficulties. In addition, even with growing cultural awareness, discrimination persists within the school system. Consider, for instance, the following disproportionate statistics. Although black children make up just 16 percent of the student population, they account for 31 percent of all corporal punishment cases, 25 percent of all student suspensions, 35 percent of those categorized as educable mentally retarded, and just 8 percent of those in gifted and talented programs (QEMP, 1990, p. 30). These figures serve as a reminder that we have a long way to go toward equity in education.

Mexican Americans

Hispanics account for a large portion of the so-called new immigrants in the United States. Often perceived inaccurately as one homogeneous group, they actually represent tremendous diversity in lifestyle and degree of ethnic identification and assimilation into mainstream society. Composed of many different subgroups—Puerto Ricans, Cubans, Mexicans, Central and South Americans—Hispanics are the second largest ethnic group in America. Mexican Americans represent the largest Hispanic subgroup in America. For the next decade or so, Hispanics will be an important group to watch, as they are the fastest growing immigrant group (both legal and undocumented) and have a higher birthrate stemming from the youthful median age of Hispanics. They are almost seven years younger than the median for the total American population. Almost 90 percent of the Hispanics in the United States live in nine states; over half are in California (34 percent) and Texas (21 percent) (McKee, 1985; QEMP, 1990).

Because of their shared border, Mexico and Texas have had their histories intertwined intimately. Mexicans populated what is now the United States before all other American groups, excluding American Indians, Aleuts, Eskimos, and Native Hawaiians (Banks, 1987). In the early 1800s, American settlers expanded to the West and eventually came into contact with Mexicans in the Southwest. These new settlers became a growing force in Texas, and by 1830, Euroamericans outnumbered Mexicans by six to one (Roberts, 1991). In 1836, Texas broke away from Mexican rule to become a separate republic, and in 1845, Mexican Americans, many of whom had been in that area for a hundred years or more, suddenly became an ethnic minority with the annexation of Texas by the United States.

Although the property rights of Mexican Americans were protected under the Treaty of Guadalupe Hidalgo, they actually encountered racism and loss of power. And so began a period where "rioting, lynchings, vigilante action, and other forms of violence were directed at America's 'newest aliens'" (Banks, 1987, p. 329). Mexican Americans entered the 20th century as second-class citizens in their own homeland.

During the 1900s, the United States often had need for unskilled labor. Mexican Americans and Mexicans from across the border filled that need. They found jobs in agricultural pursuits, in mines and industry, and on railroads. Immigrants came across the border only to be exploited on this side. Many Mexicans became migrant workers following the crops and toiling long hours in the field doing stoop labor. The migrant lifestyle had a tremendous impact on educational opportunity for the Mexican Americans.

During World War I and World War II and times of economic prosperity, Mexican laborers were welcomed. When times of economic difficulty hit during the Depression and post-World War II, Mexicans and Mexican Americans encountered another reality. In competition for scarce jobs, they confronted hostility and increased discrimination. Conflict resulted in the violation of many Mexican Americans' civil rights. Some citizens of the United States were deported "back across the border" without benefit of legal proceedings (Banks, 1987).

In the area of education, Mexican Americans fared no better than in the workforce. Despite educational gains, the Mexican Americans remained the most undereducated subgroup of Hispanics (QEMP, 1990). Segregated and inferior schooling or no

school at all was the lot of most Hispanics. Agriculture, which employed many Mexican Americans early in the century, created both political and economic barriers. "Prior to the significant urbanization after World War II, many rural areas did not offer schooling beyond sixth grade, since it was not deemed necessary for farmhands, and Mexican-origin students were discouraged from attending schools. Moreover, agricultural cycles dictated school attendance patterns" (p. 33).

As with other ethnic minorities, Mexican Americans experienced discrimination and prejudice in school. "Anglicizing the child's first or last name, forbidding the speaking of Spanish on the school grounds, and the use of curriculum that put Mexico and Mexican Americans in a bad light" compounded the educational problems of this group (Stein, 1985, p. 191). In addition, those in power worked at keeping the Mexican Americans in their "proper" place, undereducated and subordinate. As one superintendent in Texas described it, education for minorities could be dangerous (Weinberg, 1977).

> Most of our Mexicans are of the lower class. They transplant onions, harvest them, etc. The less they know about everything else, the better contented they are. You have doubtless heard that ignorance is bliss. It seems that it is so when one has to transplant onions. . . . If a man has very much sense or education, either, he is not going to stick to this kind of work. So you see it is up to the white population to keep the Mexican on his knees in an onion patch.

Language policy became an issue as well. Non-English speaking and limited English-proficient students either found themselves placed in special educational classes—based on language proficiency, not academic disability—or relegated to a sink-or-swim status in a mainstream classroom.

Tired of continued discrimination, Mexican Americans became political and pushed for their rights in the post-World War II era. Beginning in 1945, the Mexican American community started using the courts to fight their battle for educational opportunity. Cases such as *Serna v. Portales Municipal Schools* and *Lau et al. v. Nichols et al.* went a long way in protesting the segregation of schools and in providing special language program help to non-English speaking children (Banks, 1987).

Although progress has been made in opening the doors of educational opportunity to Mexican Americans, some common problems persist (QEMP, 1990). These include:

1. low expectations of Mexican American children

2. nonvaluing of the culture and language of Mexican American students
3. lack of continuity/consistency of education for children of migrant workers
4. the severe shortage of fully qualified personnel to work with non-English-speaking and limited English-proficient children

Because Mexico has been the country of origin for the majority of U.S. immigrants over the past two decades (Garcia, 1994), it is crucial to carefully examine the education provided to Mexican Americans. With a dropout rate exceeding that of either whites or blacks, these students are truly at risk in our schools.

American Indians

As with Hispanics, African Americans, and Asian Americans, the American Indians are often categorized as a unitary group. Yet nothing could be further from the truth. They display tremendous diversity. "At the time of contact with Europeans [they] exhibited great variance in economic life, political organization, religion, kinship systems, settlement patterns, and language" (QEMP, 1990, p. 27). Despite stereotypical images fostered by the media, American Indians varied physically as well, ranging from dark brown to very light. In total population, American Indians were estimated to number approximately 10 million at the time of Columbus' arrival. This large group had some 200 to 300 societies and 2,200 different languages, which anthropologists have categorized roughly into six major language families (Banks, 1987).

Contact with European explorers and settlers was more devastating to the American Indian population than the eventual physical conflict between the two groups. Exposure to illnesses and diseases foreign to this continent wiped out huge numbers. The American Indian population has grown in recent years, numbering about 1,361,869 in 1980. Of this number, at least 100 native languages were still spoken in the more than 300 tribes (Banks, 1987, QEMP, 1990).

With the arrival of Europeans to this country, the history of American Indians became one of conflict and struggle. Early encounters were generally peaceful, but with time the conflict between two cultures and two ways of life became violent. The two groups moved from trading to warring, and land was the object of conquest. The American Indian population was pushed further and further westward to land that the Europeans considered uninhabitable. Basically the policy was one of relocation or extermination. By the late 1880s, American Indians had been conquered, and the only matter remaining was the eradication of their cultures, values, and ways of life (Banks, 1987).

In Texas, as in the rest of America today, the American Indians have left their mark in the original place names given, such as Waxahachie, Anahuac, Tahoka, Seminole, Comanche, Choctaw, Kiowa, Keechi, and Quitaque. In Texas, the American Indian population has increased in recent decades, growing from 470 in 1900 to 5,750 in 1960. Of this number, the majority (4,101) are urban dwellers. Of the many tribal societies in Texas, the Tiguas and the Alabama-Coushattas have persisted in preserving their customs and traditions. The Alabama-Coushattas have the one remaining reservation in Texas (Roberts, 1991).

American Indians have had a unique relationship to the federal government over time depending on "whether their land and tribal rights were seen as needing protection, or whether these were seen as obstacles to 'civilization,' preventing assimilation into the 'American mainstream' " (QEMP, 1990, p. 27). Access to educational opportunity has shifted from one extreme to another in the relationship between the government and American Indians. "Since the 1920s, educational policy for American Indians has vacillated between strong assimilationism to self-determination and cultural pluralism" (Banks, 1988, p. 6).

Currently, approximately 531,000 American Indian students attend schools in the United States (Callahan & McIntire, 1994) and, similar to the other ethnic groups discussed previously, American Indians generally are undereducated. In fact, they are among the poorest (23.7 percent of *all* families and 42 percent of reservation families live in poverty) and most uneducated. In addition, American Indians face a higher "need for public assistance; higher probability of contact with the criminal justice system; high homicide rates; higher use of alcohol; and high unemployment" (QEMP, 1990, p. 27).

With such statistics in mind, schools need to take action and provide schooling that is relevant and in touch with American Indian children's needs. Recommendations within the literature on American Indian educational needs include the following (Roberts, 1991):

1. to provide experiences which reflect the culture and needs of the local American Indian community;
2. to ensure that instructional materials are accurate and unbiased;
3. to provide bilingual instructional materials or ones developed from an American Indian perspective which reflect the value of American Indian language and culture;

4. to provide a multisensory approach with hands-on learning activities; and finally,
5. to consider learning style differences.

Asian Americans

Asian immigrants have a long history in this country. In the mid-1880s, the Chinese came to work in the gold fields but instead were relegated to the railroads. Later the Japanese came to fill the cheap labor void created by the Chinese Exclusion Act in 1882. Following the Spanish American War, the Filipinos became the next abundant and inexpensive labor source after the Gentleman's Agreement of 1907–1908 and the Immigration Act of 1924 substantially reduced Japanese immigration (Banks, 1987). Chinese, Japanese, and Filipinos remain the three largest Asian immigrant groups, but the most recent and rapidly growing group are the Indochinese. The first wave of Indochinese hit America in 1975 in conjunction with United States' involvement in Vietnam and the fall of Saigon. This group was predominantly upper to middle class, with a wide range of educational levels and experience with urban and Western society.

From this first wave, Texas gained more than 9,000 Indochinese, second only to California. With a small nucleus of Indochinese prior to the great influx in 1975, Texas was perceived as a desirable location because of its job opportunities, warmer climate, and established Indochinese communities. Furthermore, many immigrants in this group had been employed in their home countries by the oil industry or other Texas-linked businesses (McKee, 1985).

After 1975, the second wave of Indochinese immigrants began to arrive. This group differed greatly from the first wave, which had close contact with Americans in Vietnam and were, in general, highly skilled. The second influx of Indochinese included ethnic Chinese, Vietnamese, Laotians, Hmong, and Kampucheans (Banks, 1987). These refugees fled Indochina because of starvation and food shortages, political upheaval, an unstable economy, shortage of goods, and differences with the Communist ideology. The plight of the "boat people," as they were named, drew national attention. Their journey was harsh and perilous. In contrast with earlier Indochinese arrivals, this group was generally non-English-speaking, possessed little or no education, had no marketable skills, and often had health problems and emotional trauma associated with their escape from Indochina. By 1981, the Indochinese population in Texas had increased fivefold, to 51,102.

Nationwide, the Vietnamese immigrant community grew 62 percent between 1971 and 1990 (Garcia, 1994).

Although the total number of Indochinese in the United States is small, their impact has been felt, especially in states such as California and Texas. In many school districts, the Indochinese became the largest non-English-speaking or limited-English-proficient population overnight.

In the area of education, these children sometimes have been hampered by stereotypes—not negative stereotypes such as those often associated with African Americans, American Indians, and Mexican Americans and their learning ability—but potentially an even more harmful one. Indochinese children are grouped into the Asian American success myth. Teachers assume these children will be compliant, bright, well-behaved, hard workers who will make it in our educational system. Assumptions such as these can mask a student's real needs. Like the Mexican American child, Indochinese students fall victim to the inadequate number of bilingual and English as a second language teachers and support staff available in the schools. Therefore, educators have to be culturally sensitive to *all* students and help them to make the often enormous transition to American schools.

NEEDED: A BROADER CURRICULAR VISION

Great diversity characterizes our nation and state, and in the years to come, we will only grow more pluralistic, as evidenced by the population shifts from 1980 to 1990 alone. The 1990 census results show a 13.2 percent increase for African Americans, 107.8 percent for Asian Americans, 37.9 percent for American Indians, and 53 percent for Hispanics (U.S. Bureau of the Census, 1990). By 2030, the Hispanic population in the United States is expected to double and the Asian population to more than quadruple (Hernandez, 1989). Further, conservative predictions point toward our schools serving a population of approximately 25 percent limited-English-proficient students by the year 2026 (Garcia, 1994).

The role of educators is to teach in these increasingly diverse classrooms, utilizing instruction, programs, and materials in tune with the children's needs, interests, and backgrounds. To be effective for this decade and beyond, teaching must be multicultural. Multicultural education strives "to give students a realistic perspective of the diversity of the American culture, including the numerous ethnic groups as well as religious groups, and their beliefs, . . . to the many other groups in the nation [and the world] today" (Tiedt & Tiedt, 1986, p. 3).

Implementation of multicultural education means examining both the content and the process of the classroom. First, in any consideration of content, we need to look at the curriculum. Banks (1987, p. 22) developed a continuum of four models: Mainstream-Centric, Ethnic Additive, Multiethnic, and Ethno-National. In general, Mainstream-Centric and Ethnic Additive models are characteristic of where we are today, and Multiethnic and Ethno-National models represent where we need to go for the culturally pluralistic schools of today and tomorrow.

In the Mainstream-Centric model, the most common one in our schools today, students are presented only with mainstream perspectives. This model, also labeled Eurocentric or Anglocentric, denies children exposure to alternative perspectives and sends the message that the European historical and literary tradition is the only one worthy of study.

Moving away from this narrow perspective, we arrive at the Ethnic Additive model. During the ethnic revival movement of the 1960s and more recently, we have examples of this type of curriculum. To the already existing mainstream perspective, minor ethnic modification is attempted—for example, black or Chicano studies. This model, however, has only served as a quick-fix bandage applied to an outmoded curriculum.

Banks' last two models, Multiethnic and Ethno-National, offer a broader perspective. In the Multiethnic model, students view events from multiple perspectives (e.g., mainstream, African-American, American Indian, Mexican American). Perspectives of all the groups making up our country are brought out, and no one view is considered as inferior or superior. Through these models, students gain an awareness of other perspectives and develop the skill of looking at any event from different angles.

The Ethno-National model goes a step further. Events are examined from the perspectives of ethnic groups from within as well as outside the United States. In our increasingly global society, such awareness and understanding will be invaluable. Hopefully, one of the end results of either the Multiethnic or Ethno-National model will be cross-cultural competence (Banks, 1988).

Whatever the curriculum model chosen, the content of the classroom also is impacted by the materials used. Within a multicultural classroom, the materials utilized must provide multiple perspectives reflecting the real nature of society and the subcultures within it (Hernandez, 1989). With the proliferation of new materials, teachers need to carefully examine materials for problem areas such as stereotyping, underrepresentation, selectivity and imbalance, unreality, and fragmentation and isolation (Gollnick & Chinn, 1986). Students also should develop the critical skill of analyzing what they read, see, and hear.

As far as process factors, creating a learning environment responsive to diversity requires consideration of interaction, organization, social aspects, and management (Hernandez, 1989). In interaction, teachers must be aware of the impact of ethnicity, gender, socioeconomic status, and academic achievement, as all these factors influence the manner in which children interact with each other and with the teacher. Organizing the classroom and structuring learning activities reflects sensitivity and regard for the differences among learners. Whether to use a cooperative or a competitive organization, for instance, can affect student learning. Social aspects include variables such as grouping and attitudes about language use, accent, and language variety and the impact of these variables on student performance.

Finally, management decisions are important to the multicultural classroom. In attempts to accommodate the diverse needs and interests of students, how does the teacher utilize instructional and behavioral techniques? And which behavioral techniques are most effective with different ethnic groups or learners with disabilities? In implementing multicultural education, it is important to consider content, the substance of curriculum and instruction, *and* process, the contexts and processes in the transmission of content (Hernandez, 1989).

CONCLUSION

We live in a culturally pluralistic nation and state composed of different groups that have made valuable contributions to our common culture. The rich variety of language and cultures within Texas and the United States, however, has not always been viewed as an asset. More often than not, the differences among groups were viewed as problems to be eradicated rather than as opportunities to learn and grow. In the area of education especially, the schools have failed to provide opportunities for success for *all* children. Thus, some immediate attention on the part of educational institutions is dictated.

First, educators must be aware of students' backgrounds. To ignore or to remain unaware will only result in turning off learning. If effective teaching is to take place, the gap between the experiences of students and teachers must be bridged.

Next, schools and their curriculum should be reconceptualized, moving away from a single or mainstream focus and toward a broader, global view. Multicultural education seems to provide a means to expand our curricular vision, to help students develop the knowledge, skills, and attitudes necessary for living in our culturally diverse world.

Finally, multicultural education is for everyone. It is not a course in ethnic awareness designed for a specific ethnic group or a program to be implemented in schools with a high minority population. Rather, multicultural education is an opportunity to learn about self and others and "to see others as having equal worth and dignity [because] of their diverse backgrounds" (Tiedt & Tiedt, 1986, p. 3). In short, multicultural education is just effective teaching for today's schools and their students.

REFERENCES

Armstrong, D. A., & Savage, T. V. (1990). *Secondary education: An introduction.* New York: Macmillan.

Banks, J. A. (1987). *Teaching strategies for ethnic studies* (4th ed.). Boston: Allyn & Bacon.

Banks, J. A. (1988). *Multiethnic education: Theory and practice* (2nd ed.). Boston: Allyn & Bacon.

Banks, J. A. (1989). Integrating the curriculum with ethnic content: Approaches and guidelines. In J. A. Banks & C. A. McGee Banks (Eds.), *Multiethnic education: Issues and perspectives* (pp. 189–207). Boston: Allyn & Bacon.

Callahan, C. M., & McIntire, J. A. (1994). *Identifying outstanding talent in American Indian and Alaskan Native students.* Washington, D.C.: U.S. Government Printing Office.

Cubberly, E. P. (1909). *Changing conceptions of education.* Boston: Houghton Mifflin.

From minority to majority education and the future of the Southwest. (1988). Boulder, CO: Western Interstate Compact of Higher Education (WICHE).

Garcia, E. (1994). *Understanding and meeting the challenge of student diversity.* Boston: Houghton Mifflin.

Gollnick, D., & Chinn, P. C. (1986). *Multicultural education in a pluralistic society.* Columbus, OH: Merrill.

Grant, C. A., & Sleeter, C. E. (1989a). Race, class, gender, exceptionality, and educational reform. In J. Banks & C. McGee Banks (Eds.), *Multicultural education: Issues and perspectives* (pp. 49–66). Boston: Allyn & Bacon.

Grant, C. A., & Sleeter, C. E. (1989b). *Turning on learning: Five approaches for multicultural teaching plans for race, class, gender, and disability.* Columbus, OH: Merrill.

Hadaway, N. L., & Florez, V. (1987–1988). Diversity in the classroom: Are our teachers prepared? *Teacher Education and Practice, 4* (2), 25–30.

Here they come. (1986, May). *Education Week.*

Hernandez, H. (1989). *Multicultural education: A teacher's guide to content and process.* Columbus, OH: Merrill.

Hodgkinson, H. (1988). What's ahead for education. In K. Ryan & J. M. Cooper (Eds.), *Kaleidoscope: Readings in education* (5th ed.) (pp. 475–480). Boston: Houghton Mifflin.

Hodgkinson, H. (1991). Reform versus reality. *Kappan, 73,* 8–16.

McKee, J. O. (1985). *Ethnicity in contemporary America: A geographic appraisal.* Dubuque, IA: Kendall/Hunt.

National Education Association. (1987). *NEA study of the status of public school teachers.* Washington, D.C.: NEA.

Newman, W. N. (1973). *A study of minority groups and social theory.* New York: Harper and Row.

Quality Education for Minorities Project. (1990). *Education that works: An action plan for the education of minorities.* Cambridge: Massachusetts Institute of Technology.

Roberts, L. (1991). Texas cultural and ethnic groups. In J. A. Vornberg (Ed.), *Texas public school organization and administration: 1991* (2nd ed.) (pp. 99–135). Dubuque, IA: Kendall/Hunt.

Sleeter, C. E., & Grant, C. A. (1989). *Making choices for multicultural education: Five approaches to race, class, and gender.* Columbus, OH: Merrill.

Stein Jr., C. B. (1985). Hispanic students in the sink or swim era, 1900–1960. *Urban Education, 20* (2), 189–197.

Teacher Magazine (1991, April). *You and the system: Who you will teach,* p. 32H.

Teacher, student diversity don't match, study says. (June, 1994). *Texas Education Today, 11* (9), 3–4.

Texas Education Agency. (1977, January). *Memorandum.*

Tiedt, P. L., & Tiedt, I. M. (1986). *Multicultural teaching: A handbook of activities, information, and resources.* Boston: Allyn & Bacon.

U.S. Bureau of Census. (1990). *Results of the 1990 census for selected ethnic groups.* Washington, D.C.: U.S. Government Printing Office.

Weinberg, M. (1977). *A chance to learn: A history of race and education in the United States.* New York: Cambridge University Press.

Zangwill, I. (1900). *The melting pot: A drama in four acts.* New York: Macmillan.

Zimpher, N. L. (1989). The RATE project: A profile of teacher education students. *Journal of Teacher Education, 40,* 27–30.

CHAPTER 13

Demographics of the School Population

To begin, think of the following analogy. American education is like a house. This house was beautiful and well maintained, one of the nicest houses in the world. But over time, the owners allowed the house to deteriorate. First, a leak in the roof developed, allowing water to enter the attic, then to trickle down to the second floor, and then to the main floor. Floors buckled, plaster fell from the walls, electric systems rusted, windows began to fall out. The owners, returning after a long absence, hastily repaired the windows, the plaster, and the electric motors—but they neglected to fix the roof. The owners were surprised and angry when, after all their efforts, the house continued to deteriorate.

Basically, the publication of *A Nation at Risk* marked the return of the owners after a long absence to find education's house badly deteriorated. The first major sign of deterioration was declining scores of the Scholastic Aptitude Test (SAT), which Americans often hold to be *the* single barometer of educational quality. Since that time, a blizzard of education reform proposals has fallen, and states have raised the graduation standards for high schools, installed minimum standards for moving from one grade to the next, required new teachers to pass special examinations before being allowed to teach, instituted choice and magnet school programs, and so on.

Reprinted with permission from "Reform Versus Reality," by Harold Hodgkinson, Center for Demographic Policy of the Institute for Educational Leadership and *Phi Delta Kappan*, September 1991.

But so far, there has been no change in high school graduation rates, in most test scores, or in other indicators of "quality." After nearly a decade, we have fixed the plaster in education's house, installed new windows, and repaired the electric motors. *But the roof still leaks.* Until we fix the roof, the house continues to deteriorate.

The leaky roof in our educational house is a metaphor for the spectacular changes that have occurred in the nature of the children who come to school. Until we pay attention to these changes, our tinkering with the rest of the house will continue to produce no important results. The fact is that at least one-third of the nation's children are at risk of school failure even before they enter kindergarten. The schools did not cause these deficits, and neither did the youngsters. A few examples may suffice:

- Since 1987, one-fourth of all preschool children in the U.S. have been in poverty.
- Every year, about 350,000 children are born to mothers who were addicted to cocaine during pregnancy. Those who survive birth become children with strikingly short attention spans, poor coordination, and much worse. Of course, the schools will have to teach these children, and getting such children ready for kindergarten costs around $40,000 each—about the same as for children with fetal alcohol syndrome.

- Today, 15 million children are being reared by single mothers, whose family income averages about $11,400 in 1988 dollars (within $1,000 of the poverty line). The average family income for a married couple with children is slightly over $34,000 a year.

- Twenty percent of America's preschool children have not been vaccinated against polio.
- The "Norman Rockwell" family—a working father, a housewife mother, and two children of school age—constitutes only 6% of U.S. households today.
- One-fourth of pregnant mothers receive no physical care of any sort during the crucial first trimester of pregnancy. About 20% of handicapped children would not be impaired had their mothers had one physical exam during the first trimester, which could have detected potential problems.
- At least two million school-age children have no adult supervision at all after school. Two million more are being reared by *neither* parent.
- On any given night, between 50,000 and 200,000 children have no home. (In 1988, 40% of shelter users were families with children.)
- In 1987, child protection agencies received 2.2 million reports of child abuse or neglect—triple the number received in 1976.

This is the nature of education's leaky roof: about one-third of preschool children are destined for school failure because of poverty, neglect, sickness, handicapping conditions, and lack of adult protection and nurturance. There is no point in trying to teach hungry or sick children. From this we can deduce one of the most important points in our attempts to deal with education: *educators can't fix the roof all by themselves.* It will require the efforts of many people and organizations—health and social welfare agencies, parents, business and political leaders—to even begin to repair this leaky roof. There is not time to waste in fixing blame; we need to act to fix the roof. And unless we start, the house will continue to deteriorate, and all Americans will pay the price.

Indeed, the first of the national goals for education outlined by the President and the nation's governors states that, "by the year 2000, all children in America will start school ready to learn." Three of the objectives attached to this goal read as follows:

- All disadvantaged and disabled children will have access to high-quality and developmentally appropriate preschool programs that help prepare children for school.
- Every parent in America will be a child's first teacher and devote time each day to helping his or her preschool child to learn; parents will have access to the training and support they need.
- Children will receive the nutrition and health care needed to arrive at school with healthy

minds and bodies, and the number of low-birthweight babies will be significantly reduced through enhanced prenatal health systems.

While these are noble statements about the need to fix the roof, they are not at all informative on how this should be done. (It has been estimated that meeting just the first objective would cost $30 billion to implement.) We need to know more about *why* the roof is leaking—why so many of our children are at risk of failure in school and in life.

The fact is that more than one-third of American children have the deck stacked against them long before they enter school. Although America's best students are on a par with the world's best, ours is undoubtedly the worst "bottom third" of any of the industrialized democracies. We need to take a brief look at the kinds of changes that have brought about this concentration of children at risk.

CHANGES IN THE FAMILY

During the 1980s the American family continued to undergo major changes in its structure (see Table 1). Every kind of "atypical" family increased in number during the decade, while the "typical" family—married couple with children—actually declined in number. Today, almost 50% of America's young people will spend some years before they reach age 18 being raised by a single parent. In 1988, 4.3 million children were living with a mother who had never married (up 678% since 1970). Few have studied the consequences of being a child of an unmarried mother, but it's hard to think of this situation as an advantage. The 15 million children being raised by single mothers will have about one-third as much to spend on their needs as children being raised by two parents. (When both parents work, family income does not double; it *triples*.) For young children raised by a single mother, day care becomes a *vital educational issue*, as well as a matter of family survival. The 2.5 million fathers raising children by themselves have also discovered the vital nature of day care.

Some things show up clearly in these numbers. First, only about a quarter of America's households have a child in the public schools, a fact that will make school bond issues more difficult to pass as time goes by. Second, 25 million people live by themselves or with nonrelatives, which explains why America's fertility rates are so low! Third, the feminization of poverty is not just a slogan: 23% of America's smallest children (birth to age 5) live in poverty, the highest rate of any industrialized nation. And many of them have a single parent, often a mother who works at a low-income service job. At

TABLE 1   U.S. Households, 1980–90.

	1980	1990	% Change
All households	80,467,000	93,920,000	+16.7
Family households	59,190,000	66,652,000	+12.6
Married couples	48,990,000	52,837,000	+ 7.9
Married w/o children	24,210,000	28,315,000	+17.0
Married w/ children	24,780,000	24,522,000	− 1.0
Single female head	8,205,000	11,130,000	+35.6
Single male head	1,995,000	2,575,000	+29.1
People living alone	19,202,000	22,879,000	+19.1
Living w/ nonrelatives	3,075,000	4,500,000	+46.3

present about six million workers in the U. S. earn the minimum wage, and more than five million others are within 50 cents of the minimum wage. Females over 25 with children to support—not teenage males saving for a car—account for the largest proportion of these low-wage workers. These women desperately need job skills to support their children, but they are not well represented in programs supported by the Job Training and Partnership Act or in other training programs.

We can begin to see how these areas interrelate when we think of a single mother with a low income who is raising a child. She must have a place to live; yet there are eight million qualified low-income households trying to play musical chairs with only four million low-income housing units. (Literally no one is building new low-income housing units in the U.S.) She will pay a higher percentage—in some cases more than 50%—of her income for housing than any other category of worker. It is highly unlikely that her living unit will have a quiet place for a child to study.

In addition, this woman must get to work, often on public transportation if she can't afford a car. If her child is a preschooler, she will have to get the child to day care before she gets herself to work, an arrangement that may involve four or more bus trips at the end of each day. (For women in this situation, day-care centers, housing, and jobs are not usually located close to one another.) If the child gets ill, the logistics get even more complex. A missed bus or a conked-out car can mean that the rent cannot be paid. Then the salary check must be changed for a welfare check, a switch that is painful not only to her and her child, but also to the taxpayer who must pay for the switch. (It would be much cheaper for us to prevent her from going into poverty than to pay for the very expensive consequences, including her child being in poverty and the loss of her self-esteem.)

If the President and the nation's governors are serious about the first objective associated with the first national goal, we must deal with this single parent and her child. For this woman and her child (let's call him Carlos), education services, health services, housing services, and employment services must all function together to prevent Carlos from having a diminished future. Carlos *is* education's leaky roof.

There is no way that the education system alone can be responsible for the economic difficulties of this woman and her son, although educators will have to teach the person who is at the end of the service chain: Carlos. In order for the national goals to be achieved, our leaders will have to think of a way for Carlos and his mother to have an improved base of services so that Carlos will not become a liability to the taxpayer and the nation. This may seem difficult, but Carlos' problems are much easier to solve than those of the 350,000 cocaine-addicted babies born every year. The national goals are silent about such children, although they are already showing up in the schools.

CHANGES IN ETHNIC DISTRIBUTION

One of the good things about the 1990 Census is that we already know many of the most important numbers. For example, the American population grew by 10% between 1980 and 1990, reaching a new total of 249.8 million, an addition of 23 million people. The fastest growing groups are the eldest members of our population: 57,000 Americans are at least 100 years old, according to the 1990 Census, up from 32,000 in 1980. Minority populations also grew rapidly.

Ninety percent of the 23-million-person increase occurred in the South and West, although some eastern states, such as New York and New Jersey, have

TABLE 2   Population Increases (in Millions) by Ethnic Group, 1980–90.

	1980 Total	1990 Total	% Increase
White	194.7	210.3	8
Black	26.7	31.0	16
Asian, other	5.2	8.6	65
Hispanic	14.6	21.0	44

started growing again. Only *three* states account for almost half of the nation's growth: Texas, Florida, and California increased their populations by a total of 11.7 million. We can link this growth to some political changes if we look at the increased votes in the House of Representatives by the year 2000.

It is very clear that the states with the most population growth (and the most new political clout) are states with a great deal of ethnic diversity. Table 2 shows the increases in population for various ethnic groups between 1980 and 1990.

While the white population increased by 15 million, the nonwhite population increased by 14 million. Even though whites grew by 8%, their share of the total U.S. population declined from 86% to 84%.

The numbers get even more interesting when we project changes in the youth population from 1990 to 2010 (see Figure 1). During those two decades, the nation will gain in total population, but America's youth population will decline rapidly after 2000, because of the decline in women entering the childbearing years. However, as the total youth cohort moves from 64 million to 65 million, then down to 62 million, the nonwhite component of the nation's youth cohort will increase dramatically, from 30% in 1990 to 38% in 2010. Note also that the white youth population declines during *both* decades. In fact, in 2010, 12 states and the District of Columbia will contain 30 million of our 62 million young people, with the percentages of minority youths as follows: Washington, D.C., 93.2%; Hawaii, 79.5%; New Mexico, 76.5%; Texas, 56.9%; California, 56.9%; Florida, 53.4%; New York, 52.8%; Louisiana, 50.3%; Mississippi, 49.9%; New Jersey, 45.7%; Maryland, 42.7%; Illinois, 41.7%; South Carolina, 40.1%; U. S. total, 38.7%.

Many of these are large states, with a good deal of political and economic clout. But in all of them, a new question will arise: What do we call "minorities" when they constitute a majority? It behooves us all to make sure that *every* child in America has a good education and access to a good job. We cannot,

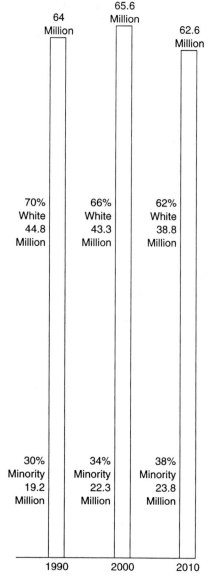

FIGURE 1   U.S. Youth (Birth–18) by Race 1990–2010. Source: *American Demographics*, May 1989, p. 37.

as a nation, afford to throw *any* child away; we need them all to become successful adults if the economy, the community, the work force, the military—indeed, the nation—are to thrive. (And who else will generate the incomes that will pay for the Social Security benefits of the readers of this article?) Of the 20 million new workers who will be added to the American economy by 2000, only 18% of the net additions will be white males born in the U.S. The rest will be a combination of women, immigrants, or minorities.

By the 1980s the equity efforts of the 1960s had begun to pay off in terms of minority populations entering the middle class (defined by college education, suburban living options, and a white-collar or professional job). About 40% of the black population can be called middle class in 1990; Hispanics are not far behind, and Asians are actually ahead. Different places in America have produced very different rates of black suburbanization, as the following list makes clear: Miami, 69%; Newark, 52.9%; Washington, D.C., 48.5%; Los Angeles, 46.5%; Atlanta, 46%; Oakland, 39.5%; St. Louis, 35.4%; Birmingham, 34.1%; Philadelphia, 27.7%; Cleveland, 27.2%; New Orleans, 24.6%; Baltimore, 23.5%; Memphis, 15.4%; Dallas, 15.3%; Detroit, 14.9%; Houston, 14%; and Chicago, 9%.

As jobs follow people to the suburbs, the ability of a city to allow either suburbanization or the development of middle-income homes and jobs within the city limits (the latter, known as "gentrification," has been a major failure in America) will have a large effect on the ability of the metropolitan area—city plus suburbs—to be economically healthy.

With money, jobs, houses, and (to some extent) brains and aspirations having moved to the suburbs, serious questions must be raised about our most serious problem: America's inner-city schools, where the highest percentage of "at-risk" students can be found; where classes are large (even though these children need the *most* individual attention); where health care, housing, transportation, personal security, and community stability are inadequate; where it is *very* hard to recruit and retain high-quality teachers and administrators; and where racial segregation still exists to an appalling degree, despite our best efforts. (It is pointless to desegregate schools if housing and jobs remain segregated.) The national education goals are conspicuous in their neglect of the special problems of inner-city schools in America.

It is particularly frustrating to realize that, if you equalize the environment in which a minority person lives (a home in the suburbs, parents who are college graduates and have managerial or professional jobs), you will tend to equalize his or her educational achievement as well. Indeed, for people of similar social and economic background, race *tends to go away as a predictor of educational achievement.* Figure 2 shows clearly that children of wealthy black families do *better* at math than do children of poor Asian families.

It is difficult to imagine a more exciting or optimistic conclusion. Nevertheless, millions of minority children and their parents are unable to enter the middle class, because they are locked into inner-city environments that offer no escape and scant possibility of improving conditions where they are. At the moment, there is no evidence of a truly permanent "underclass" in America, but give us two more generations of systematic neglect of inner-city youth,

and there will be. By then, education's leaky roof will be beyond repair. Once again, schools cannot do the job in a social vacuum. Until job opportunities, health care, housing, transportation, and personal security improve in the inner cities, it is impossible to ask schools to get better. Trying to teach sick or hungry children is an exercise in futility.

INTERNATIONAL COMPARISONS

According to a study released by the Census Bureau in March 1990, American young people are at far greater risk for social, economic, and health problems than are children in the world's other developed nations. American children were the most vulnerable in most of the dimensions covered in the study, particularly in the following areas:

- number of children affected by divorce
- youth homicide rate
- number (and percentage) of youngsters living in poverty
- infant mortality rate
- teenage pregnancy rate

From a different source, in 1988 America ranked 22nd in infant mortality, with a rate of 10 deaths per 1,000 live births. Young males in the U. S. are five times as likely to be murdered as are their counterparts in other nations. Twenty-three percent of America's youths live in poverty, and the younger the children, the higher the poverty rate.

As I mentioned above, 15 million children in this country are being reared by single parents, mostly as a result of divorce. Finally, though it might seem unlikely that any other nation could compete with our figure of 4.3 million children being reared by a mother who never married and 371,000 children being reared by a never-married father, the facts are otherwise. Although 23% of America's children are born out of wedlock today, the rate for Sweden is 48% and for Denmark, 40%. However, in Sweden and Denmark, infant mortality is low, and child hunger and poverty are virtually nonexistent.

Children can be at risk on a variety of factors, some of which reflect a social or educational problem; single-parent home (22% of eighth-graders), low-income family (21% of eighth-graders' families below the 1988 figure of $15,000), held back one or more grades (19% of eighth-graders), home alone three or more hours a day (14%), parents with a low level of education (11%), and limited English proficiency (2%).

Some children are at risk because of medical factors: fetal alcohol syndrome, no medical care in the first trimester of a mother's pregnancy, a drug-addicted

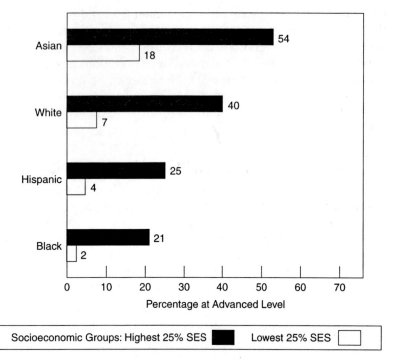

FIGURE 2   Percentage of Eighth-Graders in Low- and High-SES Groups who are Proficient in Advanced Mathematics, by Race. Source: National Center for Education Statistics, *Profile of the American Eighth-Grader* (Washington, D.C.: U.S. Department of Education, 1990).

mother, poor maternal nutrition during pregnancy, a mother who smoked during pregnancy, exposure to lead during pregnancy or in infancy, premature birth, low birthweight, having a "teenage mother," and being a victim of child abuse or neglect.

Some children are at risk because of a problem that develops in adolescence: teen pregnancy, criminal conviction, suicide attempts, and alcohol and/or drug abuse.

Indeed, many children are at risk on more than one of these factors.

Like the Reagan Administration before it, the Bush Administration made a major point of saying that Americans overspend on education. "Throwing money at problems will not make them go away" became the recurrent litany of these presidents and their advisors. However, the data they cite to show that Americans spend more than other industrialized nations on education include figures for *higher education,* on which we spend a prodigious amount. (The U.S. has 5% of the world's elementary and secondary students and 25% of the world's higher education students.)

On the other hand, if we compare the percent of its gross domestic product that America spends on K-12 education with similar expenditures in other nations, the results are spectacularly different (see Figure 3). Even with the difficulties of establishing "levels of effort" for different nations, it is clear that many nations invest a larger share of their wealth in

their children's education than we do. In addition, the discrepancies in per-pupil expenditures *within* the U.S. are unmatched by any nation with a centralized education system. In many states in the U.S., the amount spent on *some* children is three or four times the amount spent on other children in the same state. Recent court decisions in Kentucky and Texas indicate that this is an area of future concern.

This range of effort and expenditure devoted to children and youths is most characteristic of our nation. In terms of infant mortality and care, one can go from some of the best infant care in the world to some of the worst merely by taking the short drive from Scarsdale to Harlem.

These are a few of the reasons for my earlier assertion that America's "bottom third" of young people is more likely to fail than the "bottom third" of any nation with which we usually compare ourselves. If our goal is to ensure that every young person can graduate from high school with a high level of knowledge and skills, then we must concentrate a large measure of our fiscal and human resources on the children most likely to fail. At present, we concentrate our resources on those *least likely* to fail—children from relatively stable suburban families headed by parents who have high levels of education and income. The national education goals give us not a single clue as to how this reallocation of resources should be brought about. Just how do we fix the roof?

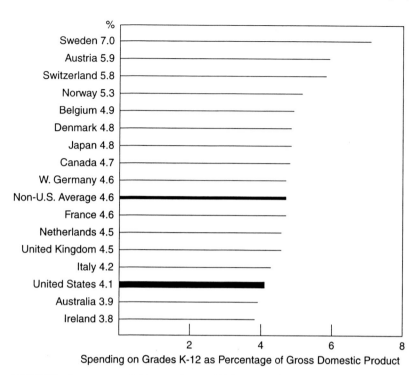

FIGURE 3   International Comparison of Education Expenditures, 1985.
Source: M. Edith Rasell and Lawrence Mishel, *Shortchanging Education* (Washington D.C.: Economic Policy Institute, 1990), p. 5.

EDUCATION—THE BEST WEAPON AGAINST POVERTY AND CRIME

Think for a moment about two young families with children. In one of the families, one or both of the parents has a high school diploma. In the other family, neither parent does. Which family is more likely to live below the poverty line? A good generalization is that increased levels of education will reduce the chances of living in poverty better than anything else. This is widely accepted.

But let's look at a different relationship. Let's look at the relationship between education and crime. Although it is not written about much, the relationship is quite strong. Today, more than 80% of America's one million prisoners are high school dropouts. Each prisoner costs taxpayers upwards of $20,000 a year. Moreover, the investment in prisoners is a bad one, in that 63% of released inmates are back in jail for serious crimes within three years. Taxpayers spend more by far on a prisoner than on *any other kind* of tax-supported individual. A college student is supported by about $3,300 of tax money—a very profitable investment indeed. Every dollar spent on a Head Start child will save taxpayers $7 in later services that the child will not need—a superb investment. Indeed, in Pennsylvania it is seven times more expensive for taxpayers to maintain someone in the *state pen* than it is to maintain someone at Penn State!

This correlation between being a high school dropout and becoming a prisoner is similar to the correlation between being a smoker and getting lung cancer. When you think about the public furor concerning the latter and the widespread ignorance concerning the former, you must wonder about America's youth policy. Table 3 shows the states with the highest and lowest high school dropout rates.[1] It is interesting to note that, with one exception, the states with the lowest dropout rates also have the lowest rates of prisoners per 100,000 people. With two exceptions, the states with the lowest graduation rates have the highest rates of prisoners per 100,000 people.

JAIL CONSTRUCTION VERSUS CRIME REDUCTION

America's prison population *doubled* in less than a decade, reaching 1.1 million prisoners in 1990. (The U.S. incarceration rate in 1991 was the highest in the

---

1. While dropout rates are notoriously unreliable as absolute numbers, comparing rates obtained from the same source—numbers with a "commonly held bias"—is a valuable exercise. Something very different is happening in Minnesota, with its 9% dropout rate, than in Florida, with its 41% rate.

TABLE 3   High School Dropout Rates, 1987.

	State (Lowest)	%		State (Highest)	%
1.	Minnesota	9.4	1.	Florida	41.4
2.	Wyoming	10.7	2.	Louisiana	39.9
3.	North Dakota	11.6	3.	Michigan	37.6
4.	Nebraska	13.3	4.	Georgia	37.5
5.	Montana	13.8	5.	New York	37.1
6.	Iowa	13.8	6.	Arizona	35.6
7.	Wisconsin	15.6	7.	Mississippi	35.2
8.	Ohio	17.2	8.	Texas	34.9
9.	Kansas	17.9	9.	California	33.9
10.	Utah	19.4	10.	Alaska	33.3
11.	Connecticut	19.5	11.	South Carolina	33.1
12.	South Dakota	20.3	12.	Kentucky	32.6

Source: *Source Education Performance Chart* (Washington, D.C.: Office of Planning, Budget, and Evaluation, U.S. Department of Education, May 1989).

world, ahead of the Soviet Union and South Africa. In fact, in 1988 a black male in the U.S. was about five times as likely to be in prison as a black male in South Africa.) Given the increase in drug-related crime and the get-tough policies now in vogue, it is very likely that the number of inmates in U.S. prisons could reach two million before the decade is over. The cost of our prisons is increasing faster than that of *any other* social service, including education and health. Yet the return on the investment is extraordinarily low.

Many governors have discovered that, in order to show that they are "tough on crime," they can build a lot of jail cells and get reelected. Jails can also be built fairly quickly, which shows that the governor is a decisive leader. But there is one major problem with a campaign of building more jail cells: it doesn't reduce the crime rate. No sensible criminal is likely to stop committing crimes because more jail cells are available! (Criminals are not stupid.) There is, however, one thing that does reduce crime rates, and that is increased levels of education.

Let's return to our high school dropout family. With no high school diploma in the household, the best a family can usually manage is a minimum-wage job at $4.25 an hour. That adds up to about $9,000 a year for a full-time worker. Is that enough for our young family even to think about buying a house? Owning a car? Putting children through college? Clearly not. For young high school dropouts working minimum-wage jobs, there is little chance that the American Dream will become reality—unless, of course, they turn to crime. In 1989, four million Americans worked full-time but were still eligible for poverty benefits! Since Ben Franklin, America's deal with its citizens has been: if you work hard,

you shouldn't be poor. Where is the reward for the work ethic for these four million people?

However, we know that as educational levels increase, so do earnings. And as earnings increase, the propensity for crime decreases. If you can make your way in the mainstream, a risky criminal "career" becomes less and less inviting. What we need to do is to work on America's crime rates, and the best policy for doing so is to make sure that *every* American child graduates from high school. Already, some school districts—e.g., Greeley, Colorado; and Springfield, Missouri—have developed strategic plans to achieve the goal of zero dropouts by 1995. To do so is to achieve a reduction in crime also, but that result won't show up for many years. Unfortunately, political pressures force elected officials to look for quick-fix solutions like jail construction rather than long-term solutions like ensuring that every young person graduates from high school.

I hope that readers take away from this article two main points. First, for the reasons I specified above, America's children are truly an "endangered species." And second, educators alone cannot "fix" the problems of education, because dealing with the root causes of poverty must involve health-care, housing, transportation, job-training, and social welfare bureaucracies.

We are left with two high-priority questions: What can educators do that they are not already doing to reduce the number of children "at risk" in America and to get them achieving well in school settings? And how can educators collaborate more closely with other service providers so that we all work together toward the urgent goal of providing services to the same client? These two questions must be answered by the nation before our schools will improve.

But we do *know* that it is possible to "fix education's leaky roof." We have the resources to reduce the proportion of at-risk children to less than 5%. We just need the will to do it.

REFERENCES

Education and Human Services Consortium. *What It Takes: Structuring Interagency Partnerships to Connect Children and Families with Comprehensive Services.* Washington, D. C., 1991.

Hodgkinson, Harold. *All One System: Demographics of Education from Kindergarten Through Graduate School.* Washington, D.C.: Institute for Educational Leadership, 1985.

Hodgkinson, Harold. *The Same Client: Demographics of Education and Service Delivery Systems.* Washington, D. C.: Institute for Educational Leadership, September 1989.

House Select Committee on Children, Youth and Families. *Children and Families.* Washington, D. C.: U.S. Government Printing Office, December 1988.

House Select Committee on Children, Youth and Families. *U.S. Children and Their Families: Current Conditions and Recent Trends, 1989.* Washington, D. C.: U.S. Government Printing Office, 1989.

National Center for Education Statistics. *Profile of the American Eighth Grader.* Washington, D. C.: U.S. Department of Education, 1990.

National Health/Education Consortium. *Crossing the Boundaries Between Health and Education.* Washington, D. C., 1990.

Statistical Abstract of the United States, 1990. Washington, D. C.: U.S. Government Printing Office, 1989.

Waldrop, Judith, and Thomas Exter. "What the 1990 Census Will Show." *American Demographics,* January 1990.

CHAPTER 14

Major Events That Shaped America's Schools

Getting an education in the years when America was about to become a nation was no problem if you were male, white, Protestant, wealthy, and well-born. For these select few there were brilliant Scottish tutors, private schools, and academies. Harvard, William and Mary, Yale, Princeton, and Brown (and a half dozen other colleges) were small but growing. Southern gentlemen traveled to England and Scotland to round out their education in the classics. Young ladies learned poetry, painting, and dancing at exclusive seminaries.

For the vast majority of the population, only the most meager schooling existed—and that schooling was rudimentary, word-dry, dominated by religious dogma. African Americans, girls, or very young children had few opportunities.

Two hundred years later, the United States supports a system of public and private schools that is the envy and wonder of the world. From the youngest to the oldest, from the richest to the poorest, opportunities exist for their education, primarily at public cost, in a range of skills, subjects, and courses undreamed of in 1776.

Thousands of events helped shape America's education during the past two centuries. They took place in the scholar's study, in legislatures, in

courts—and on riot-torn streets and campuses. There were the invention of the steel pen (replacing the quill) and publication of Noah Webster's blue-backed Spelling Book, destined for a long series of editions and many millions of copies; there were George Washington's call for a national university and a state governor standing at the schoolhouse door to block the entrance of a black student; the concept of the I.Q. (for better or for worse) and the phenomenon of 80-year-old grandparents flocking to community colleges. Education has been called America's religion, its bread, and its circus.

Out of the countless incidents and developments that have helped bring about America's educational systems, here are 12 major events of pivotal significance.

1. JEFFERSON DREAMS—AND FAILS

1779—Thomas Jefferson introduced his school bill for Virginia, the first plan for a statewide school system in the New World.

Three years after drafting the Declaration of Independence, the remarkable Mr. Jefferson, age 36, put his quill to work on another soon-to-become-historic document. He called it "A Bill for the More General Diffusion of Knowledge." Jefferson's plan, borrowed partly from French revolutionists, was for statewide public education from first grade to the university, narrowed by the notions of his time that the chief beneficiaries should be only free children.

It was an unprecedented piece of school legislation. It consisted of 19 sections, some short, some running close to a thousand words, an amalgam of high educational policy and detailed regulation.

To assure that those entrusted with power do not turn it into tyranny, Jefferson wrote in a preamble, it is necessary to illuminate the minds of the people. Education, he continued, is the means for achieving this. But since only the wealthy and well-born can afford a liberal education, the General Assembly must provide for the education of all capable, even if indigent, children at the common expense.

The bill called for the election of aldermen, county by county, to meet the first Monday in October, "if it be fair." Their task was to plan for the acquisition of land, construction of schools, hiring of teachers, supervision of instruction, testing and evaluation. All free children, male and female, were to receive free elementary education for three years in a curriculum stressing the basic skills.

The bill also called for 20 secondary schools throughout the state ("grammer" schools, Jefferson called them), "the tuition to these to be paid by the scholars." In addition to Latin and Greek, Jefferson's bill prescribed "English grammar, geography, vulgar and decimal fractions, and the extrication of the square and cube roots." Jefferson proposed scholarships for elementary pupils who were of "promising genius and dispositions, but whose parents were too poor to give them further education." He also wanted scholarships for bright but needy secondary students, who were to proceed to William and Mary, at Williamsburg, there to be "educated, boarded, and clothed for three years at public expense."

The plan was too much, too early for Virginia. Seventeen years later the legislature passed it, but, as Jefferson complained, with a provision that completely defeated his dream, "for they left it to the court of each county to determine for itself when this act should be carried into execution. . . . It was not suffered to commence in a single county."

So did Jefferson's plan for common schools fail. He was more successful in higher education. When he saw that church-controlled William and Mary would not fit into his brave schemes, he set about creating the state-controlled University of Virginia. He ranked it as one of his three greatest achievements—next to the Declaration of Independence and Virginia's statute for religious freedom.

Jefferson's educational aspirations were immense. Equally immense were the aspirations he kindled in others, down to our own day. His Virginia bill, though ignored and vitiated by his legislature, helped bring free education to New England, the Midwest, the Far West, and eventually to his own South and his native state.

2. THE GREAT REAL ESTATE GAMBIT

1787—Congress enacted the Northwest Ordinance, "forever encouraging education."

America was not yet a nation in 1784; it lacked a constitution and a strong central government. But imperishable longings were stirring even within the loose Confederation of the States. Beyond the 13 colonies lay the vast, rich lands of the Northwest. Congress knew their value. So did land grabbers and speculators, lying in wait to buy or lease at pennies per acre. Congress declared its control over and policy toward this domain in three ordinances (1784, 1785, and 1787). Essentially real estate manuals, they gave details for the surveying and sale of the lands. But they also contained a bill of rights for the inhabitants and forbade slavery. And in an immortal sentence, the Ordinance of 1787 declared: "Religion, morality, and knowledge being necessary to good government and the happiness of mankind, schools and the means of education shall forever be encouraged."

Before sale and settlement, the territory was to be mapped into townships six miles square, each divided into 36 sections. One of these, Section 16, was designated for the support of schools. Sales were to be for no less than a dollar an acre and in units of one section. This meant that Section 16 could yield at least $640—a handsome sum for raising a school and hiring a teacher.

The states which emerged from territorial lands (Ohio, Indiana, Illinois, Michigan, Wisconsin, part of Minnesota) did not rush to put their acreage to work for schools. Ohio waited for a quarter of a century before doing anything for schools, with or without Section 16 help. But an important principle had been established: federal aid to education. School aid through land grants was continued, with a few exceptions for every new state admitted to the union. Starting in 1850, two sections for school support were given newly admitted states; later, many colleges and universities came to share in the national land largesse. In all, the government donated well over 100 million acres for educational endowment.

Few could foresee the incalculable effects on education of the ordinance provisions. But it did not take long for statesmen to sense their impact. Daniel Webster, speaking of the political and educational results of the Ordinance of 1787, said: "I doubt whether any single law, ancient or modern, has produced effects of a more marked or lasting character."

3. KNOCK, KNOCK! WHO'S THERE? A WOMAN

1821—Emma Willard founded the Troy Seminary in New York; soon after, the doors to higher education for women were slowly pried loose all over the country.

The enlightened nineteenth century was in its second decade. But no college in the world admitted women. Men argued that anything beyond reading, writing, arithmetic, sewing, and cookery would unsex females; it would over-tax and probably break down their minds. Schools for girls and young ladies flourished in many parts of the new nation, but their offerings seldom rose above the rudiments, plus the decorative arts (dancing, music, painting).

Emma Hart, a dynamic young woman from Connecticut, at first accepted these limits and carried on successfully as teacher and schoolmistress in her native state and later in Middlebury, Vermont. Her intelligence and rebellious spirit soon broke through the restrictions, however. Encouraged by her husband, Dr. John Willard (28 years her senior), she drafted a Plan for Improving Female Education. It stirred protests, applause, and nationwide discussion. Jefferson read it and liked it. It was addressed primarily to the New York State legislature, because Emma Willard had set her mind on getting state support for a revolutionary women's academy and she had reason to hope for help from Albany. Her efforts as America's first woman lobbyist for education failed. But the little town of Troy, seeking new markets for its products, thought that a female academy would be good promotion. With a town appropriation of $4,000, Willard not only made Troy famous but proved that women could master mathematics, history, geography, and "natural philosophy" without losing their femininity or their minds.

Collegiate education for women pushed ahead slowly. In 1822 Catharine Beecher founded the Hartford Female Seminary; and in 1835 the Female College came in Georgia. Mary Lyon, a native of Massachusetts, bolder than her predecessors, raised $68,000 and began building what became the Mount Holyoke Seminary (1837). This institution moved further away from the decorative arts for women and sought to offer the hard disciplines—Latin, chemistry, physics. Yet, throughout the country, women's education remained separate and hardly equal to that of men. It was not until 1833, in the Ohio wilderness, that Oberlin became the first coeducational college in the world.

4. HORACE MANN: FATHER OF OUR PUBLIC SCHOOLS

1837—Horace Mann became secretary of the Massachusetts State Board of Education. In 12 years of labor in that post, he shook down the antiquated modes of colonial education and laid the foundation for America's modern school system.

Mann was a superb orator, one of the best lawyers in Massachusetts, a member of the legislature. When Massachusetts created what some thought would be a weakling state school agency, to be headed by an innocuous secretary, Mann took the job, transforming both the agency and the post into instruments of fire and brimstone. He was a furious worker—a fanatic, some said—who hated ignorance, slavery, war, and tobacco, in that order. His loves were education, school, children, teachers, and phrenology. He spent months each year visiting Massachusetts schools, liking little of what he saw. He liked more what he observed in European schools, especially those of Prussia, and this was a basis for both his glory and his anguish.

His chief duty was to prepare annual reports for the state board. He did 12 of them. In these documents, through speeches and letters (sometimes 30 a day, written with a quill), he expounded time and again the incendiary idea: Free education is the birthright of every American child. Mann brought together these principles: The common (public) schools must be tax-supported, publicly controlled, free, and compulsory. He said: "The common school is the greatest discovery ever made by man."

To assure teachers for the schools, Mann managed to establish the first teacher-training institution in America (at Lexington, 1839). To make education an instrument for modern life, he sought to free the curriculum of religious dogma and of word-dry subject matter. He brought music, a modicum of practical arts, and libraries to the schools of Massachusetts. He edited the *Massachusetts Common School Journal*, and with his wife, Mary Peabody Mann, filled its pages with lessons for classroom use and policy discussions for administrators.

After a six-month trip to Europe, Mann came back to write his famous *Seventh Report*. In it he praised the Prussian schools. By comparison, America's teachers and curriculum methods came out second best. The schoolmasters of Boston were stung. They attacked Mann's free thinking, his travels, his preachment of public education. Mann counterattacked with pamphlets and orations. The controversy brought Mann's ideas to the world's attention. But he was hurt. In anguish, he left Massachusetts and took the post of first president of Antioch College. His achievements for higher education were mediocre compared to those for the public schools. Yet his efforts made Antioch America's first truly liberal arts college. Out of his travail, almost at the end of his life, came his deathless admonition to the graduating class of 1859: "Be ashamed to die until you have won some victory for humanity."

5. TO SCHOOL—WILLINGLY OR UNWILLINGLY

1852—Massachusetts enacted the first law compelling children to attend public school.

It was a weak law. Children between 8 and 14 were required to attend school for 12 weeks a year. Nevertheless, the measure was an essential starting point for universal education.

Back in the 1500s, Martin Luther fumed that eternal damnation awaited children who were not compelled to go to school. In 1642 and again in 1647, the religious power structure in Massachusetts required the establishment of schools to teach Bible reading, but did not compel attendance of children, and little was gained for general education as a result. Almost 200 years later, in the 1840s, Horace Mann preached that compulsory education was one of the pillars of a modern public school system. But neither parent, community, nor state was zealous in compelling children to attend school.

At first, the Massachusetts law of 1852 brought little compliance; and there was weak enforcement of this meager span of schooling. Other states were slow to follow the lead. But when the cruel days of the Civil War were over, state after state enacted laws not only compelling attendance but lengthening the required school year and even prescribing what the schools were to teach. The legal machinery grinding out compulsory education was unyielding, if slow. Finally, when Mississippi passed its law in 1918, the entire nation had a blanket of compulsory attendance laws.

The blanket had holes. Some farmers, laboring families, religious groups, and rebels against state-imposed education wanted their children at work, at home, or simply away from the public schools. The blanket often failed to cover migrant families and blacks. In 1925 the U. S. Supreme Court ruled that parents did not have to send their children to public schools—private schools would do just as well. During the 1950s, South Carolina, Mississippi, and Virginia repealed their compulsory education laws—as casualties of the integration wars. But keeping children in school—public or private—had become a national habit. (South Carolina and Virginia soon reenacted compulsory education laws; Mississippi is still debating reenactment.)

Compulsory education paid off magnificently. It soon brought illiteracy in the U. S. to a level lower than that of any other major industrial nation. Immigrant children, by the millions, were brought into the mainstream of American life. And a sense of national unity developed as children from different parts of the country, from different families, lived and worked through 10 to 12 years of schooling—sharing a heritage of knowledge, goals, and attitudes and often singing the same songs from sea to sea and border to border.

6. PEOPLE'S COLLEGES FOR FARMERS AND MECHANICS

1862—President Lincoln signed the Morrill Land-Grant Act, to endow colleges for the liberal and practical education of the industrial classes.

In one of the darkest hours of the Civil War, the nation began one of its brightest chapters in American education. The Morrill Act has been praised for over a century as one of the most significant single enactments on behalf of higher education in the history of humankind.

A clamor for and against higher education under public control had been going on for generations before the land-grant act. The University of Georgia, established nine years after the Declaration of Independence, became the first state-supported institution, and a half dozen other public universities came soon thereafter. But these institutions hardly met the needs of the vast majority of people. Complaints persisted that future lawyers, doctors, and ministers had their Harvard, Yale, and Princeton, but future farmers and mechanics across the young republic had scant opportunity for higher education.

First attempts to set up "people's colleges," however, were defeated in Congress and attacked by academicians who feared the erosion of traditional classical education. The proposed "cow college," it was argued, would educate the young away from the farm, not for the farm. Plato wasn't wanted either on the farm or in factories. One farmer is alleged to have said "What you going to do with that college up there? Larn 'em to rake harder?"

Lincoln staunchly supported popular education, but it took astute leadership by Vermont's Senator Justin S. Morrill to see the land-grant bill through Congress. When it was finally passed, land grants were made to the states on a basis of 30,000 acres for each member of Congress. Income from the sale of public land was to promote agricultural and industrial education, "without excluding scientific and classical studies." Altogether, Congress eventually gave some 11.4 million acres of land, endowing at least one land-grant college in each of the 50 states, the District of Columbia, Puerto Rico, Guam, and the Virgin Islands.

Over the years, Congress was always a generous friend, enlarging and extending the activities of the land-grant institutions.

Land-grant colleges were among the first to open their doors to women. A second Morrill Act (1890) led to the creation of predominantly African-American colleges; although separate and unequal, they provided the first higher education opportunities for most African Americans. Agricultural experimental stations, tied in with the public college campuses, produced startling results in more and better food and fiber; science and engineering laboratories fed America's industrial revolution with new machines and manufacturing processes. For the farm couple unable to come to the campus, Congress set up extension courses on home and family problems.

Today, land-grant institutions are among the leaders in training not only experts for farm and industry but also teachers, doctors, lawyers, business administrators, and engineers. Most of the campuses support strong programs in painting, sculpture, drama, literature, and dance. (Since 1964, Indiana University has granted more degrees in music than any other school in the United States.) And from such institutions as Rutgers, Purdue, and the Universities of Illinois, California, Michigan, and Texas have come accomplishments that have changed the lives of all Americans: the wonder drugs, first sound motion pictures, early research in television, safe commercial canning techniques, isolation of human cancer virus, and the epoch-making findings of atomic research.

7. LITTLE FINGERS MUST BE KEPT BUSY

1873—The St. Louis Board of Education voted to include the kindergarten as a permanent part of its public school system.

The board acted on the recommendation of its superintendent, William T. Harris, one of the great school administrators of the last century, later to become U. S. commissioner of education in Washington. The idea for "a course" for very young children had been in Harris's mind for some time. He had heard of Germany's *Kleinkinderbeschaftigenanstalt* (small-children-keeping-busy-establishment) and of Froebel's mystical work with young children over-

seas. He was looking for the right person to help him start such a program in St. Louis.

Susan Blow, a pious, determined woman of social standing and means, was the person. She had advocated early childhood education for years. At age 40 she knew more about operating kindergarten than anyone in America. Harris asked her to come to St. Louis. She eagerly left New York for the Midwest to put her ideas into action.

At least two other "firsts" preceded the St. Louis kindergarten. The first kindergarten in America was opened in 1855 at Watertown, Wisconsin, by Mrs. Carl Schurz, a pupil of Froebel. It was conducted entirely in German. Chance brought Mrs. Schurz in contact with the idea-hungry, dynamic Elizabeth Peabody of Boston. Peabody forgot her transcendentalism and her interest in Chinese grammar for a while. She began to write, talk, and travel interminably on behalf of the kindergarten idea. She started the first English-speaking kindergarten privately in Boston in 1860. It spurted but soon withered. Peabody was off to other pursuits.

Susan Blow read nearly everything Peabody had written on the kindergarten, including issues of the *Kindergarten Messenger*, which Peabody had filled with essays on the magic value of ball-playing (after all, didn't the word "ball" contain the property of "all," in German and English?). And Blow knew how to put ideas into practice. Encouraged by Harris, the St. Louis kindergarten flourished. The school board was generous. Soon St. Louis was supporting more than 50 public kindergartens. Other cities took up the innovation, looking to St. Louis for ideas. And Americans trudging through the 1876 Centennial Exposition in Philadelphia came upon an intriguing demonstration: a model kindergarten, with children working, playing, and creating, instead of sitting frozen in a row reciting in unison "ba, ba, ba, da, da, da," etc.

8. THE BIRTH OF THE PUBLIC HIGH SCHOOL

1874—The Michigan Supreme Court ruled that the city of Kalamazoo had the right to establish high schools and hire a secondary school staff with public money.

The Kalamazoo case is historic. It encouraged the spread of the public high school in America. It provided the legal base for a part of the American dream—that an individual could get free, tax-supported schooling from the earliest grades to the university. The high school supplied the necessary rungs for this climb upward.

The battle for the free public high school was long and often bitter. Even while free elementary schooling was still under attack, educators and non-educators were already proposing free secondary education. The first public high school was established in Boston in 1821. A scant half-dozen years later, Massachusetts passed a law requiring a high school in every town of 500 families and over. The proposed curriculum had a touch of modernity: U. S. history, bookkeeping, algebra, geometry, surveying. Only larger towns were required to include Greek, Latin, and that colonial favorite, rhetoric.

Decades passed. The idea of the tax-supported high school languished. Labor unions fought for free secondary schools, but taxpayers' groups overwhelmed them. History records some of the arguments used against the public high school: "What a waste. . . ." "What do we want a high school for to teach the smart children for?" "What a shame to pay a man $1,800 to teach children to make x's and gabble parley vous. . . ."

When Kalamazoo voted, in 1872, to establish a free high school and hire a superintendent of schools, these arguments were among those used against the proposal. To test the issue, a citizen brought suit to prevent additional taxes for the newfangled schools. The case went to the Michigan Supreme Court. In 1874 Chief Justice Thomas Cooley gave the renowned decision: A school district cannot be restricted in its efforts to offer educational opportunities; a public education system has the right to provide the rungs necessary for climbing to the university, if citizens wish to pay for this purpose.

There was no stopping the public high school after this. In state after state, courts struck down attacks against it by following the Kalamazoo decision.

At first a city institution, the public high school began penetrating into rural areas. Arguments about the worth of the high school continued, but students flocked to its doors. By 1890 the high school was entrenched, popular, praised by most citizens. But grumbling about its costs never stopped, and at the beginning of the twentieth century public high schools enrolled only 699,000 or 11% of all youth eligible to attend.

Then came startling events. High school enrollment doubled and doubled again in each decade between 1900 and 1940. Wars and depressions affected public high school growth but little.

What and how the high school should teach continue to be issues for debate today. But the right of this truly American institution to exist was forever settled in Kalamazoo.

9. JOHN DEWEY BUYS NEW SCHOOL FURNITURE

1894—John Dewey arrived at the University of Chicago and began working out new ideas for America's schools.

It took less than two decades for John Dewey to show the world that the kinds of schooling children had been getting in the eighteenth and nineteenth centuries would not do for the twentieth. He proposed changes in method and subject matter. He provided new designs for teaching and learning. His ideas stirred, inspired, and angered Americans. He became the most influential, the best known, and the most controversial figure in American (and world) education.

Soon after Dewey decided to set up his Laboratory School, so one report goes, he went looking for furniture for his future classrooms. Nothing he saw in the stores or factories satisfied him. Finally one dealer admitted: "Professor you want something at which children can work. We have only furniture for children who sit and listen."

As a village schoolteacher in his native Vermont, Dewey knew the blank faces and blank minds of children who sat and listened while the teacher droned on. He sensed there were better ways to prepare youngsters for society, and he sought them through his study of psychology and philosophy.

When he arrived at Chicago, his job was in fact to head the Department of Philosophy, Psychology, and Pedagogy. But life, action, community, experience, practical results—these were Dewey's basic interests. Through his Laboratory School he wanted to demonstrate that children learn to swim by swimming, to talk by talking, to think by solving problems. This was later summed up in a famous dictum, "learning by doing." In his Laboratory School classrooms he ventured to connect school with life outside; to give learning a practical content; to show that for effective education children need not only books but also tools and materials, contact with nature and community, interaction with people, and experiences from which they can learn to guide future actions.

He summed up his findings and his wisdom in speeches, lectures, articles, and books. His *School and Society* (1899), *How We Think* (1909), and above all *Democracy and Education* (1916) were immediately influential, and remain towering classics in education. They are still the works most frequently quoted by education students, theorists, and practitioners. And in thousands of classrooms across the nation his ideas, or part of them, were applied or misapplied, used or misused, interpreted correctly or twisted and distorted.

Dewey left Chicago for New York (1904), and through his courses at Teachers College, Columbia, directly influenced tens of thousands of students from all parts of the United States and the world. He was called upon to advise the educational ministries of Japan and Russia. At home he became prophet, reformer, devil, savior—depending on the groups which attacked him or idolized his ideas. If he is given credit or blame for launching the Progressive Education movement, he must share it with scores of other educators and reformers. He was the best known of them all, however, and became a household and schoolhouse name. Today's schools, teachers, and administrators are different because of his career.

10. G.I.S CROWD INTO CLASSROOMS

1944—President Roosevelt signed the Servicemen's Readjustment Act, unanimously passed by Congress, ushering in an educational movement of vast scope and significance.

The soldier, sailor, or airman coming home from World War II service had before him a choice of several benefits—including schooling at Uncle Sam's expense. The G.I. Bill, as the 1944 law was known, gave veterans the opportunity to enroll in secondary schools, technical institutes, colleges, and universities. Or they could get training in industry, on the farm, or through correspondence courses.

The program was an instant success. Young men and women flocked to the nation's campuses, overcrowding classrooms, residence halls, and all temporary housing set up for them. They took up everything from elementary math to postgraduate physics. Large numbers of veterans were married and brought their wives and young families to the campus, or as close to the campus as they could move. Eager for learning, often impatient with dull professional techniques and institutional rules, the returning veterans helped change and invigorate higher education.

Below the college level and in industry, veterans enrolled in everything from shoe repair to remedial reading, from sales and auto mechanics to electronics. And whether in college, high school, or on-the-job training, the veteran was guaranteed his tuition, monthly subsistence, family allotments, free textbooks and learning materials by the federal government. The veteran's entitlement to these benefits frequently ran up to four years.

When federal officials looked at the results in 1947, a busy year for veterans' education, they found that $3.5 billion had already been spent for education and training, with more than a million former G.I.s deeply involved in their schooling programs. By 1951, $14.5 billion had been expended for World War II education and training.

Historian Edgar Knight has said that these huge sums have for the most part been wisely spent and that program outcomes have proved beneficial for veteran and country. In a later assessment, Sidney Marland, former U. S. commissioner of education, called the G.I. education movement a "golden period in our history."

With some change in practice, the principles of the G.I. education benefits have been extended to veterans of the Korean conflict (1952) and the Vietnam era (1964). And when, early in 1976, federal officials looked at results once again, they found that during the 32 years the G.I. Bills had provided education and training for a total of 16 million persons at a cost of $34 billion. "It is one of the best investments the nation has ever made," said Senator Mike Mansfield of Montana. "The G.I. Bill story is yet to be completed," said the Veterans' Administration.

11. EQUAL AND SIDE BY SIDE

1954—The U. S. Supreme Court ruled unanimously that segregation of African American and white students in public education at any level was unconstitutional.

Monday, May 17, 1954, started out as a quiet day at the United States Supreme Court in Washington. Reporters expected routine decisions. But the day became memorable in America's history when Chief Justice Earl Warren began reading the Court's judgment in *Brown* v. *Topeka*. Within a few minutes, Warren came to the momentous words: "We conclude, unanimously, that in the field of public education the doctrine of 'separate but equal' has no place. Separate educational facilities are inherently unequal." Months later, in another ruling, the Court ordered the 17 states with dual school systems to begin dismantling them "with all deliberate speed."

For generations, the South had kept the races segregated in schools, colleges, streetcars, restaurants—all public places, all areas of life. Legal power for segregation came some 30 years after Emancipation, when the U. S. Supreme Court ruled in *Plessy* v. *Ferguson* (1896) that "separate but equal" facilities for African Americans were not unconstitutional. Segregation became deeply entrenched in schools and colleges throughout the South.

Throughout the half-century after *Plessy*, African-American leaders charged that the miserable school shacks, poorly prepared teachers, and inadequate instructional materials used for the education of African Americans deprived them of their constitutional rights. Historians agree that the separate facilities were never equal.

In slow, halting steps, the U. S. Supreme Court began its retreat from the separate-but-equal doctrine. By 1950 African Americans gained admittance to law schools and graduate programs in Missouri, Texas, and Oklahoma. Doors of other graduate and professional schools slowly began opening for African Americans. But Southern and border public elementary and secondary schools held firm against integration until cases from South Carolina, Kansas, Delaware, Virginia, and Washington, D. C., were grouped together under *Brown* v. *Topeka* for decision by the Supreme Court.

Resistance to the Court's integration orders was the first response in the South. Resistance remained massive and stubborn for years. Yet, year after year, large numbers of Southern and border school districts worked out successful plans for ending their dual schools. (Louisville, Kentucky, and later Tampa, Florida, have been cited as shining examples of successful integration.)

Neither riots, parent protests, violence, nor legal maneuvers on state or local levels have halted the march of integration. By mid-1970 government figures showed that although African-American students were "at various levels of isolation," fewer than 10 percent of America's 45 million youngsters were in 100 percent African-American or minority schools.

12. UNCLE SAM—BIG PARTNER IN EDUCATION

1965—Congress enacted the Elementary and Secondary Education Act (ESEA), called "the most significant commitment to education ever made by any national government."

When President Lyndon Johnson signed the ESEA on April 11, 1965, he said: "No law I have signed or ever will sign means more to the future of America." Educators, for the most part, have agreed. The ESEA began a new era of massive federal aid to education. On its tenth anniversary, educators said that under the ESEA American education was on its way to a second decade of revolutionary changes.

The ESEA's $17 billion in 10 years has provided new schooling opportunities for children of the poor, encouraged new ways of teaching and using instructional tools, expanded library facilities, promoted research, and strengthened state departments of education. The ESEA has been amended and expanded year after year. Its basic principles continue today under the Education Amendments which are the main means for channeling federal dollars to state and local school systems.

Federal dollars, and other resources, have gone to America's public schools for 200 years. When land grants were no longer feasible, Congress used cash. In 1917, with a modest $7 million appropriation, Congress virtually started up vocational education through the Smith-Hughes Act. Congress used other resources to aid education. After each of the World Wars, Congress donated surplus property worth millions to schools and colleges. Surplus farm commodities became the basis of the federal school lunch programs starting in 1936.

When, suddenly, in 1958, the Russians launched their first rocket into space, a Sputnik-scared Congress rushed through the National Defense Education Act. Congress wanted more and better science, math, and foreign language courses, fearing the Russians might out-educate us as they had outdistanced us in space.

Despite Uncle Sam's generosity to America's schools and colleges, some school people and citizens wanted more. Bills for more ample federal aid to education showed up in Congress each year. Lobbyists, supported by blocs of teachers and the public, waged campaigns for their enactment. Yet for more than two decades (1945–1965) scores of such bills died in Congress. Main foes were church leaders, taxpayer groups, states' rights advocates, and those who feared federal control of education or education itself.

The ESEA broke the logjam. It diffused the church/state issue and by-passed the controversial formulas for giving aid to school systems. It did so simply by focusing on the needs of children from poor, black, or "culturally disadvantaged" families. The main part of the ESEA, called Title I, has become famous for its help in educating the poor in big-city ghettos as well as in the hills and hollows of Appalachia.

Side by side with Title I grants came a flood of other types of assistance to America's schools. Today, Congress supports programs for the education of the handicapped, the gifted, children who speak a non-English language at home, and children from migrant and Native American families.

The curriculum, textbooks, libraries, school statistics, research, teacher training—these and others are the objects of federal help. The "right to read" and career education are current major interests of the federal government. The U. S. Office of Education and related education agencies are operating more than 120 different programs for schools and colleges at an annual cost to the federal treasury of some $12 billion. This is about 10% of the total spent for public and private education. Some say it is too much; others that it is not enough.

37 SIGNIFICANT EVENTS IN OUR EDUCATIONAL HISTORY

1779 Thomas Jefferson introduced his school bill for Virginia, the first plan for a statewide school system in the New World.

1783 Noah Webster published the first distinctively American textbook—the phenomenally successful blue-backed Spelling Book.

1787 Congress enacted the Northwest Ordinance, with means "forever encouraging education."

1795 New York enacted a five-year experimental law to distribute $100,000 a year to its counties for school support— the first state aid to education.

1819 The U. S. Supreme Court ruled, in the famous Dartmouth case, that private institutions of higher learning may not be taken over by the state. This led to a flourishing of private colleges as well as to the spread of state universities.

1821 Emma Willard founded the Troy Seminary in New York State; soon thereafter, doors to higher education were slowly pried open for women all over the country.

1829 Samuel R. Hall published his *Lectures on School-keeping,* the first professional book for teachers published in the United States.

1836 William Holmes McGuffey, a college professor, published the first of his *Readers.* By 1920, about 122 million copies of his series had been sold—making them the most popular of all American textbooks.

1837 Horace Mann became secretary of the Massachusetts State Board of Education. In 12 years of labor at that post, he shook down the antiquated modes of colonial education and laid the foundation for America's modern school system.

1852 Massachusetts enacted the first law compelling children to attend public school.

1857 Teachers, administrators, college presidents, and educational philosophers met in Philadelphia and formed the National Teachers Association, later to become the National Education Association (NEA).

1862 President Lincoln signed the Morrill Land-Grant Act, to endow colleges for the liberal and practical education of the industrial classes.

1867 Congress created a "National Department of Education," reduced its rank to a bureau two years later, and placed it within the Department of Interior.

1873 The St. Louis Board of Education voted to include the kindergarten as a permanent part of its public school system.

1874 The Michigan Supreme Court ruled that the city of Kalamazoo had the right to establish high schools and hire a secondary school staff with public money.

1876 A scholar named Daniel Coit Gilman organized and opened Johns Hopkins University in Baltimore, the first graduate school in the United States dedicated to the discovery and advancement of knowledge, not merely its transmission.

1892 Joseph M. Rice visited 1,200 classrooms in 36 cities and published a series of influential articles charging that schools and teachers "dehumanized, immobilized, and automized the children." Historians accept this event as the first major use of investigative school reporting to bring about educational change.

1894 John Dewey arrived at the University of Chicago and began working out new ideas for America's schools.

1902 Joliet Junior College, inspired by Illinois college presidents and high school principals, started operation with 22 students. The junior and community college movement was on its way.

1907 Peak year of mass migration to the United States, a movement which brought 46 million immigrants between 1820 and 1974. "The common school changed the immigrant, but the immigrant altered the school, too," says historian David B. Tyack.

1916   Educators, impressed with methods used by organized labor to protect its interests, set up the American Federation of Teachers (AFT) in Chicago. Now affiliated with the AFL-CIO, the labor-oriented teachers are still a small group (300,000) compared to the NEA. But the AFT's use of strikes and collective bargaining have pervaded the entire profession and changed the NEA.

1916   Lewis M. Terman published *The Measurement of Intelligence,* and historian Ellwood Cubberley said, "We are now able to give each child an intelligence rating, or intelligence quotient." The age of the I.Q. was on.

1917   Congress enacted the Smith-Hughes bill and appropriated $1.7 million for promotion of home economics, agricultural education, and training for trades and industries. President Woodrow Wilson applauded the act.

1918   "The Cardinal Principles of Secondary Education" were born. The NEA Committee of Ten published what became its most famous report, calling for reorganizing secondary education to bring it in tune with the twentieth century.

1936   The U. S. Department of Agriculture began providing schools with surplus farm commodities for school lunches. By 1976 the value of food donated to schools by the federal government totaled nearly $2 billion a year.

1941   The Progressive Education Association completed its much-discussed "Eight Year Study." It showed that progressive methods and curricula gave students a slight edge for success in college; it also helped liberalize (somewhat) requirements for college entrance.

1944   President Roosevelt signed the Servicemen's Readjustment Act, which Congress had passed unanimously. It ushered in an educational movement of vast scope.

1946   In post-war euphoria, the United States joined the United Nations Educational, Cultural, and Scientific Organization (UNESCO). Schools stepped up their education for international

understanding. And educators hoped that these efforts, along with UNESCO's programs, would contribute to peace and security.

1950   At midcentury American educators launched or intensified the use of teacher aides, business/education days, teaching machines and other more mechanical devices, individualized instruction, mass testing, educational parks, citizens' advisory committees, program budgeting, performance contracting, vouchers, and alternative schools. "Innovation" became the order of the educational day.

1952   The University of Illinois Committee on School Mathematics began fashioning a new mathematics curriculum. The action inspired curricular revisions in science, social studies, and the language arts. One aim: to deemphasize facts, emphasize concepts.

1954   The U. S. Supreme Court ruled unanimously that segregation of African-American and white students in public education at any level was unconstitutional.

1963   In a decision which still remains controversial, the U. S. Supreme Court ruled (*Abington* v. *Schempp*) that laws requiring prayer recitations in the public schools were unconstitutional.

1965   Congress enacted the Elementary and Secondary Education Act (ESEA), called "the most significant commitment to education ever made by any national government."

1970   The U. S. Supreme Court ruled that the quality of a child's education cannot be dependent on the wealth of a local school district. The case, *Serrano* v. *Priest*, shook the foundations of traditional local school support.

1971   A Magna Charta for the mentally disabled? In a widely hailed decision, the Pennsylvania State Supreme Court ruled that the educational needs of the mentally disabled may not be ignored.

1972   Congress created the National Institute of Education, and for the first time educators utilized the resources of a federally financed agency totally devoted

to research into major problems of
teaching and administration.

1974 The outlay for all types and levels of
American education passed the
unprecedented sum of $100 billion a year.

EPILOGUE

For the Bicentennial, federal statisticians took a close
look at our schools and colleges and reported their
findings in *The Condition of Education,* 1976. They
started with a striking fact: Cost, bias, lack of educational resources, and sheer neglect kept most inhabitants of the new republic from any type of schooling. Today, nearly every third person is enrolled in a
class, ranging from nursery school to post-graduate
programs. Today's legion of learners and scholars,
some 62 million strong, is more than the entire 1890
U. S. population.

Four indicators reveal the distance we had to
cover to reach this point:

- One hundred years ago fewer than 35% of all
youngsters between the ages of 5 and 17 were
attending school on a regular basis. Today,
nearly 90% are attending daily for 180 days a
year. This is a legacy from that weak
Massachusetts law requiring attendance of but a
few weeks a year.
- One hundred years ago 3- and 4-year-olds were
not considered likely to gain much from
schooling, even by such enthusiasts for early
childhood education as Susan Blow and
Elizabeth Peabody. Enrollment in
prekindergarten programs has steadily increased
over the years and has taken a sharp spurt since
1964. Today more than 1.5 million children, or
21% of this population group, are in
prekindergarten programs.
- Some of the colonies supported evening schools
for a few brave souls who wanted to learn
reading, writing, and figuring. Throughout our
history, men and women over 18 have been
attracted to part-time study in lyceums,
chautauquas, Americanization schools,
extension and correspondence courses. During
the past five decades, adult education
enrollments have pushed ever upward, and
today some 18 million Americans are engaged in
one or more adult education activities.
- Emma Willard and Mary Lyon would no doubt
be impressed by the opportunities for women
interested in higher education. Of the 11,323,000
students who made up the 1975 opening fall
enrollment in all colleges and universities, more

than five million were women. In 150
institutions of higher education the chief
executive officer was a woman. This latter fact
does not impress some individuals seeking more
policy- and decision-making roles for women in
education. They look to Title IX of the Education
Amendments of 1972 to help achieve their goals.
Title IX is the federal government's main effort
to put an end to sex bias in education, and it has
led educators at all levels to reexamine sexism in
educational practices.

The increased number of students at all levels
has required ever larger expenditures for education; every generation has grumbled about it but
paid. The United States today spends $120 billion a
year for all educational efforts—not quite 10% of
the gross national product. Since 1929, expenditures for formal education have ranged from 3% to
no more than 10% of the GNP, and this is one reason that, despite taxpayer and parent complaint,
we have successfully footed the school bill year after year.

Despite the intervention of the federal government in education, its share of support for all school
programs has been traditionally low, well below 5%
of total outlay. Only in the last decade have there
been substantial increases, resulting in a 10% federal
share by 1975. But consider what the second partner,
the state governments, have done for education
since that day in 1795 when New York first distributed $100,000 in school aid to its counties: State
sources account for $41 billion a year—the largest
share of expenditures for all governments. Local
support has begun a long, slow decline, as the federal and state governments assume a large share of
the school burden.

What is America getting in return for its invest-
ments in education?

The product wasn't always appreciated by all
people, nor have all judged it to be of superior quality. That Johnny and Jane can't write, read, do the
old or new math, or even buy a can of tuna fish economically have been persistent complaints, as summaries of public opinion polls, on the one hand, and
achievement scores, on the other, have shown. But
the gross educational product is huge and diverse.
As *The Condition of Education* indicates, it includes
unprecedented programs for career education, for
the handicapped, the bilingual, the gifted, and offerings for the very young and the old. For the first time
in the history of any nation, children of the poor get
special teaching, special help, and special services.
Classrooms equipped with a dazzling array of instructional materials teach not only the basics and
the traditional, but also new math, revised social

studies, reconstructed language arts, and a new type of physical education.

"A common indicator of the extent to which we have achieved the major goal of free universal basic education is the high school graduate rate," says *The Condition of Education*. Here we see a phenomenal performance. More than 75% of the youngsters of high school age today get high school diplomas. And beyond the high school diploma? Only about one-fourth of the number of individuals who might be considered eligible received college degrees in 1974, and the future rates of college graduation may hold steady or decline. But as the statistics show, we have just been through a period of spectacular increases in the number of bachelor's degrees awarded: from 186,500 in 1940 to 977,000 in 1974.

After its massive review of American education, *The Condition of Education* concludes in its dry statistical voice: "In 1975 only 30% of the public expressed a great deal of confidence in persons running educational institutions, a drop of 10% from the year before. . . . Despite dissatisfaction with education, the public remains committed to its support. Close to 50% of the public believe that too little was being spent for education. . . ." And this despite the fact that we contribute well over $100 billion annually for its support.

CHAPTER 15

Education Since 1960

THE SIXTIES

Sputnik—The Reaction Continues

The sixties can easily and accurately be described as the decade of reaction in education. This reactive period had begun in earnest in 1957, when the Soviets launched the world's first artificial satellite, Sputnik. That event, technological competition from the-then Soviet Union, perhaps more than any other, was what caused Americans to critically examine their educational system. This microscopic critique continued in the sixties. American education was found to be "soft," especially in the areas of science and mathematics. The federal government reacted as it never had before in providing funding for education.

There was a need—indeed, a necessity—to return the United States to the apex of world technology. The route was through education, which became tied to the fibers of this country's security. This connection is illustrated concretely in section 101 of the National Defense Education Act, which was passed in 1958, right on the heels of Sputnik. The purpose was to improve higher education in this country by providing federally sponsored grants, fellowships, and loans to foster the study of the sciences and mathematics. Section 101 of the NDEA reads:

The Congress hereby finds and declares that the security of the Nation requires the fullest development of the mental resources and technical skills of its young men and women. The present emergency demands that additional and more adequate educational opportunities be made available.

The defense of this Nation depends upon the mastery of modern techniques developed from complex scientific principles.

It depends as well upon the discovery and development of new principles, new techniques, and new knowledge (PL 85–864, Section 101).

The National Science Foundation followed suit by offering financial assistance to teachers of science and mathematics for the purpose of updating and improving their skills and knowledge. As a result, American educators began to modify their methods of teaching the sciences, mathematics, and foreign languages. Even as these changes were being implemented with a view toward improving American education and placing this country once again at the frontier of technology, Yuri Gagarin, a Soviet cosmonaut, in 1961, became the first human to orbit the earth. John F. Kennedy, the nation's 35th President, responded later that same year by declaring that a goal of this country would be to put a man on the moon by the end of the decade. America, of course, would achieve that goal, but the reforming of its educational system would continue, as would federal support of those reforms.

Prepared for inclusion in this text by Bobbie Stevens Johnson, 1999.

Equal Educational Opportunities

While continuing to stress making American education equivalent or superior to that of the Soviets, Americans also came face to face with the necessity of providing equal educational opportunities to all of its citizens. The U. S. Supreme Court, in 1954, in *Brown v. Board of Education* determined that the separate but equal ruling it had set forth in 1896 in *Plessy v. Ferguson* was unconstitutional. The need to upgrade American education and the court-ordered mandate to see that all Americans have equal access to the same educational opportunities fused, and federally funded programs dedicated to bringing about the needed changes abounded.

The landmark Civil Rights Act of 1964 prohibited discrimination on the basis of race. Title IV of the act required the U. S. Commissioner of Education to survey the availability of equal educational opportunity and to provide assistance to districts that were trying to desegregate their schools.

The federal government had directed its efforts toward higher education with the National Defense Education Act in 1958. In the aftermath of *Brown v. Board of Education*, it directed its focus to early, elementary, and secondary education not only for the purpose of improvement but also to raise the educational levels of those who had been deprived under the separate but equal guidelines and to ensure equality in the arena of education.

Head Start And The Elementary And Secondary Education Act

Texas' own Lyndon Baines Johnson, the country's 36th President, directed a portion of his Great Society initiative to the nation's young, underprivileged children in the form of a program called Head Start, which began in 1964, under the Economic Opportunity Act. Children targeted to benefit from Head Start were three-to five-year-olds whose families fell below the poverty line. Head Start began as a $96,000,000 program and initially served approximately 300,000 children.

Head Start has been modified over the years, but the basic philosophy of the program, as set forth in 1965 by the Cooke Committee, chaired by Dr. Robert Cooke, then professor of pediatrics at Johns Hopkins University, has continued to be its basic guiding principles. In perusing the Cooke recommendations, one senses the obviously intended comprehensive service aspect of the program. Indeed, the original title for Head Start had been the Comprehensive Child Development Program. Some of the basic goals for Head Start put forth by the Cooke Committee include:

1. to improve the child's physical health
2. to aid the child's emotional and social development
3. to improve the child's mental processing skills
4. to establish patterns and expectations of success for the child
5. to increase the child's capacity to relate positively to family members and others
6. to develop in the child a responsible attitude toward society
7. to increase the sense of dignity and self-worth within the child (Grotberg, 1985)

One of the early criticisms of the Head Start program was directed at the requirement that, to be served by Head Start, a child had to be from a family whose income fell below the poverty line. Initially, many children who needed to be in the program were not included because of this stipulation.

Head Start is still being evaluated, but it should be mentioned here that before the end of the decade the Westinghouse Learning Corporation issued an evaluation stating that Head Start programs had little positive effect on children's long-term academic achievement. The Westinghouse report was criticized a year later by Smith and Bisell. A second analysis by Jay Magidson in 1977 found Head Start to have a positive impact.

All levels of education were being targeted for improvement and equality. In 1965, approximately three months after it was introduced, the U. S. Congress passed the Elementary and Secondary Education Act. The ESEA was designed ". . . to strengthen and improve educational quality and educational opportunities in the nation's elementary and secondary schools" (PL 89–10). This law was quite comprehensive in nature, and it made large sums of federal dollars available to schools in poverty areas, providing compensatory education for those who had been deprived previously.

In addition, funds were given to state education agencies with the understanding that they would be used to improve education at the local level. Dollars for textbooks and innovative programs were also provided (Ravitch, 1983). The ESEA thus represented a comprehensive attempt by the federal government to improve education at the more basic levels while attempting to address the deficit of educational opportunities that had existed for some of this country's children.

Landmark Court Cases

If the sixties saw massive education legislation, it was also a decade that witnessed some landmark U. S. Supreme Court cases that would become a part of the total fabric of education. The land's highest court heard cases involving familiar topics such as school prayer, Bible reading, juvenile rights, and teachers' and students' rights of expression. Jackson M. Drake of Arizona State University has compiled a list of landmark court cases that he thinks have a significant effect on school governance. The following cases are among those that he cited.

Engel v. Vitale (School Prayer), 1962. The State Board of Regents of New York state had composed a brief prayer, which it recommended for the public schools in the state of New York. The New Hyde Park School District adopted the practice of having students recite what had become known as the "Regent's Prayer." Parents of 10 students in the New Hyde Park schools then went to court to ask that the district not be allowed to order the reciting of this prayer because they felt the First Amendment of the United States Constitution was being violated by having children recite the "Regent's Prayer." When the case reached the U. S. Supreme Court, the justices ruled that the requirement to recite a state-composed prayer did indeed violate the Establishment Clause of the First Amendment. (*Engel v. Vitale*, 370 U. S. 421 (1962))

Abington School District v. Schempp (Bible Reading), 1963

Pennsylvania had a state statute that required that at least 10 verses from the Holy Bible be read, without comment, at the opening of each public school day. The statute further provided that any child could be excused from the Bible reading if his or her parent or guardian requested, in writing, such an exemption. The Edward Lewis Schempp family brought suit to request prohibition of the enforcement of the state statute that required the reading from the Bible. The U. S. Supreme Court ruled that this prescribed Bible reading violated the Establishment Clause of the Constitution's First Amendment. (*Abington School District v. Schempp*, 393 U. S. 503 (1963))

In re Gault (Constitutional Rights of Juveniles), 1967

This case does not truly fall into the realm of education, but it certainly has implications for all who deal with juveniles, and educators certainly fall into that category. A juvenile, Gerald Gault, was sent to reform school for six years for allegedly having been involved in the making of an obscene telephone call. The proceeding that resulted in his being sent to reform school was void of counsel for the defendant, advance notice of charges, and advisement that he (the defendant) could remain silent. Neither was Gault given the opportunity to confront his accusers, who had provided mostly hearsay evidence. When the case reached the U. S. Supreme Court, the justices determined that basic constitutional rights must be maintained during juvenile proceedings. According to the high court, an accused youth is entitled to his or her own counsel, the right to confront accusers, as well as the right to remain silent after appropriate warning. (*In re* Gault, 387 U. S. 1 (1967))

Pickering v. Board of Education of Township High School District 205, Will County (Teachers' Right of Expression)

After a proposal to increase school taxes was defeated by the voters in a local election, a Will County, Illinois teacher wrote a letter to the editor of the town newspaper advocating that the superintendent of schools and the school board had mishandled past proposals to increase school taxes. The teacher was dismissed because the board believed that publication of the letter would have negative effects on its ability to run the school district properly.

The U. S. Supreme Court defended the teacher's right to voice his opinion and determined that the letter, because it did not contain false statements, could not be used as cause for dismissal.

(*Pickering v. Board of Education of Township High School District 205, Will County*, 391 U. S. 563 (1968))

Tinker v. Des Moines Independent School District (Students' Right of Expression), 1969

This case occurred during the height of protests against the war in Vietnam. Some students in the Des Moines, Iowa school district chose to wear black armbands as a sign of protest against the conflict. School principals in the district had issued a regulation forbidding the students' wearing black armbands while on school property. Student violators of this rule were being suspended from school. The U. S. Supreme Court ruled that the peaceful wearing of armbands was not cause for dismissal so long as no disruption occurred. (*Tinker v. Des Moines Independent School District*, 393 U. S. 503 (1969))

Thus the decade that began with America continuing to react to the Soviets' artificial satellite and ended with our successfully putting a man on the moon saw change in the American educational system and also witnessed the use of federal dollars to finance the changes. Sputnik was the catalyst to cause us to really look at and evaluate the American educational system. *Brown v. Board of Education* (1954) caused us to continue in the sixties to strive to provide equal educational opportunities for all. Changes and adjustments are ongoing, but the sixties provide a unique window to unique change.

THE SEVENTIES

The concern with providing equal educational opportunities for all Americans that characterized the sixties continued throughout the seventies. The sixties had been primarily concerned with racial equality at the table of educational opportunities. In the seventies, the horizons expanded to include women, people with disabilities, and non-native speakers of English. Equality still was the name of the game, and the trend established in the sixties with federal legislation and funding to help achieve equality continued in the seventies.

Women

The collective voice of women had emerged in the sixties with the establishment, in 1966, of the National Organization for Women, popularly known as NOW, which has worked continually to achieve equal opportunities for women in education as well as in other areas of society. Just as the social climate in the sixties pleaded for equal opportunities for racial minorities, the social climate in the seventies was ripe for pleading for equal rights for women. Just as the U. S. Congress had heard and reacted to the need for racial equality in education in the sixties, so it heard and reacted to the need for gender equality in the seventies.

Title IX of the Education Amendments of 1972 (PL 92–318) is a piece of federal legislation that addresses the gender equity issue in that it forbids discrimination against persons on the basis of sex in any federally funded education program. Title IX, along with other legislation, is what helped athletic programs for girls and women achieve status equal to that of male athletic programs. Title IX later would serve as a guiding principle in cases of sexual harassment in educational institutions.

Another giant step toward achieving equal educational opportunities for women came two years later with the passage of the Women's Educational Equity Act of 1974 (Section 408 of Education Amendments of 1974, PL 93–380). This act, passed during the Nixon Administration, provided federal dollars to public agencies and nonprofit organizations for the purpose of seeing that women have

equal educational opportunities. Some of the specific provisions include:

1. The development, evaluation, and dissemination . . . of curricula, textbooks, and other educational materials related to educational equity
2. Preservice and inservice training for educational personnel, including guidance and counseling, with special emphasis on programs and activities designed to advance educational equity
3. Guidance and counseling activities, including the development of nondiscriminatory tests, designed to assure educational equity
4. Educational activities to increase opportunities for adult women, including continuing educational activities and programs for underemployed or unemployed women
5. The expansion and improvement of educational programs and activities for women in vocational education, career education, physical education, and educational administration. (Women's Educational Equity Act of 1974, PL 93–380, Section 408)

Thus, just as we would strive to remove racial bias from curricula, textbooks, and tests, so we would strive to remove gender bias. We would revisit the issue of gender bias when it was found that girls were not performing as well in mathematics and science as their male counterparts, and perhaps at least some of the cause would be found in bilateral expectations and treatment of the two genders.

In addition to Title IX and the Women's Educational Equity Act of 1974, Title VII of the Civil Rights Act of 1964 was revised to bar gender discrimination in educational institutions. At last women had full federal support against discrimination.

Handicaps and *Southeastern Community College v. Davis*

Significant federal strides for people with disabilities were made in the seventies. Section 504 of the Rehabilitation Act of 1973, which passed the U. S. Congress over a presidential veto, prohibits unfair treatment of individuals with disabilities in programs that receive federal funding. Any institution that receives federal dollars is required to provide full access to people with disabilities.

The Education for All Handicapped Children Act (EAHCA) (PL 94–142) followed in 1975. It requires the states to provide a "free and appropriate" education to all children with disabilities. Children with disabilities also are to be *mainstreamed*, or educated to the extent possible with nonhandicapped children in the *least restrictive environment*. Public Law 94–142 is now referred to as the Individuals with Disabilities Education Act (IDEA).

An early test of the educational provisions for the students with disabilities came in 1979 in the form of *Southeastern Community College v. Davis* (442 U.S. 397 (1979)). Davis was a deaf student who desired to enroll in the nursing program at Southeastern Community College in Whiteville, North Carolina, a state institution that received federal funding. The school, however, did not think it could, in good faith, admit Davis to its nursing program because it was believed that her handicap would prevent her from providing adequate care to patients. The high court held that Southeastern Community College had not violated Section 504 of the Rehabilitation Act of 1973 in denying admission to Davis.

Non-Native Speakers Of English and *Lau v. Nichols*

Non-native speakers of English comprised another group to benefit from federal legislation. These students were considered to be a disadvantaged population because classes in which they were enrolled were taught in English, a language in which they were not proficient. The U. S. Congress had passed the Bilingual Education Act in 1968, but virtually all it did was provide funds for local districts to use in bilingual programs. The act did not mandate that public schools offer bilingual education (Ravitch, 1983).

In 1970, however, it was decided that children who were not proficient in English were covered under Title VI of the Civil Rights Act of 1964. The Office of Civil Rights instructed the individual states to do whatever was necessary to tailor their educational programs in such a way that individuals not proficient in English could become full participants.

Interpretations of this instruction have varied, but in 1974, the U. S. Supreme Court heard *Lau v. Nichols*, which has become a landmark case in bilingual education. This case was a class action suit brought by 13 Chinese students on behalf of other Chinese-speaking students against the San Francisco United School District. The students contended that they were not being properly educated because they did not comprehend the language in which they were being taught. Echoing the separate but equal argument of the fifties, the high court established that equal access to a facility does not necessarily provide equal educational opportunities. Following the court's decision, school districts receiving federal dollars were expected to provide special instruction for non-English speaking students (*Lau v. Nichols*, 414 U. S. 563 (1974)).

Equality In School District Funding And *San Antonio Independent School District v. Rodriguez*

It is indeed significant that a seventies' U. S. Supreme Court case concerning school funding was a Texas case. Originally *Rodriguez v. San Antonio Independent School District* (337 F. Supp. 280), this suit was brought on behalf of all Texas children living in school districts with low property valuations; thus, *Rodriguez v. San Antonio ISD* challenged the method of state financing for public schools in the state of Texas. The U. S. Supreme Court, which heard the case in 1973, found that Texas' method of using property valuations as a basis for the funding of local school districts was not a violation of the U. S. Constitution. The court did not find discrimination because children of all races and all levels of wealth in a given school district would be subject to the level of funding provided by the tax base. The high court, however, did leave the door open for state courts and legislatures to reform their school funding systems. (*San Antonio Independent School District* v. *Rodriguez*, 411 U. S. 1 (1973))

This ruling came after the 1971 *Serrano v. Priest* case in which the California Supreme Court ruled, in essence, that the quality of a child's education should not be dependent on the wealth of the people who live in the school district in which the child attends school.

REVERBERATIONS FROM THE SIXTIES—THE BAKKE CASE

The University of California Medical School at Davis had the policy of annually setting aside 16 of its 100 places for new medical school students for disadvantaged individuals. Allan Bakke, a white male who was denied admission to the medical school, claimed that his denial came about as a result of the school's policy of setting aside 16 positions for the disadvantaged. He filed suit against the Regents of the University of California. The case was heard by the U. S. Supreme Court in 1978. The high court ordered that Bakke be admitted to the University of California Medical School at Davis, but the full implications of the case were not clearly discerned. Some of the justices indicated that Mr. Bakke had been discriminated against because he was white; other justices indicated that setting aside a specific number of places in the medical school for disadvantaged minorities was an acceptable way to combat past discrimination (*Regents of University of California v. Bakke*, 438 U.S. 265 (1978)). The Bakke decision would be frequently cited in the Hopwood, et al. v. State of Texas 78 F. 3rd 932 (5th Circuit 1996) regarding affirmative action policies of the University of Texas Law School.

U. S. Department Of Education

In the seventies, albeit late in the decade, the U. S. Department of Education was established, thereby granting cabinet-level status to education. As a presidential candidate in 1976, Jimmy Carter had indicated that he would favor establishing a separate Department of Education. This position generally was considered contrary to Carter's usual opposition to creating more governmental agencies. The National Education Association approved of Carter's willingness to consider creating a then-13th cabinet-level department, because the organization believed that education would then would truly take its place in the federal hierarchy and thus have a voice fully equal to that of other cabinet-level agencies.

President Carter's amended proposal for creating the U. S. Department of Education was approved by the U. S. Congress on September 27, 1979, but the unit did not become totally functional until 1980. The President named Shirley Hufstedler, a former judge on the U. S. Court of Appeals in San Francisco, the first Secretary of Education. Texas' own Lauro Cavazos was appointed U. S. Secretary of Education in 1988. He made history in that he was the first Hispanic to become a member of a President's cabinet. Cavazos was President of Texas Tech University at the time of his appointment. He resigned from the cabinet in 1990.

Although education was not granted cabinet-level status until 1979, it had been a unit of the federal government since 1867, when the Congress established a **non**-cabinet agency called the department of Education. Later, that agency became the Bureau of Education, and then the Office of Education, which was a part of the Department of the Interior. In 1953, during the Eisenhower Administration, education became a part of the then-new Department of Health, Education, and Welfare, of which Texas' own Oveta Culp Hobby was its first secretary. In 1979, with education in its very own department, the former Department of Health, Education, and Welfare became the Department of Health and Human Services.

Additional Landmark U. S. Supreme Court Cases

In addition to the cases mentioned above, others in the seventies significantly affected education. The cases that follow are among those listed by Jackson

M. Drake in his list of court cases that have affected school governance.

Due Process and Suspensions (*Goss v. Lopez*, 1975)

Ohio state law permitted school principals to suspend students for 10 days without informing them of the reasons for the suspension and without providing a hearing that would give the students an opportunity to respond to the allegations. A group of nine secondary school students challenged the constitutionality of the state statute. The U. S. Supreme Court found the statute unconstitutional and stated that students who are suspended for a period up to 10 days must be furnished with written or oral notice of the allegations. The high court further stated that a hearing must be provided that will allow the student's side of the issue to be heard. Further, if the student denies the charges against him or her, the plaintiff must provide an explanation of the evidence (*Goss v. Lopez*, 419 U. S. 565 (1975)).

Corporal Punishment (*Ingraham v. Wright, 1977*)

Students in a Dade County, Florida, Junior High School maintained that their having been subjected to corporal punishment violated their constitutional right. The U. S. Supreme Court held that the cruel and unusual punishment clause of the Eighth Amendment does not apply to disciplining with corporal punishment in the public schools (*Ingraham v. Wright*, 430 U. S. 651 (1977)).

In an earlier case, *Baker* v. *Owen* (1975), the high court had affirmed a lower court's ruling in a case in which a mother filed suit because her sixth-grade child had received corporal punishment over her (the mother's) objection. The lower court held that, although a parent's right to control the discipline of his or her child is embraced, the state has a counter interest in maintaining order in the school, and that spanking does not constitute cruel and unusual punishment (*Baker v. Owen*, 395 F. Supp 294; affirmed 423 U. S. 907 (1975)).

Mandatory Maternity Leave for Female Public School Teachers (*Cleveland Board of Education v. LaFleur*, 1974)

Pregnant public school teachers brought action challenging the constitutionality of the mandatory maternity leave rules of the Cleveland, Ohio, and Chesterfield County, Virginia school boards. The high court combined the above case with *Cohen v.*

Chesterfield County School Board and ruled that mandatory termination provisions of both school boards violated the due process clause of the Fourteenth Amendment. The court further held that the mandatory three-month period of enforced leave that the Cleveland School Board required was also in violation of the due process clause of the Fourteenth Amendment (*Cleveland Board of Education v. LaFleur, 414 U. S. 632 (1974)*).

Thus the seventies marked a period of time when women, people with disabilities, and non-native speakers of English were embraced by federal legislation and funding, as well as by significant judicial decisions.

THE EIGHTIES AND NINETIES AND INTO THE MILLENNIUM

The last two decades have really not been that different from the two previous ones. Problems continue in the educational system, and we perpetually strive to remedy same. After a while, we evaluate the attempted remedies and either continue, revise, or discard the current efforts in exchange for others. The eighties begin with concern about the low test scores of students in the nation's schools.

A Nation at Risk

Despite the efforts put forth during the sixties and seventies, the standardized test scores of U. S. students continued to decline throughout the seventies and into the early eighties. In 1983, the National Commission on Excellence in Education, a federal study group, issued *A Nation at Risk,* wherein it called for major improvement at all levels of American education. The Commission urged schools to raise their standards in specific disciplines such as mathematics, the sciences, computer science, the social sciences, and English. The body also encouraged schools to have increased hours of instruction, more homework, and additional money for teachers' salaries.

Education Reform in Texas

Individual states responded in their own ways to the Commission's findings. Texas' then-Governor Mark White appointed a Select Committee on Public Education with Dallas billionaire and future presidential candidate Ross Perot as chair. Mr. Perot and his committee made recommendations to the Texas legislature, which held a special education session in the summer of 1984. Texas eventually came to have what has become well known as House Bill 72, a

massive reform law that would, until 1995, guide public education in the state. Perhaps the part of HB 72 that received the most media coverage was that concerning "no pass, no play," which affected school athletics, and which the legislature would later amend. Although House Bill 72 certainly emphasized academics over athletics, that was only a small part of this educational reform package.

If students were doing poorly on standardized tests, perhaps the time had come to take a close look at those who teach in terms of testing, workloads, evaluations, and so forth. House Bill 72 called for teacher testing in both pedagogy and the specific discipline or disciplines taught. The Texas Examination of Current Administrators and Teachers (TECAT) and the Examination for the Certification of Educators in Texas (ExCET) are the two exams that have been designed to test teachers. The TECAT examines basic skills, and the ExCET tests one's knowledge of specific disciplines as well as of professional education.

Teachers had long complained of massive paperwork, and they were assured of a free period during which they could hold parent conferences, prepare for class, grade papers, or do whatever would enable them to become more effective in performing their job. House Bill 72 also assured teachers of a 30-minute, duty-free lunch.

Although it was dismantled in 1993, a career ladder for teachers was part of the House Bill 72 package. The theory was that teachers would be awarded higher salaries for outstanding performance. To have a uniform criteria for measuring teacher performance, House Bill 72 also mandated establishment of the Texas Teacher Appraisal System, which called for two appraisals per year by two appraisers. This system was revised in 1993, and now only one appraisal per year is required. Also, since the career ladder for teachers has been abolished, districts now have the freedom to follow the one developed by the state or develop their own appraisal system if they so desire. The current state system is The Professional Development and Appraisal System (PDAS). Districts that elect to develop their own appraisal system must have it approved by the State Commissioner of Education (Kemerer and Walsh, 1994).

Because student testing was certainly one of the keys that demonstrated that our educational system was not properly equipping children to function adequately in society, the state of Texas determined that we would use testing throughout the educational process with the hope of diagnosing problems early on with a view toward remedying them. Students are presently given the Texas Assessment of Academic Skills (TAAS) exam throughout their school years, beginning in the third grade, and high school seniors are required to pass the 10th-grade "exit" TAAS to be graduated from a Texas public high school. Entering college students who do not achieve certain required scores on the SAT, ACT, or TAAS are required to take the Texas Academic Skills Program (TASP) test. (The TASP was originally required of ALL entering college freshmen; these exceptions were established in 1993.) Scores on the TASP are also looked at in determining who is admitted to teacher certification programs. The same SAT, ACT, and TAAS exceptions apply to those seeking teacher certification.

In addition to testing, House Bill 72 mandated that each course taught in the Texas public schools be tied to specific objectives that are to be mastered by the students taking the course. These objectives, which underwent extensive revision during the 1991–1992 academic year, were popularly known as "essential elements," until 1997, when they underwent a second major revision and became known as Texas Essential Knowledge and Skills or TEKS. The theory behind the creation of course-related objectives is that if certain expectations or "outcomes" for various courses are established, and if the student succeeds in meeting those expectations, then he or she can be thought to have mastered the material.

Social promotion, as a way around a student's failure to master the subjects being taught, is being frowned upon in a big way. While most individuals involved in education agree that social promotion should not be practiced, there is a division of opinion on the criteria that should be used to determine if a student should be promoted. Some educators favor testing while others prefer for the individual teachers to make that determination. A bill ending social promotion, with a provision for exceptions determined by parents and educators, was passed by the 76th Legislature in 1999.

Examples of Troubled School Districts

Some schools, despite all efforts, retain their low-achieving label based on test scores. The state of Texas demonstrated its seriousness in dealing with troubled school districts by taking over the Wilmer-Hutchins ISD in June of 1996. The Texas Education Agency assigned state monitors to manage the school district after the Wilmer-Hutchins ISD had, over a period of time, reported low test scores and demonstrated some poor management. At this writing, the Wilmer-Hutchins ISD is well on the road to recovery. The district has a new superintendent and the monitors have departed.

The Dallas Independent School District, which has had its share of low-achieving schools, chose its first Hispanic superintendent, Dr. Yvonne Gonzalez, in January of 1997. Dr. Gonzalez' tenure was cut short when, after only eight months on the job, she pleaded guilty to the misuse of some $16,000 in public funds. She began serving a sixteen-month prison sentence in March of 1998 and was released in 1999.

School Funding

Although the U. S. Supreme Court in 1973 in *San Antonio Independent School District v. Rodriguez* (411 U.S. 1 (1973)) ruled that Texas' method of using property taxes to finance its public schools was not unconstitutional, the high court also left the door open for state legislatures to reform public school financing by acknowledging that disparities in school expenditures vary among school districts in Texas and that these disparities probably are attributable to the varying tax bases. (Judge Thurgood Marshall's Dissent, *San Antonio School District v. Rodriguez*, 411 U.S. 1 (1973))

Edgewood Independent School District was a party in *San Antonio Independent School District v. Rodriguez*, and in 1987, the case of *Edgewood v. Kirby*, in which the plaintiff pleaded that Texas' school financing system was in violation of the state constitution, was heard in state district court, where the verdict was in favor of the plaintiff. The case was appealed, and the Court of Appeals reversed the lower court's decision (761 S.W. 2d 859). The case was then appealed to the Texas Supreme Court, and the state's highest court held that the school financing system, based in part on property taxes, did indeed violate the state's constitutional provision for a "general diffusion of knowledge . . . and an efficient system of public free schools" as set forth in Article VII, Section 1 of the Texas Constitution which reads:

Public Schools to Be Established—A general diffusion of knowledge being essential to the preservation of the liberties and rights of the people, it shall be the duty of the Legislature of the State to establish and make suitable provision for the support and maintenance of an efficient system of public free schools.

Thus, the judgment of the trial court was affirmed, while that of the Court of Appeals was reversed, and the Texas state legislature began its long trek to find an equitable method of funding for all of the state's school districts. After rejecting several legislative attempts at solving the school-funding crisis, the judiciary directed the state and the individual school districts to proceed with the implementation of Senate Bill 7, which was passed late during the 1993 regular session of the state legislature.

Senate Bill 7 mandates that the wealthiest school districts must relinquish their wealth to the point of allowing a maximum of $280,000 per student. Anything over that amount per student must be relinquished. The bill allows the districts several options in determining how their wealth will be relinquished, but the most popular, as demonstrated by electorates around the state, has been for the rich districts to simply write a check to the state and thereby transfer some of their funds to the state, which will disburse the funds to poorer districts. Some of the richer school districts have unsuccessfully appealed the provisions of Senate Bill 7. The state continues to follow the mandates of Senate Bill 7 in an effort to achieve equitable funding for all of the states' school districts. Legislators were optimistic regarding the equity provisions of Senate Bill 4 passed in 1999.

Alternatives And Parental Concerns— Home Schooling

Even though efforts to improve public school education have abounded at both the state and national levels, many parents have become totally disenchanted with public schools and have turned to other alternatives. Home schooling appears to be a viable alternative to many parents throughout the country, and Texas is certainly no exception. *Leeper v. Arlington I.S.D.* (1987) is a court case that helped pave the way for the flourishing of home schooling in Texas. In that case, which challenged the compulsory school attendance law, a state district judge ruled that in the state of Texas, a home in which students are instructed qualifies as a private school (Kemerer & Walsh, 1994). Texas presently does not have any statutes governing home schools, but *Leeper v. Arlington* established that home schools must have a curriculum that is designed to meet basic educational goals. *Leeper v. Arlington* was affirmed by the Texas Court of Appeals in 1991. The case then went to the Texas Supreme Court as *Texas Education Agency v. Leeper*. The state's high court ruled that "home school can be private school within meaning of statutory exemption to compulsory attendance law, so long as children are taught in bona fide manner from curriculum designed to meet basic education goals" (893 S.W.2d 432).

Educational Vouchers and Charter Schools

Educational vouchers that allow parents to use school-tax dollars to send their children to a school of their choice have also gained a degree of support, with a number of states having approved school choice programs and with additional states considering various programs that would allow for school choice (Carnegie Foundation, 1992). By one estimate, approximately 9 percent of students in grades 3–12 are attending private schools; thus the popularity of vouchers is steadily increasing. The U. S. Congress considered a voucher bill (HR 2746) in 1997 that would have allowed the states to use federal dollars to pay for vouchers for economically-deprived students. This unsuccessful bill was the first freestanding piece of voucher legislation to make it to the House floor. It was defeated by a vote of 228 to 191 (*State Legislatures*, March 1998).

Charter schools are yet another alternative. Charter schools may be staffed by certified teachers who create their own school within a school district, with which the teachers are contracted. Charter schools are publicly funded, but they are free of many state regulations. Charter schools are expected to demonstrate student achievement in order to continue to exist. A 1995 revision of Texas' Education Code allowed school districts in Texas to establish charter schools, and Texas' State Board of Education voted in March of 1998 to expand the number of charter schools in Texas from 19 to 60. Texas originally had 20 charter schools, but one was forced to surrender its contract after receiving more than $240,000 from the state without ever opening its doors to students. A 1997 state law allows up to 100 more charter schools over a two-year period. It also allows an unlimited number of such schools if 75% of the student body consists of at-risk students (Vernon's Texas Code Annotated, Education Code, Section 12.1011, 1998).

School Safety

Academic concerns are not the sole reason that parents look for alternative methods of educating their children. Parents are concerned about violence and drugs in the schools as well. The U. S. Congress voiced its collective concern with violence in the schools by passing the Gun-Free School Zones Act of 1990 (PL 101–647). The law made it a crime to bring a firearm within 1,000 feet of a school ground.

Ironically, a Texas case is what caused the U. S. Supreme Court to agree to review the law. A San Antonio high school student, Alfonso Lopez, Jr., received a six-month prison term, combined with two years of probation, for carrying a gun into San Antonio's Edison High School. Mr. Lopez's conviction was overturned by the Fifth Circuit Court of Appeals on the grounds that the Gun-Free School Zones Act of 1990 is unconstitutional. On April 26, 1995, the U. S. Supreme Court, in *United States v. Lopez*, agreed with the Fifth Circuit Court of Appeals by declaring the Gun-Free School Zones Act unconstitutional. The vote by the U. S. Supreme Court justices was five to four, with the majority stating that Congress does not have the power to restrict guns in schools.

Regardless of the U. S. Supreme Court's decision, the very fact that the Congress of the United States passed the law underscores the basic concern that Americans have for their children's safety in the nations' schools. Their fears have certainly been justified as the country has witnessed students being accused of killing their fellow students and teachers in high-profile cases in Jonesboro, Arkansas, Pearle, Mississippi, Paducah, Kentucky, Springfield, Oregon, and Littleton, Colorado to name a few.

President Clinton voiced his desire for safe schools by having the U. S. Attorney General and the Secretary of Education produce a report card on school safety. The report, presented to the President in the spring of 1998, indicated that although most schools are safe, a lot of work remains to be done. According to the report, the number of students belonging to gangs nearly doubled between 1989 and 1995. The report also states that in 1996 alone, there were more than 10,000 physical attacks or fights with weapons in schools. In response, President Clinton has called for a Safe School Initiative, which calls for using federal funds to hire more teachers, reduce class sizes, and rehabilitate schools (Clinton , 1998).

As parents articulate their concerns with safety in the schools, some are also looking at what they consider the root causes of the violence. Some are crying out for the schools to teach moral values as a part of the curriculum. The responses from schools vary. In the Dallas-Fort Worth area, trustees of the Cedar Hill, Irving, and Plano Independent School Districts passed resolutions that allow teachers to reinforce "basic traditional moral values." A resolution is certainly not the same thing as school policy, but it is still a response to what these three school boards evidently thought was a need. There is, of course, massive disagreement on the roles of the school versus those of the home in teaching moral values, and it is a topic that is not likely to be settled soon, if ever.

In the period since the highly publicized killing of students by classmates, especially the incident at Columbine High School in Littleton, Colorado in 1999, renewed interest in public school safety has dominated the agendas of the Congress, state legislatures, and school boards throughout the country.

Changes in the Texas Education Code

In 1995, the Texas State Legislature made some major changes in the laws governing education in Texas. Senate Bill 1, whose chief sponsor was State Senator Bill Ratliff of Mount Pleasant, paved the way for charter schools in Texas and gave more control to local school authorities in the form of "home rule." Senate Bill 1 also gave students the right to transfer from "bad" to "better" public schools. Mr. Ratliff's bill also revisited the "no pass, no play" rule that was enacted in 1984 and cut in half the amount of time a student must exclude himself or herself from extracurricular activities if he or she fails an academic subject. The original legislation required a student to refrain from participating in extracurricular activities for six weeks after having failed a subject or subjects. The 1995 revision allows a student to return to extracurricular activities three weeks after having failed an academic subject or subjects.

Court Cases

Texas has continued to contribute landmark court cases in the area of education. In addition to those mentioned in the above text, the following are indeed significant.

***Irving Independent School District v. Tatro* (468 U. S. 883 (1984)).** This case has had a tremendous impact upon services school districts are expected to provide for the disabled. In 1984, Amber Tatro was an eight-year-old victim of spina bifada. One of the effects of spina bifida was that Amber Tatro was unable to empty her own bladder, and for her to attend school, catheterization (clean intermittent catheterization, or CIC) had to be performed every three or four hours. The U. S. Supreme Court found that performing the required catheterization was a "related service" covered by the Education for All Handicapped Children Act of 1975, and because the school district involved received federal funds, the district was to provide the catheterization that would enable Amber Tatro to attend school. (Amber Tatro completed high school in May of 1994.)

***Plyer, Superintendent, Tyler Independent School District, v. Doe, Guardian* (457 U. S. 202 (1982)).** This case, brought to the nation's highest court in 1982, established that children of illegal aliens could not be excluded from a tuition-free education. This case was again in the forefront in 1994, when California passed Proposition 187, which, among other provisions, denies free education to illegal aliens.

Cases Dealing With the Liability of School Districts

There have been a number of Texas cases dealing with the issue of a school district's liability for the actions of its teachers and students. Some of the noteworthy cases on this point include the following.

***Leija v. Canutillo Independent School District* (101 F3d 393 (1996)).** In this 1996 case, the Canutillo Independent School District was found not liable for the actions of one of its health/physical education teachers who had sexually molested a second-grade female student. The court based its decision on the fact that the girl's mother reported the incident to the homeroom teacher instead of to someone with authority over the accused. The U. S. Supreme Court elected not to hear the case, thus allowing the lower court's decision to stand.

***Rowinsky v. Bryan Independent School District* (80 F3d 1006).** This 1996 case concerned a male student physically and verbally abusing a female student. The U. S. Supreme Court declined to hear the case, thus letting stand the lower court's decision that the Bryan Independent School District could not be held liable for this instance of student-on-student harassment. The court stated that the district could be held liable only if it treated harassment claims made by females differently from those made by males.

J.W. v. Bryan Independent School District. This second case, filed against the Bryan Independent School District in 1997, has not actually been reported because both a District Court and the U. S. Court of Appeals for the Fifth Circuit dismissed the case, citing the Fifth Circuit's ruling in *Rowinsky v. Bryan Independent School District*, which the U. S. Supreme Court had declined to hear. *J.W. v. Bryan ISD* is significant, however, in that it is another case involving student-on-student sexual harassment. J.W. filed suit against the Bryan ISD because her daughter was being harassed by male students at one of the district's middle schools. J.W. claimed that the district's inactivity on the matter violated Title IX of the Education Amendments of 1972, which bars sexual discrimination at schools and colleges that receive federal funds (Lederman, 1997).

***Gebser v. Lago Vista Independent School District* (524 U.S. ___ (1998).[1]** This case, argued before the U. S. Supreme Court on March 25, 1998 and decided on June 22, 1998 is yet another one in which the high court found a school district <u>not</u> liable for the conduct of one of its teachers. A high school social studies teacher had been having a sexual relationship with a fifteen year old female student. When the student's mother learned of the relationship, she filed suit against the school district. The U. S. Supreme Court, in a five to four decision, found that the school district could not be held liable because school administrators did not know about the inappropriate behavior of the teacher.

SUMMARY

From the sixties through the nineties, our concerns with education have not really varied that much. Perhaps nothing so concretely illustrates the sameness of the concerns as *Goals 2000*, an articulation of six national educational goals that were unveiled by then-President George Bush in 1992. Indeed, achieving quality education for all Americans is still as much a national concern as it was in the sixties. In the early sixties, we seemingly were uncertain of our technological expertise in the face of Sputnik. The nation's forty-first President, in presenting *Goals 2000*, was speaking to a technology-driven society. Yet, the six goals that he and the nation's governors articulated in 1992 could well have been the goals of an earlier America. Only the chronological period differs. In *Goals 2000*, then-President Bush stated, for example, that by 2000, U. S. students will be first in the world in science and mathematics achievement. (We still have a ways to go before achieving that distinction.) Another goal the President stated was that by the year 2000, all schools in America will be free of drugs and violence. The latter is a goal that we would all like very much to achieve, but we know that we have a long way to go before accomplishing same. Despite the miles to go, the academic and the moral environment were addressed in *Goals 2000*, and the bilateral concerns of parents and educators were reflected at the national level. As we enter the twenty-first century, we are hopefully ready to combine what we have learned from the past with an eager anticipation of the future.

REFERENCES

Carnegie Foundation for the Advancement of Teaching. (1992). *School choice: A special report.* Princeton: Carnegie Foundation for the Advancement of Teaching.

Clinton, W. J. (1998, March 23) Remarks on the safe school initiative. *Weekly Compilation of Presidential Documents*, 34(12):464–466.

Drake, J. M. (1979). *Landmark court cases affecting school governance: A resource guide.* Tempe: Arizona State University, Bureau of Educational Research and Services.

1.Case was read as slip opinion; page number not yet assigned.

Grotberg, E. H. (1985) "Head Start Program." In H. Torsten & T. N. Postlethwaite (Eds.). *International encyclopedia of education* (Vol. 4) (pp. 2138–2141). Oxford: Pergamon Press.

Hargrove, E. C. (1988). *Jimmy Carter as president: Leadership and the politics of public good.* Baton Rouge: Louisiana State University Press.

Kemerer, F. R. & Walsh, J. (1994). *The educator's guide to Texas school law* (3rd ed.). Austin: University of Texas Press.

Lederman, D. (1997, May 23). Court denies appeal in harassment case. *Chronicle of Higher Education,* 43(37):A33.

Magidson, J. (1977). Toward a casal model approach for adjusting for preexisting differences in the nonequivalent control group situation: A general alternative to Ancova. *Evaluation Quarterly,* 1:399–414.

National Goals for Education. (1990). Washington, D. C.: U. S. Department of Education.

Ravitch, D. (1983). *The Troubled crusade: American education 1945–1980.* New York: Basic Books.

Smith, M. S. and Bissel, J. S. (1970). Report analysis: The impact of Head Start. *Harvard Educational Review,* 40:51–104.

Westinghouse Learning Corporation. (1969). *The impact of Head Start: An evaluation of the effects of Head Start on children's cognitive and affective development: executive summary.* Washington, D. C.: Clearinghouse for Federal Scientific and Technical Information.

CHAPTER 16

The Public's Attitudes Toward the Public Schools

The 1998 Phi Delta Kappa/Gallup Poll of the Public's Attitudes Toward the Public Schools includes a special focus on public funding for private and church-related schools. Along with the traditional trend questions in this area, new questions were asked regarding vouchers and tuition tax credits.

The public continues to oppose allowing students and parents to choose a private school to attend at public expense, with 44% in favor and 50% opposed. However, the public favors (51% to 45%) allowing parents to send their school-age children to any public, private, or church-related school if the government pays all or part of the tuition.

Two new questions were asked about vouchers, government-issued notes that parents can use to pay all or part of the tuition at a private or church-related school. Regarding a voucher that would pay all of the tuition, 48% of respondents are in favor, and 46% are opposed. When the question states that only *part* of the tuition would be paid, the proportion of respondents in favor rises to 52%, while the proportion who are opposed drops to 41%.

Two questions were asked regarding the obligations that should be assumed by private or church-related schools that accept government tuition payments. In response to the first question, 75% of respondents say that schools accepting such payments should be accountable to the state in the same way the public schools are accountable. In the second question, 70% say that nonpublic schools accepting public funds should be required to accept students from a wider range of backgrounds and academic ability than is now generally the case.

New questions were also asked about tuition tax credits, which would allow parents who send their children to private or church-related schools to recover all or part of the tuition paid. When the question mentions recovery of *all* tuition paid, 56% favor such credits, and 42% are opposed. When the question limits the credit to *part* of the tuition paid, 66% favor the credits, and 30% are opposed.

What do the results of this series of questions tell us? The public is deeply divided over the issue of funds going directly to private or church-related schools. Responses split almost evenly when the question implies that the public would pay *all* of the costs. The opposition seems to lessen when public schools are listed as a part of the choice option and when the funding provided pays only *part* of the cost. Tax credits for parents who send their children to private or church-related schools are supported by the public, but that support is greater if the credit covers only *part* of the tuition. Moreover, funding for private or church-related schools is conditioned on the willingness of those schools to be accountable in the same way the public schools are accountable.

The findings appear to guarantee that the issue of public funding for church-related schools will be a battleground for the foreseeable future. The public's willingness to consider aid to private and church-related schools in various forms will

---

Reprinted with permission from the 30th Annual Phi Delta Kappa/Gallup Poll of the Public's Attitudes Toward the Public Schools, by Lowell C. Rose & George Gallup, Jr., PHI DELTA KAPPAN, September, 1998.

certainly encourage those who want to see such aid provided. By the same token, the public's seeming unwillingness to provide all of the tuition involved in such programs reinforces the belief of opponents of such aid that the "haves" will be the ones who can take advantage of such programs and that the "have-nots" will be the ones left behind. The battle would seem to be joined along those lines.

With this in mind, the 1998 poll repeated an earlier question in which public school parents were asked what they would do if given the option of sending their oldest child to any public, private, or church-related school, with the tuition paid by the government. Fifty-one percent of respondents indicate that they would choose their present public school. Another 6% would choose a different public school, bringing to 57% the number of families that would remain in the public school system. Thirty-nine percent would choose a private or church-related school. Clearly, this is an issue that could affect the future of the public schools.

The poll also sought to determine the confidence Americans have in the public schools as an institution and the priority the public places on improving these schools. When asked about the amount of confidence they have in the public schools, 42% of Americans say a great deal or quite a lot of confidence. Only the church or organized religion, with a combined rating of 57%, tops the public schools. Institutions in which the public expresses less confidence include local government (a combined 37%), state government (36%), big business (31%), national government (30%), the criminal justice system (29%), and organized labor (26%).

Regarding the priority the public places on improving the public schools, respondents were asked what the states should do with the surpluses they are accumulating as a result of the booming economy. Fifty percent of respondents say spend it on the public schools, 31% say use it to reduce taxes, 14% say build a "rainy day" fund, and 4% say spend it on other state services.

This being an election year, respondents were asked which of the two major political parties they feel is more interested in improving public education. Thirty-nine percent name the Democratic Party, and 28% name the Republican Party. The corresponding percentages in 1996 were 44% and 27%. In an interesting political twist, the breakdown of responses to the voucher question that stated that *all* tuition would be paid at a private or church-related school shows that 47% of Republicans favor such vouchers, and 48% oppose them. This statistical tie is surprising given the fact that the Republican Party

is generally regarded as the party of vouchers. The picture becomes more interesting when one notes that Democrats, those from the party viewed as standing in opposition to vouchers, favor the same voucher plan by 51% to 43%. The party messages do not seem to be reaching the party faithful.

In another question, about programs with clear connections to political parties, the issues of providing funds to repair and replace older school buildings and providing funds to reduce class size in grades 1, 2, and 3—two programs associated with the Democratic Party—drew support from 86% and 80% of respondents respectively. Giving states block grants from which to fund some of the current federal programs and allowing parents to set up tax-free savings accounts to be used to pay tuition and other expenses at private or church-related schools—two programs associated with the Republican Party—drew support from 73% and 68% respectively.

Other findings in the 1998 Phi Delta Kappa/Gallup poll include the following.

- Forty-six percent of the respondents give the schools in their own community a grade of A or B. This figure increases to 52% among public school parents and to 62% when public school parents are asked to grade the school their oldest child attends.
- Americans are undecided as to whether children today get a better education than they received. Forty-one percent believe children today get a better education, 48% believe it is worse, and 8% believe there is no difference. Public school parents believe the education children get today is better by 49% to 43%.
- Approximately half of the respondents (49%) believe that the public schools in the community are about the right size. However, a significant number (30%) believe they are too big. A majority (58%) would like a child of theirs to attend a high school with less than 1,000 students.
- Almost two-thirds of respondents (62%) believe that schools in their communities are taking the necessary steps to promote understanding and tolerance among students of different racial and ethnic backgrounds.
- Fifty percent of public school parents believe that school has caused their child to become an eager learner, 34% believe it has caused their child to tolerate learning as a necessary chore, and 15% believe it has caused their child to be turned off to learning.
- The percentage of Americans who believe that public school parents should have more say in

such aspects of school operation as selection and hiring of teachers and administrators, setting of their salaries, and selection of books for school libraries has increased significantly since the question was first asked in 1990.

- There is significant public support (71%) for a voluntary national testing program, administered by the federal government, that would routinely test fourth- and eighth-grade students in order to measure the performance of the nation's public schools.
- Support for amending the U.S. Constitution to permit prayers to be spoken in the public schools remains strong, with 67% of the respondents in favor.
- The public is undecided regarding the way schools should deal with non-English-speaking students. Proposals calling for tutoring in English, providing instruction in the students' native language, and requiring students to learn English before receiving instruction in other subjects each draw support from roughly one respondent in three.
- The public is undecided about the best way to finance schools: 21% believe the means should be by local property taxes; 33%, state taxes; and 37%, federal taxes.
- Fifty percent of respondents believe that the quality of public schools is related to the amount of money spent on students in these schools.
- Sixty-three percent of public school parents say they do not fear for the safety of their oldest child when he or she is at school. This figure is down from 69% in 1977. Similarly, 68% say they do not fear for the safety of their oldest child when he or she is outside at play in the neighborhood.
- Almost two-thirds (65%) of respondents believe students with learning problems should be put in special classes.
- Eighty-seven percent of those surveyed believe sex education should be included in high school instructional programs. The respondents expressed strong support for presenting virtually all topics, including AIDS, homosexuality, and teen pregnancy.
- There is strong support for improving the nation's inner-city schools, with two-thirds of the public (66%) indicating a willingness to pay more taxes to provide the funds to do so.
- Public opinion is divided about the impact that unions have had on the quality of public education: 37% believe they have made no difference; 27% believe they have helped it; 26% believe they have hurt it.

- Almost three-fourths of respondents (73%) believe themselves to be either well informed or fairly well informed regarding local public schools.

(Editor's Note—Due allowance should be made for findings based on relatively small samples, e.g., nonpublic school parents. The sample for this group this year consists of only 33 respondents and is, therefore, subject to a sampling error of plus or minus 17 percentage points.)

PUBLIC VERSUS NONPUBLIC SCHOOLS

Choosing Private Schools at Public Expense

For the fifth year since 1993, the public was asked whether it favored allowing parents to choose a private school to attend at public expense. As in 1997, 44% of respondents are in favor. Since 1993, support has grown steadily from 24% to 44%. At the same time, the opposition has dropped steadily from 74% in 1993. This year 50% are opposed, down from 52% in 1997.

Blacks are the group most likely to support this choice, with 59% in favor. Public school parents are evenly divided: 48% in favor; 46% opposed.

The first question:

Do you favor or oppose allowing students and parents to choose a private school to attend at public expense?

	National Totals				
	'98 %	'97 %	'96 %	'95 %	'93 %
Favor	44	44	36	33	24
Oppose	50	52	61	65	74
Don't Know	6	4	3	2	2

A question posed for the fourth time since 1994 asked respondents whether they would favor allowing parents to send their school-age children to any public, private, or parochial school of their choice with the government paying part or all of the tuition. Fifty-one percent favor the idea, while 45% oppose it. This is a reversal from 1996, when 43% favored the idea, while 54% opposed it. Public school parents approve this year by a 56% to 40% margin.

Groups most likely to favor this proposal include nonwhites (68%) and 18- to 29-year-olds (63%). Groups most likely to oppose it include those in the 50- to 64-year-old age group (56%) and those in rural areas (56%).

The second question:

A proposal has been made that would allow parents to send their school-age children to any public, private, or church-related school they choose. For those parents choosing nonpublic schools, the government would pay all or part of the tuition. Would you favor or oppose this proposal in your state?

	National Totals '98 '97 '96 '94 % % % %	No Children In School '98 '97 '96 '94 % % % %	Public School Parents '98 '97 '96 '94 % % % %	Nonpublic School Parents '98 '97 '96 '94 % % % %
Favor	51 49 43 45	48 46 38 42	56 55 49 48	74 68 70 69
Oppose	45 48 54 54	48 51 59 57	40 43 49 51	21 31 28 29
Don't know	4 3 3 1	4 3 3 1	4 2 2 1	5 1 2 2

Two questions new to the poll asked specifically about the use of vouchers, government-issued notes to be used to pay tuition at a private or church-related school. A split sample design was used. Half of the sample was asked about vouchers that would pay *full tuition,* and the other half was asked about vouchers that would pay *part* of the tuition. The public is evenly divided on vouchers paying all the tuition, with 48% in favor and 46% opposed. When asked about a voucher paying part of the tuition, 52% are in favor, and 41% are opposed. Public school parents support either option.

Nonwhites (59%), 18- to 29-year-olds (57%), and manual laborers (58%) offer strong support for paying all tuition. As indicated earlier, the responses are interesting in that, with regard to vouchers to pay *all* tuition, Republicans split 47% in favor and 48% opposed, while Democrats are 51% in favor and 43% opposed.

The third question:

In the voucher system, a parent is given a voucher which can be used to pay all the tuition for attendance at a private or church-related school. Parents can then choose any private school, church-related school, or public school for their child. If a parent chooses a public school, the voucher would not apply. Would you favor or oppose the adoption of the voucher system in your state?

	National Totals %	No Children In School %	Public School Parents %	Nonpublic School Parents %
Favor	48	44	55	69
Oppose	46	50	42	22
Don't know	6	6	3	9

The fourth question:

In the voucher system, a parent is given a voucher which can be used to pay part of the tuition for at- tendance at a private or church-related school. Parents can then choose any private school, church-related school, or public school for their child. If a parent chooses a public school, the voucher would not apply. Would you favor or oppose the adoption of the voucher system in your state?

	National Totals %	No Children In School %	Public School Parents %	Nonpublic School Parents %
Favor	52	50	58	61
Oppose	41	43	37	25
Don't know	7	7	5	14

Tax Credits for Parents of Those Attending Private or Church-Related Schools

Asked for the first time in this poll were questions involving the use of tax credits at the state level for parents who send their children to private or church-related schools. Once again, a split sample design was used, with half of the sample being asked about a credit for *all* tuition and the other half about a credit for *part* of the tuition.

On the question regarding a tax credit for all tuition paid, 56% of respondents are in favor, and 42% are opposed. Public school parents favor such a credit by 63% to 35%. When asked about a credit for part of the tuition, 66% of respondents are in favor, and 30% are opposed. Support by public school parents rises to 73% for a partial tax credit, while the number opposed drops to 24%.

Groups most likely to be in favor of full tuition credits include nonwhites (71%). It is interesting to note that Republicans, whose party is supporting tax credits at the federal level, approve full tax credits (57% in favor, 42% opposed), while Democrats, whose party is opposing tax credits at the federal level, favor such credits by an even larger margin (61% in favor, 37% opposed).

The first question:

Proposals are being made in a number of states to provide a tax credit that would allow parents who send their children to private or to church-related schools to recover all of the tuition paid. Would you favor or oppose this proposal in your state?

	National Totals	No Children In School	Public School Parents	Nonpublic School Parents
Favor	56	50	63	89
Oppose	42	48	35	11
Don't know	2	2	2	*

*Less than one-half of 1%.

The second question:

Proposals are being made in a number of states to provide a tax credit that would allow parents who send their children to private or to church-related schools to recover part of the tuition paid. Would you favor or oppose this proposal in your state?

	National Totals %	No Children In School %	Public School Parents %	Nonpublic School Parents %
Favor	66	62	73	89
Oppose	30	33	24	11
Don't know	4	5	3	*

*Less than one-half of 1%.

Obligations of Private or Church-Related Schools Accepting Public Funds

Any debate over providing public funds to private or church-related schools eventually leads to the obligations schools must accept if they take the public funding. This year's poll included two questions in this area. The first asked if schools accepting such payments should be accountable to the state in the same way that public schools are accountable. In a consensus echoed by all demographic groups, 75% of respondents indicate that these schools should have the same accountability as public schools.

The second question repeated a question from the 1997 survey in which respondents were asked whether nonpublic schools accepting government tuition payments should be required to accept students from a wider range of backgrounds and academic ability than is now generally the case. Seventy percent of respondents say that nonpublic schools that accept public funding should be required to do so, while 23% say they should not. The percentage saying yes—down from 78% last year—is relatively uniform across all demographic groups.

These issues are of special significance since accountability to the state and required changes in admissions policies may be key factors in determining whether private or church-related schools choose to accept public funds if they are offered. It is certain that opponents of such aid will insist on the same kind of accountability that is required of public schools.

The first question:

Do you think private or church-related schools that accept government tuition payments should be accountable to the state in the way public schools are accountable?

	National Totals %	No Children In School %	Public School Parents %	Nonpublic School Parents %
Yes, should	75	74	80	62
No, should not	20	22	16	26
Don't know	5	4	4	12

The second question:

Do you think nonpublic schools that receive public funding should or should not be required to accept students from a wider range of backgrounds and academic ability than is now generally the case?

	National Totals		No Children In School		Public School Parents		Nonpublic School Parents	
	'98 %	'97 %	'98 %	'97 %	'98 %	'97 %	'98 %	'97 %
Yes, should	70	78	69	78	76	80	52	76
No, should not	23	18	23	17	20	17	45	22
Don't know	7	4	8	5	4	3	3	2

Impact on Public Schools of Aid To Private or Church-Related Schools

One of the arguments raised by opponents of aid to private or church-related schools is that the effect will be to encourage those with the financial means to move out of the public schools, leaving them to the disadvantaged. To test these concerns, the poll asked public school parents what they would do if they could send their oldest child to any public, private, or church-related school of their choice with tuition paid by the government. Fifty-one percent indicate that they would continue to send their oldest child to his or her present public school, while 46% say they would send the child to a different school.

A follow-up question asked the 46% who say they would select a different school what kind of school they would select. Twenty-two percent say it would be a private school, 17% a church-related school, and 6% another public school. This would indicate that 57% of public school parents would keep their children in the public schools, while 39% would leave the public school system.

The first question:

Suppose you could send your oldest child to any public, private, or church-related school of your choice, with tuition paid for by the government. Would you send your oldest child to the school he or she now attends, or to a different school?

	Public School Parents	
	'98	'96
	%	%
Present (public) school	51	55
Different school	46	44
Don't know	3	1

The second question:

Would you send your child to a private school, a church-related school, or to another public school?

	Public School Parents	
	'98	'96
	%	%
Private school	22	19
Church-related school	17	17
Another public school	6	8

GRADING THE SCHOOLS

Since 1974 respondents to the Phi Delta Kappa/Gallup education polls have been asked to grade the public schools in their communities on a scale of A to F. In 1981 a second question was added in which the public was asked to grade the "nation's public schools." Then, beginning in 1985, parents were asked to grade the public school their oldest child was attending.

The importance of this series of questions cannot be over-estimated. At a time when much criticism was being directed at the public schools, these questions provided annual evidence that people did not feel that the criticism applied to the schools in their own communities. This kept the discussion of the public schools more rational and recognized that schools vary widely and must be judged on a school-by-school and district-by-district basis.

The trends established by this series of questions have been consistent. They make it clear that the closer people are to the public schools, the higher their regard for them. The schools they rate lowest are those they do not know, the "nation's schools." These are the schools about which information comes through media reports. Ask people about the schools they do know, and the grades they assign go up. Indeed, the percentage of respondents who award the schools a grade of A or B increases almost 30 points when respondents are asked about the schools in their own community rather than about the "nation's schools." It rises again when public school parents, those closest to the schools, are asked to rate the local schools. And, finally, it increases again when public school parents are asked to grade the public school their oldest child attends.

Local Public Schools

The grades assigned to the public schools in the community remain high, as has been the case for four decades, with 46% assigning those schools a grade of A or B. Adding in those assigning a C brings to 77% the percentage giving at least a passing grade to the schools in the community.

The question:

Students are often given the grades A, B, C, D, and FAIL to denote the quality of their work. Suppose the public schools themselves, in this community, were graded in the same way. What grade would you give the public schools here—A, B, C, D, or FAIL?

	National Totals		No Children In School		Public School Parents		Nonpublic School Parents	
	'98	'97	'98	'97	'98	'97	'98	'97
	%	%	%	%	%	%	%	%
A & B	46	46	43	42	52	56	39	26
A	10	10	8	8	15	15	8	9
B	36	36	35	34	37	41	31	17
C	31	32	31	33	33	30	24	35
D	9	11	9	11	9	10	16	21
FAIL	5	6	5	7	4	3	7	13
Don't know	9	5	12	7	2	1	14	5

Public Schools Nationally

As has been true since 1981, the nation's public schools continue to be those receiving the lowest grades. In fact, the schools people are rating so low are, in many cases, the same ones receiving high marks from the people in the communities they serve. This year 18% assign the nation's schools an A or a B, down from 22% in 1997. No demographic groups assign these schools high grades, although nonwhites (24% A or B) and Democrats (25% A or B) give slightly higher grades than others.

The question:

How about the public schools in the nation as a whole? What grade would you give the public schools nationally—A, B, C, D, or FAIL?

	National Totals		No Children In School		Public School Parents		Nonpublic School Parents	
	'98	'97	'98	'97	'98	'97	'98	'97
	%	%	%	%	%	%	%	%
A & B	18	22	19	23	16	23	12	24
A	1	2	*	3	2	2	4	2
B	17	20	19	20	14	21	8	22
C	49	48	48	49	52	46	52	38
D	15	15	15	15	13	16	19	15
FAIL	5	6	6	6	4	4	7	6
Don't know	13	9	12	7	15	11	10	17

*Less than one-half of 1%.

Public School Oldest Child Attends

It would be difficult to argue that the parents of public school children would not be the best-informed people about the effectiveness of the public schools. That is why the grades that public school parents give the school their oldest child attends are so important. This year 62% assign a grade of A or B. Another 25% assign a C, bringing to 87% the proportion of parents who assign a passing grade to the school their oldest child attends.

There is some indication that the grades parents assign are somewhat affected by the success their children have had in school. For parents indicating that their child is above average in achievement, the percentage assigning an A or a B is 69%. For those indicating average or below-average achievement for their child, the percentage assigning an A or a B drops to 53%.

The question:

Using the A, B, C, D, FAIL scale again, what grade would you give the school your oldest child attends?

	Public School Parents	
	'98 %	'97 %
A & B	62	64
A	22	26
B	40	38
C	25	23
D	8	7
FAIL	3	4
Don't know	2	2

EFFECTIVENESS OF PUBLIC SCHOOLS

The 1998 survey examined the effectiveness of public schools in a number of ways. One question asked respondents whether they thought children today receive a better or worse education than they did. Another listed measures used in gauging the effectiveness of schools and asked respondents to indicate which they felt was most important. Another question probed the extent to which the public schools are taking the steps necessary to promote understanding and tolerance among students of different racial and ethnic backgrounds.

Is Education Today Better or Worse?

Americans' assessment of whether children are getting a better or worse education today than they themselves received has changed little since the question was first asked nearly two decades ago. Forty-one percent believe that children get a better education, 48% say children get a worse education, and 8% believe there is no difference. The range of opinions on this issue is great. Groups more likely to believe children are receiving a worse education include those in the West (27% better, 59% worse), political independents (33% better, 52% worse), college graduates (31% better, 51% worse), those with incomes of $50,000 and over (34% better, 55% worse), and professionals and businesspeople (33% better, 55% worse). Groups likely to feel children are getting a better education include nonwhites (53% better, 40% worse), Democrats (47% better, 42% worse), those in the South (49% better, 43% worse), and public school parents (49% better, 43% worse).

The question:

As you look on your own elementary and high school education, is it your impression that children today get a better—or worse—education than you did?

	National Totals		No Children In School		Public School Parents		Nonpublic School Parents	
	'98 %	'79 %	'98 %	'79 %	'98 %	'79 %	'98 %	'79 %
Better	41	41	38	36	49	53	38	36
Worse	48	42	49	43	43	39	55	54
No difference	8	9	10	11	6	6	3	6
Don't know	3	8	3	10	2	2	4	4

Size of School

This was the first poll in a number of years to raise the question of school size as an element relating to school effectiveness. The large comprehensive high schools that students in many communities attend today are far different from most of the schools of the past. Large elementary schools and middle schools have also become more common. It is not unusual to hear parents and students complain that the school the youngsters attend is large and impersonal. Two questions related to school size were asked.

The first question asked whether public schools in the community are too big, too small, or about the right size in terms of the number of students they serve. About half of the respondents (49%) say schools are about the right size, while 30% say they are too big. The two groups most likely to believe that public schools are about the right size are those age 50 and over (59% say they are about the right size) and rural residents (64% say they are about the right size). Since respondents were not asked the size of the schools in their communities, there is no way of identifying the size of the schools being judged as "about the right size." However, the fact that rural residents, who live where the smaller schools are located, so strongly believe that their schools are the right size and the fact that the public expresses a preference (in the second question) for smaller high schools both seem to indicate that the public thinks small is better.

The second question asked respondents to indicate how big a high school should be. Four choices were offered, ranging from less than 1,000 students to more than 2,000 students. Fifty-eight percent of respondents prefer a high school of less than 1,000 students. Only 2% prefer a high school larger than 2,000 students. The latter is, of course, the size of the high schools that a vast number of students currently attend. The preference for smaller high schools is uniform across all groups.

The first question:

In your opinion, are public schools in your community too big, too small, or about the right size in terms of the number of students?

	National Totals %	No Children In School %	Public School Parents %	Nonpublic School Parents %
Too big	30	29	29	55
Too small	15	13	21	6
About the right size	49	51	48	28
Don't know	6	7	2	11

The second question:

If you had the choice, which size high school would you prefer for a child of yours—a high school with less than 1,000 students, a high school with between 1,000 and 1,500 students, one with between 1,500 and 2,000 students, or one with more than 2,000 students?

	National Totals %	No Children In School %	Public School Parents %	Nonpublic School Parents %
Less than 1,000 students	58	56	57	84
Between 1,000 and 1,500 students	28	29	30	10
Between 1,500 and 2,000 students	6	6	7	*
More than 2,000 students	2	2	3	*
Don't know	6	7	3	6

*Less than one-half of 1%

Measuring School Effectiveness

In the public school forums conducted by Phi Delta Kappa, the National PTA, and the Center on Education Policy, participants have struggled to identify the indicators they believe should be used to measure school effectiveness. This year's poll listed six

indicators often mentioned in these forums and asked respondents to state the importance of each. The highest rating (82% very important) is given to the percentage of students who graduate from high school. Second is the percentage of high school graduates who practice good citizenship (79% very important). Third comes the percentage of high school graduates who go on to college (71% very important). The indicator rated lowest is the scores that students receive on standardized tests (50% very important).

Nonwhites show the greatest tendency to vary from the general population, with 65% saying that standardized test scores are very important, 83% rating the percentage going on to college or junior college as very important, and 86% citing the percentage graduating from college or junior college as very important.

The question:

How important do you think each of the following is for measuring the effectiveness of the public schools in your community? Would you say very important, somewhat important, not very important, or not at all important?

	Very Important %	Somewhat Important %	Not Very Important %	Not at All Important %	Don't Know %
Percentage of students who graduate from high school	83	14	2	1	1
Percentage of high school graduates who practice good citizenship	79	15	3	1	2
Percentage of high school graduates who go on to college or junior college	71	24	3	1	1
Percentage who graduate from college or junior college	69	25	3	1	2
Percentage of graduates who get jobs after completing high school	63	28	5	2	2
Scores that students receive on standardized tests	50	34	9	3	4

Understanding and Racial Tolerance

Promoting racial understanding and tolerance among students is one of the goals of the public schools. With a national commission studying racial matters, poll planners deemed this a good time to revisit a question asked in earlier polls to determine how effective Americans think the public schools are in this area. Sixty-two percent of Americans say they feel the public schools in their community are taking the necessary steps to promote understanding and tolerance among students of different racial and ethnic backgrounds. Public school parents agree. Nonwhites, a group that would be expected to be sensitive in this area, also concur, but only 56% of nonwhites believe schools are taking the necessary steps to promote tolerance and understanding.

The question:

In your opinion, are the public schools in your community taking the necessary steps to promote understanding and tolerance among students of different racial and ethnic backgrounds or not?

	National Totals		No Children In School		Public School Parents		Nonpublic School Parents	
	'98 %	'92 %	'98 %	'92 %	'98 %	'92 %	'98 %	'92 %
Yes	62	50	62	44	64	59	57	47
No	27	28	25	26	31	30	28	31
Don't know	11	22	13	30	5	11	15	22

Impact of the Public School on Students

Appropriately, the final question related to effectiveness dealt with the impact of the public schools on students. Obviously, the schools would like to have every child become an eager learner. In response to this question, 50% of public school parents say they believe the public schools have made their oldest child an eager learner. Another 34% indicate that the public schools have caused their child to tolerate learning as a necessary chore. Only 15% feel that the public schools have caused their child to be turned off to learning.

This question also separates those who say their child is an above-average learner from those who indicate their child is an average or below-average learner. Sixty percent in the former group say the public schools have made their child an eager learner, as compared to 36% in the latter category. Twenty-three percent of those who indicate that their child is an average or below-average achiever also say that the public schools have turned off their child to learning.

The question:

How would you describe the impact school has had or is having on your oldest child's attitude toward learning? Has it caused your child to become an eager learner, caused your child to tolerate learning as a necessary chore, or caused your child to be turned off to learning?

	Public School Parents %
Caused child to become eager learner	50
Caused child to tolerate learning as a necessary chore	34
Caused child to be turned off to learning	15
Don't know	1

IMPROVING THE NATION'S INNER-CITY SCHOOLS

There is much evidence to indicate that problems relating to the public schools are concentrated in the inner cities of our urban areas and in poor rural areas. While most respondents to the 1998 survey give their own schools high marks, they assign much lower grades to the nation's schools. There is every reason to suspect that the schools in the nation to which they are assigning low grades are those in the inner cities. It is not unusual for these schools to be housed in old, dilapidated buildings and to be staffed by a higher proportion of teachers who are new or lack proper credentials. In addition, teachers in these schools are likely to be short of books and other teaching materials.

Two of the questions in this poll were designed to determine whether the public is aware of the need to improve the inner-city schools and whether it has the will to do something about it. The first question asked how important respondents think it is to improve these schools. The results have to be regarded as encouraging. Eighty-six percent indicate it is very important to do so. Adding in the 10% who say the task is fairly important brings the total to 96%. This response is uniform and consistent among all demographic groups.

Moreover, support for improving the nation's inner-city schools has trended upward since 1989, when 74% thought it very important to do so. In 1993, that figure rose to 81%.

The second question asked about the public's willingness to pay more taxes to improve inner-city schools. Approximately two-thirds (66%) indicate a willingness to do so. This expressed willingness is especially high among nonwhites (79%), Democrats (74%), those between the ages of 50 and 64 (78%), and manual laborers (73%). No group indicates an unwillingness to pay taxes for this purpose.

The first question:

How important do you think it is to improve the nation's inner-city schools? Would you say very important, fairly important, not very important, or not important at all?

	National Totals			No Children In School			Public School Parents			Nonpublic School Parents		
	'98 %	'93 %	'89 %	'98 %	'93 %	'89 %	'98 %	'93 %	'89 %	'98 %	'93 %	'89 %
Very important	86	81	74	86	80	71	86	81	83	100	79	83
Fairly important	10	15	19	9	15	21	11	16	14	—	13	14
Not very important	1	2	2	1	2	2	1	2	*	—	3	1
Not important at all	1	1	*	1	1	*	*	*	*	—	4	*
Don't know	2	1	5	3	2	6	2	1	3	—	1	2

*Less than one-half of 1%.

The second question:

Would you be willing or unwilling to pay more taxes to provide funds to improve the quality of the nation's inner-city public schools?

	National Totals		No Children In School		Public School Parents		Nonpublic School Parents	
	'98 %	'93 %	'98 %	'93 %	'98 %	'93 %	'98 %	'93 %
Willing	66	60	69	59	64	62	52	52
Unwilling	30	38	26	38	34	37	46	47
Don't know	4	2	5	3	2	1	2	1

POLITICS AND THE PUBLIC SCHOOLS

The pending congressional election comes at a time when education has moved to the foreground of the national political scene. Each of the major parties is attempting to portray itself as the education party. Their approaches are different, with one focusing primarily on the public schools and the other offering such alternatives to the public schools as vouchers and tuition tax credits. Poll planners thought this was an appropriate time to ask a series of questions bearing on issues that will be resolved in the political arena.

The Major Parties and Education

Thirty-nine percent of respondents say the Democratic Party is more interested in improving public education, while 28% pick the Republican Party. A number of demographic groups assign a clear edge to the Democratic Party, including nonwhites (57%) and those in the West (47%). Only Republicans (61%) think the Republican Party is more interested in improving the public schools.

The second question asked respondents to indicate whether they favor or oppose four programs currently before Congress. The two programs associated with the Democratic Party—providing funds to repair and replace older school buildings and reducing class size in grades 1, 2, and 3—have approval ratings of 86% and 80% respectively. The two programs supported by the Republican Party—block grants that states could use in assuming responsibility for federal programs and tax-free savings accounts that parents

could use in paying tuition and other expenses at private and church-related schools—draw support from 73% and 68% respectively.[1]

The third question asked respondents to indicate how states should use the surplus funds that are being accumulated as a result of the booming economy. Fifty percent indicate that the surpluses should be spent on the public schools, 31% say they should be used to reduce taxes, and 14% say they should be used to build a "rainy day" fund for the states. Only 4% opted to spend the money on other state services. Among public school parents, 58% say that state surpluses should be spent on the public schools.

The first question:

In your opinion, which of the two major political parties is more interested in improving public education in this country—the Democratic Party or the Republican Party?

	National Totals		No Children In School		Public School Parents		Nonpublic School Parents	
	'98 %	'96 %	'98 %	'96 %	'98 %	'96 %	'98 %	'96 %
Democratic Party	39	44	42	45	38	41	18	32
Republican Party	28	27	27	26	28	29	30	36
No difference (volunteered)	18	15	18	15	17	14	29	23
Don't know	15	14	13	14	17	16	23	9

The second question:

Congress is currently considering various plans to improve the quality of the nation's public schools in kindergarten through 12th grade. As I read each of the following plans, would you tell me whether you favor or oppose that plan?

	National Totals			Public School Parents		
	Favor %	Oppose %	Don't Know %	Favor %	Oppose %	Don't Know %
Providing funds to help repair and replace older school buildings	86	13	1	89	11	0
Providing block grants to states, with the states taking the responsibility for some federal programs	73	21	6	70	25	5
Allowing parents to build tax-free accounts that they would use to pay tuition and other expenses at private and church-related schools	68	29	3	74	25	1
Providing funds to be used to reduce class size in grades 1, 2, and 3	80	17	3	88	11	1

1. The second and third questions were two of the three questions that the Gallup Organization chose to include in one of its regular polls, so as not to bias the responses by including them in an education poll.

The third question:

Because of the current strength of the nation's economy, many states have surplus budget funds available. Which one of the following do you think would be the best way to use surplus funds—1) use them to reduce taxes, 2) spend them on the public schools, 3) spend them on other state services, or 4) build a "rainy day" or emergency fund for the state?

	National Totals %	Public School Parents %
Reduce taxes	31	30
Spend them on public schools	50	58
Spend them on other state services	4	1
Build a "rainy day" or emergency fund	14	11
Don't know	1	*

*Less than one-half of 1%.

Financing the Schools

Two questions in the poll dealt with the issue of financing public schools. The first asked respondents about the best way to finance the schools. Respondents are divided, with 21% choosing local property taxes, 33% choosing state taxes, and 37% choosing federal taxes. A significant change since 1986 is that the percentage of those saying they favor federal taxes has gone up by 13%. Nonwhites (54%), 18- to 29-year-olds (45%), and Democrats (40%) express a strong preference for federal taxes as the source of funding.

The second, more basic question asked respondents whether they think the quality of the public schools is related to the amount of money spent on students in those schools. Fifty percent believe that it is. This result is generally uniform across all demographic groups.

The first question:

There is always a lot of discussion about the best way to finance the public schools. Which do you think is the best way to finance the public schools—by means of local property taxes, by state taxes, or by taxes from the federal government in Washington?

	National Totals		No Children In School		Public School Parents		Nonpublic School Parents	
	'98 %	'86 %	'98 %	'86 %	'98 %	'86 %	'98 %	'86 %
Local property taxes	21	24	22	22	19	28	34	22
State taxes	33	33	34	34	31	32	25	36
Federal taxes	37	24	35	23	41	28	28	22
Don't know	9	19	9	21	9	12	13	20

The second question:

In your opinion, is the quality of the public schools related to the amount of money spent on students in these schools, or not?

	National Totals %	No Children In School %	Public School Parents %	Nonpublic School Parents %
Yes	50	51	52	34
No	42	42	40	56
Don't know	8	7	8	10

Voluntary Testing Program

President Clinton has proposed a voluntary national testing program in which students at the fourth- and eighth-grade levels would be tested in order to measure the performance of the nation's public schools. This proposal is currently before Congress. Poll respondents were asked whether they favored or opposed the idea. The question did not identify President Clinton as the source of the proposal. Seventy-one percent say they favor the idea, and the support is uniform across all demographic groups.

The question:

A proposal has been made that the federal government administer a voluntary national testing program that would routinely test fourth- and eighth-grade students in order to measure the performance of the nation's public schools. In general, do you favor or oppose this proposal?

	National Totals %	No Children In School %	Public School Parents %	Nonpublic School Parents %
Favor	71	68	78	72
Oppose	25	28	19	21
Don't know	4	4	3	7

Prayer Amendment

The question on support for an amendment to the U.S. Constitution that would permit prayers to be spoken in public schools was first asked in 1984. It attracted support from 69% of the respondents to that year's poll. This year the same question brought a favorable response from 67% of the respondents. Groups offering particularly high support include blacks (76%), those age 50 and older (74%), Republicans (80%), those living in the South (81%), and rural residents (75%). Those less likely to favor the amendment, though still offering majority support, include those in the 18- to 29-year-old age group (55%), political independents (56%), college graduates (56%), those in the West (51%), and professionals and businesspeople (61%).

The question:

An amendment to the U.S. Constitution has been proposed that would permit prayers to be spoken in the public schools. Do you favor or oppose this amendment?

	National Totals			No Children In School			Public School Parents			Nonpublic School Parents		
	'98	'95	'84	'98	'95	'84	'98	'95	'84	'98	'95	'84
	%	%	%	%	%	%	%	%	%	%	%	%
Favor	67	71	69	64	68	68	73	75	73	85	74	68
Oppose	28	25	24	31	28	25	22	20	21	13	23	21
Don't know	5	4	7	5	4	7	5	5	6	2	3	11

PROBLEMS FACING THE PUBLIC SCHOOLS

Each of the previous Phi Delta Kappa/Gallup polls has given respondents an open-ended opportunity to identify the biggest problems with which the public schools in their communities must deal. This year poll planners decided to supplement that question with one in which seven problems frequently identified were given to respondents, who were then asked to indicate how serious they feel about each of these problems is in the local schools. And, finally, given the recent reported cases of violence in schools, respondents were asked if they believe their child is safe at school and safe when playing in the neighborhood.

Biggest Problems Facing Local Schools

Concern about fighting/violence/gangs (mentioned by 15%) replaces lack of discipline/more control and lack of financial support/funding/money at the top of the list of biggest problems mentioned by those responding to this year's poll. Lack of discipline is mentioned by 14% of this year's respondents, lack of financial support is mentioned by 12%, and use of drugs is mentioned by 10%. These are the only problems in the poll to reach double-digit figures. Nonwhites also place fighting/violence/gangs at the top of the list, with 23% identifying it as the biggest problem.

	National Totals		No Children In School		Public School Parents		Nonpublic School Parents	
	'98	'97	'98	'97	'98	'97	'98	'97
	%	%	%	%	%	%	%	%
Fighting/violence/gangs	15	12	14	12	20	12	10	16
Lack of discipline/more control	14	15	15	15	9	12	29	22
Lack of financial support/funding/money	12	15	13	15	11	14	2	4
Use of drugs/dope	10	14	10	14	12	14	8	9
Overcrowded schools	8	8	5	6	11	10	22	17
Concern about standards/quality of education	6	8	6	7	5	8	9	10
Difficulty getting good teachers/quality teachers	5	3	6	3	4	4	*	*
Pupils' lack of interest/attitudes/truancy	5	6	4	6	5	6	15	3
None	3	2	2	2	5	3	7	*
Don't know	16	10	19	13	10	6	8	4

*Less than one-half of 1%.

Seriousness of Selected Problems

In this question, respondents were given seven problems and asked to indicate how serious each is in the local public schools. In reporting the ratings, the very serious and fairly serious categories are combined. Drugs top the list, with 80% of respondents rating that problem either very serious or fairly serious. Discipline and smoking tie for second at 76%, followed by alcohol (72%), teenage pregnancy (71%), fighting (64%), and gangs (57%). Considering the combined percentages, responses are reasonably consistent across groups.

The question:

How serious a problem would you say each of the following is in the public schools in your community? Would you say a very serious problem, fairly serious, not very serious, or not at all serious?

	Very and Fairly Serious Combined %	Very Serious %	Fairly Serious %	Not Very Serious %	Not At All Serious %	Don't Know %
Drugs	80	52	28	13	3	4
Discipline	76	50	26	17	3	4
Smoking	76	50	26	15	3	6
Alcohol	72	44	28	18	4	6
Teenage pregnancy	71	43	28	19	4	6
Fighting	64	37	27	26	5	5
Gangs	57	37	20	27	11	4

Safety at School and in the Neighborhood

The recent reports of violence in schools across the country have raised questions as to how safe children are when they are at school. It seemed a good time to repeat two questions first asked in 1977, one dealing with safety while at school and the other with safety when outside playing in the neighborhood. Sixty-three percent of public school parents do not fear for their child's safety when he or she is at school. This percentage is down from 69% in 1977, while the percentage who do fear for their child's safety is up from 25% to 36%. These percentages do not vary greatly across groups. Sixty-eight percent say they do not fear for their child's safety when outside at play in the neighborhood. Thirty-one percent indicate that they do. These percentages are relatively unchanged since 1977.

The first question:

Thinking about your oldest child, when he or she is at school, do you fear for his or her physical safety?

	Public School Parents	
	'98	'77
	%	%
Yes	36	25
No	63	69
Don't know	1	6

The second question:

When your oldest child is outside at play in your own neighborhood, do you fear for his or her physical safety?

	Public School Parents	
	'98	'77
	%	%
Yes	31	28
No	68	68
Don't know	1	4

SCHOOL OPERATION/CURRICULUM

The 1998 poll dealt with a number of topics involving school operations and curriculum, including means of communication, involvement of parents, dealing with students who cannot speak English, placement of students with learning problems, and inclusion of sex education in the curriculum.

Communication

Schools and school districts use a variety of ways to communicate with parents and with the rest of the community. Some, such as open houses, neighborhood discussion groups, and school newsletters, have been around for a long time; others, such as televised school board meetings, public school news hotlines, and Internet chat rooms, are relatively new. Respondents were asked to rate the effectiveness of each of these methods.

The question:

Here are some ways in which public schools try to open lines of communication with citizens. In your opinion, how effective do you think each of the following would be? Would you say very effective, somewhat effective, not very effective, or not at all effective?

	Very and Somewhat Effective	Very Effective	Somewhat Effective	Not Very Effective	Not At All Effective	Don't Know
	%	%	%	%	%	%
Public school open houses	89	54	35	6	3	2
Public school newsletters	87	47	40	9	3	1
Open hearings	85	48	37	8	4	3
Neighborhood discussion groups	81	43	38	12	5	2
Public school news hotlines	77	35	42	13	4	6
Televised school board meetings	74	39	35	15	9	2
Internet "chat rooms" set up by your local school	63	25	38	19	9	9

Parental Control

The matter of parental control in seven areas related to the public schools has been explored just once previously in these polls. The responses in this year's poll suggest that the desire for parents to have a greater say in school matters has increased significantly since the question was first asked in 1989. (The results were not published until 1990.) Of the seven areas included in the question, the desire is highest this year for greater parental input in the allocation of school funds (57% of respondents want more say), in the selection and hiring of administrators and principals (55% want more say), and in the choice of the curriculum offered (53% want more say).

Public school parents indicate a desire for more say in each of the seven areas. Nonwhites are more likely than whites to want more say in all areas except teacher and administrator salaries and allocation of school funds, where the groups are essentially tied. College graduates are more likely than high school graduates to believe that parents have the right amount of say in each of the seven areas.

The first question:

Do you feel that parents of public school students should have more say, less say, or do they have about the right amount of say about the following areas in the public schools?

	More Say		Less Say		Right Amount		Don't Know	
	'98 %	'90 %	'98 %	'90 %	'98 %	'90 %	'98 %	'90 %
Allocation of school funds	57	59	8	10	29	27	6	4
Selection and hiring of admini- strators and principals	55	46	9	14	30	37	6	3
Curriculum, that is, the subjects offered	53	53	10	9	32	36	5	2
Selection and hiring of teachers	48	41	13	17	34	38	5	4
Teacher and administrator salaries	48	39	14	17	32	39	6	5
Selection of books and instructional materials	46	43	13	13	37	41	4	3
Books placed in school libraries	44	38	14	15	38	44	4	3

Non-English-Speaking Students

How to meet the needs of students who come to the public schools unable to speak English is a matter of controversy across the nation. The problem was highlighted recently in California when the state approved a referendum virtually banning bilingual education. This year's poll offered respondents three choices for dealing with the problem of non-English-speaking students. The first, putting them in classes taught in English with a minimum amount of tutoring in English, is supported by 34% of those polled. The second, providing public school instruction in all subjects in the students' native language while they learn English, is supported by 27%. The third, requiring students to learn English in public schools before they receive instruction in any other subjects, is supported by 37%. Nonwhites (42%) are the group most likely to choose the option of providing students with instruction in their native language. College graduates (42%) are the group most likely to opt for providing the minimum amount of tutoring needed in English.

The question:

Many families who come from other countries have school-age children who cannot speak English. Which one of the following three approaches do you think is the best way for public schools to deal with non-English-speaking students?

	National Totals %	No Children In School %	Public School Parents %	Nonpublic School Parents %
Put the students in classes taught in English with the minimum tutoring needed to help them learn English	34	33	34	40
Provide public school instruction in all subjects in the students' native language while they learn English	27	26	30	20
Require students to learn English in public schools before they receive instruction in any other subjects	37	38	34	40
Don't know	2	3	2	*

*Less than one-half of 1%.

Placement of Students with Learning Problems

There has been a trend across the country, supported by federal law and a line of court decisions, to place students with learning problems in the same classrooms with other students. In a question asked in 1995, two-thirds of the public (66%) expressed the view that students with learning problems should be in special classes. The same question was repeated in this year's poll, and the results show little change of opinion. Sixty-five percent favor placement in special classes, while 26% favor placement in the same classrooms. Groups most likely to support placement in special classes include those age

65 and older (74%), Republicans (72%), high school graduates (71%), and manual laborers (71%).

The question:

In your opinion, should children with learning problems be put in the same classrooms with other students, or should they be put in special classes of their own?

	National Totals '98 %	'95 %	No Children In School '98 %	'95 %	Public School Parents '98 %	'95 %	Nonpublic School Parents '98 %	'95 %
Yes, same classrooms	26	26	26	25	29	29	10	25
No, special classes	65	66	65	68	63	62	70	66
Don't know	9	8	9	7	8	9	20	9

The second question:

Which of the following topics, if any, should be included for high school students?

	Topics That Should Be Included '98 %	'87 %	'85 %	'81 %
Venereal disease	92	86	84	84
AIDS	92	84	*	*
Biology of reproduction	90	80	82	77
Teen pregnancy	89	84	*	*
Birth control	87	83	85	79
Premarital sex	77	66	62	60
Nature of sexual intercourse	72	61	61	53
Abortion	70	60	60	54
Homosexuality	65	56	48	45

*These topics were not included in the earlier surveys.

Including Sex Education in the Curriculum

In earlier polls, respondents were routinely asked about the inclusion of sex education in the public high school curriculum. The topic was last explored in 1987, at which time 76% of respondents favored including sex education in the curriculum. In the intervening 11 years, support has increased to 87%. It is also uniform across all groups.

A second question, also from previous polls, asked respondents about the inclusion of specific topics in the sex education curriculum. Once again, support for inclusion has increased for each of the nine topics listed. The percentage favoring inclusion varies from a high of 92% for instruction about AIDS and about venereal disease to a low of 65% for instruction about homosexuality.

The first question:

Do you feel the public high schools should or should not include sex education in their instructional programs?

	National Totals '98 '87 '85 '81 % % % %	No Children In School '98 '87 '85 '81 % % % %	Public School Parents '98 '87 '85 '81 % % % %	Nonpublic School Parents '98 '87 '85 '81 % % % %
Yes, should	87 76 75 70	87 73 72 66	89 82 81 79	78 81 80 79
No, should not	12 16 19 22	12 16 21 25	10 14 16 16	22 18 15 17
Don't know	1 8 6 8	1 11 7 9	1 4 3 5	* 1 5 4

*Less than one-half of 1%.

IMPACT OF UNIONS

The impact unions have had on the quality of public education is another area that had been explored in the early years of the poll but had not been revisited since 1976. The public remains divided in this area: 27% believe that unions have improved the quality of the public schools, 26% believe that unions have hurt the public schools, and 37% believe that unions have made no difference. These responses reflect a somewhat more positive attitude toward unions today than in 1976. Thirty-nine percent of public school parents share the view that unions have made no difference. Nonwhites (36%) are the group most likely to believe that unions have helped.

The question:

Most teachers in the nation now belong to unions or associations that bargain over salaries, working conditions, and the like. Has unionization, in your opinion, helped, hurt, or made no difference in the quality of public education in the U.S.?

	National Totals '98 %	'76 %	No Children In School '98 %	'76 %	Public School Parents '98 %	'76 %	Nonpublic School Parents '98 %	'76 %
Helped	27	22	27	22	28	23	23	24
Hurt	26	38	26	38	24	36	36	47
Made no difference	37	27	37	26	39	28	27	25
Don't know	10	13	10	14	9	13	14	4

THE PUBLIC'S KNOWLEDGE OF LOCAL SCHOOLS

The question of how well informed respondents feel about the local public schools was last asked in 1987. During this interval, the public feels it has become much better informed, with those rating themselves well informed rising from 15% to 31% and those rating themselves as fairly well informed rising from 39% to 42%. This means that 73% of respondents now consider themselves to be either well informed or fairly well informed about the local schools. It is somewhat surprising that those with no children in school feel almost as well informed as do public school parents. This is a major change since 1987. Groups most likely to consider themselves well informed include nonwhites (40%) and college graduates (42%).

The question:

Would you say you were well informed, fairly well informed, or not well informed about the local public school situation?

	National Totals '98 %	National Totals '87 %	No Children In School '98 %	No Children In School '87 %	Public School Parents '98 %	Public School Parents '87 %	Nonpublic School Parents '98 %	Nonpublic School Parents '87 %
Well informed	31	15	29	12	36	25	23	16
Fairly well informed	42	39	41	33	44	51	39	47
Not well informed	26	41	28	48	20	23	33	34
Don't know	1	5	2	7	*	1	5	3

*Less than one-half of 1%.

CONFIDENCE IN INSTITUTIONS

It seemed appropriate to close this poll with a question seeking to find out how much confidence Americans have in the institutions that serve them. This is the last of the three questions that the Gallup Organization chose to include in its regular poll in order to reduce bias. The public schools fared reasonably well in this comparison, with 42% of respondents expressing either a great deal or quite a lot of confidence in them. They came in second only to the church or organized religion (57%).

The percentage of public school parents expressing either a great deal or quite a lot of confidence in the public schools is 47%, almost identical to the 46% who award the schools in their communities a grade of A or B. In regular polls conducted by the Gallup Organization since 1980, the percentage of total respondents expressing either a great deal or quite a lot of confidence in the public schools has ranged from a high of 50% in 1987 to a low of 34% in 1994.

The question:

Now I am going to read you a list of institutions in American society. Please tell me how much confidence you, yourself, have in each one—a great deal, quite a lot, some, or very little?

	Great Deal/ Quite a Lot %	Great Deal %	Quite a Lot %	Some %	Very Little %	None (volunteered) %	Don't Know %
The church or organized religion	57	30	27	27	11	3	2
Public schools	42	16	26	35	20	2	1
Local government	37	13	24	41	20	1	1
State government	36	13	23	45	17	1	1
Big business	31	13	18	42	22	2	3
National government	30	11	19	43	22	2	3
Criminal justice system	29	12	17	37	30	4	*
Organized labor	26	13	13	39	28	3	4

*Less than one-half of 1%.

CLOSING COMMENTS

This report is an attempt to provide a factual accounting of the findings contained in the 30th Phi Delta Kappa/Gallup poll. However, what has been reported is only the tip of the iceberg in terms of the data that are available. The complete tabulations break the data down into 12 major population groups and 50 subgroups. It is possible to compare, for example, the responses given by those living in urban, suburban, and rural areas. Comparisons can be made of the responses provided by men and women or by Democrats, Republicans, and Independents.

There is not space in this report to go extensively into comparisons among groups. However, our examination suggests that nonwhites tend to provide responses that reflect greater variability and greater intensity of feeling than other groups. It is also apparent that the responses of college graduates tend to differ from those of high school graduates, those in the 18- to 29-year-old age group differ from those age 65 and older, and clerical/sales and manual workers tend to provide responses different from those of professionals and businesspeople. These kinds of comparisons add meaning to the poll results; however, they can be made only by those who have obtained the complete tabulations.

In conclusion, it is important to remember that the original reason for initiating the Phi Delta Kappa/Gallup polls was to provide those making decisions about the schools with data to be used as input in those decisions. This is not to say that educational decisions should be based on public opinion. However, in a democratic society the public schools are dependent on an informed and supportive public. If support for a worthwhile idea is not present, it becomes the responsibility of educational leaders to build the necessary support to move the public schools in the direction they need to go.

The original purpose of the poll remains as valid today as it was 30 years ago. The data contained in this report would suggest the following kinds of conclusions: public schools benefit when a large number of people have close contact with them; a significant part of the public remains to be persuaded that children today receive a better education than in the past; people tend to prefer smaller schools at a time when the trend is toward larger schools; and public school parents want more say in decisions related to the public schools. Such data-based conclusions should be useful to those who have the decision-making responsibility for the public schools.

RESEARCH PROCEDURE

The Sample.   The sample used in this survey embraced a total of 1,151 adults (18 years of age and older). A description of the sample and methodology can be found at the end of this report.

Time of Interviewing.   The fieldwork for this study was conducted during the period of 5 June to 23 June 1998.

The Report.   In the tables used in this report, "Nonpublic School Parents" includes parents of students who attend parochial schools and parents of students who attend private or independent schools.

Due allowance must be made for statistical variation, especially in the case of findings for groups consisting of relatively few respondents, e.g., nonpublic school parents.

The findings of this report apply only to the U.S. as a whole and not to individual communities. Local surveys, using the same questions, can be conducted to determine how local areas compare with the national norm.

SAMPLING TOLERANCES

In interpreting survey results, it should be borne in mind that all sample surveys are subject to sampling error, i.e., the extent to which the results may differ

from what would be obtained if the whole population surveyed had been interviewed. The size of such sampling error depends largely on the number of interviews.

The following tables may be used in estimating the sampling error of any percentage in this report. The computed allowances have taken into account the effect of the sample design upon sampling error. They may be interpreted as indicating the range (plus or minus the figure shown) within which the results of repeated samplings in the same time period could be expected to vary 95% of the time, assuming the same sampling procedure, the same interviewers, and the same questionnaire.

The first table shows how much allowance should be made for the sampling error of a percentage:

Recommended Allowance FOR Sampling Error OF A Percentage

	In Percentage Points (at 95 in 100 confidence level)* Sample Size						
	1,500	1,000	750	600	400	200	100
Percentages near 10	2	2	3	3	4	5	8
Percentages near 20	3	3	4	4	5	7	10
Percentages near 30	3	4	4	5	6	8	12
Percentages near 40	3	4	5	5	6	9	12
Percentages near 50	3	4	5	5	6	9	13
Percentages near 60	3	4	5	5	6	9	12
Percentages near 70	3	4	4	5	6	8	12
Percentages near 80	3	3	4	4	5	7	10
Percentages near 90	2	2	3	3	4	5	8

*The chances are 95 in 100 that the sampling error is not larger than the figures shown.

The table would be used in the following manner: Let us say that a reported percentage is 33 for a group that includes 1,000 respondents. We go to the row for "percentages near 30" in the table and across to the column headed "1,000."

The number at this point is 4, which means that the 33% obtained in the sample is subject to a sampling error of plus or minus four points. In other words, it is very probable (95 chances out of 100) that the true figure would be somewhere between 29% and 37%, with the most likely figure the 33% obtained.

In comparing survey results in two samples, such as, for example, men and women, the question arises as to how large a difference between them must be before one can be reasonably sure that it reflects a real difference. In the tables below, the number of points that must be allowed for in such comparisons is indicated. Two tables are provided. One is for percentages near 20 or 80; the other, for percentages near 50. For percentages in between, the error to be allowed for lies between those shown in the two tables.

Recommended Allowance for Sampling Error of the Difference

TABLE A Size of Sample	In Percentage Points (at 95 in 100 confidence level)* Percentages near 20 or percentages near 80					
	1,500	1,000	750	600	400	200
1,500	4					
1,000	4	5				
750	5	5	5			
600	5	5	6	6		
400	6	6	6	7	7	
200	8	8	8	8	9	10

TABLE B Size of Sample	Percentages near 50					
	1,500	1,000	750	600	400	200
1,500	5					
1,000	5	6				
750	6	6	7			
600	6	7	7	7		
400	7	8	8	8	9	
200	10	10	10	10	11	13

*The chances are 95 in 100 that the sampling error is not larger than the figures shown.

How to Order the Poll

The minimum order for reprints of the published version of the Phi Delta Kappa/Gallup education poll is 25 copies for $10. (Institutional purchase orders, cash, or MasterCard or VISA number required.) Additional copies are 25 cents each. This price includes postage for delivery (at the library rate). Where possible, enclose a check or money order. Address your order to Phi Delta Kappa International, P.O. Box 789, Bloomington, IN 47402-0789. Ph. 800/766-1156.

If faster delivery is desired, phone the Shipping Department at the number listed below. Persons who wish to order the 664-page document that is the basis of this report should contact Phi Delta Kappa International, P.O. Box 789, Bloomington, IN 47402-0789. Ph. 800/766-1156. The price is $95, postage included.

Here is an example of how the tables would be used: Let us say that 50% of men respond a certain way and 40% of women respond that way also, for a difference of 10 percentage points between them. Can we say with any assurance that the 10-point difference reflects a real difference between men and women on the question? Let us consider a sample that contains approximately 750 men and 750 women.

Since the percentages are near 50, we consult Table B, and, since the two samples are about 750 persons each, we look for the number in the column headed "750," which is also in the row designated "750." We find the number 7 here. This means that the allowance for error should be seven points and that, in concluding that the percentage among men is somewhere between three and 17 points higher than the percentage among women, we should be wrong only about 5% of the time. In other words, we can conclude with considerable confidence that a difference exists in the direction observed and that it amounts to at least three percentage points.

If, in another case, men's responses amount to 22%, say, and women's to 24%, we consult Table A, because these percentages are near 20. We look in the column headed "750" that is also in the "750" row and see that the number is 5. Obviously, then, the two-point difference is inconclusive.

DESIGN OF THE SAMPLE

For the 1998 survey the Gallup Organization used its standard national telephone sample, i.e., an unclustered, directory-assisted, random-digit telephone sample, based on a proportionate stratified sampling design.

The random-digit aspect of the sample was used to avoid "listing" bias. Numerous studies have shown that households with unlisted telephone numbers are different in important ways from listed households. "Unlistedness" is due to household mobility or to customer requests to prevent publication of the telephone number.

To avoid this source of bias, a random-digit procedure designed to provide representation of both listed and unlisted (including not-yet-listed) numbers was used.

Telephone numbers for the continental United States were stratified into four regions of the country and, within each region, further stratified into three size-of-community strata.

Only working banks of telephone numbers were selected. Eliminating nonworking banks from the sample increased the likelihood that any sample telephone number would be associated with a residence.

The sample of telephone numbers produced by the described method is representative of all telephone households within the continental United States.

Within each contacted household, an interview was sought with the youngest man 18 years of age or older who was at home. If no man was home, an interview was sought with the oldest woman at home. This method of respondent selection within households produced an age distribution by sex that closely approximates the age distribution by sex of the total population.

Up to three calls were made to each selected telephone number to complete an interview. The time of day and the day of the week for callbacks were varied so as to maximize the chances of finding a respondent at home. All interviews were conducted on weekends or weekday evenings in order to contact potential respondents among the working population.

The final sample was weighted so that the distribution of the sample matched current estimates derived from the U.S. Census Bureau's Current Population Survey (CPS) for the adult population living in telephone households in the continental U.S.

Composition of the Sample

Adults	%
No children in school	67
Public school parents	29
Nonpublic school parents	4

Gender	%
Men	46
Women	54

Race	
White	82
Nonwhite	15
Black	11
Undesignated	3

Age	
18-29 years	22
30-49 years	43
50 and over	34
Undesignated	1

Education	
Total college	55
College graduate	22
College incomplete	33
Total high school	44
High school graduate	28
High school incomplete	16
Undesignated	1

Income	%
$50,000 and over	29
$40,000 and over	40
$30,000-$39,999	15
$20,000-$29,999	15
Under $20,000	16
Undesignated	14

Region	
East	23
Midwest	24
South	32
West	21

Community Size	
Urban	30
Suburban	44
Rural	26

CHAPTER 17

The Condition of Public Education

The first three Bracey Reports presented a great deal of data that demolished two myths. The first myth was that a Golden Era of American education once existed, from which state of grace we have since fallen and to which state of grace we must struggle to return. The second was that the performance of American students is dreadfully low, both in comparison to Asian and European students and in comparison to the performance of American students in years past.

OF HOAXES AND MYTHS

This report continues the demolition work. But first I must take note of an even more pervasive hoax. It is one that I fell victim to, as did most of the nation. By itself, the hoax is not so important, but as a symbol it reveals how readily people believe any terrible thing about schools.

In 1986, when I took up residence in the administration building of the school district in Cherry Creek, Colorado, I noticed a sheet of green paper on the bulletin board outside my office. It listed the most pervasive school problems of the 1940s, followed by those of the 1980s. The catalogue of horrors for the 1940s included, in order, talking, chewing gum, making noise, running in the halls, getting out of place in line, wearing improper clothing, and not putting pa-

per in wastebaskets. The list for the 1980s was dramatically different: drug abuse, alcohol abuse, pregnancy, suicide, rape, robbery, and assault. The paper gave as its source the police department in Fullerton, California. That attribution made me wonder. I had spent five years as a police dispatcher and had consulted for the police department in New York City. And surveys of this sort just didn't seem to be the typical police department activity. But who knew? Maybe police work in California was closer to social science than was the case in New York.

In any case, my puzzlement led no further. Too bad. Had I but thought about it for a moment, I would have noticed that the 1980s list did not apply to the schools in Cherry Creek, a district that sends about 85% of its students on to higher education. Nor did it seem to apply in the neighboring suburban districts, nor in the approximately 150 small-town and rural districts in Colorado. Even in Denver, Colorado's only large city, the list would seem far-fetched. Moreover, there hadn't been much talk of these horrific problems during the decade I had spent in the state department of education in Virginia.

When the lists turned up on a bulletin board at Yale University, they sparked more dissonance in the mind of Professor Barry O'Neill than they had in mine. O'Neill found the 1940s list too trivial, and he was skeptical of the 1980s list. So he decided to seek the source.[1]

After collecting 250 versions of these lists, with various attributions, O'Neill found the lists to be a fabrication of one T. Cullen Davis of Fort Worth. Davis, acquitted of murdering his estranged wife's

---

Reprinted with permission from "The Fourth Bracey Report on the Condition of Public Education," by Gerald W. Bracey, *Phi Delta Kappan*, October 1994.

lover, had taken a hammer to his million-dollar collection of jade and ivory statues, smashing them as idols of false religion. He became a born-again Christian. And he used the lists to attack public schools. Cullen revealed to O'Neill his method of constructing the lists: "How did I know what the offenses in the schools were in 1940? I was there. How do I know what they are now? I read the paper."

But by the time O'Neill elicited this admission, virtually everyone in the nation had adopted the lists as gospel. On the political Right, William Bennett, Rush Limbaugh, Phyllis Schlafly, Ross Perot, and George Will dutifully cited them. On the Left, Anna Quindlen, Herb Caen, and Carl Rowan trotted them out. They turned up in *Time* and on CBS television. They were variously attributed to CBS News, *CQ Researcher,* and the Heritage Foundation. In their migration from Texas to the rest of the nation, the lists did pass through the Fullerton Police Department, which, knowing of the public's anxiety over teenage drug use, moved drugs from their original position as sixth on the 1980s list to number one.

While the problems in schools are certainly more serious today than they were four or five decades ago, they are not the problems that appear on the 1980s list. A warning many researchers receive early in their training applies here: don't trust secondary sources. Perhaps a popular bumper-sticker slogan from the 1960s applies as well: Question Authority.

Having unearthed the lists' source, O'Neill asked a more difficult question: What makes them so popular? He placed his answer in the tradition of the Puritan jeremiads. In these sermons, the preacher would remind the members of the congregation of their covenant with God, then attribute any current afflictions to God's just retribution for the broken covenant, and finally warn them to mend their ways and renew the covenant with God.

Said O'Neill, "Americans today regard their country as the richest, freest, and fairest, with the best social system, but cannot square this with the social problems of America's young. . . . The school lists are a collective moan of anxiety over the gap between ideals and reality. When Puritans or modern Americans enumerate their faults, they are declaring their dedication to their ideals, reassuring each other that at least their goals remain high."

Something similar occurs constantly in education. The state of education is never ideal, and drugs, violence, and pregnancy are problems in ways they never were 50 years ago. As with the lists, the political Right and Left agree on these problems. They part ways on how to solve them. In addition, the tradition of criticizing schools is a long one. From my forays into the history of education, it seems that in the last century such criticism has abated only during World Wars I and II and during the Great Depression, when people had more immediate and more intense things to worry about.

The hoax of the lists was not alone this year. Sam Ginn, chairman of Pacific Telesis, gave speeches declaring that his company had administered a seventh-grade reading test to 6,400 applicants for operator positions and that only 2,700 had passed with a score high enough for him to hire them. This showed, said Ginn, the need for education reform to develop "workers with skills that will allow us to be competitive in the next century."[2]

What Ginn did not say was that his jobs paid only $7 an hour. Based on a 40-hour week and a 50-week year, this works out to the princely annual income of $14,000, only about 60% of the average starting salary for teachers and a sum slightly below the official 1993 poverty level for a family of four. It's not an income likely to attract the nation's literati. Moreover, Ginn also failed to say that he had only 700 jobs to offer. His test had yielded nearly four times as many qualified applicants as he could use.

Similarly, in April 1994 a book titled *Reinventing Education* appeared.[3] The lead author was Louis Gerstner, Jr., CEO of IBM and former CEO of RJR Nabisco. The book charged that American high school students place last or next to last in international comparisons of math and science achievement; that SAT scores have fallen to historic lows; that we spend more money on education than any other nation; that, despite a decade of increasing expenditures, achievement test scores are static; and that the high school graduation rate is 72%. All of these statements are false, and below, under the heading "New Data," I will expose them for the hoaxes they are. Because high school completion is not discussed below, let me note that the First Bracey Report found the on-time completion rate to be 83%.

Benjamin Barber of Rutgers University had a different take on public education and its discontents.[4] Barber accepted the myth of school failure but proffered an alternative theory of how these miserable conditions came to be. It's not the kids, the teachers, or the administrators, he said.

I am increasingly persuaded that the reason for the country's inaction [to rescue the schools] is that Americans do not really care about education—the country has grown comfortable with the game of "let's pretend we care." . . . The children are onto this game. They know that if we really valued schooling, we'd pay teachers what we pay stockbrokers; if we valued books, we'd spend a little something on the libraries so that adults could read, too; if we valued citizenship, we'd give national service and civic education more than pilot status; if we valued children, we wouldn't let them be abused, manipulated, impoverished, and killed in their beds by gang-war crossfire and stray bullets. Schools can and should lead, but when they confront a society that in every instance tells a story exactly opposite to the one they are supposed to be teaching, their job becomes impossible.

Barber cited the writings of E. D. Hirsch, Jr., of Chester Finn, Jr., of Diane Ravitch, and of the late Allan Bloom; then he hurled his accusation: "How this captious literature reeks of hypocrisy! How sanctimonious all the hand-wringing over still another 'education crisis' seems." Given the mass of data contained in the four Bracey Reports, I must disagree with Barber's assessment of the state of education—but not so much with his assessment of our national values.

NEW DATA

Of the data that have surfaced since the Third Bracey Report was published last October, the most interesting surely were those contained in *Education in States and Nations*, a report from the National Center for Education Statistics.[5] This report compares the 19 developed nations of the Organization for Economic Cooperation and Development (OECD) on a variety of participation, input, financial, and outcome variables.

One section contains results from the Second International Assessment of Educational Progress (IAEP-2), transformed into National Assessment of Educational Progress (NAEP) scales. While these results are interesting in themselves, the picture becomes even more intriguing when one combines these data with other NAEP reporting categories used in the 1992 NAEP mathematics assessment. By so doing, we obtain the following results:

Top Finishers

1.	Asian students (U. S.)	287
2.	Taiwan	285
3.	Korea	283
4.	Advantaged urban students (U. S.)	283
5.	White students (U. S.)	277
6.	Hungary	277

Thus the great majority of American students finish at or near the top of the most recent international comparison in mathematics, a subject in which our national performance is reputed to be dismal. Whites and Asians together make up over 70% of the K–12 population of U. S. schools.

At the 1993 meeting of the American Educational Research Association, Lauren Resnick—who in 1991 was beginning all of her speeches with the message "We all know how terrible we are"—acknowledged, "We look pretty good in some areas."[6] Resnick had in mind reading and language arts, she said, but these new IAEP-2 data show many students looking good in mathematics, too.

Overall American rankings in IAEP-2 mathematics were low, though the scores were just below average. Many countries are tightly bunched together, and a small difference in scores makes a large difference in the rankings. But if most American students are near the top and the U. S. overall mean score is below the international average, this must mean that some groups are scoring low. And they are:

Bottom Scorers

Jordan	246
Mississippi	246
Hispanic students (U. S.)	245
Disadvantaged urban students (U. S.)	239
Black students (U. S.)	236

There is no NAEP category for "disadvantaged rural students," else there would doubtless be another entry in this list. Because ethnicity is a central fact of American life, we tend to overreport things in ethnic terms and underreport things in terms of class. But these low scores are largely a class-linked phenomenon. As Harold Hodgkinson has shown, while Asians usually score highest of all ethnic groups in mathematics, wealthy blacks outscore poor Asians.[7]

Paradoxically, another table in *Education in States and Nations* strongly suggests that comparing national and state school systems on the basis of average test scores is senseless. This chart shows the average scores and the range from the 5th to the 95th percentile of each country's or state's sample. As one goes from Mississippi's and Jordan's average at the bottom to Taiwan's at the top, one traverses 39 NAEP scale points. As one goes from the bottom of Taiwan's distribution (1st percentile) to the top (99th percentile), one traverses about 150 NAEP scale points.

Many states and nations show similarly large ranges. The within-country variance swamps the between-country variance. Given the enormous within-country variance, it doesn't even seem reasonable to speak of "American schools" or "Taiwanese schools" in reference to average scores. Such variability also raises an important practical question for standard-setting programs, such as the New Standards Project: Where can one place a standard that is credible as a "high" standard without failing a large proportion of students? More important than that, what happens to all the students who do fail? The answer is usually that they will be given more time to meet the standard. No one seems to have noticed that this solution may be very cruel, as well as ineffective.

While people have continued to write that test scores are falling, test scores have continued to rise. Since about 1990, scores in Iowa for all grades except 8 and 12 on the Iowa Tests of Basic Skills (ITBS) and Iowa Tests of Educational Development (ITED) have been at record highs.[8] As is the case with the SAT I, but not with other commercial achievement tests, new forms of the ITBS and ITED are equated to previous forms. This allows us to compare trends over time in the same way that we do for SAT scores.

Actually, trend data for the ITBS and ITED in Iowa are better than trend data for the SAT because the SAT average score depends on who takes the test, and the demographics of the test-taking pool have been and are still changing. Similarly, "then and now" studies of test scores, while they generally favor "now," are hard to interpret in most places because of changing demographics. Iowa, by contrast, is in some ways frozen in time. It has no large cities with their attendant problems. And it is still nearly 98% white.

Moreover, the statewide testing program in Iowa dates from the 1930s. It is a familiar aspect of schooling, not a recently imposed high-stakes endeavor. It is thus not subject to the charge that rising scores reflect curricular alignments, inappropriate administrative procedures, cheating, or other malignancies that are alleged in some quarters to have produced testing's "Lake Wobegon Effect." In sum, whatever the ITBS score represented in 1937, it probably represents much the same thing in 1994. In recent years Iowa has ranked first or second among the states in SAT scores, ACT (American College Testing) scores, and in scores on NAEP mathematics and reading tests. Such a combination of high scores would seem to confirm that they are real.

Still, some might have reservations about the generalizability of data drawn from a single state that is not really representative of the nation as a whole. It is telling, therefore, that the national norming studies for the ITBS track the Iowa data very closely. At some grade levels, national scores are actually *higher* than those in Iowa. As this article went

to press, 1992 norms for the ITBS were not yet available for formal publication, but the director of the Iowa program assured me that they would be slightly higher than the 1985 norms. It is thus possible that ITBS scores are at all-time highs.

Such record-setting performance is not so much at variance with other results as one might think at first. In 1993 the proportion of students scoring above 650 on the SAT mathematics section climbed to what appears to be an all-time high of 11%. (I say "appears" because my data go back only to 1963.) And these scores were posted before the "recentering" of SAT scores recently announced by the College Board.

This might seem like a small proportion. Indeed, a note in *Education Week* suggested that the editors of that publication think so.[9] But recall that the standards for the SAT were set in 1941 and were based on the performance of 10,654 students. Ninety-eight percent of them were white, 60% were male, 40% had attended private high schools, and most lived in the Northeast, where, by and large, they planned to attend private colleges and universities. The makers of the SAT imposed on the scores of this elite group a normal bell-shaped, or Gaussian, distribution. Thus we know from the statistical properties of the normal curve that only 6.68% of this elite group scored above 650. The current crop of SAT-takers is 30% minority and 52% female. Thirty-one percent of them report family incomes of under $30,000 annually. The test-taking pool for the SAT has been democratized, yet the proportion of high scores is at its highest point—65% above the mark obtained by the standard setters.[10]

Two factors other than general performance increases might account for this improvement at the top of the distribution: (1) an increase in the number of Asian students, who outperform all other groups and/or (2) an increase in the number of students from states where small proportions of the senior class take the SAT. If the latter were true, it would be possible that those states were adding very bright students to the test-taking pool.

Neither of these hypotheses holds up under scrutiny, however. First, while Asian students average 535 on the math portion of the SAT, they constitute only 8% of all test-takers, up from 4.5% a decade ago. This means that, of the more than 110,000 students scoring above 650, only about 14,000 are Asian Americans. Their performance exceeds that of all other groups, but the improved scores must be occurring in other groups as well. In 1993 some 10,000 more seniors took the SAT than in 1992, while 5,600 more seniors scored above 650. Moreover, even the SAT verbal scores showed an increase in the number of high scorers, with some 2,600 more seniors scoring above 650 in 1993 than in 1992.

State-by-state results reveal that the recent growth in the number of SAT test-takers has been largely in states where the test was already taken by more than 50% of the senior class. In those states whose populations are growing rapidly from immigration—e.g., Texas, Florida, and California—the proportion of the senior class taking the SAT has been stable and relatively high at 45%, 52%, and 47% respectively.

Average scores on the SAT held little interest for the media last year. They rose for the second year in a row. The *New York Times* carried the story deep in the interior of Section A.[11] The *Washington Post* buried it in the Metro section, playing it as a story of local interest.[12] The headline mentioned results for Metro Washington districts only. Not until the seventh paragraph of the piece did the story reveal national averages and trends. Of course, downturns have consistently found their way to the front pages of both papers.

Much of the information I've reported so far suggests that levels of performance on academic indicators may reflect demographic factors more strongly than they reflect the quality of the education system. Indeed, this is precisely the conclusion that Glen Robinson and David Brandon reached when they found that they could account for 89% of the variability in state-level NAEP mathematics scores by using only four variables: number of parents in the home, level of parental education, type of community, and state poverty rates for ages 5–17.[13] A rank-order correlation coefficient of actual state ranks versus predicted ranks using these same four variables was .995. Note that none of these four variables can be controlled by the school. Robinson and Brandon strongly suggest that state NAEP scores reflect not the *quality* of a state's schools, but the *difficulty* of the educational task different states face. (These findings were reported in detail in the Research column in the September 1994 *Kappan*.)

Education in States and Nations also carried information on how countries spend money for education—something that continues to be poorly reported in the U. S. As David Berliner pointed out, George Bush and virtually his whole Cabinet repeatedly pronounced some variant of "We spend more money on schools than any other country."[14] Gerstner made the same claim in the book mentioned above, as did Herbert Walberg of the University of Chicago in the *Chicago Sun Times*.[15]

Walberg's allegation is particularly curious because he serves as a consultant to the Organisation for Economic Cooperation and Development, and it is OECD data that show that the United States is not a big spender. There are a variety of ways of calculating school spending, and they all have flaws with regard to their comparability across nations. Richard Jaeger reported several calculations indicating that the U. S. is average or below average in school spending.[16] Perhaps the fairest method is to express expenditures in terms of percentage of gross domestic product. Using this method, the U. S. ranks ninth among 19 nations in spending for K–12 education, according to *Education in States and Nations*.

Yet even this figure overestimates our spending on education, because a smaller slice of the pie goes to instruction in the U. S. than in many other countries. American schools provide many services that schools in other countries do not provide or provide in reduced amounts: transportation, food, medical care, counseling, and, especially, special education. In the U. S. in 1989–90, transportation alone cost more than $8 billion.[17] As the Sandia Report showed, costs for special education have soared for the last 20 years, while costs for regular instruction have risen virtually not at all.[18] And while costs were rising, so were special education enrollments. Between 1976 and 1990, special education enrollments increased by 39%, from 8.3% of the school population to 11.6%.[19]

Money matters loomed large in 1993. The American Legislative Exchange Council, described in the *Washington Post* as a conservative group of legislators, released a study conducted by former Secretary of Education William Bennett that purported to show that there is no relationship between spending and achievement.[20] This study used per-pupil expenditures as a measure of spending, while it used SAT scores for individual states as a measure of achievement. In a column headlined "Meaningless Money Factor," George Will commented that the top five SAT states—Iowa, North Dakota, South Dakota, Utah, and Minnesota—were all relatively low spenders, while New Jersey spent more money than any other state and finished only 39th.[21]

What neither Will nor Bennett bothered to point out, of course, is that in the high-scoring states virtually no one takes the SAT. For 1993 the percentages of high school seniors taking the SAT in the top five states were 5%, 6%, 6%, 4%, and 10% respectively. Most seniors in those states take the ACT. In New Jersey, on the other hand, fully 76% of the senior class filled in the bubbles on SAT answer sheets. A state that includes three-fourths of its student body in a tested population will not look good in comparison with a state whose tested population is made up of an academic elite seeking admission to selective colleges.

The notion that money makes a difference in education outcomes has been gaining ascendancy in recent years, and new data arrived in 1994. For a number of years, school critics have claimed that education's problems cannot be solved by "throwing money at the schools." The usual source cited by these skeptics is a review of the research conducted by Eric Hanushek.[22] Although Keith Baker demonstrated in the pages of the April 1991 *Kappan* that Hanushek's data did not substantiate Hanushek's claims, Baker's analysis of the data had little impact on those who believed Hanushek to be correct.

A recent reanalysis of Hanushek's set of studies, however, might lead us to place *more* emphasis than ever before on money as an important factor in achievement. (Recall that, in the Third Bracey Report, I suggested that, if money makes no difference, someone should inform the wealthy districts so that they'll stop spending so much more of it than other folks.) Indeed, in the new analysis money seems to be the most important when used directly in the service of instruction.[23]

For his part, Hanushek now claims that he never said money makes no difference. He asserts that the reason he found no strong or systematic relationship is that some school districts find effective ways of spending money, while others do not. What we need to know is what kinds of expenditures are effective and how they exert their effect. "The available evidence," Hanushek contends, "simply indicates that the natural proclivities of school systems do not systematically lead to effective use of resources." He does not define further these "natural proclivities" of school systems, but he gives as an example the proposal that we increase the salaries of teachers by 10%. This, says Hanushek, wouldn't increase the relationship between salary and student performance. Rather it might "slow down turnover of teachers, so that policies designed to attract better people into teaching would be thwarted."[24]

In connection with teacher salaries, it is worth noting that the starting, mid-level, and maximum salaries of teachers do not compare well with the salaries of other white-collar professionals. Nor do they compare well against salaries for teachers in many other developed nations. The U. S. was seventh in comparison of teacher pay in 13 developed nations.[25]

Money for education is important in ways many people don't usually think about. A headline in the *Washington Post* told the story: "Across U. S., Schools Are Falling Apart."[26] In *Education Week* a headline ran simply: "Schoolhouse Rot."[27] Actually, though these reports were highly relevant, they weren't news. A 1990 report from the Education Writers Association told the same story, as did a 1991 survey by the American Association of School Administrators.

In September of 1993, the Educational Testing Service released *Adult Literacy in America*, a study it conducted for the U. S. Department of Education.[28]

With rare exceptions, the report was seen as further proof of education's low state. "Dumber Than We Thought" screeched the headline of a *Newsweek* story on the report.[29] One had to read much of the story to learn that the headline was not *Newsweek's* studied assessment, but a direct quote from former Secretary of Education William Bennett. Indeed, this study defined literacy in quite a complicated way, and, as Pauline Gough observed in an editorial in the *Kappan,* among those who scored low were significant numbers of the old, the foreign born, the visually impaired, or individuals who had "physical, mental, or health conditions that kept them from participating fully in work, school, housework, or other activities."[30]

Before leaving the topic of literacy, recall that the Third Bracey Report discussed an International Association for the Assessment of Educational Achievement study of reading in which American 9-year-olds finished second in the world among students from 31 nations, while U. S. 14-year-olds finished eighth and with scores as close to first place as those of the 9-year-olds. Such data are hard to square with the alarmist reactions to the adult literacy survey, unless we assume that the entire world faces a literacy crisis.

Judging from my mailbox, the U. S. Department of Education has increased the rate at which it reports statistics. I understand from officials at ED that they are striving to improve the quality as well. When ED strayed from the mere facts last year, the outcomes were less than successful. Two interpretive reports, *National Excellence: A Case for Developing America's Talent*[31] and *Prisoners of Time,*[32] left much to be desired. The former contained no new data and numerous factual errors; the latter was thin and repeated oft-made, mostly commonsensical recommendations. Given that *Prisoners of Time* was two years in production, one wonders how the researchers spent their time.

THE GEORGE WILL AFFAIR

Nothing better captured the political Right's antipathy toward public education than its campaign for Proposition 174, a referendum in the 1993 California election that would have established a $2,600 credit for parents to use at the school of their choice. The referendum apparently (the wording was so vague that even the measure's authors couldn't answer questions about its impact) would have permitted anyone who could round up 25 children to open a school. Reports cited a coven of witches that planned to do so, since their beliefs were not included in the state's Curriculum Frameworks. Even

California's Gov. Pete Wilson, generally a supporter of vouchers, came out against Proposition 174 because it would have devastating effects on the already devastated California economy. Wilson reportedly would have backed the measure if its creators had phased in the fiscal jolts over five years. But they refused, and Wilson felt obliged to oppose it.

Not so William Bennett, who stumped for it, and George Will, who dedicated several columns to it. In his column of 26 August 1992, Will wrote, "Nationally about half of urban public school teachers with school-age children send their children to private schools."[33] Three days later, Will pitched this statistic at Keith Geiger, president of the National Education Association (NEA), on "This Week with David Brinkley." Unfortunately, Geiger swung wildly and said, erroneously, "It's about 40%." Will shrugged, as if to say, "Thanks for proving my point." And a new urban legend was born.

Will's numbers look spurious to me—almost as spurious as those two lists on the bulletin board in Cherry Creek. Will's office said that the figures came from "School Choice Cases," by Clint Bolick of the Institute for Justice. Bolick, in turn, sent me to David Boaz of the Cato Institute and to his *Liberating Schools: Education in the Inner City.* Boaz passed me on to Dennis Doyle of the Hudson Institute. In 1986 Doyle and Terry Hartle, both then working for the American Enterprise Institute, had actually written a never-published paper on the topic.[34] Doyle's and Hartle's figures, which they considered to be "preliminary," in no way approached 50%. The usually cited figure of 46% (which Will interpreted as "about half") applied only to teachers in Chicago, and 80% of those teachers sent their children to parochial schools. The numbers Doyle and Hartle actually used in their paper would yield an estimated figure more like 21% for urban public school teachers and 16% for all teachers—not much above the national average for all parents.

Readers can find a complete analysis of this affair in the September 29 issue of *Education Week.*[35] Here I wish only to note further that it is inappropriate to compare teachers with the general public. All teachers have a college education, and, because so many teachers are not the sole wage earners in their families, the average annual family income for teachers is more than $70,000. Moreover, a 1992 study by James Coleman put the average income of families with children in private schools at $70,000.[36] The proper comparison would match teachers with another group of similar socioeconomic status. When the American Federation of Teachers conducted such an analysis, it found a greater proportion of teachers using public schools than was true of comparable families with similar incomes.[37]

Various versions of my analysis were sent to various media outlets. One found its way to the *Washington Post,* where Will's columns originate. It was turned down by a form letter. Another went to the *Wall Street Journal.* Daniel Henninger, the editorial page editor, sent a letter neither accepting nor rejecting the piece, but thanking me for "the Third Bracey Report and the debunking of George Will's statistic." Imagine my surprise, then, at the long lead editorial that appeared in the *Journal* of October 25 in support of Proposition 174, headed by a segment of the transcript of the Will/Geiger exchange from "This Week with David Brinkley."[38] The editorial gave no indication that either figure was in error and went on to castigate public educators for opposing Proposition 174.

My investigations failed to impress Will himself. A letter from him read, in its entirety, "Your problems multiply. Mr. Geiger, head of the teachers union, concedes 'about 40%,' which strongly suggests that my apogee may be bang on." Enclosed with the letter was the transcript from the relevant part of the Brinkley show.

Responding to my article in a letter to *Education Week,* Doyle also accepted Geiger's figure. Surely Will's and Doyle's letters marked two historic moments. Both usually hold the NEA in the same high esteem as Jim Brady holds the National Rifle Association. Yet here they were, apparently accepting on faith with no questions asked, a statistic mumbled by the president of the NEA off the top of his head. It was as if the head of the Tobacco Institute had said that nicotine was not addictive, and Garry Trudeau had agreed.

Yet another copy of my analysis went to *News & Views* of the Educational Excellence Network, a monthly compilation of articles and essays that had been initiated by Chester Finn, Jr., when he was at Vanderbilt University and that is now published by the Hudson Institute. I knew that the piece would not be published in the newsletter. My modest goal was only to preempt the reproduction of Will's essay. In a letter, Michael Heise, then director of *News & Views,* wrote, "I want to thank you for forwarding me a copy of the papers entitled 'George Will's Urban Legend' and 'The Third Bracey Report on the Condition of Public Education.' We will give them careful consideration for the next issue of *News & Views.*" The next issue contained only Will's article.

I tried to enlist the aid of media watchers in debunking this statistic. The *Washington Post* ombudsman, Joann Byrd, had been unresponsive to earlier entreaties, so I approached the *Post's* designated media watcher, Howard Kurtz. He wrote a short and accurate summary of the episode.[39] No one could account for the transformation of a statistic for Chicago into one for the nation. Kurtz quoted the Cato Institute's Boaz as saying, "All I did was repeat the findings of Doyle and Hartle." Kurtz concluded with a quote from Henninger of the *Wall Street Journal:* "The precise figures are less important than 'that public school teachers send their children to private school at a rate higher than the general population.' " This certainly was in line with the earlier editorial. In the body of that editorial, the editors had cited the figures for California public school teachers as 18%. But rather than draw attention to the distance between 18% and 50%, the *Wall Street Journal* commented only that this rate was higher than for the general public.

As I noted above, the comparison between teachers and the general public is not even the proper comparison, and the proper comparison finds the allegation false. As Shanker had said, "When teachers are compared with other college graduates, it becomes clear that they send their kids to private schools less often than other people of comparable socioeconomic status."[40]

How the figure of "nearly half" got generalized from Chicago to the nation remains a mystery. Six months earlier, Will had cited it correctly. He closed his 7 March 1993 column in support of vouchers for Chicago with "About half the Chicago public school teachers with school-age children send them to private schools."[41] Queries to Will's office to explain how half of Chicago teachers in March became half of the nation's urban teachers in August went unanswered.

EDUCATION AND THE ECONOMY

The First Bracey Report raised questions about the link between schools and the performance of the economy. The Second Bracey Report expressed those doubts more vehemently and presented some evidence that schools were *not* responsible for the economic malaise. By the Third Bracey Report, this evidence had grown to mountain size. Conditions now allow us to lay to rest, once and for all, the misbegotten notion that schools are dragging our economy down—or, for that matter, pushing it up.

It's not that people aren't still trying to make that connection. In May of this year, IBM's Gerstner took to the op-ed page of the *New York Times* to declare that "Our Schools Are Failing" and to talk about the threat posed by that dismal prospect.[42] The usually reasonable and moderate David Broder declared in the *Washington Post,* "Once again, Americans are being asked to take a gut-check on how serious we are about our children's future. If we're serious, almost everyone agrees, we have to lift the performance of the youngsters coming out of high school, so they have the skills required in the new economy."[43]

In other words, the schools haven't gotten any better, and we are still "a nation at risk." As *A Nation at Risk* had said in 1983, "If only to keep and improve on the slim competitive edge we still retain in world markets, we must dedicate ourselves to the reform of our educational system." It would seem that the economy depends on it.

Fortunately, the economy wasn't listening. It roared off to heights that—if Gerstner and Broder and *A Nation at Risk* were right—ought to be impossible. A lead article by Sylvia Nasar in the business section of the *New York Times* trumpeted this success in the headline "The American Economy, Back on Top." The *Times* waxed ecstatic:

> A three percent economic growth rate, a gain of two million jobs in the past year, and an inflation rate reminiscent of the 1960s make America the envy of the industrialized world. The amount the average American worker can produce, already the highest in the world, is growing faster than in other wealthy countries, including Japan. The United States has become the world's low-cost provider of many sophisticated products and services, from plastics to software to financial services.
>
> For the most part, these advantages will continue even after countries like Japan and Germany snap out of their recessions. It is the United States, not Japan, that is the master of the next generation of commercially important computer and communications technologies and also of leading-edge services from medicine to movie making.[44]

The *Times* article gushed on in this fashion for 2,500 euphoric words. And it was scarcely a lone voice. T. R. Reid, *Washington Post* foreign correspondent, filed a report from Tokyo, noting that Japanese business was learning from America once again.[45] The *Post* article followed an earlier *New York Times* article headlined "Now It's Japan's Turn to Play Catch-Up."[46] That article carried the subhead "From PC's to Cable TV, Tokyo Finds Itself Far Behind in the Next Electronics Revolution." And *U. S. News & World Report* carried a long feature article titled "America Cranks It Up."[47] Even *Fortune* was forced to concede, "For all the criticism of U. S. education, youngsters enter the work force far better equipped than today's mature workers."[48]

That last comment was as close as the schools came to getting any credit for the recovery. None of the other articles cited, nor myriad similar pieces published elsewhere, even mentioned the schools.

Only a couple of years ago, Marc Tucker, Lester Thurow, and Robert Reich, to name but a few, were decrying the state of our schools and our Taylorized production lines. "Japan makes television sets; we watch them," declared the Hudson Institute's Denis Doyle in 1992.[49] We might ask ourselves the question, If the schools are still awful, how on earth did the economy manage such a miraculous turnaround? According to all the articles, the new successes derived from "reengineering"—industry's equivalent of education's "restructuring"—and the application of new technologies. Companies downsized to become lean and mean. Management savvy saved the day. The schools were, at best, invisible in the process. In fact, John McClain of the Associated Press reported a survey confirming that the economy is booming but also pointing out that pervasive weaknesses in elementary and secondary education still threatened its health.[50]

Stanford University's Larry Cuban was among those to notice the asymmetry between blame for the bad economic times and credit for the good ones. "Why is it that now with a bustling economy, rising productivity, and shrinking unemployment American public schools are not receiving credit for the turnaround?" Cuban wondered.[51] Citing some of the evidence disclosed earlier in this report, he continued his questioning: "Now that America outstrips Japan and Germany in labor productivity, economic growth, and share of world merchandising exports, why haven't public schools received the equivalent of the Oscars?"

Cuban knew that his questions were rhetorical. "Not even a cheaply framed certificate of merit is in the offing for public schools. For the myth of better schools as the engine for a leaner, stronger economy was a scam from the very beginning," he concluded. Just so. In the First Bracey Report, I called *A Nation at Risk* a "xenophobic screed." These days, I simply call it a lie: much of the evidence backing its claims is highly selective; some of it doesn't even exist.

This particular economic boom comes with a most unusual downside. While Nasar's *New York Times* piece, cited earlier, spoke of the creation of two million jobs, it didn't say how many of them are good jobs. The reality is that damn few are good. In recent years, people have been indoctrinated with the argument that the fastest growing fields all require highly skilled people. This is true. But according to the Bureau of Labor Statistics, these fields account for very few jobs overall: 3,162,000 by the year 2005. On the other hand, the single largest occupation, retail sales, by itself accounts for 4,500,000. The 10 occupations with the highest numbers of workers

are largely unskilled, and these account for 30,100,000 jobs—almost 10 times more than the fastest growing fields.[52] As manufacturing lost 255,000 jobs in 1992, the restaurant industry alone added 249,000 jobs. Not many called for executive chefs.[53]

Who is taking all these new jobs? In addition to the usual new graduates and immigrants, the answer is people who already have jobs. The Labor Department reported that seven million people hold 15 million jobs, and for the first time it documented the existence of a phenomenon heretofore known mostly through anecdote: the three- and four-job couples. Some of these multi-job workers, it is true, are people trying to break into new fields, but the largest group consists of those just trying to pay their bills.[54]

Ironically, the creation of some jobs dooms others. Patte Barth, the editor of *Basic Education,* once declared in the pages of that journal that advanced algebra would soon be a basic skill, and by way of example she wrote of a restaurant that was run by only two people.[55] Barth concentrated on the breadth and depth of the skills those people would have to have and on what that implied for education. I am more impressed by the fact that there are only two of them on the premises.

Meanwhile, Richard Barnet of the Institute for Policy Studies pointed out that, "between 1979 and 1992, the Fortune 500 companies presented 4.4 million of their employees with pink slips."[56] Barnet saw two forces operating to kill jobs. One was moving the job to another locale—maybe within the U. S., maybe not. "More and more of us, from wastebasket emptiers to CEOs of multinational corporations, are waking up to the fact that we are swimming in a global labor pool," he wrote. The movement has particularly pernicious effects in the countries of Asia, Africa, and Latin America—because in those areas large numbers of women are entering the work force, and those nations have traditionally paid women much less than men.

The other force is technology. In the past year, article after article announced layoffs of a few hundred to many thousand workers, even as other articles (sometimes the very same ones) displayed curves of rising productivity. The relationship is causal: as people become more productive, fewer of them are needed in the work force. Barnet had this to say: "I have visited a variety of highly automated factories in the United States and Europe, including automobile, electronics, and printing plants. The scarcity of human beings in these places is spooky."

In 1979 Christopher Evans predicted that the microchip would end work as we know it.[57] Evans foresaw pervasive affluence and the possibility of a

25-hour work week. To date, the scenario has been more like that described 15 years earlier by Kurt Vonnegut in *God Bless You, Mr. Rosewater,* wherein one character mused, "The problem is, how to love people who have no use." As Barnet observed, "In the end, the job crisis raises the most fundamental question of human existence: What are we doing here?"

Given all of this, it is not surprising that Frank Swoboda, *Washington Post* business writer, found workers asking "one of the most fundamental questions facing the nation today: Can a worker acquire enough skills to achieve job security in a world of global competition?" Swoboda found the short-term answer to be "no." He didn't have a long-term answer.[58]

While education is at best tenuously linked to the well-being of the nation, it is becoming even more important to the well-being of the individual. That is, education is related to the likelihood of getting a job in the first place or of finding another job when you lose the one you had. Still, as Swoboda reported, it is not a guarantee. It is a necessary, but not a sufficient, condition for well-paying employment. The number of college-educated door-to-door salesmen grew from 57,000 in 1983 to 75,000 in 1990, while the number of bus drivers with bachelor's degrees increased from 99,000 to 166,000. Ross Perot wondered why all the hotel people who carried his luggage had bachelor's degrees, giving rise to the phrase "B.A. Bellhops," while in a *Washington Post* piece titled "Take This Job and Love It," a recent college graduate was quoted as saying, "We're getting jobs chimps could do."[59]

That last article described college graduates working as file clerks and photocopy makers. Compared to high school graduates, though, they had it good. "For hundreds of thousands of people graduating from high school this spring, the diploma is a one-way ticket to low-paying, part-time jobs at best," wrote Peter Kilborn.[60] The lucky ones might get full-time jobs doing what they did as part-time employees after school and on weekends.

Some companies, including large ones such as Federal Express, are taking advantage of the situation by offering only part-time work that comes without benefits. "There is a myth in this country that, if you want to be something, you can be it," said economist Richard Rothstein. "This generation is finding out it isn't true with a vengeance. And we wonder why they're cynical."[61]

In fact, high school graduates now face a new source of competition for jobs: college graduates. "Industry is shedding layers of middle-management jobs held by college graduates," wrote Kilborn, "creating an additional challenge for high school graduates: People with college degrees have invaded their blue-collar turf." Of 1993 high school graduates who tried to enter the labor market, 24% were still unemployed as of October, almost four times the national average for all workers.[62]

For those who do find jobs, whether they be college or high school graduates, wages are down. Entry-level wages fell in real dollars from just above $12 an hour for college graduates in 1973 to $11 an hour in 1991. For those with only a high school diploma, the drop was from just above $8 an hour to just above $6 an hour.[63] Alan Wurtzel, chairman of the board at Circuit City, an electronics discount chain on the East Cost, wrote that "Circuit City is a large national company that seldom hires people right out of high school. . . . In hiring new employees for our stores, warehouses, and offices, Circuit City is looking for people who are able to provide very high levels of customer service, who are honest, and who have a positive, enthusiastic, achievement-oriented work ethic."[64] These are characteristics that our high school graduates lack, Wurtzel claimed. He somehow failed to mention that Circuit City warehouse employees start at $4.25 an hour, while salespeople are paid no salary at all and work strictly on commission.

Still, education pays. The U. S. Census Bureau reported the following lifetime earnings for various levels of education:[65]

Not a high school graduate	$609,000
High school diploma	$821,000
Some college	$993,000
Associate's degree	$1,062,000
Bachelor's degree	$1,421,000
Master's degree	$1,619,000
Doctorate	$2,142,000
Professional (doctor, lawyer)	$3,013,000

Despite the turnaround in the U. S. economy since 1992, the Census Bureau also reported that the number of poor Americans continued to grow, reaching 14.7%. For children, the figure was 20%, and for African Americans and Hispanics it reached nearly 50%. These statistics seem to verify the charge that economic success in America continues to be polarized along class lines. They are all the more horrific when one considers that the threshold of poverty for a family of four is a scandalously low $14,335, according to the Census Bureau—a figure less than half of $30,786, the median American household income for a family of four. As discussed in the Third Bracey Report, children of poverty do not perform well in school.

Indeed, other studies of poverty in America suggest that we are moving away from rather than toward our first national goal: that all children begin school ready to learn. The proportion of low-income children in preschool programs is far smaller than that for upper-income children. And day-care programs that serve low-income families are more likely to be custodial than are programs serving upper-income families, which are likely to be developmental.

SCHOOL CHOICE

School choice as a one-stop solution to education's problems might have crested with California's Proposition 174, a 1993 referendum that would have created a voucher system with public funds available for use in private schools. Interest now seems to be on the wane, perhaps because interest in charter schools is waxing. While John Chubb continued to tout free-market choice,[66] while Terry Moe showed up at California's "Education Summit" in February to promise another choice referendum, and while Gerstner and his co-authors plumped for choice in their book, most other writers urged caution. So did the data.

Harold Howe II exposed choice as no more than the latest episode of what he termed "millennialist thinking"—thinking that embodies the hope that a single social reform might bring the millennium.[67] Certainly, in their book Chubb and Moe sang a most ardent paean to the free market as a panacea for most anything, especially the ills of schools:

The eighth wonder of the world is the capitalist system of economic organization. It has brought more good to more people than any other large-scale social invention. Therefore its basic assumptions are to be treasured and transferred to all possible realms of human activity. . . . The wonderful power of competition to produce quality will solve all the messy little problems like how to pay for schools, find and prepare good teachers, and motivate children to learn.[68]

This passage leaves Howe all but mute. He can declare only, "If this isn't millennial thinking, I can't imagine what is." Such gushiness coming from supposedly serious scholars certainly is bewildering.

In two similar books, sociologist Peter Cookson, Jr., of Adelphi University and political scientist Jeffrey Henig of George Washington University independently demolished the central premises of market-driven school choice. Both reviewed the history of choice as an idea and the data from choice experiments. The claims for choice are strong; the evidence, weak. Henig found most success stories to be casual claims without real substance, studies with inadequate measures to demonstrate the claims, or studies so lacking in controls as to render them impossible to

interpret.[69] Both Henig and Cookson are particularly dismissive of Chubb and Moe's analysis, which turned tiny test score gains into a scale they claimed showed years of growth. Chubb and Moe, says Cookson, "have so magnified their results by altering the unit of analysis . . . that they have lost sight of their own finding, which indicates that there are very few achievement gains between the sophomore and senior years of high school."[70]

In fact, Henig stands the market metaphor on its head. Examining the evidence, he concludes that, when choice works, it works *not* because it unshackles pent-up market demands, which often can't even be found. It works because of the much-maligned bureaucrats and government agencies:

The expanded use of choice . . . is better understood as having arisen from collective negotiation, public leadership, and authoritative government, rather than from an unleashing of individual interests and market forces. . . . Whether reactive or activist, in all cases the process of experimentation [with choice] has been public and political—mediated through collective institutions and made to work through the application of authoritative government action.[71]

Both Henig and Cookson warn that market-based choice systems would hide this collective and public discussion and would deprive schools of one of their most important qualities, their openness to public scrutiny and debate.

Henig and Cookson both favor choice, but they see it as one tool among many to improve education, not as a solution to education's problems. Henig conjectures that there might even be choice situations in which public funds would be appropriately spent in private schools.

Joe Nathan, a leading advocate of public school choice, also urged moderation. "Those who promote school choice as a 'panacea' are ignorant and/or foolish," Nathan charged. "Chubb and Moe have done more to harm the choice movement than anyone else."[72] Nathan reasons that we need school choice because there is no one best system for all children; because choice is central to teacher empowerment; because without government-sponsored choice, only the affluent can have it; and because competition stimulates improvement.

For these and other reasons, choice advocates have closely watched Milwaukee's experiment with choice, which provides public money for tuition at private schools. The data from the third year of this program are decidedly mixed. The program has never recruited as many students as it has places for, and the attrition rate is high. It might be no higher than that for low-income children elsewhere in Milwaukee, but—if people are picking schools they want—we ought to expect those schools to have stronger holding power.

Test results are mixed, too.[73] Scores have bounced around and shown no sizable increases, even when the results are statistically significant. (That tests of statistical significance are inappropriate for such program evaluations was a topic treated in the *Kappan* Research column in September 1992.)

The parents in the Milwaukee choice program are better educated, make more money, and are more involved with schools than those who are not. They were angry at their neighborhood schools and had better attitudes about the choice programs. But this finding, too, is an equivocal outcome, as the authors of the report point out: "While they look like just the kinds of parents that choice programs were designed to serve, they might have provided an even greater social good by staying behind to work to improve the neighborhood school."[74]

POVERTY

Under the heading "New Data," above, we have already seen that poverty depresses school performance. Poverty wreaks its havoc not only through home and community conditions that are antithetical to academic success, but through the underfunding of the schools themselves. Most schools are still funded largely through property taxes, thus ensuring the existence of inequities. Indeed, reports from the South, especially Mississippi, reveal the growth of "rural ghettos," communities of largely black people with little or no industrial base that are ignored by the larger white culture.[75]

There is growing interest in removing these savage inequalities. While the supreme court in Minnesota decided that that state's constitution did not require it to provide equal funds to all districts, more and more state supreme courts have found that inequitable school financing is a violation of state constitutions. One of the most recent is New Jersey, where in ordering changes the court was clearly concerned with equity in outcomes, not merely inputs. New Jersey had already made considerable progress since a similar decision in 1990. While the wealthiest districts in many states spend two or three times as much money as the poorest districts, the poorest districts in New Jersey currently receive 84% of the funding that wealthy districts receive.

Still, in interpreting New Jersey's constitutional provision for a "thorough and efficient" education, the state supreme court strongly implied that, since poor children are disadvantaged in all other aspects

of their lives, the schools must attempt to compensate for such disadvantage: "Success cannot be expected to be realized unless the department and the commission identify and implement the special supplemental programs and services that the children in these [poor] districts require." Some programs and services in poor districts will be "unique to those students, not required in wealthier districts."[76]

Although the arguments are typically cast in economic, not educational terms, the focus on poverty and welfare reform also drew attention to illegitimacy. Daniel Patrick Moynihan showed that out-of-wedlock births held at a flat 4% from 1940 to 1956, then began an accelerating upturn. Currently, 30% of all births are out-of-wedlock births, as are 80% of those to teenage mothers.[77]

Charles Murray observed that women with family incomes of more than $75,000 account for just 1% of illegitimate babies, while women with family incomes under $20,000 account for 69%.[78] The annual cost to taxpayers of illegitimate births to the poor is estimated at $34 billion. According to Murray, "Throughout human history, a single woman with a small child has not been a viable [economic] unit." Murray claims that we have been able to tolerate the demise of the black family, as horrible as that has been, because it involves only a small minority of the population. Significantly, he titles his essay "The Coming White Underclass."

Murray has performed a public service by recommending a policy of eliminating all economic support for single mothers. Few agree with this move, including me, but by framing the issue in this stark, draconian light, Murray has forced others to consider more moderate welfare reforms.

THE MEDIA

This report has already cited numerous examples of the media's misreading or misreporting the situation in education. For the most part, media attacks on schools continued as in previous years. However, there did seem to be an increase in what I have termed "gratuitous media violence" visited on the schools this year. Gratuitous violence occurs when schools are criticized in an article whose subject is something other than education.

A few examples should suffice. *Conde Nast Traveler* carries periodic contests called "Where Are You?" It provides clues, and the reader must determine his or her precise location. In the June 1994 edition, one of the clues begins, "In a nation of rampant illiteracy (no, it's not the United States). . . ." By the same token, the June 9 edition of the cartoon strip "Kudzu" contains a discussion of Generation X in which one character thinks that young adults are called that because they can't write their names. In an article about border collies, Charles Krauthammer declared that, "we have gotten used to falling SAT scores, coming in dead last in international math comparisons, [and] high schoolers who cannot locate the Civil War to the nearest half-century."[79] And so on. For the record, in none of the nine comparisons contained in the Second International Mathematics Study and in the Second International Assessment of Educational Progress does America finish "dead last." U. S. scores are, in fact, close to the international averages.

The media's indifference to good news about schools earned it a collective jibe from Project Censored, which annually names the top 10 censored stories of the year. In 1993 it gave the number-three ranking to the Sandia Report and applauded the *Kappan* for publishing an article summarizing the report. Wrote the people at Project Censored, "This report was suppressed by the Bush administration and virtually ignored by the mainstream media because it challenged the widespread view that public schools are self-destructing."[80]

The *Utne Reader*, a bimonthly collection of articles that bills itself as "the best of the alternative press," reprinted Project Censored's report,[81] but it must be said that editor Eric Utne's hands are not entirely clean in this matter either. I had sent a copy of the Sandia Report to the *Utne Reader*, and each year I also dispatched a copy of the Bracey Report. A cover letter urged the publication to give as much attention to these kinds of reports as it had to critical articles. But no response ever came from the *Utne Reader*.

In the Third Bracey Report, I noted that people tend to like their local schools and quoted Denis Doyle as saying, "That is scientific evidence that ignorance is bliss." It now looks as if another aphorism more accurately describes the situation: "Seeing is believing." Polling data from the American Association of School Administrators indicate that people get most of their information about the nation's schools from television, followed by newspapers.[82] Given the uniformly negative coverage provided by both media, a less than grim view would be hard to come by.

Television and newspapers play a major role in providing information about local schools, too, but so do friends, neighbors, children, local school officials, local school newsletters, and school visits. A lesson for schoolpeople might be to include information about the national education scene as well as local information in the materials that go home to parents.

Of course, education is not the only subject that is misreported. (Indeed, that's something I worry about when citing journalists on, say, the economy.)

Richard Harwood, former *Washington Post* ombudsman who is now retired, writes often about the general decline in journalism. He cites David Broder's comment that "citizens now perceive the press as part of the insider's world. . . . We have, through the elevation of salaries, prestige, education, and so on among reporters, distanced ourselves to a remarkable degree from the people we are writing for and have become much, much closer to the people [experts and politicians] we are writing about."[83]

In a similar vein Harwood quotes another journalist, Tom Koch, who commented, "For twenty years content analysis studies have shown that between 70 and 90 percent of our content is at heart the voice of officials and their experts, translated by reporters, into supposedly 'objective' news. People don't trust us anymore . . . because the way we quote and attribute and build factoids as if they were truth is a lie. And folks are catching on."[84] I had an inkling of this in a conversation with Broder shortly after he wrote a favorable column about *Prisoners of Time*. Although the Bracey Reports contain much more data than that slim volume—some 200 references in the first three Bracey Reports—Broder told me that he would require "more than a single voice" to be convinced of my position. Does an official government report, one commissioned by a former secretary of education who wishes to privatize public schools, constitute a chorus?

On the rare occasion when a major publication did include something good about U. S. schools, no one else seemed to notice. In December 1993, William Celis III wrote a front-page story in the *New York Times* titled "International Report Card Shows U. S. Schools Work."[85] Many statistics from the OECD study that Celis included in his story have either appeared in the Third Bracey Report or show up in this one. He found American students only slightly below international averages in math and science and almost at the top in reading. He found that more Americans get a college education than is true of citizens in any other nation. He found that a great deal of money from American school budgets goes for noninstructional programs (e.g., transportation, food), which is not the case in other nations. And no other major media outlet carried Celis' story.

One story of American educational success did appear in the *Washington Post*, but it was played only for its local angle. The American team finished first in the 1994 International Mathematics Olympiad, and one team member was from Bethesda, Maryland, just over the Maryland state line from the District of Columbia. The story was filed by the *Post's* Montgomery County, Maryland, desk and discussed the Bethesda student's achievements in more detail than those of the team.[86]

That the U. S. did well was not exactly news. Our worst finish in the Olympiad was sixth place in 1993. To finish first, the U. S. team had to outscore teams from 68 other nations. But in addition to taking first, the U. S. team truly aced the test: all six team members posted perfect scores, a first-ever occurrence for any team and something that astonished program organizers.

That small triumph aside, it is likely that only in America could a movie about a simple man who accidentally participates in events that shape the nation and achieves fortune and happiness set off a national debate about education. Many moviegoers saw *Forrest Gump* as delightful entertainment with, perhaps, another Academy Award in the offing for Tom Hanks. Many others saw it as avowing that it's good to be dumb. These people also saw its popularity as proof that Americans celebrate stupidity and passivity, that we derogate brains and hard work.[87] It's certainly true that a brainy person risks being called geek, dork, and nerd, and the celebration of our Olympiad math champions was brief. Still, the proportion of high scorers on the math section of the SAT continues to grow, more kids show up each year for and show well on the Advanced Placement tests, and as a nation we come close to the gold medal in reading. Somebody, somehow, must have been encouraging these kids.

NOTES

1. Barry O'Neill, "Anatomy of a Hoax," *New York Times Magazine*, 6 March 1994, pp. 46–49.
2. Richard Rothstein, "The Myth of Public School Failure," *The American Prospect*, Spring 1993, pp. 20–34.
3. Louis V. Gerstner, Jr., et al., *Reinventing Education* (New York: Dutton Books, 1994).
4. Benjamin R. Barber, "America Skips School," *Harper's Magazine*, November 1993, pp. 39–46.
5. *Education in States and Nations* (Washington, D.C.: National Center for Education Statistics, Report No. 93–237, 1993).
6. Lauren Resnick, "New Standards: What to Measure," symposium at the annual meeting of the American Educational Research Association, New Orleans, April 1994.
7. Harold Hodgkinson, "A Demographic Look at Tomorrow," Institute for Educational Leadership, Washington, D.C., 1992.
8. H. D. Hoover, director of the Iowa Testing Program, personal communication, July 1994.
9. Ronald A. Wolk, "Editor's Note," *Education Week*, 10 March 1993, p. 29.
10. These and other SAT-related data are from the College Board's annual publication, *Profiles of College-Bound Seniors*.
11. Karen De Witt, "Scores Improve for 2d Consecutive Year," *New York Times*, 19 August 1993, p. A-19.
12. Lisa Leff, "SAT Scores Rise in Fairfax, D.C., Drop in Alexandria, Pr. George's." *Washington Post*, 19 August 1993.
13. Glen E. Robinson and David P. Brandon, *NAEP Test Scores: Should They Be Used to Compare and Rank State Educational Quality?* (Arlington, Va.: Educational Research Service, 1994).
14. David C. Berliner, "The Author Responds," Backtalk letter, *Phi Delta Kappan*, October 1993, p. 193.
15. Herbert C. Walberg, "Are Proposed Educational Reforms Effective?," *Chicago Sun Times*, 5 February 1994, p. 16.
16. Richard M. Jaeger, "World Class Standards, Choice, and Privatization: Weak Measurement Serving Presumptive Policy," *Phi Delta Kappan*, October 1992, pp. 118–28.
17. National Center for Education Statistics, *Digest of Education Statistics 1993* (Washington, D.C.: U. S. Department of Education, 1993), Table 161, p. 159.
18. C. C. Carson, R. M. Huelskamp, and T. D. Woodall, "Perspectives on Education in America," *Journal of Educational Research*, May/June 1993, pp. 260–310.
19. *Digest of Education Statistics 1993*, Table 51, p. 65.
20. American Legislative Exchange Council, "Report Card on American Education 1993," Washington, D.C., 1993.
21. George F. Will, "Meaningless Money Factor," *Washington Post*, 26 August 1993, p. C-7.
22. Eric A. Hanushek, "The Impact of Differential Expenditures on School Performance," *Educational Researcher*, May 1989, pp. 45–65.
23. Larry V. Hedges, Richard D. Laine, and Rob Greenwald, "Does Money Matter? A Meta-Analysis of Studies of the Effects of Differential Inputs on Student Outcomes," *Educational Researcher*, April 1994, pp. 5–14.
24. Eric A. Hanushek, "Money Might Matter Somewhere: A Reply to Hedges, Laine, and Greenwald," *Educational Researcher*, May 1994, pp. 5–8.
25. William Celis III, "Teachers in U. S. Trail Those Elsewhere in Pay," *New York Times*, 18 August 1993, p. A-17.
26. Mary Jordan and Tracy Thompson, "Across U. S., Schools Are Falling Apart," *Washington Post*, 22 November 1993, p. A-1.

27. Drew Lindsay, "Schoolhouse Rot," *Education Week*, 13 July 1994, pp. 27–33.

28. *Adult Literacy in America* (Washington, D.C.: National Center for Education Statistics, U. S. Department of Education, 1993).

29. David A. Kaplan, Pat Wingert, and Farai Chideta, "Dumber Than We Thought," *Newsweek*, 20 September 1993, pp. 44–45.

30. Pauline B. Gough, "Shame on the Press," *Phi Delta Kappan*, January 1994, p. 355.

31. *National Excellence: A Case for Developing America's Talent* (Washington, D.C.: Office of Educational Research and Improvement, U. S. Department of Education, October 1993).

32. *Prisoners of Time* (Washington, D.C.: Office of Educational Research and Improvement, U. S. Department of Education, April 1994).

33. George F. Will, "Taking Back Education," *Washington Post*, 26 August 1993, p. A-27.

34. Denis Doyle and Terry Hartle, "Where Public School Teachers Send Their Children to School: A Preliminary Analysis," unpublished paper, Spring 1986.

35. Gerald W. Bracey, "George Will's Urban Legend," *Education Week*, 29 September 1993, p. 29.

36. James Coleman. "Choice in Education: Some Effects," paper presented at a conference on "Choice: What Role in American Schools?," sponsored by the Economic Policy Institute, Washington, D.C., 1 October 1992.

37. Albert Shanker, "Urban Legend," *New York Times*, 31 October 1993, p. E-7.

38. "Teacher Knows Best," *Wall Street Journal*, 25 October 1993, p. 20.

39. Howard Kurtz, "Will's Way," *Washington Post*, 6 November 1993, p. C-1.

40. Shanker, op. cit.

41. George F. Will, "When the State Fails Its Citizens," *Washington Post*, 7 March 1993, p. C-7.

42. Louis V. Gerstner, Jr., "Our Schools Are Failing: Do We Care?," *New York Times*, 27 May 1994, p. A-27.

43. David Broder, "How Serious Are We About Education?," *Washington Post*, 11 May 1994, p. A-21.

44. Sylvia Nasar, "The American Economy, Back on Top," *New York Times*, 27 February 1994, Sect. 3, p. 1.

45. T. R. Reid, "Rising Sun Meets Rising Sam," *Washington Post*, 10 February 1994, p. A-1.

46. Andrew Pollack, "Now It's Japan's Turn to Play Catch-Up," *New York Times*, 21 November 1993, Sect. 3, p. 1.

47. Sara Collins, "American Cranks It Up," *U. S. News & World Report*, 28 March 1994, pp. 57–60.

48. Louis S. Richman, "The New Work Force Builds Itself," *Fortune*, June 1994, p. 70.

49. Denis Doyle, presentation at a Junior Achievement Workshop, Colorado Springs, June 1992.

50. Cited in Craig Bowman, "What Makes for Success in School?," *Denver Post*, 14 July 1994, p. 7-B.

51. Larry Cuban, "The Great School Scam," *Education Week*, 15 June 1994, p. 44.

52. *Monthly Labor Review*, November 1991, p. 81.

53. Steven Pearlstein, "Unemployment Holds at 6.7%; Shift from Factory Jobs Continues," *Washington Post*, 9 October 1993, p. A-8.

54. Louis Uichitelle, "Moonlighting Plus: 3-Job Families on the Rise," *New York Times*, 15 August, 1994, p. A-1.

55. Patte Barth, "When Good Is Good Enough," *Basic Education*, December 1991, p. 1.

56. Richard J. Barnet, "The End of Jobs," *Harper's Magazine*, September 1993, pp. 47–52.

57. Christopher Evans, *The Micro Millennium* (New York: Viking, 1979).

58. Frank Swoboda, "At GM, Skills and Anxiety Run High," *Washington Post*, 6 July 1994, p. F-1.

59. Susan Gregory Thomas, "Take This Job and Love It," *Washington Post*, 7 December 1993, p. C-5.

60. Peter T. Kilborn, "For High School Graduates, a Job Market of Dead Ends," *New York Times*, 30 May 1994, p. A-1.

61. Richard Rothstein, presentation to the President's Professional Development Symposium, American Association of School Administrators, Arlington, Va., June 1994.

62. Kilborn, op. cit.

63. Tamar Lewin, "Low Pay and Closed Doors Greet Young in Job Market," *New York Times*, 10 March 1994, p. A-1.

64. Alan Wurtzel, "Getting from School to Work," *Washington Post*, 7 December 1993, p. A-25.

65. Melissa Lee, "When It Comes to Salary, It's Academic," *Washington Post*, 22 July 1994, p. D-1.

66. John E. Chubb, "Vouchers, Public Policy, and Educational Reformation," paper presented at the annual meeting of the American Educational Research Association, New Orleans, April 1994.

67. Harold Howe II, *Thinking About Our Kids* (New York: Free Press, 1993), p. 79.

68. Quoted in ibid., p. 79.

69. Jeffrey R. Henig, *Rethinking School Choice: Limits of the Market Metaphor* (Princeton, N.J.: Princeton University Press, 1994).

70. Peter W. Cookson, Jr., *School Choice: The Struggle for the Soul of American Education* (New Haven, Conn.: Yale University Press, 1994), p. 85.

71. Henig, p. 150.
72. Joe Nathan, "A Few Observations About School Choice," paper presented at the annual meeting of the American Educational Research Association, New Orleans, April 1994.
73. John F. Witte, Andrea B. Bailey, and Christopher A. Thorn, "Third-Year Report: Milwaukee Parental Choice Program," unpublished paper, University of Wisconsin, Madison, December 1993.
74. Ibid.
75. Peter Applebome, "Deep South and Down Home, But It's a Ghetto All the Same," *New York Times*, 21 August 1993, p. A-1.
76. Kimberly J. McLarin, "At Issue: What Is Adequate for the Poor?," *New York Times*, 13 July 1994, p. B-6.
77. David S. Broder, "Illegitimacy: An Unprecedented Catastrophe," *Washington Post*, 22 June 1994, p. A-21.
78. Charles Murray, "The Coming White Underclass," *Wall Street Journal*, 29 October 1993, p. A-14.
79. Charles Krauthammer, "Save the Border Collie," *Washington Post*, 15 July 1994, p. A-21.
80. Press release, 29 March 1994, Project Censored, Public Information Office, Sonoma State University, Rohnert Park, Calif.
81. "The Top Censored Stories of 1993," *Utne Reader*, May/June 1994, pp. 42–47.
82. Bruce Hunter, "The Public's Attitudes Toward Public Education," paper presented to the Willard Fox Seminar, Appalachian State .University, Boone, N.C., June 1994.
83. Richard Harwood, "Reporting On, By, and For an Elite," *Washington Post*, 28 May 1994, p. A-21.
84. Ibid.
85. William Celis III, "International Report Card Shows U. S. Schools Work," *New York Times*, 9 December 1993, p. A-1.
86. Chastity Pratt, "U. S. Math Team: Perfect," *Washington Post*, 20 July 1994, p. A-1.
87. Sarah Lyall, "It's 'Forrest Gump' vs. Harrumph," *New York Times*, 31 July 1994, Sect. 4, p. 2.

SECTION
III

The Curriculum

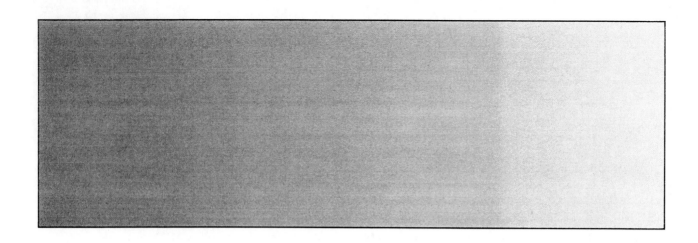

Overview

Section Three spotlights various dimensions of the curriculum and the learners in Texas public schools. The term *curriculum* refers to the subject matter that students are expected to learn as a result of schooling. That is, curriculum refers more to "what" is being taught than "how" it is being taught. Although far too simplistic, the "how" of content delivery refers more to the instructional procedures chosen and applied than to the content to be learned. For example, a teacher may choose to teach Texas history (curriculum content) by lecturing to students, by taking them to historical landmarks, or by other instructional means. The curriculum of a state, school district, or campus describes the expectations or "ends" of schooling, that is, what students must know and be able to do at given times during the educational process. The procedures employed to bring about these ends are the instructional "means."

Chapter 18 provides a historical review of the changing concepts and scope of the American curriculum. Two differing views of curriculum have emerged. The first, the subject-centered curriculum view, agrees with the definition provided above and holds that curriculum is a body of content or subject matter leading to certain goals or "ends" that ultimately can be measured in terms of student achievement. The second view, referred to as the student or learner-centered curriculum, places emphases on the learner and his or her needs and interests. This latter view is more concerned with process and the climate of the classroom and school.

A closer examination of public schools in Texas reveals that most employ some of both views in their daily routines. It is interesting to note that the format and criteria adopted by the State Board of Education to evaluate public school teachers and administrators is entitled Learner-Centered Schools for Texas: A Vision of Texas Educators it is provided in Section IV of this text.

Kathleen Kennedy Manzo observed that throughout the 20th century, the public school "curriculum would become a national preoccupation that would open up the classroom to greater scrutiny. It would at times unify the country in patriotic fervor, and at others, divide it in sectarian ferment" (Education Week, May 19, 1999). In the early decades of the 20th century, the public school curriculum reflected a relatively homogeneous student population especially in the secondary schools. As more and more adolescents enrolled in secondary schools and the economic realities of the times focused more on preparation for the real world of work than exclusively on preparation for college as had been the norm, curricular offerings began to change. Even the traditional college preparatory requirements, long held to be essential for success in higher education, would be challenged. The "Eight-Year-Study," commissioned by the Progressive Education Association followed students from 30 different high schools from around the country through their high school and collegiate experiences from 1932–1940. High schools had been encouraged to depart from the college preparatory curriculum and colleges and universities were asked to admit students who had not completed the traditional but had instead completed new courses and programs that better related to their lives. The "Study" concluded that the students who participated performed slightly better than the comparison group who completed the traditional programs.

By mid-century, the nature of the public school curriculum was to be more and more influenced by state and national governments and less a product of the school or the teachers. Concern for national security and for competing with the Russians during the Cold War led to passage of the National Defense Education Act of 1958 which encouraged scientists and public school educators to improve curricular offerings in mathematics and science. By 1965, the Elementary and Secondary Education Act dramatically increased federal financial assistance for a variety of instructional and curricular innovations. The Civil Rights movement of the 1950s, 1960s and 1970s demanded more curricular visibility for African-Americans, Hispanics, women, the disabled and others previously ignored in public school textbooks and other materials. Just as the Great Depression of the 1930's resulted in states requiring courses in economics, the Civil Rights years resulted in the inclusion of multicultural education, that history textbooks reflect the contributions of all Americans not just the Anglo males and that textbooks and other materials reflect the equality of genders.

What remains constant throughout the century is the reliance on textbooks to guide the scope and sequence of the various content components of the curriculum. However, this dependence has been weakened as the instructional technology has been improved and made available to many if not most of America's public schools.

Manzo summarizes the end of the century as "being played out in the setting of state standards and measures for holding schools, teachers, and students accountable for meeting them" (Education Week, May 19, 1999).

CURRICULUM PLANNING

Section 4.001 of the Texas Education Code states the "Public Education Mission and Objectives," which is followed by Section 4.002, the "Public Education Academic Goals." The statutory plans for implementing both are found in various sections from 28.001 through 28.051. Sections 4.001 and 4.002 are reproduced, and selected components of Section 28 are summarized in Table 1.

TABLE 1   Section 4.001

(a) The mission of the public education system of this state is to ensure that all Texas children have access to a quality education that enables them to achieve their potential and fully participate now and in the future in the social, economic, and educational opportunities of our state and nation. That mission is grounded on the conviction that a general diffusion of knowledge is essential for the welfare of this state and for the preservation of the liberties and rights of citizens. It is further grounded on the conviction that a successful public education system is directly related to a strong, dedicated, and supportive family and that parental involvement in the school is essential for the maximum educational achievement of a child.

(b) The objectives of public education are:

OBJECTIVE 1: Parents will be full partners with educators in the education of their children.

OBJECTIVE 2: Students will be encouraged and challenged to meet their full educational potential.

OBJECTIVE 3: Through enhanced dropout prevention efforts, all students will remain in school until they obtain a high school diploma.

OBJECTIVE 4: A well-balanced and appropriate curriculum will be provided to all students.

OBJECTIVE 5: Qualified and highly effective personnel will be recruited, developed, and retained.

OBJECTIVE 6: The state's students will demonstrate exemplary performance in comparison to national and international standards.

OBJECTIVE 7: School campuses will maintain a safe and disciplined environment conducive to student learning.

OBJECTIVE 8: Educators will keep abreast of the development of creative and innovative techniques in instruction and administration using those techniques as appropriate to improve student learning.

OBJECTIVE 9: Technology will be implemented and used to increase the effectiveness of student learning, instructional management, staff development, and administration.

§ 4.002. Public Education Academic Goals

To serve as a foundation for a well-balanced and appropriate education:

GOAL 1: The students in the public education system will demonstrate exemplary performance in the reading and writing of the English language.

GOAL 2: The students in the public education system will demonstrate exemplary performance in the understanding of mathematics.

GOAL 3: The students in the public education system will demonstrate exemplary performance in the understanding of science.

GOAL 4: The students in the public education system will demonstrate exemplary performance in the understanding of social studies.

COURSES OF STUDY; ADVANCEMENT

Sec. 28.001—28.005. Essential Knowledge and Skills/Curriculum.

- Defines the "foundation" (core) curriculum to include: English language arts; mathematics; science; and social studies, consisting of Texas, United States, and world history, government, and geography.
- The SBOE shall identify the essential knowledge and skills of each subject of the foundation curriculum that all students should be able to demonstrate and that will be used in evaluating textbooks and addressed on state assessment instruments; each district is required to provide instruction in the essential knowledge and skills at appropriate grade levels.
- Defines the "enrichment" curriculum to include other languages (to the extent possible), technology applications, health, P.E., fine arts, economics, and career technology education.
- The SBOE shall identify the essential knowledge and skills of each subject of the enrichment curriculum that all students should be able to demonstrate; each district is required to use the essential knowledge and skills identified by the board as guidelines for the enrichment curriculum.
- If parents of at least 22 students request a transfer to another school in the district for the purpose of enrolling in an educational program offered at that school, beginning with the following school year, the district shall offer the program at the school from which the transfers were requested or offer the program by teleconference, if available; does not include fine arts or a career and technology course.
- Requires the SBOE to consult with parents, business leaders, and educators when identifying essential knowledge and skills for courses.
- Adds a provision that course materials and instruction relating to human sexuality, sexually transmitted diseases, or HIV or AIDS shall be selected by the local board with the advice of the local health education advisory council established by the district and shall place an emphasis on abstinence; provides that a school district may not distribute condoms in connection with instruction relating to human sexuality.
- Establishes provisions for the creation of a health education advisory council in each district.

Sec. 28.021—28.022. Advancement, Placement, Credit, and Academic Achievement Record

- Repeals the curriculum mastery plan requirements.
- A teacher may not be forced to change a student's grade unless it is determined that the grade is arbitrary, capricious, or erroneous, or not in compliance with district grading policy.
- A student may be promoted only on the basis of academic achievement or demonstrated proficiency.
- Requires a district at least once every 12 weeks to give written notice of a student's performance in each class or subject.

Sec. 28.025. High School Diploma/Certificate of Coursework Completion.

- SBOE by rule will determine curriculum requirements for a minimum, recommended, and advanced high school program.
- Allows a school district to issue a certificate of coursework completion to a student who has satisfactorily completed the curriculum requirements identified by the SBOE, but who fails to perform satisfactorily on any state-required assessment instruments. The district may allow a student who receives a certificate to participate in graduation ceremonies.
- A student may graduate and receive a diploma only if the student successfully completes the SBOE identified curriculum requirements and any state-required assessment instruments or an IEP.
- Requires each district to report the academic achievement record of students who have completed a minimum, recommended, or advanced high school program on SBOE-adopted transcript forms and differentiate between types of programs.

Sec. 28.051. Advanced Placement Incentives

- Allows the commissioner to enter into an agreement with the college board and the International Baccalaureate Organization to allow students to take advanced placement tests at no charge through direct payment from the state.
- Establishes an awards program for students, teachers, and schools.

TABLE 2   The National Education Goals

1. By the year 2000, all children in America will start school ready to learn.

2. By the year 2000, the high school graduation rate will increase to at least 90 percent.

3. By the year 2000, all students will leave grades 4, 8, and 12 having demonstrated competency over challenging subject matter including English, mathematics, science, foreign languages, civics and government, economics, arts, history, and geography, and every school in America will ensure that all students learn to use their minds well, so they may be prepared for responsible citizenship, further learning, and productive employment in our Nation's modern economy.

4. By the year 2000, the Nation's teaching force will have access to programs for the continued improvement of their professional skills and the opportunity to acquire the knowledge and skills needed to instruct and prepare all American students for the next century.

5. By the year 2000, U.S. students will be first in the world in mathematics and science achievement.

6. By the year 2000, every adult American will be literate and will possess the knowledge and skills necessary to compete in a global economy and exercise the rights and responsibilities of citizenship.

7. By the year 2000, every school in the United States will be free of drugs, violence, and the unauthorized presence of firearms and alcohol and will offer a disciplined environment conducive to learning.

8. By the year 2000, every school will promote partnerships that will increase parental involvement and participation in promoting the social, emotional, and academic growth of children.

Following the legislative mandate contained in Section 28, the State Board of Education adopted the Texas Essential Knowledge and Skills (TEKS) during the summer of 1997. The process for planning and developing ultimately involved over 400 teachers, curriculum specialists, professors, business leaders, representatives of various learned societies and professional associations and organizations and parents. Chapter 19 summarizes the TEKS and is appended by examples.

In 1990, President George Bush and the governors of the United States agreed upon six National Education Goals. Their agreed-upon purpose was to improve the quality of American education by setting high standards and focusing attention on how well society is able to achieve them. Two additional goals were added during the administration of President Bill Clinton, completing what is known as the Goals 2000. The target year of 2000 was several years away from the agreement on goals, and many believed that sufficient time was available to provide evidence that all or some of the goals had been achieved. Now that 2000 has arrived, and even though significant progress has been made, the achievement remains short of the goals. The National Goals are summarized above in Table 2.

The Goals 2000: Educate America Act, passed by the U.S. Congress in 1994, was designed to codify the eight National Education Goals, authorize funds for K–12 improvement, and establish a framework to encourage state and local education agencies to develop comprehensive plans that would provide a coherent framework to integrate and implement federal education programs. Included was the intent to identify common standards or benchmarks for student achievement and school system effort. The issue of whether this kind of "nationalizing" violated the U.S. Constitutional rights of the states to conduct their own public education programs dominated the debate in both Washington, D.C. and the state capitols. Would a federal system for identifying "performance standards," "opportunity-to-learn standards" and "content standards" provide for accurate accounts that would permit comparisons of student achievement between and among the various states? Critics believed that it would and the critics, thus far, have prevailed.

Performance standards are objective degrees of mastery or levels of attainment that students must know and be able to do. For example: students must answer correctly 70% of the items on an objective test. Opportunity-to-learn standards are the basis for assessing the sufficiency and quality of resources, practices, and conditions necessary at each level of the education system for optimal learning to take place. These standards frequently focus on financial equity between and among school districts. For example, is the amount of money available in relatively poor school districts adequate enough to ensure that students attending those schools have an equal opportunity to learn as compared with those in wealthy districts? A third category, content or curriculum standards, determine the content, or "what" is being taught and what students are expected to learn. Although there won't be significant differences among the states in, for example, mathematics content standards, there may very well be differences in state content or curriculum standards that specify what students will learn in health, biology, American history, and other subjects considered "hot button" subjects in the various state legislatures and boards of education.

The standards encouraged by Goals 2000 should not be confused with national content standards adopted by the various learned societies and organizations such as the National Council of Teachers of Mathematics, National Council of Teachers of English, and the National Council for the Social Studies. The standards adopted by these organizations are referred to as National Standards but they are not standards adopted by the federal government. These standards, although voluntary, are frequently consulted in drafting state standards such as the Texas TEKS or to ensure a degree of conformity so that colleges and universities can consider that completion of Algebra II in most high schools means a degree of mastery of the knowledge and skills usually required in that course.

A planning system is the vehicle for identifying and bringing into proper relationship the interdependent elements or subparts that must function together as an organized whole to attain the ends or goals for which that system is established. From legislative mandate to Monday's lesson plan for 5th grade mathematics, the state went from general goals to specific content standards and, later in this overview, to measurable objectives, selection of books and other instructional materials, and the implementation of a teacher-appraisal program. Each link "tightly coupled" with the next and directly related, providing one of the most comprehensive education accountability systems in the nation. The model for curriculum development was provided by Ralph Tyler.

Tyler Rationale

In his seminal work entitled "Basic Principles of Curriculum and Instruction" (1949), Ralph Tyler asked four pertinent questions that must be answered before the mission, goals, and objectives of education can be established.

1. What educational purposes should the school seek to attain?
2. How can learning experiences be selected which are likely to be useful in attaining these objectives?
3. How can learning experiences be organized for effective instruction?
4. How can the effectiveness of learning experiences be evaluated?

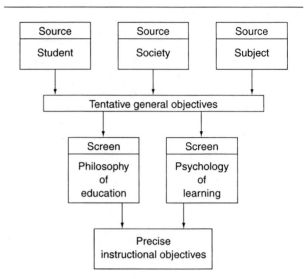

FIGURE 1   THE TYLER RATIONALE
Source: W. James Popham and Eva L. Baker, *Establishing Instructional Goals* (Upper Saddle River, NJ: Prentice-Hall, 1970), p. 87. Reprinted by permission.

Tyler suggested that studies of the *student*, the *society*, and the *subject matter* will yield important information as to what the various constituencies expect of schooling. These three data sources, according to what has become known as the Tyler Rationale, are the first considerations in determining what will ultimately be decided as the mission, goals, and objectives of public education and what must be measured in judging the effectiveness of schools in accomplishing those ends. Popham and Baker have depicted the Tyler Rationale schematically as shown in Figure 1.

The special value of the Tyler model is its systematic approach to determining the purposes of education that can ultimately be translated into objectives for application in classroom contexts.

In considering the "society" of Texas as a source for the determination of the purposes of public education, the Board reviewed the legislative mandates for the Texas curriculum. Assuming that the "people" of a state create a constitution creating a legislature, which in turn creates laws and regulatory agencies, the state government is one of society's most visible, effective, and powerful sources of influence over what is to be taught in the state's schools.

Tyler suggested that, beyond what is mandated by state law, society as a data source can be studied in terms of the following: health, family, recreation, vocation, religion, and civic affairs. There is evidence that the State Board considered the changing demographics, economics, and the nature of the workforce in the society in which students will play adult roles, the ethnic distribution of the population, and the increasingly complex expectations of citizenship. Preliminary statements of the mission, goals, and objectives reflect this consideration. Public hearings were held, consultants were employed, and research was conducted to determine the expectations of society.

Using students as a source for the determination of educational goals involves a study of both student *needs* and *interests*. A student need is the difference between where a student is and where he should be. For example, if a seventh grade student is reading at fourth grade level and should be on level, the difference or need is obvious. Learning what the student is interested in may be important in meeting that student's need. For example, if the student is interested in a military career, reading military history may help him improve his reading skill and his educational need to be reading on level.

Studying the *subject,* the third major consideration in the Tyler model, involves what should be taught in a particular course or level consistent with the essential elements mandated by law. For example, health is one of the essential elements of the public school curriculum. But does the study of health include topics such as sexually transmitted diseases? If so, and at least 28 states currently provide curriculum or curriculum guides for teaching about HIV/AIDS, how can it best be taught? Consulting the experts on (in this case) diseases may reveal an essential body of knowledge and a logical sequence of learning activities that have been proven effective in teaching about AIDS. Other sources of the subject data are the historians, mathematicians, and other specialists who can or have defined their disciplines and those who study the proper applications of those disciplines in classroom contexts.

Seldom can one study one of the Tyler sources in isolation. When it was revealed that Plano ISD high school seniors responded to a survey on consumption of alcohol and cocaine at levels above what a national study had reported, consideration of the student, society, and the subject would each be employed if the State or local board decided that substance abuse was a necessary component of the mission, goals, and objectives of the public schools. Similarly, if a Gallup poll reported and the citizens of a community agreed that teenagers needed "values education," all three data sources may be consulted. The second, or "screening" tier of the Tyler model would then come in to play.

Tyler's *Philosophy of Education* screen was designed to help facilitate decisions not just over what should be provided by the schools but equally important, what should be taught by some other institution such as the family or the church. The traditional philosophical belief which resulted in free, tax-supported, public, and compulsory schooling in America has left the door open for society to demand more and more from the schools—more, in some cases, than the schools can or should deliver.

The second screen, *Psychology of Learning,* is employed after the subject matter at issue is deemed appropriate and necessary for the schools to teach. If, for example, values education is an important responsibility of the schools, the psychology of learning screen would provide answers to the planning questions of when (at what grade level) and how (by using "values clarification" examples, "golden rules," etc.), and in what sequence. Once the mission, goals, and objectives of schooling have been determined, the learning objectives can be stated precisely for use in classrooms. The applications model provided in Figure 2 begins where the Tyler model ends, that is, the statement of precise educational objectives and the procedures to implement and evaluate the instruction.

A systematic planning model was employed by the State Board of Education in developing the state curriculum referred to as the Texas Essential Knowledge and Skills (TEKS), which is the subject of Chapter 19. The TEKS was adopted in the State Board of Education in 1997 and replaced the "essential elements," the first state curriculum, which had been in place since 1984.

ACHIEVEMENT TESTING

Texas has had about 20 years of experience in testing students using state-developed criterion-referenced tests. Beginning with the Texas Assessment of Basic Skills (TABS) in 1979–1980, students in grades 3, 5, and 9 were tested. The Texas Assessment of Minimum Skills (TEAMS) replaced the TABS in 1985–1986 and added grades 1, 7, and 11, although testing first graders was abandoned shortly thereafter. Students had to pass the 11th grade test before they could receive a diploma. The TEAMS was intended to measure student achievement of the state adopted "essential elements" of the curriculum. The 1989–1990 school year was the fifth and last year of the TEAMS. The Texas Assessment of Academic Skills (TAAS) replaced the TEAMS during the 1990–1991 academic year. Whereas TABS measured "minimum skills" and TEAMS attempted to measure student achievement of the essential elements, TAAS has been broadened in scope and better reflect academic expectations for the 21st century. Those skills that demanded little more than rote memorization have been deemphasized,

Premise of the model: The goal of teaching is to maximize the efficiency / effectiveness and minimize the anxiety with which students achieve specified objectives.
Functions of Model: (1) to guide instruction design and implementation; (2) to provide structure for viewing and studying instruction.

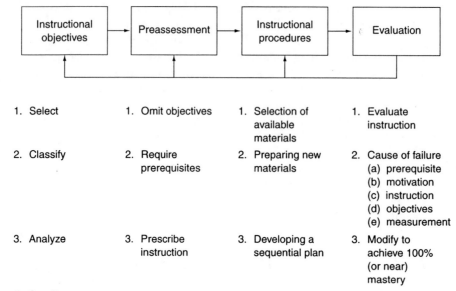

| Instructional objectives | Preassessment | Instructional procedures | Evaluation |

1. Select

2. Classify

3. Analyze

4. Specify
   (1) Use feedback information to make needed modifications in other components of the model.
   (2) Provide learners with knowledge of performance throughout instruction.

1. Omit objectives

2. Require prerequisites

3. Prescribe instruction

1. Selection of available materials

2. Preparing new materials

3. Developing a sequential plan

1. Evaluate instruction

2. Cause of failure
   (a) prerequisite
   (b) motivation
   (c) instruction
   (d) objectives
   (e) measurement

3. Modify to achieve 100% (or near) mastery

FIGURE 2 General Model of Instruction
Source: Robert J. Kibler et al., *Objectives for Instruction and Evaluation* (Boston: Allyn & Bacon, 1974), p. 28.

while those areas that improve a student's ability to think independently, read critically, write clearly, and solve problems logically received increased emphasis. This change was in keeping with the national trend in education, which stresses the importance, and even the necessity, of teaching students higher-order thinking skills.

Results of the first administration of the TAAS in October were disappointing, with a 68% pass rate. Only 39% passed in the April 1991 administration. With the years of experience with student testing, the early uses of any new test can be surprising. For example, Virginia's first-year results from the new Standards of Learning test found 97% of its schools had failed. The percentage of students who passed the new Virginia test ranged from a low of 33.8% in fifth grade history to a high of 71.1% in eighth grade science. Even though the 1999 results created severe skepticism, Virginians were unsure as to where to place the blame—with the students, teachers, parents, the school system, or the test. As more states join the standardized, state-developed test movement, more has been learned about how to publicize the testing program and how likely the results may be discouraging during the first several administra-

tions. States and their schools have to maintain the support and confidence of the public for these "high stakes" tests or risk a public-relations disaster.

Students who have not been able to pass the exit-level TAAS and those who have left school prior to graduation have been able to take the General Education Development (GED) test, generally accepted by colleges and employers as the equivalent of a high school diploma. The GED tests knowledge and skills at the 12th grade level in reading, writing, and mathematics, just as the TAAS tests do at the 10th grade exit level. In addition, the GED has a social studies and science section, content areas not previously part of the Texas tests. Some experts believe that the GED, with national standards, would be a much more appropriate exit test than those developed for and used in only Texas or Virginia or any of the other states. Texas routinely has more individuals taking the GED than any other state.

The TABS, TEAMS, and current TAAS were based on norms or standards established in and for Texas only and, as criterion-referenced tests, only measure knowledge and skills determined important by virtue of inclusion in the original "essential elements" and today in the Texas Essential Knowledge and Skills (TEKS). Norm-referenced tests, like the Iowa Test of Basic Skills (ITBS), are available for purchase, and many Texas school districts do so.

Today, if a Texas student scores well on the ITBS and some other standardized test, a relationship or "correlation" between the two exists. The degree of relationship or correlation may vary among tests but the relationship is measurable. Texas has not, with the criterion-referenced tests, had to deal with the comfort or discomfort of knowing how its students compare with others throughout the nation. However, the TAAS reveals what students know and are able to do within the framework of the TEKS. Student performance is the subject of Chapter 20.

NAEP

Called the "nation's report card," the National Assessment of Education Progress (NAEP) is the only ongoing assessment in the core academic subjects of students throughout the United States. In well over 20 years of use, the NAEP has provided longitudinal data from both public and private school student achievement. However, the test results do not identify individual students, and comparisons are not possible. During the last three years of the administration of President Bill Clinton, a proposal was developed to support a truly national test of mathematics and reading that would allow the Houston school district, for example, to compare the scores of its students with those in Seattle or Milwaukee. The proposal was approved by the U.S. Senate but denied funding by the House of Representatives. What appears to be a continuation of the movement toward improving all of the nation's schools is supported and opposed by conservatives and liberals from both rural and urban areas. However, a national test paid for and administered by the federal government may be years away. With tests such as the Third International Math and Science (TIMSS) already in use, nations can compare the test scores. However, it is impossible to compare test results from Texas with those from Iowa.

MEASUREMENT AND EVALUATION[1]

One of the major purposes in developing educational goals is to provide a basis for assessment of student achievement. Although teachers use goals

in determining the criteria by which instructional objectives, content, procedures, and evaluation measures are selected, the ultimate measure of an educational system's effectiveness is in the achievement ends and not the procedural means. As professionals, teachers are given a certain amount of freedom in determining the means by which they intend to facilitate student learning. However, student achievement will either prove or disprove the system's effectiveness much more convincingly than the methodology employed.

At some point in the history of public education in America, it was probably sufficient for a teacher to informally report student progress to parents either orally or in some form of written report card. Parents could accept the teacher's judgment and apply pressure at home when necessary to improve the academic attitude or achievement of the child. The expectations of schooling have changed significantly from that earlier period. Expectations regarding who should attend school, how long they should attend, and the purposes for which they should attend have changed dramatically.

Thirty years ago, the term *accountability* rarely appeared in the literature of the education profession. Today, it is almost always included in the mass media's coverage of all aspects of education reform, funding, and even national security. The emergence of the term, the concept, and the controversy can be attributed to the process and outcomes of schooling as well as the use of public funds to support both. Twenty years ago Ralph Tyler observed that three developments had influenced the growing emphasis and concern with accountability. Those developments included the increased proportion of the average family's income that was spent on taxes, the recognition that a considerable fraction of youth were failing to meet the standards of literacy demanded for employment in civilian and military jobs, and the development of management procedures by industry and defense that increased the effectiveness and efficiency of certain production organizations. One distressing reality is that, regardless of whether the school, the family, or some other source of responsibility is to blame, some test scores indicate that students today do not score as well as in years past or that improvements in test scores are not as significant as expected based upon reform efforts, increased financial support or other changes from earlier practices. And the teachers of today along with their supporting systems are being held accountable. In a mini-melodrama, James Popham made the following point.

The educational battlelines for impending accountability showdown are drawn as clearly as in a classic western movie. On one side we have

1. Parts of the evaluation materials were excerpted with permission from C. W. Funkhouser, et al., *Classroom Applications of the Curriculum: A Systems Approach.* Dubuque, IA: Kendall/Hunt, 1981.

the underdog public school teachers, their portable classrooms drawn into a circle. On the other side is the marauding Accountability Gang who, although they are viewed by teachers as mortal enemies, could hardly be considered "no account" bandits. The Accountability Gang is beginning to fire some pretty potent pistols at the embattled teachers. For instead of Colt six-shooters and Winchester rifles, their guns bear different markings. One is labeled "Teacher Tenure." Another is called "Teacher Evaluation." A third simply says "Taxpayer's Revolt."

It is small wonder that bullets from these guns may pick off a teacher or two. And the terrifying part of this script, at least to classroom teachers, is that there may be no cavalry over the next hill coming to the rescue.

Today it is no longer sufficient for a teacher to apprise a parent of a student's progress in terms of the teacher's judgment alone. Although reports to parents are still extremely important, the judgmental observations of the teacher are no longer sufficient in placing the student's progress in its "proper perspective." Standardized tests attempt to provide this perspective.

Standardized Norm-Referenced Tests

An estimated 400 to 500 million multiple-choice tests are administered to about one-third of the national population each year. Sales of tests, not to mention the publications associated with passing them, have been estimated at well over $300 million annually. In all, 50 major test manufacturers produce over 1,100 different standardized tests. The results of tests can determine if and when a student is promoted to the next grade or is placed in the top or bottom reading group, if an employee is "management" material, if a trainee can be licensed to drive or fly, if a graduate will be admitted to the college of his choice. The "ifs" decided by test scores are endless. Tests have taken on an increasingly important and controversial role in contemporary society. It is essential that teachers understand the uses, advantages, and limitations of standardized tests, particularly as they relate to curriculum in the classroom.

The word *standard* in standardized does not refer to the test itself. Standard refers to the sample population used to establish norms of performance or scores which can be translated into *percentiles* for more meaningful interpretation. Percentile can be defined as the point at or below which a specified percent of the scores fall, e.g., the 70th percentile is the point below which 70 percent of the scores on a test fall. This can also be used in the observation that 19 percent of the scores fall between the 70th percentile and the mean. Using this same example, the student who scored in the 70th percentile excelled 70 percent above the others in the group, and the score indicates that his is in the top 30 percent of the group.

The standardization group used in the first administration of the test is carefully selected to represent a fair cross section of the intended population. Tests can be standardized for the entire nation, for a region, for a state, a local district, a community, or for any population from within those geographical boundaries for which a normative measurement is desired. After the standard has been determined, the resulting scores of others from this population can then be translated into established *norms*.

A norm is a range of values or scores made by the group on which the test was standardized. By definition, half the scores will fall below and half will be above the *median* or 50th percentile, sometimes referred to as the *average* or *norm*. Standardization requires an arrangement whereby all students take the same test under the same conditions. Veteran test takers will recall that test administrators read the directions for taking the test from a prepared script, e.g., "We are now ready to begin work on the first test. Find the section labeled Test 7, Vocabulary, on your answer sheet near the top of the front side. (Pause.) We will read the directions at the top of page 3 to remind you of what you are to do. Read them silently while I read them aloud." It should be noted that having all students take the test under the same conditions only assists in its standardization; these conditions alone cannot attest to the worth or value of the test itself.

A standardized test is made up of carefully selected test items, "standardized" with the intended population, scored in an objective, "standardized" manner, with resulting scores translated and interpreted in terms of percentiles.

Teachers could and sometimes do standardize their tests to the degree possible within their limited student populations. The popularity of the nationally standardized tests is due to the comparisons the interpreter can make from region to region, state to state, grade level to grade level, and so forth. When a 5th grade teacher observes that a student is the best in his class of 30, it is not as authoritative as the statement that the same student is in the 50th percentile on a nationally standardized test.

Valid tests measure what they were intended to measure, or they have proven useful in accomplishing the purposes for which they were used. Tests can be validated by correlating the test scores with scores from previously validated tests designed for a similar purpose.

Tests are considered *reliable* when they accurately and consistently yield similar results time after time after a number of administrations. In short, reliability means that if the same child took the same test two days in a row the resulting scores would be similar. Seldom, even in ideal conditions, will the results be identical. A reliable test agrees with itself more often than an unreliable test.

Every test has a standard error of measurement. Jack Frymeir (*Educational Forum,* May, 1979) provides some interesting observations regarding standard errors.

The standard error of measurement is a statistic which specifies probable limits within which the true score of measurement or test of an individual actually lies. If the standard error of an IQ test is 6, for example, and if Becky Jones got a score of 107 on that test, Becky's true score can actually be assumed to be somewhere between 101 and 113 (i.e., plus or minus 6). And such an assumption will be correct two-thirds of the time. One-third of the time it will be wrong! One time out of six the score will be higher than 113, and one time out of six the score will be lower than 101.

The concept of standard error would not be particularly significant, if teachers or administrators did not use test data to make decisions about individual students in their school. However, it is one thing to say that the average sixth grader in a particular school achieved at a 5.4 grade level in reading. It is a very different thing to note that Billy Johnson achieved at a 5.4 grade level in reading.

The first bit of information can be used by evaluators or curriculum planners to make inferences regarding curriculum materials or methodologies that have been employed with the total group. The second bit of information can be used by Billy's teacher to infer that Billy's true reading achievement score lies somewhere within a range of one standard error above and one standard error below the measured score of 5.4 grade level, and that inference will be wrong one time out of three. That is, if the standard error of measurement on the reading test that Billy took was .7 grade levels, then it can be inferred that Billy's true score is actually somewhere between 4.7 and 6.1, and such an inference will be incorrect one-third of the time.

Given the possibility of making an incorrect inference a third of the time regarding a particular student's achievement, we can expand our level of confidence by expanding the range to approximately two standard errors. In other words, Billy's true level of achievement can be safely assumed to be somewhere between 4.0 and 6.8 grade level (i.e., 5.4 plus or minus 2 $\times$ 7), and the inference will be correct 95 percent of the time. Or, to cite a different example, if Becky's measured IQ score was 107, then one could assume that her true IQ is actually somewhere between 95 and 119 (i.e., 107 plus or minus 2 $\times$ 6) and be right 95 percent of the time.

Now, you may not find these examples interesting or meaningful, but I have grave concerns about the decisions that teachers and administrators make on the basis of so called "standardized objective test scores." The word "standardized" applies only to the content of the items and the conditions under which the test is administered, but it implies much more. The word "objective" suggests impartiality and fairness and adequacy, and those qualities may or may not be inherent in the instrument involved. Because the words "standardized objective test" may be used, however, those words may lull a teacher or administrator into having greater confidence in a particular student's achievement score than is warranted. It is for this reason that standard error is important.

It is not within the scope of this overview to examine any of the many nationally standardized tests available. Suffice it to say that those most frequently administered by teachers are educational achievement tests, general intellectual ability tests, academic aptitude tests and interest inventories. Generally tests were designed for administration to groups of students. Others are available for testing individuals and these are usually administered by trained school counselors, diagnosticians, or psychologists.

The overwhelming majority of the standardized tests manufactured for school use provide normative data useful for a variety of purposes. Some of the tests are produced to measure progress in specific textbooks, workbooks, and other materials published by the test publisher. This arrangement makes planning relatively simple and convenient. Other tests attempt to diminish the influence of any particular curriculum materials or grade level achievement and provide only percentile scores for the students. Tests of this kind can result in frustration because there is no clear path remaining to preparation for higher achievement on the test, if higher achievement is desirable.

Standardized tests are usually *norm-referenced* tests and can best be used to compare the score of one student with others who have taken the same test. The results of nationally standardized tests provide valuable normative information such as grade-level reading achievement, recommendations for student placement in a series of mathematics workbooks, and percentile relationships of general intellectual ability which may be used to predict success in higher education.

Criterion-Referenced Assessments

Although nationally standardized tests provide supporting evidence of student achievement of the established educational goals of a state or school district, the goals and the test results are seldom directly related. For this reason, state departments of education and local school districts have designed their own tests to more precisely measure student achievement of the stated goals. Although state and school-district-developed-tests are standardized in many ways like those mentioned above, they are seldom referred to as standardized tests. The tests are sometimes referred to as criterion-referenced assessment instruments.

In 1979, the 66th Texas Legislature called for the creation of a statewide criterion-referenced system in which annual assessment would be made of Texas students at various grade levels. The legislative architects of the law that led to the establishment of the Texas Assessment of Basic Skills (TABS), later the Texas Educational Assessment of Minimum Skills (TEAMS) and currently the Texas Assessment of Academic Skills (TAAS), anticipated that a statewide assessment program would improve the quality of instruction in the state. The tests were to be designed consistent with the goals for public education in Texas as adopted by the State Board of Education. In a sense, the establishment of the tests, to measure goals established by the State Board of Education, added the previously missing component of a state "system" of public education, that being the student achievement evaluation component.

Curriculum evaluation as it applies most directly to the teacher in the classroom seeks to answer the question, "Did the students learn the knowledge, skills, and attitudes they were supposed to learn?" Evaluation can be one of the most difficult tasks that teachers must perform. The use of instructional objectives as criteria for making judgments about students' learning involves the collection of data so that the most accurate appraisal of student progress can be made. Many varieties of grades and grading systems have been conceived and utilized for the purposes of reporting student progress. The spectrum is as broad as one's school, school board, or community will allow.

The change from the traditional A, B, C, D, F to a numerical format, or one similar, to a checklist of skills or any combination in between, has been debated many times. Such a change generally requires much effort and community involvement because, after all, it is the community that must understand the basis for measuring student academic progress.

Prior to examining specific student activities the teacher can use in pupil appraisal, it is important for the teacher to decide on an evaluation philosophy or system of determining grades. To identify a teacher's philosophy, the following questions must be answered:

1. Is the primary purpose of evaluation to judge students' performance in relation to other students' performance?
2. Is the primary purpose of evaluation to judge students' performance according to an established criterion?
3. Is the primary purpose of evaluation to compare a particular student's performance with his or her prior performance?

If the answer to the first question is "yes," a teacher would have a norm-referenced philosophy (see Figure 3). At the most basic level, norm-referenced measures ascertain an individual's performance in relationship to the performance of other individuals on the same measuring device. All pupil appraisal activities in this system would do is to discriminate in student ability and compare students with each other.

If the answer to the second question is "yes," a teacher would have a criterion-referenced philosophy. Criterion-referenced measures ascertain an individual's status with respect to some criterion or performance standard. Pupil appraisal activities in this system would be designed to measure a student's performance against established criteria (see Figure 4).

If the answer to the third question is "yes," then a teacher would have a self-referenced philosophy (see Figure 5). Pupil appraisal activities would be designed to measure cognitive growth in individuals and would require a preassessment to determine a beginning level from which to ascertain progress.

The summary of evaluation systems in Table 6 lists the advantages and disadvantages of each system.

Teacher-made Tests

The very thought of taking a test brings many students, public school and even graduate students, to a point of anxiety and fear. Perhaps it is because the student is unclear as to whether the test was designed to find out how much he or she knows or doesn't know. Taking a test can be an exciting experience; unfortunately teachers frequently use tests for a single function—the determination of grades.

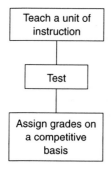

FIGURE 3   A Norm-Referenced Teaching Model
Source: Modified from Dale P. Scannell and D. B. Tracy, *Testing and Measurement in the Classroom* (Boston: Houghton Mifflin Company, 1975), p. 41.

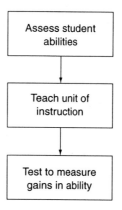

FIGURE 5   A Self-Referenced Teaching Model

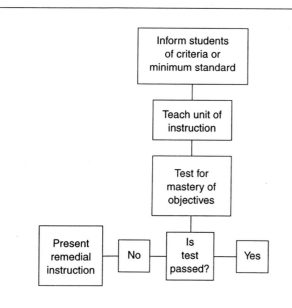

FIGURE 4   A Criterion-Referenced Teaching Model
Source: Modified from Scannell and Tracy.

Naturally that is the major use of tests in an evaluation system, but it is important to remember that grade determination is only one function of tests—not necessarily the sole or prime purpose.

Teachers should determine the evidence that they want to gather relative to the learning that has taken place and then design the diagnostic instrument accordingly. Tests should be utilized to not only determine the cognitive gain of the pupil but to determine teaching effectiveness as well as areas of weakness within the program. Poor test grades might indicate poor habits of students, but they might also suggest poor pedagogy or program

weakness. At least 20 kinds of tests can be used by the teacher for evaluating pupil progress. A summary of these kinds of tests include:[2]

1. Performance tests—a student is given a specific skill to perform, i.e., making ten consecutive free throws from the free throw line.
2. Identification tests—using stated criteria or a key, students identify objects, i.e., identifying families of plants using a key.
3. Recognition tests—without using a key, students are able to recognize objects, i.e., students can identify the food as to appropriate food group.
4. Name association tests—students can supply the name when shown or given a description of the object, i.e., students can give the title of a piece of music when they hear it played.
5. Modified recognition tests—when shown an object or given a situation students can explain the significance, i.e., when shown a protractor, students can explain its function in mathematics.
6. Picture tests—when shown a picture, students can identify or explain the significance, i.e., students would be able to identify a picture of the mushroom cloud formed from an atomic bomb explosion.
7. Diagram and model test—when given a diagram or model students can identify the parts, i.e., students would label the parts of a model of the ear.

---

2. Reference: A. T. Collette, *Teaching in the Secondary School* (Boston: Allyn & Bacon, 1973).

8. Drawing test—students make a drawing and identify the parts, i.e., students draw in and label the major rivers on a map of the United States.
9. Completion drawing test—students are given a portion of a drawing or diagram and they must complete it, i.e., students complete a partial drawing of the water cycle.
10. Essay question test—students explain, compare, or describe a situation or condition, i.e., students explain the difference between poetry and prose.
11. Short explanation test—students are given a limited or specific response length to a question, i.e., answer in one sentence.
12. Completion statement test—students fill in the blanks with the word or words that complete the statement.
13. Correction tests—students are given statements that they must correct so that they make sense, i.e., Tom went to the bus depot to catch a plane.
14. Matching tests—students are given two columns of choices to match.
15. Grouping tests—students must eliminate members from groups which do not belong, i.e., students are given the words *red, blue, yellow, car, green* and must mark out "car," which does not belong.
16. Arrangement exercise test—students are given a set of terms or situations to arrange in order, i.e., students put panels of comic strips in the correct sequence.
17. True/False tests—students determine if statements are true or false.
18. Modified True/False tests—students correct those statements they believe to be false.
19. Sometimes/Always/Never tests—another kind of true/false test where students are allowed qualifying responses.

Table 7 presents a comparison between objective and essay tests, and its author, Arnold Lein provides the following suggestions for constructing essay examinations.

1. Draft the essay question carefully, defining important directional or key words to eliminate semantic difficulties. For example, one might say: "By 'compare,' I mean to give a full answer in which you consider like and unlike factors in the situation." Each key word should be defined, for each calls for a different approach in the writing of the item.
2. Phrase the questions to give hints concerning the structure of the answer expected, unless this is inconsistent with the objectives to be

measured. The question, "Discuss the Articles of Confederation," becomes more specific for both the pupil and the teacher grading it if phrased: "Discuss the Articles of Confederation with respect to their origin, their operation in actual practice, and their relationship to the present Constitution."
3. Write questions which can be readily answered within the time allowed for the examination. Allow enough time for pupils to outline, write, and read through their answers. Suggest a time allowance for each question if more than one essay question is included in the examination.
4. Construct the questions so that they are of such a range of difficulty as will allow ALL pupils to demonstrate their level of competence.
5. Require all students to write on the same questions; avoid choices among several questions.
6. To get better sampling, increase the number of questions and reduce the length of discussion expected in each.

For scoring essay tests, Lein suggests the following steps.

1. Read over the material in the text, lesson plans, course outline, and notes that are related to the question asked.
2. Make a checklist (key) of the main points or ideas for which credit will be given in each question. Decide upon the scoring for each of the questions, as well as for the parts of each.
3. In scoring a given question, first read through the entire response to try to understand the whole response and intent of the pupil before going back to score for the important points.
4. Grade one question throughout all papers before going on to the next question.
5. The pupil's total score on the test is the sum of the credit given for each of the questions. Make a special, separate provision for consideration of sentence structure and spelling if these are to be considered in grading in relation to the objective being measured.

This list of possible kinds of tests should aid the teacher in making good use of tests to assess pupil performance on objectives, and hopefully the use of a variety of test situations can reduce some of the anxiety.

Removing the threat and anxiety associated with tests will not come overnight. It will be a slow process of moving a student conditioned to one type of behavior to another, but one worthy of attempt.

The teacher should examine the atmosphere prior to testing and discuss the parental pressures

TABLE 3   Comparison of Three Systems of Determining Grades

I. Comparison to Objective Standard

[Criterion-Referenced]

Advantages	Disadvantages
There is a pre-set standard, and everyone can know what this is.	All students could fail—but this method would *not* necessarily alert the teacher that poor teaching could have been a factor.
Makes it easier for students to prepare for tests, assignments, etc.	All students could make A's—but this method would *not* necessarily alert the teacher that the objective standard might be set unrealistically low.
Does not pit one student against another; therefore, invites cooperation instead of competition between students.	In some cases, there could be difficulty in deciding what the standard will be.
Most students do not harbor ill feelings against teacher if they score a low mark.	Can be very discouraging to slower students or students whose aptitude in this particular area is low.
Most students regard this method as the fairest means.	
Is the fairest method for the high-achieving student.	
Mitigates against a teacher's subjective assigning of grades.	
In some situations/assignments/courses students can have a part in determining what the standard will be.	
Allows for comparison of students within one class; between different classes, and with students in all courses using the same uniform standard.	

II. Comparison to Peers

[Norm-Referenced]

Advantages	Disadvantages
Allows the best student within the class to receive the highest grade.	Causes confusion or is meaningless when comparing students not in the same classes.
Is the best motivator for the externally motivated student who has been conditioned to respond primarily to direct competition.	Pits students against one another and therefore sometimes encourages hostility, throat-cutting, cheating, tattling, and other non-productive behaviors. Usually poor class morale results.
Serves as a protection for the student against poor teaching in that if the best student is only able to master enough material to make a C (under objective standard), he would still be an A in this method and not be penalized.	May cause some students to place more importance on grades than on learning.
Sometimes allows an otherwise poor achiever (under objective standard system) to be the "best student in class" for a change. Would therefore increase this student's motivation and self-esteem.	Difficult to decide the *range* of grades to be assigned.
A good system to use when teaching a particularly difficult task, or when all of your students are low achievers (as in ability grouped classes), or when your own ability to teach a task is in question.	*Mary Lynn Crow "Three Systems of Determining Grades" (Arlington, Texas). Reprinted by permission.

Continued

TABLE 3   Comparison of Three Systems of Determining Grades   *Continued*

III. Comparison to Self

[Self-Referenced]

Advantages	Disadvantages
May be the best method for the self-motivated, mature student who has no more than moderate entering proficiency in the area.	Is totally meaningless if one wants to compare one student with another.
Does not penalize the slow learner, the different learner, or the student with little aptitude in the area.	Is not helpful if the task or course is in a sequence, and the next task in line needs a required level of proficiency to be eligible to go on to the next step.
Encourages cooperation among students; good morale ensues.	Does not give the student a realistic picture of himself as he relates to others or to any objective standard; therefore may actually be harmful when student needs to make plans for the future.
Encourages the development of self-esteem and of independent goal setting; self-motivation.	
Helps make the reward and joy of learning intrinsic rather than extrinsic.	Could be a complete failure (as a motivational device) with certain students who have grown dependent upon external competition and challenge.
Serves to encourage more and more low self-esteem or low ability students to attempt a particular task or course.	Penalizes the student who already is very proficient in the area, as he cannot possibly progress as much as the one who scores low on a pretest.
Allows a student to work at his/her own pace.	
Greatly reduces external threat from teacher, or from other students.	

Source: Mary Lynn Crow "Three Systems of Determining Grades" (Arlington, Texas). Reprinted by permission.

TABLE 4   Comparison of the Objective and Essay Tests

Trait	Objective Test	Essay Test
1. Type of Structure	The pupil operates within an almost completely structured task	The pupil organizes his/her own response with a minimum of constraint
2. Type of Response	The pupil selects one of a limited number of alternatives or recalls a short answer	The pupil uses his/her own words and expression in his/her response
3. Sampling of Knowledge	The pupil responds to a relatively large number of items (extensive sampling)	The pupil responds to a relatively small number of questions (intensive sampling)
4. Credit in Scoring	The pupil receives a score for each answer according to a pre-determined key (usually right or wrong with no partial credits)	The pupil receives a score for each question depending upon the degree of completeness and accuracy
5. Learning Outcomes Measured	Very good for measuring knowledge of facts. Some types can measure higher levels of thinking. Usually inappropriate for measuring ability to select and organize ideas, writing abilities, and some types of problem-solving skills	Inappropriate for measuring knowledge of facts. Can measure higher levels of thought. Appropriate for measurement of ability to select and organize ideas, writing abilities, and problem-solving skills
6. Effect on Learning	Encourages students to develop a specific comprehensive knowledge of specific facts and to discriminate among them. Can encourage development of higher level thinking skills if properly constructed	Encourages students to learn ability to organize, integrate, and express ideas effectively. Usually asks students to concentrate on larger units of materials

Source: Arnold Lein, *Measurement and Evaluation of Learning,* Dubuque, IA: Wm. C. Brown, 1980.

(often invisible but nevertheless quite obviously real) and seek suggestions as to how to produce a more relaxed atmosphere during testing periods. After all, the test should measure the optimum knowledge and understanding of the student, so it logically should be conducted in an atmosphere conducive to this kind of output.

Caveats of Testing

Because testing is often a major evaluation tool to assess pupil performance and thereby the accomplishment of curriculum objectives, it is important to examine procedures that can be used in constructing the best test possible. According to Popham, quoted earlier, "Tests should enable a teacher to gather observations about the students' ability with respect to the instructional objective(s)." Tests are administered under "manipulated conditions—that is the teacher deliberately sets up the stimulus situation." Finally, he points out that a test administered under manipulated conditions should provide a *representative* sample of a student's behavior with respect to a particular skill or ability. Test items, generally, do not *exhaustively* measure the students' achievement. Keeping in mind these factors about testing, it is important to examine some of the other limitations of testing as well. Teachers should therefore remember that:

- Any evaluation falls short of surveying the students' understanding completely. Consequently it should be given and taken with this point in mind.
- Any evaluation reflects bias for areas included and those omitted. The emphasis on certain bias, i.e., areas emphasized in class discussion or work, should be the areas emphasized on tests, not ambiguous, vague items relegated to unimportance by lack of attention devoted to them.
- Variables should be employed in the evaluation format in order to attempt to provide students opportunities to respond according to their strong areas as well as their weak ones.

Pre and Post Testing

The process of using pre/post tests is a logical one, but probably one which is not utilized as much as it should be. Post tests alone only tell you what the student knows or doesn't know. They do not tell you if the intervention (the teaching) had any effect. The student might have known the answers to the test two weeks earlier, before the teaching took place.

A pre/post test format is designed to let the teacher know where the students are prior to the teaching and what they "learned" during the teaching. It can provide two very important facts for improving teaching:

1. It can tell a teacher where he or she needs to start with certain students.
2. It can tell a teacher where weak areas are in the teaching plans—an aid for preventing this next time.

Pre and post tests can be the same instruments, but it would probably be better if they were somewhat different in physical layout even if similar items appeared on both.

Item Writing

All tests (evaluations) require some form of asking questions, whether oral or written, and one of the keys is in the creation of the question. Some helpful hints to item writing can be found in any discussion of this important area, but for teacher-made questions the following list should be both helpful and self-explanatory:

- Decide on what the purpose of the evaluation you are about to create is for. Is it to test the cognitive gain or your teaching? Sometimes a test does both, we just don't like to admit it. You could use it purely for diagnosis skills in order to determine areas of weakness or you could use it for punishment. Be careful about wording and phraseology. You should really consider why before teaching one way and testing for another.
- Remember that the longer the question, the more variables have to be considered. Short concise statements offer the least misunderstandings.
- In decisions relative to particular items to be utilized other than objective, include specifically the points you would like the student to attend to in answering rather than making the decision after the fact. Don't ever make an exam and later give different values to the items. Let the student know so that he can address those he can accordingly.
- Consider the time necessary to evaluate a particular aspect of instruction and test accordingly. Don't make a test to last an hour if 15 minutes would cover the material.
- Avoid pre-test "anxiety-atmospheres." Try to provide as relaxed an atmosphere as possible. Some people are not bothered by pressure yet some "go-to-pieces." Try to allow for the individual differences in personalities relative to pressure situations. Excessive noise, interruptions should be avoided.
- Cheating. Most cheating can be overcome through variety in the item writing. Just make out different but similar tests. Re-arrange the

FIGURE 6   Test Development Matrix

| Test Items | Objectives of this testing period | | | | | | | |
	A	B	C	D	E	F	G	Totals
1.	1							1
2.	1		1	1				3
3.			1				1	2
4.		1			1			2
5.	1					1		2
6.								0
7.			1					1
8.	1				1			2
9.	1				1			2
10.					1			1

items in order to make direct copying difficult. Most situations when cheating occurs can be avoided by simple beforehand preparations.

If in the development of an evaluation instrument a teacher would employ a matrix for test development, the task would not only be easier but more inclusive as well. Teachers will find it helpful to utilize a matrix similar to the one in Figure 6.

In examining this example, one can see that the most questions were asked about objectives A and E, and B, F and G had the least. Test item 2 dealt with three different objectives: A, C, and D. This obvious unequal emphasis may be exactly the emphasis placed on certain objectives during the teaching period, but it's good to know this rather than just "feel" it is that way. Likewise, after testing, the teacher can plot the results on a frequency tally such as below:

1.	111	(3)
2.	11	(2)
3.	1	(1)
4.	11111	(5)
5.	11	(2)
6.	1	(1)
7.	0	(0)
8.	11111111	(8)
9.	11	(2)
10.	1	(1)
	25	25

From this the teacher can determine the areas most missed on the exam, giving some insight into the learning that took place during the teaching. As can be seen from above, question #8 was the most frequently missed. Also, by examining the Test Development Matrix, you can see that question #8 referenced objectives A and E. Likewise, five students responded incorrectly to question #4. It referred to objectives B and E. From this, the teacher might wish to re-teach objectives A, B and E.

This type of examination of testing and test-developing procedures will not only provide fairer exams for students but a wealth of diagnostic information for the teacher to use in preparing lesson plans, developing objectives and implementing the curriculum.

Measures of Central Tendency

Teachers often examine and analyze test results by arranging scores in a descending order of magnitude or an array. Figure 7 shows an array for a history test.

With a high score of 98 and a low of 57, the *range* of scores is 41. The range is the difference between the highest and lowest scores. The average score was 79. The average, also referred to as the *mean* or *arithmetic mean*, is computed by dividing the sum of all the scores by the number of scores. The average gives the teacher one measure of central tendency.

A second measure of central tendency is the *median* which, in an array such as Figure 8, is the midpoint above and below which one-half the scores fall. The median does not need to be a score per se, it is a position. Counting one-half of 37 scores, or 18.5, up or down results in a median of 80 in this example. In many cases the median portrays more accurately the position of central tendency than does any other measure.

The *mode* is the score most frequently earned by students taking the test. Like the median, it is only a measure of position and cannot be used in any mathematical calculations. The score most frequently earned in this example is 80, i.e., more students earned scores of 80 than any other score. Modal scores as a measure of central tendency can suggest many things, e.g., if most automobile buyers purchase $20,000 vehicles, a dealer would be wise to stock more of these even though the mean automobile retail price may be either $10,000 or $60,000. In some distributions, there may be more than one mode or a *bimodal* distribution, i.e., several points at which certain scores are prominent.

Seldom if ever will a teacher's students earn scores in which the mean, median, and mode will be the same. Only in a *normal distribution* might a curvilinear pattern or *curve* occur. Based upon probability, the bell-shape curve, so commonly referred to in norm-referenced observations, would seldom materialize with the test scores of students of a teacher in any assignment. Teachers may create curves by limiting the number of failing scores, "A" equivalent scores and the gradations in between to a certain percentage of the total, but these are the creations of the teacher rather than true measures of normality in the global sense. In all teacher-made evaluations, the professional judgment used rather than statistical analyses is the best determinant of student achievement. The normal distribution curve is shown in Figure 8. *Standard deviation* is the average amount that a set of scores varies from the mean.

Alternative and Authentic Assessments

The summary of the British experience with standardized testing provided by writers George F. Madaus and Thomas Kellaghan can be a lesson for or a reflection of the American experience.

> It is now widely accepted that when multiple-choice, norm-referenced, and criterion-referenced standardized tests were used as administrative devices to implement education policies during the last two decades, they adversely affected the system. Because of the high stakes associated with their use, these tests drove instruction and narrowed the curriculum. Further, the tests measured low-level knowledge and skills. Teaching to such tests eventually corrupted their validity as indicators of achievement, and test results gave the nation an incorrect picture of achievement levels and progress . . .
> (*Phi Delta Kappan*, February 1993).

According to these authors, the negative reactions to traditional testing resulted in the search for "alternative" and "authentic" devices which enable the examiner to directly assess more meaningful and complex educational performances. The three "p's" they propose are "performance, portfolios, and products" assessments. Using these, assessment is integrated "into everyday classroom practice, thus avoiding the artificial separation of assessment from teaching and learning." The approach is "direct assessment" of applied learning rather than the artificially separated "indirect assessment."

Performance assessments have long histories in the evaluation of physical education, art, music, drama and, as emphasized below, creative writing. Process and product assessments frequently utilize various forms of self-assessment. Portfolios are summarized below.

The U.S. Army used an early version of the multiple-choice aptitude examination during World War I to select candidates for military service. Unlike the oral and written examinations which were widely utilized prior to that time, the multiple-choice test only required the examinee to select from the choices available rather than create and explain a response based on prior learning and experience. From the 1970s to the present time, standardized tests, which made possible objective comparisons of one student to another, one school to another, or one district or state to others, have become the evidence of educational accountability demanded by state legislatures and the public in general. Many of these tests focused on the basic skills of reading, writing, and mathematics and were used to ensure that all students reached a minimum level of competency in each of these areas. Conveniently, these measurements drive instruction, that is, both teachers and students knew what was to be tested, and they spent the appropriate amount of time learning and practicing these skills. Unfortunately, the mandated minimum levels of competency sometimes became the maximum expectation. Teachers, systems, and states could use their test results as evidence of their effectiveness. Students who could not meet the established minimums were retained or denied diplomas, and this "high stakes" accountability system was serving its purpose even if the results provided more information on what a student couldn't do than what he or she could. The curriculum became preparation for the test even though, beyond rates of passing scores, few cared much about the results. Everyday learning experiences, other than those focused on preparation for the tests, had little to do with what was tested.

Researchers from Boston College, executing a three-year, one million dollar study sponsored by

FIGURE 7   Scores on Unit History Test*

Score	Tallies	Frequency
98	/	1
97	/	1
96		
95	/	1
94		
93	/	1
92		
91		
90	/	1
89		
88	/	1
87	//	2
86		
85	///	3
84	1	
83		
82	///	3
81		
80 Median	///// Mode	5
79 Mean		
78	///	3
77	/	1
76	//	2
75	/	1
74		
73	/	1
72	/	1
71		
70	///	3
69		
68		
67	//	2
66		
65		
64	/	1
63		
62		
61		
60	/	1
59	/	1
58		
57	/	1
Total		N = 37

*Data grouped in intervals of one.
N = total number of scores

the National Science Foundation, concluded that standardized and textbook tests emphasized only low-level thinking and knowledge and that the tests exert a profound, mostly negative effect on classroom instruction. According to the study, most of the tests did not measure the conceptual knowledge and problem-solving abilities intended. Teachers placed too much emphasis on what was to be on the tests rather than on how to apply scientific skills of analysis.

One exception to the multiple-choice tests used nationwide was the writing sample required in later versions of the basic skills tests. With the written composition, similar to the essay of pre-multiple-choice days, examinees were asked to generate correct answers rather than recognize and choose the one more correct than the others. When the composition or writing sample was added to the test, writing became the focus of preparation for the teachers and students.

As W. James Popham has observed, "If instruction is being driven by high-stakes testing—and it clearly is—then we simply need to install more praiseworthy assessment targets so that instruction can be driven toward a defensible destination." In short, if the writing sample drives teachers to require more and different kinds of writing of students and their writing is part of the accountability system and is measured accordingly, the assessment becomes "authentic." Further, "if authentic assessment becomes widespread, it will spawn more appropriate instructional emphasis in our schools."

> By making the complete array of authentic assessment tasks eligible for testing, state testing personnel can encourage educators to aim at a rich and defensible set of learner outcomes (Popham, *Phi Delta Kappan*, February 1993).

Student portfolios are perhaps the most noticeable departure from traditional assessments. In the February 1991 issue of *Education Leadership*, writers Paulson, Paulson, and Meyer define portfolios as follows.

> A portfolio is a purposeful collection of student work that exhibits the student's efforts, progress and achievements in one or more areas. The collection must include student participation in selecting contents, the criteria for selection, the criteria for judging merit, and evidence of student self-reflection.

Portfolios allow students to assume ownership in ways that few other instructional approaches allow. Portfolio assessment requires students to collect and reflect on examples of their work, providing both an instructional component to the curriculum and offering the opportunity for authentic assessments. If carefully assembled, portfolios become an intersection of instruction and assessment: they are not just instruction or just assessment but, rather,

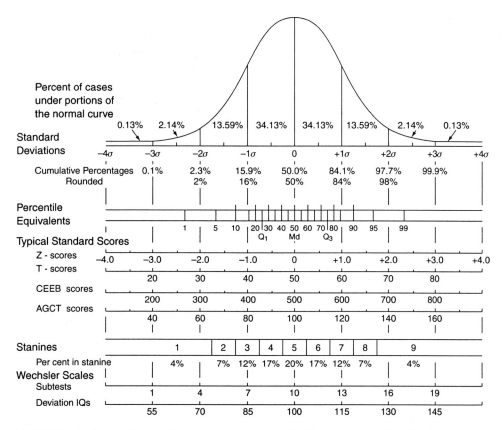

Percent of cases
under portions of
the normal curve

| | 0.13% | 2.14% | 13.59% | 34.13% | 34.13% | 13.59% | 2.14% | 0.13% |

Standard Deviations

| -4σ | -3σ | -2σ | -1σ | 0 | $+1\sigma$ | $+2\sigma$ | $+3\sigma$ | $+4\sigma$ |

Cumulative Percentages

| 0.1% | 2.3% | 15.9% | 50.0% | 84.1% | 97.7% | 99.9% |

Rounded

| 2% | 16% | 50% | 84% | 98% |

Percentile Equivalents

| 1 | 5 | 10 | 20 30 40 50 60 70 80 | 90 | 95 | 99 |
| | | | Q_1 Md Q_3 | | | |

Typical Standard Scores

Z - scores

| -4.0 | -3.0 | -2.0 | -1.0 | 0 | $+1.0$ | $+2.0$ | $+3.0$ | $+4.0$ |

T - scores

| 20 | 30 | 40 | 50 | 60 | 70 | 80 |

CEEB scores

| 200 | 300 | 400 | 500 | 600 | 700 | 800 |

AGCT scores

| 40 | 60 | 80 | 100 | 120 | 140 | 160 |

Stanines

| 1 | 2 | 3 | 4 | 5 | 6 | 7 | 8 | 9 |

Per cent in stanine

| 4% | 7% | 12% | 17% | 20% | 17% | 12% | 7% | 4% |

Wechsler Scales

Subtests

| 1 | 4 | 7 | 10 | 13 | 16 | 19 |

Deviation IQs

| 55 | 70 | 85 | 100 | 115 | 130 | 145 |

NOTE: This chart cannot be used to equate scores on one test to scores on another test. For example, both 600 on the CEEB and 120 on the AGCT are one standard deviation above their respective means, but they do not represent "equal" standings because the scores were obtained from different groups.

FIGURE 8   Normal Distribution Curve
Source: Test Service Bulletin, No. 48 (January 1955), the Psychological Corporation.

both. Together, instruction and assessment give more than either give separately.

A preface to the portfolio, as suggested by the writers, might include the example below.

To Whom It May Concern

In the pages that follow in this portfolio, you will find the work that I feel represents my strengths in my written work from my junior year at Hillsboro High School. In order that you may see the overall picture, I have included expository, informative, and creative pieces in this portfolio. All six samples were constructed in an atmosphere that provided ample time for revision and peer reviewing. Each sample represents skills that I have found to enhance the quality of my writing (*Education Leadership*, February 1991).

The portfolio does not replace the student's cumulative record or other records such as transcripts which have traditionally served other yet similar purposes. The major difference is that a portfolio provides a complex and comprehensive summary of a particular student's performance in a particular performance context. It provides the reviewer with a record of what a student has done rather than what has been done to the student; that is, the student is a participant rather than the object of assessment.

Alternative and authentic assessment will not provide the kinds of comparative data that norm-referenced tests have provided. These approaches will not show that one student's achievement places him or her in a given percentile or that he or she has mastered a given number of objectives or competencies such as is available with criterion-referenced tests, and therein lies the weakness. Accountability will be difficult to prove with such assessment approaches, and whether the public demand for objective, quantitative results is satisfied has yet to be determined.

SPECIAL EDUCATION

Chapter 21 presents a description of special education in Texas. Texas implemented its first educational program for children with specific disabilities during the 1940s, well before the much publicized federal policy contained in Public Law 94-142, the Education for All Handicapped Children Act of 1975, subsequently revised and now known as the Individuals with Disabilities Education Act (IDEA). However, the impact of Public Law 94-142 has been far more dramatic because the law obligated each of the states, for the first time in the history of public education in the United States, to provide free and appropriate individualized education for all children and youth with disabilities. This includes the obligation to provide equal educational opportunities to children and youth regardless of the severity of the disability, to educate students with disabilities with their nondisabled peers to the maximum extent possible, and to protect the procedural rights of disabled persons and their parents or guardians in all matters of school assessment and placement.

Public Law 94-142/IDEA has had the same dramatic impact on public education as the landmark Supreme Court decision in the case of *Brown v. Board of Education*, which focused on the constitutionality of racially segregated schools. In fact, the principle of the constitutional right to education of children and youth is the same in both Brown and IDEA.

IDEA defines "children with disabilities" as children with mental retardation, hearing impairments including deafness, speech or language impairments, visual impairments including blindness, serious emotional disturbance, orthopedic impairments, autism, traumatic brain injury, multidisabilities, and other health impairments or specific learning disabilities. Relatively recent interpretations and applications of Section 504 of the Rehabilitation Act of 1973 have expanded the IDEA disabilities that qualify to include drug or alcohol addiction, heart disease, dyslexia, communicable diseases such as AIDS, asymptomatic carriers of the AIDS virus (HIV), tuberculosis, short-term injuries and illnesses, behavior disorders, chronic asthma and severe allergies, spina bifida, hemophilia, required use of crutches and chronic and/or life-threatening diseases such as diabetes or cancer. Special education at the turn of the century became far more complicated as a result of the addition of Section 504 and, in 1992, the Americans with Disabilities Act (ADA). A comparison of the various aspects of IDEA and Section 504 is provided in Table 8.

With the renewed interest in educational equity in the 1990s, Texas joined other states in encouraging more "inclusion" of special education students with their regular education peers. Although placement of special education students in the least restrictive alternative had been the law of the land since 1975, "mainstreaming" of students with certain kinds of

disabilities had been limited. The national movement of the 1990s has been to educate all students with disabilities in regular classrooms, a practice called "full inclusion." The National Association of State Directors of Special Education, the National Association of State Boards of Education, and various elected officials support this move. Opposition to this dramatic change includes some teachers and parents of both regular and special education students. In Texas, full inclusion is encouraged but not mandated.

According to a study published by *U. S. News & World Report*, nationally in 1994 the cost of special education had reached $30 billion, up from $1 billion in 1977.

In 1979, the Irving Independent School District was threatened with an annual loss of $800,000 in federal funds for allegedly violating the civil rights of a disabled elementary school child. The district decided that providing the child with catheterizations so she could attend classes was beyond the district's obligation to provide free and appropriate individualized education to all disabled children. Federal law requires school districts to provide "related services" but not "medical services" to assist disabled children and youth who qualify for special education.

To benefit from special education, the Irving child, who suffers from spina bifida, requires periodic catheterization—a bladder-draining procedure that lay persons can perform with a physician's authorization. In 1979 the State Board of Education decided that clean intermittent catheterization (CIC) was a medical service, and that the school district did not have to provide it. U.S. District Judge Patrick Higginbotham agreed and refused to require the district to provide the service. But the U.S. Circuit Court of Appeals in New Orleans vacated that decision. By court order, CIC is now part of the Irving child's individualized education plan. After more than five years of controversy, administrative hearings, and litigation, the U.S. Supreme Court ruled unanimously that the Irving school district is required by federal law to provide catheterization. On July 5, 1984, Chief Justice Warren Burger, writing for the court, said that CIC was a related service that must be provided "by schools that receive federal aid." By 1993–94, catheterization in public schools had become a common practice. In June 1994, the Irving MacArther high school student walked across the stage to receive her high school diploma nearly 10 years after the Supreme Court made its landmark decision. Without the support of the school system after graduation, the future may present even more difficult challenges.

TABLE 5   A Comparison Chart: IDEA and Section 504

	IDEA	Section 504
Purpose	To ensure that all children with disabilities have available to them a free, appropriate public education.	To prohibit discrimination on the basis of disability in any program receiving federal funds.
Who Is Protected	Students who are eligible under the 13 categories of qualifying conditions.	Much broader. A student is eligible if s/he meets the definition of "qualified handicapped person"; i.e., has or has had a physical or mental impairment that substantially limits a major life activity, has a record of or is regarded as disabled by others. Parents are also protected.
Duty to Provide a Free Appropriate Education	*Both require the provision of a free appropriate education, including individually designed instruction, to students who qualify.*	
	Requires the district to provide an individualized education program. "Appropriate education" means a program designed to provide "educational benefit."	"Appropriate" means an education comparable to the education provided to students without disabilities.
Special Education vs. Regular Education	A student is eligible to receive special education services only if a multidisciplinary team determines that the student has one of the handicapping conditions and needs special education.	A student is eligible if s/he meets the definition of "qualified handicapped person"; i.e., has or has had a physical or mental impairment that substantially limits a major life activity, or is regarded as disabled by others. The student is not required to need special education in order to be protected.
Funding	Yes	No
Accessibility	Not specifically mentioned although if modifications must be made to provide a free appropriate education to a student, IDEA requires it.	Detailed regulations regarding building and program accessibility.
General Notice	*Both require child find activities.*	
	Requires notification of parental rights.	Districts must include notice of nondiscrimination in its employee, parent, and student handbooks and, if the district has more than 15 employees, must specify the district's 504 coordinator(s).
Notice and Consent	*Both require specific notice to the parent or guardian about identification, evaluation and placement.*	
	Requires written notice. Notice requirements are more comprehensive and specify what the notice must provide. Written notice is required before any change in placement.	Requires notice. (A district would be wise to give notice in writing.)
		Requires notice before a "significant change in placement."
	Requires consent for initial evaluation and placement.	Consent not required, but if a handicapping condition under IDEA is suspected, those regulations must be followed.

Continued

TABLE 5   A Comparison Chart: IDEA and Section 504   *Continued*

	IDEA	Section 504
Evaluations	*The regulations are similar.*	
	Requires consent before an initial evaluation is conducted.	Requires notice, not consent.
		Requires "periodic" reevaluations.
	Reevaluations must be conducted at least every 3 years.	Requires a reevaluation before a significant change in placement.
	No provisions	
	Provides for independent evaluations.	No provisions.
Determination of Eligibility, Program, and Placement	Done by admission, review, and dismissal committee. Parent is a member of the committee.	Done by a group of persons knowledgeable about the child, the evaluation data, and placement options. While parental participation is not mentioned in the regulations, parental notice is required.
Grievance Procedures	IDEA does not require a grievance procedure or a compliance officer.	Districts with more than 15 employees must designate an employee to be responsible for assuring district compliance with Section 504 and provide a grievance procedure (an informal hearing before a district staff member) for parents, students, and employees.
Due Process	*Both require districts to provide impartial hearings for parents or guardians who disagree with the identification, evaluation, or placement of a student with disabilities.*	
	Hearings conducted by a state hearing officer (who is an attorney). Decisions may be appealed to court.	Hearings conducted at the local level by an impartial person not connected with the school district. Person need not be an attorney. Decisions may be appealed to court.
Enforcement	Compliance is monitored by the Texas Education Agency. TEA also receives and resolves complaints regarding IDEA. Office for Civil Rights does not enforce.	Enforced by the Office for Civil Rights (Regional Office—Dallas, TX) by complaint investigation and monitoring activities.
Employment	No provisions	Employment of persons with disabilities is regulated.

The Americans with Disabilities Act of 1992 (ADA) provides even more comprehensive civil rights protection for individuals with disabilities. Title III of this act covers places of public accommodation, and therefore places of education (e.g., nursery schools, elementary, secondary, undergraduate, or postgraduate private schools). Title III is intended to provide protection to individuals with disabilities that is at least as great as that provided under Title V of the Rehabilitation Act. Title V includes provisions such as Section 504, which covers all the operations of federal executive agencies and programs receiving federal financial assistance. Title III may not be interpreted to provide a lesser degree of protection to individuals with disabilities than is provided under Section 504.

Title III does not disturb other federal laws or any state law that provides protection for individuals with disabilities at a level greater or equal to that

provided by the ADA. It does, however, prevail over any conflicting state laws.

In 1993, National Union Fire Insurance Company, a major insurer of schools, considered modifying the standard policy for special education litigation. The company provides insurance for 6,276 school districts, or 41 percent of the total. Special education litigation has become a major financial burden for schools.

Although youth with disabilities generally do not fare as well as their nondisabled peers after leaving public school, more Texas special education students are engaged productively than special education students from other states.

The report presents the preliminary findings of a study on the effectiveness of special education programs in Texas in developing the life skills needed after these students leave the public school system. The study, which included 230 former special education students, was mandated by Senate Bill 417 of the 71st Texas Legislature, and was presented to the 72nd Legislature.

The report found that the employment levels of special education students nationally tend to be lower than those of nondisabled students and that special education students do not pursue postsecondary schooling as often as the nondisabled. Nationwide, approximately one third of special education graduates were not working or pursuing additional education or training, the report said.

The rates for nonparticipation in employment, training, education or similar activities range from 17 percent to 67 percent.

In Texas, 66 percent of the state's former special education students are employed, compared to a national rate of 40 percent. Approximately 25 percent participate in some type of postsecondary education, compared with 25 percent nationally, while 21 percent are not participating in productive activity, as compared with 32 percent nationally.

Overall, 59 percent are living at home with parents, compared with 66 percent nationally, and 30 percent live independently, compared with 18 percent nationally (Texas Education Today, April 1991).

As stated in Chapter 21, the individualized education program (IEP) is the specification of learning objectives for an individual student who qualifies for special education services. The IEP requires teachers to select the most appropriate curriculum materials and instructional procedures that will most effectively enable the student to achieve specific objectives within a designated period of time.

Regardless of its successes, IDEA continues to create controversies. *U.S. News & World Report* published a special investigative report late in 1993. Entitled "Separate and Unequal,"[3] it documented a network of programs that regularly use subjective testing criteria and rely on funding formulas and identification procedures that funnel ever greater numbers of children into special programs each year. In state after state this includes disproportionately high numbers of African-American school children. The principal findings are listed below.

- *Funding.* Special education programs are often designed specifically to attract state and federal dollars to local school districts rather than serving the interests of the students. In nearly two-thirds of the 50 states, reimbursement formulas for special education programs played

a role in determining the number and type of programs funded. Texas, for example, pays local school districts 10 times more for teaching special education students in separate classrooms than in classrooms with other students. Thus, despite generally accepted evidence that many special education students benefit from general classrooms, only 5 percent of all special education students in Texas are taught in general education classrooms, the lowest rate in the nation (see Table 6).

- *Growth.* Imprecise state and federal regulations allow frequent misdesignation of special education students and also drive up the size and cost of the special education system. Since IDEA implementation, the number of special education students has increased every year without exception. Five million special education students make up 10 percent of total student enrollment.

- *Incentives.* In most states special education students are exempt from reading and math exams, so many principals have raised their schools' scores on statewide competency exams by placing low-scoring students—children who otherwise might not be in special education—in special education programs. As a result, average school test scores are higher.

- *Classification.* Special education labels are so ambiguous that classifications vary from state to state, and even from school district to school district. Of all Massachusetts students, 15 percent wind up in special education programs; only 7 percent of students in Hawaii are in special education; and just 8 percent of children in Georgia and Michigan are enrolled in special education. Classifications vary widely from state to state even within special education categories. In Alaska, only 3 percent of all special education students are classified as having retardation. The comparable figure in Alabama is 28 percent. In North Dakota, 72 percent of special education students are taught in general education classrooms. In South Dakota, a state with almost identical demographics, only 8 percent of special education students go to class with children without disabilities.

- *Race.* In 39 states African-American students are overrepresented in special education programs, compared with their percentage in the overall student population. Significantly, African-American students are most likely to be overrepresented in special education classes when attending predominantly white school districts. Tables 7, 8, and 9 illustrate the overrepresentation of minority students in special education.

3. Joseph P. Shapiro et al., "Separate and Unequal: How Special Education Programs are Cheating our Children and Costing Taxpayers Billions Each Year," *U.S. News & World Report*, December 13, 1993.

- *Oversight.* Classification problems continue because of lax enforcement by state and federal agencies. Of 10,147 discrimination complaints reviewed by the Department of Education's Office of Civil Rights since 1987, the office imposed the most severe penalty—revoking federal funds—on just one case. School districts usually are allowed to work with regulators to design corrective measures.
- *Service.* Special education classrooms often become convenient places for teachers to send struggling students they don't want in their classrooms. In such cases, education is not the priority. Special education instructors often do as much social work (life skills enhancement) as teaching. In one special education classroom in Ohio, for example, students learned how to bake a frozen pizza in an oven. Federal regulations mention 13 types of disabilities that affect learning: autism, deaf-blindness, deafness, hearing impairment, mental retardation, multiple disabilities, chronic or acute health problems (such as a heart condition or epilepsy), serious emotional disturbance, specific learning disability, speech or language impairment, traumatic brain injury, and visual impairment, including blindness. Only a few of these disabilities (such as deafness and blindness) can be measured by objective tests. The rest are highly subjective, which can result in mislabeling.

TABLE 6   States with Largest and Smallest Shares of Special Education Students in Regular Classes

Largest Share		Smallest Share	
Vermont	83%	California	27%
North Dakota	72	Colorado	24
Massachusetts	62	Iowa	22
Wyoming	62	District of Columbia	16
New Mexico	62	Minnesota	11
Nebraska	61	Arizona	10
Oregon	61	South Dakota	8
Idaho	61	New York	8
Montana	60	West Virginia	6
North Carolina	54	Texas	5

USN&WR—Basic data: Fifteenth Annual 1993 Report to Congress on the implementation of the Individuals with Disabilities Education Act.

By far the largest number of special education students are labeled learning disabled: 49.9 percent. This is the most difficult classification to identify properly. According to the U.S. Department of Education, a child with learning disabilities is one who has "a severe discrepancy between achievement and intellectual ability." The state departments of education must decide which tests and procedures to use to measure learning disabilities, so school practices vary widely. According to University of Minnesota researcher James Ysseldyke, more than 80 percent of all school children in America could qualify as having a learning disability according to one or more of the various definitions the states now use.

Likewise, the definitions of severe emotional disturbance are ambiguous. Nothing drives the special education system like money. Connecticut has the most students classified as having an emotional disturbance. People in that state do not have more stress, paranoia, or pathology; instead, the state's complex funding formula encourages school districts to send students with emotional disturbances to separate schools.

According to the *U.S. News & World Report* analysis, the federal government promised to pay 40 percent of the costs of implementing IDEA to the states. In 1994, just 7 percent of the costs to the states were reimbursed by the federal government. This unfunded mandate has contributed to the controversy surrounding special education.

Another issue is the track record of special education. For example, about one in four special education students drops out of high school; 43 percent of those who graduate remain unemployed three to five years after high school, and nearly one third—primarily those with learning and emotional disabilities—are arrested at least once after leaving high school.

Gifted and Talented

Even though the adjective "exceptional" is often used to describe any student who is different from or treated differently from others, it is probably more often associated with students who are considered above average in achievement than it is with the disabled students, even though disabled students may also achieve at above average levels. Chapter 22 summarizes various components of the Texas Plan and Guidelines for the Education of Gifted/Talented Students. Beginning with the 1990–91 school year, all school districts were required to identify and serve all gifted students at all

TABLE 7 Percentages of Students in Special Education

	African Americans Among All Students	African Americans in Special Education	Whites Among All Students	Whites In Special Education
Delaware	29%	41%	66%	54%
South Carolina	42	51	57	49
Connecticut	14	22	72	78
Louisiana	46	53	51	45
North Carolina	33	40	63	57
Nevada	12	19	70	69

USN&WR—Basic data: *USN&WR* analysis of U.S. Department of Education, Office of Civil Rights 1990 Survey of Schools.

TABLE 8 Percentages of Ethnic Groups Classified by Disability

Classification	African American	White	Hispanic
Retardation	26%	11%	18%
Learning Disabilities	43	51	55
Emotional Disturbance	8	8	4
Speech Impairment	23	30	23

USN&WR—Basic data: U.S. Department of Education, Office of Civil Rights 1990 Survey of Schools.

TABLE 9 States with Highest and Lowest Rates of Blacks Labeled as Having Retardation

States with Highest Percentages of African-American Special Education Students Labeled Retarded		States with Lowest Percentages of African-American Special Education Students Classified as Retarded	
Alabama	47%	Nevada	9%
Ohio	41	Connecticut	7
Arkansas	37	Maryland	8
Indiana	37	New Jersey	6
Georgia	36	Alaska	3

USN&WR—Basic data: *USN&WR* analysis of Department of Education, Office of Civil Rights 1990 Survey of Schools.

grade levels. Districts receive additional state funds for five percent of students identified as gifted but are obligated to provide for all who are identified.

If giftedness is usually associated with intelligence, and too often it is, how then is intelligence defined? Harvard University Professor Howard Gardner offers a broad and varied view of intelligence which includes the following seven dimensions (*Frames of Mind*, 1983):

1. *Linguistic.* The ability to communicate through language. People with this intelligence think in words and are sensitive to the order and meaning of words. Poets and writers excel in this intelligence.
2. *Mathematical–logical.* The ability to work with concepts and abstract ideas. People with this intelligence are quick to see patterns and relationships and like to experiment and solve puzzles. It is common among scientists and mathematicians.
3. *Spatial.* The ability to think in images. People with this intelligence often like to draw, work jigsaw puzzles, and read maps. They learn through pictures and images. Artists, architects, and surveyors are strong in this area.
4. *Musical.* People with this intelligence like music and are sensitive to sounds. They often study well with music in the background. They can learn by turning lessons into lyrics or rhythmic chants, like raps. Composers, singers, and musicians exhibit this intelligence.
5. *Bodily kinesthetic.* The skill of moving one's body. Those gifted in this intelligence like movement and communicate well through body language. They often learn through hands-on activities. Dancers, athletes, and surgeons have this intelligence.
6. *Interpersonal.* The ability to understand others. People with this intelligence learn through interaction. Politicians, salespeople, and teachers often exhibit this intelligence.

7. *Intrapersonal.* People with this intelligence are aware of their own abilities and their own motivations. They are often shy, but they have a strong will, confidence, and opinions. Therapists and social workers alike excel in this area.

If Professor Gardner's theory is correct, measurements traditionally considered "intelligence" tests do not measure these kinds of intelligence accurately.

Limited English Proficiency

Chapter 23 examines the historical development and current status of bilingual and English as a second language programs in Texas. The legal struggle over bilingual education nationally has been in and out of the courts for several years. The controversy is not unique to Texas. An estimated 10 percent of the population of Chicago is Spanish-speaking and one third of the Hispanic students need bilingual education. In Los Angeles about 80 languages are spoken, and Spanish-speaking families supply 45 percent of the city's school population. New York City now has about 80,000 children in bilingual classes. As far back as the 1981–82 school year, specially designed instructional programs were provided for 198,872 Texas students of limited English proficiency (LEP). The number of LEP students continues to increase rapidly.

Dyslexia

Dyslexia is the term used to describe a specific reading disability in individuals who have no other disabling condition. As the popular news media have publicized the confessions of highly successful individuals with this disability, the public has been alerted to dyslexia. In 1985, the Texas Legislature passed legislation requiring that public schools provide appropriate educational services to all students with dyslexia at all grade levels. Chapter 24 defines dyslexia and summarizes the procedures for training practitioners to implement provisions of the law.

MIDDLE SCHOOLS

Middle schools were designed to ease the transition from the security of the frequently self-contained elementary grades to the traditionally departmentalized junior high grades of 7 through 9. They are designed for teaching adolescents, usually for grades 5 or 6 through 7 or 8. Ideally, they are organized so that interdisciplinary teams of teachers with flexible schedules can maintain close contact with individ-ual students. A significant report of the Carnegie Council on Adolescent Development recommended the following.

Recommendations from Turning Points: Preparing the American Youth for the 21st Century

- Create small communities for learning where stable, close, mutually respectful relationships with adults and peers are considered fundamental for intellectual development and personal growth.
- Teach a core academic program that results in students who are literate, including in the sciences, and who know how to think critically, lead a healthy life, behave ethically, and assume the responsibilities of citizenship in a pluralistic society.
- Ensure success for all students through elimination of tracking by achievement level and promotion of cooperative learning, flexibility in arranging instructional time, and adequate resources (time, space, equipment, and materials) for teachers.
- Empower teachers and administrators to make decisions about the experiences of middle grade students through creative control by teachers over the instructional program linked to greater responsibilities for students' performance, governance committees that assist the principal in designing and coordinating school-wide programs, and autonomy and leadership within sub-schools to create environments tailored to enhance the intellectual and emotional development of all youth.
- Staff middle grade schools with teachers who are expert at teaching young adolescents and who have been specially prepared for assignment to the middle grades.
- Improve academic performance through fostering the health and fitness of young adolescents by providing a health coordinator in every middle grade school, access to health care and counseling services, and a health-promoting school environment.
- Reengage families in the education of young adolescents by giving families meaningful roles in school governance, communicating with families about the school program and students' progress, and offering families opportunities to support the learning process at home and at the school.
- Connect schools and communities, which together share responsibility for each middle grade student's success, through identifying service opportunities in the community, establishing partnerships and collaborations to

ensure students' access to health and social services, and using community resources to enrich the instructional program and opportunities for constructive after-school activities.

Traditional junior high schools (grades 7–9) now make up only 15 percent of the nation's middle school configurations, according to a 1993 report by the National Association of Secondary School Principals. In contrast, they represented 67 percent in 1966.

Although many middle schools currently operate in districts throughout the state, renewed interest in the middle school by the State Board of Education may mean that even more may be in operation in the future. Middle schools are featured in Chapter 25.

INSTRUCTION MATERIALS

The Texas Education Code and policies of the State Board of Education direct the practice of Texas instructional materials adoption. This well-defined sequence of events is summarized in Chapter 26. Although the statutes and policies that guide this process seem to be rather simple and straightforward, the actual practice has become cluttered with side issues. From time to time no other single school-related event brings Texas to the forefront in the national news as does the selection of textbooks.

One reason the selection process in Texas attracts so much attention is the magnitude of the state purchase once selections have been made. Although it is not clear as to whether Texas is the second largest or the largest purchaser of school materials in the nation, it is claimed that Texas establishes a tone for books throughout the United States by influencing how publishers design and tailor the content. For example, Scott Foresman publishers added a no pass–no play workbook to accompany and help sell its *Land of Promise* textbook to the Texas Education Agency. In addition, it included a special Texas teacher edition that matched the Texas essential elements to the contents of the text. Publishers are currently modifying their materials toward the Texas Essential Knowledge and Skills (TEKS). Publishers fear that if their materials are not purchased in Texas, they "better pray for big sales in California, New York, and all the Peorias in between." During one meeting alone, the State Board adopted materials that cost $128 million.

State Board of Education policies restricting textbook expenditures to printed materials were changed to permit the purchase of educational videodiscs in place of textbooks in elementary science beginning with the 1991–92 school year. Optical Data Corpora-

tion of Warren, New Jersey, received the contract for its videodisc program called "Windows on Science," which could radically change elementary science teaching and learning. The program relies on laser video technology and printed material and can be used with or without textbooks. One videodisc, the video version of the compact disc in the "Windows" series, contains more than 54,000 separate images that can be freeze-framed and slow-motioned at the remote control of the teacher. This videodisc program precedent could be the beginning of a dramatic change in instructional materials and methods in Texas schools. Senate Bill 1 of 1990, the enabling legislation for this change, allows publishers to submit technologies such as computer software, other computer courseware and magnetic media in addition to the interactive videodisc for state purchase in place of printed textbooks. Senate Bill 1 of 1995 expanded the definition of "textbook" to include electronic media, software, and hardware. The 1995 legislation also incorporated the $30.00 technology allotment into the textbook allotment and authorized expenditures for training district personnel (involved in student learning) in the use of electronic textbooks and technological equipment.

Other textbook-related changes to the Texas Education Code enacted by the 74th Legislature in 1995 (Senate Bill 1) include the following.

- The State Board of Education (SBOE) will review and adopt textbooks and provide the districts with two lists from which to choose.

  1. A "conforming" list which includes textbooks that cover each element of the essential knowledge and skills determined by the State Board of Education, and
  2. A "nonconforming" list that includes textbooks containing at least half of the essential knowledge and skills.

- Local districts may choose books not on either list for the "enrichment curriculum" and receive state funding for 70 percent of the costs.
- Foundation curriculum courses must use texts from either the conforming or nonconforming lists. All other courses offered by a district may be taught with texts from any list.

YEAR-ROUND SCHOOLS

Senate Bill 1 of June 1990 directed the State Board of Education to adopt rules under which school districts could operate schools year-round and implement multitrack arrangements which provide for staggered instructional blocks, usually of three semesters, with vacation periods in between. With guidelines approved, the number of year-round schools in Texas increased from one to approximately 50 from 1990–91 to 1991–92. The traditional nine-month academic year from September to June is based upon an agrarian society in which children were needed at home during the important periods for planting, harvesting, and other activities. The experimental models implemented during the 1991–92 year included both the traditional and alternative calendars offered within the same campus as well as the selection of only certain grades, such as second, third, and fourth, within the same campus or throughout a district.

Carriedo and Goren defined year-round and multitrack schools as follows:

> The year-round schedule replaces the traditional summer vacation period with shorter vacations dispersed throughout the year. Schools that implement year-round calendars do so in two forms—*singletrack* and *multitrack.* In single-track schools, all teachers and students have the same academic and vacation schedule throughout the year. Districts use singletrack year-round schools because they believe learning can be more effective if it is not interrupted by a lengthy, two-and-a-half-month summer break. The singletrack schedule does not reduce school size, nor does it allow a school to accommodate more students, since students are always in attendance at the same time.
>
> A multitrack, year-round school divides students and teachers into different groups or *tracks* of approximately the same size. Each track is assigned a different academic and vacation schedule. In all multitrack formats, one track is on vacation while the other tracks are in attendance. The tracks that are in session at the same time are independent of each other and operate as self-contained schools-within-schools, offering instruction in all or most grade levels. The most common multitrack formats are the three- and four-track systems. Students and teachers in a three-track system typically attend school 90 consecutive weekdays followed by a twenty-to-thirty day vacation. Four-track programs provide 45 consecutive weekdays of instruction followed by a 15-day break and thus are known as the "45–15" system.
>
> Multitrack, year-round schools are most often implemented to relieve overcrowding. They allow a school to house more students than would be possible on the traditional calendar. For example, imagine a community with 1,000 elementary students and a school that can house only 750. Since a four-track, year-round school has three tracks in attendance (with 250 children per track) and one track on vacation (with 250 students) at all times, this multitrack, year-round school serves 750 children at any given time while the other 250 students are on vacation.
>
> In some cases, the multitrack schedule is used to reduce the number of students on campus. If an elementary school with an enrollment of 1,000 students institutes a four-track, year-round calendar, the number of students on campus will be reduced by 250. Since only three tracks are in session at any given time and each track in a four-track, year-round school with an enrollment of 1,000 serves 250 students, the on-campus enrollment will be 750 rather than 1,000.[4]

Approximately 500 public schools in 16 states have implemented year-round schools. Most of these arrangements are in the West and Southwest. Seventy-eight percent of the year-round schools are in California, followed by Utah and Nevada. Ninety percent of the year-round schools are at the elementary level.

Opponents criticize the practice because it interrupts traditional summer vacations, complicates day care and car pool arrangements, and can split the school schedules of children within the same family. Proponents cite the following advantages of year-round education (YRE):

- YRE can save money. Fewer schools are needed because facilities are used more efficiently.
- YRE may increase student learning. Research indicates that students in year-round systems retain more of what they learn and require less review time at the start of each school year.
- YRE provides relief from overcrowded facilities and better traffic flow around schools.
- YRE may reduce student vandalism. Because the building is in almost continuous use, there are fewer days when it is unattended by school employees.
- YRE may prevent student and teacher burnout. School districts that have instituted year-round programs report that students and teachers return to school refreshed after the short, frequent breaks.
- YRE's three-week breaks provide opportunities for enrichment and tutoring programs. (Arlington ISD, 1991)

---

4. Far West Laboratory, *Policy Briefs*, No. 10, 1989.

SCHOOL EFFECTIVENESS

The school effectiveness research findings of the past two decades have provided lay and professional education leaders with many new approaches to school improvement. A summary of research on school effectiveness is provided in Chapter 27.

SCANS

Following the general theme of America 2000 and the National Goals of Education, provided earlier in this Overview, the Bush administration's Secretary of Labor Lynn Martin set up a commission to outline the skills necessary for today's students to succeed in tomorrow's workplace. The Secretary's Commission on Achieving Necessary Skills (SCANS) completed and issued a series of reports summarizing the needs of the workplace, translated those needs into skills and competencies workers must possess, and made recommendations to educators as to how they might best be taught. The recommended skills are not just for those joining the workforce after high school but for all students.

Traditional content-oriented public school teachers and university professors have found this concept somewhat troubling. For example, in the traditional high school or university English class students may be required to read prescribed literary works and compose themes and essays in styles similar to their readings. In schools where the SCANS skills are incorporated into the English course requirements, students may write brochures advertising a program or product or producing reports that summarize events such as reporting the details of a traffic accident for an insurance claim or police report. This kind of "applied learning in context," practicing workplace competencies, forces the teacher to take on a new role that may be unsettling. Learning to *know* differs significantly from learning to *do*. SCANS recommends "Reinventing Schools," which incorporates the following, by the year 2000.

- Workplace know-how (the SCANS foundation and workplace competencies) should be taught along the entire continuum of education, from kindergarten through college.
- Every student should complete middle school (about age 14) with an introduction to workplace know-how.
- Every student by about age 16 should attain initial mastery of the SCANS know-how.
- Every student should complete high school sufficiently proficient in the SCANS know-how to earn a decent living.

- All federally funded programs for youth and adults, including vocational education programs, should teach the SCANS know-how.

Chapter 28 provides the executive summary of "Learning a Living: A Blueprint for High Performance," produced by SCANS. With the momentum achieved in the first two years of SCANS, the change in presidency from Bush to Clinton will not likely slow the movement.

OUTCOMES-BASED EDUCATION

With the introduction of the SCANS recommendations in the 1990s, educators and the public at large began the periodic process of reassessing current education practices and goals of public education in general. By 1993, at least 30 states had identified, in one format or another, essential student "outcomes" that students graduating from their high schools should be able to demonstrate. One state has determined that the Carnegie Unit, the national "coin of the high school academic credit realm," is no more than a measure of "seat time" spent while waiting for graduation and has discontinued requiring districts to record it. Many of the outcomes are similar to those recommended by SCANS, and thus there is likely to be some commonality and consistency among the states and their stated outcomes.

With the rising popularity of outcomes- or results-based education versus the traditional input or process approach, Chris Pipho, in his Stateline Column entitled "Outcomes or Edubabble" for *Phi Delta Kappan* (May 1992), provided the following caveats.

THE TERMINOLOGY may differ—learner outcomes, performance-based or authentic assessment, portfolios of student work—but states and school districts are increasingly moving to adopt new programs that could change testing, teaching, and learning. Transforming education from a process that emphasizes inputs to one that stresses outcomes could be more complex than educators and policy makers realize.

Passing a law or adopting a regulation to initiate a move to focus on outcomes is the easy part. Convincing the public of the need for such a change and explaining how the new ideas will affect students in the classroom will take a coherent communications strategy. Teachers and administrators may understand the ideas behind outcomes-based education, but too much of the literature remains the domain of a cadre of theorists, and the approaches and terminology differ from one guru or group to another. When the public questions what is going on and communication via the media is unclear or not supportive, even the best programs can become targets for the critics.

Outcomes-based assessment and instruction will eventually require altering the basic premise that testing must come from outside the school and be used to check up on students and teachers. The notion that instruction can be combined with assessment and that students can progress through school by demonstrating a series of outcomes is far from being widely accepted by the general public. And if the skeptics see only bad or dubious examples that catch the attention of the media, then transforming the educational process from a focus on inputs to a focus on outputs will be slow going.

William H. Spady, perhaps the most widely known expert in the area of outcomes-based education, shares his recommendations for the process of change from traditional outcomes based to transitional and then to transformational outcomes in Chapter 29.

TOTAL QUALITY MANAGEMENT

Total Quality Management (TQM) is a philosophy of organizational improvement and practice associated with W. Edwards Deming. Deming was a consultant to the Japanese government after World War II. His continuous improvement approaches to focusing on the integrity of the process leading to the outcomes of an enterprise is credited with assisting Japan in not only its recovery after the war but its rise to the top in various measures of economic superiority in the second half of the 20th century.

American industries have adopted the philosophy, and some, such as the Saturn subsidiary to General Motors, have been able to compete successfully with the Japanese in the automobile industry. Chapter 30 responds to the rhetorical question: If TQM works so well in private business and industry, how can it be applied to public education?

Curriculum Contrasts: A Historical Review

The most fundamental concern of schooling is curriculum. Students tend to view schooling largely as subjects or courses to be taken. Teachers and professors give much attention to adoption and revision of subject matter. Parents and community members frequently express concern about what schools are for and what they should teach. In short, all of these groups are attending to one thing: curriculum.

Curriculum concepts and scope have changed over the years, and from these changes two different views of curriculum have emerged. The first sees curriculum as a body of content or subject matter leading to certain achievement outcomes or products. The second views curriculum in terms of the learner and his or her needs; the concern is with process, i.e., the climate of the classroom and school.

THE SUBJECT-CENTERED CURRICULUM

Subject matter is the oldest and most used framework for curriculum organization, primarily because it is convenient. In fact, the departmental structure of secondary schools and colleges tends to prevent us from thinking about the curriculum in other ways. Curricular changes usually occur at the departmental level. Courses are added, omitted, or modified, but faculty members rarely engage in

Reprinted by permission from "Curriculum Contrasts: A Historical Overview," by Allan C. Ornstein, *Phi Delta Kappan*, February 1982, pp. 404–408. Copyright © 1982 by Phi Delta Kappa, Inc.

comprehensive, systematic curriculum development and evaluation. Even in the elementary school, where self-contained classrooms force the teachers to be generalists, curricula are usually organized by subjects.

Proponents defend the subject-centered curriculum on four grounds: (1) that subjects are a logical way to organize and interpret learning, (2) that such organization makes it easier for people to remember information for future use, (3) that teachers (in secondary schools, at least) are trained as subject-matter specialists, and (4) that textbooks and other teaching materials are usually organized by subject. Critics, however, claim that the subject-centered curriculum is fragmented, a mass of facts and concepts learned in isolation. They see this kind of curriculum as de-emphasizing life experiences and failing to consider adequately the needs and interests of students. The emphasis, such critics argue, is on the teaching of knowledge, the recall of facts. Thus the teacher dominates the lesson, allowing little student input. Let us look at five variations on the subject-centered curriculum.

Subject-Area Curriculum

The subject area is the oldest and most widely used form of curriculum organization. It has its roots in the seven liberal arts of classical Greece and Rome: grammar, rhetoric, dialectic, arithmetic, geometry, astronomy, and music. Modern subject-area curricula trace their origins to the work of William Harris, superintendent of the St. Louis school system in the

1870s. Steeped in the classical tradition, Harris established a subject orientation that has virtually dominated U. S. curricula from his day to the present.

The modern subject-area curriculum treats each subject as a specialized and largely autonomous body of verified knowledge. These subjects can be organized into three content categories, however. Common content refers to subjects considered essential for all students; these subjects usually include the three R's at the elementary level and English, history, science, and mathematics at the secondary level. Special content refers to subjects that develop knowledge and skills for particular vocations or professions, e.g., business mathematics and physics. Finally, elective content affords the student optional offerings. Some electives are restricted to certain students, e.g., advanced auto mechanics for vocational students or fourth-year French for students enrolled in a college-preparatory program. Other electives, such as photography and human relations, are open to all students.

Perennialist Curriculum

Two conservative philosophies of education are basically subject-centered: Perennialism and Essentialism.[1] Perennialists believe that a curriculum should consist primarily of the three R's, Latin, and logic at the elementary level, to which is added the study of the classics at the secondary level. The assumption, according to Robert Hutchins, is that the best of the past—the so-called "permanent studies" or classics—is equally valid for the present.[2]

One problem with Perennialism is its fundamental premise: that the main purpose of education is the cultivation of the intellect. Further, Perennialists believe that only certain studies have this power. They reject consideration of students' personal needs and interests or the treatment of contemporary problems in the curriculum on the grounds that such concerns are frivolous and detract from the school's mission of cultivating the mind.

Essentialist Curriculum

Essentialists believe that the curriculum must consist of "disciplined study" in five areas: English (grammar, literature, and writing), mathematics, the sciences, history, and foreign languages.[3] They see the subject areas as the best way of systematizing and keeping up with the explosion of knowledge.

Essentialism shares with Perennialism the notion that the curriculum should focus on rigorous intellectual training, a training possible only through the study of certain subjects. Although the Perennialist sees no need for nonacademic subjects, the Essentialist is willing to add such studies to the curriculum, provided they receive low priority.

Both Perennialists and Essentialists advocate an educational meritocracy. They favor high academic standards and a rigorous system of testing to help schools sort students by ability. The goal is to educate each person to the limits of his or her potential.

Subject Structure Curriculum

During the fifties and sixties, the National Science Foundation and the federal government devoted sizable sums to the improvement of science and mathematics curricula at the elementary and secondary levels. The result was new curricular models formulated according to the structure of each subject or discipline. Structure includes those unifying concepts, rules, and principles that define and limit a subject and control the methods of research and inquiry. Structure brings together and organizes a body of knowledge, as well as dictating appropriate ways of thinking about the subject and of generating new data. Other subjects quickly followed the lead of mathematics and the sciences.

Those who advocated this kind of focus on the structure nonetheless rejected the idea of knowledge as fixed or permanent. They regarded teaching and learning as continuing inquiry, but they confined such inquiry within the established boundaries of subjects, ignoring or rejecting the fact that many problems cut across disciplines. Instead, they emphasized the students' cognitive abilities. They taught students the structure of a subject and its methods of inquiry so that students would learn how to learn. But they tended to dismiss learners' social and psychological needs. As Philip Phenix wrote: "There is no place in the curriculum for ideas which are regarded as suitable for teaching because of the supposed nature, needs, and interests of the learner, but which do not belong within the regular structure of the discipline."[4]

The emphasis on structure led each discipline to develop its own unifying concepts, principles, and methods of inquiry. Learning by the inquiry method in chemistry differs from learning by the inquiry method in physics, for example. Moreover, curriculum planners could not agree on how to teach the structure of the social sciences and the fine arts. Science and mathematics programs continue even today to provide the best examples of teaching the structure of a subject.

Back-to-Basics Curriculum

A strong back-to-basics movement has surfaced among parents and educators, called forth by the general relaxation of academic standards in the sixties and seventies and declining student achievement in reading, writing, and computation. Automatic promotion of marginal students, the dizzying array of elective courses, and textbooks designed more to entertain than to educate are frequently cited as sources of the decline in basic skills. Even the mass media have attacked the "soft-sell approach" to education. The concerns were voiced immediately after Sputnik. The call is less for academic excellence and rigor, however, than for a return to basics. Annual Gallup polls have asked the public to suggest ways for improving education; since 1975 "devoting more attention to teaching the basics" has either headed the list of responses or ranked no lower than third.[5]

By 1978, 33 states had set minimum standards for elementary and secondary students. All the remaining states have legislation pending or are studying the situation.[6] The National Association of Secondary School Principals (NASSP) recommends the use of certificates of proficiency for all students, whether or not minimal proficiency is made a requirement for graduation. Congress is also urging voluntary adoption by state and local education agencies of minimum competency testing programs.[7]

Although the back-to-basics movement means different things to different people, it usually connotes an Essentialist curriculum with heavy emphasis on reading, writing, and mathematics. Solid subjects—English, history, science, mathematics—are taught in all grades. History means U. S. and European history and perhaps Asian and African history, but not Afro-American history or ethnic studies. English means traditional grammar, not linguistics or nonstandard English; it means Shakespeare and Wordsworth, not *Catcher in the Rye* or *Lolita*. Creative writing is frowned upon. Science means biology, chemistry, and physics—not ecology. Mathematics means old math, not new math. Furthermore, these subjects are required. Proponents of the basics consider elective courses in such areas as scuba diving, transcendental meditation, and hiking as nonsense. Some even consider humanities or integrated social science courses too "soft." They may grudgingly admit music and art into the program—but only for half credit.[8]

These proponents believe that too many illiterate students pass from grade to grade and eventually graduate, that high school and college diplomas are meaningless as measures of graduates' abilities, that minimum standards must be set, that the basics (reading, writing, math) are essential for employment, and that students must learn survival skills to function effectively in society. Some back-to-basics advocates are college educators who would do away with open admissions or relaxed entrance re-

quirements and grade inflation; they would simply insist that their institutions require students to meet a reasonable standard in the basic disciplines—that students be able to understand homework assignments, write acceptable essays, and compute numbers accurately.[9]

Critics point out that the decline in standardized achievement test scores—a grave concern of back-to-basics enthusiasts—may be linked less to curriculum than to higher student/teacher ratios, a decrease in the number of low-achieving students who drop out of school, and the more permissive attitude of society.[10] There is no guarantee, they argue, that the student who masters specific skills for today's world will be better prepared for the world of tomorrow. They also worry that a narrow focus on basics will suppress students' creativity, encouraging instead conformity and dependence on authority.[11] Others expect the back-to-basics movement to fail because teaching and learning cannot be defined and limited precisely and because testing has too many inherent problems.

While the debate is raging, the movement is spreading quickly in response to public pressure. State legislators and state boards of education seem convinced of the merit of minimum standards. But there are also unanswered questions. If we adopt a back-to-basics approach to education, what standards should be considered minimum?[12] Who determines these standards? What do we do with students who fail to meet these standards? Are we simply punishing the victims for the schools' inability to educate them? How will the courts deal with the fact that proportionally more minority than white students fail the competency tests in nearly every state that has a testing program?[13] Is the issue minimum competence, or is it equal educational opportunity?

THE STUDENT-CENTERED CURRICULUM

If the subject-centered curriculum focuses on cognitive aspects of learning, the student-centered curriculum emphasizes students' interests and needs. The student-centered approach, at its extreme, is rooted in the philosophy of Jean Jacques Rousseau, who encouraged childhood self-expression. Implicit in Rousseau's philosophy is the necessity of leaving the child to his or her own devices; he considered creativity and freedom essential for children's growth. Moreover, he thought a child would be happier if free of teacher domination and the demands of subject matter and adult-imposed curriculum goals. This hands-off policy was Rousseau's reaction to the domineering teacher of the traditional school, whose sole purpose was to drill facts into a child's brain.

Progressive education gave impetus to the student-centered curriculum. Progressive educators believed that, when the interests and needs of learners were incorporated into the curriculum, intrinsic motivation resulted. I do not mean to imply that the student-centered curriculum is dictated by the whims of the learner. Rather, advocates believe that learning is more successful if the interests and needs of the learner are taken into account. The student-centered curriculum sometimes overlooks important cognitive content, however.

John Dewey, one of the chief advocates of the student-centered curriculum, criticized educators who overlooked the importance of subject matter. His intention was to establish a curriculum that balanced subject matter with student interests and needs. As early as 1902, he pointed out the fallacies of either extreme. The learner was neither "a docile recipient of facts" nor "the starting point, the center, and the end" of school activity.[14] More than 30 years later, Dewey was still criticizing overpermissive educators who provided little education for students under the guise of meeting their expressed and impulsive needs.[15] Dewey sought interests to enhance the cognitive learning process.

There are at least five variations of the student-centered curriculum.

Child-Centered Schools

The movement from the traditional subject-dominated curriculum toward a program emphasizing student interests and needs began in 1762 with the publication of Rousseau's *Emile*. In this book Rousseau maintained that the purpose of education is to teach people to live. Early in the next century the Swiss educator, Johann Pestalozzi, began to stress human emotions and kindness in teaching young children. Friedrich Froebel introduced the kindergarten in Germany in 1837. He emphasized a permissive atmosphere and the use of songs, stories, and games as instructional materials. Early in the 20th century Maria Montessori, working with the slum children of Rome, developed a set of didactic materials and learning exercises that successfully combined work with play. Many of her principles were introduced in the U. S. during the sixties as part of the compensatory preschool movement.

Early Progressive educators in the U.S. adopted the notion of child-centered schools, starting with Dewey's organic school (which he described in *Schools of Tomorrow*) and including many private and experimental schools—the best known of which were Columbia University's Lincoln School, Ohio State's Laboratory School, the University of Missouri Elementary School, the Pratt Play School in New York City, the Parker School in Chicago, and the Fairhope School in Alabama.[16] These schools had a common feature: their curricula stressed the needs and interests of students. Some stressed individualization; others grouped students by ability or interests.

Child-centered education is represented today by programs for such special groups as the academically talented, the disadvantaged, dropouts (actual and potential), the handicapped, and minority and ethnic groups. Many of these programs are carried on in "free" or "alternative" schools organized by parents and teachers who are dissatisfied with the public schools. Most of these new schools are considered radical and anti-Establishment, even though many of their ideas are rooted in the child-centered doctrines of Progressivism.

Summerhill, a school founded in 1921 by A.S. Neill and still in existence today, is perhaps the best-known free school. Neill's philosophy was the replacement of authority by freedom.[17] He was not concerned with formal learning; he did not believe in textbooks or examinations. He did believe that those who want to study will study and those who prefer not to study will not, regardless of how teachers teach. Neill's dual criteria for success were the ability to work joyfully and the ability to live a happy life.

Although Neill, Edgar Friedenberg, Paul Goodman, and John Holt[18] all belong to an earlier generation of school reformers, new radicals have also emerged. They include George Dennison, James Herndon, Ivan Illich, Herbert Kohl, and Jonathan Kozol. These educators stress the need for, and in many cases have established, child-centered free schools or alternative schools.[19] These schools are typified by a great deal of freedom for students and noisy classrooms that sometimes appear untidy and disorganized. The teaching/learning process is unstructured.

Critics condemn these schools as places where little cognitive learning takes place. They decry a lack of discipline and order. They feel that the radical reformers' attacks on Establishment teachers and schools are overgeneralized and unfair. Moreover, they view the radicals' idea of schooling as not feasible for mass education. Proponents counter that children do learn in these schools, which do not stress conformity but instead are made to fit the child.

Activity-Centered Curriculum

This movement, which grew out of the private child-centered schools, strongly affected the public elementary school curriculum. William Kilpatrick, a student of Dewey's, was its leader. In 1918 Kilpatrick wrote a theoretical article, "The Project Method," that catapulted him into national prominence. He advocated purposeful activities that were tied to a child's needs and interests.[20] Kilpatrick differed with Dewey's child-centered view; he believed that the interests and needs of children could not be anticipated, making a pre-planned curriculum impossible. He attacked the school curriculum as unrelated to the problems of real life and advocated purposeful activities that were as lifelike as possible.

During the twenties and thirties, many elementary schools adopted some of the ideas of the activity movement, perhaps best summarized and first put into practice by Ellsworth Collings, a doctoral student of Kilpatrick's.[21] From this movement a host of teaching strategies emerged, including lessons based on life experiences, group games, dramatizations, story projects, field trips, social enterprises, and interest centers. All of these activities involved problem solving and active student participation; they emphasized socialization and the formation of stronger school/community ties.

Recent curriculum reformers have translated ideas from this movement into community and career-based activities intended to prepare students for adult citizenship and work and into courses emphasizing social problems. They have also urged college credit for life experiences.[22] Secondary and college students often earn credit today by working in welfare agencies, early childhood programs, government institutions, hospitals, and homes for the aged.[23]

Relevant Curriculum

Unquestionably, the curriculum must reflect social change. This point is well illustrated in a satiric book on education, *The Saber-Tooth Curriculum*, written in 1939 by Harold Benjamin under the pseudonym of Abner J. Peddiwell.[24] He describes a society in which the schools continued to teach fish-catching (because it would develop agility), horse-clubbing (to develop strength), and tiger-scaring (to develop courage) long after the streams had dried up and the horses and tigers had disappeared. The wise men of the society argued that "the essence of true education is timeless . . . something that endures through changing conditions like a solid rock standing squarely and firmly in the middle of a raging torrent."[25] Benjamin's message was simple: The curriculum was no longer relevant.

There is a renewed concern today that the curriculum be relevant. But the emphasis has changed. We no longer worry so much about whether the curriculum reflects changing social conditions. Instead,

we are concerned that the curriculum be relevant to students. This shift is part of the Dewey legacy. Learners must be motivated and interested in the learning task, and the classroom should build on their real-life experiences.[26]

The new demand for relevance comes from both students and educators. In fact, the student disruptions of the late 1960s and early 1970s were related to this demand. Proponents see as needs: (1) the individualization of instruction through such teaching methods as independent inquiry, special projects, and contracts; (2) the revision of existing courses and development of new ones on such topics of student concern as environmental protection, drug addiction, urban problems, cultural pluralism, and Afro-American literature; (3) the provision of educational alternatives (e.g., electives, minicourses, open classrooms) that allow more freedom of choice; and (4) the extension of the curriculum beyond the schools' walls through such innovations as work-study programs, credit for life experiences, and external degree programs.[27]

Efforts to relate subject matter to student interests have been largely ad hoc. Many of the changes have also been fragmentary and temporary, a source of concern to advocates of relevance. In other cases, changes made in the name of relevance have led to a watered-down curriculum.

Hidden Curriculum

The notion of a hidden curriculum implies that values of the student peer group are often ignored when formal school curricula are planned. C. Wayne Gordon was one of the first educators to describe the hidden curriculum—the "informal school system" that affects what is learned.[28] Gordon argued that students' achievement and behavior are related to their status and roles in school; he also suggested that informal and unrecognized cliques of students control much of adolescent performance both inside and outside of school. These cliques or factions are sometimes in conflict with the formal school curriculum, with textbooks, and with classroom rules.

The hidden curriculum also includes the strategies adopted by students to outwit and outguess their teachers. According to John Holt, "successful" students become cunning strategists in a game of beating the system.[29] Experience has taught these students that trickery and even occasional dishonesty pay off. The implication is that teachers must become more sensitive to students' needs and feelings in order to minimize counter-productive behavior. A school that encourages personal freedom and cooperative group learning—instead of competitive individualization, lesson recitation, "right" answers, and textbook/ teacher authority—is more conducive to learning because the atmosphere is free of trickery and dishonesty. Or so the argument goes.

Another interpretation of the hidden curriculum suggests that some intentional school behavior is not formally recognized in the curriculum or discussed in the classroom because of its sensitivity or because teachers do not consider it important. At the same time, students sometimes see what is taught as phony, antiseptic, or unrelated to the real world. For example, certain ethnic or minority groups are discussed in a derogatory manner in some homes. This raises several questions. Should curriculum specialists or teachers try to suppress the hidden curriculum in order to further the purposes of the school? Or should they try to incorporate it into school life? At what age is the student mature enough to discuss such sensitive topics as racial and ethnic stereotypes? A student-oriented school, some educators contend, would try to reduce the disparity between the student's world outside of school and that within.[30]

Humanistic Curriculum

Like many other modern curriculum developments, humanistic education was a reaction to the emphasis on cognitive learning in the late fifties and early sixties. Terry Borton, a Philadelphia schoolteacher, was one of the first to write about this movement. He contended that education in the seventies had only two major purposes: subject mastery and personal growth.[31] Nearly every school's statement of objectives includes both purposes, but Borton saw the objectives related to personal growth and to values, feelings, and the happy life as "only for show. Everyone knows how little schools have done about [them]."[32] Borton believed that the time had come for schools to put their noble phrases about children's social and personal interests into practice.

In his best-selling book, *Crisis in the Classroom*, Charles Silberman also advocated the humanizing of U.S. schools.[33] He charged that schools are repressive, teaching students docility and conformity. He believed that schools must be reformed, even at the price of deemphasizing cognitive learning. He suggested that elementary schools adopt the methods of the British infant schools. At the secondary level, he suggested independent study, peer tutoring, and community and work experiences.

The humanistic model of education stems from the human potential movement in psychology. Within education it is rooted in the work of Arthur Jersild, who linked good teaching with knowledge of self and students, and in the work of Arthur Combs and Donald Snygg, who explored the impact of self-concept and motivation on achievement.[34]

Combs and Snygg considered self-concept the most important determinant of behavior.

A humanistic curriculum emphasizes affective rather than cognitive outcomes. Such a curriculum draws heavily on the work of Abraham Maslow and of Carl Rogers.[35] Its goal is to produce "self-actualizing people," in Maslow's words, or "total human beings," as Rogers puts it. The works of both psychologists are larded with such terms as maintaining, striving, enhancing, and experiencing—as well as independence, self-determination, integration, and self-actualization.

Advocates of humanistic education contend that the present school curriculum has failed miserably by humanistic standards, that teachers and schools are determined to stress cognitive behaviors and to control students not for their own good but for the good of adults.[36] Humanists emphasize more than affective processes; they seek higher domains of consciousness. But they see the schools as unconcerned about higher planes of understanding, enhancement of the mind, or self-knowledge. Students must therefore turn to such out-of-school activities as drugs, yoga, transcendental meditation, group encounters, T-groups, and psychotherapy.

Humanists would attempt to form more meaningful relationships between students and teachers; they would foster student independence and self-direction and promote greater acceptance of self and others. The teacher's role would be to help learners cope with their psychological needs and problems, to facilitate self-understanding among students, and to help them develop fully.

A drawback to humanist theory is its lack of attention to cognitive learning and intellectual development. When asked to judge the effectiveness of their curriculum, humanists generally rely on testimonials and subjective assessments by students and teachers. They may also present such materials as students' paintings and poems or talk about "marked improvement" in student behavior and attitudes. They present very little empirical evidence, however, to support their stance.

The subject-centered curriculum and the student-centered curriculum represent two extremes on a continuum. Most schooling in the U.S. falls somewhere in between—effecting a tenuous balance between subject matter and student needs, between achievement outcomes and learning climate.

NOTES

1. These two terms were coined by Theodore Brameld in *Patterns of Educational Philosophy* (New York: Holt, 1950).

2. Robert M. Hutchins, *The Higher Learning in America* (New Haven, Conn.: Yale University Press, 1936).

3. Arthur Bestor, *The Restoration of Learning* (New York: Knopf, 1956).

4. Philip H. Phenix, "The Disciplines as Curriculum Content," in A. Harry Passow, ed., *Curriculum Crossroads* (New York: Teachers College Press, 1962), p. 64.

5. See the annual Gallup polls published in the December 1975, October 1976, October 1977, September 1978, September 1979, and September 1980 issues of *Phi Delta Kappan.*

6. Ben Brodinsky, "Back to the Basics! The Movement and Its Meaning," *Phi Delta Kappan,* March 1977, pp. 522–27; Chris Pipho, "Minimum Competency Testing in 1978: A Look at State Standards," *Phi Delta Kappan,* May 1978, pp. 585–87; and Rodney P. Riegel and Ned B. Lovell, *Minimum Competency Testing* (Bloomington, Ind.: Phi Delta Kappa Educational Foundation, 1980).

7. James L. Jarrett, "I'm for Basics, But Let Me Define Them," *Phi Delta Kappan,* December 1977, pp. 235–39; and Richard M. Jaeger and Carol K. Title, eds., *Minimum Competency Achievement Testing* (Berkeley, Calif.: McCutchan, 1979).

8. Brodinsky, op. cit.; Pipho, op. cit.; and Michael Zieky and Samuel Livingston, *Manual for Setting Standards on the Basic Skills Assessment Tests* (Princeton, N.J.: Educational Testing Service, 1977).

9. Jarrett, op. cit.; and Martin Mayer, "Higher Education for All?" *Commentary,* February 1973, pp. 37–47.

10. Joyce E. Johnson, "Back to Basics? We've Been There 150 Years," *Reading Teacher,* March 1979, pp. 644–46; and Ellen V. Leininger, "Back to Basics: Concepts and Controversy," *Elementary School Journal,* January 1979, pp. 167–73.

11. Gene V. Glass, "Minimum Competence and Incompetence in Florida," *Phi Delta Kappan,* May 1979, pp. 602–5; and Arthur E. Wise, "Minimum Competency Testing: Another Case of Hyper-Rationalization," *Phi Delta Kappan,* May 1979, pp. 596–98.

12. New York is the only state currently insisting that high-school-level material be included in the minimum competences required of graduating students. This requirement will prevent several thousand New York students from graduating.

13. In Florida, a federal court postponed for an interim period the use of competency tests for graduation, because the tests seemed to be punishing the victims of past discrimination. The court did not find the test to be racially or culturally biased, however.

14. John Dewey, *The Child and the Curriculum* (Chicago: University of Chicago Press, 1902), pp. 8, 9.

15. John Dewey, *Art and Experience* (New York: Capricorn Books, 1934).

16. A number of these early experimental schools are discussed in detail by John Dewey and his daughter Evelyn in *Schools of Tomorrow,* published in 1915. Another good source is the 1926 yearbook of the National Society for the Study of Education, a two-volume work titled *The Foundations of Curriculum and Techniques of Curriculum Construction.* Lawrence Cremin's *The Transformation of the School,* published in 1961, is still another good source. Finally, Ohio State's Laboratory School is best summarized in a 1938 book titled *Were We Guinea Pigs?* written by the senior class.

17. A. S. Neill, *Summerhill: A Radical Approach to Child Rearing* (New York: Hart, 1960).

18. See Edgar Z. Friedenberg, *The Vanishing Adolescent* (Boston: Beacon, 1959); Paul Goodman, *Growing up Absurd* (New York: Random House, 1960) and *Compulsory Mis-Education* (New York: Horizon Press, 1964); and John Holt, *How Children Fail* (New York: Pitman, 1964) and *How Children Learn* (New York: Delta, 1972).

19. See George Dennison, *The Lives of Children: The Story of the First School* (New York: Random House, 1969); James Herndon, *The Way It Spozed to Be* (New York: Simon & Schuster, 1969); Ivan Illich, *Deschooling Society* (New York: Harper & Row, 1971); Herbert R. Kohl, *The Open Classroom* (New York: Random House, 1969) and *On Teaching* (New York: Schocken, 1976); and Jonathan Kozol, *Free Schools* (Boston: Houghton Mifflin, 1972).

20. William H. Kilpatrick, "The Project Method," *Teachers College Record,* September 1918, pp. 319–35.

21. Ellsworth Collings, ed., *An Experiment with a Project Curriculum* (New York: Macmillan, 1923). Another description of the activity-centered program was provided by Harold Rugg and Ann Shumaker, *The Child-Centered School: An Appraisal of the New Education* (Yonkers, N.Y.: World Book, 1928).

22. See *American Youth in the Mid-Seventies* (Washington, D.C.: National Association of Secondary School Principals, 1973); James S. Coleman et al., *Youth: Transition to Adulthood,*

Report of the Panel on Youth of the President's Science Advisory Committee (Chicago: University of Chicago Press, 1974); National Commission on the Reform of Secondary Education, *The Reform of Secondary Education* (New York: McGraw-Hill, 1973); *The New Secondary Education, a Phi Delta Kappa Task Force Report* (Bloomington, Ind.: Phi Delta Kappa, 1976); and U. S. Office of Education, *Report of the National Panel of High School and Adolescent Education* (Washington, D.C.: U.S. Government Printing Office, 1974) and *The Education of Adolescents* (U.S. Government Printing Office, 1976).

23. Mario D. Fantini, *The Reform of Urban Schools* (Washington, D.C.: National Education Association, 1970).

24. Harold Benjamin, *The Saber-Tooth Curriculum* (New York: McGraw-Hill, 1939).

25. Ibid., pp. 43, 44.

26. John Dewey, *Experience and Education* (New York: Macmillan, 1928).

27. See Donald E. Orlosky and B. Othanel Smith, *Curriculum Development: Issues and Ideas* (Chicago: Rand McNally, 1978); Louis Rubin, ed., *Curriculum Handbook: The Disciplines, Current Movements, and Instructional Methodology* (Boston: Allyn & Bacon, 1977); and Daniel Tanner and Laurel Tanner, *Curriculum Development: Theory into Practice*, 2nd ed. (New York: Macmillan, 1980).

28. C. Wayne Gordon, *The Social System of the High School* (Glencoe, Ill.: Free Press, 1957).

29. Holt, *How Children Fail.*

30. Mario D. Fantini and Gerald Weinstein, *The Disadvantaged Child* (New York: Harper & Row, 1968); Robert Goldhammer, *Clinical Supervision* (New York: Holt, 1969); and Louis E. Raths et al., *Values and Teaching,* 2nd ed. (Columbus, OH.: Merrill, 1978).

31. Terry Borton, *Reach, Touch, and Teach* (New York: McGraw-Hill, 1970).

32. Ibid., p. 28.

33. Charles A. Silberman, *Crisis in the Classroom* (New York: Random House, 1971).

34. Arthur T. Jersild, *In Search of Self* (New York: Teachers College Press, 1952) and *When Teachers Face Themselves* (New York: Teachers College Press, 1955); and Arthur Combs and Donald Snygg, *Individual Behavior,* 2nd ed. (New York: Harper & Row, 1959). See also Arthur Combs, ed., *Perceiving, Behaving, Becoming, 1962 Yearbook* (Washington, D.C.: Association for Supervision and Curriculum Development, 1962).

35. Abraham H. Maslow, *Toward a Psychology of Being* (New York: Van Nostrand Reinhold, 1962) and *Motivation and Personality,* 2nd ed. (New York: Harper & Row, 1970); and Carl R. Rogers, *Client-Centered Therapy* (Boston: Houghton Mifflin, 1951), *On Becoming a Person* (Boston: Houghton Mifflin, 1961), and *On Becoming* (New York: Delacorte, 1979).

36. Jack R. Frankel, *How to Teach About Values* (Englewood Cliffs, N.J.: Prentice-Hall, 1977); and Richard H. Willer, ed., *Humanistic Education: Visions and Realities* (Berkeley, Calif.: McCutchan, 1977).

CHAPTER 19

The Status of the State Curriculum

Since adoption of a statewide curriculum—the essential elements—in 1984, Texas has continued to increase the rigor of student knowledge and skills and raise the standards of student achievement. The state promoted these aims through:

- updating the essential elements through the textbook alignment process;
- phasing out low-level courses, such as Fundamentals of Mathematics; and
- increasing graduation requirements.

The 74th Texas Legislature in 1995 further endorsed this course of action by enacting a new law that established a required curriculum for kindergarten through Grade 12, consisting of a foundation curriculum including:

- English language arts;
- mathematics;
- science; and
- social studies, consisting of Texas, United States, and world history, government, and geography;

and an enrichment curriculum including:

- to the extent possible, languages other than English;
- health;
- physical education;
- fine arts;

Reprinted with permission from *1998 Comprehensive Biennial Report on Texas Public Schools: A Report to the 76th Texas Legislature* from the Texas Education Agency, 1998.

- economics, with emphasis on the free enterprise system and its benefits;
- career and technology education; and
- technology applications.

TEXAS ESSENTIAL KNOWLEDGE AND SKILLS (TEKS)

The 74th Texas Legislature also directed the State Board of Education (SBOE) to identify the essential knowledge and skills of each subject area with the direct participation of educators, parents, business and industry representatives, and employers.

During 1995–97, teams composed of representatives of each of these groups drafted curricula for each content area and grade level, kindergarten through Grade 12, such that the knowledge and skills would:

- ensure rigor in the curriculum;
- articulate what all students should know and be able to do;
- specify the levels of performance expected of students at particular grade levels; and
- ensure that the knowledge and skills meet the learning needs of all students.

Upon completion of the teams' work, the SBOE reviewed and revised the team's submissions and adopted the Texas Essential Knowledge and Skills (TEKS). The SBOE adopted the TEKS in Algebra I, Geometry, and Algebra II in July 1996; the SBOE adopted the remaining TEKS in April and July 1997.

The TEKS, codified in the Texas Administrative Code, Title 19 (19 TAC), Chapters 110–128, became effective in all content areas and grade levels on September 1, 1998. They replaced 19 TAC Chapter 75. Curriculum, Subchapters B–D, which contained the essential elements and which the SBOE repealed in May 1998.

By law and SBOE rule, the TEKS in the foundation areas of English language arts and reading, mathematics, science, and social studies are required to be used for instruction. Those in the enrichment areas are to be used to guide instruction. Thus, schools have more flexibility in the enrichment areas than they did under the essential elements. Another distinction between the previous curriculum and the TEKS is that whereas the essential elements stated what "students shall be provided opportunities" to learn, the TEKS specify the knowledge and skills that students will achieve, and they detail the expectations for every student. Key factors in the TEKS for each subject area are outlined later in this chapter.

To assist schools in implementing the TEKS and the public in having access to them, the TEKS are being widely distributed, and professional development is available from many sources.

Distribution of the TEKS

The agency distributed a printed copy and a CD-ROM containing the TEKS to every district and campus office, regional education service center, institution of higher education, and appropriate professional association. The TEKS are also available on the Agency web site. The Agency also distributed informational brochures on the foundation curriculum TEKS in Grades K–5 to elementary schools to be shared with parents. The TEKS are available for purchase in print and in CD-ROM.

Professional Development in the TEKS

The implementation of the TEKS in classrooms, replacing the essential elements that have been in effect since the 1985–86 school year, requires significant preparation of teachers and other educators, who are expected to raise standards, revise lesson plans, and make other adjustments. To accomplish this task, Centers for Educator Development (CEDs) in the foundation areas and statewide centers in some enrichment areas have developed and disseminated supporting materials and training. For instance, "TEKS for Leaders," a one-day seminar for district and campus administrators, pro-

vides an in-depth introduction to the TEKS and methods for planning to teach them. Many of the centers are also establishing web sites that maintain a common navigational system enabling teachers and administrators easy access to current information and materials that support the TEKS and other aspects of their respective programs. Regional education service centers also provide extensive training in the TEKS. In addition, materials for many areas in which textbooks are not yet adopted are available for teachers' use.

THE TEKS IN THE SUBJECT AREAS

English Language Arts and Reading

The TEKS in reading and English language arts emphasize such important basic skills as handwriting, spelling, grammar, language usage, and punctuation. Through listening, speaking, reading, writing, viewing and representing, Texas students use their skills in reading and language arts in purposeful ways. Texas students at all grade levels are asked to inquire into important subject areas, to make connections across books and content, to evaluate others' work as well as their own, to synthesize information gleaned from text and talk, and to produce their own error-free texts and visual representations.

The curriculum also continues an emphasis on a balanced approach to reading instruction. Students learning to read are assessed for their ability to segment and manipulate phonemes in spoken language as well as their ability to understand the relationship between letters and sounds. Instruction in the area of word identification is balanced with instructional strategies that emphasize such comprehension strategies as predicting, self-monitoring, and rereading. Students gather these skills in literature-rich classrooms. Future textbook adoptions will reflect the integration of the language arts (listening, speaking, reading, written composition, handwriting, spelling, and mechanics of writing) as well as the balanced approach to reading.

The Texas Education Agency (TEA) awarded approximately $2 million in federal Academics 2000 funds to establish the Texas Center for Reading and Language Arts at The University of Texas at Austin. Through this grant, the center has provided and will continue to provide professional development, instructional materials, and student assessment measures aligned with the TEKS.

All regional education service centers have designated reading liaisons and dyslexia contact persons. The reading liaisons work closely with the

Texas Center for Reading and Language Arts and with the Statewide Initiatives Division at Education Service Center Region XIII. Through professional development institutes in reading, provided by center staff, these reading liaisons assist local districts in the implementation of the TEKS as well as with the Governor's Reading Initiative.

Dyslexia contacts work in collaboration with the statewide dyslexia coordinators at Education Service Center Region X in Dallas. Through professional development efforts led by staff at Region X, these dyslexia contacts are able to provide information and training on a statewide basis.

The TEA field tested and benchmarked an end-of-course examination in English II in Spring 1998 and is scheduled to implement the test during the school year 1998–1999.

NOTE: The schedule for adoption of instructional materials in this subject area and others is outlined in Table 2.

Bilingual Education/English as a Second Language

Bilingual education and second language instruction programs serve students in Grades PK–12 whose primary language is not English. More than 100 languages are spoken in the homes of Texas public school students. Spanish is the language spoken in 93 percent of homes where English is not the primary language. Other frequently reported primary student languages are Vietnamese, Cambodian, Laotian, Chinese, Korean, Japanese, French and German. In 1997–1998, 519,329 limited English proficient (LEP) students were identified in Texas. The number of dual-language programs to develop bilingual literacy in all students continues to increase in all regions of the state.

Bilingual education and English as a second language (ESL) programs seek to ensure that LEP students learn English and succeed academically in school. Students participating in these programs are provided linguistically appropriate instruction. Instruction is cognitively appropriate in that creativity, problem-solving, and other thinking skills are cultivated through mathematics, science, and social studies in the language that students understand.

The TEKS for Spanish Language Arts (SLA) and English as a Second Language are based on the principle that second language learners should be expected to achieve the same high academic standards as native English speakers in our state. To demonstrate that students receiving instruction in Spanish Language Arts or English as a Second Language are learning the same knowledge and skills as students

enrolled in English Language Arts, the SLA/ESL TEKS are placed side-by-side with the TEKS for English Language Arts and Reading.

Since the adoption of the Spanish Language Arts and English as a Second Language TEKS, the TEA has developed two implementation guides in collaboration with Education Service Center Region IV. The guides, titled *Bilingual/ESL TEKS - Elementary Professional Development Manual* and *Bilingual/ESL TEKS - Secondary Professional Development Manual*, explain the structure of the SLA/ESL TEKS document, provide an analysis of the actual content of the document, and provide guidance on how to develop curriculum and lessons. Videotapes showing teachers implementing lessons and using different strategies to teach concepts in a variety of classroom environments were also developed.

The TEA has also created a web site in collaboration with Education Service Center Region IV to support the implementation of the SLA/ESL TEKS. This web site provides information to clarify curriculum and instruction. The toolkits link users to the SLA and ESL TEKS, provide information on professional development, program development, instruction and assessment, resources and technology and includes a 'parents as partners' toolkit to familiarize parents with the program rules and school system.

Texas Reading Initiative

In January 1996, Governor Bush challenged Texans to focus on the most basic of education goals—teaching children to read. The goal the governor set for the state was that all students should be able to read on grade level or higher by the end of third grade and continue to read on grade level or higher throughout their schooling. The TEA, in collaboration with the State Board for Educator Certification, regional education service centers, school districts, and teacher education programs, has undertaken a multifaceted effort aimed at providing resources and knowledge to educators as they undertake the task of teaching children to read.

Defining Good Practice The first step was to clearly identify common ground on reading issues among the diverse range of agencies and organizations in the state with a professional educational interest in and perspectives on reading. In the spring of 1996, the governor assembled representatives from various organizations to try to reach consensus on issues of good reading practice. These educators reached consensus on a set of basic principles for a balanced and comprehensive approach to reading instruction. These principles were published and distributed statewide in a brief pamphlet entitled *Good Practice: Implications for Reading Instruction—A Consensus Document of Texas Literacy Professional Organizations.*

Components of Effective Reading Programs Building on the consensus statement, TEA staff began reviewing the large volume of scientific research on reading in an effort to identify critical components of reading instruction. The resulting booklet titled *Beginning Reading Instruction: Components and Features of a Research-Based Reading Program* serves as a guide for administrators and teachers as they work to meet the governor's reading challenge. The booklet describes 12 essential components of effective beginning reading programs (Table 1) and describes features of classrooms and campuses that support effective beginning reading instruction.

Early Reading Assessment Texas Education Code (TEC), §28.006, enacted by the 75th Texas Legislature, requires school districts to measure the reading skills and comprehension development of students in kindergarten and Grades 1 and 2 beginning with the 1998–99 school year. The use of early data collection allows educators to make informed and appropriate decisions regarding students instructional needs and objectives.

The commissioner adopted several instruments to be used to measure early reading development and made recommendations for administrators, training, and local responsibilities. The TEA distributed the *1998 Reading Instruments Guide* to school districts in May 1998.

The TEA, in collaboration with the Center for Academic and Reading Skills, revised the Texas Primary Reading Inventory (TPRI). The TPRI is an informal, individually administered assessment. The Inventory is designed to provide teachers with an additional tool for collecting data to determine where along the continuum of growth students are progressing as readers. The TPRI consists of a diagnostic screen and an inventory. The reading inventory section includes tasks that ask children to demonstrate their understanding of book and print awareness, phonemic awareness, graphophonemic knowledge, oral reading ability and comprehension development.

TABLE 1   12 Essential Components of Effective Beginning Reading Programs

Children need to have opportunities to:

1. Expand their use and appreciation of oral language through a wide range of activities that involve listening, speaking, and understanding.
2. Expand their use and appreciation of printed language through activities designed to promote recognition of the important role printed language plays in the world around them.
3. Hear good stories and informational books read aloud daily to demonstrate the benefits and pleasures of good reading and to introduce children to new words and ideas.
4. Understand and manipulate the building blocks of spoken language, including phonemic awareness and the concepts of words and sentences.
5. Learn about and manipulate the building blocks of written language, including alphabetic awareness and practice in writing and manipulation of letters to make words and messages.
6. Learn the relationship between the sounds of spoken language and the letters of written language.
7. Learn decoding strategies such as those involving understanding of letter-sound relationships, word families and rhyming patterns, and blending the components of sounded out words, while also being introduced to phonetically irregular words.
8. Write and relate their writing to spelling and reading, with explicit help in understanding spelling conventions and appreciating the importance of correct spelling.
9. Practice accurate and fluent reading in decodable stories that emphasize the particular sound-letter relationships the children are learning.
10. Read and comprehend a wide assortment of books and other texts, with access to materials for self-selected reading that cover a wide range of skill levels and that can be read both during daily classroom time and taken home for reading independently or to family members.
11. Develop and comprehend new vocabulary through reading many diverse materials and direct vocabulary instruction that includes reading aloud and discussing new words as they occur.
12. Learn and apply comprehension strategies as they reflect upon and think critically about what they read through activities such as discussion with other children and reading of more difficult text with the teacher.

Reading Academies Funds were allocated by the 75th Texas Legislature to establish intensive beginning reading programs to assist districts in meeting the governor's challenge. These programs could include the purchase of diagnostic reading instruments, additional library material, instructional material, staff development and instructional staff. In August 1998, 36 school districts or education service centers were awarded funds through the Texas Reading Academies grant program. The grants range in size from approximately $57,000 to $547,000. The grants will be used to create reading programs or academies that offer as much direct intervention with students in prekindergarten through third grade as possible. Recipients of grants will use the funds for a variety of programs including after-school reading academies, professional development for teachers, a prekindergarten and kindergarten language literacy laboratory, and a family partnership.

Spotlighting Reading Excellence In 1996, the Texas Mentor School Network identified a dozen Reading Spotlight Schools that have demonstrated success in teaching elementary students to read. Each of the Spotlight Schools has conducted a self-study analysis matching their reading methods and materials with the essential components of effective reading programs identified in Beginning Reading Instruction: Components and Features of a Research-based Reading Program. The resulting document, titled *Spotlight on Reading: A Companion to Beginning Reading Instruction,* provides an analysis of their success. The Spotlight Schools serve as mentors to other schools with similar student demographics.

Parental Involvement Involving parents in their child's education is especially important in the early years. *Beginning Reading Instruction: Practical Ideas for Parents,* has been developed to provide parents with information and activities to use as they help their children learn to read. The document has been distributed to all elementary school principals and all local PTA presidents.

Focus on Professional Development The Texas Center for Reading and Language Arts was selected to lead the effort to create a coordinated system of teacher education and professional development in the area of language arts. The Center is also conducting research into the nature of phonemic awareness and its implementation in the curriculum. A web site and listserv have been developed to give teachers ready access to up-to-date information and to provide a forum for discussion. The Center is also bringing nationally known reading experts to Texas to serve as resources for the regional education service centers.

Education Service Center Liaisons Each of the 20 education service centers has identified a Texas Reading Initiative liaison. The liaison is responsible for distributing information about the initiative and answering questions from the field. Several training sessions have occurred to inform the liaisons about the latest research in reading instruction and the implications the research has on the classroom. Liaisons worked directly with 245 campuses that were identified as needing assistance with their reading programs in the 1996–97 school year.

T-STAR A series focusing on promising practices in literacy instruction was broadcast over the T-Star network from December 1996 to May 1997. Copies of the series, Creating Lifelong Readers, were distributed to the education service centers. A series planned for the 1998-99 school year will provide information on the early reading assessments and provide an update on the Texas Reading Initiative.

Read to Succeed The 75th Texas Legislature authorized creation of the "Read to Succeed" specialty license plate. The plates will feature student artwork. More than 12,000 elementary students submitted artwork for consideration. Proceeds from the sale of the specialty plate will be dedicated to purchasing early reading diagnostic materials. The "Read to Succeed" license plates are now available and are being distributed through the Department of Transportation.

Reading Summits The Governor's Business Council has organized "reading summits" around the state. The purpose of the summits is to bring together business, community, and education leaders to address the needs of local school districts. The summits also serve as opportunities to disseminate information about current research in beginning reading instruction.

Mathematics The new curriculum standards streamline the mathematics program and raise the level of rigor expected at each grade level and course. Fewer topics are addressed, and they are studied in greater depth at each level than under the essential elements. There are also fewer course options at the high school level now than previously. The high school program is designed to ensure that all students complete a course sequence that is on or above level before exiting high school. Because the SBOE eliminated all low-level high school mathematics courses, all students in Texas are required to take Algebra I and two other credits in mathematics, which can be selected from Geometry, Algebra II or Mathematical Models with Applications. Students can also take advanced mathematics courses including Precalculus, AP Calculus, AP Statistics, International Baccalaureate courses, and independent study courses. As a result of efforts to raise expectations, enrollment in and completion of core mathematics courses for the Recommended High School Program have continued to increase.

Professional development for teachers of mathematics is a critical component of implementing the TEKS. The TEA contracted with the Texas Statewide Systemic Initiative (SSI), at the Charles A. Dana Center at the University of Texas at Austin, to serve as the Center for Educator Development in mathematics. In October 1994, Texas received a four-year grant of $2 million per annum from the National Science Foundation (NSF) to support the Texas Statewide Systemic Initiative (Texas SSI). This project was funded for an additional five years beginning in 1998. Texas provides a $1 million match each year. The SSI developed a Mathematics Toolkit, an Internet resource that consists of a wealth of activities and resources for teachers and administrators designed to clarify and provide information for teaching the TEKS.

Additional professional development training and materials have been developed for mathematics through the Texas Teachers Empowered for Achievement in Mathematics and Science (TEXTEAMS) project funded by the federal Dwight D. Eisenhower Mathematics and Science Education Program. The project has produced professional development modules for all levels of mathematics. Also, professional development institutes have been developed through the project for grades 3–5, grades 6–8, Algebra I, and Geometry. TEXTEAMS professional development will be coordinated through the 20 regional education service centers. These centers will also be instrumental in providing other professional development regarding implementation of the TEKS.

Science

The Science TEKS reflect a shift in science education to include more emphasis on science content. While the essential elements focused entirely on science process skills, the TEKS emphasize both content and process skills. In keeping with the results and recommendations of the Third International Mathematics and Science Study (TIMSS), the science content is focused so that students may investigate each topic in depth. The science skills that are developed are observation, problem solving, and critical thinking. In addition, the TEKS incorporate scientific investigation skills throughout the grades and integrate the science disciplines throughout the elementary and middle school grades. The TEKS also require that all high school science courses devote 40% of their time to laboratory and field work.

Student enrollment in and completion of higher-level science courses continues to increase. The advanced science program consists of the Advanced Placement and the International Baccalaureate courses, which will prepare students for the rigor of college science courses. In addition, six courses offered through career and technology education can now be counted toward meeting high school graduation credits in science, further expanding the options for students.

As with mathematics, the science Center for Educator Development is the Statewide Systemic Initiative (SSI), located at the Charles A. Dana Center at the University of Texas at Austin. The SSI provides training, also called TEXTEAMS, on the science TEKS to science supervisors, regional education service center representatives, and master teachers in a trainer-of-trainer model. The center has also developed a Science Toolkit, a technology-based program that will assist school districts with the development of a local curriculum based on the TEKS. The Toolkit's framework, available on the Internet and CD-ROM, provides schools with access to safety regulations, equipment recommendations, certification requirements, and other components of a quality science program. In addition, the SSI sponsors several other programs that complement the TEKS implementation efforts of the Agency, including an Informal Science Network and Building a Presence for Science. The SSI works closely with the Urban Systemic Initiatives and the newly funded Rural Systemic Initiative.

Other activities also support the establishment and dissemination of quality science programs throughout the state. Regional Collaboratives for Excellence in Science Teaching, funded through the Agency by federal Dwight D. Eisenhower Mathematics and Science Education Program of the U. S. Department of Education, have the goal of empowering teachers to lead systemic reform in science education. This is done through high-quality, sustained, and intensive mentoring that includes 105–130 contact hours with educators and teacher leaders in each of the twenty collaboratives throughout the state. The focus of the staff development has been on strengthening content and pedagogy for teachers. These regional collaboratives also provide staff development on the science TEKS and the new science framework. Many collaboratives offer graduate courses leading to Master's Degrees in Science for the teachers. The Regional Collaboratives have forged strong ties to business partners that enable the collaboratives to provide state-of-the-art technology training to their members.

The Texas Environmental Education Advisory Committee (TEEAC) continues to increase professional development sites for teachers. Over 130 TEEAC sites provide environmental education staff development to Texas teachers. TEEAC representatives also receive training in the implementation of the new science TEKS. The Eye on Earth television program produced by the T-STAR television network provides teachers with resources from state natural resource agencies that will assist implementation of the TEKS.

Social Studies

The social studies TEKS in all grade levels and courses include strands in history; geography; economics; government; citizenship; culture; science, technology, and society; and social studies skills. The eight strands are intended to be integrated for instructional purposes with the history and geography strands establishing a sense of time and a sense of place. The skills strand, in particular, engages students in a greater depth of understanding of complex content material through analyzing primary and secondary sources and applying critical-thinking and decision-making skills. In addition, the science, technology, and society strand provides students with an opportunity to evaluate how major scientific and technological discoveries and innovations have affected societies throughout history.

A variety of elective courses is included in the social studies TEKS. For example, Special Topics in Social Studies and Social Studies Research Methods are one-semester elective courses. Students may repeat these courses with different course content for state graduation credits. Another new elective course is Social Studies Advanced Studies developed for students who are pursuing the Distinguished Achievement Program (DAP). This course is intended to guide students as they develop, research, and present the mentorship or independent study advanced measure of the DAP.

As in the other content areas, the Social Studies TEKS are more specific and clearer than were the Essential Elements. An example of the increased specificity of the social studies TEKS can be seen by comparing the requirements at Grade 4 from the EEs and from the TEKS regarding the Texas Revolution. Whereas the EEs stated that students should have the opportunity to "explain basic facts about the founding of Texas as a republic and state," the TEKS state that students should "analyze the causes, major events, and effects of the Texas Revolution, including the battles of the Alamo and San Jacinto."

To provide social studies educators with the professional development necessary to implement the new TEKS, the TEA established the Social Studies Center for Educator Development (SSCED), jointly directed by staff at Texas A&M University and Education Service Center Region VI. The SSCED has worked with teams of trainers from each of the 20 education service centers. Training for the teams has centered on appropriate content and pedagogy that supports the social studies TEKS, including the integration of technology into classroom instruction. Currently under development is a social studies framework that will provide additional assistance with the implementation of the TEKS.

Collaborative projects have begun between TEA social studies staff and a number of organizations desiring to provide curriculum materials and professional development opportunities for social studies teachers. These include the Texas Environmental Education Advisory Committee, the Institute of Texan Cultures, the Fort Worth Museum of Science and History, and the Lyndon Baines Johnson National Historic Park.

Economics with Emphasis on the Free Enterprise System and Its Benefits

One-half credit in Economics with Emphasis on the Free Enterprise System and Its Benefits is required in all graduation plans. The TEKS for the high school economics course reflect an emphasis on the nature of economics, the American free enterprise system and its benefits, the relationship between government and the American economic system, and international economic relations.

Languages Other Than English

The development of meaningful language proficiency remains the goal for programs in Languages Other Than English (LOTE). Program emphasis is on the development of the linguistic skills of listening, speaking, reading, and writing, and in the knowledge of culture and language. The TEKS for LOTE are described within the five areas of communication, cultures, connections, comparisons, and communities and reflect performance expectations for various lengths of learning sequences.

In addition to adoption of the TEKS, several initiatives have been undertaken. These are:

- *A Texas Framework for Languages Other Than English,* a curriculum framework developed to help teachers in schools implement the TEKS,
- *Professional Development for Language Teachers,* a document that identifies appropriate staff development models for inservice LOTE teachers implementing the TEKS,
- *Preparing Language Teachers to Implement the TEKS for Languages Other Than English,* a document

that delineates high standards for preservice LOTE teachers and programs that prepare them, and

• The Center for Educator Development in Languages Other Than English, a resource site to assist with the professional development of LOTE educators in the implementation of the TEKS.

An agreement among the TEA, the State Board for Educator Certification, and Spain's Ministry of Education and Culture has established several programs that provide Texas school districts opportunities to alleviate teacher shortages in specific content areas and teachers and students opportunities to initiate cultural exchanges.

The Languages Other Than English program in Texas schools has experienced moderate growth in enrollment at most levels in most languages, with significant increases in Spanish. New instructional materials were adopted for exploratory languages, French, German, Latin, and Spanish.

Health Education

The primary goal of the health education TEKS is to assist in the development of health literacy among students. Health literacy is the ability to obtain and understand health information to use it in ways that enhance health. Many serious health issues, including tobacco use, alcohol, and other drug use, unhealthy dietary behaviors, physical inactivity, and sexual behaviors that contribute to unintended pregnancy and sexually transmitted diseases, are established during youth and extend into adulthood. The aims of health education are to prevent such behaviors and to improve the health status of adolescents and adults. Prior to adoption of the TEKS, the SBOE adopted high school health textbooks in November 1993 that became available for classroom use at the beginning of the 1995–96 school year.

A statewide center for TEKS implementation in health education has been established at Texas A&M University. The center is developing a video series and instructional manual that districts will be able to use as part of their health education instruction. The video series will showcase examples of Texas school districts using TEKS as a curriculum framework. The instructional manual will be a collection of detailed instructional activities designed to correlate to the TEKS. These materials will be complete in August 1999 and ready for classroom use in September 1999. Also, the video series and instructional manual are designed for use at regional education service centers as a TEKS training component and at universities as a teaching tool in preservice programs.

Senate Bill 162, 75th Legislature, amended TEC, §28.002, to state that "the State Board of Education, in consultation with the Texas Department of Health and the Texas Diabetes Council, shall develop a diabetes education program that a school district may use in the health curriculum".

To comply with this statute, the Texas Department of Health and the Texas Diabetes Council recommend the Child and Adolescent Trial for Cardiovascular Health (CATCH) materials developed by the National Heart Lung and Blood Institute as a program that a school district may use in the health curriculum. CATCH materials are recommended based on age appropriateness, comprehensiveness, continuity of instruction, compliance with national school health education standards, cost effectiveness, attention to diabetes risk factors, proven effective behavioral changes, compliance with existing physical education requirements, and simple integration into existing activities.

Physical Education

Physical inactivity is one of six categories of priority health-risk behaviors that contribute to serious health problems in the population. According to research reported in the U. S. Surgeon General's report on Physical Activity and Health in 1996, 60 percent of adults do not achieve the recommended amount of regular physical activity. The TEKS in Physical Education were adopted to help address these challenges in Texas.

The TEKS emphasize traditional concepts, such as movement skills, physical fitness, and social development, as well as enjoyment of physical activities. The TEKS encourage physical education instructors to address additional wellness components, such as nutrition, safety, and making health decisions. The TEKS implementation project mentioned under Health Education also includes a video series and instructional manual involving physical education at all grade levels.

In addition, the SBOE adopted a textbook in *Physical Education called Foundation of Personal Fitness*. The textbook, which became available for classroom use in September 1997, focuses on teaching students about becoming fit for a lifetime.

Fine Arts

The subject areas encompassed by the fine arts are art, music, theatre, and dance. The TEKS in these subject areas are organized into four strands—perception, expression, historical heritage, and evaluation. At the high school level, courses provide choices for students who are studying the arts as a lifelong interest or entering a field of the arts as a career. One credit in a fine arts course is required for graduation in both the Recommended High School and the Distinguished Achievement Programs.

Beginning in the 1998–99 school year, a Center for Professional Development in the Fine Arts will be established to support TEKS implementation. The center will serve as a coordinated statewide fine arts network to support leadership in each of the four fine arts areas. Teachers and administrators will be able to obtain a variety of TEKS information, relating to general awareness about the knowledge and skills or incorporating them into effective instruction. TEA, in collaboration with Education Service Center Region XX, is developing products, processes, and strategies to assist Texas teachers in increasing student achievement in fine arts content. Regional education service centers and professional associations are expected to participate in activities of the center, including disseminating materials and conducting statewide professional development.

Technology Applications

The Technology Applications TEKS specify student proficiencies for grades kindergarten through 12. The Technology Applications TEKS were developed in response to the *Long-Range Plan for Technology, 1996–2010,* that called for the establishment of expectations for technology proficiencies by students in kindergarten through Grade 12, including computer-related skills that meet standards for each high school graduate by the year 2000 (TEC, §32.001). This is the first time in Texas that a comprehensive K–12 curriculum has focused on what students should know and be able to do through the use of computers and other related technology.

The Technology Applications TEKS expand on the keyboarding recommendations at the elementary level, computer literacy requirement at the middle school, and computer science and other courses offered at the high school. This required enrichment curriculum focuses on creating, accessing, manipulating, utilizing, communicating, and publishing information during the learning process. It is built on the premise that students acquire technology applications knowledge and skills in a continuum beginning at the elementary level and continuing through Grade 12 and that they apply them to other curriculum areas at all grade levels.

For grades K–8, the Technology Applications TEKS are organized by benchmarks rather than by grade levels. Benchmark years are grades 2, 5 and 8. Interim grade-level expectations are local definitions of strategies that build toward student success. The high school TEKS are defined in eight courses

that give students opportunities for continued development of advanced technology knowledge and skills. All students beginning with the freshmen class of 1997–1998 must have one technology applications graduation credit under all graduation plans.

To assist educators in implementing the Technology Applications TEKS, the Texas Center for Educational Technology (TCET) at the University of North Texas, with support from the TEA, has developed a project called Sharing Technology Applications Resources with Teachers (START). The resources in the START package are available in multiple formats and are designed to assist educators in implementing the Technology Applications TEKS and integrating them across the foundation and enrichment curriculum. The package includes planning and professional development resources for using technology in schools.

Several resources, highlighted in the START package, support the Technology Applications TEKS and the integration of technology throughout all curriculum areas. In addition to various local, state, and federal sources, the technology allotment has provided $30 per student per year since 1992. With this allotment, schools can buy hardware, software, and training. In addition, grant opportunities are available from many sources, including the Telecommunications Infrastructure Fund and the Technology Literacy Challenge Fund.

Through Technology Preview and Training Centers at regional education service centers, district personnel receive hands-on experience and an orientation to state-of-the-art technologies for use in the classroom. They also receive training and staff development on the integration of technology into the teaching and learning process. Technology Institutes, summer camps, and other staff development opportunities are available through the ESCs. Staff development is also available via T-STAR satellite programming and TETN video conferencing.

Career and Technology Education

The subject areas encompassed by career and technology education are home economics education, agricultural science and natural resources education, trade and industrial education, technology education/industrial technology education, marketing education, business education, and health science technology education. The TEKS for each program area within career and technology address rigorous and relevant academic skills that students need for continuing education and employment. Whenever possible, the TEKS include interdisciplinary content. Most career and technology TEKS were designed to include components that encourage students to use technology.

Strategies to assist school districts in implementing the TEKS have included web sites, TEKS implementation guides for each career and technology subject area, regional and statewide workshops, and week-long summer conferences for career and technology educators, counselors, and administrators. The workshops and conferences provided participants with information on broad educational initiatives as well as in their specific subject areas. Participants also received training in recent technological advances related to program disciplines, and current information on state and federal rules and regulations.

In addition to development of the TEKS, the agency developed the *State Plan for Career and Technology Education* as required in TEC, §29.182. The plan is based on the statutory goals for career and technology education in TEC, §29.181.

The plan was developed as a guide to assist school districts in their efforts to offer effective career and technology education programs that prepare students for further education and eventual employment. The plan rests on the premise that career and technology education should complement and enhance rigorous academic preparation by enabling students to apply academic principles to a variety of community and career situations. The plan strongly supports local control of Texas public schools by offering strategies school districts may choose to implement based on local needs and decisions.

During the 1996–98 biennium, enrollment in secondary career and technology education programs rose, from 626,783 during the 1995–96 school year to 667,350 during the 1997–98 school year (unduplicated numbers).

Kindergarten and Prekindergarten Education

The TEKS for kindergarten are found in the Texas Administrative Code for each content area (excluding Career and Technology Education). The placement of kindergarten TEKS under each discipline represents a change from the essential elements which were placed under four developmental domains—social/emotional development, intellectual development, aesthetic development, and physical development. This organizational change from developmental domains under the essential elements to subject area-specificity under the TEKS still allows for an integrated developmental approach to the kindergarten curriculum. The kindergarten TEKS focus on academic content of what five-year-

olds are expected to know and be able to do and apply to both full- and half-day programs.

Although essential elements had been adopted for students in prekindergarten in the past, there are not TEKS for this grade level. TEC, §29.153, requires that prekindergarten programs be designed to develop skills necessary for success in the regular public school curriculum, including language, mathematics, and social studies.

Because of the diversity of prekindergarten programs in the state and because the authority for these programs resides at the local level, school districts are encouraged to design these programs to best meet the needs of their students in the development of these skills. Although the essential elements for students in prekindergarten are no longer in effect, districts may consider using them as guidelines.

SCHOOL LIBRARIES

In May 1997, the Texas State Library, in consultation with the State Board of Education, adopted new standards for school libraries. These standards identify elements of the library program essential to assist students in accessing, evaluating, and using information.

In addition to helping students achieve these standards, school library programs support both integration of technology into the curriculum and teaching of the Technology Applications TEKS. Student expectations that can appropriately be taught collaboratively by librarians and classroom teachers have been identified in the foundation curriculum. In addition, the school library program, especially at the K–8 level, focuses on three strands in the Technology Applications TEKS: information acquisition, problem solving, and communications.

Over 3,000 campus libraries are using a statewide technology initiative, the Texas Library Connection (TLC), to assist in integrating the use of technology across the curriculum. The Texas Library Connection provides a virtual catalog of over 17 million items held by participating campus libraries. Students in the program can access information resources held in their library, their district, their region, or across the state from their local library, from classrooms, or from home. The Texas Library Connection also provides access to the full text of over 600 magazines, journals, newspapers, periodicals, and other sources through UMI's ProQuest Direct. Britannica Online provides access to the full text of the Encyclopedia Britannica plus hundred of thousands of web links selected by the editors of Encyclopedia Britannica. Additional information is available on the TLC web site at www.tea.state.tx.us/technology/TLC/.

IMPLEMENTING THE TEKS

In addition to the professional development opportunities cited above, implementation of the TEKS will be promoted through adoption of textbooks and through administration of the statewide assessment based on the TEKS. The TEA is also promoting TEKS implementation through T-STAR programs and TETN video conference training sessions with regional education service center staff.

Instructional Materials

Since the 1960s, Texas has followed a mixed subject-area adoption cycle for textbooks and other instructional materials. Under this cycle, books in several different content areas and grade levels were adopted in a given year.

In 1997, the SBOE voted to move to a single subject-area adoption process for kindergarten through grade 12 (Table 2). This process is designed to align adoption of instructional materials in one content area with review of the TEKS in that content area (as well as with the statewide assessment). The adoption cycle was extended from six years to eight years. In keeping with TEC, 31.002, however, textbooks in the foundation areas will be reviewed after six years to determine whether new textbooks are needed sooner.

The transition to this new approach is contained in Proclamation 1997, which focuses on two subject areas—English language arts and reading and science, grades 1–5. Books in this content area fully aligned with the TEKS will enter classrooms in fall 2000. Because the SBOE adopted Algebra I, Geometry, and Algebra II TEKS in 1996, concurrent with adoption of materials in those subjects under the previous plan, textbooks aligned with the TEKS in these subjects are in place in classrooms in fall 1998. Proclamation 1998 focuses solely on English language arts and reading, including Spanish language arts and English as a Second Language.

Texas Assessment of Academic Skills

The Texas Assessment of Academic Skills (TAAS) must be aligned with the TEKS. A key component of the alignment is that the specific skills tested on the TAAS will be stated in the exact language used in the TEKS. In addition, any skills that were previously tested under the former curriculum, the essential elements, but are not found in the TEKS will no longer be tested.

School year 1998–99 was a transitional year in the alignment process. The Spring 1999 TAAS tested only previously tested skills common to both the TEKS and the essential elements. Thus, skills found in the TEKS but not in the essential elements at a particular grade level were not tested in Spring 1999 nor were skills found in the essential elements but not in the TEKS. The test format did not change. Updates on this information, indicating which TEKS are eligible for testing have been delivered to schools.

In 1999–2000, those skills found in the TEKS but not previously tested on TAAS will be integrated into the TAAS. Students taking the TAAS administered in Spring 2000 will be tested on the TEKS that they will have studied during the previous two school years. Complete objectives and measurement specifications, including sample test items, will be distributed to schools prior to that administration.

HIGHLIGHTS OF CHANGES IN CURRICULUM RULES

Adoption of the TEKS and the subsequent repeal of the essential elements necessitated revisions to 19 TAC Chapter 74, *Curriculum Requirements*, to make course titles and other aspects of this chapter consistent with the TEKS. Following is a summary of the changes made in the required curriculum, graduation requirements, and other provisions; the revised rule is effective for students entering grade 9 in 1998–99.

Subchapter A. Required Curriculum

- References to essential elements were replaced with essential knowledge and skills, and courses that no longer exist were deleted and, where appropriate, replaced with courses that exist in the TEKS.
- Requirements to review the curriculum every five years were deleted, enabling the review to be aligned with the textbook adoption cycle.
- The new courses Mathematical Models with Applications and Integrated Physics and Chemistry were added as courses that districts must offer.
- Physical education courses that are no longer offered were replaced by physical education—Foundations of Personal Fitness and at least two of the following:
  - adventure/outdoor education;
  - aerobic activities;
  - individual sports; or
  - team sports.

TABLE 2   K–12 Instructional Materials Adoption Process

Proclamation 1996 **State Adoption 1998** **Implementation 1999–2000** Mathematics, Grades K–8 Mathematics (Spanish), Grades K–6 Geology, Meteorology & Oceanography Aquatic Science World History Studies Technical Theatre I–IV Choir 1–3	**Proclamation 1997** **State Adoption 1999** **Implementation 2000–2001** English Language Arts & Reading, Grades K–1 Reading, Grades 2–3 Spanish Language Arts & Reading, Grades K–1 Spanish Reading, Grades 2–3 Literature, Grades 9–12 Science, Grades 1–5 Science (Spanish), Grades 1–5
Proclamation 1998 **State Adoption 2000** **Implementation 2001–2002** English Language Arts, Grades 2–12 Spanish Language Arts, Grades 2–6 Reading, Grades 4–5 Spanish Reading, Grades 4–5 Literature, Grades 6–8 Spanish Literature, Grade 6 English for Speakers of Other Languages, Grades 9–12 Communication Applications English Language Arts electives	**Proclamation 1999** **State Adoption 2001** **Implementation 2002–2003** Science, Grades 6–12 Science (Spanish), Grade 6
Proclamation 2000 **State Adoption 2002** **Implementation 2003–2004** Social Studies, Grades 1–12 Social Studies (Spanish), Grades 1–6 PreKindergarten Kindergarten *Enrichment* Economics with Emphasis on Free Enterprise	**Proclamation 2001** **State Adoption 2003** **Implementation 2004–2005** *Enrichment:* Health Education, Grades 1–12 Agricultural Science & Technology Education Business Education Home Economics Education Technical Education/Industrial Technology Education Marketing Education Trade & Industrial Education Technology Applications Career Orientation Health Science Technology Applications
Proclamation 2002 **State Adoption 2004** **Implementation 2005–2006** Mathematics, Grades 6–12 Mathematics (Spanish), Grade 6	**Proclamation 2003** **State Adoption 2005** **Implementation 2006–2007** Mathematics, Grades K–5 Mathematics (Spanish), Grades K–5
Proclamation 2004 **State Adoption 2006** **Implementation 2007–2008** *Enrichment* Languages Other than English Fine Arts Physical Education	**Proclamation 2005** **State Adoption 2007** **Implementation 2008–2009** English Language Arts & Reading, Grades K–1 Spanish Language Arts & Reading, Grades K–1 Reading, Grades 2–5 Spanish Reading, Grades 2–5 Literature, Grades 6–12 Spanish Literature, Grade 6

Proclamation 2006
State Adoption 2008
Implementation 2009–10

English Language Arts, Grades 2–12
Spanish Language Arts, Grades 2–6

Proclamation 2007
State Adoption 2009
Implementation 2010–11

Science, Grades 1–12
Science (Spanish), Grades 1–6

Proclamation 2008
State Adoption 2010
Implementation 2011–12

Social Studies, Grades 1–12
Social Studies (Spanish), Grades 1–12
PreKindergarten
Kindergarten

Enrichment

Economics with Emphasis on Free Enterprise

Proclamation 2009
State Adoption 2011
Implementation 2012–13

Enrichment:

Health Education, Grades 1–12
Agricultural Science & Technology Education
Business Education
Home Economics Education
Technical Education/Industrial Technology
Education
Marketing Education
Trade & Industrial Education
Technology Applications
Career Orientation
Health Science Technology Applications

Proclamation 2010
State Adoption 2012
Implementation 2013–14

Mathematics, Grades 6–12
Mathematics (Spanish), Grade 6

Proclamation 2011
State Adoption 2013
Implementation 2014–15

Mathematics, Grades K–5
Mathematics (Spanish), Grades K–5

Proclamation 2012
State Adoption 2014
Implementation 2015–16

Languages Other Than English
Fine Arts
Physical Education

Proclamation 2013
State Adoption 2015
Implementation 2016–17

English Language Arts & Reading, Grades K–1
Spanish Language Arts & Reading, Grades K–1
Reading, Grades 2–5
Spanish Reading, Grades 2–5
Literature, Grades 6–12
Spanish Literature, Grade 6
English for Speakers of Other Languages, Grades K–12

- The language regarding fine arts was changed so that districts must offer courses selected from *at least* two of the four fine arts.
- Courses that previously met the speech requirement were removed, and Communication Applications was added as the only speech course that districts are required to offer.

Subchapter B. Graduation Requirements
Minimum High School Program

- College Board advanced placement and International Baccalaureate courses were added as courses that students may take for required courses.

- English IV (Academic) was deleted; English IV remains.
- Certain course titles were changed. English as a Second Language was replaced by English for Speakers of Other Languages and was made available to immigrant second language learners; United States History was changed to United States History Since Reconstruction; and, Introduction to Speech Communication was changed to Speech Communication.
- The requirement for health was changed to allow students to take either one-half credit of health or one credit of health science technology.
- Communication Applications was added to the list of speech courses available to meet graduation requirements.

- Language was added stating that students can take up to four credits of Reserve Officer Training Corps (ROTC) and one-half credit of driver education as an elective.
- A new one credit technology applications requirement was added beginning during the 1997–1998 school year (applicable to all graduation plans). Students may choose from eight high school technology applications TEKS courses or from selected career and technology education TEKS courses in the areas of business education and technology education.

Recommended High School Program

- Science requirements were changed so that students must choose their three required credits from the following four areas with not more than one credit available from each area:
  - Integrated Physics and Chemistry
  - Biology, AP Biology, or IB Biology
  - Chemistry, AP Chemistry, or IB Chemistry
  - Physics, Principles of Technology I, AP Physics, or IB Physics
- Language was added encouraging students who want to complete this program to take Biology, Chemistry and Physics and to study the foundation areas every year.
- The requirement for health was changed to allow students to take either one-half credit of health or one credit of health science technology.
- In *Option I: mathematics, science, elective* all mathematics course options were deleted except Precalculus, and the number of available science courses was increased.
- Language was added to say that no substitutions are allowed.

Distinguished Achievement Program

- In addition to the changes noted under the Recommended High School Program, the advanced measures were revised, as follows:
- Original research/projects may not be used for more than two of the four advanced measures.
- The provision for licenses was deleted.

Subchapter C. Other Provisions
Award of Credit

- It was made clear that out-of-country transfer students includes foreign exchange students.
- Language was added stating that a course must be considered completed, and credit must be awarded if the student has demonstrated proficiency.
- Language was added stating that students who complete one semester of a two-semester course

can be allowed, in accordance with local policy, to be awarded credit proportionately.

Innovative Courses and Programs Previously approved experimental courses underwent a sunset review during the 1997–1998 school year. The TEA has had a process for approving locally developed "experimental courses," courses designed to enable students to master knowledge, skills, and competencies not included in the essential elements.

Based on the new rules concerning graduation requirements, and based on the adoption of the TEKS, experimental courses, which had been approved in previous years for state credit toward graduation, ceased being approved on August 31, 1998.

"Innovative course" approvals replace experimental courses. During the sunset process for experimental courses, agency staff reviewed requests for approval of innovative courses in the subject areas defined in the foundation and enrichment curriculum. Requests for approval of innovative courses that did not fall within any of the subject areas in the required curriculum were reviewed and approved by the SBOE in May 1998. A total of 160 innovative courses has been approved for instruction in one or more school districts.

School districts may continue to apply for approval of innovative or other locally designed courses to enable students to master knowledge and skills not included in the TEKS. The TEA and the SBOE will continue to review innovative course applications.

ACADEMIC ACHIEVEMENT RECORD

TEC, §28.025, requires student academic achievement records to be on forms adopted by the SBOE. In addition, the statute requires that the adopted forms clearly differentiate between each of the high school diploma programs and identify whether a student received a diploma or a certificate of coursework completion.

During the 1996–97 school year, the forms were reviewed by a task force made up of agency staff and school personnel. The task force was chaired by a representative of one of the education service centers. In the past, the form of the academic achievement record had been very prescriptive. The task force focused on finding ways to allow more flexibility in the design of the forms, while still maintaining standards that would assure accuracy and consistency in student transcripts for use in transfers, for potential employers, or for application for admission to a college or university.

The proposed new forms were pilot-tested during the 1997–98 school year and were subsequently approved by the SBOE for use beginning in the 1998–99 school year. The instructions for completing the Academic Achievement Record were revised to provide alignment to the new forms. Districts were provided with samples of the new transcript forms along with the new Minimum Standards for the Academic Achievement Record in June 1998.

AGENCY CONTACT PERSON

Ann Smisko, Associate Commissioner for Curriculum, Assessment, and Technology, (512) 463-9087

OTHER SOURCES OF INFORMATION

19 Texas Administrative Code (TAC), Chapters 110–128, *Texas Essential Knowledge & Skills* (formats available include print, CD-ROM, and on the TEA web site at www.tea.state.tx.us)

19 TAC Chapter 74, *Curriculum Requirements*

Chapter 74 Handbook (including information on graduation requirements and "frequently asked questions" on Chapter 74 topics)

Chapter 74 *Questions & Answers* (on the TEA web site)

Dyslexia and Related Disorders Handbook

List of Products & Services for TEKS Implementation

Progress Report on Long-Range Plan for Technology, 1988–2000

Long-Range Plan for Technology, 1996–2010

Progress Report on Long-Range Plan for Technology, 1996–2010

The TEA Educator Resources web site at www.tea.state.tx.us/resources/.

EXAMPLES OF TEKS

Secondary

U.S. History

History

- Identify, sequence, and describe major eras, significant dates, events, and individuals in U.S. history from 1877 to the present.
- Analyze political, economic, and social issues in the United States from 1877 to 1898.
- Identify and explain significant events, individuals, and reasons for U.S. emergence as a world power between 1898 and 1920.
- Evaluate the impact of the Progressive Era, reform leaders, and third-party candidates on American Society.
- Analyze causes and effects of significant issues and the influence of significant individuals during the 1920s.
- Identify the reasons for U.S. involvement in WW II, Korea, and Vietnam; analyze the era of the Cold War; evaluate international decisions and their influence on U.S. domestic and foreign policy.
- Describe and evaluate the historical development, leaders, and social impact of the American civil rights movement.

- Create maps, graphs, charts, and models representing various aspects of the United States; explore geographic distributions and patterns shown on geographic tools.

(Continued)

Elementary

English Language Arts & Reading
Language Arts

Listening/Speaking. Students:

- analyze a speaker's message for content, persuasive technique, and tone
- distinguish between a speaker's opinion and verifiable fact
- listen to proficient models of oral reading of classic and contemporary works
- identify how language, such as labels and sayings, reflects regions and cultures

Reading. Students:

- read and comprehend a variety of fifth-grade level texts
- draw inferences from text and support these conclusions and generalizations with evidence from the text
- offer observations, make connections, react, speculate, interpret, and raise questions in response to text
- generate relevant research using multiple sources of information
- demonstrate characteristics of fluent and effective reading

(Continued)

Fifth Grade

EXAMPLES OF TEKS *(Continued)*

Geography

- Analyze, identify, and explain the reasons for and effects of physical, human, and political geographic patterns and boundaries.

- Analyze the effects of changing demographic patterns within the United States resulting from migration and immigration.

- Identify effects of population growth and distribution on the environment; trace the development of the conservation movement.

Economics

- Analyze the influence of property rights, federal legislation, economic policies, and military conflicts on U.S. economic growth between 1870 and 1920.

- Evaluate the effects of the economic cycle from WW I through WW II and the impact of New Deal programs.

- Describe the economic effects of WW II, the Cold War, and private sector expansion on American society; analyze the relationship between international trade policies and the U.S. free enterprise system.

Government

- Evaluate and explain the changes in the role of the government as a result of legislation, international events, and political incidents; predict effects of legislation.

- Evaluate the impact of events on the relationships between the legislative, judicial, and executive branches of the federal government.

- Analyze the reasons for and the effects of 20th-century Supreme Court decisions and constitutional amendments.

Citizenship

- Explain how the right to participate in the democratic process reflects our national identity; describe methods used to expand and protect this right; evaluate means of achieving political equality.

- Describe qualities of effective leadership; evaluate contributions of U. S. political and social leaders; identify contributions of U.S. presidents from Texas.

Cultural

- Describe the arts and cultural activities that reflect the times in which they were created or convey universal themes; describe the influence of cultural movements on American society; analyze the relationship of culture and the economy; explain how popular culture influences the world.

- Explain how the diverse population of the United States (racial, ethnic and religious groups, immigrants, and women) shares, adopts, and adapts native customs and ideologies to form a unique American society.

Science, Technology, and Society

- Explain and analyze the impact of scientific discoveries and technological innovations on U.S. development and how they have affected the nature of work.

(Continued)

Fifth Grade

- use a thesaurus, synonym finder, dictionary, and software to clarify meanings and usage

- support responses to readings by referring to relevant aspects of the text and their own experiences

Writing. Students:

- compose original texts applying the conventions of capitalization, punctuation, grammar, and correct spelling

- compose, organize, and revise letters, essays, records, and research papers

- use suspense, dialogue, and figurative language in original compositions

- write to persuade, argue, and request

- engage in the writing process and refine selected drafts to publish for general and specific audiences

Viewing/Representing. Students:

- describe, interpret, and use visual media to compare ideas and points of view

- analyze, critique, and contrast the messages found in visual media

- produce class newspapers, multimedia reports, and/or short films

NOTE: Students of limited English proficiency (LEP) enrolled in Spanish Language Arts and/or in English as a Second Language will be expected to learn these same knowledge and skills for this grade level; however, students in Spanish Language Arts will learn these skills through their native language, and students in English as a Second Language will apply these skills at their proficiency level in English.

SCIENCE
Third Grade Science

Third Grade

Scientific Investigations in the Field and Laboratory. Students:

- conduct safe, environmentally appropriate, and ethical investigations

- make wise choices in use, conservation, disposal or recycling of materials

Scientific Inquiry and Critical Thinking. Students:

- formulate testable hypotheses and construct reasonable explanations from evidence

- construct simple graphs, tables, maps, models, and charts to organize information

- analyze scientific explanations as to their strengths and weaknesses, using scientific evidence

(Continued)

EXAMPLES OF TEKS *(Continued)*

Social Studies Skills

- Explain and analyze how scientific discoveries and technological innovations are interrelated and continue to change the standard of living in the United States.

- Locate and identify primary and secondary sources; analyze and organize information; explain methods historians use including points of view, frame of reference, and historical context; apply historical inquiry to research, interpret, and use multiple sources of evidence; identify bias; evaluate the validity of a source; use appropriate math skills to interpret social studies information.

- Use social studies terms correctly; use standard grammar; transfer information from one media form to another; communicate social studies information in oral, written, and visual form.

- Use problem-solving and decision-making processes individually and in group settings.

Third Grade

- evaluate the impact of research on scientific thought, society, and the environment

- study the history of science and contributions of scientists

Tools and Models. Students:

- use tools, including calculators, safety goggles, microscopes, sound recorders, clocks, computers, hand-lenses, thermometers, meter sticks, magnets, balances, and compasses

- demonstrate that repeated investigations may increase reliability

Systems. Students:

- observe a simple system and describe the role of various parts

Forces Cause Change. Students:

- measure changes in an object's position when a force is applied

- know Earth's surface can be changed by forces

Physical Properties. Students:

- gather data about temperature, magnetism, and hardness

- identify matter as liquids, solids, and gases

Needs of Living Organisms. Students:

- know that organisms need food, water, light, air, and habitat

- observe organisms with similar needs that compete for resources

- describe environmental changes

- describe how organisms modify their environment

Adaptations. Students:

- analyze how adaptive characteristics help individuals survive

Inherited Traits and Learned Characteristics. Students:

- identify some inherited traits of plants and animals

Processes of the Natural World. Students:

- classify earth materials in local area as renewable, nonrenewable or inexhaustible

- identify properties of soils, such as color and texture

- identify the position of planets in relation to the Sun

CHAPTER 20

Student Performance

In 1998, Texas public school students continued an upward trend in performance by recording substantial gains on the percentages passing the Texas Assessment of Academic Skills (TAAS) tests. The increased passing rates occurred even as the number of students tested rose by over 31,000. The results from the state assessment program provide tangible evidence of continuing achievement as schools work to enable their students to meet the future and its challenges.

This chapter outlines statewide TAAS results for the 1997–1998 academic year, including results for various segments of the student population. To allow an even broader view of the assessment program's history, a five-year comparison of both the percentage passing rates and the Texas Learning Index (TLI) data is included; comparing data from five test administrations (spring 1994 through spring 1998) allows an illustration of four years' worth of gain. Also included are statewide data from the administration of the Spanish TAAS tests and the Biology I and Algebra I end-of-course examinations.

The data in this chapter represent the test results of students not in special education and include results of students in year-round education. Results for students receiving special education services can be found in a separate publication titled *Student Performance Results 1997–1998*, published by the Texas

Education Agency Division of Student Assessment. District and campus-level results can be found in the Academic Excellence Indicator System (AEIS) reports, available through the Division of Communications, or online at www.tea.state.tx.us.

Each year, the agency releases to the public all items on the TAAS and end-of-course tests used to determine student performance. It also provides districts with detailed item analysis reports to help identify strengths and weaknesses in their academic programs.

PERCENT PASSING TAAS

The 1998 TAAS results indicate the continuation of an upward trend in achievement at all grade levels. In **reading,** the percentage of students passing rose across the board, with each grade level now showing passing rates of 85 percent or higher. Reading scores ranged from 85 percent of all students passing at Grades 6, 7, and 8 to 89 percent passing at Grade 4.

In **mathematics,** most grade levels made notable gains, with the most impressive improvement at Grade 8 (an 8-point gain compared to the 1997 results) and at Grade 10 (a 6-point gain). Scores ranged from 78 percent passing at Grade 10 to 89 percent passing at Grade 5.

Writing scores improved at all three grades tested in this subject. Scores ranged from 83 percent passing at Grade 8 to 89 percent passing at Grade 10.

Reprinted with permission from *1998 Comprehensive Biennial Report on Texas Public Schools: A Report to the 76th Texas Legislature* from the Texas Education Agency, 1998.

In addition, every grade level made gains in the **all tests taken** category; for the first time, all grade levels had passing rates in the 70s or above. The percentage of students passing all tests taken (reading and mathematics at Grades 3, 5, 6, and 7 and reading, mathematics, and writing at Grades 4, 8, and 10) ranged from 72 percent at Grades 8 and 10 to 83 percent at Grade 5.

For purposes of comparison across grade levels, the all tests taken category includes the TAAS reading and mathematics tests at Grades 3, 5, 6, and 7 and the reading, writing, and mathematics tests at Grades 4, 8, and 10. The results of the science and social studies tests, administered only to students in Grade 8, are presented separately.

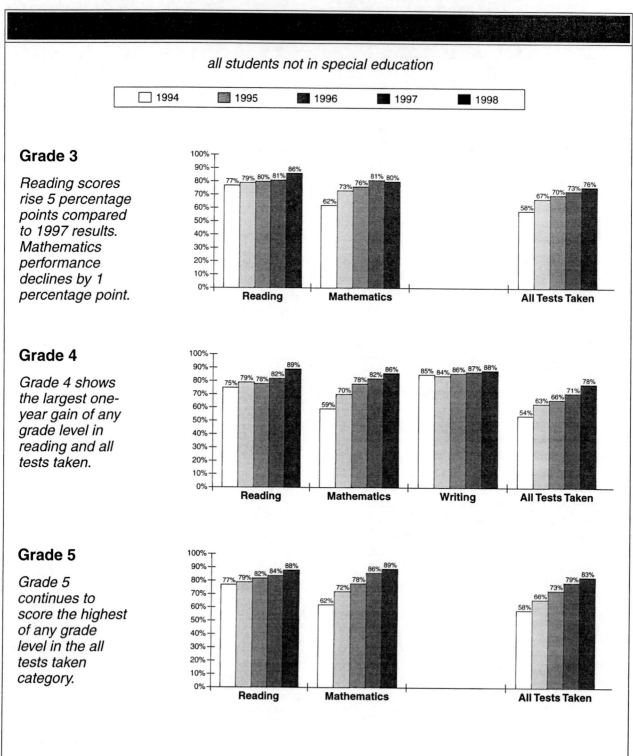

FIGURE 1

all students not in special education

□ 1994   ▨ 1995   ▨ 1996   ■ 1997   ■ 1998

Grade 6

Over four years, Grade 6 gains 26 percentage points in mathematics and 23 percentage points in all tests taken.

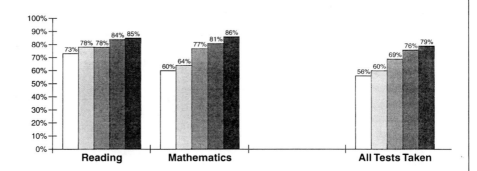

Grade 7

Mathematics scores climb into the 80s this year, while the all tests taken results continue to improve.

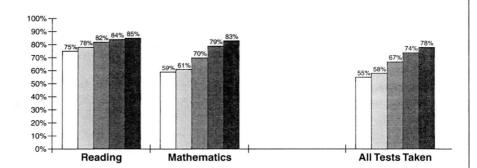

Grade 8

Between 1994 and 1998, Grade 8 exhibits an impressive 26-point rise in the mathematics passing rate.

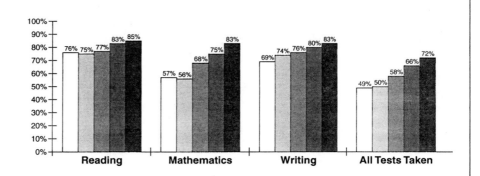

Grade 10

For the first time, the passing rate for Grade 10 in the all tests taken category rises into the 70s.

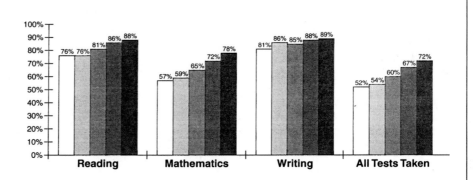

FIGURE 2

(NOTE: Only results of grades 4, 8, and 10 are compared so that writing scores can be included in the comparison).

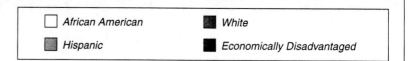

Grade 4

Reading

African American students made the biggest one-year gain, improving 11 percentage points to 80 percent passing in 1998. White students reached 95 percent passing.

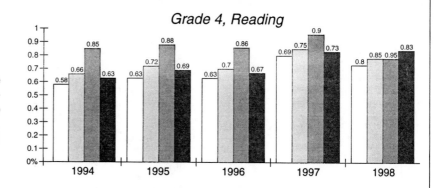

Mathematics

The comparison between 1994 and 1998 shows impressive improvement: 36 percentage points for African American students and 34 points for both economically disadvantaged and Hispanic students.

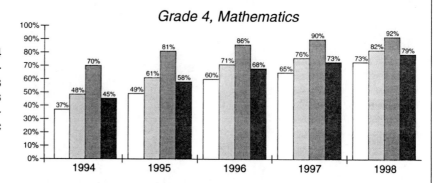

Writing

Scores rose by 5 percentage points over 1997 levels for the African American students, 3 percentage points for economically disadvantaged students, and 2 percentage points for Hispanic students; white students held steady.

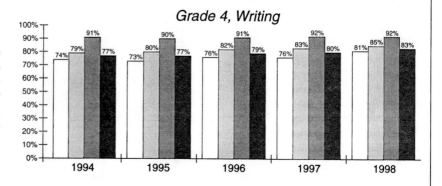

All Tests Taken

All groups showed improvement in 1998. African American students improved their performance to 63 percent passing, an increase of 10 percentage points compared to 1997 and 30 percentage points compared to 1994.

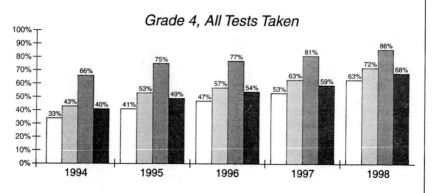

FIGURE 3

Grade 8

Reading

African American and Hispanic students reached 75 percent passing, economically disadvantaged students posted a 74 percent passing rate, and white students reached 94 percent passing. African American students made the greatest four-year gain, with an increase of 15 percentage points.

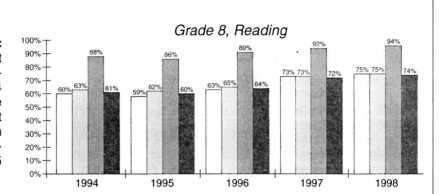

Grade 8, Reading

Mathematics

African American students showed a one-year gain of 13 percentage points; Hispanic and economically disadvantaged students each posted a gain of 11 points. The difference between passing rates of African American students and white students has fallen from 40 percentage points in 1994 to 21 points in 1998.

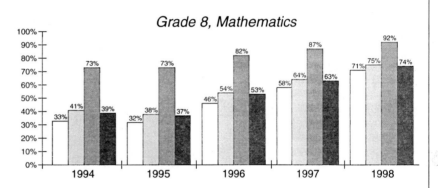

Grade 8, Mathematics

Writing

African American and Hispanic students reached passing levels of 75 percent. Economically disadvantaged students gained 5 points compared to 1997 with 74 percent passing, and white students improved to 91 percent passing.

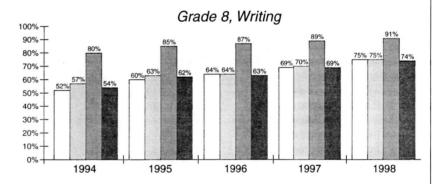

Grade 8, Writing

All Tests Taken *

All groups continue to make substantial gains; however, significant progress remains to be made to ensure that more minority and economically disadvantaged students pass all tests at Grade 8.

*excludes science and social studies results, which are presented separately

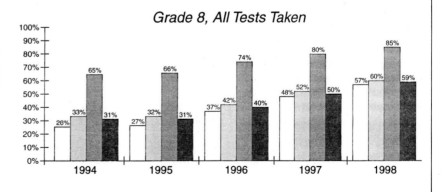

Grade 8, All Tests Taken

Legend: ☐ African American   ■ White   ▨ Hispanic   ■ Economically Disadvantaged

FIGURE 4

303

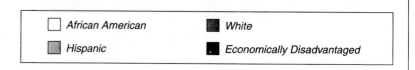

Grade 10 (Exit Level)

Reading

Hispanic and economically disadvantaged students each gained 4 percentage points compared to last year's levels. African American students, at 81 percent passing, exhibited a 3-point gain, while white students' results rose 1 point to reach 95 percent passing.

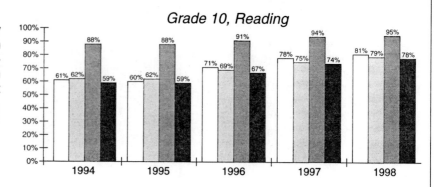

Mathematics

The comparison between 1994 and 1998 shows African American students exhibiting a gain of 28 percentage points and both the Hispanic and economically disadvantaged groups making notable gains. White students gained 18 percentage points over this four-year period.

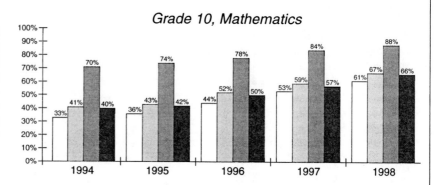

Writing

All groups exhibited passing rates of over 80 percent. Hispanic stu-dents and economically disadvantaged students reached 82 and 81 percent passing, respectively; African American students gained 2 points to reach 84 percent passing, while white students reached 96 percent passing.

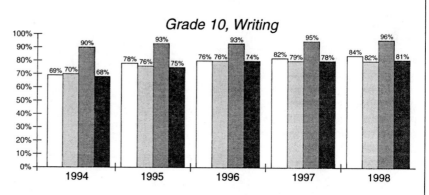

All Tests Taken

Passing rates that stood in the 30–35 percent range in 1994 have risen to almost 60 percent. While this increase is substantial, even more students must pass all sections of the exit-level TAAS, a requirement for graduation.

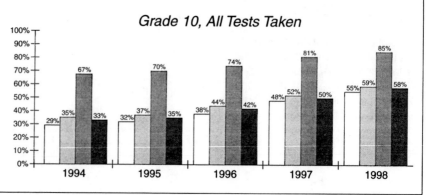

FIGURE 5

TABLE 1 TAAS Passing Results by Special Populations

all students not in special education														
ALL TESTS TAKEN														
LEP Students								**Non-LEP Students**						
						Gain							**Gain**	
	1994	1995	1996	1997	1998	97–98	94–98	1994	1995	1996	1997	1998	97–98	94–98
Grade 3	35	48	55	60	66	6	31	59	68	71	75	77	2	18
Grade 4	32	41	46	49	61	12	29	56	65	68	73	79	6	23
Grade 5	27	35	45	50	61	11	34	60	68	74	81	85	4	25
Grade 6	21	22	27	37	39	2	18	58	63	72	79	83	4	25
Grade 7	16	16	24	32	32	0	16	58	61	69	77	81	4	23
Grade 8*	13	11	15	21	26	5	13	51	52	61	69	75	6	24
Grade 10	14	14	15	22	26	4	12	54	57	62	70	75	5	21
At-Risk Students								**Not At-Risk Students**						
						Gain							**Gain**	
	1994	1995	1996	1997	1998	97–98	94–98	1994	1995	1996	1997	1998	97–98	94–98
Grade 3	32	44	48	55	58	3	26	66	74	77	80	82	2	16
Grade 4	30	37	40	45	55	10	25	69	80	80	84	88	4	19
Grade 5	34	42	47	55	62	7	28	78	84	88	91	93	2	15
Grade 6	30	32	41	49	52	3	22	70	80	86	90	92	2	22
Grade 7	29	29	39	46	47	1	18	73	78	84	89	90	1	17
Grade 8*	25	20	27	33	42	9	17	72	72	78	84	87	3	15
Grade 10	25	31	35	44	49	5	24	69	72	74	81	84	3	15

excludes results of Grade 8 science and social studies TAAS

PERCENT PASSING TAAS: RESULTS BY SPECIAL POPULATION

Table 1 provides aggregate TAAS percent passing results of limited English proficient (LEP) students and those at risk of dropping out of school and compares them to the results of students who are not LEP or at-risk.

Note that a LEP student who is not exempt from state assessments takes the English TAAS unless it is determined locally that the appropriate assessment for that student is the Spanish TAAS (available at Grades 3 through 6). This section presents results of the LEP students who took the English TAAS tests; Spanish TAAS results appear in a later section.

Table 1.1 indicates that LEP students continued making gains in performance at all grades. LEP students' 1998 scores in the *all tests taken* category ranged from 26 percent passing at Grade 8 and Grade 10 to 66 percent at Grade 3. Between 1994 and 1998, the passing rate of Grade 5 LEP students showed the greatest improvement, rising a notable 34 percentage points.

Table 1.1 also shows that at-risk students made gains in performance at all grades. Grade 4 at-risk students exhibited the greatest 1997 to 1998 improvement, rising by 10 percentage points to 55 percent passing all tests taken. Between 1994 and 1998, the passing rate of Grade 5 at-risk students registered the greatest gain, rising 28 percentage points.

GRADE 8 SCIENCE AND SOCIAL STUDIES TESTS

Science

Results of the spring 1998 administration show that, compared to the previous year, passing rates held steady, with 84 percent of all students tested passing (Table 2). This pattern of consistent results from 1997 to 1998 is repeated for most groups of students, although passing rates were down by 1 percentage point for Hispanic students, 5 points for LEP students, and 4 points for at-risk students. When comparing this year's performance to 1995 results, however, a substantial gain is apparent, with African American students posting a gain of 13 points and both the Hispanic and economically disadvantaged groups achieving 11-point gains over this period.

TABLE 2   TAAS Passing Results: Grade 8 Science & Social Studies

	all students not in special education									
	Science					Social Studies				
					Gain					Gain
STUDENT POPULATION	1995	1996	1997	1998	95–98	1995	1996	1997	1998	95–98
All Students	76	77	84	84	8	65	69	67	69	4
African American	56	59	69	69	13	46	51	49	53	7
Hispanic	63	64	75	74	11	48	54	51	53	5
White	90	90	94	94	4	80	83	82	84	4
LEP	34	33	49	44	10	20	25	21	24	4
Non-LEP	79	80	86	86	7	67	72	69	72	5
At-Risk	57	56	66	62	5	39	44	37	39	2
Not At-Risk	91	90	94	94	3	84	85	83	83	-1
Economically Disadvantaged	62	63	73	73	11	47	53	49	52	5
Not Economically Disadvantaged	85	86	91	91	6	75	80	78	80	5

Social Studies

In the spring 1998 administration, 69 percent of all students tested passed; this rate was up 2 percentage points from 1997 levels. Compared to the previous year's passing rate, all ethnic groups, special population groups, and economic groups gained from 2 to 4 percentage points with the exception of the not at-risk group, whose scores held steady. Over the period from 1995 to 1998, the at-risk group's passing rate has remained consistent and the not at-risk group's passing rate has declined by 1 percentage point; all other groups, however, have exhibited gains over this period, ranging from 4-point gains for white and LEP students to a 7-point gain for African American students.

PERCENT PASSING SPANISH TAAS

In spring 1996, the Spanish TAAS reading and mathematics tests at Grades 3 and 4 were benchmarked.

The following year, the Spanish TAAS reading and mathematics tests at Grades 5 and 6 and the Spanish TAAS writing test at Grade 4 were benchmarked. At the time of a benchmark administration, passing rates have not yet been set. As a result, data exist for a one-year comparison of results only at Grades 3 and 4 and only in mathematics and reading.

LEP students who take the Spanish TAAS are not being exempted from the statewide assessment. The students for whom Spanish TAAS is determined to be the appropriate assessment are being tested in the same manner as students taking TAAS in English because both groups must demonstrate performance on the same academic skills in reading, mathematics, and writing.

Results of the spring 1998 administration show notable gains at Grades 3 and 4 (Table 3). In reading, passing rates rose 21 percentage points at Grade 3 to 65 percent passing. Scores at Grade 4 rose 3 percentage points to 39 percent passing.

Gains in mathematics were also dramatic, with double-digit gains at both Grade 3 and Grade 4.

TABLE 3   TAAS Passing Results: Spanish

	all students not in special education								
	Reading			Mathematics			Writing		
			Gain			Gain			Gain
	1997	1998	97–98	1997	1998	97–98	1997	1998	97–98
Grade 3	44	65	21	52	66	14			
Grade 4	36	39	3	47	58	11	*	63	N/A
Grade 5	*	50	N/A	*	56	N/A			
Grade 6	*	27	N/A	*	36	N/A			

*benchmark year

TABLE 4   TAAS Passing Results: Intensive Instruction

	all students not in special education							
	One Test Only		Two Tests Only		All Three Tests		Total	
	Number	Percent	Number	Percent	Number	Percent	Number	Percent
Grade 3	37,832	15%	25,497	10%			63,329	26%
Grade 4	32,033	13%	16,482	7%	11,669	5%	60,184	25%
Grade 5	26,733	11%	16,341	7%			43,074	18%
Grade 6	31,022	13%	21,185	9%			52,207	21%
Grade 7	31,954	13%	23,643	9%			55,597	22%
Grade 8*	34,328	14%	19,881	8%	14,374	6%	68,583	28%
Grade 10	35,529	16%	15,112	7%	10,465	5%	61,106	28%

does not include results of science and social studies TAAS

The Grade 3 passing rate of 66 percent represented a rise of 14 percentage points over the previous year's results, while Grade 4, with 58 percent passing, registered a gain of 11 percentage points.

INTENSIVE INSTRUCTION

Texas Education Code, §39.024, requires that districts offer an intensive program of instruction for students who did not perform satisfactorily on an assessment instrument mandated by the code.

In the 1998–1999 school year, as Table 4 indicates, districts must offer intensive instruction in either reading, writing, mathematics, or a combination of these subject areas to between 18 percent and 28 percent of the students tested at each grade level in Grades 3 through 8. At Grade 10, 28 percent of the students tested in spring 1998 did not pass one or more tests (reading, writing, mathematics) of the exit level TAAS and must be offered intensive instruction.

The legislature also mandated that study guides be provided to assist parents in helping their children strengthen academic skills during the summer when school is in recession. Therefore, the Texas Education Agency developed *TAAS Study Guides* for all grade levels and subject areas tested on TAAS. A study guide is provided free of charge, through districts, to each student who fails one or more TAAS tests. Exit level study guides are distributed three times a year (December, May, and August), while the study guides for Grades 3 through 8 are distributed once a year, when the results from spring testing are reported.

RETESTING OPPORTUNITIES

All students who do not pass the exit level TAAS on their first attempt during the spring of their sophomore year have up to seven additional opportunities to retest before the end of their senior year. Administrations of the exit level TAAS are provided during every academic semester, including the summer. During all but the late spring administration, out-of-school examinees are also given the opportunity to retest.

The late spring TAAS administration, provided only a few weeks before the end of the school year, gives graduating students an additional opportunity to retest immediately prior to commencement. As a result of the late spring administration, an additional 3,224 students were able to satisfy the TAAS diploma requirement prior to spring 1998 graduation ceremonies.

END-OF-COURSE EXAMINATIONS

End-of-course examinations are administered at the end of the last semester of Biology I, Algebra I, U. S. History, and English II. The end-of-course tests provide statewide, regional, and district-level data on performance in the specified secondary-level courses. In addition, school districts may use the end-of-course tests for local purposes. The State Board of Education has set the passing standards for Biology I, Algebra I, U.S. History, and English II end-of-course tests at an equivalent of 70 percent of the items correct, which is represented by a scale score of 1500.

Table 5 presents the spring 1995–1998 Biology I end-of-course test results and the spring 1996– 1998 Algebra I end-of-course test results for all students not in special education. Note that no passing rates are listed for Algebra I in 1995 because the test was benchmarked in the spring of that year and the passing rate had not yet been set. The U.S. History and English II end-of-course tests were benchmarked in spring 1998 and will be implemented fully in spring 1999.

TABLE 5   TAAS Passing Results: Biology I & Algebra I

	all students not in special education												
	Biology I						Algebra I						
STUDENT POPULATION	1995	1996	1997	1998	Gain		1995	1996	1997	1998	Gain		
					97–98	95–98					97–98	96–98	
All Students	73	76	78	80	2	7	*	28	35	39	4	11	
African American	55	59	60	64	4	9	*	11	15	20	5	9	
Hispanic	56	61	62	67	5	11	*	14	20	26	6	12	
White	87	90	91	92	1	5	*	40	48	52	4	12	
LEP	28	33	28	37	9	9	*	9	10	14	4	5	
Non-LEP	76	79	81	83	2	7	*	29	37	41	4	12	
At-Risk	56	58	59	62	3	6	*	7	11	15	4	8	
Not At-Risk	84	87	88	88	0	4	*	40	48	51	3	11	
Economically Disadvantaged	56	59	60	65	5	9	*	14	19	25	6	11	
Not Economically Disadvantaged	79	83	85	87	2	8	*	35	42	47	5	12	

Biology I

Results of the spring 1998 administration showed that 80 percent of the students tested performed successfully, up from 78 percent the previous year. Compared to the previous year's passing rate, all ethnic groups, special population groups, and economic groups gained from 1 to 9 percentage points with the exception of the not at-risk group, whose scores remained consistent. Over the period from 1995 to 1998, all groups have exhibited gains, with the greatest gains achieved by Hispanic students (11 percentage points) and African American, LEP, and economically disadvantaged students (9 percentage points).

Algebra I

Although still significantly lower than the passing rate for the Biology I end-of-course test, the passing rate for the Algebra I end-of-course test continued an upward trend across all ethnic groups, special population groups, and economic groups. Spring 1998 results show that 39 percent of the students tested passed, up from 35 percent in 1997. Hispanic and economically disadvantaged students made the greatest gains (6 percentage points). Over the period from 1996 to 1998, all groups showed improvement, with double-digit gains achieved by Hispanic, white, non-LEP, not at-risk, economically disadvantaged, and not economically disadvantaged students.

TEXAS LEARNING INDEX

Spring 1998 marked the fifth year of the Texas Learning Index, or TLI. The TLI is a score that describes how far a student's performance is above or below the passing standard. The TLI was developed to allow students, parents, and schools the opportunity both to relate student performance to a passing standard and to compare student performance from year to year. Because the purpose of the TLI is to show year-to-year progress as students move toward the exit level test, the TLI is only reported for tests administered in sequential grades, i.e., English TAAS reading and mathematics tests at Grades 3 through 8 and at the exit level.

The TLI provides one indicator of whether a student is making sufficient yearly progress to be reasonably assured of passing the exit level test. The TLI can be used in this way since the passing standards for the tests administered at the lower grades are aligned with the passing standard at the exit level. In other words, it is as difficult for a third grader to pass the third-grade reading and mathematics tests as it is for an eighth grader to pass the eighth-grade reading and mathematics tests or for an exit level student to pass the exit level reading and mathematics tests. For example, a student who consistently achieves a TLI score of 70 or above at Grades 3 through 8 should be in line to succeed on the exit level test if current academic progress continues.

The results presented here are those for all students not in special education.

AVERAGE TLI

In order to pass the TAAS reading and mathematics assessments, a student must achieve a TLI of at least 70. Table 6 presents five years of average TLI scores, including the gain registered between the years 1994 and 1998 for both reading and mathematics. The

TABLE 6 Texas Learning Index: 1994–1998

	all students not in special education											
	Reading						Mathematics					
						Gain						Gain
	1994	1995	1996	1997	1998	1994–1998	1994	1995	1996	1997	1998	1994–1998
Grade 3	78.2	78.0	78.6	79.7	82.3	4.1	70.3	73.3	76.5	78.4	78.1	7.8
Grade 4	78.4	80.1	79.9	80.9	84.4	6.0	70.5	74.6	77.4	79.0	80.0	9.5
Grade 5	78.8	79.9	81.6	83.8	85.3	6.5	71.0	74.7	77.5	80.6	82.1	11.1
Grade 6	78.5	79.8	80.8	83.3	83.9	5.4	70.7	72.6	77.0	78.9	80.6	9.9
Grade 7	78.3	78.8	81.1	82.2	82.8	4.5	70.6	71.8	75.6	77.6	79.5	80.9
Grade 8	77.9	78.0	79.8	81.8	83.3	5.4	70.0	69.7	73.8	76.7	78.7	8.7
Grade 10	77.7	77.8	80.0	82.1	83.9	6.2	69.9	71.2	72.9	75.3	77.4	7.5

table indicates that at all grades, average TLI scores in both reading and mathematics have been rising since 1994. Average 1998 TLIs in **reading** were in the 80s at all grades for the first time, ranging from 82.3 at Grade 3 to 85.3 at Grade 5. Grade 5 exhibited the greatest four-year gain with an increase of 6.5 points. In **mathematics,** average TLI scores also increased at nearly every grade level, with average 1998 TLIs ranging from 77.4 at Grade 10 to 82.1 at Grade 5. Since 1994, Grade 5 has exhibited the greatest gain, with an increase in average TLI of 11.1 points.

Table 7 presents five years of average TLI scores for the same set of students. This group of 147,940 students tested in both reading and mathematics every year from 1994, when the students were in Grade 4, through 1998, when they were in Grade 8. The chart indicates that average TLI scores in both reading and mathematics have been rising steadily every year for these students. In **reading,** the group's average TLI score of 85.4 at Grade 8 represents a gain of 5.4 points over their performance on the Grade 4 test in 1994. The group's average TLI gain was even greater in mathematics, with a gain of 8.2 points when comparing their results on the Grade 4 and Grade 8 mathematics tests.

AVERAGE TLI: RESULTS BY ETHNICITY

As Table 8 indicates, average TLI scores in **reading** rose for all major ethnic groups in all grades. For African American students, average TLI scores in 1998 ranged from 77.6 at Grade 3 and Grade 7 to 80.7 at Grade 5; the greatest four-year gain (8.8 points) was at Grade 5. For Hispanic students, average TLI scores ranged from 78.2 at Grade 7 to 82.1 at Grade 5, with the greatest four-year gain (7.9 points) at Grade 5. The average TLI for white students ranged from 85.3 at Grade 3 to 88.6 at Grades 5 and 6; between 1994 and 1998, the greatest gain (5.4 points) was exhibited at Grade 5.

In **mathematics,** only Grade 3 showed a slight decline at all groups; all other grade levels exhibited improvement. For African American students, average TLI scores in 1998 ranged from 71.4 at Grade 10 to 77.0 at Grade 5; the greatest improvement since 1994 was at Grade 5, with a 13.9 gain in average TLI. For Hispanic students, average TLI scores ranged from 73.5 at Grade 10 to 80.5 at Grade 5, with the greatest four-year gain (13.3 points) at Grade 5. The average TLI for white students ranged from 81.2 at Grade 10 to 84.4 at Grade 5; the greatest improvement since 1994 (9.3 points) was exhibited at Grade 5.

TABLE 7 Texas Learning Index: 1994–1998

Reading					
Grade 4	Grade 5	Grade 6	Grade 7	Grade 8	Gain
1994	1995	1996	1997	1998	1994–1998
80.0	81.6	82.9	84.6	85.4	5.4
Mathematics					
Grade 4	Grade 5	Grade 6	Grade 7	Grade 8	Gain
1994	1995	1996	1997	1998	1994–1998
72.2	76.4	78.9	79.7	80.4	8.2

TABLE 8   Texas Learning Index: Results by Ethnicity

AFRICAN AMERICAN STUDENTS													
	Reading						Mathematics						
						Gain							Gain
	1994	1995	1996	1997	1998	97–98 94–98	1994	1995	1996	1997	1998	97–98 94–98	
Grade 3	71.7	71.5	71.9	74.1	77.6	3.5 5.9	62.5	65.9	69.9	72.3	72.2	-0.1 9.7	
Grade 4	71.2	73.2	72.9	74.7	79.2	4.5 8.0	62.6	66.9	70.6	73.0	74.8	1.8 12.2	
Grade 5	71.9	72.7	75.0	77.9	80.7	2.8 8.8	63.1	66.6	70.1	74.7	77.0	2.3 13.9	
Grade 6	71.8	73.7	74.9	77.7	79.6	1.9 7.8	62.8	65.0	71.0	73.0	75.9	2.9 13.1	
Grade 7	71.2	72.4	75.6	77.2	77.6	0.4 6.4	62.6	63.0	68.2	71.6	73.4	1.8 10.8	
Grade 8	70.8	71.4	73.3	76.7	78.4	1.7 7.6	61.7	61.5	66.3	70.4	73.9	3.5 12.2	
Grade 10	71.4	71.1	75.1	78.1	79.9	1.8 8.5	61.7	63.0	65.6	68.7	71.4	2.7 9.7	

HISPANIC STUDENTS													
	Reading						Mathematics						
						Gain							Gain
	1994	1995	1996	1997	1998	97–98 94–98	1994	1995	1996	1997	1998	97–98 94–98	
Grade 3	74.0	73.8	74.7	75.8	79.5	3.7 5.5	66.3	69.7	73.5	75.9	75.6	-0.3 9.3	
Grade 4	74.3	76.5	75.8	77.1	81.3	4.2 7.0	67.0	71.3	74.7	76.8	78.2	1.4 11.2	
Grade 5	74.2	75.5	77.3	79.6	82.1	2.5 7.9	67.2	71.4	75.0	78.5	80.5	2.0 13.3	
Grade 6	73.3	75.3	75.4	78.3	78.7	0.4 5.4	66.2	68.0	73.3	75.7	78.0	2.3 11.8	
Grade 7	72.8	73.5	76.2	77.3	78.2	0.9 5.4	65.5	66.3	71.0	74.0	76.1	2.1 10.6	
Grade 8	72.1	72.5	74.1	76.7	78.5	1.8 6.4	64.4	63.9	69.1	72.6	75.5	2.9 11.1	
Grade 10	71.7	71.9	74.3	76.8	79.4	2.6 7.7	64.6	65.5	68.4	70.6	73.5	2.9 8.9	

WHITE STUDENTS													
	Reading						Mathematics						
						Gain							Gain
	1994	1995	1996	1997	1998	97–98 94–98	1994	1995	1996	1997	1998	97–98 94–98	
Grade 3	82.2	82.0	82.7	83.5	85.3	1.8 3.1	74.5	77.3	80.1	81.5	81.3	-0.2 6.8	
Grade 4	82.6	83.9	84.1	84.9	87.8	2.9 5.2	74.4	78.3	80.6	81.9	82.5	0.6 8.1	
Grade 5	83.2	84.3	85.8	88.0	88.6	0.6 5.4	75.1	78.6	80.8	83.3	84.4	1.1 9.3	
Grade 6	83.5	84.2	85.8	88.2	88.6	0.4 5.1	75.3	77.5	80.8	82.5	83.5	1.0 8.2	
Grade 7	83.4	83.8	85.8	86.8	87.4	0.6 4.0	75.6	77.5	80.4	81.5	83.4	1.9 7.8	
Grade 8	83.1	83.0	85.2	86.5	88.0	1.5 4.9	75.3	75.3	78.7	81.0	82.1	1.1 6.8	
Grade 10	82.9	82.9	84.6	86.5	87.7	1.2 4.8	74.7	76.3	77.3	79.7	81.2	1.5 6.5	

AVERAGE TLI: RESULTS BY ECONOMIC GROUPS

As Table 9 indicates, average TLI scores of students identified as economically disadvantaged through eligibility for the free or reduced-price meal program reflected gains in **reading** across all grades. Average 1998 TLI scores for these students ranged from 77.7 at Grade 7 to 81.4 at Grade 5, with one-year gains ranging from 0.7 at Grade 7 to 4.4 at Grade 4. The average TLI of students not identified as economically disadvantaged also showed im-

provement, ranging from 85.6 at Grade 3 to 88.7 at Grade 5; one-year gains ranged from 0.6 at Grades 5, 6, and 7 to 2.8 at Grade 4. Economically disadvantaged students at Grade 10 posted the greatest gain over four years, with a rise in average TLI of 8.2 points.

In **mathematics,** both economic groups registered improvement at every grade level except at Grade 3, which exhibited a decline of 0.3 points for both groups. Average 1998 TLI scores for economically disadvantaged students ranged from 73.1 at Grade 10 to 79.5 at Grade 5, with one-year gains

TABLE 9   Texas Learning Index: Results by Economic Groups

			ECONOMICALLY DISADVANTAGED STUDENTS											
			Reading								Mathematics			
						Gain							Gain	
	1994	1995	1996	1997	1998	97–98	94–98	1994	1995	1996	1997	1998	97–98	94–98
Grade 3	73.2	72.9	73.7	75.1	78.7	3.6	5.5	65.4	68.8	72.4	74.9	74.6	−0.3	9.2
Grade 4	73.3	75.4	74.7	76.1	80.5	4.4	7.2	65.8	70.1	73.5	75.7	77.2	1.5	11.4
Grade 5	73.3	74.5	76.3	78.9	81.4	2.5	8.1	66.0	70.1	73.6	77.4	79.5	2.1	13.5
Grade 6	72.7	74.7	75.0	77.9	78.7	0.8	6.0	65.3	67.4	72.8	75.1	77.5	2.4	12.2
Grade 7	72.1	73.0	75.7	77.0	77.7	0.7	5.6	64.6	65.7	70.4	73.5	75.5	2.0	10.9
Grade 8	71.3	71.8	73.6	76.2	78.0	1.8	6.7	63.7	63.5	68.5	72.1	75.1	3.0	11.4
Grade 10	70.5	70.9	73.3	76.0	78.7	2.7	8.2	64.0	65.0	67.7	70.1	73.1	3.0	9.1
			NOT ECONOMICALLY DISADVANTAGED STUDENTS											
			Reading								Mathematics			
						Gain							Gain	
	1994	1995	1996	1997	1998	97–98	94–98	1994	1995	1996	1997	1998	97–98	94–98
Grade 3	82.2	82.2	82.9	83.8	85.6	1.8	3.4	74.3	77.1	80.1	81.6	81.3	−0.3	7.0
Grade 4	82.5	84.0	84.3	85.0	87.8	2.8	5.3	74.3	78.2	80.7	81.9	82.5	0.6	8.2
Grade 5	83.0	84.3	85.9	88.1	88.7	0.6	5.7	74.8	78.4	80.7	83.3	84.4	1.1	9.6
Grade 6	82.7	83.6	85.4	87.7	88.3	0.6	5.6	74.5	76.5	80.4	82.0	83.2	1.2	8.7
Grade 7	82.1	82.6	84.9	86.0	86.6	0.6	4.5	74.2	75.9	79.3	80.7	82.5	1.8	8.3
Grade 8	81.5	81.5	83.7	85.4	86.9	1.5	5.4	73.4	73.3	77.2	79.8	81.2	1.4	7.8
Grade 10	80.5	80.5	82.7	84.8	86.2	1.4	5.7	72.1	73.7	75.2	77.6	79.4	1.8	7.3

ranging from 1.5 at Grade 4 to 3.0 at Grades 8 and 10. The average TLI of students not identified as economically disadvantaged ranged from 79.4 at Grade 10 to 84.4 at Grade 5, with one-year gains ranging from 0.6 at Grade 4 to 1.8 at Grades 7 and 10. Between 1994 and 1998, Grade 5 students identified as economically disadvantaged registered the greatest gain, with a rise in average TLI of 13.5 points.

AVERAGE TLI: RESULTS BY SPECIAL POPULATION

Table 10 provides aggregate average TLI scores of limited English proficient (LEP) students and those at risk of dropping out of school and compares them to the results of students who are not part of these groups.

Note that a LEP student who is not exempt from state assessments takes the English TAAS unless it is determined locally that the appropriate assessment for that student is the Spanish TAAS (available at Grades 3 through 6). This section presents results of the LEP students who took the English TAAS tests.

In **reading,** LEP students achieved gains in average TLI scores in 1998 at all grades; the largest gain compared to 1997 was registered at Grade 4, with an increase of 5.3 points. Average 1998 TLI scores for LEP students ranged from 65.3 at Grade 7 to 77.9 at Grade 3, with the largest four-year gain being an increase of 9.7 points at Grade 5. The average 1998 TLI scores of non-LEP students ranged from 82.7 at Grade 3 to 86.1 at Grade 5, with the greatest four-year gain (6.6 points) posted at Grade 5.

Increases in average TLI scores for **mathematics** were registered by LEP students at all grades except Grade 3, which showed a slight decline of 0.4 points; the greatest 1997–1998 gain (3.3 points) was registered at Grade 8. Average 1998 TLI scores for LEP students ranged from 66.1 at Grade 10 to 76.8 at Grade 5; the largest four-year gain was an increase of 15.2 points at Grade 5. The average 1998 TLI scores of non-LEP students ranged from 78.2 at Grade 10 to 82.5 at Grade 5, with the greatest four-year gain (11.0 points) at Grade 5.

In comparing 1997 and 1998 TLI averages of at-risk students in **reading,** gains were recorded at all grade levels except Grade 6, which exhibited a

TABLE 10 Texas Learning Index: Results by Special Populations

LEP STUDENTS

	Reading							Mathematics						
						Gain							Gain	
	1994	1995	1996	1997	1998	97–98	94–98	1994	1995	1996	1997	1998	97–98	94–98
Grade 3	68.7	69.8	71.9	73.0	77.9	4.9	9.2	63.5	67.9	72.4	75.5	75.1	−0.4	11.6
Grade 4	68.2	71.0	70.5	71.3	76.6	5.3	8.4	62.6	67.6	72.1	74.1	75.9	1.8	13.3
Grade 5	65.4	66.9	69.0	71.3	75.1	3.8	9.7	61.6	65.7	70.5	74.2	76.8	2.6	15.2
Grade 6	63.7	66.8	64.7	67.4	67.6	0.2	3.9	59.6	60.2	66.2	68.5	71.6	3.1	12.0
Grade 7	61.4	61.5	64.8	65.1	65.3	0.2	3.9	57.3	57.5	62.5	66.7	67.3	0.6	10.0
Grade 8	60.6	61.3	61.8	65.2	65.6	0.4	5.0	56.5	56.1	60.5	64.5	67.8	3.3	11.3
Grade 9	58.3	58.7	58.7	63.1	65.6	2.5	7.3	58.0	58.5	60.0	62.9	66.1	3.2	8.1

Non-LEP STUDENTS

	Reading							Mathematics						
						Gain							Gain	
	1994	1995	1996	1997	1998	97–98	94–98	1994	1995	1996	1997	1998	97–98	94–98
Grade 3	78.8	78.5	79.1	80.3	82.7	2.4	3.9	70.8	73.7	76.8	78.7	78.4	−0.3	7.6
Grade 4	79.0	80.6	80.41	81.6	85.0	3.4	6.0	71.0	75.0	77.7	79.4	80.3	0.9	9.3
Grade 5	79.5	80.6	82.2	84.7	86.1	1.4	6.6	71.5	75.2	77.9	81.0	82.5	1.5	11.0
Grade 6	79.4	80.6	81.9	84.6	85.3	0.7	5.9	71.3	73.4	77.7	79.7	81.3	1.6	10.
Grade 7	79.2	79.8	82.1	83.4	84.0	0.6	4.8	71.3	72.6	76.4	78.4	8.03	1.9	9.0
Grade 8	78.8	78.8	80.8	82.8	84.5	1.7	5.7	70.7	70.4	74.6	77.5	79.5	2.0	8.8
Grade 10	79.0	79.0	81.2	83.4	85.1	1.7	6.1	70.7	72.0	73.7	76.2	78.2	2.0	7.5

AT-RISK STUDENTS

	Reading							Mathematics						
						Gain							Gain	
	1994	1995	1996	1997	1998	97–98	94–98	1994	1995	1996	1997	1998	97–98	94–98
Grade 3	69.7	69.7	70.5	72.1	76.2	4.1	6.5	62.0	66.2	69.5	73.0	72.5	-0.5	10.5
Grade 4	70.3	72.4	70.2	71.4	76.5	5.1	6.2	62.8	66.8	69.8	72.0	73.6	1.6	10.8
Grade 5	71.3	71.7	72.5	74.8	76.9	2.1	5.6	63.6	67.2	70.0	74.0	75.7	1.7	12.1
Grade 6	69.8	72.4	71.9	73.7	73.6	-0.1	3.8	62.5	64.5	69.4	71.1	73.4	2.3	10.9
Grade 7	70.1	70.4	73.0	72.5	72.6	0.1	2.5	62.0	62.5	66.8	69.2	70.4	1.2	8.4
Grade 8	70.7	69.3	70.6	72.6	73.4	0.8	2.7	62.5	60.5	64.6	67.3	70.7	3.4	8.2
Grade 10	69.5	71.1	73.1	75.6	77.5	1.9	8.0	61.8	63.9	65.6	67.9	70.3	2.4	8.5

NOT AT-RISK STUDENTS

	Reading							Mathematics						
						Gain							Gain	
	1994	1995	1996	1997	1998	97–98	94–98	1994	1995	1996	1997	1998	97–98	94–98
Grade 3	81.0	80.6	81.2	82.2	84.3	2.1	3.3	73.0	75.6	78.8	80.2	80.2	-0.2	7.0
Grade 4	83.5	85.0	84.07	85.5	88.0	2.5	4.5	75.2	79.6	81.1	82.4	82.9	0.5	7.7
Grade 5	85.2	85.8	87.0	88.8	89.3	0.5	4.1	77.2	80.2	82.0	84.2	85.2	1.0	8.0
Grade 6	83.2	84.9	86.1	88.2	88.4	0.2	5.2	75.0	78.3	81.6	82.9	83.8	0.9	8.8
Grade 7	83.7	84.2	86.0	87.0	87.0	0.0	3.3	76.3	77.9	80.9	81.9	83.3	1.4	7.0
Grade 8	84.5	84.3	85.6	86.8	88.0	1.2	3.5	77.0	76.5	79.7	81.9	82.5	0.6	5.5
Grade 10	83.1	82.8	83.9	85.9	87.2	1.3	4.1	75.3	76.9	77.2	79.7	81.2	1.5	5.9

decline of 0.1 points. Grade 4 achieved the largest gain compared to 1997, with an increase of 5.1 points. Average TLI scores for the at-risk students in 1998 ranged from 72.6 at Grade 7 to 77.5 at Grade 10. The largest gain between 1994 and 1998 was an increase of 8.0 points at Grade 10. The average TLI scores of not at-risk students ranged from 84.3 at Grade 3 to 89.3 at Grade 5, with the greatest four-year gain (5.2 points) posted at Grade 6.

In **mathematics,** gains in average TLI scores for at-risk students continued their upward trend at all grade levels except for a decline of 0.5 points at Grade 3; the greatest 1997–1998 gain (3.4 points) was registered at Grade 8. Average TLI scores for at-risk students in 1998 ranged from 70.3 at Grade 10 to 75.7 at Grade 5. The largest four-year gain was an increase of 12.1 points at Grade 5. The average TLI scores of not at-risk students ranged from 80.0 at Grade 3 to 85.2 at Grade 5, with the greatest four-year gain (8.8 points) at Grade 6.

A STUDY OF THE CORRELATION OF COURSE GRADES WITH STUDENT PERFORMANCE ON THE GRADE 8 TAAS SOCIAL STUDIES TEST

Texas Education Code, §39.182(a)(4), mandates biennial studies to evaluate the correlation between student grades and student performance on state-mandated assessment instruments. To comply with this statute, the Texas Education Agency has conducted periodic studies to determine the relationship between a student's classroom performance and his/her scores on statewide criterion-referenced assessments.

This section describes a study completed in 1997 which compares specific end-of-year social studies course grades of eighth-grade students with their pass/fail rates on the TAAS Grade 8 social studies test. Only students enrolled in the course described as "social studies, Grade 8" in the state-mandated curriculum were considered in this study. Passing the Grade 8 TAAS social studies test is defined as attaining a scale score of at least 1500. One large urban district, one small urban district, one rural district, and two large suburban districts, each representing a different region of the state, volunteered to participate in this study. District assistance with this study was critical since data representing specific final grades for Grade 8 social studies are not available through the Public Education Information Management System (PEIMS). All five districts used a numeric grading scale. For this study, the numerical

grades were transformed into letter grades using the following scale:

A = 90 – 100
B = 80 – 89
C = 70 – 79
D = 60 – 69
F = below 60

Each district provided data for the TAAS social studies test administered in May 1997 and for the social studies course completed in May 1997. The purpose of this case study is to examine the relationship between pass/fail rates of eighth graders on TAAS social studies and the specific letter grades issued to those same students at the end of their social studies course. This study is not intended to represent statewide patterns.

Large Urban District

This large urban district administered the May 1997 TAAS Grade 8 social studies test to more than 10,400 students who were also enrolled in Grade 8 social studies during the 1996–1997 school year. Fifty-two percent of these students were Hispanic, 32 percent were African American, 11 percent were white, and 3 percent were Asian. In addition, more than 51 percent were classified as economically disadvantaged, and 45 percent were identified as at risk of dropping out of school.

As shown in Figure 6, the higher the letter grade a student received in the Grade 8 social studies course, the more likely it was that he or she passed the TAAS social studies test. For example, students who received a final grade of A or B passed at rates of 79 and 61 percent, respectively. Similarly, the lower the letter grade, the more likely it was that a student failed the test: 27 percent of students who received an F in Grade 8 social studies passed the TAAS social studies test, and 30 percent who received a D passed the test.

Small Urban District

This district administered the May 1997 TAAS Grade 8 social studies test to approximately 750 students who were also enrolled in the Grade 8 social studies course during the 1996–1997 school year. Approximately 64 percent of these students were white, 16 percent were Hispanic, 15 percent were African American, and almost 3 percent were Asian. In addition, more than 39 percent of these students were classified as economically disadvantaged and 33 percent were at risk of dropping out of school.

As shown in Figure 7, the higher the letter grade a student received in the Grade 8 social

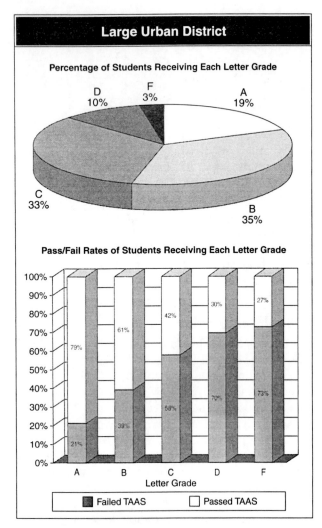

FIGURE 6   Large Urban District

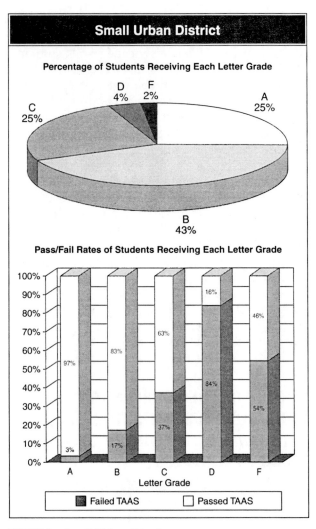

FIGURE 7   Small Urban District

studies course, the more likely it was that he or she passed the TAAS social studies test: 97 percent of students receiving an A, 83 percent receiving a B, and 63 percent receiving a C passed the TAAS social studies test. Only 16 percent of students receiving a D in the Grade 8 social studies course passed the TAAS social studies test; however, nearly half (46 percent) of students receiving an F in the course passed the TAAS.

Rural District

This district administered the May 1997 TAAS Grade 8 social studies test to over 700 students who were also enrolled in Grade 8 social studies during the 1996–1997 school year. More than 96 percent of these students were Hispanic, and 3 percent were white. Also, 87 percent of the students were classi-

fied as economically disadvantaged, and 41 percent were identified as at risk of dropping out of school.

As shown in Figure 8, students earning higher grades in the course did progressively better on the TAAS test: 23 percent who earned a C passed the test, 64 percent who earned a B passed the test, and 92 percent who earned an A passed the test. Students whose performance in the social studies course earned a grade lower than C were less likely to pass the TAAS social studies test: only 6 percent of students who received an F or a D for the Grade 8 social studies course passed the Grade 8 TAAS social studies test.

Large Suburban District I

This large suburban district administered the May 1997 TAAS Grade 8 social studies test to more than

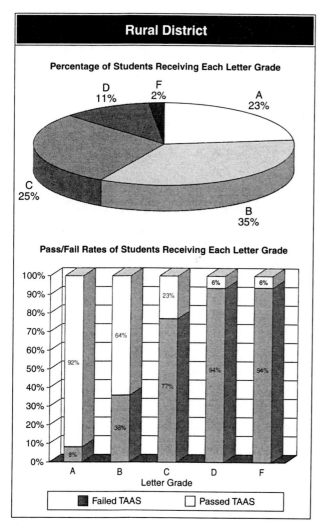

FIGURE 8   Rural District

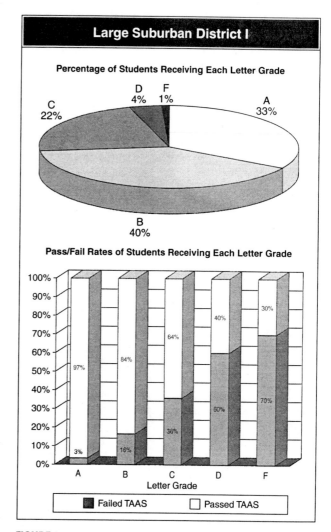

FIGURE 9   Large Suburban District I

3,200 students who were also enrolled in Grade 8 social studies during the 1996–1997 school year. More than 65 percent of these students were white, 16 percent were Hispanic, 9 percent were African American, and 8 percent were Asian. In addition, more than 14 percent of the students were classified as economically disadvantaged, and 19 percent were identified as at risk of dropping out of school.

As shown in Figure 9, students earning higher grades in the course did progressively better on the TAAS test: 64 percent who earned a C passed the test, 84 percent who earned a B passed the test, and 97 percent who earned an A passed the test. Students whose performance in the social studies course earned a D or F were less likely to pass the TAAS social studies test; 30 percent of students who received an F for the Grade 8 social studies course passed the Grade 8 TAAS social studies test, and 40 percent of students receiving a D in the course passed the test.

Large Suburban District II

This large suburban district administered the May 1997 TAAS Grade 8 social studies test to nearly 3,000 students who were also enrolled in Grade 8 social studies during the 1996–1997 school year. More than 77 percent of these students were white, 11 percent were Asian, 6 percent were Hispanic, and 6 percent were African American. More than 6 percent of the students were classified as economically disadvantaged, and 10 percent were identified as at risk of dropping out of school.

As shown in Figure 10, students earning higher grades in the course did progressively better on the TAAS test: 73 percent who earned a C passed the test, 93 percent who earned a B passed the test, and 99 percent who earned an A passed the test. Students whose performance in the social studies course earned a grade lower than C were less likely to pass the TAAS social studies test. For example, 22 percent of students who received an F for the Grade 8

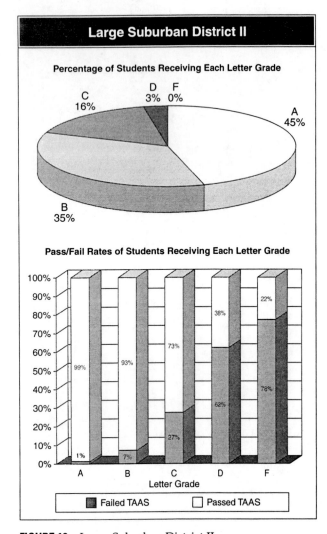

FIGURE 10   Large Suburban District II

8 social studies course passed the Grade 8 TAAS social studies test, and 38 percent of students receiving a D in the course passed the test.

AGENCY CONTACT PERSON

Keith Cruse, Senior Director of Student Assessment, (512) 463-9536.

OTHER SOURCES OF INFORMATION

Texas Student Assessment Program: Student Performance Results, 1997–98, and *Texas Student Assessment Program Technical Digest,* published by the Student Assessment Division, available in early 1999.

Special Education in Texas

Special education is the provision of specially designed child-centered educational and support services provided as a part of the total educational program of each student with a disability. These services are provided through the public school at the preschool, elementary, and secondary levels at no cost to parents. The programs and services meet the requirements set by the federal government and the Texas Education Agency and follow the goals and objectives stated in each student's individualized education plan (IEP).

Educating children with special needs presents a challenge for both general and special education teachers. Special education is a rapidly changing field, and all educators must be aware of new policies and procedures affecting the education of special needs students. Throughout this chapter, information concerning exceptional children is presented. Specifically, this information will include definitions of special education terms, background information, legislation affecting exceptional children, a description of the disabling conditions, and areas that present continuing difficulty and concern for the future.

SPECIAL EDUCATION TERMINOLOGY AND ACRONYMS

The following list of terms and acronyms are the most commonly used in special education and are presented here briefly in order to facilitate the un-

Prepared for inclusion in this text by Jan Murdock, 1999.

derstanding of the chapter. They will be expanded upon as the chapter progresses.

Exceptional children: includes children who experience difficulties learning. These students cannot benefit from the general education program without the additional support and/or services of special education. In many states, but **not** in Texas, the term *exceptional child* encompasses children whose intellectual performance is considered so superior or gifted that special education is necessary to enable them to achieve to their fullest potential.

Disability: is often used interchangeably with the term *impairment.* A disability or impairment limits the ability to perform certain tasks. A student with a disability is not handicapped unless the disability results in educational, personal, social, vocational, or other problems. If a student is confined to a wheelchair, for example, but functions in and out of school without problems, he or she is not handicapped: he or she is disabled. The term *students with disabilities* is more restrictive than the term *exceptional children* in that it does not include talented or gifted children.

Handicap: refers to a difficulty an individual with a disability confronts when interacting with the environment. A disability may be a handicap in one situation and not in another. The child in the wheelchair may be handicapped when on a field trip with his or her class but have no problems in the classroom. The word *handicapped* is derived from "cap in hand" and brings to mind the picture of a person with disabilities begging in the street.

At risk: relates to children who, although not identified as disabled, have a greater likelihood of becoming disabled because of conditions surrounding their births or home environments. The term may also identify children who are "at risk" for academic failure at school.

ADD: Attention Deficit Disorder

ADHD: Attention Deficit with Hyperactivity Disorder

ED: emotionally disturbed

ESL: English-as-a-second-language

EYS: extended year school/services

FAPE: free, appropriate public education

IDEA: Individuals with Disabilities Education Act

IEP: individualized education program

IFSP: individualized family service plan

LD: learning disabled

LEA: local education agency

LRE: least restrictive environment

MR: mentally retarded

OT: occupational therapy

PT: physical therapy

TBI: traumatic brain injury

Related Services: those developmental, corrective, and other supportive services required to assist a child with a disability to benefit from special education and include speech pathology, counseling, physical and occupational therapy, music therapy, adaptive physical education, recreational therapy, diagnostic services, transportation, the provision of adaptive equipment, and/or an interpreter for the deaf or hearing impaired.

THE DEVELOPMENT OF SPECIAL EDUCATION

If a society judges itself by the way it treats those who are different, then the American educational system has a less-than-distinguished history. Exceptional children have always been a part of society, but attention has not been paid to their special needs until the last half of the twentieth century. Recent legislation and court decisions confirm that all children with disabilities, no less than any other citizen, have the right to a *free, appropriate program of public education in the least restrictive environment.*

The provision of equitable education opportunities to exceptional children has not come about by chance. Multiple laws and litigation have had important effects on public education in general and on the education of special needs children in particular.

Brown v. Board of Education.   The education of children with disabilities was strongly influenced by the landmark case of *Brown v. Board of Education* in 1954. The case challenged the practice of segregating students by race. The U. S. Supreme Court declared that education must be made available to all children on an equal basis. The *Brown* decision initiated a period of intense interest and questioning among parents of special needs children. Numerous court cases were initiated in the 1960s and 1970s by parents and advocates displeased with the educational system that denied equal access to children with disabilities. Important judicial decisions have had far-reaching effects on special education.

Diana v. State Board of Education (California, 1970). Declared that children cannot be placed in special education classes on the basis of culturally biased tests or tests not given in the child's native language.

Mills v. Board of Education of the District of Columbia (1972).   Established the right of every child to an equal opportunity for education; declared that lack of funds was not an acceptable excuse for lack of educational opportunity.

Pennsylvania Association for Retarded Citizens v. the Commonwealth of Pennsylvania (1972).   Class action suit establishing the right to free public education for all children with mental retardation.

Larry P. v. Riles (California, 1979).   First brought to court in 1972; ruled that IQ tests cannot be used as the sole basis for placing children in special classes.

Board of Education of the Hendrik Hudson Central School District v. Rowley (New York, 1982).   First case based on PL 94–142 (IDEA) to reach the U. S. Supreme Court; while denying plaintiff's specific request, upheld for each child with disabilities the right to a personalized program of instruction and necessary supportive services.

Abrahamson v. Hershman (Massachusetts, 1983). Ruled that residential placement in a private school was necessary for a child with multiple disabilities who needed round-the-clock training; required the school district to pay for the private placement.

Irving Independent School District v. Tatro (Texas, 1984).   Ruled that catherization was necessary for a child with physical disabilities to remain in school and that it could be performed by a nonphysician, thus obligating the school district to provide that service.

Smith v. Robinson (Rhode Island, 1984). Ordered the state to pay for the placement of a child with severe disabilities into a residential program and ordered the school district to reimburse the parents' attorney fees. U. S. Supreme Court later ruled that PL 94–142 (IDEA) did not entitle parents to recover such fees, but Congress subsequently passed an "Attorney's Fees" bill, leading to the enactment of PL99–372.

Cleburne v. Cleburne Living Center (Texas, 1985). U. S. Supreme Court ruled unanimously that communities cannot use a discriminatory zoning ordinance to prevent establishment of group homes for persons with mental retardation.

Honing v. Doe (California, 1988). Ruled that children with disabilities could not be excluded from school for any misbehavior that is "disability-related" but that educational services could cease if the misbehavior is not related to the disability.

Timothy W. v. Rochester School District (New Hampshire, 1989). A U. S. Appeals Court upheld the literal interpretation that PL 94 –142 (IDEA) requires that *all* children with disabilities be provided with a free, appropriate public education. The three-judge Appeals Court overturned the decision of a District Court judge, who had ruled that the local school district was not obligated to educate a 13-year-old boy with multiple and severe disabilities because he could not "benefit" from special education.

PL 94 –142. The Individuals with Disabilities Act (IDEA).

The Individuals with Disabilities Education Act

Public Law 94–142, now known as *The Individuals with Disabilities Act* (IDEA) was passed by the United States Congress in 1975. This blockbuster legislation was hailed as the law that "will probably become known as having the greatest impact on education in history" (Stowell & Terry, 1977, p. 475). The IDEA landmark legislation has affected every school in the country and has altered the functions of every educator, parent of special needs children, and others involved in the educational process. The act requires that people with disabilities be treated

as full citizens with the same rights and privileges that all other citizens enjoy.

The IDEA mandates that all children with disabilities between the ages of 3 and 21, regardless of the type or severity of their disability, shall receive a *free and appropriate public education.* This must be provided at no cost to the child's parents. Each state education agency must comply with the law by locating and identifying all children with disabilities. Six major principles define the IDEA and have not been changed since 1975. They include:

1. *Zero reject.* Schools must enroll every child, regardless of the nature or severity of his or her disabilities; **no** child with disabilities may be excluded from a public education.
2. *Nondiscriminatory testing.* School districts must use nonbiased, multifactored methods of evaluation to determine whether a child has a disability and, if so, whether special education is needed. Testing and evaluation procedures must not discriminate on the basis of race, culture, or native language. All tests must be administered in the child's native language, and identification and placement decisions must not be made on the basis of a single test score.
3. *Appropriate education.* School districts must develop and implement an individualized education program (IEP) for each student with a disability. The IEP must be individually designed to meet the child's specific needs.
4. *Least restrictive environment (LRE).* School districts must educate students with disabilities with children who do not have disabilities to the maximum extent possible.
5. *Due process.* School districts must provide safeguards to protect the rights of children with disabilities and their parents by ensuring due process, confidentiality of records, and parental involvement in educational planning and placement decisions.
6. *Parent participation.* School districts must collaborate with the parents of students with disabilities in the design and implementation of special education service.

The Reauthorization of the IDEA

In 1997, President Clinton signed into law the reauthorization of the IDEA. The new legislation improves the IDEA through provisions that:

1. Place the emphasis on what is best educationally for children with disabilities, rather than on paperwork for paperwork's sake

2. Give professionals, especially teachers, more influence and flexibility, and school administrators and policymakers lower costs in the delivery of education to children with disabilities
3. Enhance the input of parents of children with disabilities in the decision making that affects their child's education
4. Make schools safer
5. Consolidate and target discretionary programs to strengthen the capacity of America's schools to effectively serve children, including infants and toddlers, with disabilities.

PLACEMENT OF DISABLED STUDENTS

The identification and classification of students with special needs is necessary in order to determine eligibility for special education. While the federal and state regulations list the classifications of eligibility (autism, deaf-blind, auditory impairment, mental retardation, multiple disabilities, physical disability, learning disability, speech impairment, traumatic brain injury, and visual impairment), one is not considered more or less significant than another. A sequential process must be followed by the Admission, Review, Dismissal (ARD) committee before a student can begin receiving special education services. First, eligibility must be determined through an appropriate assessment, then need for educational services must be established. After a need for special education is determined, an individual educational program (goals and objectives) is developed. Finally, placement is determined based on the most appropriate, least restrictive environment.

Least restrictive environment (LRE) is a term used to ensure that students are being educated in a setting as near normal as is appropriate. Placement options are on a wide continuum ranging from the general education classroom with appropriate modifications (least restrictive), to a content mastery setting, to a resource setting to a self contained setting (most restrictive on a general education campus). Additionally, hospital classes provide special education services for students in a hospital or residential treatment facility and homebound classes provide special education services for students who are served at home or hospital bedsides.

CLASSIFICATIONS OF ELIGIBILITY

The Texas Education Agency defines students with disabilities as those students between 3 and 21 who have disabilities which impact their ability to access educational benefits. Students between birth and 22 who are auditorially or visually impaired, or are deaf/blind and whose disability is so limiting as to require the provision of special services in place of or in addition to instruction in the regular classroom are eligible for benefits from special education. Before a student can receive any service from the special education department of a school district, the student must have had an individual assessment. An individual assessment is the data-gathering process and any testing done following a referral to special education. The student's eligibility and need for special education services are reevaluated at least every three years for as long as the student is in special education. The following is a description of each of the classifications of eligibility as recognized by the state and federal governments.

Physical Disability

Students with physical disabilities are those whose body functions or members are so impaired from any cause that they cannot be adequately or safely educated in the regular classes of the public schools without the provision of special services. Professionals responsible for therapy for students with physical disabilities include the occupational therapist (OT) and the physical therapist (PT). The OT works with the fine motor muscles of the student, training him or her to develop the fine motor skills necessary for independence, usually activities involving the use of the hands. The OT translates activities into crafts and games to promote self-help skills such as tying shoes, dressing, and pencil/pen skills. The physical therapist works with the large gross motor muscles of the student and is concerned primarily with the student's muscle strength, coordination, and mobility. In developing gross motor skills, a PT may use equipment such as parallel bars, mats, canes, and whirlpools or swimming pools.

Students with orthopedic impairments are those who have severe impairments that adversely affect educational performance. The term includes impairments caused by congenital anomaly and impairments caused by disease. Other health-impaired students are those with limited strength, vitality, or impairments, such as a heart condition, asthma, cancer, or diabetes, which adversely affect the student's educational process.

Mental Retardation

A student who has been determined by a licensed or certified psychologist, a psychological associate, or an educational diagnostician to be functioning two or more standard deviations below the mean on individually administered intelligence tests and whose adaptive behavior (the degree with which the student meets the standards of personal independence and social responsibility) is in line with the IQ is said to have mental retardation. Generally, an IQ of 70 or lower is 2 standard deviations below the mean. The extent of mental retardation, a continuum ranging from mild to moderate to severe to profound, must be specified. It is important to note that some individuals with an IQ below 70 do well in school and society. Their adaptive behavior is not subnormal, and these individuals should not be labeled as mentally retarded.

Emotional Disturbance

While there is no single, widely used definition of emotional disturbance, most definitions require a student's behavior to be extremely and chronically different from current social or cultural norms. Students displaying one or more of the following characteristics over an extended time and to a degree that affects educational performance adversely are said to be emotionally disturbed:

- An inability to learn that cannot be explained by intellectual, sensory, or health factors
- An inability to build or maintain satisfactory interpersonal relationships with peers and teachers
- Inappropriate types of behavior or feelings under normal circumstances
- A general pervasive mood of unhappiness or depression
- A tendency to develop physical symptoms or fears associated with personal or school problems

A student with emotional disturbance must have been evaluated by a licensed specialist in school psychology and determined to meet one or more of the above criteria.

It should be noted that teachers generally are well aware of and easily identify those students with severe acting out behaviors. It is the students with depressive behaviors that are often overlooked. Typical characteristics of childhood depression include having poor appetite and sleep habits, low self-esteem, low energy and poor concentration, being easily fatigued, and the inability to have fun (negative views of self, their future, and/or the world).

Learning Disability

From its inception as a category of disabilities, the definition of a learning disabilities has been controversial. The most widely accepted definition,

drafted from the Office of Education and published in the IDEA states:

> "Specific learning disability" means a disorder in one or more of the basic psychological processes involved in understanding or in using language, spoken or written, which may manifest itself in an imperfect ability to listen, think, speak, read, write, or to do mathematical calculations. The term includes such conditions as perceptual handicaps, brain injury, minimal brain dysfunction, dyslexia and developmental aphasia. The term does not include children who have learning problems which are primarily the result of visual, hearing or motor handicaps, of retardation, or of environmental, cultural, or economic disadvantages. (U. S. Office of Education, 1977b, p. 65083)

In order to be eligible for special services in Texas, a multidisciplinary assessment team must ensure that:

1. A discrepancy exists between the child's potential (the IQ score) and actual achievement (the discrepancy must be at least 15 points)
2. An exclusion criterion has not been met (the student is not being placed in special education because of a visual, hearing, or motor handicap, mental retardation, emotional disturbance, environmental, cultural or economic disadvantage)
3. There is an educational need for special education

Speech Impairment

Students with speech impairment(s) are those whose speech is so impaired that they cannot be educated adequately in general education classes without special aids or services.

A student with a speech/language impairment is one who has been determined by a certified speech and hearing pathologist to have a communication disorder such as stuttering, impaired articulation, language impairment, or voice impairment. Indicators for these disorders may include difficulty or delay with one or more of the following:

- Substitution, omission, or distortion of sounds
- Difficulty in getting words out
- Unpleasant voice quality
- Monotonous voice
- Slow, labored, jerky speech
- Difficulty understanding concepts such as between, under, over, around, top, bottom
- Incorrect interpretation of oral questions or instructions

Autism

Autism is a condition indicated by severe impairment of intellectual, social, and emotional functioning. Fundamental features of autism typically appear before 30 months of age and consist of disturbances of:

- Developmental rates and/or sequences
- Responses to sensory stimuli
- Speech, language, and cognitive capacities
- Capacities to relate to people, events, and objects

As determined by a multidisciplinary team, an autistic student may exhibit a combination of the following specific behaviors: rocking, twirling around, hand flapping, or humming; reacting strongly to changes in routines; echoing questions or statements; staring into space for long periods of time; actively avoiding eye contact; and/or engaging in tantrums and self-mutilatory behaviors. The team must also address specific recommendations for behavior management and family counseling.

Multiple Disabilities

Students with multiple disabilities are those who have two or more of the disabilities described that may result in multisensory or motor deficiencies and developmental lags in the cognitive, affective, or psychomotor areas such that they cannot be educated in the general classes of the public schools without special aids and services. The disability must be expected to continue indefinitely, and the student must require comprehensive instruction and related services (OT, PT, speech, transportation, and so on) in programs for students with severe disabilities.

Traumatic Brain Injury

Determined by a licensed physician, a traumatic brain injury is one caused by an external physical force resulting in total or partial functional disability and/or psychosocial impairment. Typical causes of head trauma include automobile, motorcycle, and bicycle accidents; falls; assaults; gunshot wounds; and child abuse. Symptoms may include cognitive and language deficits, memory loss, seizures, and perceptual disorders. Victims may also exhibit inappropriate or magnified behaviors ranging from ultra-aggressiveness to apathy. Originally, the IDEA did not mention victims of head trauma; however, when the law was amended in 1990, TBI was added as a new disability category.

Auditory Impairment

Students with auditory impairment are those who have been determined to have a profound hearing loss even after corrective medical treatment or use of amplification. This determination is made by an otologist and audiologist. Students with auditory impairment are those whose hearing is so impaired that they cannot be educated adequately in the general education classes without special aids and/or services. The term *auditory impairment* is understood to be synonymous with *hearing impairment*, and both terms are understood to include deaf and hard of hearing students.

Visual Impairment

Students with visual impairment are those who have been determined to have no vision or to have a serious visual loss after correction, as determined by a licensed ophthalmologist. In the educational setting children are expected to be able to see clearly, accurately focus on different objects, shift from near to far, have good eye-hand coordination, remember what they have seen, discriminate colors, and interpret many things simultaneously and maintain visual concentration. Students with deficits in one or more of these need special services and aids to function effectively in school.

Deaf-Blind

Students with dual sensory impairments (deaf-blind) were the first to receive special education when the government established programs funded statewide and through Regional Education Centers. This particularly challenging group of students usually experience major difficulties in acquiring communication and motor skills, mobility and appropriate social behavior. Educational programs for students with dual sensory impairments generally require materials and services similar to those for other students with severe disabilities. These generally involve multiple related services (OT, PT, speech, orientation and mobility, transportation, and so on). In order to be determined deaf/blind, a student must meet eligibility criteria for both auditory and visual impairments.

INDIVIDUALIZED EDUCATIONAL PROGRAM (IEP)

The IDEA requires that an Individual Education Program (IEP) be developed and implemented for every student with disabilities between the ages of 3 and 21. The law specifies what must be included in an IEP and those required to participate in the development of the IEP. It spells out the student's competencies, the goals and objectives for the following year, who is to implement them, when the services will begin, the duration of the services, the method of evaluating whether the goals and objectives have been met, and the frequency of the evaluation and the level of mastery the student is expected to meet. An IEP is the product of an **Admission, Review, and Dismissal** (ARD) committee. The ARD committee **must** include at least the following members: an administrator, general education teachers who have worked with the student, special education teachers who have worked with the student (or are expected to), the student's parent or guardian, an assessment specialist if assessment is to be discussed, and, as appropriate, the student. Others that may be involved in IEP process include any related service provider that is expected to work with the student. Parents may invite any advocate they wish to attend an ARD committee meeting. An IEP is a legally binding document and **must** be fulfilled exactly as specified. Only another duly constituted ARD committee can change *anything* written into an IEP. IEPs vary widely from school district to school district and are unique to each student, but each student is to have an IEP review *at least* annually.

Transition

The transition mandate in the Amendments to Education Act (IDEA, PL 101–476) requires that all students receiving special education must receive transition planning. Transition may simply be defined as movement from one stage to another, as from school to work and community living, and most significantly affects the future of students with moderate to severe disabilities. This movement may occur at graduation or completion of the IEP goals established for the student by the ARD committee.

An effective transition program requires team responsibility among educators, the student, parents or guardians, and adult services providers. Each member of the transition team has resources and services to provide in the transition process. The transition plan must be included in the IEP for all special education students 14 years of age and older.

Service Providers

Texas Rehabilitation Commission (TRC) is the primary resource for adult services during transition from school to work. TRC, as a service provider, may provide time-limited vocational rehabilitation services that lead to competitive employment and extended rehabilitation services that, over an extended time, lead to sheltered or supported employment.

The Texas Department of Mental Health and Mental Retardation provides services for persons with autism, mental retardation, and emotional disturbance. MHMR centers provide a broad range of services, including counseling and guidance, family services, case management, and vocational/day habilitation and independent living services.

The Texas Department of Human Services is the largest state agency and service provider in Texas. TDHS administers many federal programs, including Medicaid services, Food Stamps, Aid to Families with Dependent Children, and the Social Services Block Grant. TDHS also administers some state-funded programs for persons who are aged or disabled.

TRENDS AND ISSUES IN SPECIAL EDUCATION

Inclusion

Even before the reauthorization of the IDEA, the term *inclusion* was a prominent topic in both special and general education. Inclusion is the concept that all students, regardless of physical, mental, emotional, ethnic, or socioeconomic condition, are educated together in general classrooms. Various studies indicate that special education students are more likely to fare better in school if they are allowed to participate in the same educational programs as other students. Inclusion, however is not a mandate by either the federal or state government; the least restrictive environment concept continues to be the mandate. To some, inclusion means full-time placement of all students with disabilities into general education classrooms; to others, it refers to any degree of integration in the mainstream. Clearly, there is no consensus among educators as to what constitutes inclusion.

It is appropriate to place a disabled student in a general classroom if he or she will not take a disproportionate amount of the teacher's time, the program will not have to be substantially modified for the disabled student, and/or the disabled student will not require skills taught in special education classes to succeed in general education classes. The Council for Exceptional Children, the primary professional organization in special education, supports inclusion as a "meaningful goal" to be pursued by schools but believes that the continuum of services and program options must be maintained and that the ARD committee must make decisions based on the student's individual educational needs.

Discipline

The discipline of special education students is confusing to most educators because there are a number of "ifs" that must be addressed any time a special needs student is disciplined. First, it must be determined whether the ARD committee indicated that the student could follow the rules of the campus and district. If so, the student may be disciplined as any general education student might be for the same offense. If not, the behavior management plan must be addressed. An ARD committee must meet if a student is to be suspended for more than 10 days. Any time a special needs student is suspended, all services previously determined necessary for the student to benefit from the educational process must continue. It is incumbent upon the ARD committee to determine how the services will be carried out.

Teacher/Student Accountability

Accountability is a very important issue in education today. Currently, special education students may be exempted from standardized and norm-referenced testing (California Achievement Tests, Terra Nova, End of Course Exams, and TAAS) if the ARD committee determines it is appropriate for the student. The Texas Legislature has mandated that an alternative assessment be conducted for any student exempted from accountability testing. The ARD committee must determine what testing is appropriate for the student and when it will be administered. Beginning with the 1998–99 school year, school districts was required to explain any exemptions to the Texas Education Agency. The TEA intends for exemptions to be drastically reduced. This means that special education students taking state mandated tests will increase significantly, and campus scores are expected to reflect that increase. Issues such as modifications of tests, administering off grade level tests, and other test accommodations are expected to surface as parents and administrators address the issue of accountability.

REFERENCES

Bagnato, S., Neisworth, J., & Munson, S. (1989). *Linking developmental assessment and early intervention: Curriculum-based prescriptions.* Rockville, MA: Aspen Publishers.

Heward, W. L. (2000). *Exceptional children.* (6th Ed.). Upper Saddle River, NJ: Merrill/Prentice Hall.

LRP Publications. (1997). IDEA reauthorization special report.

Murdock, J. (1992). *Policy analysis of PL 94 –142.* Unpublished manuscript.

School's Advocate. (1989). *Least restrictive environment does not mean a student must be placed in regular education if* . . . Saratoga, CA: Kinghorn Press.

Texas Education Agency. (1996). *Rules and regulations for providing special education services.* Austin, TX: Agency Printing Office.

U. S. Department of Education. (1993). *To assure the free appropriate public education of all children with disabilities: Fifteenth annual report to Congress on the implementation of the Individuals with Disabilities Education Act.* Washington, DC: Government Document Service.

U. S. Office of Education. (1997b). Procedures for evaluating specific learning disabilities. *Federal Register, 42,* 65082–65085.

CHAPTER 22

Gifted/Talented Students in Texas Schools

Beginning with the 1990–91 school year, all Texas school districts were required to identify and serve gifted students at all grade levels, kindergarten through grade 12. The Texas plan was designed to incorporate the latest research in the field of gifted education as well as to allow the greatest possible flexibility for local district implementation. Because each district serves a unique population, variations, sometimes quite large variations, exist from district to district, and often even from school to school within a district.

In an attempt to encourage school districts to support services that go beyond the academic minimum and instead aim for academic excellence, the Texas State Board of Education (SBOEd) adopted the following as its goal for services for gifted learners.

Texas State Goal for Services for Gifted Students

Students who participate in services designed for gifted students will demonstrate skills in self-directed learning, thinking, research, and communication as evidenced by the development of innovative products and performances that reflect individuality and creativity and are advanced in relation to students of similar age, experience, or environment. High school graduates who have participated in services for gifted students will have produced products and performances of professional quality as part of their program services.

Prepared for inclusion in this text by Mary Lynn Crow, 1999.

According to the Senate Bill 1 of 1995, "gifted and talented students" means a child or youth who performs at or shows the potential for performing at a remarkably high level of accomplishment when compared with others of the same age, experience, or environment. Gifted/talented students are those who exhibit high performance capability in an intellectual, creative, or artistic area, who possess an unusual capacity for leadership, or who excel in a specific academic field. The national definition of the term *gifted/talented* (U.S. Office of Education, 1988) is children or youth who give evidence of high performance capability in areas such as intellectual, creative, artistic, leadership, or in specific academic fields who require services or activities not ordinarily provided by the school in order to fully develop such capabilities.

In Texas all school districts are required to adopt processes for identifying and serving these students and establishing programs for them in each grade level. All such policies must be approved by the local boards of trustees and disseminated to parents. Teachers of gifted/talented students must have a minimum of 30 clock hours of staff development (that includes the nature and needs of gifted/talented students, assessing student needs, and curriculum and instruction) but are encouraged to seek gifted/talented certification endorsement or an advanced degree. Annually there is a requirement to receive six additional clock hours of professional development. Administrators and counselors who have authority for program decisions must have a minimum of six clock hours of training and are also encouraged to seek endorsement. They too must receive six additional clock hours per year in gifted education. Although Texas sets these minimum standards, some districts require considerably more academic preparation and annual in-service training.

STUDENT IDENTIFICATION

Identifying gifted/talented students is a challenging task, partly because of the many different types of students who could be classified as gifted and/or talented, and of the variety of programs that could be available to serve them. Identification should contain three distinct steps: nomination, screening, and selection. Nomination and screening should occur at least once a year. Assessment must include measures collected from multiple sources for each area of giftedness served by the district and should include both objective and subjective information. For example, if a district provides services in the area of leadership, a minimum of three assessment criteria must be used for selection to that program. Texas also requires that a selection committee be composed of at least three qualified gifted/talent teachers but could include an administrator, a counselor, a psychologist, or diagnostician.

Special consideration should be given to ensure that groups such as the following are not overlooked during the identification process.

- Academic underachievers.
- Racial, ethnic, or minority group students.
- Recent immigrants.
- Culturally different.
- Disabled students, including the learning disabled.
- Economically disadvantaged.
- Students who do not take advantage of options because of gender stereotyping.
- Students who may do poorly on standardized tests.
- Students who display various types of classroom behavior such as disruptiveness, extreme shyness, excessively high energy levels, continuous questioning, intense anxiety, and short attention spans.

Because classroom grades are often considered, it is important to recognize that grades received by some students are not always indicative of their true ability or potential. Despite a low grade point average, the program for the gifted could still be the most appropriate educational placement for these students.

A final often-overlooked group is the profoundly gifted. Most published research on gifted/talented students and programs are based on moderately gifted students, and moderately gifted students are very different from profoundly gifted students. According to Winner (1997), Moderately gifted children perform one or two years above the level of their age mates; in IQ terms, which is often how such children are classified, a moderately gifted child has an IQ between about 130 and 150, whereas a profoundly gifted child has an IQ of about 180 or above. Recommendations derived from research with moderately gifted children, therefore, cannot be assumed to apply to profoundly gifted children because these two kinds of children are as different from one another as are moderately gifted from average children.

CHARACTERISTICS OF GIFTED STUDENTS

Stanford University psychologist Lewis Terman has been dubbed the father of the gifted education movement. In addition to his contribution of the Stanford-Binet IQ test, he also published the seminal work on gifted children. Based on the identification and longitudinal study of gifted children with Stanford-Binet IQ scores in the top 1%, his work traced their physical, psychological, social, and professional development for nearly three quarters of a century. Called "termites" in gifted education circles, these children were superior in virtually every quality examined. Terman stressed that the myth of brilliant students being weak, unattractive, or emotionally unstable was untrue. He also determined that students not allowed to accelerate in school developed poor work habits that often caused them to fail in college.

In the 1980s Walberg published his studies of historically eminent men. He reviewed the childhood characteristics of over 200 eminent men born between the 14th and 20th centuries and determined that the following traits were common to virtually all of these gifted persons:

- Versatility
- Concentration
- Superior communication skills
- At least moderately high intelligence
- Ethical
- Sensitive
- Optimistic
- Magnetic and popular

Walberg's study of gifted high school students in the arts and sciences identified the following characteristics:

- Interested in work with fine detail

- Persistent in carrying things through
- Liked school, studied hard, and completed work faster
- Enjoyed and valued creative expression
- Selected creativity rather than wealth or power as the best characteristic to develop in life
- Expected to earn higher salaries than the average
- Expected to earn graduate degrees

Many other researchers have added to the work of Terman and Walberg by identifying characteristics of gifted students:

- Early reading ability (by age 3 or 4)
- Confidence in their abilities
- Highly energetic and goal-directed
- Quick and logical thinking processes
- Curious
- May begin writing at a precocious age
- May begin counting by 5s and 10s and adding and subtracting 2-digit numbers by kindergarten
- High motivation and persistence
- High internal control
- Perfectionism
- Superior humor
- High moral thinking and empathy
- Keen sense of fair play and justice
- Interest in social issues
- Stubbornness
- Copes with several ideas at once
- Irritated and bored by the routine and obvious

INTELLIGENCE AND CREATIVITY

Intelligence and creativity are different traits, although both are frequently included as definitions of gifted/talented persons. The student who is highly intelligent may or may not be creatively gifted as well. MacKinnon (1978) describes the difference in what he calls the threshold concept: A base level of intelligence is essential for creative productivity; above that threshold [IQ score of about 120], however, there is virtually no relationship between measured intelligence and creativity. Davis and Rimm (1994) add that one important implication of distinguishing between intellectual and creative giftedness is that if students are selected for a gifted program based upon scores in the top 1% to 5% in intelligence, the large majority of creative students will be missed.

Torrance and others whose primary focus has been the study of creative persons have identified characteristics and personality traits of the creative:

- Creativity consciousness
- Confidence, risk-taking

- High energy, adventurousness
- Curiosity
- Humor, playfulness
- Idealism and reflectiveness
- Need for alone time
- Artistic and aesthetic interests
- Attraction to the novel, complex, and mysterious
- Tolerance for ambiguity
- Reflectiveness in elementary school
- Impulsiveness in adolescence
- Perceptiveness and intuitiveness
- Cynicism
- Tendency to question laws, rules, authority in general
- Temperamental
- Emotional
- Arguments that the rest of the parade is out of step
- Having an imaginary childhood playmate

PROGRAM DESIGN

"The mismatch between gifted youth and curriculum they are forced to study most of the time is nothing short of an American tragedy. The human waste, in terms of both student and faculty time is inestimable, and this waste can be found in both rich schools and poor, and even in schools that have well established programs for the gifted."

Joseph Renzulli

The establishment of a program philosophy and goals along with a needs assessment usually precedes the development of an effective gifted/talented program. What are the needs of the gifted/talented students in this district? How can a program be designed to meet the student needs while staying in alignment with the program philosophy and goals?

ACCELERATION AND ENRICHMENT

Acceleration (vertical differentiation) and enrichment (horizontal differentiation) are two main ways to meet the educational needs of gifted/talented students.

Fox (1979) defines acceleration as any strategy that results in advanced placement or credit, and enrichment as strategies that supplement or go beyond standard grade-level work but do not result in advanced placement or credit. In acceleration the student moves faster through academic content that typically includes offering standard curriculum to students at a younger-than-usual age or lower-than-usual grade. Acceleration places students with their academic rather than their chronological peers. In enrichment the student receives a richer and more varied educational experience or a curriculum that is modified to provide greater depth and breadth than is generally provided (Schiever & Maker, 1991).

Types of acceleration programs include:

- Early admission to kindergarten or first grade
- Credit by examination (or "testing out")
- Grade skipping or double promotion
- Curriculum compacting
- Concurrent or dual enrollment (e.g., in high school and college)
- Advanced placement (AP) courses—sponsored by College Board
- Early admission to college
- Telescoped programs (e.g., collapsing three academic years' work into two years or four years of high school into three).
- Residential high schools (often located on college campuses)

Types of enrichment programs include:

- Independent study and independent projects, either in-class or in resource projects
- Cluster grouping in the regular classroom
- Experimental courses
- Learning centers
- Field trips
- Saturday programs
- Summer programs
- Mentors and mentorships
- Odyssey of the Mind
- Junior Great Books
- Academic decathlon
- Mock court

GROUPING OPTIONS

Grouping options include full-time homogeneous classes (as in magnet schools for the gifted), full-time heterogeneous classes (as in cluster groups of gifted students placed with regular students or mainstreaming in the regular class), and part-time or temporary groups (as in pull-out programs or Resource Room Plans).

One of the most popular and frequently used grouping options, the pull-out program, is also severely criticized in the literature. It is, according to Davis & Rimm (1994), a part-time solution to the full-time "problem" of being gifted. It may also be more expensive due to the need to hire a gifted/talented coordinator, may cause friction between reg-

ular classroom teachers and gifted/talented teachers, and may cause problems for the students, who must either make-up or miss regular classroom work.

When gifted/talented students are mainstreamed, IEPs[1] may be used to individualize instruction. Treffinger's work provides suggestions for this option, which include using learning centers, mini-courses, independent projects, and permitting students to "test out" of material they already know. All of the various grouping options have strengths and weaknesses that must be considered when designing a program for gifted/talented students.

AFFECTIVE GROWTH

A gifted/talented student's affective growth and development may be as important as his/her cognitive growth and development. They are, certainly, inextricably intertwined. While cognitive growth refers to what you think and what you know, affective growth refers to your feelings, attitudes, beliefs, morals, biases, prejudices, values, self-concept, and social adjustment. Leadership training and skills could also be included in this category. If it is true that doing the right thing is as important as doing things right, and that a misdirected or excluded gifted/talented young person can become a gang leader as quickly as a student leader, then the affective domain becomes essential in the overall education of students with special talents and gifts.

Services and experiences that can stimulate affective growth include the use of instructional models such as the Awareness Training Model and Role Play, moral/ethical dilemmas presented for analysis and solution (such as those available in Lawrence Kohlberg's work), age-appropriate bibliotherapy, stress management skills, and assertiveness training. Training and mentoring in leadership skills is also advantageous.

COUNSELING SERVICES

As a general rule, the greater the gift, the greater the counseling need (Davis & Rimm, 1994). Used to be-

---

1. Public Law 94–142 (IDEA), the "mainstreaming law," mandated the use of an Individualized Education Program (IEP) for each student classified as having a disability. IEPs also serve that other variety of exceptional students, the gifted/talented student, particularly when they are mainstreamed in the regular classroom.

ing the best, these young people can also be the best at getting into trouble if they are not helped to find a way to be the best at something positive. Because of their mental and emotional complexity, gifted/talented children may have greater difficulty moving through their psychological developmental stages than other children. Common concerns, for example, include feeling different and not fitting in with family or peers, not understanding the nature of their "gifts," boredom, lack of motivation, deep concerns over social and moral issues, the need to hide their abilities in order to be accepted, perfectionism, stress, and reactions to jealousy or resentment by others.

Counselors who provide services to gifted/talented students must be especially sensitive to what makes them unique as well as to their special needs. In addition to individual and group counseling to meet their emotional and social needs, gifted/talents students need in-depth career counseling to help them and their families make good educational and career decisions.

INSTRUCTIONAL STRATEGIES AND MODELS

Gifted/talented students are different; their curriculum is also different. Their classroom strategies and models must also be different in that they must be geared to the learning needs, styles, and pace of the gifted/talented students. Classroom strategies and techniques should include the following characteristics in order to appropriately challenge gifted/talented students:

- Operate at higher levels on Bloom's taxonomy
- Start with questions, not answers
- Utilize achievement motivation challenges
- Leave students with some cognitive dissonance
- Are fully participatory
- End with questions, not with answers
- Utilize the inquiry method
- Utilize creativity
- Utilize critical-thinking skills
- Allow for metacognition (thinking about thinking)
- Utilize the Socratic method of questioning
- Utilize research activity and project activity
- Include analogies
- Include both inductive and deductive thinking
- Include case studies for analysis and resolution
- Include various types of problem-solving activities
- Allow for integrated content areas, ideally through multi-disciplinary team teaching
- Utilize visualizations, creative dramatics, and role play.

Whereas strategies, methods, and techniques are what a teacher does—like lead a small group discussion, ask high-order questions, or conduct a sponge activity—an instructional model is a much broader term. It refers to a series of instructional steps or procedures designed to bring about a predicted learning experience or outcome. It may involve a number of strategies and methods in a specific order and may serve as the overall design of an individual lesson or an entire unit of content. In a book devoted exclusively to instructional models, *Models of Teaching* by Joyce and Weil (1986), there are a number of models which are uniquely appropriate to use with gifted/talented students. Some of these include Group Investigation, Awareness Training, Inquiry Training, Synectics, Jurisprudential Inquiry, Simulation Games, and Role Play.

GIFTED EDUCATION: ELITISM OR EQUITY?

The purpose of school is to provide an education commensurate with each child's ability to learn and potential to achieve. "Although the belief that all people should be treated the same way is one way of interpreting the democratic ideal, another interpretation is that each person should be helped to fulfill his or her individual potential. These two interpretations of democracy lead to clashing visions of how exceptionally intelligent students should be educated" (Winner, 1997, p. 1070).

The argument that gifted education is elitist and undemocratic usually concludes that gifted students can make it on their own. Even if it is assumed by those critics that gifted/talented students should not receive *more* services, it is certainly true that they need *different* services. And if, as it is most commonly argued, a true democracy includes full individual opportunity for all, then gifted/talented students need to be educated so that they can achieve to their fullest potential. Perhaps the most convincing argument for the education of these children is that without them, society would suffer inestimable losses—in its politics, its arts, its sciences, its businesses, and its successes in all societal endeavors. When the Albert Einsteins, the Walt Disneys, the Wolfgang Mozarts, the Winston Churchills, the Sandra Day O'Connors, and the Thomas Edisons are not identified, challenged, and educated to their potential, all of society will be the losers.

REFERENCES

Clark, B. (1997). *Growing up gifted.* (5th Ed.). Upper Saddle River, NJ: Merrill/Prentice Hall.

Colangelo, N. & Davis, G. A. (Eds.) (1997). *Handbook of gifted education* (2nd Ed.). Boston: Allyn & Bacon.

Cox, C. M. (1926). *The early mental traits of three hundred geniuses.* (Vol. 2). Genetic studies of genius. Stanford, CA: Stanford Univ. Press.

Davis, G. A. & Rimm, S. B. (1994). *Education of the gifted and talented.* (3rd Ed.). Boston: Allyn & Bacon.

deBono, E. (1992). *Serious creativity.* New York: Harper Collins.

Feldhosen, J. F. (1989). Synthesis of research on gifted youth. *Educational Leadership, 46*(6), 6–11.

Fox, L. H. (1979). Programs for the gifted and talented: An overview. In A. A. Passow (Ed.), *The gifted and talented.* Chicago: National Society for the Study of Education.

Heller, K. A., Monks, F. G., & Passow, A. H. (Eds.) (1993). *International handbook of research and development of giftedness and talent.* Oxford, England: Pergamon Press.

Hollingsworth, L. (1942). *Children Above 180 IQ Stanford Binet: Origin and development.* New York: World Book.

Jackson, N. E. (1988). Precocious reading ability: What does it mean? *Gifted Child Quarterly, 32,* 196–199.

Joyce, B. & Weil, M. (1986). *Models of teaching.* (1st, 2nd or 3rd Eds only). Boston: Allyn & Bacon.

MacKinnon, D. W. (1978). Educating for creativity: A modern myth? In G. A. Davis & J. A. Scott (Eds.), *Training creative thinking.* Huntington, NY: Krieger.

Renzulli, J. S. (1991). The National Research Center on the Gifted and Talented: The dream, the design and the destination. *Gifted Child Quarterly 35,* 73–80.

Schiever, S. W. & Maker, C. G. (1991). Enrichment and acceleration: An overview and new directions. In N. Colangelo & G. A. Davis (Eds.). *Handbook of gifted education.* Needham Heights, MA: Allyn & Bacon.

Starko, A. J. (1994). *Creativity in the classroom.* Boston: Longman Publishers.

Terman, L. M. (1925). Genetic studies of genius. (Vol. 1) *Mental and physical traits of a thousand gifted children.* Stanford, CA: Stanford University Press.

Texas State Plan and Guidelines for the Education of the Gifted/Talented (1991). Texas Education Agency.

Torrance, E. P. (1981). Non-test ways of identifying the creatively gifted. In J. C. Gowan, J. Khatena, & E. P. Torrance (Eds.). *Creativity: Its educational implications* (2nd Ed.). Dubuque, IA: Kendall/Hunt.

Treffinger, D. J. (1982). Gifted students, regular students: Sixty ingredients for a better blend. *Elementary School Journal, 82,* 267–273.

Van-Tassel-Baska, J. (1994). *Comprehensive curriculum for gifted learners.* (2nd Ed.). Boston: Allyn & Bacon.

Walberg, H. J. (1982). Child traits and environmental conditions of highly eminent adults. *Gifted Child Quarterly, 25,* 103–107.

Winner, E. (1997). Exceptionally high intelligence and schooling. *American Psychologist, 52*(10), 1070–1081.

CHAPTER 23

Bilingual Education and English as a Second Language

Several early immigrant groups in Texas established schools in which both English and the group's language were used. The bilingual programs disappeared in the intense, almost xenophobic patriotism of World War I. In 1918 the Texas Legislature passed several laws to encourage the "Americanization" of the State. Among these were the mandate of daily instruction in "intelligent patriotism" (Acts 4th C.S., 1918, p. 67), and the requirement that superintendents, principals, and teachers "use the English language exclusively" in conducting the schools' business and instruction (Acts 4th C.S., 1918, p. 170).

At least as early as 1960, educators were deeply concerned with improving the educational system for Spanish-speaking students. They considered the undeniable, though unsubstantiated, dropout rate among Hispanic students (later determined to be approximately 80% in the late '60s). They recognized that the Spanish-speaking population was under-educated (even the younger Hispanics averaged only between four and five years of formal education). They admitted that the traditional approaches had not been effective. They began to seek new approaches to educating the Spanish-speaking students, many of whom came to school with little or no English. One of the alternatives discussed was bilingual education.

In 1964 bilingual education was "reborn" in Texas with the establishment of programs in the United Consolidated (Laredo) and San Antonio Independent School Districts (Andersson & Boyer, 1970, Vol. 1, pp. 18–19). To provide these programs, the districts obtained special permission to use Spanish for instruction. In United Consolidated, the program included all the children, both Spanish and English speakers, so that each child learned both English and Spanish; in San Antonio the program was directed only to the Spanish-speaking children. Both models (an enrichment approach in United; a compensatory approach in San Antonio) proved successful. These and other successful programs elsewhere in the United States provided evidence supporting the enactment of Title VII of the Elementary and Secondary Education Act (ESEA) in 1967. Texas school districts began requesting special permission for bilingual programs to take advantage of funding under Title VII.

By 1969 the Texas Legislature modified the "English only" law to permit bilingual instruction (Acts 1969, 61st Legislature, p. 2920, ch. 889). With this blanket approval, a number of districts sought funding to establish Title VII bilingual education programs. Four years later the legislature mandated bilingual education.

The Texas Bilingual Education Act of 1973 established the State policy as follows:

> English is the basic language of the State of Texas. Public schools are responsible for providing full opportunity for all students to become competent in speaking, reading, writing, and comprehending the English language. The

Prepared for inclusion in this text by Robert L. Tipton, Texas Education Agency, 1991.

legislature finds that there are large numbers of students in the state who come from environments where the primary language is other than English. Experience has shown that public school classes in which instruction is given only in English are often inadequate for the education of these students. . . . The legislature believes that bilingual education and special language programs can meet the needs of these students and facilitate their integration into the regular school curriculum (Texas Education Code).

A program of dual language instruction was required in grades one to six in districts which have "an enrollment of 20 or more students of limited English speaking ability in any language classification in the same grade level" (Acts 1973, 63rd Legislature, p. 860, ch. 392). (The phrase "limited English speaking ability" was changed to "limited English proficient" in subsequent revisions.) The next legislature amended this law to require bilingual education from kindergarten through grade three, and to fund programs through grade five (Acts 1975, 64th Legislature, p. 897, ch. 334).

The current grade levels, kindergarten through the elementary grades (at least grade five), were mandated in 1981. The State Board of Education also prescribed instruction in English as a second language for all limited English proficient students not enrolled in a bilingual education program. The amendments adopted in 1981 provided for two other major modifications in the law.

First, the 1981 amendments established Language Proficiency Assessment Committees. These committees were originally charged with identifying limited English proficient students, recommending placement in the bilingual education program (or in the English as a second language program if there were no bilingual education program available), determining when the student was no longer limited English proficient and recommending his/her placement in the all-English program, and reviewing the progress of students who had been exited from the bilingual education or English as a second language program for a period of two years. In 1991 their function was changed significantly. The committees are no longer responsible for the identification of limited English proficient students; this has become a function of the district. Instead, the committees are to (Title 19, Texas Administration Code, 89.5):

- designate the language proficiency level of each limited English proficient student
- designate the level of academic achievement of each limited English proficient student

- designate, subject to parental approval, the initial instructional placement of each limited English proficient student in the required program
- facilitate the participation of limited English proficient students in other special programs for which they are eligible
- classify students as English proficient, and recommend their exit from the bilingual education or English as a second language program

Second, the 1981 amendments required that the Texas Education Agency monitor local districts' programs more often and more thoroughly.

In 1984, the legislature enacted two important amendments to the law. The first provides that districts required to provide a bilingual education program must "offer a voluntary summer program for children of limited English proficiency who will be eligible for admission to kindergarten or the first grade at the beginning of the next school year" (Acts 1984, 68th Legislature, 2nd C.S., ch. 28, art. IV, part B). These sessions must be held during the eight weeks immediately prior to the beginning of the new school term. The focus must be on language development activities.

The second amendment "institutionalized" the programs. Prior to 1984, the programs were funded through a separate per capita allocation. The finance package adopted in the special session of 1984 provided that programs in bilingual education and English as a second language would be funded through the usual processes. A formula was established to add 10% to the allocation for each limited English proficient student served in either of the programs.

PROGRAM DESCRIPTION

The pre-1970 bilingual education programs were developed to meet the specific education needs of students; there was little or no theory or research to guide the practitioner at that time. "Common sense" and experience in the classroom with Spanish-speaking children provided the basis for developing the bilingual education programs. Practitioners relied on their discussions with other educators and the informal exchange of data. By the late '60s, the successful programs exhibited certain basic characteristics. The Texas Education Agency reviewed these programs and developed a description which specified six components for a bilingual education program. This description was published to assist districts in the development of local programs, especially if the district intended to apply for Title VII, ESEA, funding. Later they were adopted by the State Board of Education as the description of the mandated bilingual education program. These components were (Title 19, Texas Administrative Code, 77.353 adopted in 1985):

- Basic concepts starting the student in the school environment shall be taught in the student's primary language.
- Basic skills of comprehending, speaking, reading, and writing shall be developed in the student's primary language.
- Basic skills of comprehending, speaking, reading, and writing shall be developed in the English language.
- Subject matter and concepts shall be taught in the student's primary language.
- Subject matter and concepts shall be taught in the English language using English as a second language methods.
- Attention shall be given to instilling in the student confidence, self-assurance, and a positive identity with his or her cultural heritage.

The amount of time to be dedicated to each of the components was to be based on the student's proficiency in the primary language and in English. In addition, both the law and the rules provided that limited English proficient students participate in regular classes with their English-speaking peers in subjects such as art, music, and physical education.

In 1991, the description of the mandated bilingual education program was modified as follows (Title 19, Texas Administrative Code, 89.3):

The bilingual education program shall address the affective, linguistic, and cognitive needs of limited English proficient students as follows:

1. affective—limited English proficient students shall be provided instruction in their home language to introduce basic concepts of the school environment, and instruction both in their home language and in English which instills confidence, self-assurance, and a positive identity with their cultural heritages. The program shall address the history and cultural heritage associated with both the students' home language and the United States;
2. linguistic—limited English proficient students shall be provided instruction in the skills of comprehension, speaking, reading, and composition both in their home language and in English. The instruction in both languages shall be structured to ensure that the students

master the required essential elements and higher order thinking skills in all subjects; and
3. cognitive—limited English proficient students shall be provided instruction in mathematics, science, health, and social studies both in their home language and in English. The content area instruction in both languages shall be structured to ensure that the students master the required essential elements and higher order thinking skills in all subjects.

The requirement that limited English proficient students participate in regular classes with their English-speaking peers in subjects such as art, music, and physical education was retained.

English as a second language programs must be provided for limited English proficient students who are not enrolled in a bilingual education program. The program must provide specialized instruction in English which will enable the student to develop proficiency in the comprehension, speaking, reading, and composition in the English language. In prekindergarten through the elementary grades, the time afforded instruction in English as a second language may vary from a minimum of the amount of time accorded to instruction in English language arts in the regular program to total immersion. In grades seven through 12, the time afforded instruction in English as a second language may vary from one-third of the instructional day to total immersion. The amount of time dedicated to English as a second language instruction for each student is to be recommended by the Language Proficiency Assessment Committee based on the needs of the student.

PROBLEMS

There have been two major obstacles to the development of bilingual education and English as a second language programs: the shortage of appropriate materials for bilingual instruction, and the shortage of adequately trained and properly certified classroom teachers.

During the first decade, bilingual education programs had to rely on Spanish language materials designed for and produced in other countries. Teachers found it necessary to modify these materials in three ways. First, the content was based on the curricula of the country of origin so only the parts relevant to the local curriculum could be used. Second, the experiences of the children in the United States were often radically different from those of the children for whom the materials were designed. Teachers had to bridge the cultural gap between the materials and their students' experiences. Third, in some cases the Spanish dialect used, principally manifested in the choice of words, was foreign to the students in Texas schools.

With the extension of Spanish-English bilingual education programs, publishers in the United States have taken greater interest in the development and production of materials for the programs. At present, it is possible to obtain Spanish versions of many major textbook series. For this reason, the bilingual education programs in Texas use the Spanish versions of the state-adopted texts in the content areas. Special materials for Spanish language arts are available and have been adopted.

The establishment of bilingual education programs in the public schools was not anticipated by institutions of higher education. With the 1973 mandate, provision was made to certify teachers based on their prior experience in the early programs. The acute shortage of such teachers, however, led to the establishment of an institute program for training and certifying teachers based on experience rather than college/university training. By the late '70s, this approach had proved unsatisfactory. Both undergraduate and special postgraduate programs in colleges and universities were developed to train teachers. At one time there was a total of 42 colleges and universities in Texas with bilingual teacher education programs. Most of these programs, however, never attracted the number of students anticipated. For this reason, some institutions have been forced to terminate these programs.

Because of the shortage of teachers, many districts must provide alternative programs under specially granted exceptions. One of the conditions for receiving an exception is the submission of a plan to recruit and/or train an adequate number of teachers for the bilingual education and English as a second language programs. In many districts, these teachers are paid incentives. Nevertheless, the greatest problem facing districts is the shortage of trained and certified bilingual education teachers.

The shortage of trained and certified English as a second language teachers is almost as acute as the shortage of bilingual education teachers. Although the certificate does not require the knowledge or study of a language other than English, few prospective or practicing teachers have been attracted to this area.

Even if English as a second language teachers were available, the substitution of English as a second language programs for bilingual education programs would be both illegal and unwise. In the bilingual education program, the students are taught all the basic skills and higher order thinking

skills at grade level in their home language while they are learning English. When they have mastered English, therefore, they can be placed in the all-English program without being at a scholastic disadvantage. The students in English as a second language programs, even those in a total immersion program, are not taught in their home language. For this reason, they do not develop all the skills commonly taught at their grade level. By the time they have mastered enough English to be placed in the regular academic program, they have fallen behind their peers in academic skills. Bilingual education programs have proved to be a superior long term solution to the problems of educating limited English proficient students.

CONCLUSION

A great deal of progress has been made in meeting the educational needs of students who speak a language other than English. Bilingual education and English as a second language programs are not, of course, panaceas. There are still unresolved problems. Nevertheless, the State is firmly committed to providing meaningful education for all students including those of limited English proficiency.

NOTES

1. The "English only" law of 1918 was originally directed against the immigrant populations from German Empire nations. Exceptions, under certain conditions, were made for Spanish. Later policies and rules were extended indiscriminately to all languages in spite of the original intent.
2. The U. S. Supreme Court decision in *Lau v. Nichols* was not released until January 1974, several months after the adoption of the Texas Bilingual Education Act. The Court found:

   Under these state-imposed standards [the provision of instruction to ensure mastery of English by all pupils and requirement of proficiency in English as a condition for graduation] there is no equality of treatment merely by providing students with the same facilities, textbooks, teachers, and curriculum; for students who do not understand English are effectively foreclosed from any meaningful education.

   No specific remedy was asked by the plaintiffs; hence the Court did not prescribe any particular educational program. It noted, however, that options included "teaching English" (that is, English as a second language), "giving instructions . . . in Chinese" (that is, bilingual education), or some other program. The effect of this decision on Texas was a reinforcement of the already adopted state mandate.

REFERENCES

Acts (of the Texas legislature), various years.

Andersson, T. & Boyer, M. (1970) *Bilingual Schooling in the United States.* Austin: Southwest Educational Development Laboratory.

Lau et al. v. Nichols, et al., 1974.

State Board of Education, *Agenda,* February 1982.

State Board of Education, *Agenda,* May 1991.

Texas Education Code, various sections (principally Chapter 21, Subchapter L).

Title 19, Texas Administrative Code, various sections (principally Chapter 77, Subchapter R adopted in 1985 and repealed in 1991, and Chapter 89, Subchapter A adopted in 1991).

Dyslexia

Perhaps no other educational term evokes more misinterpretations and misunderstanding than that of dyslexia. According to the International Reading Association's *A Dictionary of Reading and Related Terms*, dyslexia "has come to have so many incompatible connotations that it has lost any real value for educators, except as a fancy word for a reading problem" (Harris & Hodges, 1981, p. 95). Inouye (1981) wrote, "Put all the definitions in a line and then pick every 73rd word. This would be *your* definition" (p. 3). The definitions are so varied and broad that an estimated 80 percent of U. S. students could be classified learning disabled by using one or more of the various current definitions (Ysseldyke et al., 1983).

Also associated with defining dyslexia is the seemingly indiscriminate activity of labeling children. Experts argue that labeling children does little to help teachers plan instruction, may lead to stigmatization and biased perceptions, may result in excluding children from needed services because of improper labeling, and may lead to a decline in learner self-concept (Gillis, 1994; Barry, 1993; Milich, 1992). Between the academic years 1976–77 and 1989–90, though the number of U. S. school children remained constant, the number of students identified as having learning disabilities increased approximately 150 percent; the increase may be in part a result of increased labeling for funding purposes (National Center for Educational Statistics, 1993, pp. 11, 63).

Without question, reading is one of the most critical skills humans must learn in today's society, and "[l]iteracy activity is indispensable to citizens as they negotiate their paths through society . . ." (Guthrie & Greaney, 1991, p. 68). Though becoming literate is challenging for most readers, it is even more monumental for the dyslexic child or a child with reading problems. In spite of the controversy surrounding both the definitional differences of dyslexia and the labeling of children, the 69th Texas Legislature passed House Bill 157 in 1985, providing Texas educators with both the definition of dyslexia and the clout to help those with reading problems get the needed help.

This chapter gives a brief presentation of the various definitions of dyslexia (including one for Texas) along with possible causes. It also explains House Bill 157, Texas State Board of Education (SBOE), and Texas Education Agency (TEA) policies and guidelines governing dyslexia and related disorders and gives a sampling of how Texas school districts are implementing the law and policies.

DEFINING DYSLEXIA AND POSSIBLE CAUSES

In spite of years of research, no clear consensus exists on a definition of dyslexia or its causes. The many definitions that exist basically fall into two

Prepared for inclusion in this text by John E. Jacobson, 1995.

categories—medical and psychological. The medical profession tends to regard dyslexia as a disease involving a causative constitutional factor (inborn developmental basis), whereas the psychological profession deems it a serious problem of unspecified origin (Harris & Hodges, 1981).

Though definitions date back as early as the late 1800s (Hinshelwood, 1896), from a medical perspective Samuel Orton, a neurologist, popularized the term in 1937. He proposed that severe reading problems may *not* be the result of physical, mental, or environmental causes but, rather, a hemispheric brain dominance problem with neither the left nor the right hemisphere dominating. He hypothesized that in individuals with this condition, words and letters are perceived as being mirror images of one another. He based this conclusion on his observations of readers and writers reversing letters (*b* and *d*) and words (*saw* and *was*). Though he later changed his view of dyslexia and though no evidence in brain research supports his original hypothesis, this concept of dyslexia persists (Weaver, 1994).

Orton, however, may not have been too far off. Some of today's brain specialists believe that severe reading difficulty may result from a deficiency in the functioning of one cerebral hemisphere, or from inadequate integration of the two hemispheres. Researchers studying healthy normal and abnormal brains have established that reading, writing, and other complex processes involve both hemispheres. If the left or right hemisphere was removed from individuals early in life, researchers found that individuals can compensate to a large degree, but not totally. Children with the right hemisphere remaining have problems processing graphophonemes (sounding out unfamiliar words), syntax, and literal comprehension (facts and details), whereas children with the left hemisphere remaining have problems with visual and spatial word perception and comprehending the whole or higher levels of comprehension (Dennis, 1982). (For more information on this, see Weaver, 1994.)

From a psychological perspective, some deny that neurological origins contribute in any significant way in causing dyslexia but do agree that dyslexia has a constitutional origin. In one definition Harris and Sipay (1980) stated, "Sometimes it [dyslexia] implies a constitutionally based reading disability in an individual who is free from mental defect, serious neurotic traits, and gross neurological deficits" (p. 137).

Texas defined dyslexia in House Bill 157 (now found in the Texas Education Code) as follows:

"Dyslexia" means a disorder of constitutional origin manifested by a difficulty in learning to read, write, or spell, despite conventional instruction, adequate intelligence, and sociocultural opportunity.

"Related disorders" include disorders similar to or related to dyslexia such as developmental auditory imperception, dysphasia, specific developmental dyslexia, developmental dysgraphia, and developmental spelling disability.

Based on Texas' definition of dyslexia, children are excluded from receiving dyslexia services for sociocultural factors that might contribute to reading or writing failure. Sociocultural factors dealing with children's environment must be ruled out prior to their receiving services for dyslexia. This means that ESL children would not qualify if their second language is the cause of the reading problem, nor would children who lacked sufficient exposure to print prior to entering school. In both cases children could not qualify for special help based on the state's definition of dyslexia.

Once sociocultural issues are ruled out, children still must be failing at reading and writing to receive dyslexia services. Isolating sociocultural issues as the determining factor creates confusion because virtually all available research "has failed to evaluate or adequately control for the environmental and/or educational deficits that may cause a reading disorder" (Velluntino & Denckla, 1991, p. 603). In essence, environmental factors such as sociocultural issues cannot be separated from the other conditions that may cause dyslexia.

TEXAS DYSLEXIA LAW

House Bill 157 not only provided a definition of dyslexia, but it also authorized the State Board of Education to approve a means for testing children for dyslexia and related disorders; and gave local school districts the responsibility for screening and treating students. Originally the bill required TEA to develop an inservice program to train teachers in recognizing and treating dyslexia and related reading disorders. That portion of the bill was repealed later, however, leaving school districts with both the financial and the inservice responsibilities.

In keeping with the law, the SBOE, with the help of TEA staff, created and approved dyslexia policies and guidelines. The SBOE initially approved these policies and guidelines on January 11, 1986. In March 1990, the SBOE passed a rule, or more formal directive, requiring implementation through grade 12. The new ruling is found in the document, *Dyslexia and Related Disorders: An Overview of State and Federal Requirements* (Texas Education Agency,

1992). Included in the document is information for school districts and parents pertaining to the state's dyslexia law and its relationship to the federal laws, Section 504 of the Rehabilitation Act of 1973 and the Individuals with Disabilities Education Act (IDEA), a list of dyslexia characteristics, and a four-phase process that schools must use in screening and treating children for dyslexia.

THE FOUR-PHASE PROCESS IN SCREENING AND PLACEMENT

To provide an effective program for screening and treating students who exhibit dyslexia or related disorders, the TEA (1992) developed a list of characteristics associated with dyslexia and created a four-phase process for schools to follow in providing appropriate services. The list of associated characteristics includes the following:

- problems in learning the names of the letters of the alphabet
- difficulty in learning to write the alphabet correctly in sequence
- difficulty in learning and remembering printed words
- reversal of letters or sequences of letters
- difficulty in learning to read
- difficulty in reading comprehension
- cramped or illegible handwriting
- repeated erratic spelling errors (p. 19)

The TEA provided a second list of characteristics that *may* be associated with dyslexia, which includes:

- delay in spoken language
- difficulty in finding the "right" word when speaking
- delay in establishing preferred hand for writing
- delay in learning right and left and other directionality components such as up-down, front-behind, over-under, east-west, and others
- problems in learning the concept of time and temporal sequencing, e.g., yesterday-tomorrow, days of the week and months of the year
- family history of similar problems (p. 19–20).

As a cautionary note, the TEA prefaced the characteristics by stating:

Many of the characteristics associated with dyslexia also are found in children with other specific learning disabilities or with speech/spoken language disorders. Some of the characteristics also may be present in some young children in the course of normal development.

However, when these characteristics are not age-appropriate and interfere with learning, they may be symptoms of a language or learning disorder, including dyslexia, and the child may need special assistance in academic or related areas (p. 19).

Two things emerge clearly from dyslexia research.

1. No two individuals exhibit exactly the same configuration of reading difficulties (Weaver, 1994).
2. Essentially all normally developing readers at some time or another exhibit one or more of the above characteristics.

It is obvious why so much confusion exists regarding proper identification!

Because identifying dyslexic children is so complex and difficult, the TEA developed a four-phase structure in an attempt to provide a systematic manner for screening and treating dyslexic children. In phase I initial data are gathered on those who exhibit dyslexic characteristics. Phase II allows for additional testing and outlines specific remedial programming for students identified as potentially dyslexic. If students do not make sufficient progress in phase II, they move into phase III, where additional screening and individual dyslexic instruction programs are created to meet students' needs. The final phase involves referral of students with severe dyslexia or related disorders to special education programs. A brief description of each phase of the four-phase structure follows.

Phase I: Data Gathering

Typically, data gathering takes place in the first grade. This phase, however, can take place at any grade level. Data are gathered from several sources that include:

- vision screening
- hearing screening
- speech and language screening through a referral process
- academic progress reports
- teacher reports of aptitude, behavior, and problems
- parent conferences
- Texas Assessment of Academic Skill (TAAS)
- results of basal reading series
- reading and writing portfolios (including samples of students' writing, lists of books read, audiotapes of oral reading, formal assessment, etc.)

After sufficient evaluation, school districts determine what actions are needed to ensure improved performance. Needed support actions may include, but are not limited to: vision and hearing correction, retention, rearrangement of class assignments, supportive counseling, tutoring, speech therapy, or other appropriate program modifications.

During this phase or any other phase, referral for testing through special education may occur if deemed necessary. At any time students do not make expected progress during this phase, they should be moved into phase II of the process. Students who exhibit characteristics associated with dyslexia do not have to fail phases I and II to be evaluated for dyslexia or special education.

Phase II: Remedial Programs

Phase II begins the development of special remedial programs. In determining appropriate remedial instruction, the following appraisal instruments are suggested. Results from these tests coupled with the information obtained in phase I should be used for remedial program development.

- tests to determine basic reading, reading comprehension, writing, spelling competency, and specific related problems
- an informal reading inventory to identify specific problems related to reading (TEA, p. 21)

Based on collected student assessment data, appropriate remedial instruction should be provided. TEA suggests that suitable programs could include, but are not limited to: remedial or compensatory programs, bilingual, tutorial, summer school, and the like. If students do not make satisfactory progress in these programs, the next phase should be implemented.

Phase III: Identification of Instructional Programs for Dyslexic Students

Up to this point students who satisfactorily advanced academically are not considered dyslexic. Students who have not made sufficient progress, however, are moved into this phase, where they may be identified as having dyslexia or a related disorder. The TEA gives the following guidelines for this identification process. If students who have been detected as having primary difficulties in reading, writing, and spelling do not make the necessary academic advancements in district remedial programs and all other causes have been eliminated, continued evaluation must consider identifying students as having dyslexia or a related disorder. All Section 504 federal requirements must be met in this process, including:

- notification of parents
- opportunity for parents to examine relevant records

- evaluation using validated tests
- placement by a team of persons knowledgeable about the student and about the meaning of the evaluation data and placement options (TEA, 1992, p. 5).

The original TEA policy stated that a school district's designee analyze all accumulated data, including consideration of possible problems of constitutional origin, and then judge if a child is dyslexic. However, according to federal guidelines, no single designee can make the identification and placement decision (TEA, 1992). Therefore, a team of persons knowledgeable about students and about the meaning of the evaluation data and placement options must make the decision, based on a summative analysis. The student must:

- exhibit characteristics associated with dyslexia
- lack appropriate academic progress
- have adequate intelligence
- receive conventional regular and remedial instruction
- exhibit lack of progress due to factors other than sociocultural issues such as language differences, inconsistent attendance, and lack of experiential background
- have a constitutional origin (i.e., have an inborn developmental basis) for lack of progress (TEA, 1992, p. 22)

Treatment follows the identification process and is the responsibility of the school district. The school district's specific treatment program must be offered to students in all grades, must be delivered in a remedial classroom setting by trained teachers, and must contain certain elements. The program must:

- be individualized
- be multisensory
- contain intensive phonetics (alphabetic principle understanding)
- contain synthetic phonics (learning of letters, sounds, blending, etc.)
- contain linguistic elements (words and sentences carry meaning)
- be meaning based (reading comprehension)
- be systematic (logical presentation)
- be process oriented
- be sequential
- be cumulative (Texas Education Agency, 1992, p. 22)

Phase IV: Referral to Special Education

Students found to have severe dyslexia or related disorders who do not respond adequately to programs offered in phases II and III should be referred to special education for a comprehensive assessment and possible identification as having a disability. Referral and testing procedures must comply with the federal requirements of Section 504 and follow state guidelines.

The TEA specifies that students spend a reasonable amount of time in each phase. Yet it does not advocate that students be placed in any one phase for a set period of time only to discover later that they should have proceeded immediately to the next phase.

Clarifying Guidelines

In a question-and-answer format, the TEA (1992) has provided answers to many programmatic and policy questions. Some of the questions asked most frequently, with their accompanying answers, follow.

Q: How does Section 504 of the federal law affect the way school districts implement the state law regarding dyslexia and the State Board rule?

A: Children who finally are determined to have dyslexia may or may not be considered as having a disability. Therefore, following Section 504 requirements in all phases will ensure compliance.

Q: Is every student suspected of having dyslexia also considered as having a disability within the meaning of Section 504?

A: No. Under Section 504 a disability must limit a major life activity substantially, and the student must have a record of such disability or be regarded as having such disability. The nine major life activities given include: caring for oneself, performing manual tasks, walking, seeing, hearing, speaking, breathing, learning, and working.

Q: What procedural protections are provided to parents who may not agree with the decisions a district makes?

A: If a student has a disability, the federal guidelines of IDEA apply and must be followed. Students not suspected of having a disability, however, are protected under Section 504. Under Section 504 guidelines parents may file a request for a hearing with the school district. Appeals by either the school district or the parents may be made to a court of law.

Q: May a parent refer a student?

A: Yes, but any dispute over identification or placement should follow procedures outlined in the previous answer.

Q: What monies may be used to support dyslexia programs?

A: State foundation funds, compensatory funds, or local funds. Special education funds may be used for students whose disability warrants special education services.

Q: What kind of test can be used to determine adequate intelligence, and is there a cutoff score to determine adequate intelligence?

A: Any valid individual or group standardized intelligence test may be used. There is no cutoff score to determine adequate intelligence. School districts determine what is adequate intelligence.

Q: How can the student's lack of progress be determined to be of constitutional origin?

A: By ruling out other origins that may cause the lack of progress, such as brain insult, disease, or surgery aggravating the reading problems.

Q: What certification should teachers of students with dyslexia and related disorders have?

A: A valid elementary or secondary certificate (depending upon the grade level of the students being serviced) is all that is necessary. Teachers with special coursework in reading and reading disabilities are preferred.

IMPLEMENTING DYSLEXIA POLICIES AND GUIDELINES IN TEXAS SCHOOLS

Because SBOE rules and guidelines are only partially descriptive, school districts are left with establishing their own procedures. These procedures include:

- creating a management structure
- choosing a district designee and others qualified to serve on the identifying team (number of teams depends on district's size and needs)
- setting local guidelines
- establishing referral, screening, and placement procedures
- selecting screening instruments
- determining the kinds of remedial instructional programs for the various phases
- choosing instructional staff

From the above list, perhaps one of the most monumental tasks that districts have is selecting the proper screening instruments. Confusion over symptoms and causes of dyslexia leaves educators the chore of identifying children with dyslexia. IQ tests traditionally have been a main data source. Kamhi (1992), however, reported tautological reasoning in using standardized IQ tests to determine whether a wide discrepancy exists between intelligence and reading ability, as the IQ is influenced by the necessary reading required to accomplish the IQ tasks.

In a study of 330 randomly selected school districts (33 percent of Texas school districts), Hill (in press) studied how districts identify dyslexic children. She found that districts use more than 140 different testing instruments, including formal and informal, standardized and nonstandardized, and group and individually administered tests.

Districts reported using individually administered IQ tests twice as often as group IQ tests. The individual instruments most frequently used were the Weschsler Intelligence Scale for Children, the Slosson Intelligence Test, the Test of Nonverbal Intelligence, and the Kaufman Ability Battery for Children. The group IQ tests most widely administered were the Otis Lennon, the Cognitive Abilities Test, and the Test of Cognitive Skills.

Hill also found that standardized achievement tests were a popular screening device. Group achievement tests were used twice as often as individually administered tests (just opposite of IQ tests). The top achievement group tests used were the Iowa Test of Basic Skills, the California Achievement Test, and the Texas Assessment of Academic Skills. The individually administered achievement tests used most commonly were the Woodcock-Johnson Psychoeducational Battery, the Wide Range Achievement Test Revised, and the Kaufman Test of Educational Achievement.

Hill also compared phonological awareness tests reported by districts against those suggested by reading authorities and found that districts were using only one of the recommended tests—the Decoding Skills Test. If districts are not appraising children's weaknesses and strengths accurately because of invalid testing, a potential problem exists. Given TEA's instructional requirements of using intensive phonetics and synthetic phonics in remedial programs for children with dyslexia, children who are identified improperly as having phonological weakness and placed in instructional programs with heavy doses of phonics instruction waste precious instructional time and resources on needless learning activities.

Kamhi (1992) indicated that, although individuals with dyslexia may learn to read fairly well, they always will have difficulty with phonological processing. Given what reading authorities tell us is good instructional practice (teaching to individuals' strengths rather than their weakness to help them compensate for their problems), TEA's instructional requirements of incorporating intensive phonetics and synthetic phonics in remedial dyslexia programs may be inappropriate. Instead of drill-and-practice phonics programs, Weaver (1994) suggests that the following practices are especially salient in helping special learners:

1. Learners are treated as capable and developing, not as incapable and deficient.

2. Learners' strengths are emphasized, not their weaknesses.
3. Likewise, learners' unique learning abilities and strategies are valued.
4. Students' needs and interests help guide the development of the curriculum.
5. Assessment is based much less on standardized tests than upon individual growth and upon the achievement of classroom goals, including goals for individuals that may have been established jointly by the teacher and the student.
6. The teacher promotes the learning of all students, by creating a supportive classroom community, giving students time (the whole school year) in which to grow, offering choices and ownership, providing response and structure, and gradually expecting and allowing students to take more responsibility for their work. (p. 498)

While selecting proper screening instruments is important, determining proper instructional programs is crucial. Sharon O'Neal, TEA Director of Reading, reported that a wide variety of instructional programs exists throughout the state. These programs range from being highly skill-oriented to holistic in nature. Program variances stem from philosophical differences in school district staffs as well as the influence of SBOE guidelines. Those who take a more traditional stance have dyslexia programs that typically are highly structured and involve an abundance of instruction in drill-and-practice skill mastery. Generally the programs focus on having children learn letter names, sounds, and phonetic elements of the language. Those who take a more holistic stance create programs focused more on meaning and relevancy and craft programs based on children's strengths.

Currently no data exist on either the extent of each program or its effectiveness. Although traditional programs have had some reported success, current research favors programs focusing on meaning and teaching strategies for gaining meaning rather than on the decoding aspects of learning to read (Weaver, 1994). A study of current dyslexia program offerings in Texas schools would be enlightening. An evaluation of their effectiveness is essential. Furthermore, measuring students' progress should include a broader scope of measurements than presently suggested in the TEA's guidelines—not only assessing the cognitive but the affective domain as well.

Perhaps of greater concern than the specific remediation programs being used is the prevailing philosophy toward the children with dyslexia.

Nearly all the definitions, screening devices, and remediation programs operate from the paradigm that views the child with dyslexia as deficient. Many of the definitions of dyslexia label children as such, based on their existing inabilities "even after traditional instructional practices" have been introduced. A different paradigm option offers the view that children with dyslexia are not as much *deficient* as *different*. Their learning styles vary from the norm. This paradigm creates some discomfort for educators because it demands a variation from traditional educational approaches. Instead of so much effort spent in evaluating for the dyslexic condition, educators would be asked to evaluate programs and make accommodations for learners' differences and build programs based on their strengths (Weaver, 1994).

Of final interest is how involved school districts are in identifying students as having dyslexia and how concerned they are in providing remedial programs. Many districts report being highly involved in identifying and treating children with dyslexia, whereas perhaps equally as many (or more) downplay or purposely avoid the whole business of dyslexia by approaching the treatment of dyslexia in other ways (O'Neal, 1994). This avoidance perhaps is based on the initial problem posed at the beginning of this chapter: What dyslexia really is, and how it is identified. Perhaps Kamhi (1992) summed it up best: "If nothing can be used to differentiate individuals with dyslexia from the garden variety poor reader, then we should stop using the term" (p. 50).

To date the state has defined dyslexia and established procedures to provide services to fit the state's definition. Yet, until the controversies of defining, identifying, and providing appropriate services are settled, current laws and guidelines will continue to promote current practices in which identification and labeling procedures are questionable and instruction may or may not be appropriate.

REFERENCES

Barry, A. L. (1993). What's in a name. *Reading Horizons, 34*(1), 3–12.

Dennis, M. (1982). The relationship of beginning reading instruction and miscue patterns. In W. D. Page (Ed.), *Help for the reading teacher: New directions in research* (pp. 42–51). Urbana, IL: National Conference on Research in English and the ERIC Clearinghouse on Reading and Communication Skills. (available from National Council of Teachers of English.)

Gillis, M. K. (1994). Attention deficit disorder: Just another label. *Reading and Writing Quarterly: Overcoming Learning Difficulties, 10*(2), 119–24.

Guthrie, J. T., & Greaney, V. (1991). Literacy acts. In R. Barr, M. Kamil, P. Mosenthal, & P. D. Pearson (Eds.), *Handbook of reading research, Vol. 2.* (pp. 68–96). White Plains, NY: Longman Publishing Group.

Harris, A. J., & Sipay, E. (1980). *How to increase reading ability.* New York: Longman.

Harris, T. L., & Hodges, R. E. (Eds.) (1981). *A dictionary of reading and related terms.* Newark, DE: International Reading Association.

Hill, M. The test for dyslexia! Is there one? *The State of Reading.*

Hinshelwood, J. (1896). A case of dyslexia: A peculiar form of word-blindness. *Lancet, 2,* 1451–1454.

Inouye, R. (1981). Unpublished manuscript.

Kamhi, A. G. (1992). Response to historical perspective: A developmental language perspective. *Journal of Learning Disabilities, 25*(1), 48–52.

Milich, R. (1992). Effects of stigmatizing information on children's peer relations: Believing is seeing. *School Psychology Review, 21*(3), 400–409.

National Center for Educational Statistics. (1993). *Digest of education statistics 1993.* U. S. Department of Education, Office of Educational Research and Improvement.

Texas Education Agency. (1992). *Dyslexia and related disorders: An overview of state and federal requirements.* Austin: TEA.

Velluntino, F. R., & Denckla, M. B. (1991). Cognitive and neuropsychological foundations of word identification in poor and normally developing readers. Literacy acts. In R. Barr, M. Kamil, P. Mosenthal, & P. D. Pearson (Eds.), *Handbook of reading research, Vol. 2* (pp. 571–608). New York: Longman.

Weaver, C. (1994). *Reading process and practice: From socio-psycholinguistics to whole language.* Portsmouth, NH: Heinemann.

Ysseldyke, J. E., Thurlow, M. L., Graden, J., Wesson, C., Deno, S., & Algozzine, B. (1983). Generalizations from five years of research on assessment and decision making. *Exceptional Education Quarterly, 4*(1), 75–93.

CHAPTER 25

Middle Schools in Texas

Young adolescents between the ages of 10 and 15 typically present an enigma for educators. They fidget, squirm, laugh, sulk, cry, and argue. They are lethargic, energetic, creative, helpless, invulnerable, and frustrating. Simultaneously they demand the security of childhood and the privileges of adulthood, and they continually need the acceptance and approval of parents and peers alike. They ask the most profound metaphysical questions humans ask, and above all, they demand fairness in all things. They experience more dramatic physical, emotional, social and intellectual development than at any other time in their lives after their second or third birthday. Rapid change is a drastic and dramatic way of life for them.

THE PROBLEM

The conditions and times in which young adolescents live have changed as well. Youngsters today enter a society of unprecedented choices and pressures that earlier generations did not experience. Since the 1950s, teenage suicides, substance abuse, sexual experimentation, and violence have increased while academic performance, as exemplified by Scholastic Aptitude Test (SAT) scores, has decreased. Never before have young people been so barraged with uncensored data, seduced with commercialism, and

Prepared for inclusion in this text by Thomas F. Mandeville, 1999.

maligned with faulty statistics and biased reports by the very institutions they are told to honor, respect, and emulate—government, business, religion, and the media (Males, *The Scapegoat Generation*, 1996).

Half our nation's youth are at risk of "reaching adulthood unable to meet adequately the requirements of the workplace, the commitments of relationships in families and with friends, and the responsibilities of participation in a democratic society," and for these youth, the early adolescent years offer "their last best chance to avoid a diminished future" (Carnegie Council, p. 8).

A SOLUTION

In the late 1980s the Carnegie Corporation studied 10- to 15-year-old students and the middle grade schools they attend in search of remedies for these problems. In 1989 the Carnegie Council on Adolescent Development published its report, *Turning Points: Preparing American Youth for the 21st Century,* which focuses on the significant turning points of life that young adolescents face. The report itself has become an important turning point for middle grade educators because middle grade schools are "potentially society's most powerful force to recapture millions of youth adrift, . . . [and because a] volatile mismatch exists between the organization and curriculum of middle grade schools and the intellectual and emotional needs of young adolescents" (p. 8). The *Turning Points* report lists eight specific recommendations (pp. 37–70):

1. *Creating a community for learning.* Schools should be a place where close, trusting relationships with adults and peers create a climate for students' personal growth and intellectual development.
2. *Teaching a core of common knowledge.* Every student in the middle grades should learn to think critically by mastering an appropriate body of knowledge, leading a healthy life, behaving ethically and lawfully, and assuming the responsibilities of citizenship in a pluralistic society.
3. *Ensuring success for all students.* All young adolescents should have the opportunity to succeed in every aspect of the middle grade program, regardless of previous achievement or the pace at which they learn.
4. *Empowering teachers and administrators.* Decisions concerning the experiences of middle grade students should be made by the adults who know them best.
5. *Preparing teachers for the middle grades.* Teachers in middle grade schools should be selected and educated specially to teach young adolescents.
6. *Improving academic performance through better health and fitness.* Young adolescents must be healthy in order to learn.
7. *Re-engaging families in the education of young adolescents.* If young adolescents are to succeed in school, families and middle grade schools must be allied through trust and respect.
8. *Connecting schools with communities.* Schools and community organizations should share responsibility for each middle grade student's success.

To help educators find ways to implement these recommendations, the Carnegie Corporation funded 27 Middle Grade School State Policy Initiative grants. Texas was awarded one of these grants.

THE TEXAS RESPONSE: *SPOTLIGHT ON THE MIDDLE*

With the Carnegie grant funds the Texas State Board of Education (SBOE) established a task force to study Texas' young adolescents and their schools. The task force findings were published in 1991 as *Spotlight on the Middle: The Report of the Texas Task Force on Middle School Education.* This report found that most of the state's school districts provided junior high schools for their young adolescents. In other words, the schools, the programming, and the curriculum were appropriate for older high-school age students, but not for the younger pubescents

struggling with the transition from childhood to adolescence. These younger students were being thrust into older situations before they were ready, exacerbating rather than alleviating their problems. On September 11, 1991, the State Board of Education issued a *Policy Statement on Middle Grade Education and Middle Grade Schools* calling for meaningful restructuring of middle grade schools for young adolescents. The SBOE middle grade policy is based on the philosophy that "effective middle schools serve two purposes: academic excellence and individual personal/social development. The focus is on the whole child with a balance between intellectual development and personal/social growth" (p. 16). The policy established seven goals (pp. 17–19).

Goal 1: Organizational Structure
- *Academic teams.* Four or five core subject teachers each representing a different discipline work together with 120–130 students so all students on a team have the same teachers.
- *Common planning time.* All teachers on an academic team have a common planning time to discuss students' successes and difficulties as well as for curricular and instructional team planning.
- *Flexible-block scheduling.* Block scheduling provides larger blocks of time for each subject so students meet fewer teachers and fewer new concepts each day. Further, flexible-block scheduling allows a team to adjust the amount of time devoted to each subject each day according to the amount of time needed to teach the concept. Logic and experience suggests that different concepts take different amounts of time to teach. Flexible scheduling also affords the time for active, participatory learning experiences.

Goal 2: Curriculum
- *Core of common knowledge.* The basic skills and concepts that all students need are taught by the academic team.
- *Thematic/interdisciplinary curriculum.* The academic team organizes the information and skills taught around themes that allow students to see the interrelatedness of information rather than study it in artificial segments
- *Exploratory courses.* In addition to the core of common knowledge, students are given opportunities to explore themselves, their talents, and their world through brief experiences with music, foreign language, art, athletics, mechanics, home economics, travel, and other activities.
- *Ethnic and multicultural components.* The curriculum is structured to include opportunities

for students to explore various cultures and ethnic groups as well as to understand what it means, for example, to be African Americans.

- *Relevant and challenging curriculum.* The curriculum must be challenging as well as relevant to young adolescents. One of the ways it can be relevant is for students to have some measure of choice and input. Another way is for all components of the curriculum to help students answer their most profound questions: "Who am I?" "What is life and this world all about?" and "How do I and where do I fit in?"

- *Vertical articulation.* Curriculum must be developed with elementary, middle school, and high school teachers participating together to plan a curriculum which forms a seamless web from first to twelfth grade.

Goal 3: Instruction

- *Developmentally appropriate instruction.* Instructional techniques must be appropriate to the current developmental stages and needs of middle grade students and should be targeted toward personal, social, and cognitive stages of development. Teaching techniques designed to "get them ready for high school" often are techniques appropriate for older adolescents but inappropriate for younger adolescents. For example, presentation of an abstract concept may be appropriate for high school, but most middle grade students are incapable of abstract thought without first having a concrete experience on which to develop the abstract concept.

- *Varied methodology linked to learning styles.* Instruction must be varied enough to allow all students to be successful regardless of their rates, strengths or weaknesses in learning. Note, however, that this should not be construed to mean "teach to the slowest and least able." Methods are available that allow teachers to challenge every student and to support their success in learning.

- *Flexible and heterogeneous grouping.* Grouping students by ability level is too destructive to students' self concept to be used at most grade levels and is particularly devastating to middle grade students at a time in their lives when their self-image is most fragmented and vulnerable. Further, groupings that seem "permanent" lose their effectiveness. Flexible and heterogeneous grouping and regrouping, for example, by friendships, project teams, interests, skill needs, and the like has more positive effects on learning and on personal/social development.

Goal 4: Assessment

- *Authentic assessment.* Assessments are authentic when the assessment task greatly resembles the real-world situations in which students will use the concepts and skills they learn. A large percentage of their assessments should be authentic.

- *Multiple measures.* Psychometricians know that a battery of tests provides more information than a single test in the same way that we do not evaluate the economy on a single index, but rather on the trends as exemplified by many indices. Multiple and varied measurements are essential to documenting student growth appropriately.

- *Results-focused assessment.* When designing curriculum for middle grade students, educators should begin planning with what we want the students to know and be able to do in the 21st century. We may decide, for example, that we want students to be healthy, articulate, literate, and productive citizens. Well-constructed, challenging curriculum, effective instruction, and multiple and authentic assessments lead appropriately to that result.

- *Instructional program evaluation.* Instructional programs must be evaluated regularly against and continually adapted to student success.

Goal 5: Professional Staffing and Development

- *Campus-based and student-focused professional development.* Professional development for middle grade educators should be tailored to the specific situations of individual campuses and of the communities they serve. Programs *adopted* rather than *adapted* from other campuses often fail. Options based on what is good for students should outweigh options based on funding, facilities, historical precedent, or political expediency.

- *Middle school concept.* Most middle grade teachers in Texas have either elementary or secondary certification. Few have middle grade training. Professional development for middle grade educators must be grounded in and start from the middle school concept and the needs and characteristics of early adolescents.

- *Parent-community involvement.* Parents and communities need to learn about these young people and about schools that meet their needs. Their involvement in professional staffing and development is critical to the ultimate success of the school.

Goal 6: Comprehensive Student Support

- *Network of health and human services.* Schools and teachers cannot respond adequately to all the needs of today's young adolescents. The health and human services of the community must be enlisted to assist schools.

- *Adult mentors and advisory periods.* Middle grade students need adults who will listen non-judgmentally, support, care for, and otherwise mentor them. Even the best of parents in the best of family situations cannot always meet these needs. Before the 1950s families had broad networks of relatives and neighbors to supply these caring mentors. In today's society, too many young adolescents do not have an adult mentor in their lives. Middle grade schools often provide mentors through advisory periods. Twenty to 30 minutes are set aside each day for students to meet with an adult, often a teacher, administrator, librarian, or other staff person who does not test or evaluate them. Using many adults for this advisory period allows a small student-to-adult ratio, 1 to 10 or 15 is ideal.
- *Full guidance and counseling services.* Young adolescence is a time of emotional turmoil, social difficulties, and weaning from parental authority. Teachers, mentors, and advisory staff are not counselors, nor are they trained to meet some of the more disturbing problems such as substance abuse, sexual experimentation, eating disorders, or the abandonment and abuse some experience. Full guidance and counseling services are essential.

Goal 7: Family and Community

- *Schools linked to local communities through substantive parent/community involvement.* If young adolescents are to one day become productive community members and if parents and community members are to understand and accept the younger generation, they must get to know, accept, and appreciate each other. School walls must not be barriers to students and the community interacting with one another. Programs and activities must be designed to ensure this two-way communication and interaction.

Although the goal of the Carnegie grants was to effect policy change, the Texas Task Force called for this change to be driven by innovation at the campus level rather than mandated at the state level. To this end the Texas Middle School Network was formed to assist schools implement research-based concepts and practices.

THE TEXAS MIDDLE SCHOOL NETWORK

The Network's mission was "to serve as the catalyst for middle school reform by providing leadership, staff development, and inspiration to all middle school educators of Texas" (Texas Task Force on Middle Schools, 1991). The Network identified mentor schools, those that had begun implementing some of the eight recommendations of the Carnegie Council's *Turning Points* and that were committed to continued growth. At first 19 schools became mentors, though over the next 3 years others were added.

Middle schools committed to restructuring and becoming more developmentally appropriate were invited to become Network members. A mentor school was assigned to each Network member school. The goal was to have all 1,106 schools (1993) that serve middle grade students enrolled in the network and to have a 20 to 1 ratio of network schools to each mentor school by 1996. As of May 1994, 842 schools had joined the network and 56 mentor schools had been identified.

The Texas Middle School Network is about schools helping schools, campus to campus, driven by innovation at the campus level and striving for excellence and equity for all children. It provides the technical infrastructure for reform and facilitates discussions about what is happening with and for students. Part of the infrastructure, of course, is the network of member and mentor schools. Another part of the infrastructure is the coordination of efforts and resources between the Network and the Texas Middle School Association (TMSA).

A CHANGE IN PUBLIC EDUCATIONAL POLICY IN TEXAS

With the election of Governor George W. Bush in November, 1994, changes in educational policy and priorities, perhaps inadvertently, have resulted in a dramatic slowing of the middle school movement in Texas. The governor and his new Commissioner of Education, Mike Moses, focused on reading, especially at the primary grade level. At the same time the Texas Education Agency (TEA) underwent considerable downsizing and restructuring. The Texas Middle School Network and the networks later established to serve other grade levels were moved out of TEA to the Region XIII Education Service Center. Having lost the strong backing of the previous commissioner and of TEA, the networks ground to a near standstill. The Texas Middle School Association (TMSA) struggled to keep the innovative restructuring alive, but without the network, it could not carry the burden alone.

In an effort to raise standards and increase the number of students who read on grade level, another emphasis of the newly restructured TEA and, in fact, of the state level political spectrum as a whole, has been to increase the focus on TAAS scores and on tougher standards. The scores and standards are being enforced by threatening schools with "low-performing" ratings and students with being held back. Some read these actions as unfair to minority students, in that the multiple-choice nature of the TAAS is a problematic construct for many cultures. Others read these actions as punishment instead of corrective support or remediation. Although these actions may help maintain high standards and a challenging curriculum, which is consistent with the middle school philosophy, the emphasis on a single non-authentic, non-relevant assessment undermines effective middle school restructuring.

THE APPARENT FAILURE OF THE MIDDLE SCHOOL REFORM MOVEMENT

Aside from these external forces the Texas middle school restructuring effort has also lost some of its initial vigor by failing to demonstrate improved student achievement results. A *Survey of Middle School Practices* was conducted in 1994 by Steven Rakow under the auspices of the Texas Middle School Network, TEA, and TMSA. This study sought "to determine the extent to which middle grade reforms recommended in *Turning Points, Spotlight on the Middle,* and the goals of the SBOE policy statement have been implemented throughout the state (p. 1)." There was a second purpose, which was to determine the extent to which middle school reform correlates with improvements in student performance (p. 2).

Rakow's survey, conducted in the spring of 1993, produced an 82% response rate from the 1,116 middle schools in Texas. Approximately one third of the schools implement practices that create a community of learners (academic teaming, advisories, etc.). Sixty percent of fifth and sixth grades and 40% of seventh, eighth, and ninth grades teach a core of common knowledge. More than half of the schools implement strategies designed to ensure success for all students, and 81% report teacher involvement in critical decision making. The results also indicate that 37% of the schools provide 75% of their teachers with middle grade–focused professional development. Also, 71% of the schools provide better health and fitness programs, and 65% reported some or full implementation of family involvement. Finally, more than 50% have programs and activities connecting schools with their communities.

We learn from this survey that many of the middle grade schools have fully or partially implemented some or all of the *Turning Points* guidelines. One important point to make before examining any correlation with improved student achievement is that most of the school reforms reported had been implemented for two or fewer years, that is, since the Texas Middle School Network came into existence. We cannot, and should not, expect significant achievement effects from practices implemented for only two years, and indeed that is what we find. The measure of achievement used was the seventh grade TAAS scores from the fall of 1992, which were the only TAAS scores available. Generally "the data were not able to support much relationship between the level of implementation and student performance *at this time*" (p. 10, emphasis is theirs).

These findings are predictable and must not be interpreted as a failure of the middle grade restructuring effort. In the search for quick solutions and the era of sound-bite politics, these results, whether read in the study or seen in actual practice at individual school campuses, do nothing to further the cause of middle school reform. Coincidentally, middle school reform at the national level has also had difficulty conclusively demonstrating a correlation with achievement.

EVIDENCE OF SUCCESS AT THE NATIONAL LEVEL

In 1994, at the same time that Texas was having difficulty demonstrating a positive correlation between recommended middle school practices and student achievement, the National Middle School Association (NMSA), as part of its 20th birthday celebration, published Paul George and Kathy Shewey's review, *New Evidence for the Middle School.* George and Shewey reviewed the early research, a thorough and important 1985 survey, and a 1993 survey. The early research and the 1985 study generally showed positive achievement among young adolescents in restructured middle schools, but the findings were never conclusive. Often those studies were flawed, the research methodology was weak, and/or the achievement trends did not reach the level of significance. In the 1993 study 300 middle schools across the country were surveyed. The results related to achievement were summed up this way:

> When implemented effectively, the middle school concept increasingly leads to substantially positive outcomes in virtually every area of concern to educators and parents, including academic achievement. Improvement can also

be noted in a range of aspects of student deportment, such as attendance, tardiness, referrals to the office for discipline, theft, vandalism, etc. Middle school programs improved relationships between: students of different racial and ethnic groups; parents and teachers; teachers and students; and, teachers with other teachers, especially between elementary, high school, and those at the middle level. (George & Shewey, 1994, p. 110)

While this study, like its predecessors, is not without flaws, the evidence again supports a strong implementation of middle-level practices as recommended by Carnegie, NMSA, and *Spotlight on the Middle*. Further, it appears to link these recommended practices with significant student achievement.

POSITIVE SIGNS IN TEXAS

Regardless of the disappointing lag in the middle school restructuring movement in Texas, there are some indications of a brighter future. The Texas Middle School Association remains a strong, durable organization exerting considerable influence. The annual TMSA conference is attended by nearly 10,000 teachers and principals. The Texas Middle School Journal is a respectable, widely read advocate for young adolescents and developmentally appropriate schools for them. In many ways TMSA is beginning to fill the void created when the Texas Middle School Network lost its TEA support and its influence in the state.

With the exception of a few professors scattered across the state, the teacher education programs and educational administration programs in Texas have taken little notice of middle schools and their restructuring movement. Through the commendable efforts of those few professors in collaboration with the TMSA Board of Directors, the newly created Texas State Board for Educator Certification (SBEC) is seriously considering a middle-level licensure. A middle grade teaching certificate will force the colleges and universities to include middle-level studies in their teacher education programs.

As a result of state legislative action in 1991, some teacher education programs had already begun to move in that direction. The Texas Legislature provided the funds for college and universities through competitive grants to create Centers of Professional Development and Technology (CPDTs). The objective of CPDTs was to restructure teacher education programs into field-based, technology-rich collaboratives with public schools. By 1993 the CPDTs were establishing elementary and secondary Professional Development Schools (PDS) in which college professors offered their courses in public schools with the collaboration of the faculty of the school site. Because middle schools were in the process of restructuring, they were often the most receptive to growth and change, and they often sought out or were chosen for CPDT collaborations. The middle grade PDSs fostered in colleges and universities an awakening to the middle school movement, and many teacher education programs became partners in the movement.

The next few years will probably prove to be critical to the advancement of developmentally appropriate middle grade schools to "defuse the volatile mismatch between . . . schools and the needs of young adolescents" (Carnegie, 1989).

REFERENCES

Carnegie Council on Adolescent Development (1989). *Turning points: Preparing American youth for the 21st century.* New York, NY: Carnegie Corporation.

George, P. S. & Shewey, K. (1994). *New evidence for the middle school.* Columbus, OH: National Middle School Association.

Males, M. A. (1996). *The scapegoat generation: America's war on adolescents.* Monroe, ME: Common Courage Press.

Rakow, S. J. (1994). *Survey of middle school practices: Executive summary.* Austin, TX: Texas Education Agency, Division of Middle School Education.

Texas Task Force on Middle School Education (1991). *Spotlight on the middle: Report of the Texas task force on middle school education. Executive summary and State Board of Education policy statement on middle grade education and middle grade schools.* Austin, TX: Texas Education Agency.

CHAPTER 26

The Instructional Materials Adoption Process

INTRODUCTION

Texas is one of 22 states with a process for approval or adoption of instructional materials. The Texas Constitution, Article VII, Section 3, requires that the State Board of Education (SBOE) set aside sufficient money to provide free textbooks for children attending the public schools in the state. Selection of new instructional materials for use in the state is a process that begins when the SBOE issues a proclamation calling for bids in selected subject areas and/or grade levels. The adoption process is complete with the selection and shipment of new instructional materials to school districts.

STATE LAW AND ADMINISTRATIVE RULES

Current education laws and other statutes pertaining to the operation of the public schools of the State of Texas are codified in the *Texas Education Code (TEC)*. The law concerning adoption and distribution of instructional materials appears in Title 2, Chapter 31. All rules of the SBOE are codified in Title 19 of the *Texas Administrative Code (TAC)*. The rules concerning state-level adoption and distribution appear in Title 19, Chapter 66, *State Adoption and Distribution of Instructional Materials*.

Reprinted with permission from the Texas Education Agency, 1999.

ADOPTION CYCLE

The *Texas Education Code,* Chapter 31, specifies that the SBOE adopt different cycles for subjects in the foundation and enrichment curricula. Subjects in the foundation curriculum are defined as English language arts; mathematics; science; and social studies, consisting of Texas, United States, and world history, government and geography. Subjects in the enrichment curriculum are languages other than English; health; physical education; fine arts; economics; career and technology education; and technology applications.

Chapter 31 requires that the SBOE adopt a cycle providing for a full and complete investigation of instructional materials in foundation subjects at least every six years. In addition, no more than one-sixth of the subjects in the foundation curriculum may be reviewed each year. Instructional materials in the enrichment curriculum shall be reviewed according to a cycle that the SBOE considers appropriate. In November 1997, the SBOE approved a cycle for adoption of new instructional materials for foundation and enrichment subjects.

REQUESTS FOR BIDS ON NEW INSTRUCTIONAL MATERIALS

Bids for new instructional materials from the publishing industry are solicited by means of a proclamation issued by the SBOE approximately 24 months prior to scheduled adoption of new materials. The proclamation identifies subject areas scheduled for review in a given year and contains content requirements based on the Texas Essential Knowledge and Skills adopted by the SBOE, maximum per-student costs to the state for adopted materials, an estimated number of units to be purchased during the first contract year for each of the subject areas and/or grade levels, and a detailed calendar of adoption procedures. In addition, specifications for providing computerized files to produce Braille versions of adopted materials and a schedule for the adoption process are contained in the proclamation. Proclamations do not specify the type or configuration of instructional materials to be submitted for review. Submissions of traditional textbooks or electronic media are allowed in all subjects in any combination of media.

SUBMISSION OF INSTRUCTIONAL MATERIALS FOR ADOPTION

Publishers who plan to offer instructional materials for adoption in the state must complete and file a Statement of Intent to Bid on or before the deadline established in the proclamation. Instructional materials may be withdrawn from the process after an intent to bid is filed, but no materials may be added after the deadline. Publishers later provide finished-format review samples of materials to the Texas Education Agency, each of the 20 regional education service centers, and each member of the appropriate state review panels. In most cases, instructional materials filed by publishers are pre-publication samples, and participating publishers file lists of editorial corrections which would be made in materials adopted by the SBOE prior to distribution to school districts.

CONFORMING AND NONCONFORMING INSTRUCTIONAL MATERIALS

The *Texas Education Code*, Chapter 31, provides for adoption of two separate lists of instructional materials. The "conforming" list is to consist of instructional materials submitted that meet manufacturing standards adopted by the SBOE, contain material covering each element of essential knowledge and skills, and are free of factual errors. The "nonconforming" list is to consist of instructional materials submitted that meet manufacturing standards adopted by the SBOE, contain material covering at least half, but not all, of the elements of essential knowledge and skills, and are free of factual errors. Both conforming and nonconforming adopted instructional materials are eligible for purchase by the state.

EVALUATION AND RECOMMENDATION OF INSTRUCTIONAL MATERIALS

In accordance with 19 *Texas Administrative Code*, Chapter 66, the commissioner of education appoints members of state review panels. Nominations are solicited from the SBOE, school districts and open-enrollment charter schools, and educational organizations throughout the state. Members of state review panels will be charged with evaluating instructional materials to determine coverage of essential knowledge and skills and with identifying factual errors.

Each state review panel will be allowed to request a meeting with publishers to obtain responses to questions. At the close of the review period, panel members will submit evaluation instruments and lists of factual errors to the commissioner of education. Based on these evaluations, the commissioner will prepare a preliminary report recommending that instructional materials be placed on the conforming list, be placed on the nonconforming list, or be rejected. Publishers will be allowed to request show-cause hearings in the event that they elect to protest the commissioner's initial recommendations.

PUBLIC COMMENT

Samples of all materials under consideration for adoption are provided to each of the regional education service centers for public review. Texas residents will be allowed to file written comments regarding instructional materials submitted for adoption. However, since state review panel members have no authority to reject materials or to recommend changes to materials under consideration, no public hearings will be held before the panels. A public hearing will be held before the SBOE approximately two months before scheduled adoption. Publishers will be given the opportunity to respond orally or in writing to any comments made by the public.

ADOPTION BY THE STATE BOARD OF EDUCATION

After consideration of evaluations submitted by state review panel members, information provided by publishers, and staff recommendations, the commissioner of education will submit a final report to the SBOE recommending that instructional materials submitted be placed on the conforming list, placed on the nonconforming list, or rejected. A report detailing factual errors to be corrected in instructional materials will also be submitted to the SBOE for action. A publisher who continues to disagree with the commissioner's final recommendations will be allowed the opportunity to request to withdraw a submission at this point in the process.

LOCAL SELECTION

Publishers will be required to provide descriptions of newly adopted instructional materials to all school districts and open-enrollment charter schools; however, a district retains the option of requesting one complete official sample. Publishers are responsible for all aspects of the shipment and retrieval of sample materials and bear all costs of the sampling process.

Each local board of trustees is responsible for determining appropriate local policy for selecting instructional materials. However, with the exception detailed in the following paragraph, only state-adopted instructional materials ratified by a school district's board of trustees will be purchased by the state for districts.

In enrichment subjects, school districts will be allowed to select non-adopted instructional materials. The state will pay the district the lesser of: (1) 70 percent of the cost of the materials to the district based on the applicable quota for adopted materials in the subject; or (2) 70 percent of the maximum cost to the state established in the proclamation for the subject based on the applicable quota for adopted materials in the subject. School districts electing to order nonadopted instructional materials will be responsible for the remainder of the cost. It should also be noted that the *Texas Education Code*, Chapter 31, does not allow the SBOE to reject an instructional material submission because the bid price exceeds the limit established in the proclamation. If instructional materials are adopted that exceed the maximum cost, the state's payment to the publisher will not exceed the maximum cost. School districts electing to order instructional materials with prices that exceed the maximum cost to the state will bear responsibility for the portion of the cost that exceeds the state maximum.

ANCILLARY MATERIALS

Most publishers also provide free "ancillary" materials to school districts that select their adopted materials. However, ancillary materials are not part of a publisher's bid or contract, and are not purchased by the state. Therefore, these items are not reviewed at the state level, and are not adopted or sanctioned by the SBOE. Decisions regarding selection and use of free ancillary materials are entirely the province of local boards of trustees, as is the decision to purchase non-adopted instructional materials with local funds.

DISTRIBUTION OF STATE-ADOPTED MATERIALS

Orders for new instructional materials are transmitted to the agency for processing. Local adoption, requisition, and membership data are entered into an automated system for verification based on the enrollment of the district and the distribution quota for the course or subject.

State-approved instructional materials are shipped from one or more of the textbook depositories. Publishers are required to have adopted materials in stock in a depository available for immediate shipment to districts. Shipments are made to school districts throughout the summer based on the district's preferred shipment date. After the first day of school, requisitions are processed within one day of receipt and depositories are instructed to ship materials as soon as the orders are received from the agency. Districts are allowed to submit orders throughout the school year, as necessary. Instructional materials are usually shipped within seven days of receipt of a requisition.

BRAILLE, LARGE TYPE AND AUDIOTAPE INSTRUCTIONAL MATERIALS

The SBOE is authorized to acquire, purchase, and contract for free instructional materials for the education of blind and visually impaired public school students. Publishers are required to provide the agency with computerized files for rapid production of adopted Braille instructional materials whenever such files are requested by the SBOE. Local school districts submit orders for Braille and large type materials to the agency, which manages acquisition from producers. Teachers who are blind or visually impaired are provided with Braille or large type teacher materials to accompany materials the teacher uses in the instruction of students.

STATE TEXTBOOK DEPOSITORY

Surplus instructional materials are shipped by school districts to the State Textbook Depository in Austin for redistribution. In addition, "worn-out" instructional materials are shipped to the depository by schools, and when possible, these materials are refurbished and redistributed. Instructional materials that are too worn for reconditioning are sent to a recycling center. The State Textbook Depository also serves as a warehouse for receipt and redistribution of Braille and large type materials.

SUBCHAPTER B. STATE ADOPTION OF INSTRUCTIONAL MATERIALS

§66.21. Review and Adoption Cycles.

(a) The State Board of Education (SBOE) shall adopt a six-year review and adoption cycle for subjects in the foundation curriculum. No more than one-sixth of the subjects in the foundation curriculum may be reviewed each year. Placement of a subject in the cycle shall be based on the need for up-to-date materials due to changes in essential knowledge and skills, changing information, and/or changing technology. Estimated expenditures shall also be considered when determining placement of subjects in the cycle.

(b) The SBOE shall adopt a review and adoption cycle for subjects in the enrichment curriculum. Placement of a subject in the cycle shall be based on the need for up-to-date materials due to changes in essential knowledge and skills, changing information, and/or changing technology. Estimated expenditures shall also be considered when determining placement of subjects in the cycle.

§66.24. Review and Renewal of Contracts.

(a) The commissioner of education shall review contracts for instructional materials and recommend which contracts should be renewed for terms not to exceed four years and which contracts should not be renewed.

(b) The State Board of Education (SBOE) shall decide to renew existing contracts upon determining that the renewal would be in the best interest of the state and after considering the following factors:

(1) placement of subject areas in the foundation and enrichment review and adoption cycles;

(2) availability of new instructional materials; and

(3) willingness of publishers to offer materials for readoption and renewal of contracts.

(c) Publishers awarded new contracts shall be prepared to make the adopted instructional materials available for at least one extended contract period of not more than four years at prices the commissioner of education approves. The SBOE may consider refusing to award future contracts to a publisher who, after receiving written notice to do so, refuses to rebid instructional materials at least one time. Failure of a publisher to negotiate an acceptable price for an extended contract shall not be considered failure to rebid instructional materials.

§66.27. Proclamation, Public Notice, and Schedule for Adopting Instructional Materials.

(a) The State Board of Education (SBOE) shall issue a proclamation calling for new instructional materials according to the review and adoption cycles for foundation and enrichment subjects adopted by the SBOE. The proclamation shall serve as notice to all registered publishers and to the public that bids to furnish new materials to the state are being invited. The proclamation shall be issued at least 24 months before the scheduled adoption of the new instructional materials by the SBOE.

(b) The proclamation shall contain the following:

(1) specifications for essential knowledge and skills in each subject for which bids are being invited;

(2) a maximum cost to the state per student for adopted instructional materials in each subject for which bids are being invited;

(3) an estimated number of units to be purchased during the first contract year for each subject in the proclamation;

(4) specifications for providing computerized files to produce braille versions of adopted instructional materials; and

(5) a schedule for the adoption process.

(c) A draft copy of the proclamation shall be provided to each member of the SBOE and

Source: The provisions of this §66.21 adopted to be effective September 1, 1996, 21 TexReg 7236.

Source: The provisions of this §66.24 adopted to be effective September 1, 1996, 21 TexReg 7236.

to designated representatives of the publishing industry to solicit input on maximum costs before the SBOE considers the proclamation. In addition, the Texas Education Agency shall hold a public meeting regarding the draft proclamation with representatives of the publishing industry 60-90 days prior to the scheduled adoption of the proclamation by the SBOE. Any revisions recommended as a result of the meeting with publishers shall be presented to the SBOE along with the subsequent draft of the proclamation.

(d) Under extraordinary circumstances, the SBOE may adopt an emergency, supplementary, or revised proclamation without complying with the time lines and other requirements of this section.

§66.28. Adoption by Reference.

The sections titled "Content Requirements" in the *1997 Proclamation of the State Board of Education Advertising for Bids on Instructional Materials* are adopted by this reference as the agency's official rule governing essential knowledge and skills that shall be used to evaluate instructional materials submitted for consideration under Proclamation 1997. A copy of the *1997 Proclamation of the State Board of Education Advertising for Bids on Instructional Materials* is available for examination during regular office hours, 8:00 a.m. to 5:00 p.m., except holidays, Saturdays, and Sundays, at the Texas Education Agency, 1701 North Congress Avenue, Austin, Texas 78701.

§66.30. State Review Panels: Eligibility.

A person is not eligible to serve on a state review panel if, during the three years immediately preceding the appointment, the person:

(1) was employed by or received funds from any individual or entity in any way affiliated with a publishing company participating in the adoption under which the state review panel will evaluate instructional materials; or

Source: The provisions of this §66.27 adopted to be effective September 1, 1996, 21 TexReg 7236; amended to be effective September 1, 1997, 22 TexReg 3779.

Statutory Authority: The provisions of this §66.28 issued under the Texas Education Code, §28.002.

Source: The provisions of this §66.28 adopted to be effective February 15, 1998, 23 TexReg 1019.

(2) owned or controlled, directly or indirectly, any interest in a publishing company or an entity receiving funds from a publishing company.

§66.33. State Review Panels: Appointment.

(a) The commissioner of education shall: determine the number of review panels needed to review instructional materials under consideration for adoption, determine the number of persons to serve on each panel, and determine the criteria for selecting panel members. Each appointment to a state review panel shall be made by the commissioner of education with the advice and consent of the State Board of Education (SBOE) member whose district is to be represented.

(b) The commissioner of education shall solicit recommendations for possible appointees to state review panels from the State Board of Education (SBOE), school districts, open-enrollment charter schools, and educational organizations in the state. Recommendations may be accepted from any Texas resident. Nominations shall not be made by or accepted from any publishers; authors; depositories; agents for publishers, authors, or depositories; or any person who holds any official position with a publisher, author, depository, or agent.

(c) The SBOE shall be notified of appointments made by the commissioner of education to state review panels.

(d) Members of a state review panel may be removed at the discretion of the commissioner of education.

§66.36. State Review Panels: Duties and Conduct.

(a) The duties of each member of a state review panel are to:

(1) evaluate all instructional materials submitted for adoption in each subject assigned to the panel to determine if essential knowledge and skills are covered;

(2) make recommendations to the commissioner of education that each submission assigned to be evaluated by the state review panel be placed on the conforming list, nonconforming list, or rejected;

Source: The provisions of this §66.30 adopted to be effective September 1, 1996, 21 TexReg 7236.

Source: The provisions of this §66.33 adopted to be effective September 1, 1996, 21 TexReg 7236.

(3) submit to the commissioner of education a list of any factual errors in instructional materials assigned to be evaluated by the state review panel; and

(4) as appropriate to a subject area and/or grade level, ascertain that instructional materials submitted for adoption do not contain content that clearly conflicts with the stated purpose of the Texas Education Code, §28.002(h).

(b) State review panel members shall not accept meals, entertainment, gifts, or gratuities in any form from publishers, authors, or depositories; agents for publishers, authors, or depositories; any person who holds any official position with publishers, authors, depositories, or agents; or any person or organization interested in influencing the selection of instructional materials.

(c) Before presenting recommendations to the commissioner of education, state review panel members shall be given an opportunity to request a meeting with a publisher to obtain responses to questions regarding instructional materials being evaluated by the state review panel. Questions shall be provided to publishers in advance of the meeting.

(d) A member of a state review panel shall have no contact with other members of the panel except during official meetings. State review panel members shall not discuss instructional materials being evaluated with any party having a direct or indirect interest in adoption of instructional materials.

(e) Members of each state review panel may be required to be present at the State Board of Education (SBOE) meeting at which instructional materials are adopted.

§66.39. State Review Panels: Expenses.

(a) State review panel members shall be reimbursed for expenses incurred in attending official meetings according to the applicable provisions of the General Appropriations Act.

(b) Expenses shall be paid for designated state review panel members to attend the State Board of Education (SBOE) meeting at which instructional materials are considered for adoption.

§66.42. State Review Panels: Orientation.

State review panel members shall receive an orientation including at least the following:

(1) the responsibilities of a state review panel member;

(2) statutes and rules pertaining to the state adoption process;

(3) essential knowledge and skills specified for subjects included in the proclamation;

(4) identifying factual errors;

(5) the schedule for the adoption process;

(6) training in technology appropriate to media submitted for adoption; and

(7) regulatory requirements, including the Government Code, §572.051 (relating to Standards of Conduct), and the Texas Penal Code, §36.02 (relating to Bribery). Copies of the statutes mentioned in this section shall be supplied to each state review panel member.

§66.45. State Review Panels: No-Contact Periods.

(a) State review panel members shall observe a no-contact period that shall begin with the initial communication regarding possible appointment to a state review panel and end after recommendations have been made to the commissioner of education that each submission assigned to be evaluated by the state review panel be placed on the conforming list, nonconforming list, or rejected. During this period, state review panel members shall not be contacted either directly or indirectly by any person having an interest in the adoption process regarding content of instructional materials under evaluation by the panel. This restriction is not intended to prohibit members of the state review panels from seeking advice regarding materials under consideration from the State Board of Education (SBOE).

(b) State review panel members shall report immediately to the commissioner of education any communication or attempted communication by any person regarding instruc-

Source: The provisions of this §66.36 adopted to be effective September 1, 1996, 21 TexReg 7236.

Source: The provisions of this §66.39 adopted to be effective September 1, 1996, 21 TexReg 7236.

Source: The provisions of this §66.42 adopted to be effective September 1, 1996, 21 TexReg 7236.

tional materials being evaluated by the panel.

(c) State review panel members shall not discuss content of instructional materials under consideration with any subject area staff member of the Texas Education Agency (TEA), except during the official orientation meeting. Additional requests for information or clarification shall be directed to the commissioner of education or his designee. Copies of all questions from individual members shall be distributed with responses to all members of the appropriate state review panel. This restriction is not intended to prohibit members of the state review panels from contacting designated staff of the TEA regarding adoption procedures.

§66.48. Statement of Intent to Bid Instructional Materials.

(a) Each publisher who intends to offer instructional materials for adoption shall submit a statement of intent to bid on or before the date specified in the schedule for the adoption process. The statement of intent shall be accompanied by publisher's data submitted in a form approved by the commissioner of education.

(b) A publisher shall designate instructional materials submitted as appropriate for placement on the conforming list or non-conforming list.

(c) If a student or teacher component of a submission consists of more than one item, a publisher shall provide complete and correct titles of each item included in the student and/or teacher component at the time the statement of intent is filed.

(d) A publisher shall specify hardware or special equipment needed to review any item included in an instructional materials submission.

(e) Additions to a publisher's submission shall not be accepted after the deadline for filing statements of intent established in the schedule for the adoption process. A publisher who wishes to withdraw an instructional materials submission after having filed a statement of intent to bid shall notify the commissioner of education in writing on or before the date specified in the schedule for the adoption process.

§66.51. Instructional Materials Purchased by the State.

(a) Instructional materials offered for adoption by the State Board of Education (SBOE).

(1) Publishers may not submit instructional materials for adoption that have been authored by an employee of the Texas Education Agency (TEA).

(2) The official bid price of an instructional material submission shall not exceed the price included with the official sample filed under §66.54 of this title (relating to Samples).

(3) A teacher's component submitted to accompany student instructional materials under consideration for adoption shall be part of the publisher's official bid and shall be provided for the duration of the original contract and any contract extensions at no cost to every teacher that uses the adopted student materials in a school district or open-enrollment charter school.

(4) Under the Texas Education Code, §31.025, the official bid price for an instructional material submission may exceed the maximum cost per student to the state that is established in the proclamation. The state shall only be responsible for payment to the publisher in an amount equal to the maximum cost. A school district ordering instructional materials is responsible for the portion of the cost that exceeds the state maximum.

(5) Any discounts offered for volume purchases of adopted instructional materials shall be included in price information submitted with official samples and in the official bid.

(6) The official bid filed by a publisher shall include separate prices for each item included in an instructional material submission. The publisher shall guarantee that individual items included in the student and/or teacher component shall be available for local

Source: The provisions of this §66.45 adopted to be effective September 1, 1996, 21 TexReg 7236.

Source: The provisions of this §66.48 adopted to be effective September 1, 1996, 21 TexReg 7236.

purchase at the individual prices listed for the entire contract period.

(7) Instructional materials submitted for adoption shall be self-sufficient for the period of adoption. Nonconsumable components shall be replaced by the publisher during the warranty period. Consumable materials included in a student or teacher component of a submission shall be clearly marked as consumable. The cost of such consumables to the state for the entire contract period shall not exceed the maximum cost established in the proclamation.

(8) On or before the deadline established in the schedule of adoption procedures, publishers shall submit correlations of instructional materials submitted for adoption with essential knowledge and skills required by the proclamation. Correlations shall be submitted in a format approved by the commissioner of education.

(b) Non-adopted instructional materials. A publisher of non-adopted instructional materials selected and purchased by school districts or open-enrollment charter schools under §66.104(c)-(f) of this title (relating to Selection of Instructional Materials by School Districts) shall meet all applicable requirements of the Texas Education Code, §31.151.

§66.54. Samples.

(a) Samples of student and teacher components of instructional materials submitted for adoption shall be complete as to content and representative of finished-format binding.

(b) Two sample copies of the student and teacher components of each instructional materials submission shall be filed with each of the 20 regional education service centers (ESCs) on or before the date specified in the schedule for the adoption process. These samples shall be available for public review.

(c) If it is determined that good cause exists, the commissioner of education may extend the deadline for filing samples with ESCs. At its

discretion, the State Board of Education (SBOE) may remove from consideration any materials proposed for adoption that were not properly deposited with the ESCs, the Texas Education Agency (TEA), or members of the state review panel.

(d) Two official sample copies of each student and teacher component of an instructional materials submission shall be filed with the TEA on or before the date specified in the schedule for the adoption process. Price information required by the commissioner of education shall be included in each sample. In addition, the publisher shall provide a complete description of all items included in a student and teacher component of an instructional materials submission.

(e) One sample copy of each student and teacher component of an instructional materials submission shall be filed with each member of the appropriate state review panel on or before the date specified in the schedule for the adoption process. To ensure that the evaluations of state review panel members are limited to student and teacher components submitted for adoption, publishers shall not provide ancillary materials, supplementary materials, or descriptions of ancillary or supplementary materials to state review panel members.

(f) The TEA, ESCs, and affected publishing companies shall work together to ensure that hardware or special equipment necessary for review of any item included in a student and/or teacher component of an instructional materials submission is available in each ESC. Affected publishers may be required to loan such hardware or special equipment to any member of a state review panel who does not have access to the necessary hardware or special equipment.

(g) A publisher shall provide a list of all corrections necessary to each student and teacher component of an instructional materials submission. The list must be in a format designated by the commissioner of education and filed on or before the deadline specified in the schedule for the adoption process. If no corrections are necessary, the publisher shall file a letter stating this on or before the deadline in the schedule for submitting the list of corrections. On or before the deadline for submitting lists of corrections, publishers shall submit certification that all instructional materials have been edited for accu-

Source: The provisions of this §66.51 adopted to be effective September 1, 1996, 21 TexReg 7236.

racy, content, and compliance with requirements of the proclamation.

(h) Two complete sample copies of each student and teacher component of adopted instructional materials that incorporate all corrections required by the SBOE shall be filed with the commissioner of education on or before the date specified in the schedule for the adoption process. In addition, each publisher shall file an affidavit signed by an official of the company verifying that all corrections required by the commissioner of education and SBOE have been made. Corrected samples shall be identical to materials that will be provided to school districts after purchase.

(i) Publishers participating in the adoption process are responsible for all expenses incurred by their participation. The state does not guarantee return of sample instructional materials.

§66.57. Regional Education Service Centers: Procedures for Handling Samples; Public Access to Samples.

(a) Handling procedures.

(1) Each regional education service center (ESC) executive director shall designate one person to supervise all shipments of instructional materials. The Texas Education Agency (TEA) shall provide to each designated person forms to be used in reporting receipt of sample shipments.

(2) On or before the date specified in the schedule for the adoption process, each ESC representative shall notify the commissioner of education of all irregularities in sample shipments. The appropriate publisher shall be notified of any sample shipment irregularities reported by the ESCs.

(b) Public access to samples.

(1) One sample of all instructional materials under consideration for adoption shall be retained in each ESC for review by interested persons until notification is received from the TEA. One sample shall be made available to be checked out according to rules established by each ESC based on demand.

(2) Regional ESCs shall ensure reasonable public access to sample instructional materials, including access outside of normal working hours that shall be scheduled by appointment.

(3) On or before the date specified in the schedule for the adoption process, each ESC shall issue a news release publicizing the date on which sample instructional materials will be available for review at the center and shall notify all school districts in the region of the schedule.

§66.60. Public Comment on Instructional Materials.

(a) Written comments.

(1) Any resident of Texas may submit written comments for, against, or about any instructional materials submitted for adoption.

(2) Written comments and lists of factual errors shall be submitted to the commissioner of education on or before the deadlines specified in the schedule for the adoption process.

(3) Copies of written comments and lists of factual errors shall be provided to the State Board of Education (SBOE), participating publishers, regional education service centers (ESCs), and persons who have filed written requests.

(b) Public hearing before the SBOE. On a date specified in the schedule for the adoption process, the SBOE shall hold a hearing on instructional materials submitted for adoption that may, at the discretion of the SBOE chair, be designated an official meeting of the SBOE.

(1) Testimony at the hearing shall be accepted only from residents of Texas. Copies of speeches made at the hearing may be distributed to SBOE members. No other written material may be distributed during the hearings. Persons who wish to testify must notify the commissioner of education on or before the date specified in the schedule for the adoption process. The notice must identify the subject areas and titles about which testimony will be presented. The

Source: The provisions of this §66.54 adopted to be effective September 1, 1996, 21 TexReg 7236.

Source: The provisions of this §66.57 adopted to be effective September 1, 1996, 21 TexReg 7236.

SBOE may limit the time available for each person to testify.

(2) Oral responses to testimony at the hearing may be made by official representatives of publishing companies who have requested time to present responses on or before the date specified in the schedule for the adoption process.

(3) The commissioner of education shall have a complete record of the hearing made and transcribed. The transcript of the hearing shall be provided to the SBOE, ESCs, participating publishers, and persons who have filed written requests. The official record shall be held open for 14 calendar days after the close of the hearings. During this period, any person who participated in a hearing before the SBOE and any official representative of a publishing company may submit a written response to written comments and/or oral testimony presented at the hearing.

(4) Within 10 days after the record is closed, the commissioner shall send copies of responses to written and/or oral testimony to members of the SBOE, ESCs, participating publishers, and persons who have filed written requests.

(c) Public comment on instructional materials not adopted on schedule. Public comment on instructional materials not adopted by the SBOE on the date specified in the schedule for the adoption process shall be accepted according to the SBOE Operating Rules, §2.10 (relating to Public Testimony).

§66.63. Report of the Commissioner of Education.

(a) The commissioner of education shall review all instructional materials submitted for consideration for adoption. The commissioner's review shall include the following:

(1) evaluations of instructional materials prepared by state review panel members, including recommendations that instructional materials be: placed on the conforming list, placed on the nonconforming list, or rejected;

(2) compliance with established manufacturing standards and specifications;

(3) recommended corrections of factual errors identified by state review panels;

(4) prices of instructional materials submitted for adoption; and

(5) whether instructional materials are offered by a publisher who refuses to rebid instructional materials according to §66.24 of this title (relating to Review and Renewal of Contracts).

(b) Based on the review specified in subsection (a) of this section, the commissioner of education shall prepare preliminary recommendations that instructional materials under consideration be: placed on the conforming list, placed on the nonconforming list, or rejected. According to the schedule for the adoption process, a publisher shall be given an opportunity for a show-cause hearing if the publisher elects to protest the commissioner's preliminary recommendation.

(c) The commissioner of education shall submit to the State Board of Education (SBOE) final recommendations that instructional materials under consideration be: placed on the conforming list, placed on the nonconforming list, or rejected.

(d) The commissioner of education shall submit for SBOE approval a report on corrections of factual errors that should be required in instructional materials submitted for consideration. The report on recommended corrections shall be sent to the SBOE, affected publishers, regional education service centers (ESCs), and other persons, such as braillists, needing immediate access to the information. The commissioner shall obtain written confirmation from publishers that they would be willing to make all identified corrections should they be required by the SBOE.

§66.66. Consideration and Adoption of Instructional Materials by the State Board of Education.

(a) Publishers shall file the following documents with the commissioner of education according to the schedule for the adoption process:

(1) three copies of the official bid form; and

(2) appropriate proof of authority to do business in the State of Texas.

Source: The provisions of this §66.60 adopted to be effective September 1, 1996, 21 TexReg 7236; amended to be effective September 1, 1997, 22 TexReg 3779.

Source: The provisions of this §66.63 adopted to be effective September 1, 1996, 21 TexReg 7236.

(b) A committee of the State Board of Education (SBOE) shall be designated by the SBOE chair to review the commissioner's report concerning instructional materials recommended for state adoption. The committee shall report the results of its review to the SBOE.

(c) By a vote of a majority of the SBOE, the SBOE shall adopt a list of conforming instructional materials and a list of nonconforming instructional materials under the Texas Education Code, §31.023 and §31.024. Instructional materials may be rejected for:

  (1) failure to meet essential knowledge and skills specified in the proclamation. In determining the percentage of elements of the essential knowledge and skill covered by instructional materials, each performance description shall count as an independent element of the essential knowledge and skills of the subject;

  (2) failure to meet established manufacturing standards and specifications recognized by the SBOE;

  (3) failure to correct errors of fact; or

  (4) content that clearly conflicts with the stated purpose of the Texas Education Code, §28.002(h).

(d) The SBOE may allow a publisher to withdraw from the adoption process after the date specified in the proclamation due to recommended placement on a conforming or nonconforming list, manufacturing specifications required as a condition of adoption by the SBOE that the publisher states cannot be met, or failure to agree to make corrections required by the SBOE.

Source: The provisions of this §66.66 adopted to be effective September 1, 1996, 21 TexReg 7236; amended to be effective September 1, 1997, 22 TexReg 3779.

CHAPTER 27

Elements of School Effectiveness

Serious concerns have surfaced concerning the validity of the original five *effective schools factors*. A number of the early reviewers cautioned that some of the conclusions drawn from this research were questionable. Recent studies of effective schools have produced a more diversified list of characteristics. Research on effective teaching and administration, as well as studies on school culture, illustrate the critical nature of the interaction between the school and the socioeconomic environment in which it functions. In addition, decision-making authority and collegial relations at the school level appear to have a strong impact on effectiveness. The essential lesson from the research is that there is really no blueprint for excellence that can be transported from school to school. Excellence is the result of "inspired leadership, committed personnel, and adequate resources" applied to the conditions found in each school.

EFFECTIVE SCHOOLS RESEARCH RECONSIDERED

Edmonds' School Effectiveness Formula

The effective schools formula that was popularized by Edmonds (1979) and other researchers consists of

Reprinted with permission from "Organizing for Excellence," sponsored by Office of Exceptional Research and Improvement; published by Southwest Educational Development Laboratory; prepared by P. C. Duttweiler, 1988.

five factors: (1) strong leadership by the principal, particularly in instructional matters; (2) high expectations for student achievement on the part of teachers; (3) an emphasis on basic skills; (4) an orderly environment; and (5) the frequent, systematic evaluation of students. The formula has been translated into an Effective Schools Model and the program has been widely embraced throughout the nation on the assumption that adoption of these factors would increase the achievement of minority students in inner-city schools (Stedman, 1987). There are, however, a number of researchers and practitioners who have reservations about such widespread acceptance of an overall prescription for improving schools.

A serious concern shared by many researchers is the low degree of fit between some of the effective-school studies' findings and the conclusions drawn by their authors. D'Amico (1982) suggests that some authors seem to have done a good deal of interpretation when translating their findings into conclusions. For example, Edmonds listed the five *indispensable* characteristics of effective schools. However, these characteristics were not the ones that Edmonds and Frederiksen identified in their 1979 study. The list from that study was both longer and more specific. The authors were not clear about what research was used to arrive at these five characteristics (D'Amico, 1982).

Reviews of the Early Studies

Purkey and Smith (1982) conducted a major review of the early effective school studies. Their comments highlight the commonalities and the problems found in those early studies. For example, they examined the findings of the *outlier* studies and suggested that variations in the findings should serve as a caution to those who would reduce the findings of such disparate literature to five or six variables. In addition, they cautioned that those variations suggest that no variable in particular is crucial. They did, however, point out some consistency in the results. The consistent, common elements found by outlier studies were "better control or discipline" and "high staff expectations for student achievement." Each of these variables showed up in four of the seven studies. An emphasis on "instructional leadership by the principal or another important staff member" was found to be important in only three out of the seven studies.

Purkey and Smith (1982) examined six school case studies cited in various school effectiveness reviews. Taken together, the studies looked closely at a total of 43 schools, an average of a little over seven schools per study. In Purkey and Smith's opinion, the inherent weaknesses of the case-study approach and the small samples seemed "a frail reed upon which to base a movement of school improvement." They did, however, point out that the commonality of findings among the case studies and their similarity to other kinds of studies tended to increase their credibility. The five case-study factors that were common to most, but not all, of the six case studies were (1) strong leadership by the principal or another staff member, (2) high expectations by staff for student achievement, (3) a clear set of goals and emphasis for the school, (4) a school-wide effective staff training program, and (5) a system for monitoring student progress. It should be noted that the five factors the case studies uncovered are not identical to the five Edmonds factors.

Purkey and Smith (1982) looked at a third category of school effectiveness research—program evaluation, which was considered methodologically stronger than the outlier or case-study research. However, the findings of the program-evaluation studies were consistent with the findings of other types of studies. Most schools with effective programs were characterized by (1) high staff expectations and morale, (2) a considerable degree of control by the staff over instructional and training decisions in the school, (3) clear leadership from the principal or other instructional figure, (4) clear goals for the school, and (5) a sense of order in the school.

Two findings were consistent across the three types of studies:

1. strong instructional leadership from the principal or other instructional figure

2. high expectations by the staff for student achievement

These are also two of the variables identified by Edmonds. It should be noted, however, that in all three types of studies, instructional leadership is a function that can be performed by the principal *or another instructional figure.* "Clear goals for the school" was a common element in the findings from the case studies and the program evaluation studies. The case-studies findings shared the characteristic of "a system for the monitoring of student progress" with the Edmonds' list while the program evaluation studies shared "a sense of order in the school" with the Edmonds' list. There were also findings that seem to have been overlooked in subsequent discussions of the effective schools research. "A school-wide effective staff training program" and "a considerable degree of control by the staff over instruction and training decisions in the school" are two of the findings that have failed to make the more popular lists of effective schools characteristics.

"Effectiveness Factors" Questioned

Stedman (1987) points out that the vast majority of the early studies provide little support for the *effectiveness factors* to be adopted as models for school improvement. He argues that:

1. Many of the schools characterized by the factors still had extremely low levels of achievement, with students averaging several years below grade level. This suggests that merely adopting the formula is not sufficient to produce effectiveness. In a widely cited study by the New York State Department of Education, for example, researchers credited strong instructional leadership with producing the success of a school they called Urban A. Yet two-thirds of Urban A's sixth-graders were performing two or more years below grade level. Even after three years of improvement, four of the six schools counted fewer than 39% of their students at or above the 75% level in reading. Furthermore, between one-fourth and one-half of their students could not pass 25% of the state objectives.

2. Researchers for the Maryland State Department of Education found that the teachers in high- and low-performing schools rated the quality of instructional leadership equally high. And, although principals of the effective schools reported spending slightly more of their time in classrooms, they spent less of their overall time in an instructional role. There were no differences in teachers'

expectations for student achievement and little difference in teachers' classroom behavior.

3. Time-on-task data also failed to distinguish clearly between effective and ineffective schools: effective schools spent only three minutes more per day on reading and math, and their overall teaching time was not statistically greater than that of ineffective schools.

There are also problems with how *effectiveness* is defined and measured. Good and Brophy (1986) point out that there are a number of problems in using student achievement on standardized tests as a measure of effectiveness. For example, when defining an effective school, researchers have commonly used test results for only a single grade level. In addition, information about student achievement is only one of many dimensions of schooling that would have to be considered in assessing the general concept of effectiveness since schools are asked to influence many aspects of students' behavior and attitudes. Also, in attempting to explain differences between schools' average level of student achievement, most of the previous research fails to note that the greater part of the variance in student achievement (between 70% and 90%) actually occurs *within* schools (Good & Brophy, 1986).

Criticism of the Effective Schools Model

The criticisms of the *Effective Schools Model* have been summed up by Wayson and his associates (1988) in *Up From Excellence: The Impact of the Excellence Movement on Schools.* The criticisms point out some of the pitfalls to be avoided when developing a program to improve schools. Wayson cites the following (pp. 168–169):

- The Effective Schools formula is too simplistic. Defining effective schools by a brief list of general characteristics obscures what it really takes to make good schools.
- The research base of the Effective Schools Model is not as solid as is claimed. A common overstatement is, "Research now shows what needs to be done to create effective schools." In fact, the research is spotty and claims of success and miracle cures have not been substantiated.
- The Effective Schools movement has been overpromoted with the promise of quick results. Many entrepreneurs have climbed aboard the bandwagon to sell services or products that promise to create effective schools overnight.
- The Effective Schools program has been tried mostly in elementary schools in large city systems with a large number of disadvantaged

students, where it has been considered as an appealing alternative to busing students in order to desegregate schools.
- The educational outcomes of Effective Schools programs are too narrow. By focusing primarily on improving standardized achievement test scores, the curriculum is restricted and teachers' creativity and initiative are diminished. Instruction becomes inflexible; curriculum materials are unexciting. Sometimes the drive to improve achievement scores results in punitive practices with children.
- The Effective Schools program calls for a controlling form of supervision. The Effective Schools characteristic of "a strong principal dedicated to improving achievement" can be interpreted by a naive or insensitive administrator to mean heavy-handed, top-down control over both teachers and students. Such an authoritarian view of supervision is contrary to a participative leadership role in which an administrator works cooperatively with staff to help them develop the commitment and gain the skills needed to help children improve achievement.
- The Effective Schools program, with its stress on improving achievement test scores, could lead to manipulating test data to show quick results. Such pressure, when combined with competition among schools in a district to improve scores, creates conditions that encourage cheating in both subtle and blatant ways.
- In implementing the Effective Schools Model, some administrators confuse standards with expectations. Expectations come from the teacher's belief that every child can learn. If a child is not learning, then the teacher diagnoses the reasons for failure and devises more effective instructional techniques to help the child learn. Standards, as commonly used in schools, impose the responsibility for achievement on students and punish them when they fail, even though they might not have had effective instruction.

Despite problems with the data base available for designing school improvement plans based on the Effective Schools Model, many projects are in progress. Major cities including Chicago, Milwaukee, Minneapolis, New York, San Diego, St. Louis, and Washington, D.C., have established school improvement projects. Several community action groups monitor school performance using effective school check lists and many state departments of education have established effective schools programs based on the effective schools formula (Stedman, 1987). Although most researchers agree that schools or school districts should develop plans in response to their unique situations, some districts have simply taken plans developed in other districts and applied them with few, if any, modifications (Good & Brophy, 1986). Many researchers and practitioners question the wisdom of this approach. Finn (1983) reasons that effective schools have become so because they have developed their own goals, norms, and expectations.

ANOTHER LOOK AT EFFECTIVE SCHOOLS RESEARCH

Effective Schools Practices

A number of researchers and reviewers have cited a more diversified set of characteristics in schools identified as effective and those which have been given awards for *excellence.* Stedman (1987) concentrated on case studies of those effective schools that had achieved grade-level success with low-income students for several years. His analysis found that successful schools incorporated practices that fell into nine broad categories:

Ethnic and Racial Pluralism   Teachers and principals in the effective schools committed themselves to breaking down institutional and community barriers to equality. They created a learning environment that was open, friendly, and culturally inviting. Using community resources, they acknowledged the ethnic and racial identity of their students. The schools also displayed a great deal of sensitivity toward linguistic minorities.

Parent Participation   Effective schools involved parents in three major ways. First, they established good communication between the school and the home. Second, these effective schools made sure that parents were involved in their children's learning. Several schools required parents to sign their children's homework, and many schools stressed home learning and did not consider the parents' lack of education to be a barrier. And, the effective schools in the literature often included parents in the governance of the school.

Shared Governance with Teachers and Parents   Instructional leadership at most of the effective schools did not depend solely on the principal. For example, various techniques included an executive team or steering committee composed of teachers to help run the instructional program and the use of team teaching and team planning. Parents shared in the governance of several schools, as well.

Academically Rich Programs   Student development and the provision of a well-rounded academic program were the primary goals in many of the schools. Teaching was neither narrow, standardized, nor drill-based. These schools engaged students in their learning. Success in the basics was not achieved by abandoning a liberal arts education.

Skilled Use and Training of Teachers   Effective schools placed their best teachers in what they considered to be the most important positions. Most made extensive use of inservice training. They used practical, on-the-job training that was tailored to specific needs of staff members and students. The emphasis was on the exchange of practical teaching techniques and on making training an integral part of a collaborative educational environment.

Personal Attention to Students   Effective schools used community volunteers, parents, teacher aides, and peer tutors so that they could provide close, personal attention to students. They lowered student/teacher ratios, provided more time for adults and students to interact, and improved the monitoring of students' academic progress. Students were often grouped according to ability—both across grades and across classrooms. However, the grouping was quite fluid, students were frequently moved between groups, and extra attention was given to slower students.

Student Responsibility for School Affairs   Effective schools involved students in many of the day-to-day activities of running a school. Giving students responsibility produced several benefits, including improvements in discipline, self-esteem, and learning.

An Accepting and Supportive Environment   Good discipline was the result of the schools' organization and positive learning environments. Effective schools were described as happy places, as providing encouragement and not accepting teacher unkindness, as having no written rules, and as taking a more relaxed approach to discipline. The approach of these effective schools was quite different from that of the typical school. The effective schools also took more steps to minimize discipline problems.

Teaching Aimed at Preventing Academic Problems   Effective schools designed their programs to insure academic success and to head off academic problems. Many of these effective schools assigned their best teachers to the early grades, sponsored home learning programs, lowered the adult/pupil ratio, provided personal attention to students, and alerted parents to their children's minor academic difficulties before they became serious problems.

Stedman (1987) suggests that these factors should be thought of as a set of highly interrelated practices where efforts in one area will generally facilitate efforts in the others. For example, schools that are more responsive to students' ethnic and racial identities foster greater community support. As more parents become involved in the life of the school there is a greater pool of community resources and volunteers to draw on. Consequently, the school can enrich its academic programs and provide more individual attention to its students. As a result, its students are likely to learn at higher levels.

U.S. Department of Education Excellence Award Schools

In taking an in-depth look at those schools that received the U.S. Department of Education 1983 Excellence School Awards, Roueche and Baker (1986) found that the schools selected as outstanding were not necessarily unusual nor was there anything atypical about the student populations they served. However, the schools in their study did exceptional things with average students and transformed typical environments into prototypical institutions. They found that people were the key variable in building excellent schools. This focus on people resulted in hard work, team effort, and a strong commitment to shared values and goals. Together, teachers and principals created a positive atmosphere conducive to student growth and achievement.

While every school had its own character, Roueche and Baker (1986) found certain common climate factors in effective schools that formed the foundation for student success. Those common factors included:

Effective Schools Possess a Sense of Order, Purpose, Direction, and Coherence   This climate of order generates student achievement, a collective sense of identity, and a sense of decisive purpose. Overall coherence is achieved through clearly articulated goals expressed in a "plan of action" known to the whole organization.

Effective Schools Contain Orderly Classrooms Teachers actively organize and plan for efficiency in a quest for more time to spend on instruction and learning.

Effective Schools are Student-Centered   Student needs are given priority over other concerns. An atmosphere of cooperation and trust is created through a high level of interaction between students and teachers. While standardized assessment and careful monitoring of student progress is typical, the daily, face-to-face interaction within effective schools is personal, warm, and supportive.

Effective Schools Maintain Quality in Both Academics and Co-Curricular Activities   Student activities supported by the principal and faculty members create an excitement and school spirit necessary to establishing a positive school climate.

Effective Schools Have a Climate of Optimism and High Expectations   Teachers in high-achieving schools firmly believe that all students can learn and feel responsible for seeing that they do. Furthermore, teachers in effective schools believe in their own ability to influence students' learning.

Effective Schools Possess Organizational Health The administrative characteristics contributing to a climate of success are strong leadership, accountability, clear commitment to instructional excellence through inservice education and evaluation, and community involvement.

"Excellent" School Practices

Wayson and his associates (1988) reported their findings of what *excellent* schools did. Excellent schools focused on student learning in both basic and critical thinking skills. They established a foundation for learning by engaging students in experiences that required them to use basic skills in real-life situations. Such schools helped children who were not achieving; they did not reject or retain reluctant or slow students. A characteristic of many of the schools was their effort to serve all students. The staff in these schools created a positive climate that communicated to students that they were wanted and could succeed and created ways to involve students in the life of the school. Many of these schools created support networks to give students personal assistance in meeting academic expectations, knowing that students learn as much or more from one another as they learn in their classes. These excellent schools had programs that helped students meet their individual needs (Wayson, 1988).

The excellent schools also provided special programs for academically talented students, and some provided students with experiences specifically designed to teach critical thinking and creative problem solving. These schools attempted to broaden and enrich the curriculum with special in-depth courses, field trips, and independent study options. Not surprisingly, these *excellent* schools maintained extensive extracurricular programs for students (Wayson, 1988).

Excellent schools closely examined their testing programs to ensure that they were testing what was being taught in the school. The schools devised ways to diagnose student learning and to evaluate both individual student progress and instructional effectiveness on a continuing basis. They engaged in curriculum planning and evaluation on a systematic basis and some of the schools created new curricular structures by integrating traditional disciplines. Excellent schools acknowledged that time on task is important but recognized that time alone will not ensure more student learning. Curriculum planners in these schools emphasized interesting instructional activities, while also making sure that students had ample *chunks* of concentrated time for in-depth learning (Wayson, 1988).

Teachers in the excellent schools worked together in instruction, in planning curriculum, in solving problems, and in improving the school or organization. These cooperative working relationships clearly set these schools apart from the average schools. Excellent schools used teacher evaluation systems to help teachers improve their skills, and initiated and often implemented high-quality staff development programs geared to identify problems and program needs (Wayson, 1988).

Parents were involved in volunteer programs, which extended resources for the curriculum and increased support for the schools. In addition, parents and the community provided resources to supplement what the district provided and to provide what the district could or did not provide. The staff in excellent schools communicated in a variety of ways with parents about the school's programs and about their children (Wayson, 1988).

CHARACTERISTICS OF EFFECTIVE TEACHING

Schools that are effective or achieve excellence provide a supportive environment for teaching and student learning and foster the development of teachers who are effective. Good teachers become even better teachers in an environment that values and rewards them. "It is possible to develop an image of the good teacher as a thoughtful practitioner who operates with considerable autonomy yet purposefully works toward a set of goals that is simultaneously differentiated and integrated" was the conclusion drawn by Porter and Brophy (1988, p. 81) from their review of the effective teaching literature. They pointed out that effective schools require professionals who exercise judgment in planning and delivering the education of their students.

Effective Teachers Accept Responsibility for Student Learning

Teachers' classroom practices are directed by their perceptions of the goals of education and by the responsibilities they accept for student learning. Teacher classroom autonomy accounts for important variations in the type of goals that teachers adopt and the differences in teacher practices and student accomplishments. Teachers who believe they have a responsibility for student outcomes are more effective than teachers who believe their students (or students' family backgrounds) are responsible for what students learn. For example, those teachers who have been identified as the most effective in coping with students who present sustained problems in personal adjustment or behavior, viewed the problems as something to be corrected rather than merely endured. In contrast, less effective teachers try to turn over responsibility for the problem to someone else or confine their personal responses to attempts to control student behavior through demands backed by threats of punishment (Porter & Brophy, 1988). Research in secondary science classes has shown that low-aptitude students have higher achievement if their teachers accept responsibility for seeing that all students learn science than they do if their teachers attribute the degree of science mastery primarily to student ability and motivation factors (Lee & Gallagher, 1986).

Effective Teachers Motivate Student Learning

Teachers motivate their students to learn by communicating to them what is expected and why. They do this by beginning their lessons with explicit statements about what is to be learned in the future, by providing explanations that go beyond the immediate school context, and by monitoring student understanding of the reasons behind assignments as well as how to complete the assignments. Teachers provide their students with strategies for monitoring and improving students' own learning efforts. Teachers also provide students with structured opportunities for independent learning so that students develop skills and procedures for learning independently. In order to accomplish this, teachers explicitly model and instruct students in information processing, sense making, comprehension monitoring and correction, problem solving, and other metacognitive strategies for purposeful learning. Teachers also provide their students with opportunities to practice the strategies individually and in groups (Porter & Brophy, 1988).

Effective Teachers Teach for Conceptual Change

Effective teachers have a firm command of the subject matter and the strategies required to teach it. They adapt instruction to the needs of the students and the situation. Active instruction requires professional planning, thinking, and decision making by teachers (Clark & Peterson, 1986). Research has revealed that students who participate in active instruction and whose work is supervised by their teachers achieve more than those students who spend most of their time working through curriculum materials on their own (Brophy & Good, 1986). Effective teachers are aware of the misconceptions their students bring to the classroom that will interfere with student learning and adapt their instruction to students' preexisting knowledge and beliefs about the subject matter. The literature on *conceptual change teaching* points out that teaching is not a process of pouring knowledge into the empty brain of a student but involves inducing change in an existing body of knowledge and beliefs (Anderson & Smith, 1987). Conceptual change teaching confronts and changes students' misconceptions. Although sometimes useful in teaching other subject matter, these strategies are essential to instruction in science, where student misconceptions abound (Porter & Brophy, 1988).

Teachers Choose, Adapt, and Use Materials Effectively

Porter and Brophy (1988) suggest that effective teachers use published instructional materials in ways that contribute to instructional quality. While published instructional materials clearly have their faults, some researchers suggest that teachers have neither the time nor the training to develop their own materials and, therefore, choose and adapt material that is already available. It has been pointed out that the constraints of the typical teaching assignment and the meager financial resources available make it questionable that teachers can achieve better results on their own (Ball & Feiman-Nemser, 1986). Porter & Brophy, therefore, assert that teachers (those who have the authority to choose their own materials) who select instructional materials that fit the curriculum goals and that are appropriate for their students will be able to devote most of their time and energy to practices that enrich the content. However, Wayson (1988) found that teachers in *excellent* schools tend to develop their own instructional materials rather than purchase commercial packages.

Characteristics of Effective Teachers Summarized

Based on ten years of studies at the Institute for Research on Teaching, Porter and Brophy (1988, p. 75) have painted a picture of effective teachers as semi-autonomous professionals who:

- are clear about their instructional goals
- are knowledgeable about their content and the strategies for teaching it
- communicate to their students what is expected of them—and why
- make expert use of existing instructional materials in order to devote more time to practices that enrich and clarify the content
- are knowledgeable about their students, adapting instruction to their needs and anticipating misconceptions in their existing knowledge
- teach students metacognitive strategies and give them opportunities to master them
- address higher- as well as lower-level cognitive objectives
- monitor students' understanding by offering regular appropriate feedback
- integrate their instruction with that in other subject areas
- accept responsibility for student outcomes
- are thoughtful and reflective about their practice

LEADERSHIP IN EFFECTIVE SCHOOLS

The importance of school leadership is underscored by Richard Andrews' concluding remarks in an interview by Ron Brandt (1987). Andrews, who is at the University of Washington, was interviewed about his research on teachers' perceptions of their principals' leadership. Andrews concluded with:

> Frankly, I never anticipated that we would find such a powerful relationship between leadership of the principal and student outcomes. . . . But what we found is: the teachers' perception of their work environment is so important, the power of the principal's leadership so pervasive, that it has a measurable impact on student learning.

Principals Affect Culture of Schools

Successful leaders in both schools and the private sector recognize that organizational enterprises operate far more loosely than the organizational chart depicts. Despite the efforts of management, most enterprises are characterized, in practice, by a great deal of autonomy for workers. Successful leaders realize that traditional management controls and other bureaucratic linkages do not always bring about coordination. Instead, such leaders emphasize cultural dimensions that function as *bonds* to provide the necessary connections. They recognize the task of the leader is to create a bond between people through a common culture rather than to link people and events through management design (Blase, 1987).

Sergiovanni (1987a) has identified these leaders as having a *Clockworks II* mindscape. In spite of the mechanical metaphor, a Clockworks II mindscape is one that is fluid, adaptable, and open to change. While the *Clockworks I* mindscape seeks to establish the teacher's relation to the work system through hierarchical controls, the Clockworks II mindscape views teaching more as a vocation engaged in by professionals. Quality control relates to what teachers and other school professionals believe, their commitment to quality, their sense of pride, how much they identify with their work, the ownership they feel for what they are doing, and the intrinsic satisfaction they derive from the work itself.

Management and Leadership

The Maryland Commission on School-Based Administration (1987) insists that principals must provide both educational leadership and managerial direction for the school. The Commission defined educational leadership as the initiation, implementation, and institutionalization of school-wide change that results in improvement in student educational achievement and opportunity. Principals of effective schools, for example, provide leadership by establishing a sense of purpose and direction through well-developed and clearly articulated goals. Educational management was defined by the Commission as maintenance of the stability and security of an organization as it is directed and controlled on its given course. Effective principals are also resourceful managers. Although both more- and less-effective principals tend to exhibit similar work patterns, effective principals have learned to be proactive within their work environment (Manasse, 1985). The Commission's definitions of leadership (fostering and guiding change) and management (maintaining stability) portray a principalship that is dynamic and involves interplay between change and stability.

Leadership without management can result in little other than rhetoric and disappointment, while management without leadership rarely results in substantive or lasting changes (Sergiovanni, 1987b). However, the Maryland Commission counseled that a reduction in management activity combined with an increase in leadership activity is absolutely necessary to achieve school improvement. As managers, administrators must ensure the effective use of fiscal and human resources in accomplishing organization goals. As leaders, they "must display the vision and skills necessary to create and maintain a suitable teaching and learning environment, to develop school goals, and to inspire others to achieve these goals" (Guthrie & Reed, 1986, p. 199).

Research supports those who look to school leadership to influence the social and cultural structures of schools. Blase's (1987) research found that dramatic changes in the culture of a school result from changes in leadership. In a case study (1983–1986) of factors that contribute to changes in teachers' work perspectives over time, Blase found that teachers' attitudes and behaviors tended to change significantly in response to changes in leadership. School principals seen as effective by the teachers appeared to contribute to cohesive school cultures. Interactions between those principals and teachers and between teachers and others were viewed as cooperative, empathetic, supportive, respectful, equitable, and productive. In contrast, principals seen as ineffective tended to create fragmented cultures. Interactions between those principals and teachers and between teachers and others were defined as distant, uncaring, non-supportive, conflictive, inequitable, and in many ways nonproductive.

Rather than images of *heroic leadership* or *gatekeeper of change*, however, teachers portray the principal's role as one of *enabling* effective instruction by teachers. Teachers identify the principal as the central actor in shaping the environment around their classroom. In a study of the sources of teacher effectiveness and job satisfaction, a research team interviewed 85 classroom teachers in five school districts in the San Francisco bay area (Pfeifer, 1986). More than 95% of the teachers responded that their school was different in some way as a direct result of its principal. From the teachers' perspectives, leadership in schools is a task of *enablement*, a task of providing the conditions that allow competent teachers to flourish and to maximize their effectiveness. The teachers expressed a need for principals to shape the norms and attitudes shared by staff and students in a manner that provides an enabling, affective school climate. This challenges school administrators to become problem solvers, not recipe followers, in their efforts to increase teachers' efficacy (Pfeifer, 1986).

Behaviors Characteristic of Leadership Effectiveness

Effective leadership entails making the bureaucracy work by constructing an environment that minimizes uncertainty and assures emotional support for teachers (Pfeifer, 1986). While different situations may require different actions, Roueche and Baker (1986) summarized the principal behaviors that appear to form the foundation for leadership effectiveness. Among those behaviors were the following:

- Effective principals are flexible in their approach to leadership and use an appropriate type of control for professionals who have specialized expertise in various areas. They encourage innovation and at the same time tolerate failure.
- Teachers are trusted as responsible professionals, and collaborative planning, direction, and order are established and maintained even while important changes and transformations are continually occurring.
- Effective principals build cohesiveness within the organization by communicating values shared by those within the school. They cultivate cohesiveness through open dialogue and friendly interaction with staff and students.
- Effective principals recognize and reward staff accomplishments as well as willingly confront unacceptable performance and behavior.
- Effective principals solve problems through collaboration. They are willing to communicate honestly and openly with staff for the purpose of arriving at solutions that work. They see the members of the staff as valuable resources when seeking viable answers for solving conflicts and meeting demands.
- Effective principals know their staff well and delegate tasks appropriately. Delegation is done clearly and efficiently. Autonomy in getting the job done is granted with minimal supervision. Follow-up clarifies any confusion and ensures quality of task completion.

Indispensable Attitudes

Harlan Cleveland (1987), Dean of the Hubert H. Humphrey Institute of Public Affairs at the University of Minnesota, has pointed out that the leaders in our society have developed how-to-get-things-done skills. They recognize, in addition, that the most difficult part is not learning *skills* but changing *attitudes*. He cites the following attitudes as indispensable to the management of complexity:

- a lively intellectual curiosity, an interest in everything
- a genuine interest in what other people think and what makes them tick
- an attitude that risks are there not to be avoided but to be taken
- the feeling that crises are normal, tensions can be promising, and complexity is fun

- the realization that paranoia and self-pity are reserved for people who *don't* want to be leaders
- the quality of unwarranted optimism—the conviction that there must be some more upbeat outcome that would result from adding together the available expert advice
- a sense of personal responsibility for the general outcome of your efforts

FACTORS THAT INFLUENCE SCHOOL EFFECTIVENESS

The Cultural Perspective

There are four critical functions to which any organization must effectively attend in order to survive. An organization must (Sashkin & Huddle, 1986):

- adapt to change in the environment
- identify goals that meet clients' needs
- coordinate ongoing activities of the people who operate the organization
- maintain a pattern of actions with respect to adapting, attaining goals, and coordinating people's activities

School systems are confronted daily with problems that call these functions into play—coping with the fact of limited funding; identifying goals; and developing the internal structures (committees, departments, etc.) that are needed to support norms of collegial cooperation and contact in the school. The patterns of actions needed to maintain these functions are developed through a set of common values, beliefs, and norms of behavior that form a shared organizational *culture*. The culture determines how (and if) the organization adapts to change, what goals are chosen, and the way people are dealt with and deal with one another in order to link or coordinate their organizational activities (Sashkin & Huddle, 1986).

Culture is made up, in part, of the recurrent and predictable behavior patterns of a social group. This normative structure defines both *what is* and *what ought to be* (Firestone & Corbett, 1988). Culture infuses life with meaning; provides stability, certainty, and predictability; and through symbols, creates a sense of efficacy and control (Deal, 1987). Within the culture of a school, there are norms that define the *way we do things around here*. While regarded as the customary way, they are open to variation and to change. Certain norms, however, become *sacred* in that they form the foundation for professional identities and give meaning to organizational activity. Changes that tamper with the sacred norms elicit a reaction out of all proportion to the apparent importance of the issue (Corbett, Firestone, & Rossman, 1987).

The importance of culture is evident when examining the characteristics of effective schools—individual characteristics or practices often have little explanatory value alone. Their power comes from the way they combine to form a common *ethos* or culture (Rutter, Maugham, Mortimer, Ousten, & Smith, 1979). This culture is a widely shared understanding of what is and what ought to be symbolized in student, teacher, and administrator acts. What sets the highly achieving school apart from the less effective one is not simply the presence of particular norms and values but the fact that most members support them in work and deed. Therefore, the most productive schools have a distinctive normative structure that supports quality instruction (Firestone & Corbett, 1988).

Research by Rutter and his colleagues (1979) identified a cluster of characteristics associated with the school culture as the differentiating aspect of effective schools. The study stands out in four respects: it was a longitudinal study carried out from 1970–74; it examined secondary schools; it looked at 12 inner-city schools in London; and it attempted to measure school outcomes in terms of students' in-school behavior, attendance, examination success, and delinquency. The authors found that variations in the outcomes were associated with the characteristics of schools as *social institutions,* and that a school's *ethos* influenced students as a group. School ethos was defined as the *style and quality* of school life, patterns of student and teacher behavior, how students were treated as a group, the management of groups of students within the school, and the care and maintenance of buildings and grounds (Purkey & Smith, 1982).

As Little and Bird (1984) have pointed out, schools that prove successful, even under difficult circumstances, have certain characteristics, habits, and perspectives that make up the culture of the school. The staffs of these schools exhibit norms of collegiality and norms of continuous improvement. Teachers (and others) work closely together as colleagues, and teaching practices are openly scrutinized, discussed, and refined. These norms are part of the school's culture and the ability to build and sustain these norms is a measure of the school administrator's instructional leadership.

Berman and McLaughlin (1978) found that especially innovative school districts had cultures with the following characteristics:

- an emphasis on diversity in services delivered
- the primacy of improved educational service over *bureaucratic or political* concerns

- open boundaries to the environment that allowed for learning about new approaches and new resources
- norms of mutual trust and encouragement for risk taking

Viewing effective schools from a school-culture perspective emphasizes that changing schools requires changing people, their behaviors and attitudes, as well as school organization and norms. It makes it clear that consensus among the staff of a school is more powerful than overt control; that school leadership should promote collaborative planning, collegial work, and a school atmosphere conducive to experimentation and evaluation (Purkey & Smith, 1982). Teachers and administrators, together, can shape a school's culture in favor of learning, but no single teacher's or administrator's effort is likely to exert much influence. Only a concerted faculty effort is likely to develop a firm, fair, and consistent system of discipline or a climate of favorable expectations for students (Bird, 1984).

Social Context Factors Affect School Culture

A school is affected by the social context of the community it serves and by the distribution of academic skills, social skills, work habits, perceptions, and behavior that its students bring with them into the school. These student behaviors are formed, in part, by the environment that surrounds them. That environment includes norms that define expected behavior, values that determine what is worthwhile, and attitudes that shape responses to people and events. These norms, values, and attitudes are first learned in the environment of infancy and early childhood—long before the educational system sees the child (Bird, 1984).

Understanding the effects of the school social context is important to understanding the effective organization and management of schools. The research from urban elementary schools identified strong instructional leadership as a characteristic of effective schools. This finding has been consistently interpreted to mean that strong leadership by the principal is a prerequisite for improving schools, and school improvement programs typically carve out a uniform role for the principal regardless of the school context. Even if strong instructional leadership is necessary to generate improvement in low-income, urban, elementary schools, the appropriate style of instructional leadership in other schools may vary depending on both organizational and environmental factors (Hallinger & Murphy, 1987). For example, a study by Martinko and Gardner

(1983) found that principals' behaviors varied significantly with grade level, staff size, district size, geographic location, socioeconomic status, and relative urbanization.

Instructional leadership in effective secondary schools, for example, differs from that in effective elementary schools. In high schools, the principal's ability to be personally involved in all aspects of instructional management is limited by the size of staff and student populations, the multi-leveled organizational structure, and the specialized subject areas. Instead, the principal relies more on indirect, facilitative, and symbolic modes of expression, directly intervening only in selected situations (Hallinger & Murphy, 1987). Actions by a principal that are appropriate in one school might produce resentment or confusion in another (Pfeifer, 1986).

Socio-economic status has a pervasive influence on the conduct of education. Measures of student socio-economic status (SES) correlate highly with measures of student achievement and educational attainment. The findings in a study by Walberg and Fowler (1987) are typical. They found a correlation of 0.84 between student SES and ninth-grade writing scores. This means that the variance in student achievement scores accounted for by student SES was 71%—not an unusual finding. The influence of the socio-economic environment goes beyond conditioning individual behavior; however, it also provides a cultural context in which the school functions.

Social class has a significant effect on the educational expectations and preferences of parents. These varying preferences influence the goals that schools actually pursue and the corresponding structure of their educational programs (Hallinger & Murphy, 1987). Parents of different social classes prefer schools to address different educational goals. In lower-class communities, parents often prefer an emphasis on social and vocational goals. Effective low-SES schools focus on improving instruction in basic reading and mathematics skills. This highly limited mission is often translated into a few explicitly stated, school-wide academic goals and the delineation of a few, specific priorities. Parents in wealthier districts are more concerned with the development of students' intellectual abilities. Evidence from a California effective school study indicates that successful schools in wealthy communities maintain an academically oriented mission that addresses a broad array of intellectual skills. Mastery of basic cognitive skills is accepted almost as a given. Successful higher-SES schools pursue more generally defined goals that require less consensus concerning the actual content of the school's mission and the specific means for achieving it (Hallinger & Murphy, 1987).

Parental involvement in schools varies according to SES. In general, parents in higher-SES communities are more involved in the school program than parents in lower-SES communities. In the high-SES schools, principals are constantly seeking efficient ways to involve a group of parents that takes great interest in the school and that has substantial resources to offer. Principals in these schools spend more time mediating relationships between demanding parents and teachers, tend to be more open to group activities involving staff and community, and use more participatory decision making (Lortie, Crow, & Prolman, 1983). In low-SES schools, even those that have been labeled *effective*, there is a history of limited parental interest in the school, and school staff expect relatively little from the community in terms of support. In low-income schools in the California study, the principals acted as buffers, carefully controlling access to the school and filtering outside influences (Hallinger & Murphy, 1987).

Teachers generally accommodate their teaching styles to student subcultures (Metz, 1978). Corwin and Borman (1988) cite Everhart's studies at Harold Spencer Junior High, a blue-collar, predominantly white school of about a thousand students. Classrooms were punctuated by acts designed to *bug* teachers who were disliked because they enforced many trivial rules and treated students like babies. Teachers who were not the targets of these episodes of laughing, gum chewing, and pencil tapping were those who varied the curriculum and allowed students to talk among themselves. These teachers were most successful, however, with higher-track students who enjoyed class discussion and a lively classroom atmosphere. The lower-track students liked teachers who didn't yell, provided highly structured seatwork, and kept students quiet and busy.

The social context also influences the structure of school-wide reward systems. Students from low income families generally come to school with few of the skills necessary for academic success and, in many cases, do not value schooling very highly. In such cases, the school must take systematic measures to reward and publicly recognize students for the behavior that the school seeks to promote. Principals in lower-status schools are often preoccupied with discipline issues and have more problematic relationships with faculty (Lortie, Crow, & Prolman, 1983). Students from wealthier families generally come to school with more of those skills necessary for academic success, a more positive attitude toward schooling, and higher parental expectations. Because of this combination of factors, students from higher-SES families experience success in school more quickly and learning becomes rewarding and less dependent upon frequent extrinsic rewards. The school in a high-SES community may need to resort to fewer concrete rewards in order to promote high expectations (Hallinger & Murphy, 1987).

Perhaps the most often quoted finding from the effective schools literature is that in effective low-SES schools, the principal and teachers hold reasonably high expectations for their students to master basic reading and math skills. The principal, however, must instill those high expectations without the benefit of continuing input from parents, who are less well schooled and who often are only peripherally involved in the life of the schools. The principal often becomes the key actor in developing and sustaining high expectations on the part of school staff. Their expectations are not as high, however, as those of staff in schools serving students in wealthier communities. The source of expectations also seems to differ in schools located in high-SES communities. Principals and teachers in these schools identify parents as the primary source of the school's expectations. There is an implicit assumption that the children of professional parents will succeed in school and the principal's job is to sustain the high expectations that prevail in the community. Since high expectations already exist, the principal's tasks are to ensure that the expectations are clear and consistent, and to translate the high expectations into appropriate school policies and programs (Hallinger & Murphy, 1987).

Principals of effective low-SES schools have a clear vision of how the school should be organized. They play a highly directive role in the selection, development, and implementation of curriculum and instructional programs and tend to exercise relatively tight control over classroom instruction. They are forceful in establishing high expectations and standards for staff and students and in holding themselves and staff accountable for student achievement. Teachers describe these principals as being a major factor in the school's success. On the other hand, principals in effective high-SES schools exercise less direct control over classroom instruction, coordinate more from the background, and allow teachers greater autonomy with respect to instructional decision-making. Although they maintain a close watch over student outcomes, they tend to exert control over classroom instruction only when results fall below expected levels. Teachers describe these principals as strong instructional leaders but they do not identify them as *the key* to school success. Both formal and informal norms within the schools allow the principal in a low-SES school to assume greater authority than the principal in a higher-SES school (Hallinger & Murphy, 1987). Mar-

tinko and Gardner (1983) found that principals in high-SES schools used skills in delegating authority, managing change, and interacting with central administrative staff. Those in middle-SES schools more often used human relations approaches to leadership, while those principals in lower-SES schools had more knowledge of minority culture and more classroom teaching skills.

Lessons from Inner-City Schools

In reviewing current directions in urban school reform, Oakes (1987) concluded that the central lesson of the effective-schools research is that, under the right conditions, inner-city poor and minority children can learn. She cautioned, however, that those conditions are not necessarily the same for inner-city children as for more-advantaged, middle-class children, nor are they the same for urban children in one school as they are for children in another. Her analysis suggested several promising strategies for urban districts attempting to help inner-city students break the cycle of school failure, unemployment, and social disintegration. These strategies included the following:

- Build capacity at local school sites.
- Provide school autonomy and flexibility in designing and implementing improvement plans.
- Take a broad rather than a narrow view of curriculum and instruction.
- Reorganize classroom teaching and learning to promote urban children's positive self-perceptions, effort, and school performance.
- Provide real-life incentives for urban children to achieve at school.
- Coordinate efforts with the self-interests of other institutions and agencies to provide social and economic opportunities beyond the reach of the school.

Developing Conditions That Foster Excellence

Attaining educational excellence is difficult under the current organizational structure of public schools. That excellence is possible is proved by the fact that so many excellent schools exist in so many different settings. Yet the excellent schools are not models that can be duplicated and mass produced. "No formula exists to guarantee excellence; it is born of a persisting commitment to do well and to do well by others; it develops from a blend of inspired leadership, committed personnel, and adequate resources; it occurs as a result of initiative, perseverance, faith, and pluck" (Wayson, 1988, p. 202). Wayson identified the following common characteristics exhibited by good schools:

- They are not rigid; they are flexible and relaxed.
- They are not punitive; they accentuate the positive.
- They are not elitist; they welcome and encourage all students.
- They do not have a narrow curriculum limited to the basics; they offer a varied curriculum that is flexible and adapted to students' needs.
- They are not test-driven; their students do achieve well because they teach higher-order thinking processes.
- They do not rely on packaged programs; they do rely on their staffs' commitment and creativity.
- They do not have authoritarian principals; rather they have principals who have a vision of what the school should be and the determination to accomplish that mission.
- They recruit and keep staff members on the basis of merit and have procedures for removing those who do not contribute to the school's mission.
- They have intensive staff development.
- They know what they are trying to accomplish and have ways for assessing how well they are doing and for correcting any shortcomings they detect.
- They believe in themselves and their students and hold themselves responsible for instructing all children.
- They put student welfare above all other concerns.
- They have structures that foster decision making and problem solving by staff members as groups, not as individuals.
- They have a *cheerleader* who generates staff enthusiasm and participation and who solicits support from outsiders.
- They celebrate their successes and give recognition to staff and students for their achievements.
- They are loose (flexible) about means and tight (demanding) about ends.

SUMMARY AND IMPLICATIONS

The five factors of the *Effective Schools Formula* have been widely embraced throughout the nation in the belief that adoption of these factors would increase the achievement of students. In a major review of the early effective school studies, however, Purkey and Smith (1982) found only two findings that were consistent across the studies:

1. strong instructional leadership from the principal or other instructional figure
2. high expectations by the staff for student achievement

While they were not present in all the studies, there were two important findings that were overlooked in subsequent discussions of the effective schools research. "A school-wide effective staff training program" and "a considerable degree of control by the staff over instruction and training decisions in the school" failed to make the more popular lists of effective schools characteristics. Yet, current research is finding that these also are critical to school improvement and to school excellence.

Although most researchers agree that schools or school districts should develop plans in response to their unique situations, some districts have simply taken plans developed in other districts and applied them with few, if any, modifications. A number of researchers and practitioners have reservations about such widespread acceptance of an overall prescription for improving schools. Finn (1983) reasons that effective schools have become so because they have developed their own goals, norms, and expectations.

New insights have been gained from more recent research studies and reviews. Stedman (1987) concentrated on case studies of those effective schools that had achieved grade-level success with low-income students for several years. His analysis found that successful schools incorporated practices that fell into broad categories. He suggested that these categories should be thought of as a set of highly interrelated practices where efforts in one area will generally facilitate efforts in the others.

While every school had its own character, Roueche and Baker (1986) found certain common climate factors in effective schools that formed the foundation for student success. Those common factors included: a sense of order, purpose, direction, and coherence; orderly classrooms; a student-centered focus; quality in both academics and co-curricular activities; a climate of optimism and high expectations; and organizational health. Wayson and his associates (1988) reported that excellent schools focused on student learning in both basic and critical thinking skills. He stressed that "cooperative working relationships among the staff" clearly set the effective schools apart from the average schools.

The importance of culture is evident when examining the characteristics of effective schools. Individual characteristics or practices often have little explanatory value alone. Their power comes from the way they combine to form a common *ethos* or culture. The culture determines how (and if) the organization adapts to change, what goals are chosen, and the way people interact in order to link or coordinate their organizational activities. The culture of a school is affected by the social context of the community it serves and by the distribution of academic skills, social skills, work habits, perceptions, and behavior that its students bring with them into the school.

Research by Rutter and his colleagues (1979) identified a cluster of characteristics associated with the school culture as the differentiating aspect between those schools identified as effective schools and those that were not. The authors found that schools which prove successful, even under difficult circumstances, have certain characteristics, habits, and perspectives that make up the culture of the school. The staffs of these schools exhibit norms of collegiality and norms of continuous improvement.

Socio-economic status has a pervasive influence on the conduct of education. Measures of student socio-economic status (SES) correlate highly with measures of student achievement and educational attainment. Social class has a significant effect on the educational expectations and preferences of parents. These varying preferences influence the goals that schools actually pursue and the corresponding structure of their educational programs. Teachers generally accommodate their teaching styles to student subcultures and the social context influences the structure of school-wide reward systems. Principals in lower-status schools are often preoccupied with discipline issues and must take systematic measures to reward and publicly recognize students for the behavior that the school seeks to promote.

A clear picture of an effective school forms from the previous discussion of the factors that influence school effectiveness. Looking at the recent findings from research on effective schools, effective teaching, and effective school administrators, the following characteristics emerge:

- *Effective schools are student centered.* They make an effort to serve all students; create support networks to assist students; involve students in school affairs; respect and celebrate the ethnic and linguistic differences among students; and have student welfare as a first priority.
- *Effective schools offer academically rich programs.* They address higher- as well as lower-order cognitive objectives; provide an enriched environment through a variety of options; have an active cocurricular program; provide in-depth coverage of content; and appropriately monitor student progress and provide feedback.
- *Effective schools provide instruction that promotes student learning.* Teachers communicate expectations to students; hold themselves responsible for student learning; provide focused and organized instructional sessions; adapt instruction to student needs; anticipate and correct student misconceptions; and use a variety of teaching strategies.
- *Effective schools have a positive school climate.* They have a distinctive normative structure that supports instruction. They have a sense of order, purpose, and direction fostered by consistency among teachers; an atmosphere of encouragement where students are praised and rewarded; a work-centered environment; and high optimism and expectations for student learning.
- *Effective schools foster collegial interaction.* Teachers work together as colleagues in instruction, to plan curriculum, and to refine teaching practices.
- *Effective schools have extensive staff development.* The teacher evaluation system is used to help teachers improve their skills. Inservice is practical, on-the-job training that is tailored to meet the specific needs of staff members. Teachers are encouraged to reflect on their practices.
- *Effective schools practice shared leadership.* School administrators understand and use a leadership style appropriate for professionals; solve problems through collaboration, team, or group decision making; know their staff and delegate authority; communicate and build cohesiveness; and use their position to recognize and reward accomplishments of both staff and students.
- *Effective schools involve parents.* They establish methods for communicating with parents, involve parents in the activities of the school, include parents in the decision-making process, use parents as resources to extend the efforts of the school, and depend on parents to provide good public relations for the school.

The above distillation suggests that effective schools respond to the needs of students in their schools, build programs that will encourage responsibility and learning in their students, and adjust the workings of the school in order to help students function to their capacity. Such schools are not test driven, regulation bound, or focused on control. They are striving to meet the needs of all their students and all the needs of their students. Schools that build collegial norms, share authority and leadership, and use the results of teacher evaluation to improve performance are schools that are able to adapt to the changing requirements of both staff and students. It is highly probable, however, that schools which incorporate the above factors are expending a great deal of energy bypassing the bureaucratic constraints built into most school systems. And, increasingly, these schools are having to contend with mandates from legislatures or state boards of education that make the job of being effective even harder. It is imperative that the organizational structure within which administrators and teachers function be designed to facilitate rather than constrain teaching and learning.

REFERENCES

Anderson, C. W. and Smith, E. L. (1987). Teaching Science. In V. Koehler (Ed.), *The educator's handbook: A research perspective.* New York: Longman.

Ball, D. L. and Feiman-Nemser, S. (1986). *Using textbooks and teachers guides: What beginning elementary teachers learn and what they need to know.* (Research Series No. 174). East Lansing, MI: Michigan State University, Institute for Research on Teaching.

Berman, P. and McLaughlin, M. W. (1978). *Federal programs supporting educational change, Vol. VIII: Implementing and sustaining innovations.* (R-1589/8-HEW). Santa Monica, CA: The Rand Corp.

Bird, T. (1984, Dec.) *School organization and the rewards of teaching.* Education Commission of the States, Denver, CO.

Blase, J. J. (1987, Winter). Dimensions of effective school leadership: The teacher's perspective. *American Educational Research Journal, 24*(4): 589–610.

Brandt, R. (1987, Sept.). On leadership and student achievement: A conversation with Richard Andrews. *Educational Leadership 45*(1): 9–17.

Clark, C. M. and Peterson, P. M. (1986). Teachers thought processes. In C. Wittrock, *Handbook of research on teaching* (3rd ed., pp. 255–296). New York: Macmillan.

Cleveland, H. (1987). *The public manager in an information society* (Occasional paper on leadership issues/2). Washington, D.C.: The Institute for Educational Leadership.

Corbett, H. D., Firestone, W. A., and Rossman, G. B. (1987, Nov.). Resistance to planned change and the sacred in school cultures. *Educational Administration Quarterly, 23*(4): 36–59.

Corwin, R. G. and Borman, K. M. (1988). School as a workplace: Structural constraints on administration. In N. J. Boyan (Ed.), *Handbook of research on educational administration* (pp. 209–237). New York: Longman.

D'Amico, J. (1982, Dec.). Using effective schools studies to create effective schools: No recipes yet. *Educational Leadership, 40*(3): 61–69.

Deal, T. E. (1987). The culture of schools. In L. T. Sheive and M. B. Schoenheit (Eds.), *Leadership: Examining the elusive* (pp. 3–15). Washington, D.C.: Association for Supervision and Curriculum Development.

Edmonds, R. (1979). Effective schools for the urban poor. *Educational Leadership, 37*(1): 15–24.

Finn, G. (1983, June). *Toward strategic independence: Policy considerations for enhancing school effectiveness* (Final report, Grant NIE 400–79–0035). Washington, D.C.: National Institute of Education.

Firestone, W. A. and Corbett, H. D. (1988). Planned organizational change. In N. J. Boyan (Ed.), *Handbook of research on educational administration* (pp. 321–338). New York: Longman.

Good, T. L. and Brophy, J. E. (1986). School effects. In M. C. Whittrock (Ed.), *Handbook of research on training* (3rd ed., pp. 570–602). New York: Macmillan.

Guthrie, J. W. and Reed, R. J. (1986). *Educational administration and policy: Effective leadership for American education.* Upper Saddle River, N.J.: Prentice Hall.

Hallinger, P. and Murphy, J. (1987, April). *Organizational and social context and the instructional leadership role of the school principal.* Paper presented at the annual meeting of the American Educational Research Association, Washington, D.C.

Lee, O. and Gallagher, J. J. (1986, March 28). *Differential treatment of individual students and whole cases by middle school science teachers: Causes and consequences.* Paper presented at the National Association for Research in Science Teaching, San Francisco.

Little J. W. and Bird, T. D. (1984). *Is there instructional leadership in high schools? First findings from a study of secondary school administrators and their influence on teachers' professional norms.* Paper presented at the annual meeting of the American Educational Research Association, New Orleans.

Lortie, D. C., Crow, G., and Prolman, S. (1983). *Elementary principals in suburbia: An occupational and organizational study* (Final report). Washington, D.C.: National Institute of Education.

Manasse, A. L. (1985, March). Effective principals: Effective at what? *Principal, 61*(4): 10–15.

Martinko, M. J. and Gardiner, W. L. (1983). *An executive summary of: The behavior of high performing educational managers: An observational study.* Tallahassee, FL: The Florida State University.

Maryland Commission on School-Based Administration. (1987, Feb.). *Improving the effectiveness of school-based administration in Maryland.* Baltimore: Maryland State Dept. of Education.

Metz, M. H. (1978). *Classrooms and corridors.* Berkeley, CA: University of California Press.

Oakes, J. (1987). *Improving inner-city schools: Current directions in urban district reform.* New Brunswick, NJ: Center for Policy Research in Education, Rutgers University.

Pfeifer, R. S. (1986, April). *Enabling teacher effectiveness: Teachers' perspectives on instructional management.* Paper presented at the annual meeting of the American Research Association, San Francisco.

Porter, A. C. and Brophy, J. (1988). Synthesis of research on good teaching: Insights from work of the Institute for Research on Teaching, *Educational Leadership, 45*(8): 74–85.

Purkey, S. C. and Smith, M. S. (1982, Dec.). Synthesis of research on effective schools. *Educational Leadership, 40*(3): 64–69.

Roueche, J. E. and Baker, III, G. A. (1986). *Profiling excellence in American schools.* Arlington, VA: American Association of School Administrators.

Rutter, M., Maughan, B., Mortimore, P., and Ouston, J. (1979). *Fifteen thousand hours: Secondary schools and their effects on children.* Cambridge, MA: Harvard University Press.

Sashkin, M. and Huddle, G. (1986). *The principal's leadership role in creating effective schools.* Draft, unpublished manuscript.

Sergiovanni, T. J. (1987a). The theoretical basis for cultural leadership. In L. T. Sheive and M. B. Schoenheit (Eds.), *Leadership: Examining the elusive* (pp. 116–129). Association for Supervision and Curriculum Development.

Sergiovanni, T. J. (1987b). *The principals: A reflective practice perspective.* Boston: Allyn & Bacon.

Stedman, L. C. (1987, Nov.). It's time we changed the effective schools formula. *Phi Delta Kappan, 69*(3): 215–227.

Walberg, H. J. and Fowler, Jr., W. J. (1987, Oct.). Expenditure and size efficiencies of public school districts. *Educational Researcher, 16*(7): 5–13.

Wayson, W. W. (1988). *Up from excellence: The impact of the excellence movement on schools.* Bloomington, IN: Phi Delta Kappa Educational Foundation.

CHAPTER 28

SCANS Report: Learning a Living

PRINCIPLES FOR RECOMMENDATIONS

The Secretary's Commission on Achieving Necessary Skills (SCANS) was appointed by the Secretary of Labor to determine the skills our young people need to succeed in the world of work. The Commission's fundamental purpose is to encourage a high-performance economy characterized by high-skill, high-wage employment.

Our primary message to schools is this: Look beyond the schoolhouse to the roles students will play when they leave to become workers, parents, and citizens.

Our message to teachers is this: Look beyond your discipline and your classroom to the other courses your students take, to your community, and to the lives of your students outside school. Help your students connect what they learn in class to the world outside.

Our message to employers is this: Look outside your company and change your view of your responsibilities for human resource development. Your old responsibilities were to select the best available applicants and to retain those you hired. Your new responsibilities must be to improve the way you organize work and to develop the human resources in your community, your firm, and your nation.

Reprinted with permission from "Learning a Living: A Blueprint for High Performance, A SCANS Report for America 2000." U. S. Department of Labor, April 1992.

We want to state at the outset that the well-being of the nation—and its citizens—is not synonymous with economic status. There is much more to life than earning a living, and we want more from schools than productive workers. We want citizens who can discharge the responsibilities that go with living in a democratic society and with being parents. As we said in our first report: "A solid education is its own reward and has value beyond specific skills." We are not talking about turning our high schools into trade schools. Nor do we suggest that schools ignore the beauty of literature and scientific theories or the lessons of history and geography.

SCANS has focused on one important aspect of schooling: what we call the "learning a living" system. In 1991 we issued our initial report, *What Work Requires of Schools*. As outlined in that report, a high-performance workplace requires workers who have a solid foundation in the basic literacy and computational skills, in the thinking skills necessary to put knowledge to work, and in the personal qualities that make workers dedicated and trustworthy.

But a solid foundation is not enough. High-performance workplaces also require competencies: the ability to manage resources, to work amicably and productively with others, to acquire and use information, to master complex systems, and to work with a variety of technologies. This combination of foundation skills and workplace competencies—"workplace know-how" (see Figure 1)—is not taught in many schools or required for most diplomas.

The time when a high school diploma was a sure ticket to a job is within the memory of workers who

The know-how identified by SCANS is made up of five workplace competencies and a three-part foundation of skills and personal qualities that are needed for solid job performance. These are:

WORKPLACE COMPETENCIES—Effective workers can productively use:

- **Resources**—They know how to allocate time, money, materials, space, and staff.
- **Interpersonal skills**—They can work on teams, teach others, serve customers, lead, negotiate, and work well with people from culturally diverse backgrounds.
- **Information**—They can acquire and evaluate data, organize and maintain files, interpret and communicate, and use computers to process information.
- **Systems**—They understand social, organizational, and technological systems; they can monitor and correct performance; and they can design or improve systems.
- **Technology**—They can select equipment and tools, apply technology to specific tasks, and maintain and troubleshoot equipment

FOUNDATION SKILLS—Computer workers in the high-performance workplace need:

- **Basic Skills**–reading, writing, arithmetic, and mathematics, speaking, and listening.
- **Thinking Skills**—the ability to learn, to reason, to think creatively, to make decisions, and to solve problems.
- **Personal Qualities**—individual responsibility, self-esteem and self-management, sociability, and integrity.

FIGURE 1   Workplace Know-How

have not yet retired; yet in many places today a high school diploma is little more than a certificate of attendance. As a result, employers discount the value of all diplomas, and many students do not work hard in high school.

As shown in Figure 2, the market value of a high school diploma is falling. The proportion of men between the ages of 25 and 54 with high school diplomas who earn less than enough to support a family of four above the poverty line is growing alarmingly. Among African-American men with 12 years of schooling, the proportion with low earnings rose from 20 percent in 1969 to 42.7 percent in 1989; among Hispanic men, from 16.4 to 35.9 percent; and among white men, from 8.3 percent to 22.6 percent. That is, in 1989 more than two in five African-American men, one in three Hispanic men, and one in five white men, all with high school diplomas, did not earn enough to lift a family of four above poverty. Unless there is a

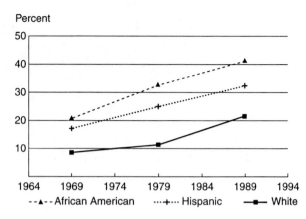

Percent

Source: Sheldon Danziger, "The Poor," in David Hornbeck and Lester Solamon, *Human Capital and America's Future.* (Baltimore: John Hopkins Press, 1991), p. 148, and unpublished data for 1989.

FIGURE 2   The Proportion of Male High School Graduates Unable to Support a Family of Four is Growing[1]

second earner, their families will not have what most would call a decent living.

The workplace know-how SCANS has defined is related both to competent performance and to higher earnings for the people who possess it. Figure 3 compares the know-how required in 23 high-wage jobs with the requirements of 23 low-wage jobs. The conclusion is inescapable: workers with more know-how command a higher wage—on average, 58 percent, or $11,200 a year, higher.

Everyone must have the opportunity to reach the higher levels of skills and competencies shown in Figure 3. To that end, the Commission has recast the broad principles set forth in *What Work Requires of Schools* as the context for our recommendations:

- The qualities of high performance that today characterize our most competitive companies must become the standard for the vast majority of our employers, public and private, large and small, local and global.
- The nation's schools must be transformed into high-performance organizations.
- All Americans should be entitled to multiple opportunities to learn the SCANS know-how well enough to earn a decent living.

To make this a reality we recommend:

1. The nation's school systems should make the SCANS foundation skills and workplace competencies explicit objectives of instruction at all levels.

---

1. Males ages, 25–54, with 12 years of education whose earnings are less than the poverty level for a family of four. Family income may be higher.

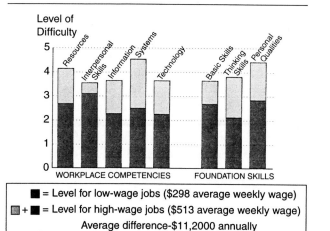

FIGURE 3   High-Wage Jobs Require Higher Levels of the SCANS Know-How

2. Assessment systems should provide students and workers with a resume documenting attainment of the SCANS know-how.
3. All employers, public and private, should incorporate the SCANS know-how into all their human resource development efforts.
4. The Federal Government should continue to bridge the gap between school and the high-performance workplace, by advancing the SCANS agenda.
5. Every employer in America should create its own strategic vision around the principles of the high-performance workplace.

Implementation

The Commission recognizes that nationwide policies are of little value until they are carried out by people on the front line. Cities such as Fort Worth, Los Angeles, Pittsburgh, Tampa, and Louisville and states such as Florida, Indiana, New York, and Oregon have taken steps to put the broad SCANS principles in place in their school systems at the local and state levels. In the corporate sector, TGI Friday's, MCI, Gannett, Motorola, NationsBank, and AT&T (and its major unions) are taking action. A number of trade organizations in the hospitality field have joined together to introduce the SCANS language into their industry. The U. S. Department of Labor is moving to build SCANS into various aspects of Job Training Partnership Act programs. The Federal Government's Office of Personnel Management (OPM) is seeking ways to apply SCANS findings in skills centers for Federal employees.

These leaders and those who follow them can begin the systemic change to a high-performance fu-

ture. In the process they will have to reinvent education, reorganize work and work-based learning, and restructure educational assessment.

Reinventing K–12 Education   During the 1980s the United States, seeking to improve public schools, tried to get more results through tighter curricula, higher certification standards for teachers, and more testing of everyone. Despite the effort, students were performing essentially no better at the end of the decade than they were at the beginning. More of the same was not a successful strategy.

As this Commission argued in *What Work Requires of Schools,* American society today requires that elementary and secondary schools meet drastically different goals. The job now is to bring all students to a level that, in the past, only a small minority reached. Experts universally agree that this job requires reinventing elementary and secondary education.

President Bush and the nation's governors agreed on a set of six goals for education. These goals have been generally agreed to by state governments, education leaders, and business groups such as the Business Roundtable. SCANS supports all six goals; its recommendations are particularly pertinent to the two goals that refer to preparing youth and adults for productive employment in our competitive economy.

The experience of schools, districts, and states that are advancing toward high-performance schooling provides important lessons for educators wishing to teach the SCANS know-how:

- Teaching should be offered "in context," that is, students should learn content while solving realistic problems. "Learning in order to know" should not be separated from "learning in order to do."
- Improving the match between what work requires and what students are taught requires changing how instruction is delivered and how students learn.
- High performance requires a new system of school administration and assessment.
- The entire community must be involved.

Table 1, drawn from experience in Fort Worth, Texas, outlines how the traditional classroom differs from the SCANS classroom. The conventions of today's classroom (teacher omniscience, student passivity and isolation, rigid disciplinary borders, and "abstracted" knowledge and facts) are replaced with sophisticated and more realistic concepts of instruction and learning (the teacher may not know all the answers, students often learn best in groups, and knowledge is related to real problems).

Resources. Of all the resources required for reinventing schools around the SCANS ends, none is more important than those devoted to teacher training and staff development. Providing training opportunities for instructional staff will be costly, especially if teachers and administrators are to be given the time they need during the school day and summers for training. But teachers, noninstructional staff, and building and school-district administrators need time if they are to:

- develop new pedagogical skills required to teach in context and to develop active, collaborative learning environments
- learn new instructional management skills and use new instructional technologies to develop new ways of interacting with students
- gain experience with the principles of high performance as applied in restructured workplaces

Emerging instructional technologies promise to revolutionize teaching and learning by enabling teachers and students to change their traditional roles. When technology dispenses information, teachers are free to teach and facilitate student learning. With technology monitoring learning, students can become active learners, working to acquire new skills.

The SCANS competencies cannot be widely taught unless teachers have instructional materials: textbooks and other print materials, and computer-based and multimedia materials. Video and multimedia materials are essential to creating the realistic contexts in which the competencies are used.

Equity and Diversity. The changes advocated by the Commission promise great benefits to minority and low-income Americans. One-third of new entrants into the American labor force are members of minority groups; they are entitled to an education that will let them learn and will equip them to find and hold a decent job. Because children vary, not only as individuals but also as members of different cultural, racial, and ethnic groups, education must take into account three basic elements that contribute to this diversity:

1. differences in family income
2. limited English-speaking proficiency (LEP)
3. differences in learning styles

Variation and diversity are not the enemies of high-quality education. The enemy is rigid insistence on a factory model of schooling, a prescription for failure that refuses to accommodate diversity or to allow those students with special strengths to function productively.

TABLE 1   The Conventional Classroom Compared with the SCANS Classroom

From the Conventional Classroom	To the SCANS Classroom
Teacher knows answer.	More than one solution may be available, and teacher may not have it in advance.
Students routinely work alone.	Students routinely work with teachers, peers, and community members.
Teacher plans all activities.	Students and teachers plan and negotiate activities.
Teacher makes all assessments.	Students routinely assess themselves.
Information is organized, evaluated, interpreted and communicated to students by teacher.	Information is acquired, evaluated, organized, interpreted, and communicated by students to appropriate audiences.
Organizing system of the classroom is simple: one teacher teaches 30 students.	Organizing systems are complex: teacher and students both reach out beyond school for additional information.
Reading, writing, and math are treated as separate disciplines; listening and speaking often are missing from curriculum.	Disciplines needed for problem solving are integrated; listening and speaking are fundamental parts of learning.
Thinking is usually theoretical and "academic."	Thinking involves problem solving, reasoning, and decision making.
Students are expected to conform to teacher's behavioral expectations; integrity and honesty are monitored by teacher; student self-esteem is often poor.	Students are expected to be responsible, sociable, self-managing, and resourceful; integrity and honesty are monitored within the social context of the classroom; students' self-esteem is high because they are in charge of their own learning.

Source: Fort Worth public schools.

Reorganizing for High-Performance Work and Work-Based Learning Both high-performance workplaces and highly trained workers are needed if we are to build a high-skilled, high-wage economy. Reinventing K–12 education is necessary but not sufficient because about 80 percent of the workers on whom American employers will depend as we enter the 21st century are already on the job. To create high-performance workplaces, employers must actively work to develop the skills and competencies of these workers. Only in this way can they constantly improve the quality of the goods and services they provide and satisfy their customers' needs.

Every American employer, public or private, large or small, local or global, must consider the human resources needed for high performance and high quality. Yet today, American companies do much less training than some of our international competitors; in fact, fewer than 10 percent of front-line American workers now receive training of any kind.

The Commission believes that employer-sponsored training, both public and private, must be upgraded and organized around the SCANS know-how. As a useful first step, coalitions of trade associations, business organizations, labor unions, and industry-specific groups could develop training strategies and materials around the SCANS know-how for use by all businesses, particularly small firms.

Many young people between the ages of 16 to 25 today are frustrated because their high schools talked of English and geometry, but their workplace speaks a different language. In a system that serves people beyond high school, employers would describe job requirements in terms of the SCANS workplace competencies and use these for recruitment and employee development. Human resource and training managers would reorient their education and training offerings to include not only job-specific skills but also the SCANS workplace competencies and foundation skills.

Providers of education—vocational schools, proprietary schools, community colleges, adult education, and work-based programs—would offer instruction and certification in SCANS workplace competencies. Referral agencies—job counselors in high schools, in employment agencies and the Employment Service, or in the skill centers newly recommended by the Administration—would assess their clients' SCANS workplace competencies, understand job and educational requirements and opportunities in the same terms, and refer clients to career-enhancing work and education.

Restructuring Educational Assessment A system for assessing and certifying the SCANS workplace know-how is essential. If employers and colleges pay

attention to the SCANS foundation skills and workplace competencies, students will work to acquire them. If teachers have to certify that the know-how is acquired, they will make the effort to teach it. If parents and community groups understand the standards that graduates are expected to attain, they will demand that their children reach these levels.

The Commission supports the emerging national consensus calling for a new, nationwide, voluntary assessment system. The Commission believes the system should incorporate new techniques of judging performance—not "tests" as traditionally understood, but assessment tied to learning goals. The National Council on Education Standards and Testing has endorsed including SCANS workplace competencies in the system it recommended, stating that the SCANS competencies "can and should be integrated into the national standards and assessments."[2] The Commission hopes that the curriculum development work of several groups—the National Council of Teachers of Mathematics, the National Council of Teachers of English, the National Science Teachers Association, and others—will follow this advice.

The Commission believes that a national system, as recommended by the National Council on Education Standards and Testing, should integrate assessment of proficiency in SCANS know-how with other equally important outcomes of schooling. Such a system is needed to:

- communicate world-class standards of curriculum content and student performance
- certify individual performance and thereby motivate students and their teachers to meet these standards

The challenge is to design a system that clearly establishes that all young people in our nation have the right to an education up to a recognized performance standard—without putting the burden of failure on students' backs.

The Commission suggests establishing for all students, beginning in middle school, a cumulative resume. The resume would contain information about courses taken, projects completed, and proficiency levels attained in each competency. A student who accomplishes enough to meet an overall standard would be awarded a certificate of initial mastery (CIM), a universally recognized statement of experience and accomplishment. The information would mean the same thing to everybody: this

2. Raising Standards for American Education (Washington, D.C.: National Council on Education Standards and Testing. January 1992).

Jane Smith
19 Main Street
Anytown

Home Phone: (817) 777-3333 Age: 20

Date of Report 5/1/92
Soc. Sec.: 599-46-1234
Date of Birth: 3/7/73

SCANS Workplace Competency	Date	Proficiency Level
Resources	10/91	1
Interpersonal Skills	12/91	2
Information	11/92	3
Technology	1/92	2
Systems	4/92	3

Core Academic and Elective Courses	Date	Proficiency Level
English	11/91	3
Mathematics	12/91	3
Science	2/91	3
History	4/91	2
Geography	8/91	1
Fine Arts	11/91	4
Vocational/Industrial Education	4/92	2

SCANS Personal Qualities	Average Rating	No. of Ratings
Responsibility	Excellent	10
Self-Esteem	Excellent	10
Sociability	Excellent	8
Self-Management	Excellent	7
Integrity/Honesty	Good	6

Portfolios and Other Materials Available		Reference
1. Report on Grounds Keeping (Chemistry)		Mr. Kent
2. Video on Architectural Styles (Social Studies)		Ms. Jones
3. Newspaper Article Written		Ms. French

Extracurricular Activities	Role	Date	Reference
Newspaper	Reporter	9/89–1/90	Frank Jones (Advisor)
Basketball Varsity	Center	9/90–6/91	Dean Smith (Coach)

Awards and Honors	Date	Source	Reference
Teen Volunteer of the Year	6/91	Rotary Club	John Grove
Class Secretary	9/91–1/92	Lincoln High School	Emma Rice

	Earned	Required
POINTS TOWARD CERTIFICATE OF INITIAL MASTERY	300	500

(Supplied by Student)

Work Experience	Date	Place	Reference
Volunteer Work	6/88–6/89	St. Joseph Homeless Shelter	Father John O'Connell (508) 296-3304
Summer Camp Counselor	6/91–8/91	Camp Kiowa	Susan Miller (508) 628-5128
Office (Word Processor)	1/90–5/92	PDQ Secretarial Help	Myrna Copper (508) 389-0202

FIGURE 4   Hypothetical Resume

person has the SCANS workplace know-how noted here. (See Figure 4 for a hypothetical resume.)

Students would be free to use their resumes in seeking employment or further education at any time. Employers could be expected to demand from students the highest level of certification that the job demands (i.e., high-performance workplaces can demand high skills, including, but not limited to, those required for the CIM). It would be up to the consumers of this information—employers, colleges, the military, or others—to decide what weight to give each element in the resume, using their own needs and criteria as guides.

In addition to the education-based assessment, a way to assess and certify persons who are already in the workforce (an experience-based assessment) is needed. The Federal Government, some private firms, and a coalition of trade associations in the hospitality industry have begun the hard work that will lead to the needed assessment tools.

Improving the "Learning a Living" System   The Commission understands that preparation for work is only part of the mission of schools, and that school is only part of the learning process. President Bush spoke of the need for America to be a nation of learners and for the "education revolution" to extend beyond the schools into the community. This report is concerned with those parts of education and work that form the "learning a living" system (see Figure 5).

The box on the left side of Figure 5 represents education. Within it, at least through the second year of high school, students learn the SCANS know-how in English, math, science, history, and geography; in other classes (e.g., art); and in extracurricular activities.

The basic idea is that all students follow a common academic program, a single track, until they are about 16. After age 16, some students are more likely to be learning the SCANS know-how in the context of work, perhaps by specializing in the application of the competencies to a particular industry, such as manufacturing or hospitality.

Some of these students will go on to community colleges in a 2+2 tech-prep program, a program that begins with the last two years of high school and leads to an associate degree after two years of college. Other students will continue to learn the SCANS know-how in academic courses as they move toward a four-year college program. Others will, after graduating, go directly to work and work-based learning, including apprenticeship.

The box on the right side of Figure 5 represents employers and work-based education. Within it, workers pursue learning that continues for a lifetime. This box includes the human resource functions of recruiting, developing, and retaining employees. Workplace education produces portable certificates that are valued in many workplaces.

Information should flow from employers to educators through recruiting and employee development activities, including the ways in which employees progress up career ladders. Educators, in turn, should inform employers of the workplace competencies that students have attained. Today, neither employers nor educators receive or deliver

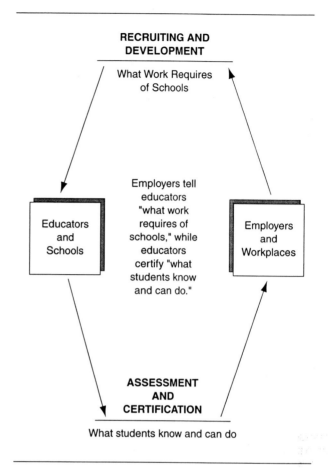

FIGURE 5   Information Flow in the "Learning a Living" System.

information effectively. The SCANS aim is to improve the information flow (and the learning and earning) so that the economy will deliver the high productivity and wage increases that characterized the United States in the years from 1937 to 1973.

Figure 6 outlines the actions that are needed to reach the SCANS goals. Unless the nation takes forceful action on this agenda, the nation's schools, employers, students, and workers will not fare well in the next century.

This, the SCANS final report, provides a blueprint for groups at the national, state, and local levels. Each community must decide what resources will be allocated to create a system that will meet its specific goals. But first, each must become involved in a conversation about its place in a fast-changing world as we approach the year 2000. Our nation's ability to lead in a global economy will depend on the outcome of those conversations. This Commission is confident that once they are informed, communities will commit themselves to maintaining the American dream for themselves and their children.

Reinventing Schools

- Workplace know-how (the SCANS foundation skills and workplace competencies) should be taught along the entire continuum of education, from kindergarten through college.
- Every student should complete middle school (about age 14) with an introduction to workplace know-how.
- Every student by about age 16 should attain initial mastery of the SCANS how-how.
- Every student should complete high school sufficiently proficient in the SCANS know-how to earn a decent living.
- All federally funded programs for youth and adults, including vocational education programs, should teach the SCANS know-how.

Fostering Work-Based Learning

- Federal, state, and local agencies should incorporate SCANS workplace competencies into their own employee programs.
- Private-sector work-based training programs should incorporate training in the SCANS workplace competencies.

- Coalitions of businesses, associations, government employers, and labor organizations should teach the SCANS competencies to the current workforce, including employees of small businesses.

Reorganizing the Workplace

- The vast majority of employers should adopt the standards of quality and high performance that now characterize our most competitive companies.
- Firms should develop internal training programs to bring employees to the proficiency in the SCANS competencies needed for high-performance work organizations.

Restructuring Assessment

- A national education-based assessment system should be implemented that will permit educational institutions to certify the levels of the SCANS competencies that their students have achieved.
- Public and private employers should define requirements for higher-level competencies.
- Employment-based assessments should permit diagnoses of individual learning needs.

FIGURE 6   The Commission's Recommendations For Full Implementation By The Year 2000

SCANS IN THE SCHOOLS

Introduction

This paper addresses the question: How will schools enable students to acquire the SCANS skills? The specific shape and substance of SCANS implementation will vary, of course, from school to school. But it is important to lay out the key dimensions within each SCANS competency, specify what students need to learn, and consider where in the curriculum the skills will be taught. We will also take a look at some of the innovative methods educators are beginning to use to help students acquire necessary skills within each competency.

Figure 7 provides the definitions for the five SCANS competencies—resources, information, interpersonal, systems, and technology. It also includes examples of tasks or performances that illustrate the use of each skill. Before examining each of the competencies in turn, let us consider a few general points about integrating SCANS into the curriculum.

One of the first questions principals, teachers, curriculum developers, and parents will ask is "Where?"—**Where within the curriculum will SCANS be taught?** Are educators to develop new courses—SCANS 101—or incorporate the learning of SCANS skills into existing courses?

Although a new course or two might be designed at some schools (Principles of Technology, for instance), the primary place to teach SCANS skills is within the existing curriculum. SCANS skills can and should be integrated into each subject in the core curriculum. The matrix displayed in Table 2 illustrates how each subject-matter area can be used to develop each competency.

The skills identified by SCANS as necessary for work are already taught to a limited extent in existing courses. For instance, students may learn about ecological systems in a science class. But even when such knowledge is embedded in the current curriculum, it typically is not made "intellectually explicit." In addition, teachers and students are not connecting a particular isolated piece of knowledge (the forest as an ecological system) to the broader competency (learning how systems function). When such connections are not made explicit, students are less likely to generalize skills and knowledge and apply them in new situations.

It is important, in particular, to connect knowledge and skills to workplace applications so students can see how they will use them. Creating such connections leads to the "How?" question: **How are SCANS skills best taught and learned?** Do we need different instructional methods as well as different curricula?

FIGURE 7   Definitions: The Competencies

Resources

Allocated time. Selects relevant, goal-related activities, ranks them in order of importance, allocates time to activities, and understands, prepares, and follows schedules.

Examples:
- construct a timeline charge, e.g., Gantt, PERT;
- understand the concept of a critical path;
- estimate the time required to complete a project by task; or
- use computer software, e.g., Harvard Project Planner, to plan a project.

Allocates money. Use or prepares budgets, including cost and revenue forecasts; keeps detailed records to track budget performance; and makes appropriate adjustments.

Examples:
- estimate costs;
- prepare a multi-year budget using a spreadsheet; or
- do a cost analysis.

Allocates material and facility resources. Acquires, stores, and distributes materials, supplies, parts, equipment, space, or final products in order to make the best use of them.

Examples:
- lay out a workspace document with narrative and graphics using desktop publishing software;
- demonstrate understanding of First In First Out (FIFO) and Just-in-Time (JIT) inventory systems; or
- design a request for proposal (RFP) process.

Allocates human resources. Assesses knowledge and skills and distributes work accordingly, evaluates performance, and provides feedback.

Examples:
- develop a staffing plan;
- write a job description; or
- conduct a performance evaluation.

Information

Acquires and evaluates information. Identifies need for date, obtains it from existing sources or creates it, and evaluates its relevance and accuracy.

Examples:
- develop a form to collect data;
- research and collect data from appropriate sources (library, on-line data bases, field research); or
- develop validation instrument for determining accuracy of data collected.

Organizes and maintains information. Organizes, processes, and maintains written or computerized records and other forms of information in asystematic fashion.

Examples:
- develop a filing system for storing information (printed or computerized);
- develop an inventory record-keeping system; or
- develop a bill processing system.

Interprets and communicates information. Selects and analyzes information and communicates the results to others using oral, written, graphic, pictorial, or multi-media methods.

Examples:
- produce a report using graphics to interpret and illustrate associated narrative information;
- make an oral presentation using several different media to present information (overheads, slides, film, audio); or
- develop material for communicating information to be used during a teleconference call.

Uses computers to process information. Employs computers to acquire, organize, analyze, and communicate information.

Examples:
- use a computer spreadsheet, e.g., Lotus 1-2-3, to develop a budget;
- use a computer graphics program, e.g., Harvard Graphics, to prepare overheads for a report; or
- use on-line computer databases, e.g., Lexus, New York Times, ERIC, to research a report.

Interpersonal

Participates as a member of a team. Works cooperatively with others and contributes to group with ideas, suggestions, and effort.

Examples:
- collaborate with group members to solve a problem;
- develop strategies for accomplishing team objectives; or
- work through a group conflict situation.

Teaches others. Helps others learn.

Examples:
- train a colleague on-the-job; or
- explore possible solutions to a problem in a formal group situation.

continued

FIGURE 7 Definitions: The Competencies *(continued)*

Serves clients/customers. Works and communicates with clients and customers to satisfy their expectations.

Examples:
- demonstrate an understanding of who the customer is in a work situation;
- deal with a dissatisfied customer in person; or
- respond to a telephone complaint about a product.

Exercises leadership. Communicates thoughts, feelings, and ideas to justify a position; and encourages, persuades, convinces, or otherwise motivates an individual or group, including responsibly challenging existing procedures, policies, or authority.

Examples:
- use specific team-building concepts to develop a work group;
- select and use an appropriate leadership style for different situations; or
- use effective delegation techniques.

Negotiates. Works toward an agreement that may involve exchanging specific resources or resolving divergent interests.

Examples:
- develop an action plan for negotiating; or
- write strategies for negotiating; or
- conduct an individual and a team negotiation.

Works with cultural diversity. Works well with men and women and with a variety of ethnic, social, or educational backgrounds.

Examples:
- demonstrate an understanding of how people with differing cultural/ethnic backgrounds behave in various situations (work, public places, social gatherings); or
- demonstrate the use of positive techniques for resolving cultural/ethnic problem situations.

Systems

Understands systems. Knows how social, organizational, and technological systems work and operates effectively with them.

Examples:
- draw and interpret an organization chart;
- develop a chart that illustrates an understanding of stocks and flows; or
- draw a diagram that illustrates a technological problem definition and problem-solving process.

Monitors and corrects performance. Distinguishes trends, predicts impact of actions on system operations, diagnoses deviations in the function of a system/organization, and takes necessary action to correct performance.

Examples:
- generate a statistical process control (SPC) chart;
- develop a forecasting model; or
- develop a monitoring process.

Improves and designs systems. Makes suggestions to modify existing systems to improve products or services, and develops new or alternative systems.

Examples:
- draw a diagram showing an improved organizational system based on Deming's 14 points; or
- choose a situation needing improvement, break it down, examine it, propose an improvement, and implement it.

Technology

Selects technology. Judges which set of procedures, tools, or machines, including computers and their programs will produce the desired results.

Example:
- read equipment descriptions and technical specifications to select equipment to meet needs.

Applies technology to task. Understands the overall intent and the proper procedures for setting up and operating machines, including computers and their programming systems.

Example:
- set up/assemble appropriate equipment from instructions.

Maintains and troubleshoots technology. Prevents, identifies, or solves problems in machines, computers, and other technologies.

Examples:
- read and follow instructions for troubleshooting and repairing relevant equipment; or
- read and follow maintenance instructions for keeping relevant equipment in good working order.

TABLE 2 Assignments That Integrate the SCANS Competencies into the Core Curriculum Areas

			Curriculum Area		
Competency	**English/Writing**	**Mathematics**	**Science**	**Social Studies/Geography**	**History**
Resources	Write a proposal for an after-school career lecture series that schedules speakers, coordinates audio-visual aids, and estimates costs.	Develop a monthly family budget taking into account family expenses and revenues and using information from the budget plan, schedule a vacation trip that stays within the resources available.	Plan the material and time requirements for a chemistry experiment, to be performed over a two-day period, that demonstrates a natural growth process in terms of resource needs.	Design a chart of resource needs for a community of African Zulus. Analyze the reasons why three major cities grew to their current size.	Study the Vietnam War, researching and orally presenting findings on the timing and logistics of transporting materials and troops to Vietnam and on the impact of the war on the Federal budget.
Interpersonal	Discuss the pros and cons of the argument that Shakespeare's *Merchant of Venice* is a "racist" play and should be banned from the school curriculum.	Present the results of a survey to the class, and justify the use of specific statistics to analyze and represent the data.	Work in a group to design an experiment to analyze the lead content in the school's water. Teach the results to an elementary school class.	Debate the issue of withdrawing U. S. military support from Japan in front of a peer panel. Engage in a mock urban planning exercise for Paris.	Study the American Constitution and role-play the negotiation of the wording of the free states/slave states clause by different signers.
Information	Identify and abstract passages from a novel to support an assertion about the values of a key character.	Design and carry out a survey and analyze the data in a spreadsheet program using algebraic formulas. Develop a table and a graphic display to communicate the results.	In an entrepreneurship project, present statistical data pertaining to a high-tech company's production and sales. Use a computer to develop the statistical charts.	Using numerical data and charts, develop and present conclusions about the effects of economic conditions on the quality of life in several countries.	Research and present papers on the effect of the Industrial Revolution on the class structure in Britain, citing data sources used to arrive at conclusions.

continued

TABLE 2 Assignments That Integrate the SCANS Competencies into the Core Curriculum Areas

| Competency | Curriculum Area | | | |
	English/Writing	Mathematics	Science	Social Studies/Geography	History
Systems	Develop a computer model that analyzes the motivation of Shakespeare's *Hamlet*. Plot the events that increase or decrease Hamlet's motivation to avenge the death of his father by killing Claudius.	Develop a system to monitor and correct the heating/cooling process in a computer laboratory, using principles of statistical process control.	Build a model of human population growth that includes the impact of the amount of food available, on birth and death rates, etc. Do the same for a growth model for insects.	Analyze the accumulation of capital in industrialized nations in systems terms (as a reinforcing process with stocks and flows).	Develop a model of the social forces that led to the American Revolution. Then explore the fit between that model and other revolutions.
Technology	Write an article showing the relationship between technology and the environment. Use word processing to write and edit papers after receiving teacher feedback.	Read manuals for several data-processing programs and write a memo recommending the best programs to handle a series of mathematical situations.	Calibrate a scale to weigh accurate portions of chemicals for an experiment. Trace the development of this technology from earliest uses to today.	Research and report on the development and functions of the seismograph and its role in earthquake prediction and detection.	Analyze the effects of wars on technological development. Use computer graphics to plot the relationship of the country's economic growth to periods of peace and war.

Chapter 4 of the SCANS report *Learning a Living: A Blueprint for High Performance* outlines the instructional implications of SCANS. A major emphasis is teaching skills "in context." This means placing learning objectives within real environments rather than insisting that students first learn in the abstract what they will later be expected to apply. Teaching in context implies that schools will provide students with the opportunities to apply knowledge in real-life situations or simulations; e.g., problems or projects related to workplace situations, as well as internships, mentorships, and "shadowing" workers on the job.

Along with the SCANS emphasis on learning in context is the focus on students becoming more active in their own learning. In the view of the Commission, students do not learn to grapple with problems and to apply skills if teachers are always directing the learning and doing the talking. Working together on problems, students are more responsible for their own learning, more actively involved. Most importantly, they are functioning as they will in the workplace.

Integrating All the SCANS Competencies In the workplace, we do not use one skill at a time in isolation from other skills; effective performance requires many different skills used in combination. It stands to reason, then, that students benefit from working on tasks and problems that call on a range of skills. Here's an example (adapted from a chemistry class in the Fort Worth Independent School District).

> A high school chemistry teacher gave his students a problem: to determine the best lawn fertilizer for the school to use. Students worked together in small groups, and each group tackled the problem in its own way. They designed experiments to investigate the effects of fertilizers differing in chemical composition. When they needed more information, they called on experts from industry or academia. Their recommendations were not based only on applying chemistry and using scientific methods; they also had to weigh costs and other feasibility factors. Once they reached conclusions, students had to develop reports, including charts and computer graphics, which would present their conclusions and persuade school decision-makers to accept their recommendations. They studied how such decisions are made within the institution, determined how to inform and convince key players, and participated in the negotiation process.

Clearly, such a project develops skills within the five SCANS competencies of resources, interpersonal, information, systems, and technology. Teachers with different skills and/or subject-matter expertise (writing, computer graphics, etc.) will probably participate at various junctures, along with experts from the community. Working on such a project, students acquire and practice skills in ways they will actually use them on the job; they use many skills in combination, and all skills are directed toward a purpose.

This project, it should be noted, is not based on a problem neatly defined in advance with an answer that the teacher knows and the students must arrive at. New complexities and side issues arise as the students wade into the problem—like the problems adults encounter in real jobs.

Moreover, there are real-world outcomes of students' work. The soundness of the students' research, the degree to which they consider the full range of relevant factors, the cogency with which they present their recommendations, and the savvy with which they deal with the powers-that-be will determine whether their recommendations are accepted. The motivation to perform each task well does not rest solely on a grade but is intrinsic to the enterprise—the better a task is carried out, the more likely a successful final outcome. These elements are all important for effective education.

SCANS in the K–12 Curriculum The details of what to teach at the elementary, middle school, and secondary levels (as well as in postsecondary settings) will need to be worked out for each competency and will take much careful thought and experimentation by teachers and curriculum developers. This introduction simply offers a few generalizations about the developmental progression in teaching SCANS-related skills and knowledge and ends by offering an example of how one set of skills, acquiring and using information, might be taught in elementary, middle, and secondary school levels.

In considering the timing for introducing SCANS skills, one rule of thumb is that students should not specialize too early, that is, pursue a specific occupation or field to the exclusion of others. Rather, **all students should begin by developing the fundamental conceptual foundation and skills that will allow them to acquire more specialized skills later on.** From the beginning, instruction in this conceptual foundation should be integrated with the core subject areas.

In a model dropout prevention program designed by the National Academy Foundation, for instance, eleventh graders may opt to enter one of the specialized programs designed to prepare them for a specific field (e.g., finance, travel and tourism, public affairs), but up through tenth grade they acquire skills applicable in all occupations and jobs. In the interpersonal area, for instance, they learn to participate in a group, assess group effectiveness, give and receive constructive criticism, and teach others new skills. These "generic" skills—useful and important in every field and job—belong in every student's course of study and should precede instruction in more specialized skills.

This observation leads to the next key point about sequences of instruction. Students usually do not acquire Skill A only at a single point in time—for example, learn the skill of participating in a group in fourth grade—and then move on to other skills. Rather, they keep developing group participation skills—or any set of skills—**at successively more advanced levels**. The model is that of a spiral, with each competency developed throughout the K–12 curriculum. Students in the elementary grades have a range of experiences with developing data forms, such as the one described, that give them the sense that they can develop forms to serve their purposes and show them how to go about doing this. By middle school, their experience base, as well as their higher stage of cognitive development, allows them to tackle more complex and advanced tasks in gathering and presenting data. Still more sophisticated tasks and procedures, such as sampling, are introduced at the high school level. Spirals of this kind—with a greater number and complexity of skills drawn into learning activities at higher grade levels—can be designed for any set of skills within the SCANS competencies. The factors noted here are not exhaustive lists of all aspects of development that educators will need to consider; they only illustrate the kinds of developmental issues that arise in planning a coherent curriculum across the K–12 span.

DEFINITIONS: THE FOUNDATION

Basic Skills

Reading. Locates, understands, and interprets written information in prose and documents—including manuals, graphs, and schedules—to perform tasks, learns from text by determining the main idea or essential message; identifies relevant details, facts, and specifications; infers or locates the meaning of unknown or technical vocabulary; and judges the accuracy, appropriateness, style, and plausibility of reports, proposals, or theories of other writers.

Writing. Communicates thoughts, ideas, information, and messages in writing; records information completely and accurately; composes and creates documents such as letters, directions, manuals, reports, proposals, graphs, flow charts; uses language, style, organization, and format appropriate to the subject matter, purpose, and audience. Includes supporting documentation and attends to level of detail; checks, edits, and revises for correct information, appropriate emphasis, form, grammar, spelling, and punctuation.

Arithmetic. Performs basic computations; uses basic numerical concepts such as whole numbers and percentages in practical situations; makes reasonable estimates of arithmetic results without a calculator; and uses tables, graphs, diagrams, and charts to obtain or convey quantitative information.

Mathematics. Approaches practical problems by choosing appropriately from a variety of mathematical techniques; uses quantitative data to construct logical explanations for real world situations; expresses mathematical ideas and concepts orally and in writing; and understands the role of chance in the occurrence and prediction of events.

Listening. Receives, attends to, interprets, and responds to verbal messages and other cues such as body language in ways that are appropriate to the purpose; for example, to comprehend; to learn; to critically evaluate; to appreciate; or to support the speaker.

Speaking. Organizes ideas and communicates oral messages appropriate to listeners and situations; participates in conversation, discussion, and group presentations; selects an appropriate medium for conveying a message; uses verbal language and other cues such as body language appropriate in style, tone, and level of complexity to the audience and the occasion; speaks clearly and communicates a message; understands and responds to listener feedback; and asks questions when needed.

Thinking Skills

Creative Thinking. Uses imagination freely, combines ideas or information in new ways, makes connections between seemingly unrelated ideas, and reshapes goals in ways that reveal new possibilities.

Decision Making. Specifies goals and constraints, generates alternatives, considers risk, and evaluates and chooses best alternatives.

Problem Solving. Recognizes that a problem exists (i.e., there is a discrepancy between what is and what should or could be), identifies possible reasons for the discrepancy, and devises and implements a plan of action to resolve it. Evaluates and monitors progress, and revises plan as indicated by findings.

Seeing Things in the Mind's Eye. Organizes and processes symbols, pictures, graphs, objects, or other information; for example, sees a building from a blueprint, a system's operation from schematics, the flow of work activities from narrative descriptions, or the taste of food from reading a recipe.

Knowing How to Learn. Recognizes and can use learning techniques to apply and adapt new knowledge and skills in both familiar and changing situations. Involves being aware of learning tools such as personal learning styles (visual, aural, etc.), formal learning strategies (notetaking or clustering items that share some characteristics), and informal learning strategies (awareness of unidentified false assumptions that may lead to faulty conclusions).

Reasoning. Discovers a rule or principle underlying the relationship between two or more objects and applies it in solving a problem. For example, uses logic to draw conclusions from available information, extracts rules or principles from a set of objects or written text; applies rules and principles to a new situation, or determines which conclusions are correct when given a set of facts and a set of conclusions.

Personal Qualities

Responsibility. Exerts a high level of effort and perseverance toward goal attainment. Works hard to become excellent at doing tasks by setting high standards, paying attention to details, working well, and displaying a high level of concentration even when assigned an unpleasant task. Displays high standards of attendance, punctuality, enthusiasm, vitality, and optimism in approaching and completing tasks.

Self-Esteem. Believes in own self-worth and maintains a positive view of self; demonstrates knowledge of own skills and abilities; is aware of impact on others; and knows own emotional capacity and needs and how to address them.

Sociability. Demonstrates understanding, friendliness, adaptability, empathy, and politeness in new and ongoing group settings. Asserts self in familiar and unfamiliar social situations; relates well to others; responds appropriately as the situation requires; and takes an interest in what others say and do.

Self-Management. Assesses own knowledge, skills, and abilities accurately; sets well-defined and realistic personal goals; monitors progress toward goal attainment and motivates self through goal achievement; exhibits self-control and responds to feedback unemotionally and non-defensively; is a "self-starter."

Integrity/Honesty. Can be trusted. Recognizes when faced with making a decision or exhibiting behavior that may break with commonly held personal or societal values; understands the impact of violating these beliefs and codes on an organization, self, and others; and chooses an ethical course of action.

CHAPTER 29

Outcome-Based Education

Outcome-Based Education (OBE) is founded on three basic premises:

- All students can learn and succeed (but not on the same day in the same way).
- Success breeds success.
- Schools control the conditions of success.

OBE is growing at an astounding rate throughout North America. The emphasis on student success has come about for many reasons, including evidence of lagging U. S. student achievement compared with that of many other developed countries. Three forces have combined to attract a large educational following to this restructuring of the way we teach our youngsters.

First, in the past decade, several states and districts have fostered major improvements in student learning through OBE in schools and subject areas of all kinds. Whether operating under the label Mastery Learning, Outcome-Based Instruction, Outcomes-Driven Developmental Model, OBE, or something else, these efforts have attracted many educators and have validated all three philosophical premises.

Second, regional and state policy-making bodies (along with the President and governors) in the 1991 National Goals for America's Schools are demanding improved student outcomes and placing them at the center of major efforts to improve all as-

pects of schooling: curriculum, instruction, assessment, attendance, credentialing, accreditation, and accountability. Major examples include legislation in Kentucky, Michigan, Minnesota, and Washington. This emphasis on improving student learning and demonstrating student success is mainly the result of the strident criticisms that have been heaped on the public schools by a host of business people, legislators, and journalists. Successful outcomes are now both the starting points and the bottom lines of educational policy thinking and action in both the United States and Canada.

Third, our educational system needs a new theoretical and operating paradigm; and a growing consensus of prominent educators, business executives, and political leaders supports this notion. These leaders, among them educational reformers Philip Schlechty and Theodore Sizer—all call for a new, restructured system of education—a necessity if either the United States or public education is to survive the flood of internal and external economic, social, and political problems making daily headlines. They argue that our educational system needs to shed its archaic, Industrial Age assumptions and structures and, as modern corporations have done, find a new way of doing business. These reformers strongly agree that "more, longer, and harder" must give way to "different, smarter, and better," and that the new paradigm must be success-based in philosophy and outcome-based in practice.

The biggest single factor accounting for differences in OBE approaches involves the concept of "culminating demonstration." This issue has two aspects.

By William G. Spady and Kit J. Marshall. Reprinted with permission from *Educational Leadership*, October 1991. CC by ASCD.

One involves the nature of the demonstration (the substance, processes, and setting that are brought into play); the other is the scope of learning to which it applies. Consequently, we routinely say that "Outcomes of Significance" require *substance* of significance applied through *processes* of significance in *settings* of significance.

Substance can range from very specific content details to broad, complex concepts and their interrelations. Processes can range from relatively simple cognitive or psychomotor skills to complex, higher-order syntheses and applications. Settings are both the places where learning is to occur (such as the classroom) and those where it is applied and demonstrated (real life).

The scope of these outcomes can range from relatively small segments of learning, such as lessons and units, to large arenas of learning or performance demonstration, such as entire subject areas, whole programs of study, or even the total K–12 schooling experience. The trend in the past few years is definitely toward expanding the nature and scope of demonstrations: more significant substance, processes, and settings, which involve larger scopes of learning. OBE is evolving from a microcurriculum and instructional design approach to a more comprehensive approach.

APPLICATIONS AND IMPLICATIONS

We in the High Success Program on OBE believe that most of the fundamental features of reform proposals can easily be incorporated within the "success for all" restructuring principles of what we call "Transformational Outcome-Based Education." Transformational OBE, like Schlechty's and Sizer's school restructuring efforts, is a collaborative, flexible, transdisciplinary, outcome-based, open-system,empowerment-oriented approach to schooling. Figure 1 contrasts 10 attributes of traditional (and current) education to 10 alternatives advocated by Transformational OBE supporters.

Advocates of Transformational OBE are people whose thinking is future oriented and visionary. They are optimistic, and oriented to growth and success. They embrace, rather than fear, change in education; they are what futurist Joel Barker calls "paradigm pioneers."

As the rapid growth of the OBE movement attests, people are drawn to an outcome-based approach in different ways and with different understandings of its potential applications and implications for curriculum design, instructional delivery, and student assessment and credentialing. Some of these approaches we call

Traditional OBE; others are genuinely Transformational; and yet others lie somewhere in between, what we call Transitional OBE.

TRADITIONAL OBE

The irony about Traditional OBE is this: it characterizes almost all of the current OBE approaches in local districts in the United States and Canada, and it is highly effective in improving student achievement. Yet it is not, strictly speaking, outcome-based. The reason is simple: the starting point for almost all district OBE efforts over the past 20 years has been the existing curriculum, not a clear picture of intended Outcomes of Significance for students that lie beyond the curriculum. What is taking place in most OBE districts today should actually be labeled CBO (for Curriculum-Based Objectives) rather than OBE, because the curriculum actually precedes the outcomes in the design process.

Traditional OBE typically encourages local staff to take their existing curriculum content and structure—lessons, units, courses, and programs—and determine what is truly important for students to learn to a high level of performance. (We view this as an inherently internal, micro, and limiting approach to addressing the issue of significance.) Once these CBO priorities have been set, they are used as the basis of curriculum, instruction, and assessment design and alignment. After teachers begin to apply OBE's principles in their classrooms to these aligned instructional components, they routinely experience major increases in student learning success, even within the time and programmatic constraints imposed by the traditional school structure.

The downside of this Traditional OBE approach is reflected in five issues:

- The concept of culminating demonstration is often limited to individual units or small segments of instruction, which makes each unit or segment an end unto itself and its substance and processes quite specific.
- The content and structure of the curriculum remains the same as before; the units and courses that already existed are still there, albeit with a clearer focus. Thus outcomes are synonymous with traditional, content-dominated categories that do not relate to real-life demands and living experiences.
- Such programs typically are silent concerning the context or setting of intended role performances. The school and classroom are assumed to be the only contexts in which preparation, performance, and assessment are to occur.

FIGURE 1   What is Transformational OBE?

In contrast to 10 attributes of traditional (and current) education, advocates of
Transformational OBE propose 10 alternatives:

Transformational OBE *is not:*	Transformational OBE *is:*
1. Calendar defined (schools, programs, processes, credentialing, and decision-making priorities);	Outcome defined (schools, programs, processes, credentialing, and decision-making priorities);
2. Constrained in opportunity (which limits time for teaching and successful learning to occur);	Expanded in opportunity (which enables successful teaching and learning for all to occur);
3. Custodial in credentialing (credit based on seat-time attendance and ambiguous criteria);	Based on performance credentialing (credit through accomplishment, using clear criteria, and demonstrating success of priority outcomes);
4. Tied to curriculum coverage (approach to teaching and testing);	Aided by instructional coaching (fostering successful performance for all students on essential outcomes);
5. Segmented in content (curriculum structure, instructional delivery, testing, and credentialing);	Integrated in concepts (cross-curriculum approach to outcomes, curriculum structure, instructional delivery, and assessment);
6. Based on cumulative achievement (approach to curriculum planning, teaching, testing, and grading);	Based on culminating achievement ("end-result" approach to outcomes, curriculum design, instruction, assessment, and grading);
7. Selection oriented (opportunity structures, grading, and curriculum tracking);	Oriented to inclusionary success (structure of curriculum cross-groupings, learning, assessment, and credentialing opportunities);
8. Characterized by contest learning (students compete for scarce rewards);	Characterized by cooperative learning (to foster learning success for all);
9. Dependent on comparative evaluation (emphasizing relative quality of work accomplished and grades assigned);	Confirmed by criterion validation (expectations of high-level performance on clearly defined outcomes and standards);
10. Composed of cellular structures (school and curriculum organization, learning environments, and credentialing).	Formed on collaborative structures (for curriculum planning, instructional delivery, and student learning).

- These approaches rarely are driven by a framework of exit outcomes or a clear concept of the graduate as a total person. Their guiding metaphor of the graduate is simply an "academically competent student."
- Traditional OBE rarely addresses or challenges the traditional nature of schooling today, including the time-defined structuring of curriculum content and its attendant nine-month delivery, credentialing, and placement structures. By focusing primarily on unit and course outcomes, it seeks, and gets, greater success within these arbitrary constraints, rather than seeking to modify or eliminate them. Most of the state-level OBE reforms reflect a strong traditional bias.

TRANSITIONAL OBE

As its name implies, Transitional OBE lies in the Twilight Zone between traditional subject-matter curriculum structures and planning processes and the future-role priorities inherent in Transformational OBE. It is a viable approach for districts seeking to extend their vision beyond existing subject area content in defining outcomes of significance because (1) these districts usually address higher-order competencies that are essential in virtually all life and learning settings, and (2) they can at least initially postpone the overwhelming challenge of rethinking and restructuring everything about their curriculum and delivery structures while getting into OBE.

This approach is primarily concerned with students' culminating capabilities at graduation time and centers curriculum and assessment design around higher-order exit outcomes. Having graduates who are broadly competent persons best reflects its vision. Transitional OBE districts usually generate exit outcomes in a process that places less emphasis on the exact nature of future conditions but takes them into account informally in addressing the question: *What is most essential for our students to know, be able to do, and be like in order to be successful once they've graduated?*

In answering this question, Transitional OBE staff and community members almost universally emphasize broad attitudinal, affective, motivational, and relational qualities or orientations. These schools give priority to higher-level competencies, such as critical thinking, effective communications, technological applications, and complex problem solving, rather than particular kinds of knowledge or information.

Two pioneering OBE districts have been studied by thousands of educators interested in their Transitional Exit Outcomes. One pioneer is Township High School District 214 in Arlington Heights, Illinois, a large district serving grades 9–12 near Chicago. The other is the Johnson City Central School District in Johnson City, New York. The most recent version of District 214's General Learner Outcomes framework requires all graduates, regardless of courses taken or programs pursued, to successfully demonstrate 11 kinds of competency or role performance. The Johnson City framework consists of five key competence and affective arenas that guide all curriculum and instructional decisions.

As prime examples of Transitional OBE, both frameworks are virtually silent regarding subject matter content or subject-specific skills. Ultimately, the purpose of programs and courses is to adapt content to the explicit development of the higher-order competencies and orientations in the exit outcomes, rather than to foster subject knowledge in isolation.

It is our experience that districts go through three stages of maturity in implementing Transitional Exit Outcomes:

Incorporation. The typical need involves getting staff to recognize that textbooks and subject matter outlines are neither the only nor the primary focus of their instructional efforts. OBE staff development shows teachers how to focus on these outcomes with their existing content as the base.

Integration. In curriculum redirection and redesign, Transitional Exit Outcomes become the prime goal of all departments and programs; teachers use content as the support base for addressing and facilitating these outcomes. Interdisciplinary work becomes much easier because people with different specialties can jointly integrate their work and address the same outcomes.

Redefinition. The most advanced stage of Transitional OBE begins to open the door to Transformational approaches. Schools and districts further subordinate subject content priorities to the emergence of key concepts, issues, problems, and processes. With this broader focus, the purpose and meaning of the content take on a higher form. Here, shared concepts and problems, not content per se, are linked to ever higher-order forms of demonstration and application in the fulfillment of what truly do become Outcomes of Significance.

TRANSFORMATIONAL OBE

This paradigm represents the highest evolution of the OBE concept, and it contrasts sharply with both the prevailing educational system and with Traditional OBE. Its implications for curriculum design and the structuring of schools is profound. It fully embraces and embodies the spirit and substance of the four OBE operational principles (see "Success for All," at end of chapter). It is grounded on the question: Why do schools exist in this day and age?

The Transformational OBE answer to this question is bold: "To equip all students with the knowledge, competence, and orientations needed for success after they leave school." Hence, its guiding vision of the graduate is that of competent future citizen. When viewed from this future-oriented, life-role perspective, success in school is of limited benefit unless students are equipped to transfer that success to life in a complex, challenging, high-tech future. Our prevailing, century-old, Industrial Age curriculum structure and delivery model lack credibility and the capacity to generate these kinds of results.

Transformational OBE takes nothing about schooling today as a given; no existing features are considered untouchable in carrying out a curriculum design. Instead, Transformational OBE districts set their existing curriculum frameworks aside when addressing the issue of future-driven exit outcomes. But because these districts have few examples of mature OBE designs on which to model their efforts, these pioneers are building a new legacy of work whose designs and results are not yet certain.

Transformational OBE has its roots in the future-scanning procedures found in well-designed strategic planning and design models. We ask districts to form strategic design teams to thoroughly examine, critique, and synthesize the best available information about the conditions of life students are likely to encounter in their future. These carefully developed descriptions of future conditions serve as the starting point for their OBE design. Three districts provide outstanding examples of careful design work in OBE.

U. S. Department of Defense Dependents Schools. In April 1990, a task force of parents, teachers and administrators from the U. S. Department of Defense Dependent Schools (DODDS) in the Mediterranean

Region developed these statements about some future conditions they needed to address:

> Based upon an assessment of the future, we believe our students will face challenges and opportunities in a world characterized by:

- Worldwide economic competition and interdependence which create ever-increasing requirements for job related performance and a need to transcend language, cultural, national, and racial differences. . . .
- An increasing pluralization and polarization of social, cultural, political, and economic life that demand understanding and that require innovative approaches to leadership, policy-making, resource distributions, and conflict resolution.

The DODDS group developed seven such statements and systematically used them to develop an outcome-based mission for their schools. Then, from the mission statement and the seven conditions, they drew a series of critical inferences and implications they translated into a framework of 10 role-based Transformational Exit Outcomes. This framework, in turn, was to become the template against which all curriculum design and evaluation in their schools would proceed and the success of their mission would be judged.

Certainly not all exit outcome frameworks capture the life-role essence inherent in this future-oriented approach, but two early 1991 efforts in Colorado and Wyoming have come close.

Aurora Public Schools. Educators in the Aurora, Colorado, Public Schools began a serious strategic planning effort in 1990, which resulted in (1) a set of future conditions that drove both their district mission and a set of 28 key learning goals and (2) a set of five role-based exit outcomes that were derived systematically from the mission and the goals. Both role context and role demonstration elements are evident in their exit outcome framing statement and their outcome statements, two of which are:

> We will know we are accomplishing our mission when all of our students are:

- Collaborative Workers, who use effective leadership and group skills to develop and manage interpersonal relationships within culturally and organizationally diverse settings.
- Quality Producers, who create intellectual, artistic, practical, and physical products which reflect originality, high standards, and the use of advanced technologies.

Aurora's other statements refer to Self-Directed Learners, Complex Thinkers, and Community Con-

tributors. Work is now underway in Aurora to frame each existing curriculum area around this set of five exit outcomes so that the outcomes serve as the key organizers of all their programs and courses. The district also is developing performance indicators for assessment purposes.

Hot Springs County School District. The third example involves the Hot Springs County School District in Thermopolis, Wyoming, which initiated a similar outcome-based strategic planning process in 1990. This district's planning team reviewed many district and state exit outcome frameworks and found the power, persuasiveness and role grounding of the Aurora framework to be most impressive. The Hot Springs Team used the Aurora framework as a general template for defining their own priority future conditions. The team wrote six role-grounded exit outcomes very similar in nature to Aurora's. Three of them are:

- Involved Citizens, who take the initiative to contribute their time, energies, and talents to improve the welfare of themselves and others and the quality of life in their local and global environments.
- Self-Directed Achievers, who formulate positive core values in order to create a vision for their future, set priorities and goals, create options and take responsibility for pursuing these goals, and monitor and evaluate their progress on them.
- Adaptable Problem Solvers, who anticipate, assess, and resolve the problems and challenges that accompany the rapidly changing political, economic, environmental, and social conditions of modern life.

The other three outcomes describe students as Perceptive Thinkers, Collaborative Contributors, and Innovative Producers. Hot Springs has formed a design task force for each outcome, composed of staff members representing a variety of grade levels and subject areas. Each task force will determine:

- the essential learning components that must be developed to assure student success on the outcome
- the instructional methods and learning contexts appropriate to each
- the performance indicators and assessment strategies consistent with each

We have found in all three of these districts—DODDS, Aurora, and Hot Springs—a comprehensive, deliberate pursuit of Transformational OBE: that is, to have all exit outcomes serve as the "bottom line" of teaching and assessment in every area of study that any student pursues, starting the first day of kindergarten and continuing until graduation day. Why? Because having all students succeed on these Transformational Exit Outcomes is now viewed as the reason the district and all its programs exist.

Changes in each district's program content and structure are sure to follow as the emphasis shifts from completion of traditional subject areas, courses, content, and skills to these higher-order, life-role performances. Current programs and courses will facilitate, rather than define, each district's exit outcomes. Strategic decision making, program planning, and resource allocations will all directly reflect the nature and scope of these outcomes.

With its focus on the future, its philosophical commitment to success for all students on Outcomes of Significance in life, and its implications for fundamentally redefining the curriculum, instructional delivery, assessment, and credentialing components of schooling, Transformational OBE gives schools a profoundly different means for restructuring themselves. But it takes vision and a willingness to step beyond the given of curriculum thinking and program design that have left us mired in an Industrial Age model governed by an Agricultural Age calendar.

SUCCESS FOR ALL

Advocates of (OBE) agree that an *outcome* is a successful demonstration of learning that occurs at the culminating point of a set of learning experiences. The term *culminating* refers to the completion point of a segment of curriculum—what students are ultimately able to do at the end, once all formal instruction is over and can be synthesized and applied successfully.

Adherents of OBE seek to apply four key principles to the design, delivery, documentation, and decision-making work of schooling:

- *Ensure clarity of focus on outcomes of significance.* Culminating demonstrations become the starting point, focal point, and ultimate goal of curriculum design and instruction. Schools and districts work to carefully align (or match) curriculum, instruction, assessment, and credentialing with the substance (criteria) and processes of the intended demonstration.
- *Design down from ultimate outcomes.* Curriculum and instructional design inherently should carefully proceed backward from the culminating demonstrations (outcomes) on which everything ultimately focuses and rests, thereby ensuring that all components of a successful culminating demonstration are in place.
- *Emphasize high expectations for all to succeed.* Outcomes should represent a high level of challenge for students, and all should be expected to accomplish them eventually at high performance levels and be given credit for their performance whenever it occurs.
- *Provide expanded opportunity and support for learning success.* Time should be used as a flexible resource rather than a predefined absolute in both instructional design and delivery (to better match differences in student learning rates and aptitudes). Educators should deliberately allow students more than one uniform, routine chance to receive needed instruction and to demonstrate their learning successfully.

TABLE 1   Models for Designing Outcome-Based Education

	Traditional	**Transitional**	**Transformational**
Envisioned outcome:	Academically competent students	Broadly competent persons	Competent future citizens
Outcomes derived from:	Existing academic subjects (no exits)	Higher-order generic competencies	Future role contexts, challenges and opportunities
Intended curriculum result:	Subject structure maintained	Subject structure integrated	Subject structure redefined
Use of outcomes:	Focus and align existing programs	Incorporate across programs	Fundamentally restructure programs
Predominant demonstrations/assessments:	Bloom's knowledge and comprehension	Bloom's analysis and evaluation	Bloom's synthesis and application
Predominant measures/indicators:	Test results and papers	Problems and observable processes	Projects, products, and performances

CHAPTER

30

Total Quality Management

The same evils that have brought our economy to destruction also afflict and affect education. Our system of rewards has ruined both.
—W. Edwards Deming, 1989

The task of transforming our schools is today within our reach. We can find direction in the theories and principles that guide our most advanced corporations. Many of these organizations are making a sustained effort to apply the philosophy of W. Edwards Deming, the man who helped Japanese industry achieve world-class standards of quality.

You may wonder what the management philosophy of companies has to do with running schools. Schools, after all, are not "businesses," and the challenges of educating children are different from those of operating a company. But as Al Shanker (1990), John Goodlad (1984), and other educational leaders have pointed out, schools are modeled after the *old* business paradigm of Taylorism—the basis for the assembly-line method that permitted mass production of automobiles—a system that is no longer functional.

As David Kerns, former CEO of Xerox and now Deputy Secretary of Education, suggested, we need a design for schools that is relevant for present times:

The modern school should look less like a factory and more like our best high-tech companies, with lean structures, flat organizations, and decision making pushed to the lowest pos-

sible level . . . [withn] fewer middle managers, and those that remain act[ing] less like controllers and more like colleagues and collaborators (in Doyle and Kearns 1988, p. 38).

This recommendation is in sync with Deming's philosophy, which provides a framework that can integrate many positive developments in education. Without such a framework, teacher participation, team-teaching, site-based management, and cooperative learning, for example, remain individual elements lacking the cohesiveness necessary to transform our schools. Deming's 14 principles are powerful, universal axioms based on the assumptions that individuals want to do their best and that it is management's job to enable them to do so by constantly improving the *system* in which they work (Deming, 1988). They are:

1. Create constancy of purpose for improvement of product and service.
2. Adopt the new (Deming) philosophy.
3. Cease dependence on inspection to achieve quality. Build in quality in the first place.
4. End the practice of awarding business on the basis of price alone.
5. Improve constantly and forever every process.
6. Institute training on the job.
7. Adopt and institute leadership.
8. Drive out fear.
9. Break down barriers between staff areas.
10. Eliminate slogans, exhortations, and targets for the staff.

By Alan M. Blankstein. Reprinted with permission from *Educational Leadership*, March 1992. CC by ASCD.

11. Eliminate numerical quotas for the staff and goals for management.
12. Remove barriers that rob people of pride of workmanship.
13. Institute a vigorous program of education and self-improvement for everyone.
14. Put everybody in the organization to work to accomplish the transformation.

In order to see how Deming's principles, which were originally developed for business, might apply to schools, we need to translate a few of his terms. Principals and superintendents can be considered "management" or "leadership." Teachers are "employees," "leaders," and "managers" of students. Students are "employees," and the knowledge they gain and later contribute to society is the "product." Parents and society are the "customers." Legislators are the "board of directors."

In Japan, where Deming's principles were first adopted, managers have a broad view of their "system," which encompasses both the individual company and the whole nation. It would be ideal, and ultimately necessary, to include the entire community of legislators, parents, businesses, universities, and social service agencies in implementing the principles. Communities like Ware Shoals, South Carolina, are doing this. However, since garnering such broad support may initially be difficult, the "system" for our purposes will include only what can be directly influenced at the district and school level.

Although all of Deming's principles are important and interrelated, here I will focus on just a few (1, 2, 3, 5, and 11), restating them slightly.

MAINTAIN CONSTANCY OF PURPOSE

The first principle we might apply to improve schools is maintaining a constancy of purpose. American management's focus on short-term goals and outcomes is evidenced in an emphasis on quarterly profits, wide acceptance of corporate takeovers for quick profit, and a view of quality and training as an "expense" rather than an "investment." This shortsightedness is also evident in schools; for example, when students who are not learning are promoted and when teachers teach to the test. These are *not* the fault of the teachers, however, but, rather, inherent flaws in the *system*.

One prerequisite to long-range planning, of course, is reasonable confidence that one will have the resources to carry out the plan. Unfortunately, many administrators are forced from year to year to reevaluate their budgets and school policies in light of laws passed by legislators who are often distant from the real process of education. This is contrary to Deming's belief that innovations in the system come from the input of those who are most intimately familiar with the work: the employees, not the board of directors.

Constancy of purpose is most severely undermined, however, by the enormous turnover of management.

According to the American Association of School Administrators, 45 percent of their members leave their jobs within three years (1990). Losing one's district leader every few years is a major blow to experience-based innovation, ongoing efforts, and maintenance of institutional memory.

ADOPT THE NEW PHILOSOPHY

The second Deming principle that we might apply to schools is assuring that all policies and procedures are consistent with the new point of view. Instituting Deming's principles are difficult. They require rethinking a school's priorities, with everyone in agreement on them.

For example, who are the school's "customers"? For teachers, are they the principal, students, or parents? For principals, are they parents or the superintendent? It's important that everyone agree on who the customers are and what their needs are. As noted earlier, I contend that the customers for the entire school organization are the parents and the community. Their needs should drive the organization.

BUILD IN QUALITY NOW

"Quality comes not from inspection," writes Deming, "but from improvement of the process" (1988, p. 29). The next principle we'll look at is: do not depend on inspections and examinations to assure quality: do things right in the first place. It *always* costs more to fix a problem than to prevent one.

This principle's clear application to education can be illustrated in NEA President Keith Geiger's remark:

> We worry about kids when they reach 14, 15, or 16 years old and discover they don't have enough math or science. . . . If we concentrated more of our time and energy on kids in kindergarten to 3rd grade, then we wouldn't have to invest so much time and money [later] (Geiger, 1989).

An example of an effective preventive approach is Head Start, conceived of by Edward Aigler at Yale University.

IMPROVE THE ENTIRE SYSTEM

Working continuously to improve the entire system—another of Deming's principles—requires extensive collection and analysis of data to determine which systems need attention. An individual (student or teacher) whose record of performance falls consistently within a certain range is part of a "stable system." Most of the opportunities for improvement of a stable system, Deming advises, come from altering the system itself, which is primarily the job of management, not those who work within that system.

The ultimate intent of improving the system is to narrow the amount of variation within it, bringing *everyone* toward the goal of perfection. This is the primary task of leadership (principle 7, Deming 1988, pp. 248–249). Having good data on people's performance is essential.

In education, the data currently collected, such as standardized test scores, are notoriously inadequate. Even teachers' grades are not necessarily valid indicators of student learning, because they may be based on other factors, such as attendance, classroom conduct, or completion of homework and tests. The need to have better data on actual student performance related directly to valued outcomes goes beyond the scope of this article, but it must be solved if schools are to make sound use of the Deming philosophy.

In fact, full application of Deming's ideas requires shifting to a paradigm very different from that found in most schools today. His philosophy assumes an educational system in which desired outcomes are clearly defined and understood by all. The teacher's responsibility is to assist all students to improve processes toward achieving the outcomes. Teachers do not collect grades on homework and tests and average them at the end of the marking period; instead they maintain records of what students have achieved, with the intent to *decrease variability*.

When problems arise, those directly involved (teachers, parents, students, the principal) may form a *quality circle*. Rather than blaming any individual, they collect relevant data on the situation, define a possible opportunity to improve the process, test the change in the system, observe the results, and permanently implement the change, if it proves effective (Sherkenbach, 1988).

DO NOT USE QUOTAS OR NUMERICAL GOALS

In recent years educators have been pressured, often by people outside the schools, to use quantitative goals, highly structured teacher evaluation systems, and merit pay. Deming's concept of these practices is critical to understanding all of his work. The problems with setting goals and evaluating people by quantifiable output are many. Let's examine them.

1. *The goals are usually arbitrarily set.* A superintendent once proudly told me that he and his staff set a goal of a 90 percent high school graduation rate for the district. When I asked him how they decided on that figure, he replied that at a staff meeting everyone had decided that it was achievable.

The problem with this approach is that it does not take into account information from the current system. The questions to ask this superintendent are: "Did you graduate 90 percent of last year's students? If not, why not? What will you do differently *this* year? Why aim for only *90 percent?*" The focus should be on improvement of the process based on what the process is currently producing.

"If you have a stable system," Deming advises, "then there is no use to specify a goal. You will get whatever the system will deliver. If you have not a stable system, then there is again no point in setting a goal. . . . Focusing on outcome is not an effective way to improve a process or an activity" (1988, p. 76).

2. *Setting quotas leads to marginal work.* If teachers are evaluated on how many of their students receive a passing grade of 60 percent, then they will strive to have as many as possible do just that. They will not be as inclined to help those who are way below or well above that mark, or to move *everyone* toward excellence. This leads to the "finish Mao Tse-tung by Friday" syndrome (Sizer, 1991), in which mastery is *not* the goal.

According to Glasser, minimum standards are as common in schools as in industry: "The goals on their [teachers'] minds are those of the top-level management: raise the test scores a little, get more students through, and keep discipline problems low" (1990, p. 434). Setting goals of this nature crowds out the intrinsic motivation that leads to pride in work (Deming 1988; Glickman 1991, p. 6).

3. *Appraisal of individual performance is unfair and misguided.* Any system, Deming explains, has two types of variability, which occur as a result of common or special causes. Most variability within a stable system comes from common or natural causes, beyond the purview of any single worker.

Variation between different people's performance is natural and unavoidable. One-half of all people will *always*, by definition, perform below median. It is not management's job to tell this half that they are in fact performing below average. It is also counterproductive to try to get them to "do better" if they are performing within the system.

Management's job, rather, is to improve *everyone's* performance through training and education and improvement of the entire system. Management should also *help* those who represent "special" causes of variation. As Deming explains, doing anything less is failing to take responsibility for one's role as leader.

4. *Merit pay destroys teamwork.* The notion that excellence requires formal evaluation of individuals is deeply embedded in educational practice and in current management theory—both in and out of schools. Carried to its logical extreme, such a system rewards those judged to be superior. Among Deming's reasons for supporting those who oppose merit pay is that it is difficult for a team to work together toward a common goal when the members will receive individual rewards at the end of the year. "Who did what?" becomes the issue, leading to divisiveness on evaluation day.

Like American businesses, schools are *functionally* oriented. This often leads to mutually exclusive goals (for example, superintendents have to show high test scores, while teachers may want to foster higher-order thinking skills). The reward system in this case reinforces people for doing well *within* a faulty, divisive system, not for improving that system.

5. *Individual appraisal nourishes fear.* If a teacher is to be evaluated, and the system for evaluation is ultimately subjective, then the teacher's fate is in the hands of the principal. This leads to politics, concealment of mediocre work, and mindless adherence to regulations. It also stifles innovation or improvement of the system. Deming points out that "the 80 American Nobel prize winners all had tenure, security. They were answerable only to themselves" (1988, p. 109). (Readers may wish to become more familiar with Deming's principle 8 on driving out fear. Fear creates an insurmountable obstacle to *any* improvement.)

6. *A system of individual appraisal increases variability in the desired performance.* Deming's arguments against appraising individual performance call into question the entire grading and marking system that is basic to the operation of most schools. Such a system, he explains, increases variability because of the implied preciseness of the rating system (What is the real difference between a test score of 88 percent and one of 90 percent?). Students may not really desire to earn higher grades, but even if they did, the results would be undesirable. With half the people trying to change their outcomes, the variability of the organization is doubled.

A ROAD MAP

It took U. S. auto and electronics industries decades to realize how performance appraisals, fear-driven incentives, short-term measures, and externally imposed quotas destroy people and the organizations they served. The leaders of these industries had time to spend learning the value of Deming's principles. Our youth, and the schools and societal structures that determine their future, don't have that luxury.

The changes necessary to transform our schools are massive but attainable. Deming provides a road map for success.

Author's note: Special thanks to W. Edwards Deming, Stuart Rankin, Larry Barber, Anne Meek, Nancy Shin, Ernest Mueller, Tom Koerner, William Sherkenbach, Warren Lewis, and Julie Pareles.

REFERENCES

American Association of School Administrators. (1990). Membership survey. Arlington, VA. AASA.

Deming, W. E. (1988) *Out of the Crisis.* Cambridge, Mass.: Massachusetts Institute of Technology.

Deming, W. E. (February 3, 1989). From a speech delivered at a national forum on "Shaping America's Future I." New York City.

Doyle, D., and D. Kearns. (1988). *Winning the Brain Race.* San Francisco: ICS Press.

Geiger, K. (September 25, 1989). From a speech delivered at a national forum on "Shaping America's Future II." New York City.

Glasser, W. (February 1990). "The Quality School." *Kappan* 47: 434–435.

Glickman, C. (May 1991). "Pretending Not to Know What We Know." *Educational Leadership* 48: 4–10.

Goodlad, J. I. (1984). *A Place Called School.* New York: McGraw-Hill.

National Educational Service Transcripts. (1989). *Shaping America's Future I and Shaping America's Future II.* Bloomington, Ind.: National Educational Service.

Shanker, A. (January 1990). "The End of the Traditional Model of Schooling—and a Proposal for Using Incentives to Restructure Our Public Schools." *Kappan* 71: 344–357.

Sherkenbach, W. (1988). *The Deming Route to Quality and Productivity.* Washington, D. C.: CEE Press Books.

Sizer, T. (May 1991). "No Pain. No Gain." *Educational Leadership* 48: 32–34.

SECTION IV

The Education Profession

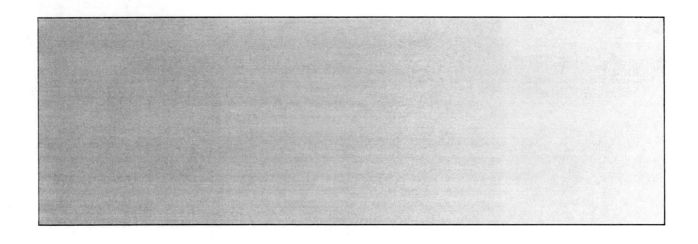

Overview

Section Four focuses on education as a profession. *Pedagogy* is the term used to describe the art and science of teaching. Whereas the engineering profession, for example, is based upon the application of physics and mathematics, pedagogy is undergirded by disciplines such as psychology, sociology, anthropology, philosophy, and an emerging body of knowledge based upon empirically derived research findings from studies of teaching and learning in school settings. More about the "knowledge base" for teaching is provided later in this overview. Teachers apply pedagogical principles and skills, their professional knowledge, in presenting content or subject matter to learners. Effective teachers must possess a mastery of both pedagogy and the subject matter to be taught and both are tested in the Examinations for the Certification of Educators in Texas (ExCET), which candidates must pass prior to the issuance of a certificate to practice.

Although it is recognized that engineers, nurses, attorneys, biologists, and other professionals may also engage in teaching, the focus of this section is on educators who must be certified or licensed by the State of Texas before they may practice their profession in the public elementary and secondary schools. Generally, this certification must be earned by public school teachers, administrators, and other specialists such as counselors and diagnosticians.

EDUCATOR CERTIFICATION

As summarized in Chapter 3, the State Board for Educator Certification (SBEC) was created by Senate

Bill 1 in 1995 to establish and administer the standards of the education profession. The 15 member SBEC oversees all aspects of public school educator preparation, certification, and continuing education and enforces the Code of Ethics and Standard Practices. SBEC describes several routes to educator certification.

1. SBEC-approved college or university-based programs.

    a. These programs are usually offered as part of a degree program that requires emphases in general education, academic specialization, and usually an applied professional component with experiences in public school contexts. Seventy institutions of higher education have been approved by the SBEC to offer programs leading to educator certification. These teacher certification programs are sometimes referred to as "traditional" although each may vary significantly from institution to institution. The SBEC reports that two thirds of these programs have restructured their requirements to permit more "field-based" experiences.

    b. Some institutions of higher education have developed special teacher certification programs for those who have earned baccalaureate and higher degrees. These programs, sometimes referred to as "post-baccalaureate," encourage those who may have tried other careers, early retirees such as those from the military and others, and usually provide more convenient opportunities for entry into the teaching profession.

2. Alternative certification programs.

   a. A variety of designs for alternative, or non-traditional educator certification, have been cooperatively developed by school districts and institutions of higher education. Some require university coursework followed by school district induction and mentoring. Others utilize district personnel in preparing candidates for the first year of teaching. Larger school districts approved to offer alternative programs for teacher certification have found this route to be an excellent source for the recruitment of minority teachers. For example, the 28 alternative programs in Texas produce nearly half of all the newly certified minority teachers. In a California example, between 25 percent and 40 percent of the graduates who complete traditional teacher training never take a teaching position within the state. Eighty-seven percent of those certified via alternative programs take positions in California schools. However, it appears that those certified through alternative programs leave the profession at about the same rate as those certified in traditional, university-based programs (see Education Week, Oct. 21, 1998, p. 13). Some sort of alternative teacher certification program now is available in 41 states.

3. Certification by examination.

   a. An opportunity for certified teachers to earn additional certification is available to those who successfully complete the appropriate ExCET, Texas Oral Proficiency Test (TOPT), Texas Assessment of Sign Communication (TASC) examinations. For example, a teacher certified to teach secondary English may take the Mathematics ExCET and, if the teacher receives a passing score, is then eligible to add Mathematics to his or her credential. If the same secondary, now mathematics, teacher wants to be certified for elementary teaching, a year of supervised teaching at that level is required for certification. Certification by examination is not available for initial certification, professional (graduate level certificaion for administrator, counselor, diagnostician, etc.), and career and technology certificates based on experience.

4. Recognition of certification earned in other states or countries.

   a. SBEC staff review applications and convert appropriate out-of-state certification to Texas certification on an individual review and evaluation basis.

   b. Out-of-country applicants must apply directly to an SBEC-approved college, university, or alternative certification program for a review of their foreign credentials. Certification plans are prepared for each individual applicant.

5. Teaching without certification and school district teaching permits.

   a. The SBEC description of teaching opportunities for those not certified directs the interested applicant to contact a local school district for information. In the midst of a shortage of teachers in specializations such as special education, bilingual education, mathematics, and science, school districts can employ individuals under a variety of temporary arrangements.

   b. Section 21.055 of the Texas Education Code states that a school district may issue a teaching permit and employ as a teacher a person who holds a baccalaureate degree. "Promptly after employing the person," the district must send to the Commissioner of Education a statement identifying the person and his or her qualifications for teaching the subject or class the person will teach. The Commissioner has 30 days to accept or reject the recommendation of the district. If accepted, the teacher may only teach in that district or, if approved by another district following the same procedure, any other district which seeks the teacher's services.

The form used by educator preparation entities to recommend candidates to SBEC is provided at the end of this overview.

Supply and demand for teachers frequently dictate the degree of control over certification of new members by the profession. In 1999, the Secretary of the U. S. Department of Education estimated that 2.2 million new teachers would be needed by 2009. The teacher shortage, particularly in fields such as math, science, special education, and bilingual education is especially acute in Texas. In Texas, with such a variety of opportunities for individuals with collegiate degrees to enter the profession, insistence on "input" expectations prior to certification is difficult. Input characteristics can be described as those academic and applied pre-professional experiences required by SBEC-approved institutions of higher education that have been approved as centers for professional development and technology. Examples of input criteria might include a course in student diversity, exceptionalities, educational technology or classroom management as well as extensive field experiences. Input requirements and prerequisites are those believed to be important in the initial success of the beginning teacher as well as continued success overtime. "Output," or product characteristics (for example, in Texas the ExCET scores) do not emphasize what precedes a passing score on the ExCET. Focusing on output alone suggests that what is important is passing the test and that of lesser importance are the other ascribed input characteristics, if any, believed to be appropriate prior to taking the test. Passing the ExCET alone as a condition for certification may suggest that preparation for the profession is more "on the job training" than pre-professional study and experience.

SBEC has approved 70 institutions of higher education, 28 alternative teacher certification programs and 6 alternative administrator certification programs for Texas educator certification. The "product" quality of each approved program is monitored through the Accountability System for Educator Preparation (ASEP), which has similar characteristics to the Academic Excellence Indicator System (AEIS) used for the ranking and accreditation of independent school districts. AEIS criteria are provided in Chapter 5. ASEP, based on ExCET results, created considerable controversy when the results of the Fall 1998 scores were released. Approximately one third of the entities authorized by SBEC to grant teacher certification were initially given an "accredited-under review" status, not unconditional accreditation as expected. Among those entities were several prestigious public and private universities unaccustomed to academic embarrassment. For most of the one third, the solution was to work toward improving the scores of one or two of the demographic groups now that ExCET disaggregated results are reported and considered in the state's accreditation of certification programs. The categories in which disaggregated ExCET results are reported are ethnicity (African American, Hispanic, other, and white) and gender.

Believing that only educators should set standards for their profession, SBEC has, with recommendations from practicing professionals, established high standards that educators must rigorously uphold. In the early stages of planning, SBEC members and their advisory committees reviewed proposed changes in light of the existing Learner-Centered Proficiencies for Teachers and Administrators, which is the basic framework for the evaluations of these educators, and the Texas Essential Knowledge and Skills (TEKS) which is the state curriculum for elementary and secondary schools. The

TEKS are summarized in Chapter 19. The Learner-Centered Proficiencies are presented in Chapter 35.

SBEC's first major certification change came with the adoption of a "Standard Certificate" for all classes of certificates, which will be subject to renewal every five years. "All classes" of certificates includes superintendent, principal, teacher, and other education professionals. Educators certified prior to the effective date of September 1, 1999 hold certificates that are good for life even though some are stamped "provisional." An educator who fails to renew the new Standard Certificate issued after September 1, 1999 is assigned an inactive status and no longer holds a valid certification and thus cannot be employed by the public schools. According to SBEC publications, to be eligible for renewal, the educator must:

1. Hold a valid standard certificate that has not been sanctioned
2. not be a defendant in a hearing where SBEC is seeking to sanction the educator's certificate—in such cases, the renewal will be stayed pending the outcome of the hearing
3. successfully complete a criminal history review
4. not be in default on a guaranteed student loan—this includes defaults where the educator co-signed the loan
5. not be in arrears of child support
6. pay the renewal fee
7. complete 150 clock hours of continuing professional education (CPE) every five years within the following guidelines
   a. minimum of 20 clock hours each year
   b. at least 80% of CPE hours must be directly related to the certificate(s) being renewed—focus on maintaining currency in the knowledge and skills relevant to each certificate being renewed
   c. a minimum of 5 CPE hours each year in content area knowledge for each certificate being renewed (i.e., if an educator is renewing in English, government and special education, a minimum of 5 CPE hours in each is required each year)
   d. acceptable CPE activities include workshops, conferences, in-staff development given by an approved provider or sponsor; post-graduate work through an accredited institution of higher education (1 semester credit hour is equivalent to 15 CPE clock hours) and a variety of other activities which meet SBEC expectations

Educators will be responsible for maintaining documentation of CPE hours with the expectation that a given number would be audited each year.

Those proposing to deliver CPE programs have to receive approval from SBEC and also are subject to audit periodically.

THE PROFESSION OF TEACHING

The State Board for Educator Certification's mission is to ensure the highest level of educator preparation and practice to achieve student excellence. Further, the SBEC recognizes its responsibility to regulate the preparation and certification system to ensure that all students interact with appropriately certified educators. SBEC values ethical leadership and conduct, innovation, efficiency, and accountability (SBEC Strategic Plan, 1999). But what are the common characteristics among "professions" and how does SBEC's challenge and its role in the "professionalization of education" in Texas compare?

The use of the term *professional* has a wide variety of applications and evaluations. A person who can perform difficult procedures with a Yo-Yo is sometimes referred to as "a real pro." Promising collegiate football players are drafted into the "pros" of the National Football League. For some, whatever their job might be, it is their profession, i.e., job and profession are interchangeable terms. Chapter 31 lists the following as characteristics common to professions as follows:

- A defined body of knowledge beyond the grasp of the layman
- Control of entry requirements, i.e., who gets to practice and under what conditions
- Autonomy in spheres of work, i.e., within some legal limits, professionals alone decide how to conduct professional practice
- Prestige and economic standing long associated with the "established" professions

Characteristics of professions frequently blend together and although each may sound unique each shares similar qualities. For example, control of entry requirements is similar to monopolizing the delivery of services. Prestige and economic standing are sometimes associated with the nature of the client served; that is, psychiatrists have more prestige and are better paid than social workers even though both may utilize similar counseling techniques. Regarding compensation, Table 1 provides a state-by-state comparison of average teacher salaries. Table 2 allows for another dimension of comparison, that of average beginning teacher salaries among states; Texas ranks in the top 10 of the states in terms of first-year teachers as a percentage of the total number of teachers, i.e., in excess of 5%; a consideration when analyzing comparative

salaries for new teachers. As indicated in the data provided by the American Federation of Teachers, the average Texas teacher salary was 84.4% of the national average. However, cost of living in the various states, whether the salary stated does or does not include benefits such as medical and dental insurance, and a variety of other factors make direct comparisons difficult if not impossible. Additional educator salary data is appended to Chapter 4 and is also included in Chapter 11. The American Federation of Teachers and the National Education Association collaborate on salary studies and have documented that Connecticut paid the highest average salary ($51,181) in 1996–1997, and South Dakota's average was the lowest ($27,072) during the same year, in which the national average was $38,436, the average in Texas was $32,426. Teachers began the 1999–2000 school year with an increase of at least $3,000 per year as mandated by the 76th legislature. Although still below the national average, it was the most dramatic mandatory increase in a decade. Significant differences in what districts offer are also important as is indicated in Chapter 4. There are a number of other caveats in comparing teacher salaries with other professions and occupations that require baccalaureate degrees. Public school teachers are employees of state and local independent school districts. Salary comparisons with other employees of the state and local governments may prove teaching is far more favorable than comparisons with surgeons or very successful attorneys in private practice.

Add to the list of characteristics of professions the following:

1. standards for judging or evaluating the quality of performance
2. control of professional preparation programs
3. a recognized body of literature that conceptualizes the methodology and the knowledge base of the profession
4. authority to issue and revoke licenses or certificates
5. professional associations specifically devoted to the professional specialization.

The creation of an empowered State Board for Educator Certification with specific statutory authority to address numbers 2 and 4 is significant. Characteristic 1 can be considered addressed in the Commissioner's recommended Professional Development and Appraisal System (PDAS), which was also mandated by the same Senate Bill 1 of 1995 that created SBEC. The PDAS is the subject of Chapter 38. Characteristic 3 and 5 are acknowledged realities, and professional organizations are listed and described in Chapter 34.

TABLE 1 The Average Teacher Salary in 1996-97 State Rankings

Rank	State	Average Salary	Percent of U.S. Average
1	Connecticut	51,181	133.2%
2	New Jersey	49,786	129.5%
3	Alaska	49,140	127.8%
4	New York	48,000 c	124.9%
5	Michigan	47,769 b	124.3%
6	Pennsylvania	47,147	122.7%
7	Massachusetts	44,101 b	114.7%
8	Rhode Island	43,084 b	121.1%
9	California	42,992	111.9%
10	D.C.	42,424 b	110.4%
11	Illinois	42,339 e	110.2%
12	Delaware	41,436	107.8%
13	Maryland	41,257	107.3%
14	Oregon	41,093 e	106.9%
15	Nevada	40,817 e	106.2%
16	Ohio	38,944	101.3%
17	Indiana	38,722	100.7%
18	Minnesota	38,276	99.6%
19	Hawaii	38,105 e	99.1%
20	Wisconsin	37,878	98.5%
21	Washington	37,860 a	98.5%
22	Colorado	36,271	94.4%
23	Virginia	36,116	94.0%
24	Vermont	36,053	93.8%
25	New Hampshire	36,029	93.7%
26	Georgia	35,679	92.8%
27	Tennessee	34,267	89.2%
28	Florida	33,885	88.2%
29	Kentucky	33,802 a	87.9%
30	Maine	33,676	87.6%
31	Iowa	33,272	86.6%
32	West Virginia	33,258	86.5%
33	Arizona	33,208	86.4%
34	Kansas	33,150 d	86.2%
35	Missouri	33,143	86.2%
36	South Carolina	32,659	85.0%
37	Alabama	32,470	84.5%
38	Texas	32,426	84.4%
39	Idaho	31,818	82.8%
40	Nebraska	31,768	82.7%
41	Wyoming	31,716 e	82.5%
42	Utah	31,310 a	81.5%
43	North Carolina	31,019 b	80.7%
44	Arkansas	30,987	80.6%
45	Oklahoma	30,187	78.5%
46	Montana	29,958	77.9%
47	New Mexico	29,715	77.3%
48	Louisiana	28,347	73.8%
49	North Dakota	27,709	72.1%
50	Mississippi	27,662	72.0%
51	South Dakota	27,072	70.4%
	U.S. Average	$38,436	100.0%
	Virgin Islands	33,216 e	86.4%
	Guam	33,854	88.1%

a, estimate or preliminary; *b*, AFT estimate; *c*, median; *d*, estimated to exclude fringe benefits (at 8%); *e*, includes employer pick-up of employee pension contribution, where applicable.

Source: American Federation of Teachers.

TABLE 2 Actual Average Beginning BA Teacher Salaries, 1995-96 and 1996-97

State	Beginning Salary 1996–97	Average Salary 1996–97	Beginning To Average Salary Ratio	Beginning Salary 1995–96	Increase in: Beginning Salary	Increase in: Average Salary
1 Alabama	26,171	32,470	82.3%	25,568	4.5%	3.7%
2 Alaska	32,502	49,140	66.1%	32,638	-0.4%	0.0%
3 Arizona	24,286	33,208	73.1%	24,042	1.0%	1.1%
4 Arkansas	20,680 b	30,987	66.7%	20,000	3.4%	3.4%
5 California	26,684	42,992	62.1%	25,711	3.8%	1.7%
6 Colorado	23,068	36,271	63.6%	21,472	7.4%	2.6%
7 Connecticut	29,154	51,181	57.0%	28,961	0.7%	0.5%
8 D.C.	25,937 b	42,424 b	61.1%	25,937 b	0.0%	0.0%
9 Delaware	24,349	41,436	58.8%	24,300	0.2%	2.2%
10 Florida	24,736	33,885	73.0%	23,609	4.8%	1.7%
11 Georgia	25,434 b	35,679	71.3%	24,693	3.0%	5.3%
12 Hawaii	25,965 e	38,105 e	68.1%	25,436 e	2.1%	2.9%
13 Idaho	19,715	31,818	62.0%	19,328	2.0%	3.0%
14 Illinois	27,210 e	42,339 e	64.3%	26,294 e	3.5%	3.5%
15 Indiana	24,172	38,722	62.4%	23,530	2.7%	2.8%
16 Iowa	21,884	33,272	65.8%	21,338	2.6%	2.8%
17 Kansas	21,909 d	33,150 d	66.1%	21,607 d	1.4%	2.2%
18 Kentucky	23,018 d	33,802 d	68.1%	22,457	2.5%	2.6%
19 Louisiana	21,087	28,347	74.4%	19,406	8.7%	5.8%
20 Maine	21,108	33,676	62.7%	20,781	1.6%	2.5%
21 Maryland	26,548	41,257	64.3%	26,160	1.5%	0.2%
22 Massachusetts	25,445 b	44,101 b	60.0%	25,800 b	2.5%	2.5%
23 Michigan	26,404 b	47,769 b	55.3%	25,635 b	3.0%	2.0%
24 Minnesota	25,600 b	38,276	66.9%	24,850 b	3.0%	3.0%
25 Mississippi	20,264	27,662	73.3%	20,240	0.1%	-0.1%
26 Missouri	23,205	33,143	70.0%	22,308	4.0%	2.5%
27 Montana	20,592 b	29,958	68.7%	20,000 b	3.0%	2.0%
28 Nebraska	21,189	31,768	66.7%	21,299	-0.5%	0.9%
29 Nevada	28,538 e	40,817 e	69.9%	27,539 e	3.6%	3.2%
30 New Hampshire	23,690 b	36,029	65.8%	23,000 b	3.0%	0.7%
31 New Jersey	28,039	49,786	56.3%	28,219	-0.6%	2.1%
32 New Mexico	22,840	29,715	76.9%	22,500	1.5%	1.5%
33 New York	28,749 c	48,000 c	59.9%	28,749 c	0.0%	-0.2%
34 North Carolina	21,136 b	31,167	67.8%	20,620	2.5%	2.5%
35 North Dakota	18,889	27,709	68.2%	18,225	3.6%	2.8%
36 Ohio	22,146	38,944	56.9%	20,394	8.6%	2.3%
37 Oklahoma	23,847	30,187	79.0%	24,187	-1.4%	3.5%
38 Oregon	25,373 e	41,093 e	61.7%	24,592 e	3.2%	3.5%
39 Pennsylvania	29,426	47,147	62.4%	28,892	1.8%	2.3%
40 Rhode Island	25,497 b	43,084 b	59.2%	24,754	3.0%	3.0%
41 South Carolina	22,681	32,659	69.4%	21,940	3.4%	3.3%
42 South Dakota	19,820	27,072	73.2%	19,609	1.1%	2.8%
43 Tennessee	21,705	34,267	63.3%	21,500 b	1.0%	3.4%
44 Texas	24,079	32,426	74.3%	22,782	5.7%	3.3%
45 Utah	21,475	31,310 a	68.6%	20,544	4.5%	2.4%
46 Vermont	24,934 b	36,053	69.2%	24,445 b	2.0%	1.5%
47 Virginia	24,774	36,116	68.6%	24,267	2.1%	3.8%
48 Washington	23,933	37,860 a	63.2%	23,091	3.6%	0.0%
49 West Virginia	22,278	33,258	67.0%	22,011	1.2%	3.4%
50 Wisconsin	24,830	37,878	65.6%	24,350	2.0%	2.5%
51 Wyoming	22,010 b	31,716 e	69.4%	21,900 b	0.5%	0.5%
U.S. Average	$25,012	$38,436	65.1%	$24,285	3.0%	2.4%
Virgin Islands	21,913	33,216	66.0%	20,226	8.3%	0.0%
Guam	26,197	33,854	77.4%	26,197	0.0%	0.0%

a, estimate or preliminary; *b,* AFT estimate; *c,* median; *d,* estimated to exclude fringe benefits (at 8%); *e,* includes employer pick-up of employee pension, contribution, where applicable.

Source: American Federation of Teachers.

The degree of, need for, and nature of governmental regulation of licensing may be directly related to the public's perception of the importance of the service or profession. All physicians and dentists must be licensed by the state regardless of any shortage of specialists that may exist. Not all teachers need state certification. Teachers in Texas private schools need not be certified, nor do parents or others who school their children at home. As stated above, applicants for teacher certification have five different options to choose from. SBEC has only varying degrees of control over who gets certified and how. As one wag observed, states pay more attention to the requirements for certifying veterinarians who treat dogs and cats than they do those who teach their children. On the other hand, the legislative creation of an empowered State Board for Educator Certification is the most positive act toward the professionalization of teaching in the history of the state.

TEACHER APPRAISAL

The Professional Development and Appraisal System (PDAS), recommended by the Commissioner and adopted by over 90% of the school districts in Texas, addresses most of the contemporary issues of teacher evaluation and (critics claim) then some. Perhaps the most significant difference between (PDAS) and its predecessor, the Texas Teacher Appraisal System (TTAS), is the emphasis on what the student is doing while the teacher is teaching and less emphasis on teacher behavior. Also at issue is the consideration of student performance on the TAAS as part of the teacher's evaluation. Chapter 38 documents the statutory (Texas Education Code) and administrative (Texas Administrative Code) provisions for teacher evaluation and provides the criteria for PDAS. Adoption of the PDAS is an option for local school districts, not a requirement. The Commissioner must approve district-created appraisal systems used in lieu of the PDAS.

SITE-BASED DECISION MAKING

The movement or trend against top-down education mandates from Austin to more autonomy for the local districts began in the 1980s and was strengthening in the 1990s. Often referred to as restructuring or empowerment, this trend focused on creating new ways to lead, manage and govern schools through greater involvement on the part of teachers and other education stakeholders. Even those at the top realized that reforms mandated at that level were frequently misunderstood at the local level, obstructed or ignored by those at the local level, or unworkable in the realities of the public school context. This later reform movement was launched with the recognition that change must take place at the local level and that the logical locus of authority, as well as responsibility, is at the campus level. More on restructuring and professional knowledge is provided in Chapter 32.

Since 1990, state law has required site-based management approaches that enable the campus faculty, administration, and appropriate others to make decisions unique to their particular needs, an example of a degree of autonomy in the workplace. Texas Education Code 11.251 (d) requires that the campus level committee be involved in decisions in the areas of planning, budgeting, curriculum, staffing patterns, staff development, and school organization. The degree of involvement of the faculty may vary from campus to campus but the principle behind teacher involvement is sound. The legislative guidelines for site-based decision-making are reprinted in Chapter 33.

Advocates of site-based management argue that education decisions will improve and are more likely to be implemented if they are made by those closest to the effects of the decision. Site-based management creates an avenue for the input of teachers, support staff, parents, and the community—those with first-hand knowledge of the issues. It instills a sense of ownership in those involved and improves teachers' morale and motivation by formally recognizing the merit and worth of their professional opinions and judgments. Proponents also contend that increased authority at the school site will lead to greater accountability because school improvement plans will be locally developed and specific with clear lines of responsibility established for each program element. As school boards and central offices become more comfortable with relinquishing authority to the campuses the real effectiveness of this approach can be evaluated. Figure 1 compares components of traditional and site-based management.

TEACHER TESTING FOR CERTIFICATION

After May 1, 1984, all students applying for admission to a Texas educator preparation program were required to provide evidence of passing scores on the Pre-Professional Skills Test (PPST), developed by the Education Testing Service of Princeton, New Jersey. The PPST was administered for the last time in Texas in October 1989. Beginning in March 1989, the reading, writing, and mathematics tests of the Texas Academic Skills Program (TASP) were used for admission to teacher education programs. After September 1, 1989, all new Texas college students

FIGURE 1   Components of Site-Based Decision Making

Traditional	Site-Based Decision Making
Goals are dictated by district priorities and districtwide needs assessment.	Goals are determined based on campus-level staff perceptions of needs and analysis of campus-level outcome data.
Implementation activities are initiated and given direction from district-level administration.	Implementation activities are self-directed and initiated by campus staff.
Budget development and decisions about the allocation of resources flow from a central source based on the priorities of administrators with a broad view of districtwide needs and priorities.	Budget development and decisions about the allocation of resources are controlled at the campus level, based on local campus needs and priorities.
Evaluation of student performance is aggregated by campus, subject, and grade levels to provide comparisons of groups for administrative purposes.	Evaluation of student performance is individualized and ongoing to provide information relevant to instructional decisions.
Selection of staff is directed from central office personnel whose criteria reflect qualifications and characteristics valued by policy makers.	Selection of staff is guided by criteria developed by faculty that reflect the team needs for instructional expertise.
Curriculum revisions are standardized across grade levels at all campuses to ensure transferability of students and to reflect research and practices valued by central office staff and board members.	Curriculum revisions and instructional methods are coordinated at the campus level to meet the unique instructional needs of the students they serve.
Campus organizational structure is arranged hierarchically to facilitate top-down communications and supervision.	Campus organizational structure is arranged functionally to allow for shared team decision making and input into campuswide decisions.
Superintendents and administrators think and believe that they already have collaborative decision making in place.	Staff will attest that they have site-based decision making in place.

were required to pass the TASP, and passing scores for those seeking admission to teacher certification programs were the same as for those seeking regular college admission. In 1993, the Texas Legislature directed the State Board of Education and the Texas Higher Education Coordinating Board to develop policies for using Scholastic Achievement Test (SAT), American College Test (ACT), or Texas Assessment of Academic Skills (TAAS) scores in lieu of the TASP for admission to college and admission to teacher certification programs. The policy developed is summarized below.

Students seeking admission to teacher preparation and post graduate programs at private colleges or alternative certification programs will be exempted from the TASP test if they achieve certain scores on either the ACT, the SAT, or the TAAS test.

Under the new standards, students may be exempted from the TASP Test if they earn a composite score of 26 on the ACT, with a minimum of 22 on both the English and the mathematics tests. Previous standards required a composite score of 29 or higher with English and math scores equal to or greater than 27.

Students may also be exempted if they earn a combined verbal and mathematics score of 1090 on the SAT, with a minimum of 470 on the verbal test and 530 on the mathematics test (for tests taken prior to April 1995); or a combined verbal and mathematics score of 1180, with a minimum of 550 on both the verbal and mathematical tests. Previous standards required a passing score of 1200 or higher, with verbal and math scores equal to or greater than 550 for the TASP Test exemption.

Exemptions from the TASP Test also are granted if students pass the TAAS test with a minimum score of 1780 on the writing test and a Texas Learning Index (TLI) of 86 on the mathematics test and an 89 on the reading test. Under the previous standards, students had to have a TLI of 90 or higher in reading, 87 or higher in math and score 1800 or higher in writing to be exempt.

Exemptions will be effective for five years from the date the ACT or SAT was taken and for three years from the date the TAAS was taken. The new standards were effective in fall 1995.

Under the previous standards, only 3 percent of students were exempted from the TASP Test for entrance to state colleges and universities. Projections show the new standards will allow for 15 percent to be exempted. (*Texas Education Today*, June 1995.)

Since May 1, 1986, all teacher, administrator, and other professional educator candidates applying for Texas certification have had to pass proficiency tests in their fields of certification or endorsement. The tests, collectively entitled the Examination for the Certification of Educators in Texas (ExCET), were developed by National Evaluation Systems of Amherst, Massachusetts. The first ExCET tests were administered in May 1986 and have been continuously reviewed, evaluated and revised since. The 3 domains and 15 competencies of the Professional Development, both elementary and secondary, are provided. These competencies are described in greater detail, sample questions are provided and test-taking hints are explained in the State Board for Educator Certification's "Examination for the Certification of Educators in Texas (ExCET) Preparation Manual (Professional Development)" which is available at each educator preparation entity.

The ExCET examination scores of candidates completing their requirements not only determine their eligibility for state certification but also affect the accreditation, status, and reputation of the educator preparation entities recommending their certification. With the Accountability System for Educator Preparation (ASEP), certification entities face accountability pressures similar to those the elementary and secondary schools have experienced for years. And, given the high stakes of accreditation depending on ExCET scores, entities will probably be more cautious as to who is admitted to their programs and who will be declared eligible to take the ExCET examinations.

NATIONAL CERTIFICATION

Teacher certification granted and issued by the State of Texas via the State Board for Educator Certification is, at a minimum, a governmental assurance that the individual certified has met certain expectations, the most important of which is, as the adage from the medical profession admonishes, "first, do no harm." Certification to teach in Texas should assure the students, parents, and community at large that some sort of systematic preparation and/or review of the candidate has determined that he or she is safe to practice the profession in the public schools. This review process, regardless of the option for certification chosen, as described above, includes a criminal records check. Private schools may or may not require any pedagogical or academic preparation for their teacher employees but private schools do not represent the "government" as do public school educators.

A 1986 report of the Carnegie Corporation's Forum on Education and the Economy entitled *A Nation Prepared: Teachers for the 21st Century* called for the formation of a non-profit, non-partisan, non-governmental National Board for Professional Teaching Standards. The Carnegie proposal was in response to a highly critical assessment of American public education stated in *A Nation at Risk: The Imperative for Education Reform* prepared by the President's Commission on Excellence in Education in 1983. In that report, the Commission defined the seriousness of their interpretation of the problem as follows: "If an unfriendly foreign power had attempted to impose on America the mediocre educational performance that exists today, we might well have viewed it as an act of war." Although experts disagree as to the accuracy and objectivity of the findings, the report kicked off an intensive search for better ways of educating America's youth that persists today, i.e., the current and seemingly endless generation of educational reform.

The National Board for Professional Teaching Standards was established in 1987 as an independent, non-profit, non-partisan organization governed by a 63-member board of directors. The Board of Directors is composed of a majority of classroom elementary and secondary teachers; 14 of these are selected solely upon their outstanding performance records as teachers, a second 14 is made up of teachers recognized as leaders in their teaching fields, and the final 14 are teacher representatives of local, state, or national teacher unions and/or organizations. The remaining 21 members are from a variety of fields, but at least half must be public officials with governance or management responsibilities for public schools. Board members may serve two 3-year terms. Nominations for membership are solicited from the various constituent organizations, such as the National Education Association.

The main purpose of the National Board was to establish high and rigorous standards for what teachers should know and be able to do and to certify teachers who could voluntarily meet those standards. Accordingly, teachers who can perform at the prescribed levels have demonstrated that they can effectively exercise independent professional judgment on a variety of instructional policy matters that affect the education of young people. In this way, the Board's requirements will be similar in many respects to the standards that other professionals must meet.

The five core propositions or standards of accomplished teaching that are endorsed by the Board as the basis for national certification are summarized as follows.

- Teachers are committed to students and their learning.

FIGURE 2

DOMAIN I—UNDERSTANDING LEARNERS

Competency 001

    The teacher uses an understanding of human developmental processes to nurture student growth through developmentally appropriate instruction.

Competency 002

    The teacher considers environmental factors that may affect learning in designing a supportive and responsive classroom community that promotes all students' learning and self-esteem.

Competency 003

    The teacher appreciates human diversity, recognizing how diversity in the classroom and the community may affect learning and creating a classroom environment in which both the diversity of groups and the uniqueness of individuals are recognized and celebrated.

Competency 004

    The teacher understands how learning occurs and can apply this understanding to design and implement effective instruction.

Competency 005

    The teacher understands how motivation affects group and individual behavior and learning and can apply this understanding to promote student learning.

DOMAIN II—ENHANCING STUDENT ACHIEVEMENT

Competency 006

    The teacher uses planning processes to design outcome-oriented learning experiences that foster understanding and encourage self-directed thinking and learning in both individual and collaborative settings.

Competency 007

    The teacher uses effective verbal, nonverbal, and media communication techniques to shape the classroom into a community of learners engaged in active inquiry, collaborative exploration, and supportive interactions.

Competency 008

    The teacher uses a variety of instructional strategies and roles to facilitate learning and to help students become independent thinkers and problem solvers who use higher-order thinking in the classroom and the real world.

Competency 009

    The teacher uses a variety of instructional materials and resources (including human and technological resources) to support individual and group learning.

Competency 010

    The teacher uses processes of informal and formal assessment to understand individual learners, monitor instructional effectiveness, and shape instruction.

Competency 011

    The teacher structures and manages the learning environment to maintain a classroom climate that promotes the lifelong pursuit of learning and encourages cooperation, leadership, and mutual respect.

DOMAIN III—UNDERSTANDING THE TEACHING ENVIRONMENT

Competency 012

    The teacher is a reflective practitioner who knows how to promote his or her own professional growth and can work cooperatively with other professionals in the system to create a school culture that enhances learning and encourages positive change.

Competency 013

    The teacher knows how to foster strong school–home relationships that support student achievement of desired learning outcomes.

Competency 014

    The teacher understands how the school relates to the larger community and knows strategies for making interactions between school and community mutually supportive and beneficial.

Competency 015

    The teacher understands requirements, expectations, and constraints associated with teaching in Texas, and can apply this understanding in a variety of contexts.

Source: Texas Education Agency

- Teachers know the subjects they teach and how to teach those subjects to students
- Teachers are responsible for managing and monitoring student learning
- Teachers think systematically about their practice and learn from experience
- Teachers are members of learning communities.

A two-part assessment process for measuring mastery of these standards has been developed by the NBPTS. The first component is completed at the teacher's school. The candidate must also prepare a portfolio containing videotapes of the candidate's teaching, lesson plans, samples of student work, and written reflections on the candidate's instructional choices or responses to student work or behavior. Part two takes place at an assessment center. During a one-day session exams in the teacher's field, interviews, evaluation of other teachers, reactions to instructional scenarios, and other structured activities are completed.

The National Board for Professional Teaching Standards launched National Board Certification (NBC) during the 1994–1995. At the outset, only Early Adolescence/English Language Arts and Early Adolescence Generalist were available for English Language Arts teachers of students between the ages of 11 and 15. Generalist teachers are those who may be assigned to teach a single subject or multiple subjects that represent the early adolescence curriculum, e.g., mathematics, English language arts, social studies/history, science, health, and the arts. The National Board has since developed certification categories in the following:

- Early childhood generalist (ages 3–8)
- Middle childhood generalist (ages 7–12)
- Early Adolescence/Generalist (ages 11–15)
- Early Adolescence/English Language Arts
- Early Adolescence through Young Adulthood/Art (ages 11–18+)
- Adolescence and Young Adulthood/Math (ages 14–18+)
- Adolescence and Young Adulthood/Science
- Early Adolescence/Science
- Early Adolescence/Math
- Early Adolescence/Social Studies-History
- Adolescence and Young Adulthood/English Language Arts
- Adolescence and Young Adulthood/Social Studies—History
- Early and Middle Childhood/English as a New Language (ages 3–12)
- Early and Middle Childhood/Exceptional Needs
- Early Adolescence through Young Adulthood/English as a New Language
- Early Adolescence through Young Adulthood/Vocational Education
- Early Adolescence through Young Adulthood/Exceptional Needs

According to various publications of the National Board, the 17 certification areas listed above cover about 80% of the classroom teachers currently assigned. The NBPTS plans for a total of 30 certificates by the year 2007.

The cost for the 10-year national certificate is $2,000, and Texas has been encouraged to involve more teacher candidates, with the NBPTS waiving half that fee for a limited number and for a limited time. Beyond being able to pass the rigorous assessments, candidates must have a baccalaureate degree and at least three years of teaching experience. Public school teachers are required to hold state certification, and private school teachers are required to have at least three years experience in schools recognized and approved by the state. Between 1994, the first year, and 1999, NBPTS anticipated that approximately 7,000 teachers would participate nationally. Both the National Education Association (NEA) and the American Federation of Teachers (AFT) have endorsed the concept and in 1999 jointly prepared a 60-page manual for teachers interested in preparing for the NBC. According to the "National Board Certification: A Guide for Candidates," the manual provides a step-by-step guide to help teachers get ready for the process, understand the standards, prepare their portfolios, and undergo assessment-center activities.

In Texas, the Corpus Christie school district has decided to reward teachers who have earned NBC with a $1,500 salary increase. Payment of the $2,000 fee for serious candidates was the incentive offered by the San Antonio school district in addition to a $1,000 salary supplement for four years or $500 for 10 years (teacher's choice) to those who earn NBC.

PROFESSIONAL ORGANIZATIONS

Professional organizations for educators are summarized in Chapter 34. The list of both major and minor organizations formed by educators must be viewed as in progress rather than complete, for whenever two or more educators agree and organize, a new one is created. Conversely, whenever a single-cause organization accomplishes or decides not to pursue it further, it disintegrates without fanfare. Even so, the major national and state organizations, associations, and unions endure and frequently engage in spirited competition for leadership and membership.

TEACHING

In early 1994, the State Board of Education approved a new format and criteria for evaluating both teachers and administrators. Adoption of "Learner-Centered Schools for Texas: A Vision of Texas Educators," was the first step in what was to become, in time, the Accountability System for Educator Preparation (ASEP) cited above. The proficiencies contained in Learner-Centered Schools are provided in Chapter 35. Each proficiency is provided in two parts: (1) a declarative statement of the proficiency, and (2) a descriptive narrative further illustrating the proficiency. These proficiencies provide the framework for the Professional Development and Appraisal System (PDAS) cited above and provided in Chapter 38. In addition, whether the district decides to use PDAS or a system of its own design, the Texas Education Code requires that all teacher appraisals include evaluation of the teachers' discipline management policies and performance of the teachers' students.

Districts that chose to continue use of the Texas Teacher Appraisal System (TTAS) find that direct or explicit instruction fares well in teacher evaluations.

Explicit teaching is the subject of Chapter 36 and the lesson cycle is featured in Chapter 37. Several states and a multitude of school districts throughout the states have adopted various forms of what has been attributed to Madeline Hunter, of the University of California at Los Angeles, and dubbed the "Hunter model." Teachers who have been "Hunterized" follow her design for effective instruction, which includes the following seven steps.

1. anticipatory set
2. objectives and purposes
3. input
4. modeling
5. checking for understanding
6. guided practice
7. independent practice

The Lesson Cycle described in Chapter 37 follows the Hunter model.

Instructional approaches change over time and no one "model" or approach suits every teacher in every teaching situation. However, whatever gets evaluated gets modeled on evaluation day.

STATE BOARD FOR EDUCATOR CERTIFICATION
College/University Recommendation and Application for Certification
APPLICANT: See instructions on back of application form for items 1-16, 31-34

CRT

1. Social Security Number

2. Date of Birth
M M D D Y Y

3. Gender
☐ Male
☐ Female

4. Ethnic Group
☐ Native American
☐ Asian ☐ Hispanic
☐ African American ☐ White

5. First Name

6. Middle Name

7. Last Name

8. Generation

9. Permanent Address

10. City

11. State

12. Zip Code

13. Area Code and Telephone Number

14. E-mail Address (optional)

15. Have you ever been the subject of an arrest that has resulted in deferred adjudication, probation or a conviction? ☐ Yes ☐ No
If YES, attach a statement with the date and place of arrest, nature of charge, date and court of trial, and subsequent disposition.

16. Have you ever had a teaching certificate revoked, denied, suspended or subject to any sanctions in Texas or any other state?
☐ Yes ☐ No   If YES, attach a statement providing the school district, the state, and detailed information.

APPLICANT: Continue at Item 31 on the back of this application form.

INFORMATION BELOW TO BE COMPLETED BY Recommending Teacher Education Program Administrator

17. HIGHEST DEGREE EARNED
☐ Bachelor's
☐ Master's
☐ Doctorate

18. Date Degree was Conferred
M M D D Y Y

19. State Abbrev.

20. Org. ID for College/University where Degree was Conferred (if in Texas)

22. CERTIFICATE

☐ Provisional

☐ Professional

21. Name of College/University where Degree was Conferred

23. PROGRAM COMPLETED
☐ Standard Program
☐ Vocational (based on Skill and Experience)
☐ Post-Baccalaureate
☐ Center for Professional Development & Technology

24. STANDARDS GOVERNING APPROVED PROGRAM
☐ 1955
☐ 1972
☐ 1984
☐ 1987
☐ Center for Professional Development & Technology

25. RECOMMENDED CERTIFICATIONS

Type	Area	Subject		Type	Area	Subject
Type	Area	Subject		Type	Area	Subject

26. EXAMINATION EXCEPTIONS

1. ☐ Applicant completed requirements for teacher preparation program under **Secondary Option II**, but passed only professional development ExCET and content specialization exam(s) for the secondary certificate recommended.

2. ☐ Applicant completed requirements for teacher preparation program under **Elementary Option II, III, or IV**, but passed professional development and elementary comprehensive exams only. Recommended Certification is Elementary General Option I.

3. ☐ Applicant completed all academic, degree and experience requirements under 1955, 1972 or 1984 Standards **prior to September 1, 1991**, but did not pass all appropriate examinations until **after September 1, 1991**.

27. DATE CERTIFICATION REQUIREMENTS COMPLETED
M M D D Y Y

28. RECOMMENDING INSTITUTION Organization ID for College/University
2 2 0 5 0 3

29. Print Certification Officer's Name & Phone
Thomas John Bedell Graca
817/272-2956

30. ▼ CERTIFICATION OFFICER SIGNATURE HERE

Date _____

The evidence secured by this institution indicates the applicant is of good moral character. The applicant has fulfilled all requirements for certificate(s) described herein and is judged to have the competencies for service in the area(s) for which certification is recommended. This institution recommends that the applicant be certified as described herein.

SBEC-008R98

418

STATE BOARD FOR EDUCATOR CERTIFICATION
College/University Recommendation and Application for Certification

31. Have you ever held a Texas teacher certificate? ☐ Yes ☐ No   If YES, when was it issued?_____ Certificate #_____

32. As far as you know, do you have any records in our office under a different name than your current name? ☐ Yes ☐ No
If YES, please provide information which may help us locate all your previous records. _____

33. For Vocational Certification based on skill and experience, provide a service record, certified by Superintendent of employing district(s)

School Year	School District	Assignment	Grades Taught	No. Days Employed	Full Time Part Time	Authorized Signature of Superintendent or Representative

34. **Applicant's Affidavit:** (*All applicants must execute this affidavit*)

"I do hereby agree, consent and direct that any person or entity maintaining information in any form relating to my criminal history shall release all such information upon the request of the State Board for Educator Certification.

"I do further hereby agree and permit the State Board for Educator Certification to obtain from any person or entity information relating to my personal background, my moral character and my worthiness to instruct the youth of this state, and do hereby expressly direct that any such person or entity release such information upon the request of the State Board for Educator Certification.

"I do hereby release, discharge, and exonerate the State Board for Educator Certification, its agents or representatives, and any person or entity so furnishing information from any and all liability of every kind arising therefrom.

"The foregoing consent and release is valid and binding so long as I hold or seek any certificate, license, permit, or other credential issued under the authority of the Texas Education Code.

"I understand that any credential issued to me by the State Board for Educator Certification is the property of the State of Texas. I agree that I will tender my credential to the State Board for Educator Certification if I am ordered to do so by the State Board for Educator Certification.

"I understand that a copy of this affidavit shall have the same force as the original.

"I have reviewed this application and I affirm that all of the information which I have provided on the application and attached documents is true."

▼ DRIVER'S LICENSE/STATE ID NUMBER HERE | APPLICANT'S SIGNATURE HERE ▼

_____ Issuing State: _____ | _____ Date: _____

This application must be submitted directly by certification officer at recommending preparation program.

This form will be scanned using automatic character recognition. HANDWRITTEN: Write with a black pen. Print each letter or number neatly within a blue box. Use a blue box for each space or punctuation mark. Answer multiple choice questions by filling box completely. Print letters and numbers as shown below. TYPEWRITTEN: Type normally in area provided. Do not space letters to fit in blue boxes.

Write Alphabetic Characters Like This

A B C D E F G H I J K L M N O P Q R S T U V W X Y Z

Write Numbers Like This

1 2 3 4 5 6 7 8 9 0

Detailed Instructions for Applicant Items:

1. Social Security Number - Unique number assigned by Social Security Administration. Certification files are kept by Social Security Number.
2. Date of Birth - (m m d d y y)
3. Gender - Fill in box beside the appropriate gender choice.
4. Ethnic Group - Fill in box to select ethnic background. Leave blank = "other".
5. First Name - First word of your full legal name. This name is the first name that will print on your certificate.
6. Middle Name - Second word of your full legal name. This name is the second name that will print on your certificate. You may substitute a maiden name or previous married name for the middle name, if you prefer.
7. Last Name - Final word of your full legal name. This name is the last name that will print on your certificate. See item 8 for suffix, such as Jr. or Sr. or III.
8. Generation - Optional suffix to name (Jr., Sr., III, IV, etc.)
9. Permanent Address - Street address or post office box for mailing.
10. City - City portion of permanent mailing address.
11. State - Abbreviation for state portion of mailing address.
12. Zip Code - U.S. Postal Service zip code for mailing address.
13. Telephone Number - Optional area code and phone number we could call.
14. E-mail Address - Optional address for internet mail if we have a question.
15. Arrest Information - Provide details if your answer is YES.
16. Certificate Sanction Information - Provide details if answer is YES.
31. Previous Certificate - This information will help us locate your files.
32. Previous Names - This information will also help us to locate your files.
33. Service Record - Required for vocational certification based on experience.
34. Applicant's Affidavit - Affidavit must be affirmed and signed by applicant.

Detailed Instructions for Recommending Entity Items:

17. Highest Degree Earned - Indicate degree by filling in the box.
18. Date Degree Was Conferred - (m m d d y y) If day is unknown, enter '01' for day. For example, graduation in May 1992, enter '050192'.

19. State Abbrev. - Abbreviation of state where college/university is located.
20. Org. ID for College/University - If college / university that conferred highest degree is in Texas, provide the organization ID number of the institution.
21. Name of College/University - If the college / university that conferred highest degree is not in Texas, provide name of the institution. (may be abbreviated)
22. Certificate - Fill in box for certificate to be issued to applicant. Remit appropriate fee to SBEC-CRT so recommended certificate can be issued:
$75 Provisional Certificate $75 Professional Certificate
23. Program Completed - Fill in the box beside the correct educator preparation program which was completed by the applicant.
24. Standards Governing Approved Program - Fill in correct box.
25. Recommended Certifications - Enter the appropriate codes for each certification for which the applicant completed requirements and is being recommended. The Teacher Certification Handbook, Section XX Appendix C has details about these codes.
26. Examination Exceptions - Teacher Certification Handbook Section VI provides additional information about examination requirements and exceptions.
27. Date Certification Requirements Completed - (m m d d y y) When did applicant complete preparation program and pass all required tests?
28. Recommending Institution - Certification Officer MUST fill in the correct organization ID number for your institution.
29. Certification Officer Name & Phone Number - Name and phone number of person at recommending institution responsible for validity of the information provided in this application.
30. Signature of Certification Officer - Signature of Certification Officer affirms statement about moral character and qualifications of applicant.

> **If you have questions** about this form, contact the Certification Officer at your preparation program.

CHAPTER 31

Teaching as a Profession

Whether teaching can be considered a profession in the fullest sense has concerned educators and education scholars for decades. Some have tried to identify the ideal characteristics of professionals and, by matching teaching against them, to determine whether teaching qualifies as a profession. A synthesis of the thinking of three writers on this subject, whose work spans the decades from the fifties to the seventies, produces a list of 13 distinct characteristics of a true profession, each mentioned by at least one of them.[1] These writers arrive at similar conclusions: Teaching is not a profession in the fullest sense; it lacks some of the defining characteristics of professions: and it may be viewed as a semi-profession on its way to achieving full professional status.

Of the 13 characteristics cited by at least one of these three writers, four are perhaps most important: (a) a defined body of knowledge beyond the grasp of the lay public, (b) control over licensing standards and/or entry requirements, (c) autonomy in making decisions about selected spheres of work, and (d) high prestige and economic standing. In this article I shall argue that teaching does not exhibit all of these characteristics and that it lags substantially behind such professions as the law and medicine in the degree to which it exhibits any of them.

A DEFINED BODY OF KNOWLEDGE

All professions have a monopoly on certain knowledge. Their members are set apart from the general public and given control over their vocation, in exchange for which the public is protected from quacks, untrained amateurs, and special interest groups. But there is no agreed-upon specialized body of knowledge that is "education" or "teaching."

Education lacks a well-defined body of knowledge that is applicable to the real world of teaching[2] or that has been validated and agreed upon by most authorities. Thus the content of teacher education courses varies from state to state and from institution to institution within states. As late as 1946 only 15 states required a bachelor's degree for elementary teachers; in 1976 only three states required that teachers hold a master's degree.[3] In 1975 as many as 40% of the 1,350 colleges involved in training teachers were not accredited by the national accrediting agency.[4]

CONTROL OF ENTRY REQUIREMENTS

Most professions enforce uniform standards to ensure minimum competence, but this is not the case in the teaching profession. The problem concerns both those who enter teacher education programs and those who are ultimately certified to teach.

At one time, students who entered teacher training programs had lower aptitude scores than students in most other fields,[5] and there were no widely accepted tests used to determine whether the graduate of a teacher training program was adequately prepared to be a teacher. In addition, state certification requirements vary greatly.

Whatever they may think about these differing requirements, teachers do not have much say in the matter. Thus their mobility is limited from state to state by the different licensing procedures. Most people, including teachers, reject teacher regulation of licensing requirements, but the exercise of professional autonomy would be enhanced if teachers could establish licensing laws and if state certification standards were more uniform. It is in the public interest to vest control of professional standards and requirements partly in educators rather than to continue to leave such decisions entirely to laypeople.

AUTONOMY IN SPHERES OF WORK

Every member of a profession, but no outsider, is assumed competent to judge the specific work of that profession. Professions usually establish laws of exclusive jurisdiction in a given area of competence, and custom and tradition control matters relating to work and clients. Indeed, lay control is the natural enemy of professions; it limits the power of the professional and opens the door to outside interference.

Teachers acquiesce in the belief that local and state officials have the right to decide on the subjects they teach and on the instructional materials and books they use. They sometimes question how wisely the community exercises such rights, but the legitimacy of these rights is rarely questioned. At best, teachers are accorded minimum input in curriculum decisions.

The problem is that teachers and the general public believe that the democratic process entitles the public to decide what books to use and what content to teach. Any parent or taxpayer may challenge a teacher, and the community may dictate curriculum in opposition to the teacher's professional judgments. Taxpayers are said to "reasonably" claim a share in decision making, since they pay the bills and provide the clients.

But physicians and lawyers are paid by their clients, yet no one expects clients to prescribe drugs or write the clauses in contracts. When a client interferes with the decision of the practicing physician or lawyer, the professional/client relationship ends. This protects clients from being victimized by their own lack of knowledge and safeguards the professional from the unreasonable judgments of the public. Peter Blau and W. Richard Scott observe that "professional service . . . requires that the [professional] maintain independence of judgment and not permit the clients' wishes as distinguished from

their interests to influence his decisions." Professionals have the knowledge and expertise to make judgments, "and the client is not qualified to evaluate the services he needs." Professionals who permit their clients to tell them what to do "fail to provide optimum service."[6]

Teachers are not professionals in this sense. They can be told what to do by parents, other citizens, principals, superintendents, and school board members. Although collective bargaining has resulted in new distributions of power among teachers and administrators, most people still feel that teachers, as public servants, are accountable to the people and to the school officials who are hired, elected, or appointed by the people. Teachers must not lose sight of the welfare of their clients or the desires of the public, but they should not completely surrender the power to determine the nature of the service they render. To err in the first direction is to become rigid and despotic; to err in the second is to become subservient and impotent.

Professional autonomy does not mean that no control is exercised over the performance of professionals. On the contrary, it means that controls requiring technical competence must be imposed by people who possess such competence. There are many ways of ensuring that competent people have a say in governing the teaching profession. Collective negotiations can define those areas in which teachers can make use of their experiences and competencies to control their profession; teacher representation on local school boards and on state licensing and governing boards could be increased. Professional organizations could also help to elect political candidates who are pro-teacher and pro-education.

PRESTIGE AND ECONOMIC STANDING

Teachers have registered major gains in salary and status during the past 50 years. In 1930 the average teacher earned $1,420; in 1950, $3,126; in 1970, $16,001. In 1996–97 the average teacher earned $38,436. Much of this increase is the result of inflation, but real gains were registered, especially between 1960 and 1970. This period corresponds to the growth of teacher militancy, and salaries for teachers during the sixties rose 44% while prices rose 28%. Since the mid-1970s, however, teacher salary increases have not kept pace with inflation.[7]

Nevertheless, teacher pay remains lower than that of the average college graduate.[8] In addition, teachers earn far less than do lawyers, business executives, and some other professionals with similar levels of formal education.

Although the prestige and income of teachers have risen relative to their past station, teachers remain only slightly better off than the average worker and not nearly as well off as other professionals with similar levels of education. The "status-consistency hypothesis" holds that a group tends to compare its rewards (prestige and salary) with those of other groups and will strive to raise them to a level consistent with people who have similar jobs, even similar years of education.[9] If this is true, we should expect teachers to make comparisons with other professional groups, to remain dissatisfied, and to express this dissatisfaction through militance. In fact, this has been one of the major reasons for teacher militance since the mid-1960s.

TRENDS TOWARD PROFESSIONALISM

It is not likely that educators will be given complete autonomy in setting standards for professional practice, but one way of increasing the role of teachers in setting professional standards has been the establishment of teacher standards and practices commissions. These commissions are usually made up of a majority or plurality of teachers and set standards for teacher preparation and minimal competence in professional practice.[10]

Professional practices commissions are moving to establish requirements for content and skills to be covered in teacher education programs and, with the National Council for the Accreditation of Teacher Education (NCATE) and the American Association of Colleges for Teacher Education (AACTE), to approve teacher education programs. The movement is spearheaded by the National Education Association (NEA), and standards of excellence in teacher education is one item on the NEA's 1982 convention agenda. But the American Federation of Teachers (AFT) also takes the position that an insufficient relationship exists between teacher education and classroom reality.

These professional practices commissions also have placed a few teachers on probation, suspended certificates, and reprimanded teachers for unprofessional or illegal behavior.

Some people see a serious conflict of interest in permitting teachers to influence certification standards—a marked contrast to the privilege of self-regulation accorded to other professions. Many colleges and universities oppose these commissions, because the commissions are usually staffed by a majority of teachers and a minority of college-based representatives. In addition, the AFT is aware that state professional practices commissions would most likely be controlled by the NEA in most states,

since the majority of teachers belong to the NEA. Both teacher organizations should try to work out their differences on this matter, because the profession can only benefit by teachers playing a major role in setting certification and licensing standards.

The spread of collective bargaining during the seventies has also had an impact on the professional status of teachers. Many people consider collective bargaining and contract negotiations as non-professional or even unprofessional activities, and in many of the professions (e.g., law, medicine, the ministry) few practitioners work in organizations that have anything to do with collective bargaining. From another point of view, however, the spread of collective bargaining has significantly enhanced teachers' control over the conditions of their employment and their effectiveness in the classroom. The trend in collective bargaining—depending partly on any government action to extend bargaining rights to all public employees or withhold them—has been to include in the negotiations more and broader concerns than salary issues.

In the future, teachers will face a bargaining dilemma. Even before the Reagan Administration's hard-line stand against the Professional Air Traffic Controllers' Organization (PATCO), public officials had begun to take firmer positions in the face of threatened job actions by the unions. These tougher stands have been partly the result of mounting taxpayer dissatisfaction with increasing local and state taxes and partly the result of the continuing squeeze of inflation. In order to maintain some control over working conditions and to ensure professional status, salary gains, and jobs, teacher unions will have to work together on collective bargaining—organizing statewide, regional, and national strikes. Otherwise, teachers will find themselves settling for conditions only marginally better than before they began to bargain.

Another way in which teachers are achieving greater professional status by exercising greater control over their own affairs is in the area of staff development. To stay up to date and to acquire new professional skills, teachers traditionally have participated in various kinds of inservice training. Most of this training has been provided on college campuses, frequently to meet school district requirements for additional college credit for continuing certification. Many observers view this kind of inservice training as unrelated to job roles and student needs.[12]

Lately a growing number of inservice training opportunities have been provided by teacher centers—governed partly by teachers themselves. Teacher centers are designed to make staff development more relevant to teachers' actual classroom needs. As providers of inservice training, teacher centers may represent a significant move toward teachers' participation in making professional decisions.

Teacher centers have existed for years as information exchange centers where teachers could obtain ideas about new instructional practices and talk with colleagues about how to apply appropriate methods in their classrooms. Centers of this kind have provided valuable services to teachers, but their funding has been unstable. Consequently, they have not been able to undertake systematic efforts at improving instructional practice in the schools. With the advent of federal funding, teacher centers have been able to offer recertification courses, graduate courses for credit, community education workshops, and even small instructional development grants.[13] If teacher centers can escape the federal budget cuts, they will become increasingly important centers of professional development in the 1980s.

Also, the practice of inducting persons into a profession through carefully supervised stages, known as mediated entry, has proven successful for some professions and holds promise of similar success for teaching. In the medical profession, for example, aspiring physicians serve one or more years beyond their minimal professional training as interns and then as residents before they are considered full-fledged professionals.

Dan Lortie has studied teaching from a sociological perspective and has concluded that, on the spectrum of sequenced professional entry, teaching ranks in between occupations characterized by "casual" entry and those that place protracted and difficult demands on the would-be members.[14] The lack of more carefully mediated entry restricts the depth and practicality of preservice training. Teachers frequently report that experience has been their main teacher and that they have learned through trial and error in the classroom.

Efforts to provide more effective induction of new teachers into the profession have not been widespread or systematic enough. Most school districts, for example, require a probationary period for new teachers, but in too many cases relatively little concrete assistance is provided in developing and refining skills during probation. Many school districts and a few states require a fifth year of preparation beyond the traditional bachelor's degree and initial certificate, but too often this requirement means that new teachers take a few more courses that may or may not help them improve professionally. Most new teachers still find themselves largely on their own in their first professional position.

The future of mediated entry into teaching may be brighter, however. School district officials no longer feel compelled to put new teachers to work immediately, as was done during the teacher shortage of the 1960s.

In the past, various segments of the teaching profession, particularly leaders of the NEA and the AFT, have been unable to agree on qualitative issues of education. Consequently, they have not worked well together on issues of power and policy. But times have changed. Today the worsening economic situation of the education profession, the public attitude toward reducing education spending, force various professional groups and all levels of education to cooperate rather than compete. Strategies to improve the teaching profession exist. But, if members of the profession continue to squabble, their professional status will continue to suffer. The choice is not new, but the stakes have been raised.

NOTES

1. Myron Lieberman, *Education as a Profession* (Upper Saddle River, N.J.: Prentice-Hall, 1958); Ronald G. Corwin, *Sociology of Education* (New York: Appleton-Century-Crofts, 1965); and Allan C. Ornstein, *Teaching in a New Era* (Champaign, Ill.: Stipes Publishing Co., 1976).

2. M. L. Cushman, *The Governance of Teacher Education* (Berkeley, Calif.: McCutchan, 1977); and Dan C. Lortie, *Schoolteacher: A Sociological Study* (Chicago: University of Chicago Press, 1975).

3. Allan C. Ornstein, "Characteristics of a Profession," *Illinois School Journal*, Winter 1976–77, pp. 12–21.

4. Egon, G. Guba and David Clark, "Selected Demographic Data About Teacher Education Institutions," paper presented at the first annual Conference on Teacher Education, Indiana University, Indianapolis, November, 1975; and Allan C. Ornstein, "Educational Poverty in the Midst of Educational Abundance: Status and Policy Implications of Teacher Supply/Demand," *Educational Researcher*, April 1976, pp. 13–16.

5. Mark Borinsky, *Survey of Recent College Graduates* (Washington, D. C.: U. S. Government Printing Office, 1977); Robert P. Hilldrup, "What Are You Doing About Your Illiterate Teachers?" *American School Board Journal*, April 1978, pp. 27–29; George Nolfi et al., *Experiences of Recent High School Graduates: The Transition to Work or Post-Secondary Education* (Cambridge, Mass.: University Consultants, 1977); and W. Timothy Weaver,

"Educators in Supply and Demand: Effects on Quality," *School Review,* August 1978, pp. 552–93.

6. Peter Blau and W. Richard Scott, *Formal Organizations* (San Francisco: Chandler, 1965), pp. 51, 52.

7. Allan C. Ornstein, *Education and Social Inquiry* (Itasca, Ill.: Peacock, 1978); idem, "Teacher Salaries: Past, Present, Future," *Phi Delta Kappan,* June 1980, pp. 677–79.

8. Frank S. Endicott, *Trends in Employment of College and University Graduates in Business and Industry* (Evanston, Ill.: Northwestern University Press, 1980).

9. Ronald G. Corwin, *Militant Professionalism: A Study of Militant Conflict in High Schools* (New York: Appleton-Century-Crofts, 1970).

10. See Peter L. LoPresti, "California: The Impact of the Commission for Teacher Preparation and Licensing," *Phi Delta Kappan,* May 1977, pp. 674–77; Russell B. Vlaanderen, "State Review: Focus on Certification, Teacher Education, and Governance," *Legislative Review,* October 1979, pp. 4, 5; and James M. Wallace, "The Making of a Profession: An Oregon Case Study," *Phi Delta Kappan,* May 1977, pp. 671–73.

11. Allan C. Ornstein and Harry L. Miller, *Looking into Teaching* (Chicago: Rand-McNally, 1980); *Teacher Standards and Licensing Boards* (Washington, D. C.: National Education Association, 1976); and telephone conversation with NEA officials of the Standing Committee on Instruction and Professional Development, 7 September 1981.

12. Arnold M. Gallegos, "Politics and Realities of Staff Development," *Educational Leadership,* January/February 1980, p. 21; and Bruce Joyce, "The Ecology of Staff Development," paper presented at the annual meeting of the American Educational Research Association, Boston, April 1980.

13. The functioning of teacher centers is described in Kathleen Devaney, ed., *Building a Teachers' Center* (New York: Teachers College Press, 1979). Several specific centers are described in some detail in Charlotte K. Hoffman, "Teacher Training Inside Out," *American Education,* August/September 1979, pp. 6–17.

14. Lortie, pp. 15–21.

CHAPTER 32

Restructuring and Professional Knowledge

Calls for the "restructuring" of schools raise questions as to what knowledge should guide our efforts. I've become aware, as a participant in an effort known as The League of Professional Schools, that restructuring needs to begin with confrontation of our own professional knowledge. For too long, professionals have gone about the business of teaching and operating schools in ways they privately admit are not in the best interests of students. The reasons for doing so are plentiful—we all live with district policies, state regulations, traditional school structures, mandated curriculum alignment, community pressures, and limited resources. Then, too, we can, by pretending not to know what is known, live with dissonance between our internal values and our behavior (Festinger, 1957).

Today, as we answer the calls for restructuring, school faculties can begin by opening up their suppressed knowledge, thus creating debate and fostering their own value-driven enthusiasm for "doing the right thing" for students rather than simply for "doing things right" (Sergiovanni, 1991). We have the opportunity to stop pretending not to know.

Let us spend the rest of this essay describing what we know, summarized in 11 statements in 3 categories. (I admit to no higher enlightenment than other educators, and I'm confident that there will be disagreement with my claims.) I will conclude with

Reprinted with permission from "Pretending Not to Know What We Know," by Carl Glickman, *Educational Leadership,* May 1991.

a discussion about the need for "elite" schools to pioneer a new era of intellectual confrontation. If we don't confront what we know, the rhetoric of innovation-for-its-own-sake will drive the underlying values away; and this reform movement will become another fad to endure for a few years, to be replaced by the next (Slavin, 1989).

TEACHING AND LEARNING

Let's begin by looking at what we know about teaching and learning.

1. *Tracking students does not help students.* We know that the evidence shows no benefits are gained by tracking students into ability groups, as shown by Oakes (1985), Slavin (1987, 1990), George (1987), and Garmoran and Berends (1987). Higher-achieving students do not do better when together, and lower-achieving students do much worse when together. Tracking clearly discriminates and clearly perpetuates inequities among students; higher-track students tend to be white, wealthy, and from highly educated families; and lower-track students tend to be black and Hispanic, poor, and from poorly educated families. Students tend to be put into ability groups less on their academic abilities and more as a result of their socioeconomic status. Once assigned to a low track, very few move into higher tracks; and their performance as low achievers becomes self-perpetuating. Consequently, tracking often results in resegregation of students by socioeconomic status and/or race. That may not be the intent, but it is the result.

In responding to these findings, some schools have eliminated or dramatically reduced homogeneous grouping and have eliminated separate classroom programs such as Gifted and Chapter 1. The San Diego schools, for example, no longer have remedial education. In British Columbia, a phased-in elimination of tracking or "streaming" (through the 11th year of schooling) has begun, leaving tracking for the last two years, when students will specialize in vocational or college-bound programs.

But in many places tracking continues even when the evidence is overwhelmingly against it. Perhaps it benefits a few individual students and placates some parents; but more often tracking continues because it's easier to manage classrooms and schools when the range of abilities is restricted rather than if they are expansive and students need to be taught in multiple ways. Recently, the National Education Association (1990) and the Quality Education for Minorities Network (Henry, 1990), as well as the National Governors' Association (1990), have asked for the elimination of ability grouping in the United States.

2. *Retention does not help students.* Thomas Holmes (1990, p. 28), in an update of his classic meta-analysis of studies comparing the education of students who were retained with students of comparable achievement and maturity who were promoted, concluded that in longitudinal studies ". . . retained students were no better off in relation to their younger at-risk controls who went on immediately to the next grade."

In the past 15 years, study after study has shown rather conclusively that there is little benefit of retention (Shepard & Smith, 1989). Students retained one year have only a 50 percent chance of graduating, and students retained twice have little if any chance to graduate (Gastright, 1989). It stands to reason that a student who starts high school at the age of 16 is not going to stay in school until he or she is 20.

As Holmes (1990) concluded, "Those who continue to retain pupils at grade level do so *despite* [italics mine] the cumulative research evidence" (p. 78). The task of schools is not to sort and thwart students but instead to assist them to move along from year to year with the knowledge, concepts, and skills which allow them to graduate in 12 years with the prerequisites to be productive citizens.

3. *Corporal punishment does not help students.* As one who spent his earlier years as a researcher on the effects of various discipline approaches and continues to keep up on this literature, I find no research that shows any long-term benefits from paddling students. In fact, there is research (The Fifteen Thou-

sand Hours Study, Rutter et al. 1979) that shows the least successful schools are the most punitive. At its best, what corporal punishment does is make students comply out of fear, become subversive in their misbehavior, and learn the lesson that physical might is the way to resolve problems. At the worst, the students who are big enough simply rebel and physically attack back.

Schools and states that eliminate corporal punishment are helping students to learn self-control. Still, 31 states allow corporal punishment, and more than 1.1 million paddlings are administered in a year (White, 1990). The United States is one of the few countries remaining in the world where corporal punishment is still practiced.

4. *Students learn from real activities.* In a century of public schools, little structural change has occurred in classroom teaching (Cuban, 1984). The majority of classroom time is spent on teachers lecturing, students listening, students reading textbooks, or students filling out work sheets. To observe classrooms now is to observe them 50 years ago: a teacher standing and talking, students sitting and daydreaming (Goodlad, 1984, p. 105). Perhaps the last real structural change occurred when the desks were unbolted.

Yet we know that real projects, with primary sources, real problems to solve, and real discussions show dramatic and significant gains in student achievement and motivation (see Slavin and Madden's [1989] summary of instructional approaches and Brophy, 1987). Teachers need to learn multiple ways of teaching students that engage their minds, their bodies, and their souls (Joyce, 1990). Teachers need to think about how students think, listen to students describe what helps them learn, and share with their colleagues activities and methods that get closer to active learning.

5. *Effective teaching is not a set of generic practices, but instead is a set of context-driven decisions about teaching.* Effective teachers do not use the same set of practices for every lesson (Porter & Brophy, 1988). They do not—as mindless automatons—review the previous day's lessons, state their objectives, present, demonstrate, model, check for understanding, provide guided practice, and use closure. Instead, what effective teachers do is constantly reflect about their work, observe whether students are learning or not, and then adjust their practices accordingly.

Effective teaching, then, is a set of decisions about the use of a variety of classroom materials and methods used to achieve certain learning goals. Researchers and theorists from Madeline Hunter, to Barak Rosenshine, to David Berliner, to Jere Brophy have disclaimed any responsibility for the application of their own research as simple-minded pre-scriptions of uniform criteria for monitoring and evaluating teachers. Such prescriptions are driven by psychometricians looking for objectivity and reliability. The problem is that such concepts of teaching are divorced from reality, simply not valid.

6. *There is nothing inherently sacred about Carnegie units, classroom size, and grade levels!* A leading school reformer, Phil Schlechty (1990a), has expressed what we know about this eloquently, as follows:

> There are, at present, a number of structural elements in schools that preclude flexibility in the allocation of human resources. Chief among these are the concepts of *school class, grade level,* and the *Carnegie unit* in high school. . . . Arranging schools in classes and classrooms, and grouping children by age or ability or sex or any other characteristic, represents only a few of the possibilities for grouping children for schoolwork. One could just as well group children according to the tasks that must be performed to carry out a particular piece of schoolwork or according to any of a number of other grouping arrangements one might conceive. The Carnegie unit is another convention. Invented primarily as a means of satisfying the interest of higher education in having a basis for judging college preparedness among youth, the Carnegie unit became a standard measure in American education just as the pound, the quart, and the inch are standard measures in American commerce.
>
> The problem with these conventions is not that they exist. . . . The problem arises when upholding the convention becomes an end in itself (pp. 64–65).

Schlechty explains that alternatives to these conventions are not necessarily better but they might be. The point is we'll never know unless we try.

TEACHERS AND WORK CONDITIONS

Now let's move on to what we know about teachers.

7. Outstanding teachers do not teach for external incentives but for the pleasure of seeing the effects of their decisions on students. Incentives, career ladders, and merit pay plans are not inducements for great teachers. Garret Keizer (1988) wrote about receiving the Star Teacher of the Year:

> Last year my freshman student Jessica Davis took a first prize of a thousand dollars in the Honors Competition for Excellence in Writing. I taught composition in Jessica's English class,

and when we learned of her candidacy, I gave her extra coaching outside of class, which she graciously acknowledged in the newspaper articles about her. But the fact is, I did not make Jessica Davis a good writer. Somewhere on the scale of merit between me and God are at least eight elementary and middle school teachers. . . .

> Another teacher, who works in a local elementary school, starts her summer by tearing up every note, exercise, and handout that she has used the preceding year. In the fall, she will begin from scratch. Just the thought that I might be forced by theft or fire to adopt this woman's standards makes me light-headed. How does one quantify that kind of integrity?
>
> As I write, one of our 1st grade teachers is adjusting the last hem of the authentic Pilgrim costumes she has sewn for every student in her class. A girl so poor that she has on occasion come to school without underwear stands smoothing down the folds of her long dress in wonderment. "See my dress!" she calls out to the visitor. It may be the cleanest, newest, handsomest thing she has ever worn—this garment of another age's austerity. How many hours this teacher must have spent at home behind a sewing machine—how many seconds will it take to punch her dedication into someone's business-model, performance-oriented, incentive-based, computerized version of how schools ought to run (pp. 117–119).

After interviewing and studying outstanding teachers of the past 50 years, Duval (1990) concluded that these teachers spent up to $2,000 a year out of their own pockets for supplies, materials, and trips for students. He wrote:

> This group of teachers spent their own money knowingly and for maximum effect . . . being able to secure materials, services, and other things of use . . . without having to go through a tiring, tedious bureaucratic process is something prized by all of the excellent teachers (p. 192).

Eliot Wigginton, past Teacher of the Year in Georgia and founder of the renowned Foxfire program, wrote this:

> I am a public high school English teacher. Occasionally, on gloomy nights, my mood shifts in subtle ways, and familiar questions rise in my throat: in social situations, confronted by those whose lives seem somehow more dramatic, an implication in the air is that I will have little of interest to contribute to the conversation; many people with fewer years of formal education

make more money. Then the mood passes, for I know that surface appearance is deceitful and salary is a bogus yardstick of worth.

Actually, if the truth be told, it is only rarely that I wonder why I am still teaching. I know why. I teach because it is something I do well; it is a craft I enjoy and am intrigued by; there is room within its certain boundaries for infinite variety and flexibility of approach, and so if I become bored or my work becomes routine, I have no one to blame but myself; and unlike other jobs I could have, I sometimes receive indications that I am making a difference in the quality of people's lives. That, and one more thing; I genuinely enjoy daily contact with the majority of the people with whom I work (Wigginton, 1985, Intro.)

So what do we know about what motivates excellent teachers? We know that it has to do with discretion and control over resources, time, instructional materials, and teaching strategies so as to make better educational decisions.

How have we responded to what we know, over the past 17 years? It is amazing that in 1991, with the technology available to us, most teachers have to wait in line in the school office to make a phone call to a parent. What other professional is left without a phone in his or her work station? At a time where personal computers are essential to almost every knowledgeable worker, teachers don't even have phones! Instead, 96 percent of teachers spend an average of $250 per year *of their own money* on teaching supplies because they lack control over the teaching budget. What's more, the recent Carnegie Foundation study (1990) found more than 70 percent of all teachers in the U. S. are not involved deeply in decisions about curriculum, staff development, grouping of students, promotion and retention policies, or school budgets.

SCHOOL IMPROVEMENT

Now let's look at what we know about improving schools.

8. *Teacher evaluation does not relate to schoolwide instructional improvement.* The evaluation boondoggle has been perhaps the greatest robbery of educational resources in our times. There is little research that establishes a clear link between the amount and type of teacher evaluation with the attainment of schoolwide priorities. Yet policymakers have poured millions of dollars into evaluation systems while ignoring the daily support needs of teachers.

Blankenship and Irvine (1985) found, for example, that a majority of all experienced teachers in Georgia had never been observed, given feedback, or had a conference focused on thinking critically about ways to improve teaching. Throughout their careers, all classroom visits by observers were for the purpose of being judged and rated. Furthermore, 90 percent of teachers had never had a chance to observe a peer teacher and discuss what they could learn from each other. The lack of helpful and supportive assistance has been underscored by conclusions of The Fifteen Thousand Hours Study:

> It was striking, however, that in the less successful schools teachers were often left completely alone to plan what to teach, with little guidance or supervision from their . . . colleagues and little coordination with other teachers to ensure a coherent course from year to year (Rutter et al., 1979, p. 136).

Uniform systems of teacher evaluation have cost millions of dollars and millions of hours—and for what? To rid the profession of fewer than 2 *percent* of our teachers. Imagine what could happen if the bulk of that money and time were reshifted to help competent teachers become even more thoughtful and skillful in the craft and art of teaching through peer coaching, group problem-solving sessions, curriculum work, staff development, and clinical supervision.

Teacher evaluation may be a necessary control function of an organization; but it improves a school *only* when the majority of people border on incompetence—they either shape up or get out. Most of our schools do not employ a majority of incompetent people; rather, we employ people who could use more help and assistance to think through the long-term and short-term decisions they are making on behalf of students.

9. *The principal of a successful school is not the instructional leader but the coordinator of teachers as instructional leaders.* The arrogance by which the education community has embraced the concept of "principal as instructional leader" is mind-boggling. We really want to believe—as my friend Ed Pajak (1985) suggests—in the principal as Rambo, leading a school up the path of glory. This concept—the principal as all knowing, all wise, and transcendent in vision, who can lead the staff development council and the curriculum council, be an expert on group facilitation and organizational change, can spend 50 percent of his or her time in classrooms with uncanny analytical and conferencing abilities, deal with all manner of students, staff, parents, and communities, plus fill out all necessary forms, run all the schedules, and take care of maintaining the air conditioner and furnace—this is an incomprehensible idea for supporting school reform.

Let me express what we all know about powerful, successful schools. In such schools, the people who are seen as most credible with the greatest expertise about teaching and learning are the teachers themselves. There are teachers in our schools who are beyond those of us in formal leadership positions in their knowledge, skills, and applications of curriculum and instruction. In successful schools, principals aren't threatened by the wisdom of others: instead, they cherish it by distributing leadership. The principal of successful schools is not the instructional leader but the educational leader who mobilizes the expertise, talent, and care of others. He or she is the person who symbolizes, supports, distributes, and coordinates the work of teachers as instructional leaders (see Chubb and Moe, 1990, p. 86).

10. *Successful schools don't work off prescriptive lists; they work off professional judgments!* Roland Barth, in his 1990 book *Improving Schools from Within,* says that:

> Our public schools have come to be dominated and driven by a conception of educational improvement that might be called *list logic.* The assumption of many outside of schools seems to be that if they can create lists of desirable school characteristics, if they can only be clear enough about directives and regulations, then these things will happen in schools. . . . The vivid lack of congruence between the way schools are and the way others' lists would have them be cause most school people to feel overwhelmed, insulted, and inadequate—hardly building blocks for improving schools or professional relationships. . . . Moreover, I doubt that we would find that many teachers, principals, and students in high-achieving schools comply closely with anybody's list. As Ronald Edmonds often said, we know far more about the features that characterize an effective school than we know about how a school becomes effective in the first place. Why, then, do we try to force schools we do not like to resemble those we do like by employing means that have little to do with the evolution of the kind of schools we like? (Barth, 1990, pp. 37–40).

11. *The measure of school worth is not how students score on standardized achievement tests but rather the learning they can display in authentic or real settings.* The fixation with test scores has recently come under a storm of criticism. George Hanford, past president of the College Board (which is the developer of the Scholastic Aptitude Test), wrote that the scores produced by tests exude "an aura of precision out of proportion to their significance, which in turn fosters an unsuitable reliance on them, to the exclusion or neglect of other indicators that are equally important and useful" (Hanford, 1986, p. 9).

It is not that standardized tests are useless. They do provide a source of information about what groups of students know. How much weight should be put on that source of knowledge, rather than other sources of knowledge, is the issue of dispute. Wise (1988) warns, "Many schools no longer teach reading, they teach reading skills; no longer do they teach important reading skills; instead, they teach only reading skills measured on the achievement tests."

The task force on education of the National Governors' Association states that:

> The present system requires too many teachers who focus "largely on the mastery of discrete, low-level skills and isolated facts . . . By doing so . . . the system denies opportunities for students to master subject matter in depth, learn more complex problem solving skills, or apply the skills they do learn (Henry, 1990, IE, p. IA).

The task force goes on to say that top priority needs to be given "to developing new tools for assessing student performance" and "that portfolios, essays, or other open-ended problems that require students to synthesize, integrate, and apply knowledge and data need to be developed as alternatives to the exclusive use of conventional multiple-choice tests" (Henry, 1990, 8A).

This indeed is the rationale for why such states and provinces as California, Connecticut, Utah, Vermont, and British Columbia, and such school districts as Dade County, Florida, and Rochester, New York, have employed teams of teachers to develop alternative assessments (Wiggins, 1989) and have moved to eliminate or severely reduce the use of standardized tests. This also is the reason that, as part of the Coalition of Essential Schools, many public high schools are developing new performance exhibits to replace Carnegie units and basic skill tests for graduation requirements.

WHAT DO WE DO WITH WHAT WE KNOW?

These 11 statements are my views of what we know—schools might develop different statements. My point is that we must confront our knowledge and use it to guide our efforts; then we must operate our schools in different ways, using our knowledge.

We ask our districts and states to pilot new teacher evaluation and supervision systems. We ask to develop new assessment measures, create new curriculum, new grading and grouping organizations, new discipline and management systems, and our own staff development plans. We ask that teachers be given equal voice in all decisions about teaching and learning, and we include parents and students as participants in such discussions. Above all, we ask that the school be the center for professional decisions where teachers and administrators control the priorities and means of helping students to learn.

Beginning now, we ask that existing resources be reallocated to the school level to assist us. In those districts and states where schools are being given the power to change themselves, most of the money that previously went into centralized and controlling functions are now being reallocated to the local school. Instead of having curriculum specialists at the central office, teachers are given extended contracts to do curriculum work. Instead of having central office supervisors, teachers are given released time to function in master, mentor, and coaching roles. Instead of staff developers, teachers and administrators are given time to plan their own staff development. Instead of following a state or district formula of funding per classroom size, faculties are rethinking the roles of teachers, counselors, administrators, and specialists. (For example, rather than hire another teacher for 25 students, a school might hire three paraprofessionals; rather than replace an assistant principal, a school might use the money for a part-time bookkeeper and use the balance for specialized group work for students.)

Basically, the idea is to flatten and streamline centralized bureaucracies and redistribute the curriculum, staff development, personnel, and administrative budgets to the schools. In Dade County, as site-based management and shared governance increased to more than 100 schools in 3 years, the central office has been dramatically reduced, with the salaries and budgets reallocated to the local schools. Thus, decentralized school-based initiatives can expect to expend no greater amount of money but to increase the amount of state and district monies going directly into schools to support instructional services to faculty and students.

In many cases where districts are small, we are not going to reduce our central office positions. Instead, the monies that central office controls will need to be rethought. The point is, if we are serious about the school's being the unit of change and if we are serious that the time has come for teachers to make decisions about their professional work of teaching and learning, then the current organizations of centralized control, monitoring, and distri-

bution of money need to be changed. And this is why, initially we need to think of this reform movement as one dealing with elite schools only.

THE ELITE—A FEW GOOD SCHOOLS

The decentralization, deregulation, site-based, empowerment movement is on the right track because it uses what we know. But ultimately it will be right only if the quality of education improves, and the quality of education will not improve if we don't first move with "elite" schools.

By *elite*, I don't mean schools that are necessarily rich or poor, suburban, urban, or rural. I don't mean schools where all students have high IQs or all teachers have advanced degrees. Instead, elite schools are places where central office people, building administrators, and teachers trust each other to share in decisions about teaching and learning. Elite schools are places where those with formal leadership responsibilities know, as Schlechty has remarked, "In democratic environments power is achieved by giving it away rather than struggling for more" (1990b).

So, elite schools are those where the faculty wants to share in the choice and responsibilities of school-wide decisions and where administrators and supervisors likewise want them to share—my caution is that there are few such schools in the nation, perhaps 10 to 20 percent. In most places, each party is suspicious of the other, and people fight to protect their own domains. The leaders think that to empower teachers will lead to anarchy and evil, and most of the teachers think that administrators and supervisors who talk about empowerment are giving paternalistic lip service to listening to their suggestions rather than truly sitting with them as co-equals in real decisions.

So for teachers, schools, and central offices who don't see this chance to deregulate and decentralize as an opportunity for students but instead see it as a threat to current jobs—and it is a threat to many of our jobs as we currently function—they should not get involved, nor should they be forced to operate in such a manner. All of our current legislation and centralized monitoring should continue to direct them. These schools and districts should sit on the sidelines and watch what elite schools can do for and with kids. Only then will we discover whether those schools willing to use what they know can usher in a far better future for students, educators, and public education.

REFERENCES

Barth, R. S. (1990). *Improving Schools from Within: Teachers, Parents, and Principals Can Make a Difference.* San Francisco: Jossey-Bass.

Blankenship, G., Jr., & J. J. Irvine. (1985). "Georgia Teachers' Perceptions of Prescriptive and Descriptive Observations of Teaching by Instructional Supervisors." *Georgia Educational Leadership 1*, 1: 7–10.

Brophy, J. (1987). "Synthesis of Research on Strategies for Motivating Students to Learn." *Educational Leadership 45*, 2: 40–48.

The Carnegie Foundation for the Advancement of Teaching. (1990). *The Conditions of Teaching: A State by State Analysis.* (1990). Princeton, N.J.: The Carnegie Foundation for the Advancement of Teaching.

Chubb, J. E., & J. M. Moe. (1990). *Politics, Markets, and America's Schools.* Washington, D. C.: The Brookings Institution.

Cuban, L. (1984). *How Teachers Taught: Constancy and Change in American Classrooms.* New York: Longman.

Darling-Hammond, L. (1991). "Supervision and Policy." In *Supervision in Transition: 1991 ASCD Yearbook*, edited by C. Glickman. Alexandria, Va.: Association for Supervision and Curriculum Development.

Duval, J. H. (1990). "Dedication/Commitment: A Study of Their Relationship to Teaching Excellence." Doctoral diss., University of Vermont.

Festinger, L. (1957). *A Theory of Cognitive Dissonance.* Stanford, Calif.: Stanford University Press.

Garmoran A., and M. Berends. (1987). "The Efforts of Stratification in Secondary Schools." *Review of Educational Research 57*, 415–435.

Gastright, J. F. (April 1989). "Don't Base Your Dropout Program on Somebody Else's Program." *Research Bulletin 8.*

George, P. S. (1987). *What's the Truth about Tracking and Ability Grouping Really???* Gainesville, Fla.: Teacher Education Resource.

Goodlad, J. I. (1984). *A Place Called School: Prospects for the Future.* New York: McGraw-Hill.

Hanford, G. H. (1986). "The SAT and Statewide Assessment: Sorting the Uses and Caveats." In *Commentaries on Testing*, Princeton, N.J.: College Entrance Examination Board.

Henry, T. (July 29, 1990). "Governors Access Education: Report Asks States to Redesign System." Associated Press. *The Burlington Free Press.* 1E.

Holmes, C. T. (1990). "Grade Level Retention Effects: A Meta-Analysis of Research Studies." In *Flunking Grades: Research and Policies on Retention*, edited by L. A. Shepard & M. L. Smith. New York: The Falmer Press.

Joyce, B., ed. (1990). *Changing School Culture Through Staff Development: 1990 ASCD Yearbook.* Alexandria, Va.: Association for Supervision and Curriculum Development.

Keizer, G. (1988). *No Place But Here: A Teacher's Vocation in a Rural Community.* New York: Viking Penguin.

National Education Association. *Academic Tracking.* (1990). Washington, D. C.: NEA.

National Governors' Association (1990). *Educating America: State Strategies for Achieving the National Education Goals.* Washington, D. C.: National Governors' Association.

Oakes, J. (1985). *Keeping Track: How Schools Structure Inequality.* New Haven, Conn.: Yale University Press.

Oates, J. C. (1989). "Excerpts from a Journal." *The Georgia Review XLIV*, 1–2: 121–134.

Pajak, E. F. (1985). "Implications of the Education Reform Movement for School-Based Instructional Leadership." Presentation at the Alabama Association for Supervision and Curriculum Development. Birmingham.

Porter, A. C., and J. Brophy. (1988). "Synthesis of Research on Good Teaching: Insights from the Work of the Institute for Research on Teaching." *Educational Leadership 45*, 8: 74–85.

Rutter, M., B. Maughan, P. Mortimore, J. Ouston, & A. Smith. (1979). *Fifteen Thousand Hours: Secondary Schools and Their Effects on Children.* Cambridge, Mass.: Harvard University Press.

Schlechty, P. S. (1990a). *Schools for the 21st Century.* San Francisco: Jossey-Bass.

Schlechty, P. S. (1990b). Presentation to the Educational Futures Conference, ASCD Institute, Alexandria, Va.

Sergiovanni, T. J. (1991). "The Dark Side of Professionalism in Educational Administration." *Kappan 72*, 7: 524.

Shepard, L. A., & M. L. Smith, eds. (1989). *Flunking Grades: Research and Policies on Retention.* London and New York: The Falmer Press.

Slavin, R. E. (1987). "Ability Grouping and Student Achievement in Elementary Schools: A Best-Evidence Synthesis." *Review of Educational Research 57*: 293–336.

Slavin, R. E. (1989). "PET and the Pendulum: Faddism in Education and How to Stop It." *Phi Delta Kappan 70*, 10: 752–758.

Slavin, R. E. (1990). "Achievement Effects of Ability Grouping in Secondary Schools: A Best-Evidence Synthesis." *Review of Educational Research 60*: 471–499.

Slavin, R. E., & N. A. Madden. (1989). "What Works for Students At Risk: A Research Synthesis." *Educational Leadership 46*, 5: 4–13.

White, B. (February 4, 1990). "School Paddles Say They Could Do Without It." *The Atlanta Journal and Constitution*, p. 5.

Wiggins, G. (1989). "Teaching to the (Authentic) Test." *Educational Leadership 46*, 7: 41–47.

Wigginton, E. (1985). *Sometimes a Shining Moment: The Foxfire Experience*. Garden City, N.Y.: Anchor Press/Doubleday.

Wise, A. (June 1988). "Restructuring Schools." Presentation to the Annual Georgia Leadership Institute, Athens.

CHAPTER

33

Site-Based Decision-Making

TEXAS EDUCATION CODE

Subchapter F. District-Level and Site-Based Decision-Making

§ 11.251. Planning and Decision-Making Process

(a) The board of trustees of each independent school district shall ensure that a district improvement plan and improvement plans for each campus are developed, reviewed, and revised annually for the purpose of improving the performance of all students. The board shall annually approve district and campus performance objectives and shall ensure that the district and campus plans:

   (1) are mutually supportive to accomplish the identified objectives; and

   (2) at a minimum, support the state goals and objectives under Chapter 4.

(b) The board shall adopt a policy to establish a district- and campus-level planning and decision-making process that will involve the professional staff of the district, parents, and community members in establishing and reviewing the district's and campuses' educational plans, goals, performance objectives, and major classroom instructional programs. The board shall establish a proce-

dure under which meetings are held regularly by district- and campus-level planning and decision-making committees that include representative professional staff, parents of students enrolled in the district, and community members. The committees shall include business representatives, without regard to whether a business representative resides in the district or whether the business the person represents is located in the district. The board, or the board's designee, shall periodically meet with the district-level committee to review the district-level committee's deliberations.

(c) For purposes of establishing the composition of committees under this section:

   (1) a person who stands in parental relation to a student is considered a parent;

   (2) a parent who is an employee of the school district is not considered a parent representative on the committee;

   (3) a parent is not considered a representative of community members on the committee; and

   (4) community members must reside in the district and must be at least 18 years of age.

(d) The board shall also ensure that an administrative procedure is provided to clearly define the respective roles and responsibilities of the superintendent, central office staff, principals,

Reprinted with permission from the Texas Education Code, 1998.

teachers, district-level committee members, and campus-level committee members in the areas of planning, budgeting, curriculum, staffing patterns, staff development, and school organization. The board shall ensure that the district-level planning and decision-making committee will be actively involved in establishing the administrative procedure that defines the respective roles and responsibilities pertaining to planning and decision-making at the district and campus levels.

(e) The board shall adopt a procedure, consistent with Section 21.407(a), for the professional staff in the district to nominate and elect the professional staff representatives who shall meet with the board or the board designee as required under this section. At least two-thirds of the elected professional staff representatives must be classroom teachers. The remaining staff representatives shall include both campus- and district-level professional staff members. Board policy must provide procedures for:

(1) the selection of parents to the district-level and campus-level committees; and

(2) the selection of community members and business representatives to serve on the district-level committee in a manner that provides for appropriate representation of the community's diversity.

(f) The district policy must provide that all pertinent federal planning requirements are addressed through the district- and campus-level planning process.

(g) This section does not:

(1) prohibit the board from conducting meetings with teachers or groups of teachers other than the meetings described by this section;

(2) prohibit the board from establishing policies providing avenues for input from others, including students or paraprofessional staff, in district- or campus-level planning and decision-making;

(3) limit or affect the power of the board to govern the public schools; or

(4) create a new cause of action or require collective bargaining.

§ 11.252. District-Level Planning and Decision-Making

(a) Each school district shall have a district improvement plan that is developed, evalu-

ated, and revised annually, in accordance with district policy, by the superintendent with the assistance of the district-level committee established under Section 11.251. The purpose of the district improvement plan is to guide district and campus staff in the improvement of student performance for all student groups in order to attain state standards in respect to the academic excellence indicators adopted under Section 39.051. The district improvement plan must include provisions for:

(1) a comprehensive needs assessment addressing district student performance on the academic excellence indicators, and other appropriate measures of performance, that are disaggregated by all student groups served by the district, including categories of ethnicity, socioeconomic status, sex, and populations served by special programs;

(2) measurable district performance objectives for all appropriate academic excellence indicators for all student populations, appropriate objectives for special needs populations, and other measures of student performance that may be identified through the comprehensive needs assessment;

(3) strategies for improvement of student performance that include:

(A) instructional methods for addressing the needs of student groups not achieving their full potential;

(B) methods for addressing the needs of students for special programs, such as suicide prevention, conflict resolution, violence prevention, or dyslexia treatment programs;

(C) dropout reduction;

(D) integration of technology in instructional and administrative programs;

(E) discipline management;

(F) staff development for professional staff of the district;

(G) career education to assist students in developing the knowledge, skills, and competencies necessary for a broad range of career opportunities; and

(H) accelerated education;

(4) resources needed to implement identified strategies;

(5) staff responsible for ensuring the accomplishment of each strategy;

(6) timelines for ongoing monitoring of the implementation of each improvement strategy; and

(7) formative evaluation criteria for determining periodically whether strategies are resulting in intended improvement of student performance.

(b) A district's plan for the improvement of student performance is not filed with the agency, but the district must make the plan available to the agency on request.

(c) In a district that has only one campus, the district- and campus-level committees may be one committee and the district and campus plans may be one plan.

(d) At least every two years, each district shall evaluate the effectiveness of the district's decision-making and planning policies, procedures, and staff development activities related to district- and campus-level decision-making and planning to ensure that they are effectively structured to positively impact student performance.

(e) The district-level committee established under Section 11.251 shall hold at least one public meeting per year. The required meeting shall be held after receipt of the annual district performance report from the agency for the purpose of discussing the performance of the district and the district performance objectives. District policy and procedures must be established to ensure that systematic communications measures are in place to periodically obtain broad-based community, parent, and staff input and to provide information to those persons regarding the recommendations of the district-level committee. This section does not create a new cause of action or require collective bargaining.

(f) A superintendent shall regularly consult the district-level committee in the planning, operation, supervision, and evaluation of the district educational program.

§ 11.253. Campus Planning and Site-Based Decision-Making

(a) Each school district shall maintain current policies and procedures to ensure that effective planning and site-based decision-making occur at each campus to direct and support the improvement of student performance for all students.

(b) Each district's policy and procedures shall establish campus-level planning and decision-making committees as provided for through the procedures provided by Sections 11.251(b)–(e).

(c) Each school year, the principal of each school campus, with the assistance of the campus-level committee, shall develop, review, and revise the campus improvement plan for the purpose of improving student performance for all student populations with respect to the academic excellence indicators adopted under Section 39.051 and any other appropriate performance measures for special needs populations.

(d) Each campus improvement plan must:

(1) assess the academic achievement for each student in the school using the academic excellence indicator system as described by Section 39.051;

(2) set the campus performance objectives based on the academic excellence indicator system, including objectives for special needs populations;

(3) identify how the campus goals will be met for each student;

(4) determine the resources needed to implement the plan;

(5) identify staff needed to implement the plan;

(6) set timelines for reaching the goals; and

(7) measure progress toward the performance objectives periodically to ensure that the plan is resulting in academic improvement.

(e) In accordance with the administrative procedures established under Section 11.251(b), the campus-level committee shall be involved in decisions in the areas of planning, budgeting, curriculum, staffing patterns, staff development, and school organization. The campus-level committee must approve the portions of the campus plan addressing campus staff development needs.

(f) This section does not create a new cause of action or require collective bargaining.

(g) Each campus-level committee shall hold at least one public meeting per year. The required meeting shall be held after receipt of the annual campus rating from the agency to discuss the performance of the campus and the campus performance objectives. District policy and campus procedures must be established to ensure that systematic communications measures are in place to periodically obtain broad-based community, parent, and staff input, and to provide information to those persons regarding the recommendations of the campus-level committees.

(h) A principal shall regularly consult the campus-level committee in the planning, operation, supervision, and evaluation of the campus educational program.

§ 11.254. State Responsibilities for the Planning and Decision-Making Process

(a) The commissioner shall oversee the provision of training and technical support to all districts and campuses in respect to planning and site-based decision-making through one or more sources, including regional education service centers, for school board trustees, superintendents, principals, teachers, parents, and other members of school committees.

(b) The agency shall conduct an annual statewide survey of the types of district- and campus-level decision-making and planning structures that exist, the extent of involvement of various stakeholders in district- and campus-level planning and decision-making, and the perceptions of those persons of the quality and effectiveness of decisions related to their impact on student performance.

Added by Acts 1995, 74th Leg., ch. 260, § 1, eff. May 30, 1995.

CHAPTER
34

Professional Organizations

Should future and practicing teachers join professional organizations? Which ones are available and what are their purposes and benefits? How large is the membership and how much are dues? Questions such as these often arise when deciding on which associations are best to join, especially when prospective members consider the proliferation of organizations within the last 13 years. While the 1978 *Directory of Education Associations* named approximately eleven hundred groups, the 1990–91 *Yearbook of International Organizations* and the *Encyclopedia of World Problems and Human Potential* lists 2,823 international educational societies (U. S. Department of Health, Education, and Welfare, 1978 and the Union of International Associations, 1991). According to another source, the *Encyclopedia of Associations,* over 2,000 education associations exist (Burek, 1991). Among these groups, the two largest teacher organizations, the National Education Association and the American Federation of Teachers, have worked for improved working conditions, better teacher salaries, and more voice in legislative matters. Along with examining the roles of these two national groups, this chapter will explain the functions of four state teacher organizations. Then, a list of 87 other associations follows with a brief account of the purposes, benefits, affiliations, membership statistics, dues requirements, and addresses for each one. Information is based on recent survey results compiled for this chapter. Directors/presidents were asked to complete a two-page questionnaire which provided up-to-date information about the organizations. Whenever answers were not supplied, the authors have deleted that segment from the data. Benefits, such as lower cost liability and auto insurance packages for members, help individuals decide on which organizations have greater offerings. For purposes of organization, associations are grouped under categorical headings such as early childhood, vocational education, and parent/ teacher/volunteer organizations.

NATIONAL TEACHER ORGANIZATIONS
National Education Association
With a 1999 membership of over 2.3 million, the National Education Association is the largest of the professional education organizations. It was established in 1857 to promote educational excellence and to assist the nation's teachers to unite behind common goals. Horace Mann, who established the first normal school in Lexington, Massachusetts, became one of the first members (Ryan, Cooper, 1988).

Today the general purpose of the NEA is to promote the cause of quality education and advance the profession of education, expand rights and further the interests of educational employees, and advocate human, civil, and economic rights for all. Benefits include a journal, *Today's Education,* newsletters, national conferences, a variety of workshops, and

Prepared for inclusion in this text by Patricia Williams and Carl Harris, 1999.

liability insurance. Through the NEA special services, members have access to auto insurance, life insurance, health insurance, travel packages, and discounts on purchases.

In addition to the national organization, NEA consists of 50 state affiliates, a Puerto Rico chapter, and an Overseas Education Association. Along with these groups, there are about 13,250 local associations.

Governance follows democratic principles and consists of a representative assembly, a board of directors and an executive committee. A large representative assembly meets each summer. For example, during the 1999 assembly over 9000 delegates, elected using a ratio of one individual for each 150 members, were present. The Board of Directors consists of 144 members. This body meets five times each year and is concerned primarily with Association policies. The president, vice president, secretary, treasurer, and six members elected from the representative assembly serve on the executive committee and meet 10 times each year.

Two programs of particular interest are the Innovation Center and Uniserv. The National Center for Innovation is a nation-wide network concerned with the restructuring of schools. Its primary purpose is to assist in ensuring that every student in the nation has the knowledge, skills, and self-confidence to compete well in today's world. A significant portion of the NEA's resources are directed to Uniserv which provides local professional staff to assist teachers with NEA's various service programs. Since its inception in 1970, Uniserv has expanded beyond expectation.

For $10 per year, plus state and local dues, elementary and secondary teachers, higher education faculty, educational support personnel, retired educators, and students preparing to become teachers may join the NEA. In doing so they will belong to the world's largest educational organization, one that is both a union and a powerful lobbying agent at both national and state levels. NEA is concerned with the development of the finest educational system possible and with the welfare of the students and educational personnel of this nation.

American Federation of Teachers

The American Federation of Teachers was formed in 1916 when the Chicago Teachers' Federation merged with eight other locals. The renowned American educator, John Dewey, was one of the first members and maintained his interest throughout most of his professional career.

Currently the AFT enrolls about 984,000 members, which makes the National Education Association over two and one-half times larger than the AFT. The American Federation of Teachers, however, is a part of the labor movement in this country and is affiliated with the AFL-CIO, with some 14 million members.

The American Federation of Teachers historically has advocated that unionism and professionalism are compatible, and, indeed, are strongly linked. Albert Shanker, the long-time President, indicates that currently the organization's primary goal is the professionalization of teaching (Ryan, Cooper, 1988). To realize this goal the AFT seeks higher salaries, smaller classes, relief from non-teaching assignments, and the empowerment of teachers. Empowerment would give teachers more control of the workplace and a greater voice in establishing standards for their profession.

Historically the AFT has called for collective bargaining and has used strikes on numerous occasions. The organization believes that collective bargaining and strikes have benefitted the profession in a number of ways, not the least of which is increased salaries. A bargaining unit is a group of employees who have organized and have the right to bargain, through their representatives, with their employer. The landmark collective bargaining contract in education was negotiated in 1962 by the teachers of New York City. Currently over three-fourths of the states have collective bargaining laws that apply to teachers (Rebore, 1991).

Differences between these two groups are depicted in the organizations' literature. The American Federation of Teachers is smaller in numbers than the NEA; from its beginning it has advocated unionism; its major power base is in the large urban areas; its scope of activities is not as large as the NEA; and the AFT is noted for its hard bargaining on basic issues.

Over the years these two major, national unions have had an adversarial relationship, but there have been times when they have talked of a merger. Currently leaders of the organizations are hinting of this possibility (Bradley & Diegmueller, 1990). And indeed, the San Francisco chapters of the NEA and AFT recently merged (Bradley, 1989). Such a merger on the national level would create an organization wielding unprecedented educational and political power.

STATE ORGANIZATIONS

Texas State Teachers Association

The Texas State Teachers Association, with offices located at 316 West 12th Street, Austin, Texas, 78701, is an affiliate of the National Education Association. Currently TSTA has about 95,000 members and 600 chapters across the state.

Any person actively engaged in the profession of teaching or in other educational work and persons interested in advancing the course of public education may become members. Whereas annual dues for teachers, $309, might seem rather steep for beginning teachers, individuals who are undergraduate members receive a discounted rate for their first year. Students preparing to teach may become members through the Texas Student Education Association, with dues of $20 plus the local chapter charge. Also, the Texas Future Teachers of America, a high school organization, is affiliated with both TSTA and NEA.

Texas State Teachers Association works to promote the progress of education in Texas and to obtain for its members the benefits of an independent, united teaching profession. Current issues of primary concern include teacher salaries, statewide health insurance, on-site management, and the equalization of funding.

Members enjoy numerous benefits. The reduced-cost insurance program includes automobiles, health care, dental care, life, and disability options. Other benefits include a journal, newsletters, conferences, workshops, a legal defense fund, travel packages, and discounts on purchases.

TSTA is, then, a large, active organization concerned with the improvement of education in Texas and the well being of students and teachers alike. To this end it maintains close contact with state legislators and the State Board of Education in its efforts to shape the course of education.

Texas Federation of Teachers

The Texas Federation of Teachers is an affiliate of the American Federation of Teachers and the AFL-CIO. Its headquarters are located at 1717 W. Sixth St., Suite 230, Austin, Texas, 78703.

This organization's purpose is to represent educational employees in an effort to bring about improvements in wages, hours, and other conditions of employment. Currently the TFT is concerned with educational reform, especially as it promotes shared decision making and site-based management.

Non-supervisory public school employees and college students preparing to teach are eligible to join the TFT. For example, dues for full-service members in the Dallas ISD are $32.68 per month. Students pay annual dues of $10. In 1999, the organization had some 27,000 members and 40 local chapters in Texas.

Benefits provided include journals, newsletters, conferences, workshops, a legal defense fund, liability and life insurance, travel packages, and discounts on some purchases. In addition, representatives continuously lobby for their membership. For instance, at the local level, TFT works in school board campaigns to elect board members who are union oriented.

As at the national level, the greatest support for the TFT is found in urban settings. As an example, the Houston Federation of Teachers is the majority organization in Houston, Texas. Both local and state affiliates support the AFT's efforts to bring about professionalism and power for teachers.

Association of Texas Professional Educators

The Association of Texas Professional Educators is one of the newest organizations in the state. In 1980 the Association of Texas Educators and the Texas Professional Educators joined together to form ATPE. This association advocates that it is an alternative to the negative influence of the national unions. It has grown rapidly and currently enrolls over 87,000 members. The main office is located at 505 E. Huntland Drive, Suite 280, Austin, Texas 78752.

Association of Texas Professional Educators' purposes are: (a) to further education as a service and as a profession through support of public control of public schools in Texas, (b) to promote activities, services, and training for educators, and (c) to develop and maintain high standards among all educators. Current issues of concern to the organization include equity funding for the public schools, increased funding for student programs and educator benefits, and the preservation of a non-union professional environment in the public school.

An individual actively engaged in, or any individual interested in, the education of Texas youth is eligible for membership. Dues for a professional member, that is, a full-time school employee, are $95 yearly. Student teachers may become members with annual dues of $17, and college students may join for $11 per year.

Members of ATPE receive a professional journal and newsletters and have a variety of workshops and conferences available to them. They may purchase automobile insurance and liability insurance and are entitled to discounts on selected purchases.

In response to a questionnaire an ATPE official commented that "in order for the public schools to be respected and to be a viable institution for learning in the eyes of the public, organizations will have to discontinue the practice of fostering strife and disrespect among educators and focus on teamwork approaches to instruction accountability." The Association of Texas Professional Educators has adopted a strong anti-union stance and claims that the organization's actions are based on a philosophy of cooperation rather than confrontation. The Association of Texas Professional Educators believes that all educators should join in shaping a successful, productive educational community (ATPE, 1990).

Texas Classroom Teachers Association

The Texas Classroom Teachers Association has some 40,000 members and reports that 220 chapters are located across the state. The address of the state office is P.O. Box 1489, Austin, Texas 78767.

The purpose of the TCTA is to promote quality service to both the student and the community by encouraging democratic teacher participation in the formulation of educational policies. These policies should lead to high standards, improvements in teaching conditions, professional growth, high teacher morale, and security within the profession.

Yearly dues vary according to status, i.e., and an optional liability insurance plan is available for an additional $15.

1. **Active: $75**
   Certified classroom teachers, counselors, education diagnosticians, librarians, speech pathologists, social workers, school nurses and other professional nonadministrative personnel
2. **First-Year Texas Teacher: $45**
   Individuals eligible for Active membership who are teaching their first year in Texas
3. **Associate: $40**
   Public school substitute teachers, teachers' aides, education secretaries and paraprofessionals
4. **Student: $15**
   College students seeking certification as teachers in the state of Texas
5. **Retired: $15**
   Retired school employees whose former position qualified them for Active or Associate TCTA membership

Teachers in state-supported higher education institutions are eligible for membership too.

In 1991 issues of primary concern to TCTA included the school finance system, the teacher appraisal system, group health insurance for public school employees, preparation for the Texas Master Teacher Examination, the district-level decision-making process, teacher compensation, and improvement of the career ladder system.

Benefits offered through membership in TCTA include a journal, newsletters, conferences, workshops, a legal defense fund, and discounts on purchases. Also the organization does lobby at sessions of the state legislature and claims to have passed more legislation than any other teachers' association during the Texas 71st Legislative Session.

ADDITIONAL ORGANIZATIONS[1]

Administration/Supervision/ Counseling
American Association of School Administrators

Membership: 16,500 Yearly Dues: $189, Student: $50

Affiliations: National, State

Benefits: journals, newsletter, legal defense fund

Purpose Statement: to improve education through the development of its leaders; to serve the public interest through the availability of high quality education for all; to provide knowledgeable, ethical, and effective administrators to achieve educational excellence

Address: 1801 North Moore Street

Arlington, VA 22209

Association for Supervision and Curriculum Development

Membership: 200,000 Yearly Dues: $65

Undergraduate Students' Yearly Dues: $49

Affiliations: International, National, State, Local

Benefits: journals, newsletters, conferences, discounts on purchases

Purpose Statement: to develop quality education for all students. Current issues of concern are cooperative learning and schools of choice

Address: 1250 N. Pitt Street

Alexandria, VA 22314

Council of Administrators of Special Education

Membership: 5,300 Yearly Dues: $60 + CEC membership

Undergraduate Students' Yearly Dues: $20

Affiliations: International, State

Benefits: journals, newsletters, reduced rates at conferences/workshops, discounts on purchases

Purpose Statement: to provide leadership and support to members by shaping policies and practices which impact the quality of education

---

1.Listed under alphabetized, categorical headings.

Address: 615 16th Street, NW

Albuquerque, NM 87104

National Association of Secondary School Principals

Membership: 46,000 Yearly Dues: $125 Student, $49

Affiliations: International, National, State

Benefits: journals, newsletters, conferences, workshops, legal defense fund, liability, life and health insurance, travel packages

Purpose Statement: to advance the effectiveness of middle level and high school administrators and support their pursuit of quality education for youth; to advocate the continuing improvement of the conditions under which students learn and grow to adulthood

Address: 1904 Association Drive

Reston, VA 22091

National Association of Supervisors of Agricultural Education

Membership: 152 Yearly Dues: $25–$35

Benefits: newsletters, conferences

Purpose Statement: to provide for a better understanding of vocational education in agriculture; to foster fellowship and understanding among members; to serve as a medium to exchange ideas, philosophy, and materials; to help determine program direction, needed research and encouragement of professional advancement of its members; to discuss plans and policies with the U. S. Department of Education staff members; and to promote professional relationships with other agencies, organizations, and institutions concerned with agriculture and agricultural education

Address: P.O. Box 68860

Indianapolis, IN 46268-0889

National Science Supervisors Association

Membership: 1,200 Yearly Dues: $20

Undergraduate Students' Yearly Dues: $20

Affiliations: National, State, Local

Benefits: journals, newsletters, conferences, workshops, travel packages, discounts on purchases

Purpose Statement: to improve science education through supervision. Current issues include humane treatment of animals, sanitary environment, creationism, minorities and women, safety, and leadership skills

Address: P.O. Box AL

Amagansett, NY 11930

Texas Association of Counseling and Development

Membership: 6,000 Yearly Dues: $75

Undergraduate Students' Yearly Dues: $37.50

Affiliations: National, State

Benefits: journals, newsletters

Purpose Statement: to enhance individual human development and to advance the counseling and human development profession. Current issues include those affecting youth, such as child abuse, teen pregnancy, alcohol and drug abuse, school dropouts, and those concerns affecting licensed professional counselors

Address: 316 West 12th Street

Suite 402

Austin, TX 78701

Texas Association for Supervision and Curriculum Development

Membership: 1,485 Yearly Dues: $49 to $65

Undergraduate Students' Yearly Dues: $20

Affiliations: National, State, Local

Benefits: newsletters, monograph, conferences, workshops

Purpose Statement: to promote curriculum study and improvement of instruction; to stimulate growth in the field of education; to establish professional standards for persons in positions of responsibility for supervision and/or curriculum development; to work cooperatively with other organizations seeking to improve education

Address: 1101 Trinity

Austin, TX 78701

Texas Association of School Boards

Membership: over 1,049 school districts Yearly Dues: $500–$10,000

Affiliation: State

Benefits: journals, newsletters, conferences, workshops

Purpose Statement: to provide visionary leadership to Texas school boards and to support, through quality services, their pursuit of educational excellence for each student. Current issues include finance, personnel, and legislative concerns

Address: P.O. Box 400

Austin, TX 78767

Texas Association of Secondary School Principals

Membership: 3,950 Yearly Dues: $93

Affiliations: International, National, State, District

Benefits: journals, newsletters, conferences, workshops, legal defense fund, life insurance

Purpose Statement: to promote secondary education; to provide a clearinghouse for ideas related to secondary education; to sponsor the Texas Association of Student Councils. Current issues include graduation rates, student achievement, and collaborative decision making

Address:1833 South IH 35

Austin, TX 78741

Texas Elementary Principals and Supervisors Association

Membership: 4,250 Yearly Dues: $118

Undergraduate Students' Yearly Dues: $15

Affiliations: National, State

Benefits: journals, newsletters, conferences, workshops, legal defense fund, liability insurance

Purpose Statement: to improve the elementary and middle schools of Texas. Current issues include instructional leadership development, school funding and accountability

Address: 501 East 10th Street

Austin, TX 78701

Business
American Economic Association

Membership: 20,000 Yearly Dues: Depends on Income Level

Undergraduate Students' Yearly Dues: $21

Benefits: journals, life insurance

Purpose Statement: to encourage economic research, especially the historical and statistical study of the actual conditions of industrial life; to encourage the perfect freedom of economic discussion

Address: 2014 Broadway

Suite 305

Nashville, TN 37203

Phi Beta Lambda

Membership: 21,044 Yearly Dues: $23

Undergraduate Students' Yearly Dues: $10

Affiliations: National, State

Benefits: journals, newsletters, conferences, workshops

Purpose Statement: to provide opportunities for post-secondary students to develop vocational competencies for business and office operations and business teacher education; to promote a sense of civic and personal responsibility

Address: P.O. Box 17417-Dulles

Washington, D.C. 20041

Early Childhood
Association for Childhood Education International

Membership: 15,000 Yearly Dues: $45

Undergraduate Students' Yearly Dues: $26

Affiliations: International, National, State, Local

Benefits: journals, newsletters, reduced rates on conferences, workshops, liability, life, and health insurance, travel packages

Purpose Statement: to establish and maintain the highest standards for child growth, development, and learning; to identify and address the current issues and concerns that affect the development of early childhood

Address: 11141 Georgia Avenue

Suite 200

Wheaton, MD 20902

National Association for the Education of Young Children

Membership: 103,000 Yearly Dues: $25

Undergraduate Students' Yearly Dues: $25

Affiliations: International, National, State, Local

Benefits: journals

Purpose Statement: to aid in the professional development of those in the early childhood field; to develop standards of excellence; to promote public support for quality services

Address: 1834 Connecticut Avenue, N.W.

Washington, D.C. 20009

English, Speech, Journalism, Reading

Association for Education in Journalism and Mass Communication

Membership: 3,300 Yearly Dues: $85

Undergraduate Students' Yearly Dues: $40

Affiliations: National

Benefits: journals, newsletters

Purpose Statement: to promote journalism. Current issues include First Amendment issues and diversity

Address: 1621 College Street

Columbia, SC 29308-0251

International Reading Association

Membership: 94,012 Yearly Dues: $30–$105

Undergraduate Students' Yearly Dues: $19–$96

Affiliations: International, State, Local

Benefits: journals, newsletters, discounts on purchases

Purpose Statement: to extend professional knowledge about reading instruction; and to promote literacy programs in all areas of the world represented in the IRA membership. Current issues include legislation affecting reading and literacy programs, assessment relating to reading and literacy, and staff development programs being developed for literacy educators

Address: 800 Barksdale Road
Newark, DE 19714-8139

Modern Language Association

Membership: 32,927 Yearly Dues: Varies by Income

Undergraduate Students' Yearly Dues: $20

Affiliations: National

Benefits: journals, newsletters, reduced rates at conferences, reduced rates for travel packages to conferences, discounts on purchases

Purpose Statement: to assess public schools and higher education institutions; to promote scholarship and criticism in the modern languages and literatures; to study curricular developments in modern languages and literatures

Address: 10 Astor Place

New York, NY 10003

National Council of Teachers of English

Membership: 100,000 Yearly Dues: $30

Undergraduate Students' Yearly Dues: $15

Affiliations: National, State, Local

Benefits: journals, reduced rates at conferences, optional life and health insurance, travel packages, and discounts on purchases

Purpose Statement: to provide professional resources to English/language arts teachers; to improve the quality of teaching at all grade levels. Current issues include censorship, curriculum guidelines, research, a working definition of English language arts, and minority teacher recruitment

Address: 1111 Kenyon Road

Urbana, IL 61801

Speech Communications Association

Membership: 6,200 Yearly Dues: $50–$110

Undergraduate Students' Yearly Dues: $25

Affiliations: National

Benefits: journals, newsletters, placement service

Purpose Statement: to promote study, criticism, research, teaching, and application of the artistic, humanistic, and scientific principles of communication

Address: 5105 Backlick Road, Bldg. E

Annandale, VA 22003

Texas Joint Council of Teachers of English

Membership: 2,892 Yearly Dues: $15

Undergraduate Students' Yearly Dues: $15

Affiliations: National, State, Local

Benefits: journals, newsletters, reduced rates at conferences/workshops

Purpose Statement: to improve the teaching of English. Current issues include the Texas statewide test, the teacher evaluation instrument, and the integrated approach to language arts

Address: 909 Elms Road

Killeen, TX 76542

Fine Arts
The American College of Musicians

Membership: 14,867 Yearly Dues: $22

Undergraduate Students' Yearly Dues: $22

Affiliations: International, National, Local

Benefits: journals, workshops, life and health insurance

Purpose Statement: to provide yearly auditions for piano students worldwide; to give one hundred and fifty scholarships to high school seniors who meet the requirements specified in the Guild syllabus; to help teachers work toward national certification

Address: P.O. Box 1807

Austin, TX 78767

American String Teachers Association

Membership: 9,600 Yearly Dues: $54

Undergraduate Students' Yearly Dues: $20

Affiliations: International, National, State

Benefits: journals, newsletters, conferences, workshops, instrument protection insurance, discounts on purchases

Purpose Statement: to support the teaching and playing of stringed instruments

Address: 1806 Robert Fulton Dr.

Suite 300

Reston, VA 20191

Delta Omicron International Music Fraternity

Membership: 24,000 Yearly Dues: $20

Undergraduate Students' Yearly Dues: $10

Affiliations: International

Purpose Statement: to create and foster fellowship among musicians

Address: 1352 Redwood Court

Columbus, OH 43229

National Art Education Association

Membership: 17,000 Yearly Dues: $60

Undergraduate Students' Yearly Dues: $20

Affiliations: National, Regional, State

Benefits: journals, newsletters, conferences, travel packages

Purpose Statement: to promote art education

Address: 1916 Association Drive

Reston, VA 22091

National Band Association

Membership: 3,000 Yearly Dues: $40

Undergraduate Students' Yearly Dues: $40

Affiliations: International, National

Benefits: journals, newsletters, conferences, workshops, awards

Purpose Statement: to promote the excellence of band performance; to encourage the composition and performance of quality band music; to assist directors at all levels; to enhance the spirit of cooperation

Address: 1916 Association Drive

Reston, VA 20191

Texas Association of Music Schools

Membership: 93 Universities and Colleges

Yearly Dues: Member School Dues

Affiliations: National, State

Purpose Statement: to advance the cause of music in higher education; to improve the quality and program of the music educational system in Texas through the promotion of cooperation and exercise of leadership

Address: College of Music

University of North Texas

P.O. Box 13887

Denton, TX 76203

Texas Music Educators Association

Membership: 10,000 Yearly Dues: $40

Undergraduate Students' Yearly Dues: $10

Affiliations: National, Regional

Purpose Statement: to keep music education in the public schools; to help music teachers to become effective educators. Current issues include keeping the fine arts in the mandated curriculum and gaining public support for fine arts education

Address: 4507 North I-35

Austin, TX 78722

Texas Music Educators Conference

Membership: 750 Yearly Dues: $54

Undergraduate Students' Yearly Dues: $12

Affiliations: International, National, Local

Benefits: journals, newsletters, conferences, workshops, liability and instrument protection insurance, discounts on purchases

Purpose Statement: to promote the advancement of music education in the schools

Address: 213 Sam Bass Road

Weatherford, TX 76087

Foreign Languages
American Association of Teachers of French

Membership: 11,000 Yearly Dues: $45–$67

Undergraduate Students' Yearly Dues: $22

Affiliations: National, State

Benefits: journals, newsletters

Purpose Statement: to serve teachers of French at all levels. Current issues concern teacher proficiency standards, legislation, and technology

Address: 4510 So. Ill. Univ.

Carbondale, IL 82901-4510

American Association of Teachers of Spanish and Portuguese

Membership: 13,000 Yearly Dues: $40

Undergraduate Students' Yearly Dues: $15

Affiliations: National, State, Local

Benefits: journals, newsletters, conferences, workshops, liability, life, and health insurance, travel packages

Purpose Statement: to advance the study of the Hispanic and Luso-Brazilian languages and literatures through the promotion of friendly relations among its members; to publish articles and make presentations about the results of studies of its members

Address: Frasier Hall

Room 8

University of Northern Colorado

Greeley, CO 80639

Geography and History
Association of American Geographers

Membership: 7,000 Yearly Dues: $55–$129

Undergraduate Students' Yearly Dues: $45

Affiliations: International, National, Regional

Benefits: journals, newsletters, reduced rates at conferences, liability, life, and health insurance, discounts on purchases

Purpose Statement: to advance professional studies in geography and to encourage the applications of geographic research in education, government, and business. Current issues include hazards such as acid rain and waste disposal and problems such as world population growth

Address: 1710 16th Street, NW

Washington, D.C. 20009-3198

National Council for Geographic Education

Membership: 2,561 Yearly Dues: $35–$75

Undergraduate Students' Yearly Dues: $20

Affiliations: National

Benefits: journals, newsletters, conferences

Purpose Statement: to encourage the training of teachers in geographic concepts, methods, skills, techniques, practices, and teaching methods; to provide active leadership in formulating education policies; to develop effective geographic education programs; to stimulate the production and use of accurate understandable teaching materials and media; to cooperate with other organizations which share a concern for advancing the understanding of human societies in a spatial and environmental context; to enhance public awareness of and appreciation for geography and geographers

Address: 16A Leonard Hall

Indiana University of Pennsylvania

Indiana, PA 15705

National Council for the Social Studies

Membership: 26,000 Yearly Dues: $50–$79

Undergraduate Students' Yearly Dues: $27

Affiliations: National, State, Local

Benefits: journals, newsletters, reduced rates at conferences, workshops, credit card

Purpose Statement: to provide leadership in the social studies education field; to provide professional development for social studies educators; to strengthen the advancement of social studies education

Address: 3501 Newark Street, NW

Washington, D.C. 20016

Organization of American Historians

Membership: 12,000 Yearly Dues: $30–$90

Undergraduate Students' Yearly Dues: $15

Affiliations: National

Benefits: journals, newsletters, conferences, workshops, liability, life, and health insurance, travel packages

Purpose Statement: to promote the historical study and research in American history. Current issues include history education reform, minority recruitment, and graduate education

Address: 112 North Bryant Street

Bloomington, IN 47408-4199

Honor Societies
Alpha Chi

Membership: 174,817 Yearly Dues: $25 lifetime

Undergraduate Students' Yearly Dues: $25 lifetime

Affiliations: National, Regional, Local

Benefits: journals, newsletters, conferences

Purpose Statement: to honor the top 10 percent of the junior and senior classes

Address: Harding University

Searcy, AR 72143-5590

Association for Library and Information Science Education

Membership: 722 Yearly Dues: $40–$90

Benefits: journals, newsletters, reduced rates at conferences

Purpose Statement: to promote excellence in research, teaching, and service to library and information science education

Address: PO Box 7640

Arlington, VA 22207

Delta Kappa Gamma

Membership: 169,000 Yearly Dues: $35

Affiliations: International, State, Local

Benefits: journals, newsletters, conferences, workshops, life and health insurance, travel packages

Purpose Statement: to unite women educators in a genuine spiritual fellowship; to honor women who have given or who evidence a potential for distinctive service in education; to initiate, endorse, and support desirable legislation; to endow scholarships; to inform the members of current economic, social, political, and educational issues

Address: P.O. Box 1589

Austin, TX

Kappa Delta Pi

Membership: 56,000 Yearly Dues: $26 plus chapter dues

Undergraduate Students' Yearly Dues: $21 plus chapter dues

Affiliations: International, National, Local

Benefits: journals, newsletters

Purpose Statement: to promote excellence in and recognize outstanding contributions to education. Current issues concern certifying teachers through non-traditional means, attracting and retaining superior educators, and restoring prestige to the profession

Address: 1601 West State St.

PO Box 2669

West Lafayette, IN 47996-2669

Kappa Kappa Iota

Membership: 10,164 Yearly Dues: $10

Affiliations: National, State, Local

Benefits: newsletters, conferences, workshops, travel packages

Purpose Statement: to promote good fellowship and fraternal cooperation among teachers; to strive for the elevation and dignity of the teaching profession; to oppose all forces detrimental to the schools of the United States. Current concerns include support for battered adults and the children's foundation

Address: 1875 East 15th Street

Tulsa, OK 74104

Kappa Tau Alpha

Membership: 48,000 Yearly Dues: $10 lifetime

Undergraduate Students' Yearly Dues: $10 lifetime

Affiliations: National, State, Local

Benefits: newsletters

Purpose Statement: to recognize the top 10 percent of journalism/communication students who are seniors or graduate students

Address: Univ. of Missouri School of Journalism

Columbia, MO 65211

Phi Delta Kappa

Membership: 112,000 Yearly Dues: $50 plus chapter dues

Affiliations: International, Local

Benefits: journals, newsletters, conferences, workshops, life insurance, travel packages

Purpose Statement: to promote quality education with emphasis on public education through research, leadership, and service

Address: P.O. Box 789

Bloomington, IN 47402

Pi Lambda Theta

Membership: 12,500 Yearly Dues: $35

Undergraduate Students' Yearly Dues: $25

Affiliations: International, National

Benefits: journals, newsletters, conferences, workshops, liability insurance, discounts on purchases, career network service

Purpose Statement: to promote excellence in education at all levels; to recognize outstanding students and professionals in education

Address: 4101 East 3rd Street

P.O. Box 6626

Bloomington, IN 47407-6626

Library

Quill & Scroll Society

Membership: 13,780 Charters Yearly Dues: Contact School of Journalism, University of Iowa

Affiliations: International, Local

Benefits: magazines

Purpose Statement: to honor high school journalists; to sponsor journalism contests, scholarships, and publications. Current concern is censorship for high school publications

Address: School of Journalism

University of Iowa

Iowa City, IA 52242

Sigma Gamma Epsilon

Membership: 75,000 Yearly Dues: $15

Affiliations: National, State

Benefits: journals, newsletters

Purpose Statement: to promote scholastic and scientific advancement of its members; to extend friendship and offer assistance to colleges, universities, and scientific schools which are devoted to the advancement of the earth sciences

Address: 100 East Boyd

Room N-131

Norman, OK 73019-0628

Sigma Tau Delta

Membership: 135,000 Yearly Dues: $20

Undergraduate Students' Yearly Dues: $20

Affiliations: International, Local

Benefits: journals, newsletters, conferences, workshops

Purpose Statement: to promote excellence in English studies. Current issues concern maintaining high standards and finding ways to reward high academic achievement in English

Address: NIU-English

DeKalb, IL 60115

Sigma Zeta

Membership: 20,000 Yearly Dues: $15

Undergraduate Students' Yearly Dues: $15

Affiliations: National, Local

Benefits: journals, conferences

Purpose Statement: to honor undergraduate students who excel in math and science

Address: Malone College

Canton, OH 44709

National Organizations Not Listed Under Other Headings
National Alliance of Black School Educators

Membership: 5,000 Yearly Dues: $60

Undergraduate Students' Yearly Dues: $20

Affiliations: International, National, State

Benefits: journals, newsletters, conferences, workshops

Purpose Statement: to improve the achievement of African American learners in the public schools

Address: 2816 Georgia Avenue, NW

Washington, D.C. 20001

National Catholic Educational Association

Membership: 20,000 Yearly Dues: $75

Undergraduate Students' Yearly Dues: $75

Affiliations: International, National, State, Local

Benefits: journals, newsletters, conferences, workshops, legal defense fund, liability, auto, life, and health insurance, credit card

Purpose Statement: to proclaim the uniqueness of Catholic education; to serve as a single voice for Catholic educators

Address: 1077 30th Street, NW

#100

Washington, D.C. 20007

National Organization on Legal Problems of Education

Membership: 2,500 Yearly Dues: $75

Undergraduate Students' Yearly Dues: $25

Affiliations: International, National

Benefits: journals, newsletters, conferences, workshops, discounts on purchases

Purpose Statement: to provide a vehicle for the dissemination of unbiased information about current issues in school law

Address: 3601 SW 29th

Suite 223

Topeka, KS 66614

Parent/Teacher/Volunteer Organizations
National Association of Partners in Education

Membership: 7,500 Yearly Dues: $75

Affiliations: National, State

Benefits: newsletters, conferences, workshops, liability insurance, discounts on purchases

Purpose Statement: to promote the concepts of partnerships in education, school volunteerism and citizen-parent participation involvement as quality components of effective educational programs; to advocate to policymakers, educational leaders and the public the benefits provided by educational partnerships

Address: 209 Madison Street

Suite 401

Alexandria, VA 22314

National Parent Teacher Association

Membership: 6.8 million Yearly Dues: Established at the local level

Undergraduate Students' Yearly Dues: Established at the local level

Affiliations: National, State, Local

Benefits: journals, newsletters, conferences, workshops, leadership training

Purpose Statement: to be an advocate for the education, health, and safety needs of children and youth

Address: 700 N. Rush Street

Chicago, IL 60611

Texas Congress of Parents and Teachers

Membership: 815,000 Yearly Dues: $.75

Undergraduate Students' Yearly Dues: $.75

Affiliations: National, Councils, Local

Benefits: journals, newsletters, conferences, workshops, legal defense fund, liability auto, life and health insurance, travel packages

Purpose Statement: to promote the welfare of children and youth in home, school, community, and place of worship; to raise standards of home life; to secure adequate laws for the care and protection of children and youth; to bring into closer relation the home and the school; to develop unified efforts between educators and the general public

Address: 408 W. Eleventh Street

Austin, TX 78701

Physical Education, Health, Dance
The American Alliance of Health, Physical Education, Recreation, and Dance

Membership: 26,000 Yearly Dues: $100–$175

Undergraduate Students' Yearly Dues: $30–$105

Affiliations: International, National, State, Local

Benefits: journals, newsletters, conferences, workshops, liability, life and health insurance, travel packages, discounts on purchases

Purpose Statement: to assist member groups as they seek to initiate, develop, and conduct programs in health, leisure, and movement-related activities for the enrichment of human life

Address: 1900 Association Drive

Reston, VA 22091

American Driver & Traffic Safety Education

Membership: 1,000 Yearly Dues: $50–$150

Undergraduate Students' Yearly Dues: $10

Affiliations: National, Regional, State

Benefits: journals, newsletters, conferences, workshops

Purpose Statement: to promote quality driver education; to train high school driver educators

Address: Highway Safety Center IUP

Indiana, PA 15705

American School Health Association

Membership: 3,000 Yearly Dues: $65

Undergraduate Students' Yearly Dues: $35

Affiliations: National, State

Benefits: journals, newsletters, conferences, workshops, discounts on purchases

Purpose Statement: to protect and improve the well being of children and youth by supporting comprehensive school health programs

Address: 7263 State Route 43

P.O. Box 708

Kent, OH 44240

Association for the Advancement of Health Education

Membership: 10,000 Yearly Dues: $60

Undergraduate Students' Yearly Dues: $22

Affiliations: National, State

Benefits: journals, newsletters, conferences, workshops, life and health insurance

Purpose Statement: to preserve health through education by providing information, resource material, and services

Address: 1900 Association Drive

Reston, VA 22091

Texas Association for Health, Physical Education, Recreation, and Dance

Membership: 5,000 Yearly Dues: $39

Undergraduate Students' Yearly Dues: $18

Affiliations: International, National, State, Local

Benefits: journals, newsletters, conferences, workshops

Purpose Statement: to enhance the quality of programs and instruction in health, physical education, recreation, and dance in our schools. Current issues concern quality daily instruction, manageable class size, and teacher certification

Address: Box 7578

Austin, TX 78713

Texas Driver & Traffic Safety Education Association

Membership: 500 Yearly Dues: $10

Undergraduate Students' Yearly Dues: $5

Affiliations: National, State

Benefits: journals, conferences, workshops

Purpose Statement: to promote quality driver education programs and traffic safety

Address: P.O. Box 213

Austin, TX 78767

Texas Public Health Association

Membership: 1,100 Yearly Dues: $30

Undergraduate Students' Yearly Dues: $15

Affiliations: National, State

Benefits: journals, newsletters, reduced rates at conferences and workshops, dental health insurance, discounts on purchases

Purpose Statement: to promote and protect the health of Texas citizens; to offer continuing education

Address: 3724 Jefferson St. #309

Austin, TX 78731-6222

Texas School Health Association

Membership: 200 Yearly Dues: $15

Undergraduate Students' Yearly Dues: $5

Affiliations: National, State, Local

Benefits: newsletters, conferences, workshops

Purpose Statement: to promote better health for school children; to serve as a forum for current health issues and research

Address: 7954 Glenheath Street

Houston, TX 77061

Research
American Educational Research Association

Membership: 22,000 Yearly Dues: $45

Undergraduate Students' Yearly Dues: $20

Benefits: journals, conferences, workshops, liability and health insurance, travel packages

Purpose Statement: to improve the educational process through scholarly inquiry and dissemination of the results

Address: 1230 17th Street, NW

Washington, D.C. 20036

Science and Mathematics
American Association of Physics Teachers

Membership: 11,000 Yearly Dues: $84–$154

Undergraduate Students' Yearly Dues: $30.50–$57.50

Affiliations: National, Regional

Benefits: journals, reduced rates for conferences, workshops, liability, life, and health insurance, discounts on purchases

Purpose Statement: to advance the teaching of physics and the appreciation of physics in our culture

Address: 1 Physics Ellipse

College Park, MD 20740-3842

Mu Alpha Theta

Membership: 50,000 Yearly Dues: $2 lifetime

Undergraduate Students' Yearly Dues: $2 lifetime

Affiliations: International, State

Benefits: newsletters, conferences

Purpose Statement: to provide public recognition of superior mathematical scholarship, especially for high school and junior college students; to promote various mathematical activities

Address: 601 Elm Avenue

Room 423

Norman, OK 73019

National Association of Geoscience Teachers

Membership: 2,000 Yearly Dues: $35

Undergraduate Students' Yearly Dues: $20

Benefits: journals, conferences

Purpose Statement: to promote excellence in earth science teaching

Address: P.O. Box 5443

Bellingham, WA 98227-5443

National Science Teachers Association

Membership: 53,000 Yearly Dues: $60

Undergraduate Students' Yearly Dues: $30

Affiliations: National, State

Benefits: journals, newsletters, reduced rates for conferences, liability, auto, life, and health insurance, travel packages, discounts on purchases

Purpose Statement: to further science education. Current concerns include science education curriculum reform, science and society, and the federal budget

Address: 1840 Wilson Blvd.

Arlington, VA 22201-3000

School Science and Mathematics Association

Membership: 1,100 Yearly Dues: $35

Undergraduate Students' Yearly Dues: $17.50

Benefits: journals, newsletters, conferences, workshops, discounts on purchases

Purpose Statement: to emphasize the interrelationships between science and mathematics in the curriculum

Address: 400 E. 2nd St.

Bloomsburg, PA 17815

Science Teachers Association of Texas

Membership: 5,000 Yearly Dues: $10

Undergraduate Students' Yearly Dues: $7

Benefits: journals, newsletters, conferences, workshops

Purpose Statement: to serve as a unified voice for science teachers in the state; to keep science teachers and others informed about current trends in science education. Current issues include restructuring of science education, lab requirements, and lab safety

Address: 1502 Lewis Drive

Garland, TX 75041

Texas Section of the Mathematical Association of America

Membership: 1,436 Yearly Dues: Part of National Dues

Undergraduate Students' Yearly Dues: $32

Affiliations: National, State

Benefits: journals, annual meetings, short courses, free renewal membership for students making presentations at annual meetings, discounts on purchases

Purpose Statement: to promote the improvement of mathematical sciences at the collegiate level

Address: HSU Box 1170

2200 Hickory

Hardin Simmons University

Abilene, TX 79698

Special Populations
Association for Compensatory Educators of Texas

Membership: 345 Yearly Dues: $20

Affiliations: National, State, Local

Benefits: newsletters, conferences, workshops

Purpose Statement: to provide updated information on all compensatory programs to supervising administrators

Address: P.O. Box 50033

Austin, TX 78763

The National Association for Gifted Children

Membership: 8,000 Yearly Dues: $50

Undergraduate Students' Yearly Dues: $25

Affiliations: International, National, State

Benefits: journals, newsletters, conferences, travel packages, discounts on purchases

Purpose Statement: to promote an appropriate education for gifted and talented children and youth; to disseminate and encourage research and new information in the area of gifted and talented education

Address: 1707 L St. NW #550

Washington, D.C. 20036

National Association for Visually Handicapped

Membership: 5,000 Yearly Dues: $40

Undergraduate Students' Yearly Dues: $35

Affiliations: International, National, State

Benefits: newsletters

Purpose Statement: to serve the partially seeing with large print loan libraries, informational literature, and newsletters; to make the plight of the partially seeing more understandable to normally sighted people; and to offer current technology to help adults and children who have partial vision

Address: 22 West 21st Street

New York, NY 10010

Texas Association for Bilingual Education

Membership: 1,350 Yearly Dues: $30

Undergraduate Students' Yearly Dues: $20

Affiliations: State, Local

Benefits: newsletters, conferences, workshops

Purpose Statement: to promote the effective implementation of the six components of bilingual/bicultural education in Texas schools; to address legislative issues; to promote consultation with policy making bodies

Address: Laredo State University

1 West End Washington Street

Laredo, TX 78040

Texas Association for Children and Adults with Learning Disabilities

Membership: 1,705 Yearly Dues: $20

Undergraduate Students' Yearly Dues: $20

Affiliations: National, State, Local

Benefits: newsletters, conferences, workshops, information packets, speaker's bureau

Purpose Statement: to advance the education and general welfare of learning disabled individuals. Current issues include funding for special education least restrictive environment, dyslexia law in Texas, attention deficit hyperactivity disorder, and PL 94-142

Address: 1101 West 31st Street

Austin, TX 78705

Texas Federation of the Council for Exceptional Children

Membership: 2,000 Yearly Dues: $60

Undergraduate Students' Yearly Dues: $24.50

Affiliations: National, State, Local

Benefits: journals, newsletters, reduced rates at conferences/workshops, liability, auto, life, and health insurance, travel packages, discounts on purchases

Purpose Statement: to improve the quality of education for all exceptional children, both handicapped and gifted

Address: 825 West 11th Street

Box 76

Austin, TX 78701

University
American Association of University Professors

Membership: 45,000 Yearly Dues: $100–$130

Affiliations: National, State, Local

Benefits: journals, newsletters, conferences, legal defense fund

Purpose Statement: to maintain and advance the standards and ideals of the profession and to ensure academic freedom and shared governance

Address: 1012 14th Street, NW

Suite 500

Washington, D.C. 20005

Association of Teacher Educators

Membership: 3,500 Yearly Dues: $90

Undergraduate Students' Yearly Dues: $25

Affiliations: National, State

Benefits: journals, newsletters, reduced rates for conferences/workshops, liability and life insurance, discounts on purchases

Purpose Statement: to improve teacher education, especially the quality of field experiences for preservice teachers and programs for beginning teachers

Address: 1900 Association Drive

Reston, VA 22091-1599

Texas Association of College Teachers

Membership: 1,200 Yearly Dues: $60

Undergraduate Students' Yearly Dues: $60

Affiliations: State, Local

Benefits: journals, newsletters, conferences, legal defense fund, free consultations about retirement funds

Purpose Statement: to promote faculty ideas and concerns, and to speak before policy-making bodies concerning salaries, benefits, and teaching conditions

Address: 9513 Burnet Rd. #206

Austin, TX 78758-5248

Vocational
American Vocational Association

Membership: 38,000 Yearly Dues: $40

Undergraduate Students' Yearly Dues: $10

Affiliations: National, State

Benefits: journals, newsletters, discount on conferences, workshops, liability, auto, life, health insurance, travel packages, discounts on purchases

Purpose Statement: to maintain leadership in vocational-technical education; to render service to state and local communities in promoting vocational education; to cooperate with other nations in developing vocational education; to encourage the promotion, improvement, and expansion of programs of vocational part-time and adult education

Address: 1410 King Street

Alexandria, VA 22314

Home Economics Education Association

Membership: 3,700 Yearly Dues: $20

Undergraduate Students' Yearly Dues: $10

Affiliations: National, State, Local

Benefits: newsletter, conferences, monograph

Purpose Statement: to promote effective home economics programs and publish materials of interest

Address: 1201 Sixteenth Street, NW

Washington, D.C. 20036

International Technology Education Association

Membership: 40,000 Yearly Dues: $60

Undergraduate Students' Yearly Dues: $30

Affiliations: International, State

Benefits: journals, newsletters, conferences, workshops, liability and life insurance, placement service

Purpose Statement: to represent technology teachers and teacher educators

Address: 1914 Association Drive #201

Reston, VA 22091-1539

National Association for Industry–Education Cooperation

Membership: 1,180 Yearly Dues: $35

Undergraduate Students' Yearly Dues: $35

Affiliations: National

Benefits: newsletters, conferences, workshops, discounts on purchases, award programs

Purpose Statement: to further industry-education joint efforts in school improvement; to prepare for work and human resources/economic development

Address: 235 Hendricks Boulevard

Buffalo, NY 14226

National FFA Organization

Membership: 449,814 Yearly Dues: $5.00

Undergraduate Students' Yearly Dues: $5.00

Affiliations: National, State, Local

Benefits: journals

Purpose Statement: to develop agricultural leadership, cooperation, and citizenship; to learn how to speak in public, conduct meetings, handle financial matters, solve problems, and assume civic responsibility

Address: 5632 Mt. Vernon Memorial Highway

P.O. Box 15160

Alexandria, VA 22309-0160

National Vocational Agricultural Teachers' Association

Membership: 7,250 Yearly Dues: $35

Undergraduate Students' Yearly Dues: $3

Affiliations: National, State

Benefits: newsletters, conferences, workshops

Purpose Statement: to provide professional leadership and service for vocational educators in agriculture

Address: 5632 Mt. Vernon Memorial Highway

P.O. Box 15440

Alexandria, VA 22309

Technology Student Association

Membership: 100,000 Yearly Dues: $5 (elementary and secondary students)

Affiliations: National, Local

Benefits: journals, newsletters, conferences, workshops, liability insurance, travel packages, discounts on purchases

Purpose Statement: to promote leadership and personal growth in a technical world; to enhance student's knowledge and exposure to technology

Address: 1914 Association Drive

Reston, VA 22091

Texas Industrial Vocational Association

Membership: 700 Yearly Dues: $106

Undergraduate Students' Yearly Dues: $9

Affiliations: National, State

Benefits: newsletters, conferences, workshops, liability insurance, accidental death and dismemberment coverage

Purpose Statement: to represent the interests of trade and industrial teachers before decision-making bodies. Current issues concern the

expansion of vocational education courses at grades 9 and 10 and reinstatement of vocational program standards statewide.

Address: 316 W. 12th Street

Suite 319

Austin, TX 78701

REFERENCES

Bradley, A. (1989). "Teachers' Unions in San Francisco Decide to Merge." *Education Week, 18,* October, 1989, 1, 9.

Bradley, A., & Diegmueller, K. (1990). "Glimmers of Unification." *Teacher Magazine, 9:* 18–19.

Burek, D. M. (Ed.). (1991). *Encyclopedia of Associations.* (Vol. 1) (25th ed.). Detroit: Gale Research.

Mauer, Christine and Sheets, Tara. (1999). *Encyclopedia of Associations.* (Vol. I & II) (34th ed.). Detroit: Gale Research.

Rebore, Ronald W. (1991). *Personnel Administration in Education: A Management Approach.* Upper Saddle River, N.J.: Prentice Hall.

Ryan, Kevin and James Cooper. (1988). *Those Who Can, Teach.* 5th ed. Boston: Houghton, Mifflin.

Union of International Associations (Ed.) (1990). *Yearbook of International Organizations.* (Vol. 3) (8th ed.). New York: K. G. Saur Munchen.

U. S. Department of Health, Education, and Welfare. (1978). *Directory of Education Associations.* Washington, D.C.: Government Printing Office.

Write, Rita. (1991). *Texas Trade & Professional Associations.* Bureau of Business Research, The Univ. of TX at Austin.

CHAPTER 35

Learner-Centered Schools

PROFICIENCES FOR TEACHERS

Learner-Centered Knowledge

The teacher possesses and draws on a rich knowledge base of content, pedagogy, and technology to provide relevant and meaningful learning experiences for all students.

The teacher exhibits a strong working knowledge of subject matter and enables students to better understand patterns of thinking specific to a discipline. The teacher stays abreast of current knowledge and practice within the content area, related disciplines, and technology; participates in professional development activities; and collaborates with other professionals. Moreover, the teacher contributes to the knowledge base and understands the pedagogy of the discipline.

As the teacher guides learners to construct knowledge through experiences, they learn about relationships among and within the central themes of various disciplines while also learning how to learn. Recognizing the dynamic nature of knowledge, the teacher selects and organizes topics so students make clear connections between what is taught in the classroom and what they experience outside the classroom. As students probe these relationships, the teacher encourages discussion in which both the teacher's and the students' opinions are valued. To further develop multiple perspectives, the teacher integrates other disciplines, learn-

ers' interests, and technological resources so that learners consider the central themes of the subject matter from as many different cultural and intellectual viewpoints as possible.

Learner-Centered Instruction

To create a learner-centered community, the teacher collaboratively identifies needs; and plans, implements, and assesses instruction using technology and other resources.

The teacher is a leader of a learner-centered community, in which an atmosphere of trust and openness produces a stimulating exchange of ideas and mutual respect. The teacher is a critical thinker and problem solver who plays a variety of roles when teaching. As a coach, the teacher observes, evaluates, and changes directions and strategies whenever necessary. As a facilitator, the teacher helps students link ideas in the content area to familiar ideas, to prior experiences, and to relevant problems. As a manager, the teacher effectively acquires, allocates, and conserves resources. By encouraging self-directed learning and by modeling respectful behavior, the teacher effectively manages the learning environment so that optimal learning occurs.

Assessment is used to guide the learner community. By using assessment as an integral part of instruction, the teacher responds to the needs of all learners. In addition, the teacher guides learners to develop personally meaningful forms of self-assessment.

The teacher selects materials, technology, activities, and space that are developmentally appropriate

Reprinted with permission from Texas Administrative Code, 1995.

and designed to engage interest in learning. As a result, learners work independently and cooperatively in a positive and stimulating learning climate fueled by self-discipline and motivation.

Although the teacher has a vision for the destination of learning, students set individual goals and plan how to reach the destination. As a result, they take responsibility for their own learning, develop a sense of the importance of learning for understanding, and begin to understand themselves as learners. The teacher's plans integrate learning experiences and various forms of assessment that take into consideration the unique characteristics of the learner community. The teacher shares responsibility for the results of this process with all members of the learning community.

Together, learners and teachers take risks in trying out innovative ideas for learning. To facilitate learning, the teacher encourages various types of learners to shape their own learning through active engagement, manipulation, and examination of ideas and materials. Critical thinking, creativity, and problem solving spark further learning. Consequently, there is an appreciation of learning as a lifelong process that builds a greater understanding of the world and a feeling of responsibility toward it.

Equity in Excellence for All Learners

The teacher responds appropriately to diverse groups of learners.

The teacher not only respects and is sensitive to all learners but also encourages the use of all their skills and talents. As the facilitator of learning, the teacher models and encourages appreciation for students' cultural heritage, unique endowments, learning styles, interests, and needs. The teacher also designs learning experiences that show consideration for these student characteristics.

Because the teacher views differences as opportunities for learning, cross-cultural experiences are an integral part of the learner-centered community. In addition, the teacher establishes a relationship between the curriculum and community cultures. While making this connection, the teacher and students explore attitudes that foster unity. As a result, the teacher creates an environment in which learners work cooperatively and purposefully using a variety of resources to understand themselves, their immediate community, and the global society in which they live.

Learner-Centered Communication

While acting as an advocate for all students and the school, the teacher demonstrates effective professional and interpersonal communication skills.

As a leader, the teacher communicates the mission of the school with learners, professionals, families, and community members. With colleagues, the teacher works to create an environment in which taking risks, sharing new ideas, and innovative problem solving are supported and encouraged. With citizens, the teacher works to establish strong and positive ties between the school and the community.

Because the teacher is a compelling communicator, students begin to appreciate the importance of expressing their views clearly. The teacher uses verbal, nonverbal, and media techniques so that students explore ideas collaboratively, pose questions, and support one another in their learning. The teacher and students listen, speak, read, and write in a variety of contexts; give multimedia and artistic presentations; and use technology as a resource for building communication skills. The teacher incorporates techniques of inquiry that enable students to use different levels of thinking.

The teacher also communicates effectively as an advocate for each learner. The teacher is sensitive to concerns that affect learners and takes advantage of community strengths and resources for the learners' welfare.

Learner-Centered Professional Development

The teacher, as a reflective practitioner dedicated to all students' success, demonstrates a commitment to learn, to improve the profession, and to maintain professional ethics and personal integrity.

As a learner, the teacher works within a framework of clearly defined professional goals to plan for and profit from a wide variety of relevant learning opportunities. The teacher develops an identity as a professional, interacts effectively with colleagues, and takes a role in setting standards for teacher accountability. In addition, the teacher uses technological and other resources to facilitate continual professional growth.

To strengthen the effectiveness and quality of teaching, the teacher actively engages in an exchange of ideas with colleagues, observes peers, and encourages feedback from learners to establish a successful learning community. As a member of a collaborative team, the teacher identifies and uses group processes to make decisions and solve problems.

The teacher exhibits the highest standard of professionalism and bases daily decisions on ethical principles. To support the needs of learners, the teacher knows and uses community resources, school services, and laws relating to teacher responsibilities and student rights. Through these activities, the teacher contributes to the improvement of comprehensive educational programs as well as programs within specific disciplines.

PROFICIENCIES FOR ADMINISTRATORS

Learner-Centered Leadership

Through inspiring leadership, the administrator maximizes learning for all students while maintaining professional ethics and personal integrity.

The administrator guides the learning community in the development of a vision that reflects students' needs for academic achievement and success in life and makes that vision tangible for others through positive action. The administrator encourages the collaborative planning, implementation, assessment, and ongoing modification of strategies to achieve this mission. While continually striving to expand the base of support for the learning community, the administrator also creatively allocates resources such as money, time, facilities, technology, and volunteers. In addition, the administrator uses innovative governance structures and methods to further the mission of the learning community.

As a risk-taker, the administrator not only encourages innovation but also expects and handles the ambiguity inherent in the process of school change, including that involved in continual assessment and ongoing improvement. The administrator also consistently examines and questions routine ways of doing things.

To foster a continued commitment to the vision of the learner-centered community, the administrator empowers others not only by delegating authority but also through team building, creative problem solving, and the development of consensus. To support this effort, the administrator involves others in the selection and the delegation of roles of staff members. So that others respond from a sense of mission, the administrator encourages self-management and facilitates the development of leadership among all members of the learning community. The administrator builds relationships within this community and seeks to enlarge it by including parents, businesses, neighborhoods, and other kinds of resources.

The administrator exhibits and encourages the highest standard of professional conduct and bases daily decisions on ethical principles. In addition, the administrator ensures that the Code of Ethics and Standard Practices for Texas Educators is followed and uses an understanding of legal issues to make sound decisions.

Learner-Centered Climate

The administrator establishes a climate of mutual trust and respect which enables all members of the learning community to seek and attain excellence.

In a learner-centered community, an atmosphere of openness and mutual respect fosters optimal academic, social, and personal growth for all community members. Within this open environment, people not only share resources but also a dynamic exchange of ideas. To continually assess and improve this climate, the administrator seeks and uses feedback from the members of the learning community.

While encouraging others to creatively solve problems, the administrator celebrates innovation and accomplishments, acknowledges excellence, and views unsuccessful experiences as opportunities to learn. The administrator models and supports responsible risk-taking so that all community members take chances and try out new ideas. As a result, every person in the learner-centered community teaches, encourages, and learns from others.

The administrator shares responsibility for the well-being of the entire learning community. In addition, the administrator acts appropriately to ensure the safety and welfare of community members while they are in school and also removes barriers that impede success for any person.

Learner-Centered Curriculum and Instruction

The administrator facilitates the implementation of a sound curriculum and appropriate instructional strategies designed to promote optimal learning for all students.

The administrator applies a thorough understanding of human development, learning theories, and educational philosophy to the structure of the curriculum and to the implementation of appropriate learning experiences. The administrator is also aware of influences such as social issues, political forces, and future trends on curriculum and instruction and understands their implications for life-long learning.

The administrator employs collaborative planning processes to facilitate curricular change. While recognizing the interests and needs of learners, members of the learning community select, modify, and design developmentally appropriate curricular materials. The administrator also incorporates technology, practical arts, liberal arts, and co- and extra-curricular activities into the comprehensive curriculum. To create an environment in which students learn how to learn, the administrator encourages all members of the learner community to use critical thinking, creativity, and problem solving as tools that build a greater understanding of the world.

The administrator systematically assesses curriculum and instruction to ensure that both are continually updated and adjusted to achieve optimal student learning. To support members of the learning community, the administrator encourages a variety of learning experiences, facilitates effective use of time and resources to benefit all community members, observes classroom instruction in order to support teacher and student goals, and collaboratively plans for systematic instructional improvement. Additionally, the administrator encourages teachers to integrate assessment and teaching to ensure that relevant learning opportunities are provided for all learners. The administrator engages all members of the community in sharing knowledge about the curriculum and learners to ensure continuity as students progress through the school system.

Learner-Centered Professional Development

The administrator demonstrates a commitment to student learning through a personal growth plan and fosters the professional development of all staff in the learning community.

The administrator actively promotes the growth and wellness of every individual of the learning community. Based on the learning community's vision, the administrator works with the school staff to create a comprehensive plan for professional development and encourages participation in appropriate activities through the allocation of time and other resources. The administrator also schedules time for staff members to reflect, to work together, and to plan for their own professional growth. The administrator uses ongoing assessment to ensure that professional development activities are based on the changing needs of the learning community and that they are effective in promoting student learning.

In the interest of improvement in education, the administrator uses self-assessment to identify areas for professional growth. To enhance teaching and learning, the administrator pursues professional development activities such as attending local, state, and national conferences; staying current with professional literature and research; and visiting other campuses. As a result, the administrator develops an identity as a professional, interacts with other professionals, and develops a personal commitment to growth which is aligned with student, campus, district, and state needs.

Equity in Excellence for All Learners

The administrator promotes equity in excellence for all by acknowledging, respecting, and responding to diversity among students and staff while building on shared values and other similarities that bond all people.

The administrator is committed to a diverse learning community in which all members learn to live and work together while holding high expectations for the pursuit of excellence. The administrator ensures that all members of this learning community have an equitable opportunity to achieve. Recognizing that a diverse population enhances the learning environment, the administrator respects all learners, is sensitive to their needs, and encourages them to use all their skills and talents.

While honoring and appreciating diversity in the learning community, the administrator also emphasizes how similarities foster unity among all people. In addition, the administrator actively seeks to eliminate racism, sexism, and other forms of discrimination in the learning community.

Because the administrator views differences as opportunities for learning, cross-cultural experiences are an integral part of the learner-centered community, and the cultures of school families are affirmed. In addition, the administrator follows changes in demographics to better understand the community and uses this information to make decisions about contemporary conditions. As a result, all members of the learner community develop an appreciation of diversity, an awareness of common needs, and the ability to communicate and work collaboratively toward common ends.

Learner-Centered Communication

The administrator effectively communicates the learning community's vision as well as its policies and successes in interactions with staff, students, parents, community members, and the media.

As an effective communicator, the administrator demonstrates the power of language in self-identity, expression, and influence. The administrator continually practices active listening and encourages honest and open communication. Communicating with empathy to a variety of audiences, the administrator shares decision making, seeks consensus, and resolves conflicts by capitalizing on knowledge of group processes and the differences that occur during any group effort.

In addition, the administrator recognizes that schools are part of the public domain and responds to the public's right to know through a systematic plan for communication developed and implemented by all members of the learning community.

Through effective oral and written presentations, the administrator clearly defines what is expected and hoped for in order to accomplish the school's mission.

As a spokesperson for public education, the administrator uses technology and establishes formal and informal networks to explain and enhance the vision for the school. The administrator accepts responsibility for the flow of communication among various groups that affect and are affected by educational policies and seeks to shape these policies at the local, state, and national levels. The administrator assesses the needs of various groups and the social, political, and economic aspects of the community at large. Recognizing the impact that mass media have in shaping opinions, the administrator proactively influences the media to enhance the learning community's mission.

CHAPTER

36

Explicit Teaching

The terms *explicit teaching* or *direct instruction* are summary terms for recent findings on effective teaching. They refer to a systematic method of teaching with emphasis on proceeding in small steps, checking for student understanding, and achieving active and successful participation by all students.

Although the findings on effective teaching come primarily from reading and mathematics research conducted in urban elementary and junior high schools, the procedures seem relevant to any instruction where the objective is to teach skilled performance or mastery of a body of knowledge. Specifically, they seem applicable to reading, mathematics, foreign language, English grammar, science, and parts of social studies and language arts. These procedures seem less applicable to areas that cannot be broken into smaller parts such as analysis of literature or discussion of social science issues. However, investigators are currently developing explicit procedures to teach implicit skills in reading comprehension (Brown & Palinscar, 1982; Paris, Cross, & Lipson, 1984; Raphael and Pearson, 1985).

Researchers have found that teachers effective in these procedures use most of the following skills:

- Begin a lesson with a short statement of goals.
- Begin with a short review of previous, prerequisite learning.

Reprinted by permission from "Explicit Teaching and Teacher Education," by Barak Rosenshine, *Journal of Teacher Education,* May–June, 1987, pp. 34–36.

- Present new material in small steps, with student practice after each step.
- Give clear and detailed instructions and explanations.
- Provide a high level of active practice for all students.
- Guide students during initial practice.
- Ask a large number of questions, check for student understanding, and obtain responses from all students.
- Provide systematic feedback and corrections.
- Obtain a student success rate of 80 percent or higher during initial practice.
- Provide explicit instruction for seatwork exercises, and, where possible, monitor and help students during seatwork.
- Provide for spaced review and testing.

In explicit teaching, the emphasis is on teaching in small steps, providing for student practice after each step, guiding students during initial practice, and providing all students with a high level of successful practice. All teachers utilize some of these behaviors some of the time, but the most effective teachers use most of them almost all of the time.

THE STEPS IN EXPLICIT TEACHING

Some investigators (Gagne, 1970; Good & Grouws, 1979; Hunter & Russell, 1981) present these findings as a set of teaching steps or functions. The following six functions are one way to summarize the research on explicit teaching or direct instruction.

1. *Review and check previous work.* When teaching skill subjects such as reading, mathematics, foreign language, and grammar, effective teachers begin with correction of the homework and a short review of previous work so that students will be firm in their knowledge and able to apply it to the current lesson. During this time, some teachers review new vocabulary or new skills by asking questions or asking students to solve problems, while other teachers review by giving a short quiz. These activities usually take from two to eight minutes.

Effective teachers also review the prerequisite materials for new learning. They review previous material, for example, before proceeding with science and social studies instruction, or they review the steps in effective writing before the class starts an assignment. Less effective teachers review less often.

2. *Present new material in small steps.* At the start of a presentation of new material, effective teachers focus the learners on what they are to learn and structure the material so that the students can proceed with minimum confusion. The teachers do this by starting with clear objectives, recalling relevant background information, and providing an outline, when relevant. They then teach the new material in small steps. They elaborate the material by providing many examples, providing additional explanations, making the points explicit and vivid, and summarizing one point before proceeding to the next. When teaching the students a skill, the teacher models each step explicitly. Complex material is not introduced before the students have mastered the earlier material.

After each step, the teacher checks for student understanding by asking students to summarize parts of the presentation, to answer specific questions, to repeat directions or procedures, to give new examples, and then by asking other students whether they agree or disagree with the first student's answers. This checking tells the teacher whether there is a need to reteach the material. It is important to check the entire class, or at least the lower achieving students. However, it is inappropriate to ask a few questions, call on volunteers to hear their usually correct answers, and then assume that the other students understand or have learned from hearing the volunteers.

Deciding on the appropriate size of each step is an important area of teacher decision making. Generally, when the material is difficult and the learners are slower, the size of each step is smaller, and the size of each step increases when the material is easier and the learners are quicker.

3. *Guided practice.* After the presentation, or after small steps of the presentation, the teacher leads the students through guided practice on the new material. This guidance helps the students as they begin to integrate the material. For example, if the students are learning to write sentences with colorful adjectives, the guided practice could consist of the class as a group attempting to write a few sentences together.

When teaching skills and content, teachers also use varied techniques to provide for active participation by *all* students. These include having students (a) tell the answer to their neighbor, (b) raise their thumb if they know the answer, (c) raise their thumb if they think the answer was correct, or (d) summarize the content in two or three sentences and share it with their neighbor. The more effective teachers spend about half the class period presenting new material and guiding student practice, whereas the less effective teachers spend less time.

4. *Provide feedback and correctives.* When students make errors during guided practice, effective teachers provide hints, break the questions down, and/or re-explain the steps to be followed. Less effective teachers simply give the answer or call on another student.

5. *Supervise independent practice.* When most of the students can work alone without error, independent practice begins. Independent work is facilitated by sufficient *guided practice.* The purpose of independent practice is to help the students integrate the material and achieve a confident, smooth, fluid performance. Effective teachers circulate during independent practice, or, if they are working with a second group, show students how to get help if they need it. Frequently, independent practice is continued as homework.

6. *Review, weekly and monthly.* Effective teachers have weekly and monthly reviews and testing. The reviews provide the additional, successful practice that the students need to become smooth performers, capable of applying their skills to new areas. Having tests ensures that students will do the reviewing and deep processing.

SOME SUBJECT EXAMPLES

These explicit teaching procedures can best be applied to areas of the curriculum that can be broken down into small steps—this includes mathematical computation, grammar concepts such as subject and predicate, literature concepts such as metaphor and simile, foreign language learning, balancing chemical equations, playing musical instruments, and many procedures in vocational education. These procedures can also be used, with modification, for the teaching of content in social studies and science. In such a case, the presentation of new material is followed by guided practice that contains questions and discussion. These activities help the students encode and elaborate the new material so it can later be used for higher level thinking.

These teaching procedures also can be used to teach some aspects of writing. For example, if a teacher wanted students to write essays using colorful adjectives, she or he could incorporate a good deal of guided practice into the lesson. A lesson could begin with a review of colorful adjectives, and then require students to list more adjectives and check their work (or have students check each other). Then the teacher might present a model paragraph using colorful adjectives and ask students to write single sentences using these adjectives. When all students have demonstrated that they can form these sentences and have been checked for understanding, they would begin independent practice.

Although explicit teaching is most appropriate for teaching a skill, modeling a process, and presenting new content, it is not appropriate for less structured activities such as analyzing literature, discussing social issues, or activities where students are exploring new ideas or defending their views. Even here, however, it would be appropriate to use explicit teaching *before* the less structured activity to ensure that students have mastered the basic material upon which the discussion and inquiry are based.

IMPLICATIONS FOR TEACHER TRAINING

One implication of this research would be to have the education students do extensive reading, conduct discussion, and receive frequent tests in the area of explicit teaching. This is done so that the students can develop a knowledge base, can understand the research behind these ideas, can overlearn the findings, and can develop rich, cognitive networks of the basic concepts. The students will be better able to transfer this material to practice when the material is well-connected and easily accessible. Articles on this topic appear regularly in *Elementary School Journal* and *Educational Leadership.* One of the best summaries of this research is by Brophy and Good (1986), especially the last section (see also Brophy, 1986; Rosenshine & Stevens, 1986). Such knowledge will help provide the intellectual tools teachers need for classroom decision making.

Preservice teachers should also have a great deal of guided practice and independent practice in applying these skills. In such training, they would study and practice how to teach various areas of explicit teaching such as lists (e.g., parts of a castle, parts of a plant, countries of South America), concepts (e.g., parts of speech, and distinguishing fact and opinion), and procedures (e.g., adding decimals, completing and balancing a chemical equation, computing the area of a rectangle). The same procedures of explicit presentation, guided practice, and independent practice would be used to teach these skills to preservice teachers.

Preservice teachers would benefit by seeing models of the skills to be learned. These models might be videotapes, transcripts, or vignettes of effective practice. In these models, different teacher behaviors such as small-step presentation, guided practice, and checking for understanding would be labeled to facilitate student learning. Thus, these models would illustrate the teaching concepts and also provide teachers with models which they could refer to and use in their own teaching.

The next step in training would be to provide the preservice teachers with guided practice as they practice the teaching of lists, concepts, and procedures. This could be done in a microteaching setting. Finally, the preservice teachers would do independent practice by writing lessons and presenting them to students.

This initial learning needs to be followed by extensive practice in each area so that teachers go through the explicit teaching steps automatically. Then they can use more of their processing capacity to monitor individual students and make revisions in the lesson. Finally, in order to facilitate transfer to classrooms, the preservice teachers need to practice on a wide variety of different lessons so that they can develop the rich cognitive networks that will facilitate transfer to the classroom.

In the course of such study of explicit skills, it is likely that some preservice teachers will want to apply some of these ideas to the teaching of implicit skills such as the writing of a term paper or teaching students how to answer higher level questions. They should be allowed to try developing methods for teaching these implicit skills. There has been promising work in teaching reading comprehension, which shows that learners can learn implicit skills through models and guided practice (Brown and Palinscar, 1982; Raphael and Pearson, 1985).

In sum, we have made a great deal of progress by learning how effectively to teach explicit facts, concepts, and procedures to students. Today, we should not only provide preservice and inservice teachers with this information, but should use the same successful procedures to teach them how to apply this knowledge to their classrooms.

REFERENCES

Brophy, J. (1986). Teacher influences on student achievement. *American Psychologist, 41,* 1069–1078.

Brophy, J. E., & Good, T. L. (1986). Teacher behavior and student achievement. In M. C. Wittrock (Ed.), *Handbook of research on teaching* (3rd ed.) (pp. 328–375). New York: Macmillan.

Brown, A. L., & Palinscar, A. S. (1982). Inducing strategic learning from texts by means of informed, self-control training. *Topics in Learning and Learning Disabilities, 2,* 1–17.

Gagne, R. (1970). *The conditions of learning.* New York: Holt, Rinehart, & Winston.

Good, T. L., & Grouws, D. A. (1979). The Missouri mathematics effectiveness project. *Journal of Educational Psychology, 71,* 143–155.

Hunter, M., & Russell, D. (1981). Planning for effective instruction: Lesson design. In *Increasing your teaching effectiveness.* Palo Alto, CA: The Learning Institute.

Paris, S., Cross, D., & Lipson, M. (1984). Informed strategies for learning: A program to improve children's reading awareness and comprehension. *Journal of Educational Psychology, 76,* 1239–1252.

Raphael, T. E., & Pearson, D. P. (1985). Increasing students' awareness of sources of information for answering questions. *American Educational Research Journal, 22,* 217–237.

Rosenshine, B., & Stevens, R. (1986). Teaching functions. In M. C. Wittrock (Ed.), *Handbook of research on teaching* (3rd ed.) (pp. 376–391). New York: Macmillan.

CHAPTER 37

The Lesson Cycle

The scene was the faculty workroom in a large high school in the state of Texas. One of the most respected and effective teachers in the school entered the workroom, dropped an arm load of books and exclaimed, "It just won't work!"

"What won't work?" called out another teacher from across the room.

At this point, the first teacher began to describe her frustration with the Lesson Cycle (Figure 1). She taught a number of honors classes in American History and was having great difficulty incorporating her very successful methodology into the structure directed by the Lesson Cycle as currently practiced in Texas. After surviving her two appraisals, she decided to shelve the Lesson Cycle because she was convinced that her honors students were motivated and were learning by her previous approach.

This teacher felt restricted not only by the Lesson Cycle but also by the appraisal system. This teacher, like those cited by Cuban, reacted negatively to a sequential step approach, feeling ". . . like technicians—low level bureaucrats who need only to push this button or pull that lever. The can-do spirit of such formulas annoys teachers who recognize the complexity of the teaching act."[1] The Texas Teacher Appraisal System, although not structured

around the Lesson Cycle per se, includes criteria and indicators in a sequential step approach which clearly reflects the cycle. It is what Shulman called a "generic checklist used by administrators to rate teachers according to an unchanging scale of uniform behaviors."[2] Thus, in the interest of high appraisals and Career Ladder advancement, Texas teachers follow this prescribed teaching model. Teachers across the nation also share frustration with teaching under such prescribed regimen. Glickman, referring to Boyer in *Report on School Reform: The Teachers Speak*, wrote,

> I [have] read surveys showing that teachers as a group have had it up to their ears with paperwork, lesson alignment, teaching to test objectives, and being monitored and evaluated according to how closely they follow a lockstep sequence of instruction.[3]

He criticized the reforms for adding ". . . fuel to the scientific reductionist view of reform: the need for installing "best practice" in the schools."[4]

As a result of numerous teachers' stories similar to the one described initially and their own frustrations with the Lesson Cycle while teaching at the high school level, the authors of this article decided to take a critical look at the Lesson Cycle and its connection with the Texas Teacher Appraisal System, especially in regard to process and methodology used in the classroom. Instructional Leadership Training sessions presented across the state indicated that the process dictated by the Lesson Cycle and the criteria for teacher appraisal were research

Reprinted with permission from "The Lesson Cycle: A Direct Instruction Teaching Model," by Carolyn Cartwright and Terry L. Simpson. Original version appeared in the *Baylor Educator*, Winter 1989.

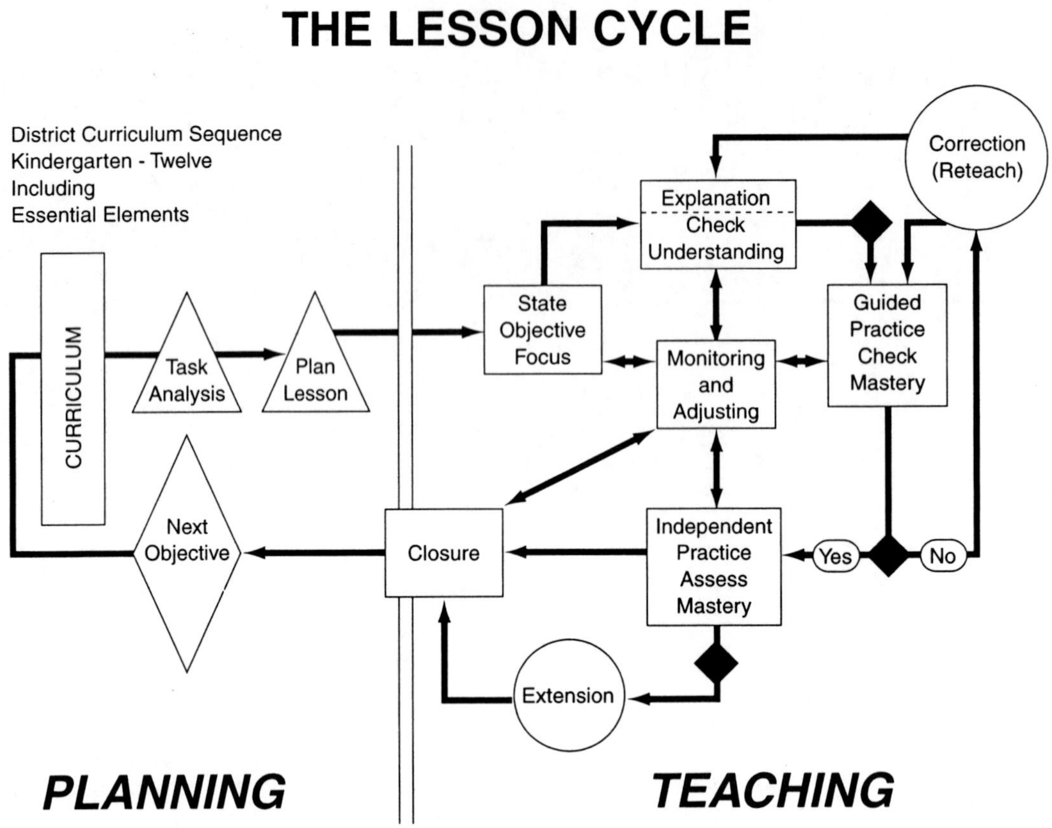

THE LESSON CYCLE

FIGURE 1   Model for Effective Teaching.

based.[5] The question is whether all teachers should be rated according to uniform criteria. Shulman questioned such a procedure: "How could someone go in with a generic rating scale, someone whose own training may be in industrial arts or in history, and make sense of the teaching in a Spanish class, or a trigonometry class, or a poetry class?"[6] After reviewing the research on such directed teaching models, the authors became convinced that the Lesson Cycle process was not always appropriate for certain classes and courses. Their goal was to determine whether or not the process dictated by the Lesson Cycle was curriculum free and appropriate for all classes kindergarten through grade 12.

THE LESSON CYCLE

The development of the Lesson Cycle in Texas and the Texas Teacher Appraisal System was a direct result of the educational reform movement in that state. A part of the initial reform legislation in 1984, the Texas Teacher Appraisal System was introduced and placed additional pressure on teachers to con-

form to the process of the Lesson Cycle. It became necessary to follow that process if the teacher wanted to receive as high a score as possible on the appraisal instrument.

In order to tie the Lesson Cycle to earlier research, it is necessary to describe briefly the teaching process as described in the Lesson Cycle.[7]

Step 1: State Objective and Focus

Teachers are instructed to secure the attention of the students and also verbally state or display in writing the objectives for the class period.

Step 2: Explanation and Check for Understanding

This step encompasses the presentation of the information to the learner. The task of the teacher is to divide the learning into its most basic elements or into its smallest units. After the presentation of each element or unit, the teacher should use various procedures, such as questioning, to check for understanding.

Step 3: Guided Practice of Learning

This step is to determine whether or not the student can demonstrate the learning. As the students practice the learning, they are directly monitored by the teacher. If needed, reteaching occurs. When the teacher determines that the learning is secure, the students proceed to the next step.

Step 4: Independent Practice

This step is practice of the learning that is not directly monitored by the teacher. It is used to reinforce learning and may be classwork/homework or may be for assessment/evaluation.

Step 5: Closure

This step involves bringing the lesson to an appropriate conclusion through a summary of the learning.

RESEARCH ON EFFECTIVE TEACHING PRACTICES

Rosenshine and Stevens, noted researchers on effective teaching practices, noted that, in numerous successful experimental studies, specific teaching functions will result in increased student achievement when teachers are trained in the following functions:

- Begin a lesson with a short review of previous, prerequisite learning.
- Begin a lesson with a short statement of goals.
- Present new material in small steps, with student practice after each step.
- Give clear and detailed instructions and explanations.
- Provide a high level of active practice for all students.
- Ask a large number of questions, check for student understanding, and obtain responses from all students.
- Guide students during initial practice.
- Provide systematic feedback and corrections.
- Provide explicit instruction and practice for seatwork exercises and, where necessary, monitor students during seatwork.[8]

Clearly these functions, as outlined by Rosenshine and Stevens, are very similar to the steps in the Lesson Cycle. The major components in both models include teaching in small steps with student practice after each step, guiding students during initial practice, and providing all students with a large

amount of successful practice. Rosenshine and Stevens were explicit in the importance that they attached to their list of teaching functions by stating, "... the most effective teachers use most of them all the time."[9]

The question as to whether or not the Lesson Cycle was always appropriate to all classes kindergarten through grade 12, however, was still not answered; thus, a survey was made of the research described as "noteworthy" by Rosenshine and Stevens. One of the most extensive studies was completed by the Southwest Educational Development Laboratory in Austin, Texas. Those researchers concluded the following: "... A coherent picture is emerging, a picture of effective teaching in one setting-instruction in basic skills in the primary grades."[10] Out of this study came an instructional model with a set of 22 guidelines for teacher behavior in the classroom. Only six of those guidelines are applicable to direct instruction as outlined in the Lesson Cycle:

- The introduction to the lesson should give an overview of what is to come in order to prepare the students mentally for the presentation.
- It is also at the beginning of the lesson that new words and sounds should be presented to the children so that they can use them later when they are reading or answering questions.
- The teacher should have the children repeat new words or sounds until they are said satisfactorily.
- After moving into the lesson, but before asking the children to use new material or undertake new tasks, the teacher should present a demonstration or an explanation of any new activity.
- At some point during the lesson, the teacher must make a fundamental decision about whether the group as a whole can or cannot meet the objectives of a lesson.
- If the teacher decides that the group as a whole cannot reach the objectives at the same time because of large individual differences in comprehension of the material, she should teach the more able students through to the end of the lesson, dismiss them, and keep in the group those few who need extra help.[11]

It is evident that the six guidelines listed above are quite similar to the components of the Lesson Cycle. Even though the researchers contended that the instructional model was curriculum free and that it did not focus on the content of the materials used in teaching reading but only on teachers' behaviors involved in managing the group as a whole, it must be noted that the subjects of the research were first-grade reading groups.[12] This study had its main application to teaching basic reading skills in the primary grades, the content and level of instruction which lend themselves to a direct instruction model.

A second noteworthy study, entitled Project Follow Through, began in 1967 and employed the University of Oregon's Direct Instructional Model.[13] This model was similar to the previously mentioned models with a few distinctive features. It called for scripted presentation of lessons, for criterion-referenced tests developed to monitor the progress of the children, and for signals and choral response to be used during questioning. Again, the subjects of the study must be emphasized, namely disadvantaged youngsters being taught reading and language in the first three grades. Furthermore, the procedures were said to be essential for compensatory education.[14]

As other noteworthy studies were investigated, the subjects of each study became of primary importance. "Improving Classroom Management and Organization in Junior High Schools: An Experimental Investigation," conducted by the Research and Development Center for Teacher Education and the University of Texas, described a study which involved two urban school districts in two southwestern cities during the 1981–82 school year.[15] "Organizing and Managing the Elementary School Classroom" described a study also conducted by the Research and Development Center for Teacher Education at the University of Texas. The study included 41 teachers in grades one through six in 14 schools.[16] "The Missouri Mathematics Effectiveness Project: An Experimental Study in Fourth-Grade Classrooms," a study that focused entirely on instructional behavior, resulted in a significant difference in student progress in mathematics. The students, however, were fourth graders and most of the teachers and classrooms selected were in low socioeconomic status areas.[17] All of these research projects dealt with teaching basic skills, and a direct instruction model is tailored to that teaching situation.

CONCLUSION

It is clear that the Lesson Cycle as presently used in Texas has evolved from well-documented research the past twenty years. It is also evident that this direct instruction model has resulted in significant learning in the majority of these studies. It is, however, inappropriate to conclude that the Lesson Cycle is curriculum free and applicable for all teaching situations in all classrooms, kindergarten through grade 12. First of all, the overwhelming bulk of this research was conducted in elementary schools

teaching basic reading, math, and language skills. Secondly, even the studies conducted in higher grades were concerned with lower socioeconomic students with an emphasis on basic skills. Therefore, the question is whether the teaching model for junior high basic mathematics class should be the same as the teaching model for an honors class in American Literature. Rosenshine and Stevens noted that these procedures are most applicable for the "well-structured" parts of a content area where the skills to be taught do not follow explicit steps, or areas which lack a general skill that is applied repeatedly. They also concluded the following:

> The results of this research are less relevant for teaching composition, and writing of term papers, analysis of literature, problem solving in specific content areas, discussion of social issues, or the development of unique or creative responses.[18]

This small-step, direct instruction approach, whether it be the Lesson Cycle or some other direct instruction approach, is useful when teaching younger students and basic skills to slower students, but one model is not always applicable for all content, for all teachers, and in all classes.

At issue in Texas, as in other states, is the need for a reconceptualization of teacher education—namely, in methods courses where teaching is addressed as a science. One primary example is the teaching of the Lesson Cycle. As reported by Pinar, all the attempts at formulating a science of teaching have failed and such attempts have resulted in the conversion of teacher evaluation into an assessment by standardized instruments, such as the Texas Teacher Appraisal System and subsequent reliance on the Lesson Cycle for mechanized instruction.[19] Pinar further noted: "Standardized instruments are best avoided, as they force a mechanization of teaching."[20] The authors concur and also agree with Pinar's contention that "(p)seudoscientific, 'practice-oriented' teacher preparation emphasizes a narrow vocationalism over the cultivation of professional judgement." In Texas the result has been the "deskilling" and "disempowering" of teachers and the subsequent decline in education in this state. Reforms which were implemented to improve instruction have, in fact, limited those Texas teachers who aspire to teach higher level skills in their classrooms.

Although at present the Texas Teacher Appraisal System relies heavily on this direct instruction model, progress is occurring. In Instructional Leadership Training (the first part of Texas Teacher Appraisal Training), the addition of a Model Component by several trainers is significant. As more research on different models of instruction becomes available, the present emphasis on a direct instruction model (the Lesson Cycle in Texas) will expand to include other models and the subsequent application of TTAS to those models.

Extensive coverage of models of instruction is provided by Gunter, Estes, and Schwab. Specific models discussed are the following:

- Concept Attainment Model
- Concept Development Model
- The Synectics Model
- The Suchman Inquiry Model
- The Classroom Discussion Model
- Cooperative Learning Models
- Exploration of Feelings and Resolution of Conflict Model (an affective model)[21]

Expanding the knowledge and expertise of both teachers and appraisers to include all models of instruction and the subsequent adaptation of such models to the Texas Teacher Appraisal System would seem advisable and inevitable. Then, teachers' frustrations with a model that "won't always work" could be alleviated, and master teachers would no longer, behind closed doors, feel out-of-step as they continue to teach with variety and creativity that have been the keys to effective teaching for centuries. In fact, all teachers would have some extremely effective models to utilize in varying content and level of challenge to meet the needs of an increasingly diverse population of learners.

NOTES

1. Larry Cuban, "Persistent Instruction: Another Look at Constancy in the Classroom," *Phi Delta Kappan* (September 1986): 10.
2. Lee Shulman, "Challenge," *ASCD Update* (May 1988): 1.
3. Carl D. Glickman, "Has Sam and Samantha's Time Come at Last?" *Educational Leadership* (May 1989): 5.
4. Glickman, 5.
5. John A. Crain et al., *Effective Teaching and Supervision Institute* (Richardson: Education Service Center, Region 10, 1986).
6. Shulman, 1.
7. Crain.
8. Barak Rosenshine and Robert Stevens, "Teaching Functions," *Handbook of Research on Teaching*, ed. Merlin C. Wittrock (New York: Macmillan Publishing Company, 1986), 375–380.
9. Rosenshine and Stevens, 377.
10. L. M. Anderson, C. M. Evertson, and J. E. Brophy, "An Experimental Study of Effective Teaching in First Grade Reading Groups," *The Elementary School Journal* 79 (1979): 194.
11. Anderson et al., 198.
12. Anderson et al.
13. Wesley C. Becker, "Teaching Reading and Language to the Disadvantaged—What We Have Learned From Field Research," *Harvard Educational Review* 7 (1977): 518–543.
14. Becker.
15. E. T. Emmer et al., "Improving Classroom Management: An Experimental Study in Junior High Classrooms," (Austin: Research and Development Center for Teacher Education, 1986).
16. C. Evertson et al., "Organizing and Managing the Elementary School Classroom," (Austin: Research and Development Center for Teacher Education, 1981).
17. Thomas L. Good and Douglas A. Grous, "The Missouri Mathematics Effectiveness Project," *Journal of Educational Psychology* 71 (1979): 355–362.
18. Rosenshine and Stevens, 377.
19. William F. Pinar, "A Reconceptualization of Teacher Education," *Journal of Teacher Education* (January–February 1989): 9–12.
20. Pinar, 11.
21. M. A. Gunter, Thomas H. Estes, and Jan Hasbrouch Schwab, *Instruction: A Model Approach* (Boston: Allyn & Bacon, 1990).

CHAPTER

38

Professional Development Appraisal System

TEXAS ADMINISTRATIVE CODE

Chapter 150. Commissioner's Rules Concerning Educator Appraisal

Subchapter AA. Teacher Appraisal

§150.1001. General Provisions.

(a) Beginning with the 1997-1998 school year, all school districts have two choices in selecting a method to appraise teachers: a teacher-appraisal system recommended by the Texas commissioner of education or a local teacher-appraisal system.

(b) The commissioner's recommended teacher-appraisal system, the Professional Development and Appraisal System (PDAS), was developed in accordance with Texas Education Code (TEC), §21.351.

(c) The superintendent of each school district, with the approval of the school district board of trustees, may select the PDAS. Each school district or campus wanting to select or develop an alternative teacher-appraisal system must follow TEC, §21.352.

§150.1002. Assessment of Teacher Performance.

(a) The teacher proficiencies described in *Learner-Centered Schools for Texas: A Vision of Texas Educators*, approved by the State

Board of Education on February 11, 1994, shall be the foundation for the Professional Development and Appraisal System (PDAS).

(b) Each teacher shall be appraised on the following domains:

(1) Domain I: Active, successful student participation in the learning process;

(2) Domain II: Learner-centered instruction;

(3) Domain III: Evaluation and feedback on student progress;

(4) Domain IV: Management of student discipline, instructional strategies, time and materials;

(5) Domain V: Professional communication;

(6) Domain VI: Professional development;

(7) Domain VII: Compliance with policies, operating procedures and requirements; and

(8) Domain VIII: Improvement of academic performance of all students on the campus (based on indicators included in the Academic Excellence Indicator System (AEIS)).

(c) Each domain shall be scored independently. The evaluation of each of the domains shall consider all data generated in the appraisal process. The data for the appraisal of each

Reprinted with permission from Texas Administrative Code, 1999.

domain shall be gathered from observations, the Teacher Self-Report Form, and other documented sources. The data shall describe teacher contributions in increasing student achievement, making the whole school safe and orderly, and creating a stimulating learning environment for children.

(d) Each teacher shall be evaluated on Domains I through VIII using the following categories:

(1) exceeds expectations;

(2) proficient;

(3) below expectations, and

(4) unsatisfactory.

(e) The teacher evaluation in Domain VIII shall include the following areas:

(1) efforts to enhance academic performance;

(2) efforts to enhance student attendance;

(3) efforts to identify and assist students in at-risk situations; and

(4) campus performance rating.

(f) Campus performance rating data for Domain VIII shall be reported (not scored) by a campus or district for the first year of the PDAS implementation and/or during the first year for new teachers to a campus.

§150.1003. Appraisals, Data Sources, and Conferences.

(a) Each teacher must be appraised each school year. Whenever possible, an appraisal shall be based on the teacher's performance in fields and teaching assignments for which he or she is certified.

(b) The annual teacher appraisal shall include:

(1) at least one classroom observation of a minimum of 45 minutes as identified in subsection (g) of this section, with additional walk-throughs and observations conducted at the discretion of the appraiser;

(2) a written summary of each observation, which shall be given to teachers within 10 working days after the completion of an observation, with a pre- and post-observation conference conducted at the request of the teacher or appraiser;

(3) completion of Section I of the Teacher Self-Report Form that shall be presented to the principal within the first three weeks after the Professional Develop-

ment and Appraisal System (PDAS) orientation;

(4) revision of Section I (if necessary) and completion of Sections II and III of the Teacher Self-Report Form that shall be presented to the principal at least two weeks prior to the annual summative conference;

(5) cumulative data of written documentation collected regarding job-related teacher performance, in addition to formal classroom observations;

(6) a written summative annual appraisal report; and

(7) a summative annual conference.

(c) A teacher may be given advance notice of the date or time of an appraisal, but advance notice is not required.

(d) Each school district shall establish a calendar for the appraisal of teachers. The appraisal period for each teacher must include all of the days of a teacher's contract. Observations during the appraisal period must be conducted during the required days of instruction for students during one school year. The appraisal period:

(1) shall exclude the first two weeks of instruction;

(2) shall prohibit observations on the last day of instruction before any official school holiday or on any other day deemed inappropriate by the school district board of trustees; and

(3) shall indicate a period for summative annual conferences which ends no later than 15 working days before the last day of instruction for students.

(e) During the appraisal period, the appraiser shall evaluate and document teacher performance specifically related to the domain criteria as identified in §150.1002(b) of this title (relating to Assessment of Teacher Performance).

(f) The appraiser is responsible for documentation of the cumulative data identified in subsection (b) (5) of this section. Any third-party information from a source other than the teacher's supervisor that the appraiser wishes to include as cumulative data shall be verified and documented by the appraiser. Any documentation that will influence the teacher's summative annual appraisal report must be shared in writing with the teacher within ten working days of the appraiser's knowledge of the occurrence. The principal shall also be notified in writing when the appraiser is not the teacher's principal.

(g) By mutual consent of the teacher and the appraiser, the required minimum of 45 minutes of observation may be conducted in shorter time segments. The time segments must aggregate to at least 45 minutes.

(h) A written annual summative report shall be shared with the teacher no later than five working days before the summative conference and no later than 15 working days before the last day of instruction for students. The written annual summative report shall be placed in the teacher's personnel file by the end of the appraisal period.

(i) Unless waived in writing by the teacher, a summative conference shall be held within a time frame specified on the school district calendar and no later than 15 working days before the last day of instruction for students. The summative conference shall focus on the written summative report and related data sources.

(j) In cases where the appraiser is not an administrator on the teacher's campus, either the principal, assistant principal, or another supervisory staff member designated as an administrator on the campus will participate in the summative annual conference.

(k) Any documentation collected after the summative conference but before the end of the contract term during one school year may be considered as part of the appraisal of a teacher. If the documentation affects the teacher's evaluation in any domain, another summative report shall be developed and another summative conference shall be held to inform the teacher of the change(s).

§150.1004. Teacher in Need of Assistance.

(a) A teacher whose performance meets any of the following circumstances will be designated as a "teacher in need of assistance":

(1) a teacher who is evaluated as unsatisfactory in one or more domains; or

(2) a teacher who is evaluated as below expectations in two or more domains.

(b) When a teacher is designated as a teacher in need of assistance, the appraiser and/or the teacher's supervisor shall, in consultation

with the teacher, develop an intervention plan that includes the following:

(1) domain(s) that designate a teacher as a teacher in need of assistance;

(2) directives or recommendations for professional improvement activities;

(3) evidence that is used to determine successful completion of professional improvement activities;

(4) directives for changes in teacher behavior;

(5) evidence that is used to determine if teacher behavior has changed; and

(6) specific time line for successful completion.

(c) In cases when the teacher's appraiser is not the teacher's principal, the principal shall be involved in the development and evaluation of the intervention plan.

(d) A teacher who has not met all requirements of the intervention plan for teachers in need of assistance by the time specified may be considered for separation from the assignment, campus, and/or district.

(e) The intervention plan shall include options for professional development activities designed to enhance teacher proficiency. At least one option shall not place significant financial burden on either the teacher or the school district.

(f) An intervention plan may be developed at any time at the discretion of the appraiser when the appraiser has documentation that would potentially produce an evaluation rating of "below expectations" or "unsatisfactory."

§150.1005. Teacher Response and Appeals.

(a) A teacher may submit a written response or rebuttal at the following times:

(1) after receiving a written observation summary; or any other written documentation associated with the teacher's appraisal; and/or

(2) after receiving a written annual summative report.

(b) Any written response or rebuttal must be submitted within 10 working days of receiving a written observation summary, a written annual summative report, or any other written documentation associated with the teacher's appraisal. At the discretion of the appraiser, the time period may be extended to 15 working days.

(c) A teacher may request a second appraisal by another appraiser at the following times:

(1) after receiving a written observation summary with which the teacher disagrees; and/or

(2) after receiving a written annual summative report with which the teacher disagrees.

(d) The second appraisal must be requested within 10 working days of receiving a written observation summary or a written annual summative report. At the discretion of the appraiser, the time period may be extended to 15 working days.

(e) A teacher may be given advance notice of the date or time of a second appraisal, but advance notice is not required.

(f) The second appraiser shall appraise the teacher in all domains. The second appraiser shall make observations and walk-throughs as necessary to evaluate Domains I through V. The second appraiser shall use the Teacher Self-Report Form and cumulative data from the first appraisal to evaluate Domains VI through VIII. Cumulative data may also be used by the second appraiser to evaluate other domains.

(g) Each school district shall adopt written procedures for a teacher to present grievances and receive written comments in response to the written annual report. Each district shall also adopt written procedures for determining the selection of second appraisers. These procedures shall be disseminated to each teacher at the time of employment and updated annually or as needed.

§150.1006. Appraiser Qualifications.

(a) The teacher-appraisal process requires at least one appraiser.

(b) The teacher's supervisor shall conduct the teacher's appraisal and must hold a superintendent, mid-management (principal), or supervisor certification, or must hold comparable certificates established by the State Board for Educator Certification. An appraiser other than the teacher's supervisor must be approved by the school district board of trustees, hold a valid teaching certificate, and have at least three years of prekindergarten, elementary, or secondary teaching experience.

(c) An appraiser who is a classroom teacher may not appraise the performance of another classroom teacher who teaches at the same school campus at which the appraiser teaches, unless it is impractical because of the number of campuses or unless the appraiser is the chair of a department or grade-level whose job description includes classroom observation responsibilities.

(d) Before conducting an appraisal, an appraiser must be certified by having satisfactorily completed uniform appraiser training, including required Instructional Leadership Training (ILT), with a trainer and curriculum approved by the commissioner of education. Periodic recertification and training shall be required.

(1) Educators certified as appraisers for the Texas Teacher Appraisal System (TTAS) before January 1997, shall be required to take only the Professional Development and Appraisal System (PDAS) training to qualify as a certified appraiser for the new system.

(2) Educators seeking certification as an appraiser for the PDAS after January 1, 1997, holding no prior TTAS certification, shall be required to complete the ILT and the PDAS training.

§150.1007. Teacher Orientation.

(a) A school district shall ensure that all teachers are provided with an orientation of the Professional Development and Appraisal System (PDAS) no later than the final day of the first three weeks of school and at least three weeks before the first observation.

(1) Additional orientations shall be provided any time substantial changes occur in the PDAS.

(2) A teacher new to the district shall be provided with an orientation of the PDAS at least three weeks before the teacher's first observation.

(b) Teachers' orientation shall include materials approved by the commissioner of education. These materials shall include all state and local appraisal policies, the local appraisal calendar, and information on the requirements for the completion of the Teacher Self-Report Form. In addition to the orientation, campuses may hold other sessions sufficient in length allowing teachers to actively participate in a discussion of the PDAS specifics and to have their questions answered.

§150.1008. Training of Teacher Participants.

(a) In the initial year of adoption and implementation of the Professional Development and Appraisal System (PDAS), selected teachers from each campus shall be given the opportunity to participate in the appraisal training for purposes of disseminating information to colleagues on their campus and assisting, at the discretion of the principal, in the orientation of all campus teachers. These teachers shall be designated as appraisal-orientation facilitators.

   (1) Each campus shall offer the opportunity to participate in appraisal training to a number of teachers equal to the number of campus administrators; however, each campus shall have at least one teacher participant.

   (2) The principal shall select representative teachers from nominations submitted by the site-based decision making (SBDM) committee created in accordance with Texas Education Code (TEC), §11.251. The principal may select representatives other than those nominated by the SBDM committee when nominated teachers are unable to attend appraisal training.

   (3) Each school district shall pay the training fees for its teachers attending the PDAS appraisal training.

(b) School districts and regional education service centers shall make available additional training for teachers as part of the district's and education service center's menu of professional development opportunities. All teachers are eligible to participate in appraisal and/or Instructional Leadership Training (ILT) at their own expense. Executive directors of regional education service centers may prescribe appropriate registration fees to offset the cost of providing these services.

§150.1009. Alternatives to the Commissioner's Recommended Appraisal System.

(a) District option. Beginning with the 1997-1998 school year, a school district not wanting to use the commissioner's recom-

mended Professional Development and Appraisal System (PDAS) must develop its own teacher-appraisal system supported by locally adopted policy and procedures and by the processes outlined in Texas Education Code (TEC), §21.352. The Texas Teacher Appraisal System (TTAS) is no longer a state-recommended system; however, it may become a local option governed by the process outlined in TEC, §21.352. If adopted as a local option, the TTAS must be modified to comply with TEC, §21.351(a)(1) and (2).

   (1) The school district-level planning and decision-making committee shall:

      (A) develop an appraisal process;

      (B) develop evaluation criteria, including discipline management and performance of the teachers' students; and

      (C) consult with the campus planning and decision-making committee on each campus in the school district.

   (2) The appraisal process shall include:

      (A) at least one appraisal each year;

      (B) a conference between the teacher and the appraiser that is diagnostic and prescriptive with regard to remediation needed in overall performance by category; and

      (C) criteria based on observable, job-related behavior, including:

         (i) teachers' implementation of discipline management procedures; and

         (ii) performance of the teachers' students.

   (3) The school district-level planning and decision-making committee shall submit the appraisal process and criteria to the superintendent, who shall submit the appraisal process and criteria to the school district board of trustees with a recommendation to accept or reject. The school district board of trustees may accept or reject an appraisal process and performance criteria, with comments, but may not modify the process or criteria.

(b) Campus option. A campus within a school district may choose to develop a local system as provided in this section.

(1) The campus planning and decision-making committee shall:

  (A) develop an appraisal process;

  (B) develop evaluation criteria, including discipline management and performance of the teachers' students; and

  (C) submit the process and criteria to the district-level planning and decision-making committee.

(2) The appraisal process shall include:

  (A) at least one appraisal each year;

  (B) a conference between the teacher and the appraiser that is diagnostic and prescriptive with regard to remediation needed in overall performance by category; and

  (C) criteria based on observable, job-related behavior, including:

    (i) teachers' implementation of discipline management procedures; and

    (ii) performance of the teachers' students.

(3) Upon submission of the appraisal process and criteria to the school district-level planning and decision-making committee, the committee shall make a recommendation to accept or reject the appraisal process and criteria and transmit that recommendation to the superintendent.

(4) The superintendent shall submit the recommended campus appraisal process and criteria, the school district-level planning and decision-making committee's recommendation, and the superintendent's recommendation to the school district board of trustees. The school district board of trustees may accept or reject, with comments, an appraisal process and performance criteria, but may not modify the process or criteria.

§150.1010. District Notification to Regional Education Service Center.

For purposes of providing training and support, the superintendent shall notify the executive director of the regional education service center of the district's choice of appraisal system(s) by a time designated by the commissioner of education.

RELATED STATUTORY CITATIONS IN THE TEXAS EDUCATION CODE

The following statutory citations in the Texas Education Code relate to the new 19 TAC, Chapter 150, Subchapter AA, Teacher Appraisal

Chapter 21. Educators

Subchapter H. Appraisals and Incentives
§21.351. Recommended Appraisal Process and Performance Criteria.

(a) The commissioner shall adopt a recommended appraisal process and criteria on which to appraise the performance of teachers. The criteria must be based on observable, job-related behavior, including:

  (1) teachers' implementation of discipline management procedures, and

  (2) the performance of teachers' students

(b) The commissioner shall solicit and consider the advice of teachers in developing the recommended appraisal process and performance criteria.

(c) Under the recommended appraisal process, an appraiser must be the teacher's supervisor or a person approved by the board of trustees. An appraiser who is a classroom teacher may not appraise the performance of another classroom teacher who teaches at the same school campus at which the appraiser teaches, unless it is impractical because of the number of campuses or unless the appraiser is the chair of a department or grade level whose job description includes classroom observation responsibilities.

(d) Under the recommended appraisal process, appraisal for teachers must be detailed by category of professional skill and characteristic and must provide for separate ratings for each category. The appraisal process shall guarantee a conference between the teacher and the appraiser. The conference shall be diagnostic and prescriptive with regard to remediation needed in overall performance and by category.

§21.352. Local Role.

(a) In appraising teachers, each school district shall use:

  (1) the appraisal process and performance criteria developed by the commissioner, or

(2) an appraisal process and performance criteria:

    (A) developed by the district- and campus-level committees established under Section 11.251

    (B) containing the items described by Sections 21.351(a)(1) and (2), and

    (C) adopted by the board of trustees

(b) The board of trustees may reject an appraisal process and performance criteria developed by the district- and campus-level committees but may not modify the process or criteria.

(c) Appraisal must be done at least once during each school year. The district shall maintain a written copy of the evaluation of each teacher's performance in the teacher's personnel file. Each teacher is entitled to receive a written copy of the evaluation on its completion. After receiving a written copy of the evaluation, a teacher is entitled to a second appraisal by a different appraiser or to submit a written rebuttal to the evaluation to be attached to the evaluation in the teacher's personnel file. The evaluation and any rebuttal may be given to another school district at which the teacher has applied for employment at the request of that district.

(d) A teacher may be given advance notice of the date or time of an appraisal, but advance notice is not required.

§21.451. Statutes Regarding Professional Development.

(a) The staff development provided by a school district must be conducted in accordance with minimum standards developed by the commissioner for program planning, preparation, and improvement. The staff development:

    (1) must include technology training and training in conflict resolution and discipline strategies; and

    (2) may include instruction as to what is permissible under law, including opinions of the United States Supreme Court, in regard to prayers in public school.

(b) The staff development must be predominantly campus-based, related to achieving campus performance objectives established under Section 11.253, and developed and approved by the campus-level committee established under Section 11.251. Campus staff development may include activities that enable the campus staff to plan together to enhance existing skills, to share effective strategies, to reflect on curricular and instructional issues, to analyze student achievement results, to reflect on means of increasing student achievement, to study research, to practice new methods, to identify students' strengths and needs, to develop meaningful programs for students, to appropriately implement site-based decision-making, and to conduct action research. The campus staff development activities may be conducted using study teams, individual research, peer coaching, workshops, seminars, conferences, or other reasonable methods that have the potential to improve student achievement.

(c) A school district may use district-wide staff development developed and approved through the district-level decision process under Section 11.251.

PROFESSIONAL DEVELOPMENT AND APPRAISAL SYSTEM

APPRAISAL FRAMEWORK

Domain I: Active, Successful Student Participation in the Learning Process

Evaluation Dimensions:
a. Quantity and quality of active student participation in the learning process is evident.
b. Students are challenged by instruction and make connections to work and life applications, both within the discipline and with other disciplines.

Evaluation Criteria

Exceeds Expectations **ALMOST ALL OF THE**	*Proficient* **MOST OF THE**	*Below Expectations* **SOME OF THE**	*Unsatisfactory* **LESS THAN HALF OF THE**
1. Students are actively engaged in learning.	1. Students are actively engaged in learning.	1. Students are actively engaged in learning.	1. Students are actively engaged in learning.
2. Students are successful in learning.	2. Students are successful in learning.	2. Students are successful in learning.	2. Students are successful in learning.
3. Student behaviors indicate learning is at a high cognitive level (e.g., critical thinking, creative thinking, problem solving, etc.).	3. Student behaviors indicate learning is at a high cognitive level (e.g., critical thinking, creative thinking, problem solving, etc.).	3. Student behaviors indicate learning is at a high cognitive level (e.g., critical thinking, creative thinking, problem solving, etc.).	3. Student behaviors indicate learning is at a high cognitive level (e.g., critical thinking, creative thinking, problem solving, etc.).
4. Students are self-directed/self-initiated as appropriate to the lesson objectives.	4. Students are self-directed/self-initiated as appropriate to the lesson objectives.	4. Students are self-directed/self-initiated as appropriate to the lesson objectives.	4. Students are self-directed/self-initiated as appropriate to the lesson objectives.
5. Students are connecting learning to work and life applications, both within the discipline and with other disciplines.	5. Students are connecting learning to work and life applications, both within the discipline and with other disciplines.	5. Students are connecting learning to work and life applications, both within the discipline and with other disciplines.	5. Students are connecting learning to work and life applications, both within the discipline and with other disciplines.

Domain II: Learner-Centered Instruction

Evaluation Dimensions:

a. The instructional content is based on appropriate goals and objectives.
b. The instructional content includes basic knowledge and skills, as well as central themes and concepts, both within the discipline and with other disciplines.
c. The instructional strategies are aligned with learning objectives and activities, student needs, and work and life applications, both within the discipline and with other disciplines.
d. The instructional strategies promote application of learning through critical thinking and problem solving.
e. The teacher uses appropriate motivational and instructional strategies which successfully and actively engage students in the learning process.

Evaluation Criteria

Exceeds Expectations **ALMOST ALL OF THE TIME**	*Proficient* **MOST OF THE TIME**	*Below Expectations* **SOME OF THE TIME**	*Unsatisfactory* **LESS THAN HALF OF THE TIME**
1. Objectives and goals include basic knowledge/skills and central themes/concepts of the discipline.	1. Objectives and goals include basic knowledge/skills and central themes/concepts of the discipline.	1. Objectives and goals include basic knowledge/skills and central themes/concepts of the discipline.	1. Objectives and goals include basic knowledge/skills and central themes/concepts of the discipline.
2. Instructional content is learner-centered (e.g., relates to the interests and varied characteristics of students).	2. Instructional content is learner-centered (e.g., relates to the interests and varied characteristics of students).	2. Instructional content is learner-centered (e.g., relates to the interests and varied characteristics of students).	2. Instructional content is learner-centered (e.g., relates to the interests and varied characteristics of students).
3. Instructional strategies promote critical thinking and problem solving.	3. Instructional strategies promote critical thinking and problem solving.	3. Instructional strategies promote critical thinking and problem solving.	3. Instructional strategies promote critical thinking and problem solving.
4. Instructional strategies include motivational techniques to successfully and actively engage students in the learning process.	4. Instructional strategies include motivational techniques to successfully and actively engage students in the learning process.	4. Instructional strategies include motivational techniques to successfully and actively engage students in the learning process.	4. Instructional strategies include motivational techniques to successfully and actively engage students in the learning process.
5. Instructional strategies are aligned with the objectives, activities, student characteristics, prior learning, and work and life applications, both within the discipline and with other disciplines.	5. Instructional strategies are aligned with the objectives, activities, student characteristics, prior learning, and work and life applications, both within the discipline and with other disciplines.	5. Instructional strategies are aligned with the objectives, activities, student characteristics, prior learning, and work and life applications, both within the discipline and with other disciplines.	5. Instructional strategies are aligned with the objectives, activities, student characteristics, prior learning, and work and life applications, both within the discipline and with other disciplines.
6. The teacher varies activities appropriately and maintains appropriate pacing and sequencing of instruction.	6. The teacher varies activities appropriately and maintains appropriate pacing and sequencing of instruction.	6. The teacher varies activities appropriately and maintains appropriate pacing and sequencing of instruction.	6. The teacher varies activities appropriately and maintains appropriate pacing and sequencing of instruction.
7. The teacher emphasizes the value and importance of the activity/content.	7. The teacher emphasizes the value and importance of the activity/content.	7. The teacher emphasizes the value and importance of the activity/content.	7. The teacher emphasizes the value and importance of the activity/content.
8. The teacher uses appropriate questioning and inquiry techniques to challenge students.	8. The teacher uses appropriate questioning and inquiry techniques to challenge students.	8. The teacher uses appropriate questioning and inquiry techniques to challenge students.	8. The teacher uses appropriate questioning and inquiry techniques to challenge students.
9. The teacher makes appropriate and effective use of available technology as a part of the instructional process.	9. The teacher makes appropriate and effective use of available technology as a part of the instructional process.	9. The teacher makes appropriate and effective use of available technology as a part of the instructional process.	9. The teacher makes appropriate and effective use of available technology as a part of the instructional process.

Domain III: Evaluation and Feedback on Student Progress

Evaluation Dimensions:
a. The teacher aligns assessment and feedback with goals and objectives and instructional strategies.
b. The teacher uses a variety of evaluation and feedback strategies which are appropriate to the varied characteristics of the students.

Evaluation Criteria

Exceeds Expectations	*Proficient*	*Below Expectations*	*Unsatisfactory*
ALMOST ALL OF THE TIME	**MOST OF THE TIME**	**SOME OF THE TIME**	**LESS THAN HALF OF THE TIME**
1. Academic progress of students is monitored and assessed.	1. Academic progress of students is monitored and assessed.	1. Academic progress of students is monitored and assessed.	1. Academic progress of students is monitored and assessed.
2. Assessment and feedback are aligned with goals and objectives and instructional strategies.	2. Assessment and feedback are aligned with goals and objectives and instructional strategies.	2. Assessment and feedback are aligned with goals and objectives and instructional strategies.	2. Assessment and feedback are aligned with goals and objectives and instructional strategies.
3. Assessment strategies are appropriate to the varied characteristics of students.	3. Assessment strategies are appropriate to the varied characteristics of students.	3. Assessment strategies are appropriate to the varied characteristics of students.	3. Assessment strategies are appropriate to the varied characteristics of students.
4. Student learning is reinforced.	4. Student learning is reinforced.	4. Student learning is reinforced.	4. Student learning is reinforced.
5. Students receive specific constructive feedback.	5. Students receive specific constructive feedback.	5. Students receive specific constructive feedback.	5. Students receive specific constructive feedback.
6. The teacher provides opportunities for relearning and re-evaluation of material.	6. The teacher provides opportunities for relearning and re-evaluation of material.	6. The teacher provides opportunities for relearning and re-evaluation of material.	6. The teacher provides opportunities for relearning and re-evaluation of material.

Domain IV: Management of Student Discipline, Instructional Strategies, Time, and Materials

Evaluation Dimensions:
a. The teacher effectively implements the discipline-management procedures approved by the district.
b. The teacher establishes a classroom environment which promotes and encourages self-discipline and self-directed learning.
c. The teacher selects instructional materials which are equitable and acknowledge the varied characteristics of all students.
d. The teacher effectively and efficiently manages time and materials.

Evaluation Criteria

Exceeds Expectations **ALMOST ALL OF THE TIME**	*Proficient* **MOST OF THE TIME**	*Below Expectations* **SOME OF THE TIME**	*Unsatisfactory* **LESS THAN HALF OF THE TIME**
1. The teacher effectively implements the discipline-management procedures approved by the campus. The teacher participates in the development of discipline management procedures and offers suggestions for improvement.	1. The teacher effectively implements the discipline-management procedures approved by the campus. Any lack of effective implementation is rare, inadvertent, and does not seriously compromise the needs of students or the effective operation of the classroom or campus.	1. The teacher effectively implements the discipline-management procedures approved by the campus. Any lack of effective implementation is rare, inadvertent, and does not seriously compromise the needs of students or the effective operation of the classroom or campus.	1. The teacher effectively implements the discipline-management procedures approved by the campus. Any lack of effective implementation is rare, inadvertent, and does not seriously compromise the needs of students or the effective operation of the classroom or campus.
2. The teacher establishes a classroom environment which promotes and encourages self-discipline and self-directed learning as appropriate.	2. The teacher establishes a classroom environment which promotes and encourages self-discipline and self-directed learning as appropriate.	2. The teacher establishes a classroom environment which promotes and encourages self-discipline and self-directed learning as appropriate.	2. The teacher establishes a classroom environment which promotes and encourages self-discipline and self-directed learning as appropriate.
3. The teacher interacts with students in an equitable manner, including the fair application of rules.	3. The teacher interacts with students in an equitable manner, including the fair application of rules.	3. The teacher interacts with students in an equitable manner, including the fair application of rules.	3. The teacher interacts with students in an equitable manner, including the fair application of rules.
4. The teacher specifies expectations for desired behavior.	4. The teacher specifies expectations for desired behavior.	4. The teacher specifies expectations for desired behavior.	4. The teacher specifies expectations for desired behavior.
5. The teacher intervenes and re-directs off-task, inappropriate or disruptive behavior as needed.	5. The teacher intervenes and re-directs off-task, inappropriate or disruptive behavior as needed.	5. The teacher intervenes and re-directs off-task, inappropriate or disruptive behavior as needed.	5. The teacher intervenes and re-directs off-task, inappropriate or disruptive behavior as needed.
6. The teacher reinforces desired behavior when appropriate.	6. The teacher reinforces desired behavior when appropriate.	6. The teacher reinforces desired behavior when appropriate.	6. The teacher reinforces desired behavior when appropriate.
7. The instructional materials selected by the teacher are equitable and acknowledge the varied characteristics of all students.	7. The instructional materials selected by the teacher are equitable and acknowledge the varied characteristics of all students.	7. The instructional materials selected by the teacher are equitable and acknowledge the varied characteristics of all students.	7. The instructional materials selected by the teacher are equitable and acknowledge the varied characteristics of all students.
8. The teacher effectively and efficiently manages time and materials.	8. The teacher effectively and efficiently manages time and materials.	8. The teacher effectively and efficiently manages time and materials.	8. The teacher effectively and efficiently manages time and materials.

Domain V: Professional Communication

Evaluation Dimensions:
a. The teacher uses appropriate and accurate written, verbal, and non-verbal modes of communication with students.
b. The teacher uses appropriate and accurate written, verbal, and non-verbal modes of communication with parents, staff, community members, and other professionals.
c. The teacher's interactions are supportive, courteous, respectful, and encouraging to students who are reluctant and having difficulty.

Evaluation Criteria

Exceeds Expectations **ALMOST ALL OF THE TIME**	*Proficient* **MOST OF THE TIME**	*Below Expectations* **SOME OF THE TIME**	*Unsatisfactory* **LESS THAN HALF OF THE TIME**
1. The teacher uses appropriate and accurate written communication with students.	1. The teacher uses appropriate and accurate written communication with students.	1. The teacher uses appropriate and accurate written communication with students.	1. The teacher uses appropriate and accurate written communication with students.
2. The teacher uses appropriate and accurate verbal and non-verbal communication with students.	2. The teacher uses appropriate and accurate verbal and non-verbal communication with students.	2. The teacher uses appropriate and accurate verbal and non-verbal communication with students.	2. The teacher uses appropriate and accurate verbal and non-verbal communication with students.
3. The teacher encourages and supports students who are reluctant or having difficulty.	3. The teacher encourages and supports students who are reluctant or having difficulty.	3. The teacher encourages and supports students who are reluctant or having difficulty.	3. The teacher encourages and supports students who are reluctant or having difficulty.
4. The teacher uses appropriate and accurate written communication with parents, staff, community members, and other professionals.	4. The teacher uses appropriate and accurate written communication with parents, staff, community members, and other professionals.	4. The teacher uses appropriate and accurate written communication with parents, staff, community members, and other professionals.	4. The teacher uses appropriate and accurate written communication with parents, staff, community members, and other professionals.
5. The teacher uses appropriate and accurate verbal and non-verbal communication with parents, staff, community members, and other professionals.	5. The teacher uses appropriate and accurate verbal and non-verbal communication with parents, staff, community members, and other professionals.	5. The teacher uses appropriate and accurate verbal and non-verbal communication with parents, staff, community members, and other professionals.	5. The teacher uses appropriate and accurate verbal and non-verbal communication with parents, staff, community members, and other professionals.
6. The teacher's interactions are supportive, courteous, and respectful with students, parents, staff, community members, and other professionals.	6. The teacher's interactions are supportive, courteous, and respectful with students, parents, staff, community members, and other professionals.	6. The teacher's interactions are supportive, courteous, and respectful with students, parents, staff, community members, and other professionals.	6. The teacher's interactions are supportive, courteous, and respectful with students, parents, staff, community members, and other professionals.

Domain VI: Professional Development

Evaluation Dimensions:
a. The teacher determines and participates in professional development goals and activities that are aligned with the goals of the campus and the goals of the district.
b. The teacher correlates professional development activities with assigned subject content and the varied needs of students.
c. The teacher exhibits a willingness to collaborate with colleagues and other professionals for continuous growth and development.
d. The teacher correlates professional development activities with the prior performance appraisal.

Evaluation Criteria

Exceeds Expectations ALMOST ALL OF THE TIME	Proficient MOST OF THE TIME	Below Expectations SOME OF THE TIME	Unsatisfactory LESS THAN HALF OF THE TIME
1. The teacher successfully seeks out and engages in professional development activities that positively correlate with the goals of the campus and district.	1. The teacher successfully engages in professional development activities that positively correlate with the goals of the campus and district.	1. The teacher successfully engages in professional development activities that positively correlate with the goals of the campus and district.	1. The teacher successfully engages in professional development activities that positively correlate with the goals of the campus and district.
2. The teacher successfully correlates professional development activities with assigned subject content and the varied needs of students.	2. The teacher successfully correlates professional development activities with assigned subject content and the varied needs of students.	2. The teacher successfully correlates professional development activities with assigned subject content and the varied needs of students.	2. The teacher successfully correlates professional development activities with assigned subject content and the varied needs of students.
3. The teacher successfully engages in professional development activities that positively correlate with the prior performance appraisal.	3. The teacher successfully engages in professional development activities that positively correlate with the prior performance appraisal.	3. The teacher successfully engages in professional development activities that positively correlate with the prior performance appraisal.	3. The teacher successfully engages in professional development activities that positively correlate with the prior performance appraisal.
4. The teacher works collaboratively and constructively with colleagues and other professionals toward the overall improvement of student performance.	4. The teacher works collaboratively and constructively with colleagues and other professionals toward the overall improvement of student performance.	4. The teacher works collaboratively and constructively with colleagues and other professionals toward the overall improvement of student performance.	4. The teacher works collaboratively and constructively with colleagues and other professionals toward the overall improvement of student performance.

Domain VII: Compliance With Policies, Operating Procedures, and Requirements

Evaluation Dimensions:
a. The teacher contributes to making the whole school safe and orderly, and a stimulating learning environment for children.
b. The teacher respects the rights of students, parents, colleagues, and the community.

Evaluation Criteria

Exceeds Expectations	*Proficient*	*Below Expectations*	*Unsatisfactory*
1. The teacher complies with all policies, operating procedures, and legal requirements (national, state, district, and campus). The teacher participates in the development of operating procedures and offers suggestions for improvement.	1. The teacher complies with all of the policies, operating procedures, and legal requirements (national, state, district, and campus). Any lack of compliance is rare, inadvertent, and does not seriously compromise the needs of students or the effective operations of the campus/district.	1. The teacher occasionally does not comply with policies, operating procedures, or legal requirements (national, state, district, and campus). In instances of non-compliance, the needs of the students or the effective operations of the campus/district may be compromised.	1. The teacher frequently does not comply with policies, operating procedures, or legal requirements (national, state, district, and campus). In instances of non-compliance, the needs of the students or the effective operations of the campus/district are seriously compromised.
2. The teacher complies with all verbal and written directives, participates in the development of operating procedures, and offers suggestions for improvement.	2. The teacher complies with all verbal and written directives. Any lack of compliance is rare, inadvertent, and does not seriously compromise the needs of students or the effective operations of the campus/district.	2. The teacher occasionally does not comply with all verbal or written directives. In instances of non-compliance, the needs of the students or the effective operations of the campus/district may be compromised.	2. The teacher frequently does not comply with all verbal or written directives. In instances of non-compliance, the needs of the students or the effective operations of the campus/district are seriously compromised.
3. Apart from classroom responsibilities, the teacher consistently contributes to making the whole school safe and orderly, and a stimulating learning environment for all students.	3. Apart from classroom responsibilities, the teacher generally contributes to making the whole school safe and orderly, and a stimulating learning environment for all students.	3. Apart from classroom responsibilities, the teacher seldom contributes to making the whole school safe and orderly, and a stimulating learning environment for all students.	3. Apart from classroom responsibilities, the teacher rarely contributes to making the whole school safe and orderly, and a stimulating learning environment for all students.

Domain VIII: Improvement of Academic Performance of All Students On The Campus (Based on Indicators included in the AEIS)

Evaluation Dimensions:
a. The teacher diagnoses student needs and provides performance feedback related to all appropriate TAAS-related objectives.
b. The teacher aligns the planning and delivery of instruction to all appropriate TAAS-related objectives.
c. The teacher collaborates with other faculty and administration to improve TAAS-related performance of all students on the campus.
d. The teacher identifies students who are at risk and develops appropriate strategies to assist these students.
e. The teacher monitors the attendance of all students and intervenes to promote regular attendance.

Evaluation Criteria

(A) Efforts to Enhance Academic Performance*

Exceeds Expectations **ALMOST ALL OF THE TIME**	*Proficient* **MOST OF THE TIME**	*Below Expectations* **SOME OF THE TIME**	*Unsatisfactory* **LESS THAN HALF OF THE TIME**
1. The teacher works with colleagues to align instruction to include appropriate TAAS-related objectives to support student achievement in all assigned classes.	1. The teacher aligns instruction to include appropriate TAAS-related objectives to support student achievement in all assigned classes.	1. The teacher aligns instruction to include appropriate TAAS-related objectives to support student achievement in all assigned classes.	1. The teacher aligns instruction to include appropriate TAAS-related objectives to support student achievement in all assigned classes.
2. The teacher works with colleagues to analyze TAAS performance data relevant to all students in assigned classes prior to beginning instruction.	2. The teacher analyzes TAAS performance data relevant to all students in assigned classes prior to beginning instruction.	2. The teacher analyzes TAAS performance data relevant to all students in assigned classes prior to beginning instruction.	2. The teacher analyzes TAAS performance data relevant to all students in assigned classes prior to beginning instruction.
3. The teacher coordinates with others within and outside the teacher's discipline to determine the sequencing of classroom instruction to appropriately incorporate TAAS-related objectives.	3. The teacher adjusts the sequencing of classroom instruction to appropriately incorporate TAAS-related objectives.	3. The teacher adjusts the sequencing of classroom instruction to appropriately incorporate TAAS-related objectives.	3. The teacher adjusts the sequencing of classroom instruction to appropriately incorporate TAAS-related objectives.
4. The teacher collaborates with others within and outside the teacher's discipline to select/adapt instructional materials and activities which are correlated with appropriate TAAS-related objectives.	4. The teacher selects/adapts instructional materials and activities which are correlated with appropriate TAAS-related objectives.	4. The teacher selects/adapts instructional materials and activities which are correlated with appropriate TAAS-related objectives.	4. The teacher selects/adapts instructional materials and activities which are correlated with appropriate TAAS-related objectives.
5. The teacher provides feedback to all students regarding their learning progress on appropriate TAAS-related objectives.	5. The teacher provides feedback to all students regarding their learning progress on appropriate TAAS-related objectives.	5. The teacher provides feedback to all students regarding their learning progress on appropriate TAAS-related objectives.	5. The teacher provides feedback to all students regarding their learning progress on appropriate TAAS-related objectives.

* For Section A only, with approval of the principal, certain high school teachers may substitute other standardized measures and related objectives which are addressed in the AEIS system. This may include SAT/ACT, AP, TASP, and end-of-course examinations. The substitutions should be reflected in teacher responses on the Teacher Self-Report Form.

(Appraisal Framework for Domain VIII continues.)

Exceeds Expectations ALMOST ALL OF THE TIME	Proficient MOST OF THE TIME	Below Expectations SOME OF THE TIME	Unsatisfactory LESS THAN HALF OF THE TIME
(B) Efforts to Enhance Student Attendance			
6. The teacher monitors attendance of all students in assigned classes and contacts parents, counselors, or other school officials regarding an intervention plan for students with serious attendance problems.	6. The teacher monitors attendance of all students in assigned classes and contacts parents, counselors, or other school officials for students with serious attendance problems.	6. The teacher monitors attendance of all students in assigned classes and contacts parents, counselors, or other school officials for students with serious attendance problems.	6. The teacher monitors attendance of all students in assigned classes and contacts parents, counselors, or other school officials for students with serious attendance problems.
(C) Efforts to Identify and Assist Students in At-Risk Situations			
7. The teacher works with teachers, counselors, and other school professionals to seek information to identify and assess the needs of assigned students in at-risk situations.	7. The teacher identifies and assesses the needs of assigned students in at-risk situations.	7. The teacher identifies and assesses the needs of assigned students in at-risk situations.	7. The teacher identifies and assesses the needs of assigned students in at-risk situations.
8. The teacher meets with parents and/or other teachers of students who are failing or in danger of failing to develop an appropriate plan for intervention.	8. The teacher meets with students who are failing or in danger of failing and develops an appropriate plan for intervention.	8. The teacher meets with students who are failing or in danger of failing and develops an appropriate plan for intervention.	8. The teacher meets with students who are failing or in danger of failing and develops an appropriate plan for intervention.
9. The teacher participates in and/or contributes to campus-wide programs to modify and adapt classroom materials and/or instruction for students in at-risk situations.	9. The teacher modifies and adapts classroom materials and/or instruction for students in at-risk situations.	9. The teacher modifies and adapts classroom materials and/or instruction for students in at-risk situations.	9. The teacher modifies and adapts classroom materials and/or instruction for students in at-risk situations.

(D) Campus Performance Rating

10. The campus performance rating consists of three factors including: (a) student performance on the Texas Assessment of Academic Skills (TAAS), (b) student attendance, and (c) drop-out rates. All teachers make contributions toward this overall performance rating of the school, and therefore this is included among the criteria for improved academic excellence. The commissioner of education will issue a policy directive concerning the campus performance rating used in Domain VIII for teachers on campuses not rated under the Standard Accountability System. Beginning with the 1998-99 School Year, the following scale is used to score the campus performance rating:

Exemplary = 5
Recognized = 4
Acceptable = 3
Low Performing = 2 (if quartile 1 or 2 on comparable improvement)*
1 (if quartile 3 on comparable improvement)*
0 (if quartile 4 on comparable improvement)*

*currently under review.

Name: _____   **Appraisal Year:** _____

Appraiser: _____   **Date Submitted:** _____

Campus: _____   **Assignment/Grade:** _____

PROFESSIONAL DEVELOPMENT AND APPRAISAL SYSTEM

TEACHER SELF-REPORT FORM

Contributions to The Improvement of Academic Performance
of All Students on Campus

The following are general rules for use of the Teacher Self-Report (TSR):

(1) Based upon the nature of the teaching assignment, TAAS-related objectives may vary in content and level of difficulty.

(2) Context for the objectives include (1) teaching field, (2) assignment and/or (3) varying characteristics of the teacher's students.

(3) Depending upon the classroom contest, targeted objectives may be developed for:

    (a) a subset of the TAAS-related objectives.

    (b) a subset of classes assigned to the teacher.

    (c) a subset of the teacher's students.

(4) The TSR requires the least amount of writing necessary to communicate the point or make the example (limited to one-half page per item).

Section I*

The data requested in Section I must be presented to the principal within the first three weeks after the orientation. The teacher may elect to revise this section prior to the annual summative conference.

1. Which academic skills (TAAS-related **objectives**) do you directly teach or reinforce in your classes? Check all that apply.

READING (Six Objectives)
Reading Comprehension
ALL OBJECTIVES .... _____

Objective 1:	The student will determine the meaning of words in a variety of contexts.	_____
Objective 2:	The student will identify supporting ideas in a variety of written texts.	_____
Objective 3:	The student will summarize a variety of written texts.	_____
Objective 4:	The student will perceive relationships and recognize outcomes in a variety of written texts.	_____
Objective 5:	The student will analyze information in a variety of written texts in order to make inferences and generalizations.	_____
Objective 6:	The student will recognize points of view, propaganda, and/or statements of fact and nonfact in a variety of written texts.	_____

WRITING (Seven Objectives)
Written Communication
ALL OBJECTIVES .... _____

Objective 1:	The student will respond appropriately in a written composition to the purpose/audience specified in a given topic.	_____
Objective 2:	The student will organize ideas in a written composition on a given topic.	_____
Objective 3:	The student will demonstrate control of the English language in a written composition on a given topic.	_____
Objective 4:	The student will generate a written composition that develops/supports/elaborates the central idea stated on a given topic.	_____
Objective 5:	The student will recognize appropriate sentence construction within the context of a written passage.	_____
Objective 6:	The student will recognize appropriate English usage within the context of a written passage.	_____
Objective 7:	The student will recognize appropriate spelling, capitalization, and punctuation within the context of a written passage.	_____

*Information primarily related to Domain VIII

MATHEMATICS (Thirteen Objectives)
Mathematics Concepts
ALL OBJECTIVES .... _____

Objective 1:   The student will demonstrate an understanding of number concepts. _____

Objective 2:   The student will demonstrate an understanding of mathematical relations, functions, and other algebraic concepts. _____

Objective 3:   The student will demonstrate an understanding of geometric properties and relationships. _____

Objective 4:   The student will demonstrate an understanding of measurement concepts using metric and customary units. _____

Objective 5:   The student will demonstrate an understanding of probability and statistics. _____

Mathematical Operations
ALL OBJECTIVES .... _____

Objective 6:   The student will use the operation of addition to solve problems. _____

Objective 7:   The student will use the operation of subtraction to solve problems. _____

Objective 8:   The student will use the operation of multiplication to solve problems. _____

Objective 9:   The student will use the operation of division to solve problems. _____

Problem Solving
ALL OBJECTIVES .... _____

Objective 10:   The student will estimate solutions to a problem situation. _____

Objective 11:   The student will determine solution strategies and will analyze or solve problems. _____

Objective 12:   The student will express or solve problems using mathematical representation. _____

Objective 13:   The student will evaluate the reasonableness of a solution to a problem situation. _____

OTHER OBJECTIVES _____

With the approval of the principal, certain high school teachers may substitute other standardized measures and related objectives which are addressed in the AEIS system. This may include SAT/ACT, AP, TASP, and end-of-course examinations. Specify below.

2. What process do you use to assess the needs of your students with regard to academic skills (TAAS-related objectives)?

Disaggregated TAAS data _____

Curriculum-correlated assessment materials _____

Teacher-designed assessment process/materials _____

Diagnostic observations _____

Other standardized test results _____

Cumulative classroom performance data _____

Other (describe) _____

Name: _____   **Appraisal Year:** _____

Appraiser: _____   **Date Submitted:** _____

Campus: _____   **Assignment/Grade:** _____

PROFESSIONAL DEVELOPMENT AND APPRAISAL SYSTEM

TEACHER SELF-REPORT FORM

Contributions to the Improvement of Academic Performance
of All Students on Campus

Section II[1]

The data requested in Sections II and III must be presented to the principal at least two weeks before the annual summative conference. Limit all responses to one-half page per response.

3. Describe a specific instructional adjustment (e.g., materials, sequencing, etc.) which you have made based on the needs assessment of your students.

4. Describe the approaches you have used to monitor classroom performance and provided feedback to students regarding their progress in academic skills (TAAS-related objectives).

5. Describe how you assisted your students who were experiencing serious attendance problems.

6. Describe your approach in working with students who were failing or in danger of failing.

1.Information primarily related to Domain VIII

Provide the information requested in the space below.

7. List or describe your professional development activities for the past year related to campus/district goals, assigned subject/content, needs of students, or prior appraisal performance in the following areas: inservice, team planning, mentoring, collaboration with colleagues, self-study, video coursework or distance learning, university-level coursework, professional conferences, and other non-traditional activities.

8. As a result of your professional development activities described above, what have you been able to use in your classroom that has positively impacted the learning of students?

9. Be prepared to discuss the following in the summative annual conference: Identify three target areas for continued professional growth. In order to organize your thoughts, you may wish to make notes below, but it is not required.

---

2. Information primarily related to Domain VIII

Name: _____ Appraiser: _____ Date: _____ Campus: _____ Assignment/Grade: _____

Beginning Time: _____ Ending Time: _____

PROFESSIONAL DEVELOPMENT AND APPRAISAL SYSTEM

☐ Observation Summary
☐ Summative Annual Appraisal

Domain I: Active, Successful Student Participation in the Learning Process

	Exceeds (x 5)	Proficient (x 3)	Below (x 1)	Unsatis-factory (x 0)
1. Engaged in learning	1. ___	1. ___	1. ___	1. ___
2. Successful in learning	2. ___	2. ___	2. ___	2. ___
3. Critical thinking/ problem solving	3. ___	3. ___	3. ___	3. ___
4. Self-directed	4. ___	4. ___	4. ___	4. ___
5. Connects learning	5. ___	5. ___	5. ___	5. ___
SUBTOTAL				

TOTAL [ ]

Total: 20 to 25   Exceeds Expectations
12 to 19   Proficient
4 to 11   Below Expectations
0 to 3   Unsatisfactory

Comments:

Domain II: Learner-Centered Instruction

	Exceeds (x 5)	Proficient (x 3)	Below (x 1)	Unsatis-factory (x 0)
1. Goals and objectives	1. ___	1. ___	1. ___	1. ___
2. Learner-centered	2. ___	2. ___	2. ___	2. ___
3. Critical thinking and problem solving	3. ___	3. ___	3. ___	3. ___
4. Motivational strategies	4. ___	4. ___	4. ___	4. ___
5. Alignment	5. ___	5. ___	5. ___	5. ___
6. Pacing/sequencing	6. ___	6. ___	6. ___	6. ___
7. Value and importance	7. ___	7. ___	7. ___	7. ___
8. Appropriate questioning and inquiry	8. ___	8. ___	8. ___	8. ___
9. Use of technology	9. ___	9. ___	9. ___	9. ___
SUBTOTAL				

TOTAL [ ]

Total: 37 to 45   Exceeds Expectations
23 to 36   Proficient
7 to 22   Below Expectations
0 to 6   Unsatisfactory

Comments:

Strengths   Areas to Address

Strengths   Areas to Address

Name: _____ Appraiser: _____ Date: _____ Campus: _____ Assignment/Grade: _____

Beginning Time: _____ Ending Time: _____

PROFESSIONAL DEVELOPMENT AND APPRAISAL SYSTEM

☐ Observation Summary
☐ Summative Annual Appraisal

Domain III: Evaluation and Feedback on Student Progress

	Exceeds (x 5)	Proficient (x 3)	Below (x 1)	Unsatis-factory (x 0)
1. Monitored and assessed	1. ____	1. ____	1. ____	1. ____
2. Assessment and instruction are aligned	2. ____	2. ____	2. ____	2. ____
3. Appropriate assessment	3. ____	3. ____	3. ____	3. ____
4. Learning reinforced	4. ____	4. ____	4. ____	4. ____
5. Constructive feedback	5. ____	5. ____	5. ____	5. ____
6. Relearning and re-evaluation	6. ____	6. ____	6. ____	6. ____
SUBTOTAL				TOTAL

Total:
25 to 30 Exceeds Expectations
15 to 24 Proficient
5 to 14 Below Expectations
0 to 4 Unsatisfactory

Comments:

Strengths   Areas to Address

Domain IV: Management of Student Discipline, Instructional Strategies, Time, and Materials

	Exceeds (x 5)	Proficient (x 3)	Below (x 1)	Unsatis-factory (x 0)
1. Discipline procedures	1. ____	1. ____	1. ____	1. ____
2. Self-discipline and self-directed learning	2. ____	2. ____	2. ____	2. ____
3. Equitable teacher-student interaction	3. ____	3. ____	3. ____	3. ____
4. Expectations for behavior	4. ____	4. ____	4. ____	4. ____
5. Redirects disruptive behavior	5. ____	5. ____	5. ____	5. ____
6. Reinforces desired behavior	6. ____	6. ____	6. ____	6. ____
7. Equitable and varied characteristics	7. ____	7. ____	7. ____	7. ____
8. Manages time and materials	8. ____	8. ____	8. ____	8. ____
SUBTOTAL				TOTAL

Total:
34 to 40 Exceeds Expectations
20 to 33 Proficient
6 to 19 Below Expectations
0 to 5 Unsatisfactory

Comments:

Strengths   Areas to Address

Name: _____ Appraiser: _____ Date: _____ Campus: _____ Assignment/Grade: _____

Beginning Time: _____ Ending Time: _____

PROFESSIONAL DEVELOPMENT AND APPRAISAL SYSTEM

☐ Observation Summary
☐ Summative Annual Appraisal

Domain V: Professional Communication

	Exceeds (x 5)	Proficient (x 3)	Below (x 1)	Unsatis- factory (x 0)
1. Written with students	1. _____	1. _____	1. _____	1. _____
2. Verbal/non-verbal with students	2. _____	2. _____	2. _____	2. _____
3. Reluctant students	3. _____	3. _____	3. _____	3. _____
4. Written with parents, staff, community members, and other professionals	4. _____	4. _____	4. _____	4. _____
5. Verbal/non-verbal with parents, staff, community members and other professionals.	5. _____	5. _____	5. _____	5. _____
6. Supportive, courteous	6. _____	6. _____	6. _____	6. _____
SUBTOTAL				TOTAL

Total: 25 to 30 Exceeds Expectations
15 to 24 Proficient
5 to 14 Below Expectations
0 to 4 Unsatisfactory

Comments:

Strengths   Areas to Address

Domain VI: Professional Development

	Exceeds (x 5)	Proficient (x 3)	Below (x 1)	Unsatis- factory (x 0)
1. Campus/district goals	1. _____	1. _____	1. _____	1. _____
2. Student needs	2. _____	2. _____	2. _____	2. _____
3. Prior performance appraisal	3. _____	3. _____	3. _____	3. _____
4. Improvement of student performance	4. _____	4. _____	4. _____	4. _____
SUBTOTAL				TOTAL

Total: 16 to 20 Exceeds Expectations
9 to 15 Proficient
3 to 8 Below Expectations
0 to 2 Unsatisfactory

Comments:

Strengths   Areas to Address

Name: _____ Appraiser: _____ Date: _____ Campus: _____ Assignment/Grade: _____

Beginning Time: _____ Ending Time: _____

PROFESSIONAL DEVELOPMENT AND APPRAISAL SYSTEM

☐ Observation Summary
☐ Summative Annual Appraisal

Domain VII: Compliance With Policies, Operating Procedures, and Requirements

	Exceeds (x 5)	Proficient (x 3)	Below (x 1)	Unsatis-factory (x 0)
1. Policies, procedures, and legal requirements	1. _____	1. _____	1. _____	1. _____
2. Verbal/written directives	2. _____	2. _____	2. _____	2. _____
3. Environment	3. _____	3. _____	3. _____	3. _____
SUBTOTAL				
TOTAL				

Total: 13 to 15 Exceeds Expectations
9 to 12 Proficient
5 to 8 Below Expectations
0 to 4 Unsatisfactory

Comments:

Strengths

Areas to Address

Name: _____   Appraiser: _____   Date: _____   Campus: _____   Assignment/Grade: _____

Beginning Time: _____   Ending Time: _____

PROFESSIONAL DEVELOPMENT AND APPRAISAL SYSTEM

☐ Observation Summary
☐ Summative Annual Appraisal

Domain VIII: Improvement of Academic Performance of All Students on The Campus (Based on Indicators Included in the AEIS)

	Exceeds (x 5)	Proficient (x 3)	Below (x 1)	Unsatis-factory (x 0)
1. Aligns instruction	1. ___	1. ___	1. ___	1. ___
2. Analyzes TAAS data	2. ___	2. ___	2. ___	2. ___
3. Appropriate sequence	3. ___	3. ___	3. ___	3. ___
4. Appropriate materials	4. ___	4. ___	4. ___	4. ___
5. Monitors student performance	5. ___	5. ___	5. ___	5. ___
6. Monitors attendance	6. ___	6. ___	6. ___	6. ___
7. Students in at-risk situations	7. ___	7. ___	7. ___	7. ___
8. Appropriate plans for intervention	8. ___	8. ___	8. ___	8. ___
9. Modifies and adapts	9. ___	9. ___	9. ___	9. ___
SUBTOTAL 1-9				

SUB TOTAL 1-9 _____

Comments:

Strengths

Areas to Address

PLUS 10. Campus Performance Rating of: Reported only _____   Scored _____

Exemplary = 5
Recognized = 4
Acceptable = 3 (if quartile 1 or 2 on comparable improvement)
         = 2 (if quartile 3 or 4 on comparable improvement)
Low Performing = 2 (if quartile 1 or 2 on comparable improvement)
         = 1 (if quartile 3 on comparable improvement)
         = 0 (if quartile 4 on comparable improvement)

Total Domain VIII Score:

	1ST YEAR	2ND YEAR
Total:	Exceeds Expectations	37 to 45	40 to 50
	Proficient	23 to 36	24 to 39
	Below Expectations	7 to 22	8 to 23
	Unsatisfactory	0 to 6	0 to 7

Signature of Appraiser: _____   Date: _____

My appraiser and I have discussed this annual summative appraisal.

Signature of Teacher: _____   Date: _____

497

Name: _____ Appraiser: _____ Date: _____ Campus: _____ Assignment/Grade: _____

Beginning Time: _____ Ending Time: _____

Example - 1st Year (1997-98), Reported but Not Counted

PROFESSIONAL DEVELOPMENT AND APPRAISAL SYSTEM

☐ Observation Summary   ☐ Summative Annual Appraisal

Domain VIII: Improvement of Academic Performance of All Students on The Campus (Based on Indicators Included in the AEIS)

	Exceeds (x 5)	Proficient (x 3)	Below (x 1)	Unsatisfactory (x 0)
1. Aligns instruction	1. ___	1. ✓	1. ___	1. ___
2. Analyzes TAAS data	2. ___	2. ✓	2. ___	2. ___
3. Appropriate sequence	3. ✓	3. ___	3. ___	3. ___
4. Appropriate materials	4. ___	4. ✓	4. ___	4. ___
5. Monitors student performance	5. ___	5. ✓	5. ___	5. ___
6. Monitors attendance	6. ✓	6. ___	6. ___	6. ___
7. Students in at-risk situations	7. ___	7. ✓	7. ___	7. ___
8. Appropriate plans for intervention	8. ___	8. ___	8. ✓	8. ___
9. Modifies and adapts	9. ___	9. ✓	9. ___	9. ___
SUBTOTAL for ITEMS 1-9	10	18	1	0

SUB TOTAL 1-9
29

PLUS 10. Campus Performance Rating of: Reported only __ X __ Scored _____

Exemplary = 5 _____
Recognized = 4 _____
Acceptable = 3 (if quartile 1 or 2 on comparable improvement) _____
= 2 (if quartile 3 or 4 on comparable improvement) __2__
Low Performing = 2 (if quartile 1 or 2 on comparable improvement) _____
= 1 (if quartile 3 on comparable improvement) _____
= 0 (if quartile 4 on comparable improvement) _____

Total Domain VIII Score:
29

	1ST YEAR	2ND YEAR
Total:	Exceeds Expectations	37 to 45	40 to 50
	Proficient	23 to 36	24 to 39
	Below Expectations	7 to 22	8 to 23
	Unsatisfactory	0 to 6	0 to 7

Comments:

Mrs. Jones is a very good teacher. She is growing each year.

Strengths

Ms. Jones is beginning to really specify the learning needs of her students. She is now preparing better instruction and materials. She has also done quite well in monitoring and increasing the attendance of her students.

Areas to Address

Ms. Jones needs to provide more appropriate learning situations for at-risk students.

Signature of Appraiser: _____ Date: _____

My appraiser and I have discussed this annual summative appraisal.

Signature of Teacher: _____ Date: _____

Name: _____ Appraiser: _____ Date: _____ Campus: _____ Assignment/Grade: _____

Beginning Time: _____ Ending Time: _____

Example - 2nd Year (1998-99), Reported but Not Counted

PROFESSIONAL DEVELOPMENT AND APPRAISAL SYSTEM

☐ Observation Summary ☐ Summative Annual Appraisal

Domain VIII: Improvement of Academic Performance of All Students on The Campus (Based on Indicators Included in the AEIS)

	Exceeds (x 5)	Proficient (x 3)	Below (x 1)	Unsatisfactory (x 0)
1. Aligns instruction	1. ___	1. ✓	1. ___	1. ___
2. Analyzes TAAS data	2. ___	2. ✓	2. ___	2. ___
3. Appropriate sequence	3. ✓	3. ___	3. ___	3. ___
4. Appropriate materials	4. ___	4. ✓	4. ___	4. ___
5. Monitors student performance	5. ___	5. ✓	5. ___	5. ___
6. Monitors attendance	6. ✓	6. ___	6. ___	6. ___
7. Students in at-risk situations	7. ___	7. ✓	7. ___	7. ___
8. Appropriate plans for intervention	8. ✓	8. ___	8. ___	8. ___
9. Campus-wide programs	9. ___	9. ✓	9. ___	9. ___
SUBTOTAL for ITEMS 1-9	15	18	0	0

SUB TOTAL 1-9
33

PLUS 10. Campus Performance Rating of: Reported only ___ Scored _X_

Exemplary = 5 ___
Recognized = 4 ___
Acceptable = 3 (if quartile 1 or 2 on comparable improvement) 3
 = 2 (if quartile 3 or 4 on comparable improvement) ___
Low Performing = 2 (if quartile 1 or 2 on comparable improvement) ___
 = 1 (if quartile 3 on comparable improvement) ___
 = 0 (if quartile 4 on comparable improvement) ___

Total Domain VIII Score:
36

	1ST YEAR	2ND YEAR
Exceeds Expectations	37 to 45	40 to 50
Proficient	23 to 36	24 to 39
Below Expectations	7 to 22	8 to 23
Unsatisfactory	0 to 6	0 to 7

Total:

Comments:

Mrs. Jones continues to be a solid member of our faculty. She makes efforts to improve that have paid off this year.

Strengths

Ms. Jones has focused on working with students in at-risk situations, developing specific plans for intervention, which she has successfully carried out.

Areas to Address

Ms. Jones has selected the continued alignment of instruction with TAAS-related objectives as an area to focus on for the next year. She intends to increase her collaboration with colleagues as she works in this area.

Signature of Appraiser: _____ Date: _____

My appraiser and I have discussed this annual summative appraisal.

Signature of Teacher: _____ Date: _____

INTERVENTION PLAN FOR TEACHER IN NEED OF ASSISTANCE

Name: _____   Appraiser: _____

Campus: _____   Assignment/Grade: _____

Period of Intervention: From: _____   To: _____

PROFESSIONAL DEVELOPMENT AND APPRAISAL SYSTEM

INTERVENTION PLAN FOR TEACHER IN NEED OF ASSISTANCE

1. Domain(s) in which the teacher is in need of assistance.

2. Professional-improvement activities and dates for completion.

3. Evidence that will be used to determine that professional-improvement activities have been completed.

4. Directives for changes in teacher behavior and time lines.

5. Evidence that will be used to determine if teacher behavior has changed.

_____   _____
Signature of Appraiser   Date

_____   _____
Signature of Principal   Date

My appraiser, principal, and I have discussed this intervention plan. My signature does not indicate whether I agree or disagree with this plan.

_____   _____
Signature of Teacher   Date

Final proof. April 11, 1997.

Name: _____   Appraiser: _____

Campus: _____   Assignment/Grade: _____

Period of Intervention: From: _____   To: _____

INTERVENTION PLAN FOR TEACHER IN NEED OF ASSISTANCE

This plan has been successfully completed.   _____

This plan has not been successfully completed.   _____

This plan was not successfully completed for the following reasons:

Further action to be taken:

_____   _____
Signature of Appraiser   Date

_____   _____
Signature of Principal   Date

My appraiser, and I have discussed this intervention plan. My signature does not indicate whether I agree or disagree with this plan.

_____   _____
Signature of Teacher   Date

Final proof. April 11, 1997.

502

Professional Development and Appraisal System
Standard of Proficiency
Scoring Guidelines Continuum by Criteria over Time

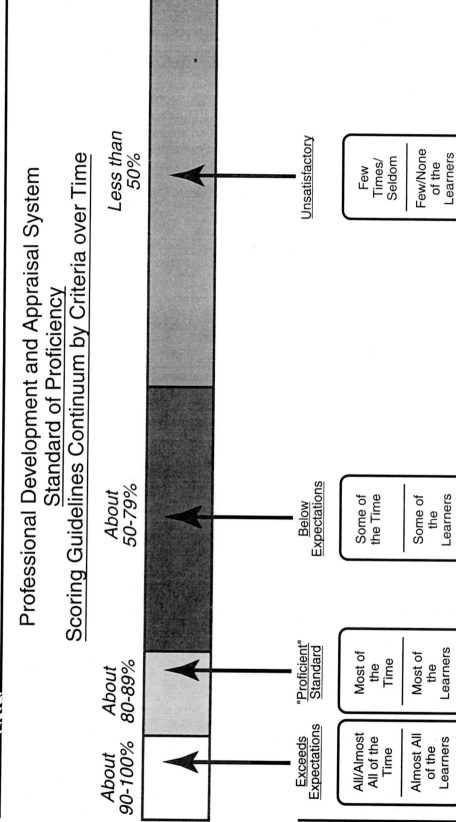

About
90-100%

About
80-89%

About
50-79%

Less than
50%

Exceeds
Expectations

"Proficient"
Standard

Below
Expectations

Unsatisfactory

All/Almost
All of the
Time

Almost All
of the Learners

Most of
the
Time

Most of
the
Learners

Some of
the Time

Some of
the
Learners

Few
Times/
Seldom

Few/None
of the
Learners

High Inference

Low Inference:
Student Performance

Professional Development and Appraisal System

Scoring Factors:

A. Critical Attributes	B. Quality of the Application	C. Quantity of Time/Students With Which the Attributes are Exhibited

A. **CRITICAL ATTRIBUTES** *are described in the appraisal framework.*

B. Scoring standards for **QUALITY**

KEY WORDS	Exceeds Expectations	Proficient	Below Expectations	Unsatisfactory
	All/Almost All	Most	Some	Less than Half
GUIDELINE	**Great:** • strength • impact • variety • alignment	**Considerable:** • strength • impact • variety • alignment	**Limited:** • strength • impact • variety • alignment	**Little or None:** • strength • impact • variety • alignment

Strength

- multidimensional
- depth and complexity
- significant content knowledge
- powerful
- effective
- clarity
- accurate
- substantive

Impact

- promotes student success
- over time
- productive
- promotes student responsibility /investment
- timely
- challenging
- promotes reflection

Variety

- appropriate to meet the varied characteristics of students
- promotes engagement/ learning
- appropriate to the lesson objective

Alignment

- connection to a set of objectives and expectations external to the classroom
- congruent
- progression
- leads to understanding of unified whole
- appropriate to varied characteristics of students
- relevant

C. Scoring Standards for **QUANTITY**
1. For criteria primarily judged by **FREQUENCY COUNTS/PERCENTAGE OF TIME.**

KEY WORDS	Exceeds Expectations	Proficient	Below Expectations	Unsatisfactory
	All/Almost All	Most	Some	Less than Half
GUIDELINE	*About 90-100%*	*About 80-89%*	*About 50-79%*	*About 49% or less*

2. For criteria primarily judged by **REPEATED EVIDENCE.**

KEY WORDS	Exceeds Expectations	Proficient	Below Expectations	Unsatisfactory
	All/Almost All	Most	Some	Less than Half
GUIDELINE	**Consistently:** • uniformly • see it from the beginning to the end • highly predictable • routines are seamless	**Generally:** • common practice • predictable • typical prevalent • as a rule	**Occasionally:** • sporadic • random • moderately • more often than not • irregular	**Rarely:** • seldom • infrequent • nonexistent • not attempted • minimal • hardly ever

SCORING INDICATORS GUIDE

Final Proof

Domain I: Active, Successful Student Participation in the Learning Process

Performance at the "Proficient" Level is primarily based upon formal classroom observation(s).
Other documentary evidence, as needed, may be collected over the entire appraisal period.
*Performance at the "Proficient" Level **MAY** be inferred for a criterion if 80% of the criteria in the Domain **ARE** documented at the "Proficient" or Exceeds Expectations Levels and **NO** criteria are documented at Below Expectations Levels or Unsatisfactory.*

Evaluation Criteria "Proficient" Standard	Scoring Indicators "Proficient" Standard	Observation/Documentation "Proficient" Standard Examples	Quantity and Quality Key Words/Concepts
I-1. Students are actively engaged in learning.	*Most of the students* are focused on the learning objective more than 80% of the academic learning time.	• <u>Count</u> reveals that <u>85% of students</u> are engaged at <u>regular intervals</u> during academic learning time. [Appraiser must be cognizant of objective(s).]	<u>Quantity</u>: *Most of the students. . . . .:80% of the . . . time.* _<u>Quality</u>: . . . engaged. . ._
I-2. Students are successful in learning.	*Most of the students demonstrate success* with the stated, implied or written learning objective.	• Learning objective stated and taught, more than 80% of students pass <u>teacher's</u> <u>assessment</u> of objective.	<u>Quantity</u>: _Most of the students . . ._ <u>Quality</u>: . . .*demonstrate success.* . . .
I-3. Student behaviors indicate learning is at a high cognitive level (e.g., critical thinking, creative thinking, problem solving, etc.)	*Most of the students* are involved in learning activities at the *application level or higher* on Bloom's Taxonomy which produce a logic, an innovative approach, or a solution to a problem or concern.	• Guided practice leads students to apply newly acquired knowledge, skill or concept to an <u>application</u> scenario.	<u>Quality</u>: *Most of the students. . .* <u>Quality</u>: . . .involved in learning activities at the *application level or higher. . .*
I-4. Students are self-directed/self-initiated as appropriate to the lesson objectives.	*As appropriate,* students <u>generally</u> create or extend a skill, knowledge or concept connected to the learning objective; students demonstrate task commitment, often without further prompting.	• Students, *as a rule,* create or extend a newly acquired skill, knowledge or concept, such as, using "onomatopoeia" in a personal essay or story; teacher values the engagement through appropriate feedback.	<u>Quantity</u>: . . . <u>generally</u>. . . _<u>Quality</u>: As appropriate. . ._

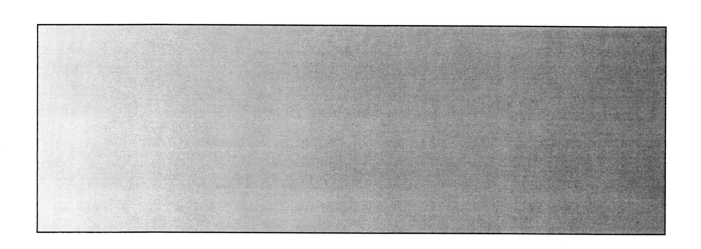

Index

Texas State Teachers Association
(TSTA), 440–41
Texas Statewide Systemic Initiative
(Texas SSI), 286
Texas Task Force, 348
Texas Teacher Appraisal System
(TTAS), 199, 412, 417, 467, 468
Texas Teachers Empowered for
Achievement in Mathematics
and Science (TEXTEAMS),
286
thinking skills, and SCANS, 392–93
"Third Bracey Report on the
Condition of Public
Education" (Bracey), 227, 231,
232, 234, 237
Third International Mathematics and
Science Study (TIMSS), 14,
249, 286
"This Week with David Brinkley,"
231
Thurow, Lester, 233
Timothy W. v. Rochester School District,
319
*Tinker v. Des Moines Independent
School District,* 195–96
Title IX (Education Amendments), 7,
30, 125, 196
Today's Education, 439
Total Quality Management (TQM),
272, 401–4
tracking, 427–28
Traditional OBE, 396–97
Transformational OBE, 398–400
Transitional OBE, 397–98
transportation, disruption of, 113
traumatic brain injury, 322
true/false tests, 254
T-Star, 285
Tucker, Marc, 233

Turning Points (Carnegie Council on
Adolescent Development),
345–46, 348
Tyler, Ralph, 246–47, 249
Tyler Rationale, 246–47

unions, public assessment poll, 219
U.S. Census Bureau, 234
U.S. Constitution, 2, 8, 17–18, 28–29,
195, 198
U.S. Department of Defense
Dependent Schools (DODDS),
398–99
U.S. Department of Education, 198,
230, 367–68
U.S. Department of Health and
Human Services, 198
U.S. Department of Health,
Education, and Welfare, 198
U.S. News & World Report, 232, 265–66
United States v. Lopez, 201–2
University of California Medical
School at Davis, 197
University of Chicago, 186
University of Georgia, 184
University of Missouri, Elementary
School, 276
university organizations, 454–55
Up From Excellence (Wayson), 365
Utne, Eric, 237
Utne Reader, 237

vertical articulation, 347
visual impairment, 322
vocational organizations, 455–56
voluntary testing program, 215
volunteers, professional
organizations, 450–51
vouchers. *See* charter schools; school
choice

Walberg, Herbert, 229
Waldrop, Frank, 127
Wall Street Journal, 232
Warren, Earl, 187
Washington, George, 181
Washington, D.C., charter schools in,
96
Washington Post, 230, 231, 232, 234,
237–38
Webster, Daniel, 182
Webster, Noah, 181
Weighted Average Daily Allowance
(WADA), 53
Westinghouse Learning Corporation,
194
White, Mark, 199
Whittle, Chris, 24, 51
Wigginton, Eliot, 429
Will, George, 226, 229, 230–32
Willard, Emma, 183
Willard, John, 183
Wilmer-Hutchins ISD, 200
Wilson, Pete, 231
"Windows on Science," 269
Wisconsin, charter schools in, 96
women
and educational history, 183
educational opportunities
for, 196
See also Education Amendments;
sexual discrimination; sexual
harassment; Title IX
Women's Educational Equity Act of
1974, 196
work-based learning, 383
writing, and SCANS, 392
Wurtzel, Alan, 234
Wyoming, charter schools in, 96

year-round schools, 269–70